FALLEN FOUNDER

FALLEN FOUNDER

The Life of Aaron Burr

NANCY ISENBERG

VIKING

VIKING
Published by the Penguin Group
Penguin Group (USA) Inc., 375 Hudson Street, New York, New York 10014, U.S.A.
Penguin Group (Canada), 90 Eglinton Avenue East, Suite 700, Toronto, Ontario, Canada M4P 2Y3
(a division of Pearson Penguin Canada Inc.)
Penguin Books Ltd, 80 Strand, London WC2R 0RL, England
Penguin Ireland, 25 St. Stephen's Green, Dublin 2, Ireland (a division of Penguin Books Ltd)
Penguin Books Australia Ltd, 250 Camberwell Road, Camberwell, Victoria 3124, Australia
(a division of Pearson Australia Group Pty Ltd)
Penguin Books India Pvt Ltd, 11 Community Centre, Panchsheel Park, New Dehli –110 017, India
Penguin Group (NZ), 67 Apollo Drive, Mairangi Bay, Auckland 1311, New Zealand (a division of
Pearson New Zealand Ltd)
Penguin Books (South Africa) (Pty) Ltd, 24 Sturdee Avenue, Rosebank, Johannesburg 2196
South Africa

Penguin Books Ltd, Registered Offices:
80 Strand, London WC2R 0RL, England

First published in 2007 by Viking Penguin,
a member of Penguin Group (USA) Inc.

10 9 8 7 6 5 4 3 2 1

Map illustrations by Adrian Kitzinger

ISBN: 978–0–670–06352–9

Printed in the United States of America
Set in Berkeley Oldstyle with P22 Declaration
Designed by Daniel Lagin

For Andy

PREFACE

*A*aron Burr (1756–1836) stands apart from the other founders—then and now. He is remembered, first, as the man who shot and killed Alexander Hamilton; second, as a vice president turned traitor; and third, as a womanizer. Historians have favored "nation builders" George Washington, John Adams, and Thomas Jefferson, whose published papers are voluminous. Burr has been left chiefly in the hands of imaginative writers: popularizers of history, novelists, playwrights, producers of cheap gothic romances, and even a pornographer. This is just the beginning of an explanation for why Aaron Burr has been mishandled by students of history—and textbook writers—for almost two centuries.[1]

Non-historians have written biographies of Burr, but this book marks the first time a professional historian has undertaken to tell his life story. Oddly, even the most recent, and most respected, interpreters of the founding generation have unconsciously mimicked fictional portrayals of Burr. Historians have failed to do the legwork; that is, to read the bulk of Burr's papers on microfilm, scour old newspapers, and track down documents in archives.[2] For too long, prejudiced characterizations of Burr have been repeated as received wisdom. Burr has been called many things, in ascending order of dangerousness: mysterious, mentally unstable, and congenitally evil—a shallow opportunist devoid of political principles. Moralizing has substituted for historical analysis. And yet, despite all the vitriol thrown at Burr, he had many reliable friends and large numbers of supporters, something his detractors still find difficult to explain. During his lifetime, friends and foes alike recognized that Burr was a skilled politician and an enlightened thinker; this underscores why he was considered a genuine national leader and a dangerous opponent, and why he rose to the U.S. Senate and the vice presidency.

Unlike those founders who acted to secure their records in late life and who allowed aides to publicize their personal and political morals, Burr did not toot his own horn, nor did he defend himself with an eye to posterity. As his wife and daughter did not survive him, they could not do so either. Many of Burr's papers were lost in a shipwreck, and others were sold off, making a fuller reconstruction of his life difficult. Because of all that was said against him, and because he was, and is, admittedly, hard to know, attempting a fair assessment of Aaron Burr is a demanding task.

Many of the lies and exaggerations that obscure the real Burr focus on his relationship to Alexander Hamilton. Historians have been too trusting of Hamilton's portrait of Burr, discounting his partisan motives in blackening Burr's name. Only half of that story has been told. Hamilton, an extremely motivated political thinker, was also a master of backroom politics. He was known for his poison-tipped pen, viciously attacking anyone he believed stood in the way of his political dominance. When it came to his sense of Burr as a competent rival, first in New York politics and later in presidential politics, Hamilton overreacted. He systematically sought, over a period of many years, to ruin Burr's chances through insults, slights, and writing campaigns. The great irony is that Hamilton routinely accused Burr of lacking a moral compass, when no evidence exists that the self-possessed Burr ever insulted Hamilton.

The essential problem in Americans' understanding of the Burr-Hamilton relationship is that it has only been described to them in personal, pathological, or sexual terms. The relationship has been removed from politics, where it rightly belongs. To put it succinctly, it was not any issue relating to moral character, but Hamilton's aggressive style of politics that led to his duel with Burr. At the dueling ground itself, Hamilton gave Burr every indication that he intended to fire in earnest; not to waste his shot, as Hamilton apologists continue to insist to this day.

How can history have gotten Burr so wrong? I can offer several suggestions. First, Burr was ganged up on by politically powerful combinations during his lifetime, his morals attacked merely as a political dirty trick.

Next, he lacked a sympathetic posterity, whereas the other founders had legions of descendants responsible for celebratory publications. Finally, shoddy research over the years has plagued the study of both Burr the politician and Burr the man, reducing his legacy to oversimplifications, for which popular biographers are principally at fault. Writers tend to have an unconscious need to construct a narrative that features noble minds, courageous arms, and a foil (or black sheep) against whom the "good guys" are to be compared. The truth about most popular history is that even when it is not patriotically inspired, it is made up of dangerous shortcuts. As things stand, popular treatments disparaging Burr have proven quite seductive.[3]

History is not a bedtime story. It is a comprehensive engagement with often obscure documents and books no longer read—books shelved in old archives, and fragile pamphlets contemporaneous with the subject under study—all of which reflect a world view not ours. We cannot make eighteenth-century men and women "familiar" by endowing them and their families with the emotions we prefer to universalize; nor should we try to equate their politics with politics we understand. But this is what popular biographers do, and as a result, everything we think we know about Aaron Burr is untrue. It is time to start over.

ACKNOWLEDGMENTS

This book began because I was curious about scandalous trials in American history. I was eventually drawn to the scandal-bound Burr, who had been sketched many times, but whose mixed reputation has never been convincingly analyzed. I have had a lot of help along the way from other historians who desired a fresh study of Burr. As the editor of Burr's political correspondence, Mary-Jo Kline deserves my particular gratitude, because she and her team did a tremendous job in preparing two superb volumes and putting together the guide to the microfilm collection. Mary-Jo patiently fielded many queries, and gave me much useful advice. Talented editors are invaluable partners in historical scholarship.

Several institutions have funded my work, and afforded me access to some wonderful archives. I would like to thank John Hench and the staff at the American Antiquarian Society (AAS), in Worcester, Massachusetts, for granting me a Kate B. and Hall J. Peterson fellowship. Multiple trips to the AAS led to rare finds in their manuscript and early American newspaper collections. Though I might have been viewed as an enemy invading the tranquil retreat of Monticello, Daniel P. Jordan and the International Center for Jefferson Studies gave me a fellowship and greeted me warmly. The new Jefferson Library was a joy to work in. Other institutions that aided my research include the New-York Historical Society; the New York Public Library; the Special Collections adjoining the Alderman Library at the University of Virginia; the Huntington Library in San Marino, California; the Historical Society of Pennsylvania and Philadelphia Library Company;

the Rare Books and Special Collections, Princeton University Library; the Virginia Historical Society in Richmond, Virginia; and the Library of Congress in Washington, D.C.

Friends and fellow scholars generously shared their research. I begin by thanking the always obliging Barbara Oberg, editor of the Jefferson Papers at Princeton University. David B. Mattern, Senior Editor of the Papers of James Madison, kindly sent me an important letter dealing with Burr's filibuster. Cynthia D. Earman let me read her wonderful work on boardinghouse culture in Washington, D.C. I had several profitable conversations and e-mail exchanges with art historian Katherine C. Woltz, who is writing an original thesis on Burr's protégé John Vanderlyn. Roland Baumann addressed my questions about John Swanwick, and his work was particularly useful for sorting out the mysterious caricature, "A Peep into the Antifederal Club." Fellow early republican scholar Jeff Pasley discovered Matthew Livingston Davis's manuscript in the New-York Historical Society, which provided new insights into the election of 1800 and the relationship between Jefferson and Burr. Bruce Kirby, Manuscript Reference Librarian at the Library of Congress, was good enough to track down a letter about Burr and Humboldt's maps. And I especially appreciate Philip Lapsansky's willingness to share his research on Lenora Sansay, a fascinating woman who deserves her own biography.

One of the most enjoyable excursions in the course of writing this book was visiting Blennerhassett Island on the Ohio River, and meeting the historian Ray Swick, whose enthusiasm and generosity are unmatched. I appreciate, as well, a pair of research assistants who took the time to gather important materials from the Chicago Historical Society and Newberry Library: Nick Tate, a graduate student at the University of Tulsa, and Shannon Grady at Northwestern University. At the University of Tulsa's McFarlin Library, the energetic Andy Lupardus assisted in uncovering details relating to Catherine Thompson. Brian D. Hardison generously prepared the photograph of Burr's watch, and sent me copies of several Burr letters from his private collection. Finally, T. J. Stiles, a fellow biographer, kindly sent me an obscure newspaper article concerning Burr's death.

My deep appreciation extends to my literary agent, Geri Thoma, who carefully read and commented on the manuscript and helped at every stage of production. My editor at Viking Penguin, Wendy Wolf, had complete faith in the value of this project from the beginning, which kept me focused. She and her assistant Hilary Redmon offered very useful suggestions for manuscript revisions. I wish also to express thanks to David Waldstreicher and Peter Onuf, who read chapters and offered intellectual support; and to Michael Zuckerman at the University of Pennsylvania for inviting me to talk about the book-in-progress at the McNeil Center for Early American Studies.

This book is far better because of Andrew Burstein. I am lucky to have a partner who not only shares my interest in the world of books but also has been a perfect sparring partner as I engaged with the knotty political issues chronicled in this biography. As a Jefferson scholar and early American specialist, Andy played devil's advocate on a daily basis, encouraging me to refine arguments and improve the narrative. At the University of Tulsa, we have been afforded the time and resources to pursue our fascination with history and culture. I hope that this book will serve to highlight the value of the archive and the work of historians more generally.

CONTENTS

ILLUSTRATIONS

The College of New Jersey in 1776

Chapter One

A MAN OF PROMISING PARTS

> People are always looking for the man in the child without
> considering what he is before he becomes a man.
> —Jean-Jacques Rousseau, *Emile, or On Education* (1762)

In 1793–94, Gilbert Stuart, best known today for his unfinished likeness of George Washington, painted a portrait of a promising politician. There is something unconventional about this particular canvas: age and authority do not quite coincide. The perfectly proportioned face, its flawless skin rose-tinted and glowing, suggests a man in his early twenties. Only the receding hairline hints that he might be older. One other pronounced feature stands out: the large hazel eyes, with coal black pupils, that gaze intently from the canvas. (See the book's jacket for portrait.)

The man in the portrait is thirty-seven-year-old Senator Aaron Burr of New York. Two years earlier, he had come into office by defeating Philip Schuyler, a powerful, wealthy landholder twenty-three years his senior. Schuyler was deeply resentful about the unexpected turn of events. These two men could not have been more unalike: the elder was hulking and unapproachable, his victorious opponent not just younger but elegant and engaging.[1]

Appearances mattered in the politically tumultuous 1790s, and Burr's decision to commission the portrait marked more than the entry of a newcomer into the republican ruling class. Stuart's carefully composed image of Burr announced a new democratic ethos: none of the outward emblems of social status appears in the portrait. The youthful Burr is without a wig. His dress is remarkably plain: no lacy frills, no gold buttons, no richly dyed satin cloth. Stuart tellingly observed that his American clients demanded accurate and realistic representations of themselves—none of the costumes, insignia of office, and "Grand Manner" setting associated with British portraiture.[2]

Burr represented a new era. So-called "natural aristocrats" had stepped in, where before the Revolution only the traditional landed elite had stood. The new leadership core was composed of enlightened readers, disciples of an American nationalism, whose rise coincided with the adoption of the federal Constitution. Aaron Burr projected the image of a man of possibilities, a mirror of the energetic young nation that he represented in the Senate. At the same time, the political world that Burr entered was fiercely competitive, as a new partisan climate emerged that relied on nasty public attacks, the circulation of vicious rumors, and occasionally led to duels. A young man of promise could just as easily provoke envy and anger, if he became too prominent, or was perceived as threatening other politicians, especially those who already were in power.

The new ruling elite consciously fashioned themselves as suitable leaders. Though the image of defiant children rebelling against the "mother country" had been a seductive metaphor during the long war for American independence, celebrating youthful rebellion was a less compelling refrain once the new United States government tried to shore up its symbols of national authority. Indeed, though the Revolution had been waged by young men, the act of nation building became enshrined as the province of fathers. As George Washington assumed the presidency in 1789, he was styled the "friend and father" of his country. Today we still idolize the founders as austere and wise, and long past their days of youthful excess and indulgence. Burr, in contrast, is almost always portrayed as a man who still exudes a romantic vitality.[3]

Stuart was not alone in fashioning an image of Burr that emphasized his youth. As he grew older, Burr was pleased to recall several childish escapades from which later biographers took their cue. Thus, he was often described as defiant and mischievous. A favorite story he told concerned the time he tried at the age of ten to run off to sea. He had outmaneuvered his uncle and guardian, who then climbed aboard ship to fetch his errant ward. Hoisting himself to the top of the ship's mast, the lithe young boy skillfully negotiated a truce on his terms: His uncle agreed to let him return home without a beating. Here was a childhood memory to preview his future as a courtroom attorney—that is, as a master of rhetorical persuasion, active and tireless, who was prepared to go to great lengths (or heights) in order to gain the upper hand.[4]

Burr's unusual relationship with his older wife Theodosia Prevost (she was ten years his senior) further reinforced the notion of his perpetual youthfulness. By marrying a mature woman, he appeared to have skipped over the "normal" stages of development. The contrast between them must have made him appear even younger. Burr was considered for the vice presidency as early as 1792, to contest the incumbent vice president, John Adams, nearly a quarter century his elder; but his name was ultimately dropped because of his relative youth. As his political career went forward, Burr surrounded himself with a corps of energetic younger men. They, too, celebrated his youthful exploits, still praising him in 1804 for having joined the army as a mere "boy," and standing in the forefront of those who "drew their swords at the opening of the revolution." The "boy" was a man of forty-eight when his "little band" issued this reminder of his adolescent feats.[5]

Youth, age, and appearance had political significance, conditioning how public and private character was judged and measured. Burr's youthfulness was relevant, as personality itself became a more crucial quality in shaping electoral politics in the nascent American democracy. Burr became known as a man who achieved a lot early in life; his precocity set him apart. In that sense, his childhood had lasting consequences.

"A LITTLE DIRTY NOISY BOY"

Aaron Burr was born in Newark, New Jersey, on February 6, 1756, in the middle of winter. His mother, Esther Burr, recorded in her journal that he arrived "unexpectedly." Presumably, she had wanted her husband to be present for the birth, but it had "pleased God" that her son should make his entrance when his father was away from home. She found this birth a "gloomy" event, enduring labor "destitute of Earthly friends—no Mother—no Husband."[6]

Burr's family was a rather unusual, and extremely tight-knit, family. His father, Aaron Burr, Sr., had been educated at Yale. A Presbyterian minister since 1736, he was now president of the College of New Jersey (today's Princeton University). On assuming his duties in 1748, only three other men in the American colonies were serving as presidents of colleges. Despite his small stature, the senior Burr was known for preaching in a "powerful manner" to the large flock that gathered at his meetinghouse. His wife described her husband's performance this way: "nature seems to bubble up and overflow into expression."[7]

Burr's mother was a remarkable woman. She was the daughter of the Reverend Jonathan Edwards, the most influential theologian in America, and herself an independent spirit. One contemporary said she possessed an "unaffected, natural freedom," and that "her genius was more than common." She had "a lively, sprightly imagination, a quick and penetrating discernment," the same observer added. "She knew how to be facetious and sportive, without trespassing on the bounds of decorum." The Burrs did not fit the typical profile of a dour Calvinist family. Esther Burr displayed a passion for life. She was not shy about expressing her opinions, nor could she be categorized as a retiring matron. She was deeply religious, without being stuffy, a clever conversationalist with a mind of her own.[8]

Esther's detailed journal, almost 300 pages long, was filled with witty comments on religion, literature, and politics. In these pages, she defended her sex, in one case opposing a tutor at the college for making disparaging comments about women. She found it appalling that the man had insisted that women were incapable of understanding "anything so cool and rational as friendship." She would hear none of it, noting that she had "retorted several severe things upon him," which made him flustered and caused him to go off in a huff. Her confidence was unusual, but not out of character. She came from a proud family, and her father had closely supervised the education of every one of his children. She could be quick to act—it took her only five days to accept her future husband's proposal of marriage. She was twenty, he was thirty-six, but she willingly left Massachusetts for a new life in New Jersey.[9]

The Burrs were living in Newark at the time Esther gave birth to her son. Aaron had a sister, Sally, who was two years older. By the end of his first year, when the college building was nearing completion, the family moved to Princeton. Esther Burr wrote with a rare candor in her journal, saying that "Aaron is a little dirty noisy boy" and "very different from Sally in almost everything. He has more sprightliness than Sally & most say he is handsomer, but not so good tempered." Her childrearing methods were rigid and unyielding; her "mischievous" little son was "very resolute and requires a good governor to bring him to terms." Physical punishment was readily applied to both children.[10]

At the same time, Burr's mother looked at her son as special—a survivor. At eight months, he had become gravely ill. She had little hope, but somehow he recovered. She wrote powerful lines in her journal: "I look on the Child as one given to me from the dead. What obligations are we laid under to bring up this Child in a peculiar manner for God?" Before he was old enough to talk, he was thought to be a fortunate soul.[11]

The Burr household would not continue to be so blessed. On September 4, 1757, Aaron Burr, Sr., rode to Elizabethtown, New Jersey, to preach the governor's funeral sermon. When he returned the following day, he became seriously ill, and never summoned enough energy to leave his bed. He died on September 23. A few weeks later, Esther recorded that "my little son has been sick . . . and has been brought to the brink of the grave." But little Aaron survived once more. After her husband's death, Esther's own father, the Reverend Jonathan Edwards, moved to Princeton to replace him as president of the college; yet he was next, struck down by smallpox in March 1758. Though Esther Burr and her children had all been inoculated, she barely outlasted her father, dying on April 7. If that was not enough tragedy for one family, Sarah Edwards, Esther's mother, came to Princeton to collect the family's belongings and to take charge of her grandchildren, when she, too, became ill with dysentery, and died on October 2. In little over a year, Burr had lost his parents and his grandparents. Aaron and his sister Sally were now orphans.[12]

"AND LEARNS BRAVELY"

Burr left few memories about his childhood, and he wrote nothing about his parents. Precocity and perseverance—achieving well beyond one's age or assumed capacity—nevertheless marked his youth. In everything he later wrote to his own daughter, he voiced an urgency, intensity, and insistence on her "determination and perseverance in every laudable under-taking." His sense of personal calling and inner resolve give us some clue about his early education. Time or talents could not be wasted. Nothing could be left to chance. Burr's urgency, a desire to excel at an early age, reveals something essential about his childhood.[13]

A family friend, Dr. William Shippen of Philadelphia, temporarily cared for the two orphans. In 1760, two years after the death of his parents, Aaron and his sister were placed under the guardianship of their uncle, Timothy Edwards, Esther's younger brother. The two children suddenly found themselves in a large alternative family. In addition to Aaron and Sally, Timothy and his new wife Rhoda Ogden gained custody of all of Timothy's surviving siblings. As it turned out, death had dissolved two families—Burr's immediate family, and that of his grandparents. In the re-constituted Edwards household, presided over by Timothy, Burr was the youngest, surrounded by five aunts and uncles, who ranged in age from twenty to ten years old. Almost immediately, Timothy Edwards's brood in-creased again. He took in two additional charges, his wife's younger brothers, Matthias and Aaron Ogden.[14]

Death is a potent reminder that life is short and the future is unpredict-able. Burr learned this lesson early. Competing for recognition in a crowded household, he grew in determination. When Burr was seven, his uncle Pierpont Edwards described him as an avid scholar, writing that he was "hearty, goes to school, *and learns bravely*." Burr's most vivid childhood memories curiously focused on episodes in which he ran away from home. The young Burr was always eager to prove himself to his family.[15]

Burr's family background reinforced his commitment to education. The exacting theologian Jonathan Edwards had professed a personally de-manding religious faith to those around him. The grandfather's "awakened" gospel commanded a full knowledge of salvation at an early age. The theo-logian had been openly criticized in 1740 for "frightening poor innocent children, with talk of hell fire, and damnation." But he withstood this criti-cism: to hold onto naive views, Edwards believed, only left children vulnerable to suffering an eternity in hell. Children were not simply sinners in God's eyes; they were intelligent beings capable of persuasion and reflection. Jon-athan Edwards treated his own children—including Esther and Timothy—as pupils, instructing them according to their "age and capacity," training their agile minds as quickly as possible. With death looming large, there was a real urgency to save children before it was too late. It seems likely, then, that Timothy Edwards shared the same urgency about education as his father and instructed Aaron and his sister accordingly.[16]

Burr's childhood was unusual in another sense. Though they died when he was little more than an infant, he could read testimonials to his parents' uncommon virtues. In death, his father was eulogized for his "industry, integrity, strict honesty, and pure undissembled piety." He was a Christian man of action—scrupulously honest and endowed with an unblemished moral character. Such glowing memorials offer a startling contrast to his son's eventual reputation, for the promising Aaron Burr would be tarred and feathered in historic memory as a ruthlessly ambitious, dishonest, dissembling public official, and a hedonist in his private life.[17]

Timothy Edwards raised Burr to follow in his father's footsteps. There was little social mobility in the eighteenth century, and few young men imagined selecting a career that was different from their fathers. The rather remarkable achievements of Benjamin Franklin, moving in leaps and bounds from his father's status of tradesman to that of international celebrity and one of the wealthiest men in America, were rare indeed.[18]

Aaron Senior and Junior both grew up as orphans of means. Aaron's father had been the youngest of the thirteen children of Daniel Burr, a wealthy and respected landowner in Fairfield, Connecticut. His father died when he was six, and his father's patrimony allowed him to attend Yale College. Burr Senior left his namesake an inheritance of £3,679, which was used to support his son's education. Neither Aaron truly knew his father, though each knew of his father's reputation as a gentleman. They understood, as young men, that they were expected to become "men of letters." One chose the church, the other the bar, but both honed their manners and skills of persuasion so as to maintain their standing among the elite of society.[19]

KITH AND KIN

Burr spent his first two years under Timothy Edwards's roof in Stockbridge, Massachusetts, and the remainder of his early years in Elizabethtown, New Jersey. Edwards appears to have been a devoted guardian. In 1762, upon returning to New Jersey, he took up the practice of law. He was clearly prosperous enough to support his growing family, as he and his wife would eventually have fifteen children. His uncle nevertheless made sure that young Aaron gained a solid education. He took the unusual step of hiring a Princeton graduate, Tapping Reeve, to supervise the instruction of both Aaron and Sally. Reeve was appointed master at the local Presbyterian academy, Edwards served on the board of visitors, and Aaron enrolled at the age of seven.[20]

Situated along the river of the same name, Elizabethtown was a fairly prosperous colonial town. It was later the home of William Livingston, longtime governor of New Jersey, who served from 1776 until his death in 1790. He had been a close friend of Aaron's father, giving the eulogy at his funeral. A native New Yorker, Livingston was a member of the one of the largest landholding "manor" families in the Empire State. Livingston was an avid supporter of the College of New Jersey (Princeton), and the first classes of the institution were held in Elizabethtown. Not unlike many of the other elite members of the community, he sided with the "New Light" Presbyterians, or "Dissenters," as the branch that followed Jonathan Edwards were called. The Elizabethtown Presbyterian Church became a symbol of the town's Revolutionary as well as dissenting religious heritage.[21]

Presbyterianism, the college, and a conservative political ruling class represented the three pillars of the social order in Elizabethtown before and after the Revolutionary War. Burr's stepmother was Rhoda Ogden Edwards. Her father, Robert Ogden, was a leading member of the political and religious elite in Elizabethtown. His sons, Robert, Matthias, and Aaron, all attended Princeton, fought for the patriots' cause, and went on to practice law—taking the same professional path as their cousin Aaron Burr.[22]

In this small but influential Revolutionary community, Burr made lasting connections with the sons of the town fathers. Matthias and Aaron Ogden, who were close to him in age, grew up in the same household. They were more like brothers than cousins. Another boyhood friend from Elizabethtown was Jonathan Dayton (Dayton shared Burr's youthful ambition, and would later be the youngest delegate sent to the Constitutional Convention in 1787). The bond of friendship among Burr, Dayton, and the Ogden boys was sealed when Matthias married Hannah Dayton, Jonathan's sister. As two of the most prosperous families in town, the Daytons and Ogdens occupied the best pews in the Presbyterian Church. Dayton attended Princeton, which completed the inner ring of Burr's boyhood band.[23]

It was in Elizabethtown that Burr may have first crossed paths with his future political rival Hamilton. Both spent time there in 1773, as teenagers. Burr was living in Princeton that year, but regularly visited Elizabethtown, pursuing a leisurely pace of reading while eagerly socializing. Hamilton, recently arrived from his native West Indies in order to attend college, enrolled in the Presbyterian Academy, the same grammar school in which Burr had studied under the tutelage of Tapping Reeve. Here is where Hamilton prepared himself for Princeton, to which he applied a short time later. Once he passed the entrance exam, he proceeded to offend the college president and several trustees by demanding too many exemptions from the rules of promotion and class standing. His request denied, the self-confident Hamilton turned to New York's King's College (later Columbia), where he commenced study in late 1773 or early 1774.[24]

Elizabethtown was a small community, and Burr most likely retained some connection to the local academy from which he had graduated and where Hamilton studied before moving on to King's. There is no extant record of their having met here. But it is more than idle speculation to consider what might have happened if Hamilton had matriculated at Princeton rather than Columbia. Might Hamilton have looked at Burr differently if, under impressionable circumstances, the two had joined the same college club and shared a fraternal bond? That is, would their relationship have been altered if Hamilton had been one of that influential coterie of early Princeton alumni who invariably relied on each other for political and personal favors in later years?

NASSAU HALL

Burr submitted an application to the College of New Jersey at the age of eleven. Colonial colleges were more like today's preparatory schools, and Princeton's student body had young men of all ages. Though he had the proper academic qualifications, the trustees and faculty still rejected him because of his age. He spent the next two years studying the college curriculum on his own, and in 1769 reapplied for examination and requested to enter as a junior. As with Hamilton's later request, the trustees turned him down, offering to admit him as a sophomore. At thirteen, Burr was still four years younger than most of his classmates, and his youth set him apart. His college nickname was "Little Burr," affectionately mocking his unusual precocity as much as his small stature.[25]

When the college's Nassau Hall was completed in 1756, the impressive Georgian-style structure was the largest building in British North America. Three stories high, with sixty rooms, Nassau Hall included everything under one roof—library, chapel, dormitory rooms, and recitation halls. The college was founded as a non-denominational institution. The initial plan for the school was to train "New Light" ministers, but by the time Burr arrived there in 1769, the curriculum had changed. It was no longer a training ground for ministers alone but a place for inspiring young men with enlightened ideals.[26]

Leading these reforms was John Witherspoon, the new president of the college. In person, the Presbyterian divine hardly cut a striking figure. One visitor described him as an "intolerably homely Scotchman," and he was known for his personal eccentricities, such as constantly changing the position of his hands and feet, and pulling his large eyebrows when excited. He always dressed in his clerical gown when he preached at Princeton, and looked like a plump medieval monk. Although his fame derived from his powerful oratory, Witherspoon's heavy Scottish burr made him almost incomprehensible to those in his audience who were unfamiliar with the accent.[27]

As a proponent of "common sense" philosophy, Witherspoon was the embodiment of the Scottish Enlightenment. He believed that the main purpose of education was to cultivate common sense—to join thought to action—and to promote virtuous actions for the improvement of society. His curriculum stressed the practical subjects of history, science, geography, French, and English composition. Whether lecturing on moral philosophy or writing advice to the lovelorn in the *Pennsylvania Magazine,* Witherspoon advanced an enlightened pedagogy that viewed ethical behavior as a product of human nature rather than the gift of divine grace. His lecture style seemed unconventional to certain observers. He was said to resemble an eloquent lawyer rather than a fire-and-brimstone Presbyterian preacher.[28]

Burr found himself deeply immersed in his studies. He and his classmates at Princeton were required to recite in geography, mathematics, and history every day, and were expected to compose and memorize an oration every other week. Burr studied incessantly, up to eighteen hours a day, and like his fellow students, he was restricted to his room during long study periods, forbidden to go out for more than ten minutes at a time.[29]

What might appear a harsh or repressive regime for a young teen nevertheless offered clear advantages over other colonial colleges. Princeton embraced the idea of "liberty" far more readily than other institutions. Unlike the presidents at Harvard and Yale, Witherspoon supported the liberal policy of opening the library stacks to the students; he encouraged curiosity, while adding titles on contemporary and social affairs. He allowed students to select their own oration topics, placing less emphasis on Latin oratory, preferring instead speeches on current issues. While his students continued to wear caps and gowns in the Old World tradition, under Witherspoon's direction, new ideas about society and politics flourished.[30]

The colonial college experience involved more than a monkish existence. Students frequently engaged in boyish pranks. Philip Fithian, a member of Burr's graduating class, recorded in his diary the kinds of shenanigans common on campus. Occasionally his chums might steal "a plump fat Hen" from the neighborhood, or parade prostitutes across the campus, to upset the strait-laced faculty. And some ingenious lads displayed their penchant for discovery by "ogling Women with the Telescope."[31]

The most important socializing occurred in the college clubs. The College of New Jersey had two clubs at this time: the American Whig Society and the Cliosophic Society. Burr was unusual because he belonged to both clubs—the Whigs, until he switched to the Clios. The clubs were what one scholar has called the "college within the college," offering male camaraderie and competition. Far more than the classroom, clubs polished character, encouraged verbal contests, and created intense, highly emotional fraternal bonds.[32]

Amid the pre-Revolutionary political excitement, the clubs served the unique purpose of creating a proving ground for future American statesmen. A president (Madison), a vice president (Burr), several Supreme Court justices, senators, and congressmen all came from Princeton's fraternal ranks. There is evidence to suggest that college clubs laid the foundation for later political parties. In direct contrast to the dangerous portrait of "factions," which Madison famously wrote about in *Federalist* No. 10 in 1787, clubs presented a positive model for male association. United by feelings of brotherhood, the Whigs and Clios shared a set of principles, while they engaged in a public rivalry. Much like the informal rules that sustained the partisan political culture that emerged in the 1790s, club members in the 1770s were bound by secret confidences, a code of honor, and rules of polite deportment. At Princeton, Philip Fithian astutely described the club style as a "secret polite manner."[33]

Burr's popularity is apparent from an incident that his friends in later years recounted: Taking his turn as the club president, he sat in the customary armchair, one so big that the diminutive Burr had a hard time keeping his two elbows balanced on the wooden arms. A professor arrived at the meeting late, and the good-natured club president spontaneously poked fun at him for being tardy, upsetting the normal teacher-pupil chain of command. Burr was the sort of fellow, at least at this stage in his life, who could turn the tables on his professor and get away with it.[34]

The clubs fostered rivalry, which was, unmistakably, preparation for political battles to come. In one typical foray of 1771, Hugh Henry Brackenridge, later known nationally for his satirical talent, directed his venom against one Samuel Spring, considered "the Poet-Laureate of Clio." Brackenridge engaged in an unremitting barrage of ridicule, calling the college as a whole a "den of scribing boys and wicked men." He mocked Spring for his lack of literary finesse and his caustic temper. Brackenridge charged that Spring was both childish and boring, because Spring was trying to "put a stop to Whiggish writing by roaring, snoring, swearing, and fighting." Spring had challenged Brackenridge to a fight for insulting him. Then the cowardly poet had run to a tutor for safety, and was rescued just as the fight was about to begin.[35]

"MY DEAR LITTLE FELLOW"

Burr was very much a part of this club world. It was the camaraderie, much more than the spirited competition, that drew him. In 1772, a "brother" Clio and classmate, Moses Allen, characterized club friendships in a letter to Burr. He mentioned the plight of Samuel McCorkle, whom he described as "much dejected" at the idea of graduating, for the very thought of "leaving the Society kills him." Allen stressed the commitment, the benevolence, which fellow Clios gamely upheld: "We, being brothers, should submit to some inconveniences, for the peace and happiness of each other." Allen openly expressed his affection: "I long, My Dear little fellow, (pardon the expression of fondness) for an opportunity to requite your kindness, and make you sensible of my tender regard."[36]

In other fraternal societies, as in the Cliosophic club, there surfaced, according to one member, a "relish for friendship" that was "like a violent appetite." Luther Martin and William Paterson, both Clios, confessed their strong feelings for classmate John MacPherson. As Martin put it, "few brothers were ever bound together by stronger bonds of affection." Paterson maintained a correspondence with MacPherson after graduation, pestering his friend for more letters: "He knows I love him, he knows I am pleased to hear of his good fortune . . . why is he so remiss in answering my last letter?" Both men gossiped about friends in their correspondence. MacPherson, for his part, shared the scandalous story of a classmate who had been forced to the altar. Having "made free" with a doctor's daughter, MacPherson wrote, his friend had sadly suffered the fate for his "known virility."[37]

This kind of male banter was a crucial element in solidifying club relations. Though he graduated Princeton in 1763, earning a master's degree in 1766, Paterson was a permanent fixture in the life of the Clios right up to the Revolution. His role as unofficial mentor to younger members was unique. By the time he took Burr under his wing, there was an eleven-year gap between graduate mentor and student protégé. Paterson shared compositions with Burr, and wrote gossipy letters when Burr went home, gently mocking his handwriting, and giving the youth practical advice about speaking too fast. In one letter, Paterson claimed that Burr's "hand" was too "sleek, & lady-like," and that anyone who saw a letter addressed by him would assume a woman had written it.[38]

In this way, sexual innuendo was often a part of club members' playful prose. In the same letter in which he ridiculed Burr's feminine hand, Paterson, who remained a bachelor for fourteen years after his graduation, compared his own "scribbling" to masturbation: "When the state of scribbling seizes me I hardly know when to stop. The fits indeed seldom comes upon me; but when it does, though I sit down with the desire to be short, yet my letter immeasurably slides into length & swells perhaps into an enormous size. I know not how it happens, but on such occasions I have a knack of throwing myself out on paper, that I cannot readily get the letter off." This punning exchange was not unusual. The most popular English novelist of the day, Laurence Sterne, author of the risqué, multivolume *Tristram Shandy* (1760–67), routinely made sexual allusions to "rash jerks" and "squirts," and "spurting ink about on thy table and thy books."[39]

In the Clio Society, Burr was fondly called "My Dear little fellow" by Allen, and was made a confidant of Paterson's sexual fantasies. Theirs was a male-centered world: men like Paterson, who clearly preferred the company of men to women, fostered platonic friendships through their literary exercises, combining witty banter and sexual gossip. Intense same-sex friendships temporarily substituted for the emotional ties that these same young men would go on to forge with women when they were of an age to marry and have children.

Young men's banter was not a temporary phenomenon—it stayed with Burr's cohort as they went off to war and eventually sought political careers. From his Revolutionary exploits to his quest for national office, Aaron Burr would always be associated with intense fraternal bonds, and his name linked to a kind of hypersexuality that conveniently explained his appeal to young and politically aggressive men. The same label would ultimately be used to tar him as a devious and untrustworthy libertine—and traitor.

"ON HONOR"

In the letter Burr received from Moses Allen, another phrase stands out: "Be happy in life and glorious in death." The subject was honor. This friend was alluding to Burr's oration "On Honor," delivered in 1772 to his classmates. William Paterson had generously lent his own oration on this subject, from which Burr cribbed freely. In Burr's version (as in Paterson's), the pacifistic ideas of the Scottish Enlightenment somehow merged with a prophetic militancy. Burr's rather undemocratic theme was that "Men of action," as a political elect, were the divinely called and naturally gifted leaders of society. These specially chosen men of action "nourish those hidden sparks of genius . . . so capable of enlightening the world." As enlightened prophets given a calling, such men of honor deserved to occupy the public stage; they combined noble ambition with discretion. Doing everything to avoid the stigma of dishonor, they even, in Burr's words, concealed their "natural defects" from the "scorn and ridicule of the less honorable part of mankind." The teenage Burr fully agreed with Witherspoon's assumptions that men of genius and action could become *"invincible."*[40]

The concluding thought in Burr's oration is worth repeating, because it takes as its subject the practice of dueling. The parable concerns a certain Colonel Gardiner, a man of action who best displayed the virtues of "the Christian hero and the true warlike man." Gardiner refused to engage in a duel with a man who had challenged him on a trivial matter. "With all the boldness and intrepidity of a warrior and all the godlike reverence of the Christian," Burr explained, the colonel briskly replied to his rash antagonist: "You know . . . that I have courage to fight with a feeble man but I am afraid to sin against almighty God."[41]

What is striking about this passage, besides its reference to dueling, is Burr's selection of the qualities he feels are suited to a political leader. Colonel Gardiner embodied manly courage, common sense, and Christian heroism. Gardiner's reason and respect for God informed his sense of honor, enabling his self-respect, yet he refused to engage in a senseless duel. Manly dignity overrode brute aggression. Honor was never simply a matter of revenge over a personal grievance. Rather, it was meant to comprise one's public duty, in following at once the dictates of reason and a higher moral law.

This Christian martial spirit and Burr's faith in common sense were nurtured at Princeton, where in 1770, students openly joined in public protests against the British Parliament. In support of the boycott of British goods, Princetonians denounced tea and textiles. The graduating class of 1770 made homespun their choice of apparel for commencement. In 1774, after Burr had graduated, students would take even bolder action, burning the Massachusetts royal governor Thomas Hutchison in effigy, before gathering the college's store of tea and setting it afire. By February 1774, Princeton students had formed their own militia. And in 1775, as Burr and Matthias Ogden headed to Boston to join the Continental Army, many of their former classmates left college in droves to join the New Jersey militia.[42]

MARKS OF DESTINY

In his speech on honor, Burr did not contemplate what happened when bold and intrepid Christian warriors and statesmen faced disappointment or failure. What should occur if one of the elect was denied the public stage that he truly deserved? What if his reputation could not be preserved, despite his repeat attempts to "conceal his natural defects" from the ridicule of the masses?

During his last oration as an undergraduate, Burr explored this dilemma. His commencement address, "Building Castles in the Air," was a secular jeremiad against the dangers of wild dreams and far-fetched schemes. His mentor William Paterson reported favorably on Burr's performance to another classmate: "Our young friend Burr made a graceful appearance; he was excelled by none, except perhaps Bradford"—that is, William Bradford, destined to be George Washington's second attorney general.[43]

Many years later, Dr. Benjamin Rush, a signer of the Declaration of Independence and another graduate of Princeton, remembered Burr's "elegant oration" differently. Thinking back from the perspective of 1807, when Burr was standing trial for treason, the wild dreams and far-fetched schemes seemed to have augured ill. "There is often something said or done by men in their youth that marks their destiny," Rush told John Adams, as he listed every political defeat in Burr's career. "To be unfortunate," Rush observed, "is to be imprudent." He imagined signs of future missteps in the ancient oration.[44]

But in 1772, Burr was neither a tragic figure nor a fallen angel. He was imbued with heroic ideals and the duty of leadership. At this point, he still considered that he would follow his father's calling and enter the ministry. So he spent an additional year of study at Princeton, and then pursued a rigorous regime of theological training with the Presbyterian divine Joseph Bellamy, accomplishing all of this before he reached the age of twenty. Burr left college at a proud moment, with the support of friends and family.

Looking back on Burr's early life, Rush's comment is nonetheless a telling reminder of how memory clouds a clear understanding of childhood. Looking for the man in the child, as Jean-Jacques Rousseau put it, Rush forgot the young man he once knew. He failed to remember Aaron Burr as a boy of sixteen, plainly marked for success.

John Trumbull's *The Death of General Montgomery in the Attack on Quebec, December 31, 1775* (1786)

Chapter Two

TO CONCERT WITH
MY BROTHER OFFICERS

All things are mortal, but the warriors fame;
This lives eternal, in the mouths of men.
> —Hugh Henry Brackenridge,
> "The Death of General Montgomery" (1777)

There remains a special reverence for the soldier. . . .
War itself . . . has something sublime about it.
> —Immanuel Kant, *Critique of Judgment* (1790)

John Trumbull's *Death of General Montgomery in the Attack on Quebec, December 31, 1775* (1786), is certainly one of the most famous of the Revolutionary War paintings. General Richard Montgomery, Burr's commander, falls languidly into the arms of a devoted aide. Before him lie the bodies of two of his officers, one of whom is still clutching his sword as he stretches across the lifeless remains of his brother officer. Darkening clouds hover above the fallen, and dramatically announce their glorious deaths. For some reason, Trumbull decided to paint Burr's close friend Matthias Ogden into the scene, where Burr should have been. Ogden, earlier wounded, was not there as Montgomery fell. But Burr was.[1]

Now the story gets even more intriguing. Nine years before Trumbull's painting, and less than two years after Montgomery's death, Princetonian

Hugh Henry Brackenridge had praised his classmate Aaron Burr as the hero of the scene. In Brackenridge's well-known poem, "The Death of General Montgomery, in the Storming of the City of Quebec," it is Burr who, after the initial attack, discovers what remains of the commander. He falls upon Montgomery's body, embraces and kisses the corpse. And it is Burr who hoists the martyred general's onto his shoulders, to bring the body back for burial.[2]

In his poem, Brackenridge expresses the passion that surrounded the general's death. He has Burr espy John MacPherson and Jacob Cheesman (the two officers slain, along with Montgomery, in Trumbull's painting). Gazing down at the once graceful MacPherson, Burr is made to lament the loss of this man's "comely beauty, ravishing the heart." Brackenridge wished to recover the intensity of fraternal feeling that was commonly evoked by his college peers. It was the same MacPherson who had once captured the hearts of students William Paterson and Luther Martin.[3]

Montgomery marched into history after leading the 1775 invasion of Canada, but it was in death that he became the foremost hero and martyr of the American Revolution. In the process, Burr, too, achieved "warrior's fame" (to use Brackenridge's term) as news spread of his role in the siege of Quebec. The Continental Congress commended the young captain when it appropriated funds to commission a monument to General Montgomery. In fact, for a while, the clamor over Burr the survivor nearly rivaled the strains of mourning over Montgomery. General David Wooster, another member of the Canada expedition, sent an emissary to Congress, who spread the news of Burr's bravery. Princeton classmate and member of Congress William Bradford, Jr., wrote to Burr of his battlefield performance: "'Tis said you behaved well—you behaved gallantly. I never doubted but you would distinguish yourself, and your praise is now in every man's mouth."[4]

That Burr's accomplishment was lost to public memory in less than a decade, when Trumbull's painting was first exhibited, tells us something important about Burr's military career. A "warrior's fame" was not "immortal," as the poet preferred to tell it; it was, in fact, highly politicized. Though Bradford had told Burr that he would soon receive a promotion for his action, he was wrong. Two years passed before Burr was promoted.

During those two years, the war changed. At first, volunteers like Burr rushed to fight, inspired by what the French called a *rage militaire*—a "passion for arms." Zealous devotion to the patriots' cause reached its peak in the early stages of the war. As the conflict progressed, Commander in Chief George Washington saw generals come and go, and he found himself defending his military reputation as often as he was defending his country. In this new political environment, factions formed around competing generals, and the young men who were tied to these generals advanced their careers by fighting duels, spreading gossip, and riding on the coattails of their commanding officer. Burr soon realized that his college ideal of "Christian heroism" was no more than a fantasy, and that backbiting and malicious public attacks could ruin an officer's reputation.[5]

Often pictured as a courtier, Burr in fact was quite the opposite. He cultivated an independent style of leadership, determined to find solutions, without being beholden to others. He believed that audacity could be a virtue, as it was for General Montgomery; but at the same time, he was critical of the overblown demonstrations of ego he saw others use to advance themselves. And, probably because he tasted war—and received accolades—earlier than many of his glory-seeking peers, he understood sooner than most how quickly military valor could disappear into the morass of political infighting.

FORTUNE FAVORS THE AUDACIOUS

When Burr graduated from Princeton, he was uncertain about a career. In 1772, his good friend and fellow Clio Samuel Spring urged him to answer the "prayer" of his parents and enter the ministry. Spring was intent on becoming a clergyman, as were many of their classmates. Tarrying in Princeton one more year, in the fall of 1773, Burr did what was expected of him: he headed to Bethlehem, Connecticut, to train with the Reverend Joseph Bellamy, a fire-and-brimstone preacher like Burr's grandfather, the Reverend Jonathan Edwards. As he had at Princeton, he again adopted an intensive course of study. But after six months, he changed his mind, writing to his uncle Timothy that he now wished to pursue a legal career. His sister Sally had married their former tutor, Tapping Reeve, who would become a leading legal scholar. Burr now agreed to read law with his new brother-in-law, and make his home with the couple in Litchfield.[6]

He was restless. News of the colonial protests in Boston reached him in Litchfield, along with reports on the recently convened Continental Congress. Upon learning of the battles of Lexington and Concord in April 1775, he excitedly wrote to his friend Matthias Ogden in Elizabethtown. He was ready to join the army, he said, and he pleaded with Ogden to pack his belongings and accompany him to New England. Yet several more months passed until the two young men abandoned their studies for the life of a soldier. That August, they arrived in Cambridge, Massachusetts, along with 16,000 other untested volunteers. It was there that Burr learned of the expedition to Canada.[7]

Benedict Arnold urged an invasion of Canada through Maine—the infamous traitor was as yet a patriotic hero. In spring 1775, the Connecticut colonel had carried out a raid on a British fort in St. Johns, Quebec, which suddenly created the possibility that Americans would engage in an offensive war. At first, the Continental Congress hesitated to back such a daring plan, but it soon agreed to support a full-scale preemptive strike against the British in Canada. That summer, Arnold began gathering recruits in New England for a long trek through Maine to Quebec. Meanwhile, General Richard Montgomery, that same autumn, initiated the invasion of the sparsely populated Canadian province, securing the Continental Army its first major victories. After capturing two British forts, and forcing Montreal to surrender, Montgomery headed for the last crucial outpost in Canada: Quebec, where he planned to join forces with Arnold and his men.[8]

Arnold's expedition to Quebec began with much fanfare. One thousand volunteers arrived in Newburyport, Massachusetts, and set sail on September 19 for the Kennebec River, in Maine, where they would begin their march northward. Burr and Ogden were there. On the Sabbath before their departure, Burr's pal Samuel Spring gave a rousing sermon in the First Presbyterian Church in Newburyport. Displaying their flying colors, soldiers paraded into the vestibule and formed two lines; then, the six-foot-tall chaplain passed the rows of gallant men, as they presented their arms and drums rolled in a solemn but jubilant procession. Burr had written of something similar in one of his college essays, and now his earlier fantasy materialized before his eyes: he felt the rapturous sensations of martial music and religious devotion animate men with the glow of honor and an ardor for daring enterprise.[9]

Following the service, Spring, Arnold, and several of the officers, most likely including Burr, asked to visit the tomb of the British evangelist

George Whitefield. Burr's father had been a friend and supporter of White-field when he preached in the colonies. The minister's son surely understood how the dead could inspire the living. Requesting that the sexton remove the lid of the coffin, the men discovered that little remained of the great itinerate preacher; there was only dust, and remnants of clothing. Taking up Whitefield's collar and wristbands, they cut the fabric into pieces and divided it among themselves. Possessing this religious relic, the officers turned the expedition into a quasi-religious crusade.[10]

Burr and Ogden were just two of countless young volunteers taking part in Arnold's expedition. Beginning what contemporaries likened to Hannibal's crossing of the Alps, Arnold and his men embarked on a 350-mile trek through the Maine wilderness. When they finally came within reach of Quebec in November 1775, over one third of Arnold's men were gone: an entire battalion had turned back, due mostly to illness and food shortages, and the survivors, after a harrowing six-week march, verged on starvation.[11]

Better built than his slight and fragile friend, Ogden worried that Burr might not withstand the hardships of the journey. Family and friends had sent him letters before he left that were filled with similar warnings, pleading with him to forego the trip. He could be excused from the expedition, as one friend advised, "without any risk of being reported timid." After his thirty-five-mile march to Newburyport, Burr wrote to his sister, and assured her that he was none the worse for wear; he wanted to convince her and his family that he "was equal to the undertaking." He had no intention of em-barrassing himself, and probably, at that moment, relished the challenge ahead.[12]

Concerns for his "delicate" constitution proved unwarranted. Burr's intense determination served him well as he trudged through the forbid-ding terrain of lakes, swamps, rivers, and dense woodlands. Ogden kept a journal, noting that they traveled on "bad roads" and "sometimes climb[ed] on all fours," being "scarcely able to see for the thickness of the bramble and small fir shrubs." Ogden's boots were so worn that he made a cover for them from a bag of flour. Burr and Ogden watched starving men greedily devour dog meat.[13]

It was Burr's family name as much as his fortitude that caught the at-tention of Colonel Arnold. In fact, Arnold went out of his way to show favor to Burr, and he was even more solicitous of Ogden. Apparently Ogden was quite adept at making a good impression on his superior, and secured a promotion to captain before Burr. Yet Burr wasted little time in trying to set himself apart from the other volunteers. On November 30, Arnold sent him as a messenger to General Montgomery, who was a day's march away. In his brief letter, Arnold introduced Burr as "a volunteer in the army and son to the former president of the college of New Jersey"; he then recommended Burr as "a young man of much life and activity [who] has acted with great spirit and resolution on our fatiguing march." Immediately pleased with the young man, Montgomery attached Burr to his staff, making the cadet a captain and one of his aides-de-camp.[14]

Richard Montgomery was a tall, slender man. He was considered handsome, despite a pockmarked face. Like Horatio Gates and Charles Lee, two other generals in the Continental Army, Montgomery had been a career British officer. Unable to secure the promotion he felt he deserved in the British army, he sold his commission, retired, and sailed for the colonies in 1772. Taking up the life of a gentleman farmer in New York, he married Janet Livingston, and so aligned himself with one of the wealthiest and most influential families in the Hudson Valley. Family connections quickly secured his election to New York's provincial congress, and when war commenced in the spring of 1775, congress appointed him brigadier general.[15]

With fifteen years of military service behind him, Montgomery had no problem displaying the expertise of a professional officer or the personal style of a gentleman. Much later, Washington Irving (who also admired Burr's dashing demeanor) claimed that Montgomery was "the *beau idéal* of the soldier." Montgomery seemed to embody what young and inexperienced volunteers like Burr expected from a genuine leader. The general was "beloved," a fellow soldier of Burr's wrote, because of "his manliness of soul, heroic bravery, and suavity of manners."[16]

What is clear is that Montgomery knew how to carry himself. In his years as a British officer, he had learned that a certain style was necessary to win over the troops, to ensure both their loyalty and their deference. To his men, he had to appear fearless. He had nearly been killed three times during the invasion of Canada. In the siege of St. Johns, while he was examining an artillery battery, a cannonball ripped through his coattail, threw him from the breastwork, and yet he landed on his feet, to the utter amazement of his men. He had two other close encounters in Quebec. His sled was destroyed by a cannonball just after he left it; seven days later, a shell barely missed him as he inspected another battery. Montgomery's calm under fire enhanced his reputation.[17]

A later letter to Burr from Montgomery's widow hints at what his opinion of her husband might have been. Acknowledging the praises he bestowed on her dead husband, she recited what were probably Burr's original words: "He was, indeed, an angel sent us for a moment." If her husband had lived, she observed, "*his friends* [would be] *in stations more equal to their merit.*" It was her opinion that Burr would well have risen faster and further serving under Montgomery, a general who possessed flair to rival Washington.[18]

While gentility and decorum were important to Montgomery, he still faced trying times attempting to maintain discipline among his troops. He complained in October 1775 about the "wretches" he had as officers, histrionically regretting he had ever accepted his commission. He believed that his reputation was at stake, because the men were nothing more than "ragamuffins," prone to "beastly" drunkenness, cowardice, blunders, and arrogance. He told his father-in-law that "the privates are all generals but not soldiers." He added ominously: "Honor, the very soul of the soldier, has no existence among us." A month later, he continued to voice disappointment in his officers and in the general lack of discipline, writing to General Philip Schuyler that he wished "some method could be fallen upon of engaging *Gentlemen* to serve—a point of honour and more knowledge of the world to be found in that Class of men would greatly reform discipline and render the troops much more tractable."[19]

When Montgomery finally joined up with Arnold's troops, he liked what he saw. He remarked that there was "a style of discipline among them, much superior to what I have been used to" in this campaign.[20] Obviously, he sought "gentlemen." Burr was only nineteen at the time, but his Princeton training and family background had imparted to him the manner of a gentleman. A fellow soldier, John Henry, upon meeting the "amiable youth" Aaron Burr on the march northward, found him to be a model soldier.[21]

The one close aide to Montgomery who probably set the standard for a subaltern was John MacPherson. He was the eldest son of Captain John MacPherson, a former British officer, and his family was one of the most prominent and wealthy in Philadelphia. After graduating from Princeton in 1766, he traveled in Europe, polishing his manners and acquiring, in

Montgomery's words, "more knowledge of the world." Burr must have met expectations, too, because, in the general's eyes, he resembled MacPherson with his polish and learning. Indeed, as a close friend of William Paterson, Burr's former college mentor, it was probably MacPherson who recommended Burr to the general's attention.[22]

Montgomery may have been inspired by the sight of Arnold's troops, but he faced enormous pressures at Quebec. After his appeals for surrender were ignored, he realized that an assault was his only option. He had little time to waste; the terms of enlistment for Arnold's men expired on January 1, 1776, and this forced him to take action before the new year. Three companies in Arnold's battalion vocally opposed the assault; dissensions threatened to weaken the army. Just before Christmas, in an attempt to quell growing dissent, the commander gave a rousing speech, calling for the men to pursue "immortal honor." Four days later, he had to abort the first night attack, when the weather changed and it was no longer dark enough to conceal the army's approach. Montgomery then learned that an informer had divulged his plan to the British, forcing him to abandon it. This last-minute change of strategy worried the men. Aide Jacob Cheesman had a premonition of his own death. In the *Memoirs,* Matthew Livingston Davis claims that Burr, too, "entertained strong apprehensions of the result."[23]

The actual siege, of course, bore little resemblance to Trumbull's glorified interpretation on canvas. In the early hours of December 31, 1775, Montgomery and his troops approached the city along a narrow riverside path. After cutting through two stockades, and meeting no resistance, they discovered a blockhouse that appeared empty. Leading the charge, Montgomery ordered his men to advance. But Canadian militiamen, hiding in the blockhouse, opened fire when the Continentals came within forty yards of the building. At such close range, the entire head of the column was "mowed down like grass," killing the general, MacPherson, Cheesman, and at least ten others.[24]

What happened next is a matter of dispute. In a letter to Montgomery's father-in-law Robert Livingston, Colonel Donald Campbell offered his account of the deadly encounter. It is the most complete report written in the period just after the assault. Campbell placed Burr at the head of the troops as they reached the first stockade. After the fatal blast had eliminated Montgomery and the others, Lieutenant Richard Platt informed Campbell (who was to assume command) that his general was dead. After discussion with his remaining officers, Campbell ordered a retreat. Only Captain Gershom Mott contested the decision, and he was voted down. Burr, along with Mott and Campbell, remained behind to cover the withdrawal. None of the bodies was recovered.[25]

Campbell's version is challenged by Chaplain Spring's claim that Burr tried to recover the general's body. Much later, in 1807, Spring told Senator William Plumer: "Burr returned back alone & attempted, amidst a shower of musquetry, to bring on his shoulder, the body of Montgomery— But the general being a large man, & Burr small, & the snow deep, prevented him." According to English records, Montgomery's corpse was found on New Year's Day, buried under heavy snow, and lying on its side ("curled in a fetal position"). One arm protruded above the snow.[26]

It is worth asking: Did Burr try to save the general's body or not? Why would Spring spread such a story, if he felt uncertain of its veracity? It is clear that the chaplain was not present at the site of the initial assault. At that time he was in the hospital, nowhere near the place where Montgomery's troops attempted to enter the city. His version nevertheless had early on gained currency, for it appeared in Brackenridge's 1777 poem. In all likelihood, the poet heard it from Spring, Burr, Bradford, or some other Princetonian. Surely Bradford would have been privy to the same favorable report about Burr that was being circulated in Congress. If Burr's heroic gesture had not been widely disseminated, then the poet would not have repeated it.[27]

Strangely enough, Matthew Davis did not include the incident in his authorized Burr biography of 1836. He incorrectly described the scene in Trumbull's painting, asserting that the artist had drawn the general falling into Burr's arms. In an earlier testimonial concerning Burr's military career, written in 1814, Richard Platt, present at the assault and later Burr's business associate, made no mention of Burr trying to save the body. Platt contended that Burr—not Gershom Mott—had opposed the retreat. He had "animated the troops, and made many efforts to lead them on," and would have succeeded, if not for Campbell's orders. Platt's opinion that Burr's efforts might have "saved Arnold's division from capture" reconfirmed the rumors that had circulated among the soldiers in Quebec. John Henry (who wrote his version of the assault) called Campbell a cowardly "poltroon," whose retreat and failure to recover the bodies was unpardonable. To shield himself from criticism, the vulnerable Campbell had every reason to diminish Burr's role.[28]

Rumor and report—what really happened during and after the fateful assault? Why did Platt, who claimed to have seen everything, fail to mention Burr's valiant act? Why is Davis silent, if he wished to portray Burr positively? We know that if Burr had tried to recover the body, he would have been placing himself in an extremely vulnerable position. The Canadian militiamen in the blockhouse would have had a clear shot at him, especially as he struggled to lift the heavy corpse. Unless he decided to rush headlong, imprudently, this version seems suspect.

One tantalizing fact remains: the position of the corpse. Wounded in both thighs, groin, and face, Montgomery might have collapsed in pain into a "fetal position." But why was his arm in the air? Perhaps Burr indeed had tried to lift him, and had draped the arm over his back. Was the chaplain Spring telling tales, or was Campbell, a jealous junior officer, ignoring Burr's valor by putting his pride before the truth? As with many stories about Burr, the truth remains elusive.

The defeat in Quebec was devastating. The commander, five other officers, and 46 privates died in the assault; 34 were wounded, 372 captured. Almost all of Arnold's command were taken prisoner. By the spring of 1776, the small, sickly, humiliated force that remained was driven from Canada, removing all trace of Montgomery's victories of the previous year. General Montgomery had refused to contemplate such a fate. Because fortune favors the audacious (as he had confidently written to his father-in-law in December 1775), he assumed he would prevail. And he added that he anticipated no "fatal consequences." He was, of course, wrong on both accounts. Fortune did not favor him, except, perhaps, with "warrior's fame." Even that, it seems, was not eternal.[29]

"MY DEAREST SOLDIER"

In the aftermath of the defeat, friends and family waited anxiously for news. Burr's brother-in-law, Tapping Reeve, expressed both relief and satisfaction when he learned that Burr had escaped "imminent danger" and had been commended for his "intrepid conduct." Uncle Timothy showed his ap-

proval of Burr's actions by claiming that he, too, wanted to enlist. Others of
Burr's admirers were saying the same thing. One of them, Jonathan Bellamy
(the son of Reverend Joseph Bellamy), opened his letter to Burr with the
salutation "My Dearest Soldier," and recounted a dream he had had of visiting Burr in his tent. He described the Burr of his imagination as a man who
was "agitated by every emotion," in having "come to the resolution to risk
his life for his country's freedom." In his dream, Bellamy watched Burr
"stand up, clasp your hand upon your sword, look so fiercely . . . it almost
frightened me." It was Quebec, and Burr's recent reputation for gallantry,
that filled the dreamer with "exquisite delight."[30]

Other men fawned over Burr in their prose. Future U.S. Attorney General William Bradford claimed that Burr had so inspired him that he had
"thrown away his books & taken up the sword." Another acquaintance, future Hamilton ally Theodore Sedgwick, despite being ten years Burr's
senior, assumed a self-deprecating tone in one of his letters: he wondered
whether he merited Burr's attention, as he went on to praise the "young,
gay, enterprising martial genius."[31]

Clearly, Burr invoked among his friends what the philosopher Imman-
uel Kant had called "a special reverence for the soldier." Perhaps they most
admired his ability to carve out his own destiny: he had become both a
bold and enterprising "martial genius" and the master of his passions. There
was no more noble energy in the well-established masculine code of conduct
that arose during the age of the Enlightenment. As the eighteenth-century
Scottish intellectual Hugh Blair contended, passion, in this sense, "renders
the mind infinitely more enlightened, more penetrating, more vigorous
and masterly than it is in its calm moments." A man actuated by passion
becomes "greater than he is at other times," "is conscious of more strength
and force . . . conceives higher designs, and executes them with a boldness
and a felicity." To return to Kant's description, Burr's actions acquired, in
the eyes of his friends, "something sublime." In a few short months, he had
lost all traces of that effeminacy that the eighteenth-century gentlemen associated with an overly civilized existence. He had shed the weakness and
selfishness that his friends now associated primarily with their domesti-
cated lives on the homefront.[32]

A similar hyperbolic praise attached to George Washington throughout his public career. Burr's fan club was echoing the prevailing fascination

with the "citizen-soldier." Lacking a strong military tradition, the Revolutionaries instead chose to celebrate the idea of the noble and enlightened volunteer. The volunteer put aside his books or his plow, to engage in what General Washington described as a "vigorous and manly exertion." In this way, patriots could claim that the American military was different from the British army. A future secretary of state, Timothy Pickering, made the case in his popular military manual of 1775: American soldiers did not need the "trappings (as well as tricks) of the parade" nor the "splendor of equipage and dress" to be "awed into servility." Mindless manipulation would never inspire Americans to fight, as it did less enlightened populations, who, Pickering reminded, could be "duped by a glittering outside." American patriotism did not have to be coaxed. Citizens took to military discipline, to the command structure, on the basis of virtuous example.[33]

Burr imbibed this culture, in which officers were taxed to perform before their peers. Unlike the English officer who was "born to his station," acquiring rank through class background, the American officer could not rely solely upon such fragile props as class and gentility. Many did not come from the upper crust of colonial society; recall General Montgomery's bitter complaint that so few of his officers were "gentlemen." Insecure officers found themselves needing to defend their reputation—especially their masculine rectitude. Because class alone could not make a man into an officer, Revolutionary soldiers took masculinity as their proving ground, and defense of honor as the means of asserting leadership qualities.[34]

In letters to his family during the march to Quebec, Burr described the daring feats of his comrades, despite "insuperable" obstacles. He also stressed the kindness and courtesy of people he met along the way. Two hundred miles outside Boston, at Fort Weston on the Kennebec River, he appreciated the hospitality he received from complete strangers, simply because he was a soldier. For his sister, he painted a humorous portrait of himself in his Continental outfit. He described a fringed coat, topped with a foxtail and feather in his hat, and asked her to imagine him carrying tomahawk, gun, and bayonet, plus a blanket slung over his back. He doffed his hat to her: "And pray how do you like him?"[35]

At the same time, he was quick to acknowledge that a soldier's life could lose its luster. While camping outside Quebec in 1776, a month after the failed assault, he described himself as "dirty, ragged, moneyless and friendless." In this candid letter to his sister and her husband, he voiced a sudden cynicism for the war effort. Congress was "either drunk or crazy," he wrote, for sending such a small army to blockade the city. And he dismissed the patriotic fervor that called for converting Canadians to the American cause. Catholic priests, "our unalterable enemies," had had generations to indoctrinate their neighbors. "To think of instilling any principles of belief of liberty into the Canadians is perfectly idle." Neither Protestantism nor patriotic cant would sway the Canadians to declare independence on American terms.[36]

Burr's perspective on military life was changing. Women still toyed and teased, he wrote once again to his sister, but instead of enjoying a verbal repartee with them, he reported that he behaved with "natural bluntness." No "dirty and "ragged" officer, as he now referred to himself, could play the part of the gentleman convincingly. Just as his dress now failed to suggest his rank, so did the sermons and speeches about liberty seem out of touch with actual conditions in Quebec. Burr was showing signs of disenchantment with military life at the same time as he was being touted as a hero back home.[37]

The real war, then, was rarely glorious, and most of the time boring. He had lost none of his Revolutionary ardor, but the stalemate at Quebec offered little hope. The 600 men who remained on the outskirts of the garrisoned city were waiting for their inevitable withdrawal, occasionally embarking on pointless raids, designed to alarm the inhabitants. Yet Burr's deeper source of discontent was that he felt friendless. While he was left behind in Quebec, wasting his time and talents, his friend Ogden had been selected by Benedict Arnold to deliver news of the defeat to Congress.

Ogden had been gone since the end of January 1776, and informed Burr in March that General Washington had asked him to join his staff. Was Ogden boasting? Burr must have felt so. He sent Ogden an angry response, accusing his friend of having a "fickle heart," enjoying the "caresses of the great, and the flatteries of the low," while forgetting his real friend in Quebec. Both men were ambitious, yet Burr resented that Ogden had put his career ambition before honor and sincerity—two qualities that Burr valued greatly.[38]

The breach between the young men healed. Yet the following year Burr wrote Ogden with equal candor, again, on the subject of ambition. He said he had few expectations of promotion, whereas most of his "former equals, and even inferiors in rank" had already passed him by. He had been given "assurances from those in power," which he did not request, though none of these promises was fulfilled. His reputation was in the hands of unpredictable others, but he claimed he still found satisfaction in public service. "We are not to judge our own merit," he demurred, "and I am content to contribute my mite to any station."[39]

This was more than mere posturing. Burr had no intention of groveling for a promotion. As he wrote to Ogden, "I have never made any application, and, as you know me, you know I never shall." He knew how the game was played. It was not a game he was prepared to participate in, and he knew that Ogden had—willingly.[40]

Honor, as Burr understood the concept, curbed the excesses of ambition—curbed, that is, vanity and fickleness. This was how proud men of the eighteenth century were saved from being womanish. Burr and Ogden lived in a culture in which weakness was measured in gendered terms. As Burr was discovering, the military tended to reward the womanish traits of gossiping, displaying vanity in one's appearance, and engaging in petty quarrels over exaggerated slights of honor. It is not insignificant that Burr steered clear of duels throughout his career in the military. His unwillingness to play the game of the courtier was an integral part of who he was. His determination to pursue his own destiny without relying on the "caresses of the great" was an unabashed part of him.

"MY GOOD OLD GENERAL"

While Burr worried about his future prospects in Quebec, the British army left Boston and headed for New York. General Charles Lee had been sent ahead in February 1776 to fortify what he considered an indefensible city. In mid-April, Washington set up his headquarters in Manhattan. In a few short months, the city became a military fortress: breastworks blocked the streets that led to the water, artillery batteries were set up along the Hudson River, streets were torn apart, and sunken ships were placed in the rivers to deter the British fleet. As hundreds of residents fled the city, American military forces occupied the abandoned homes. By the time Burr arrived in June, Washington's staff occupied a Greenwich Village mansion known as

Richmond Hill—a house that Burr would later purchase as he began building his legal and political career in New York.[41]

After forcing the British to abandon Boston in March, Washington exuded confidence, as he anticipated a massive battle in New York City. He seemed somehow certain that his untried troops would repulse the British. A modern biographer has termed him optimistic, if not utterly naive. In fact, New York would prove to be one of Washington's most embarrassing defeats. The British armada moved into New York Bay on June 29, just as final debate ended in Philadelphia and the Declaration of Independence was put on parchment. Over the next two months, 353 enemy warships took control of the harbor, causing one contemporary observer to remark that masts were "as thick as trees in the forest." The two armies were mismatched from the start: the British commander, General William Howe, fielded a total of 30,000 professional British soldiers and German mercenaries, while Washington could muster only two thirds that number, perhaps even less, and they were poorly trained.[42]

When, on August 22, Howe finally made his move, he landed some 15,000 soldiers on Long Island, feinted in one direction, then divided his forces and marched unopposed along two different routes, successfully surrounding the American army four days later. Exposing Washington's relative lack of experience, Howe caught the Continentals completely by surprise, resulting in a British rout of the Americans in less than half a day's fighting. Three hundred Americans were killed, 900 were taken captive, and two of Washington's generals, John Sullivan and William Alexander (known as Lord Stirling), were taken prisoner. It was a demoralizing defeat. Overcome with fear, the American forces broke ranks and scattered in confusion. Some drowned as they desperately sought to escape the British juggernaut.[43]

Burr watched these events unfold. His friend Ogden had helped Burr secure a temporary post on Washington's staff until June 22, when he was transferred to General Israel Putnam's force, assuming the position of the general's aide-de-camp. Putnam, a hero of the June 1775 Battle of Bunker Hill, was Washington's second-in-command, in charge of Long Island, and would play a pivotal role in the evacuation of American troops.[44]

Though much has been made of Burr's initial encounter with Washington, there is absolutely no evidence to support the claim that the two men took an instant dislike to each other.[45] Burr simply wanted a more active role in the war. He wished to leave Washington's staff even before he met the general. Assigned to Putnam, Burr stood to exercise more influence. As Putnam's right-hand man, he would not have to compete for attention in the way he would have as one of several aides in Washington's large military family.

Writing to Ogden, Burr defended his "good old general," as he affectionately referred to Putnam. The farmer-warrior had few pretensions; their relationship, according to Burr, was based on mutuality, on utter honesty. A canny and fearless fighter known for his drinking stories and lack of polish, the Connecticut Yankee stood in stark contrast to the unapproachable, aristocratic Washington.[46]

Burr did not dismiss Washington or disparage his abilities at this early date, though he would come to distance himself from the insular world of the commander's staff. Burr was unwilling to pursue success if it demanded that he pander or feign respect (as he wrote to Ogden), in which case it would not suit him to link his career to Washington's rise. The events that produced Washington's visceral hatred for Burr, and the younger man's utter disdain for the general, did not occur until the 1790s, when the two were prominently identified with opposing political factions. By then, both men viewed the past through a somewhat warped political lens, employing historic memory of the Revolution as a weapon of partisan warfare. But at this point, they had no reason to dislike or distrust one another.

Even so, as Putnam's aide, Burr was able to gain firsthand knowledge of Washington's questionable decision making. After the disaster on Long Island, the commander in chief wavered back and forth over whether to abandon or defend New York. He asked his generals for advice, and seemed willing to support Congress's wish to safeguard the city, but then he reversed himself. Despite this indecision, Washington must be credited with having orchestrated the daring operation by which 12,000 of his remaining troops were spirited off Long Island in the middle of the night. Putnam assisted in this stealthy retreat. As an old Indian fighter, he called upon the Native Americans in his service to wail their war chants, which caused the neighborhood dogs to howl, and effectively concealed the noise made by the escaping American soldiers.[47]

Washington dangerously hesitated before making his next move and finally ordering the retreat. Luckily, the British were in no hurry, and waited until mid-September to invade Manhattan. On the morning of the 15th, amid another embarrassing defeat, the Continentals benefited from the slow movement of British reinforcements, giving Putnam the time he needed to lead the American army out of the city.[48]

Burr assisted Putnam in this daring retreat. More familiar with the city than his commander, Burr pointed out a safe route along Bloomingdale Road, salvaging some of the army's artillery while guiding 5,000 men to safety. During this exodus from Manhattan, Burr rescued Colonel Gold Selleck Silliman's party at Bayard's Hill Redoubt at Grand and Mulberry Streets, just as these men were about to be surrounded by the British.[49]

According to an account based on an interview with Burr and later published by Silliman's son, Burr urged the men to withdraw, but the brave colonel refused. He would not abandon his post until he received orders to do so. So, with little time to waste, Burr improvised. He rode away from the vulnerable redoubt, then galloped back, yelling to the colonel that he had just been ordered to retreat. He had a rare talent for solving logistical problems quickly and skillfully, without offending a superior officer. Young officers tended to lack prudence, but Burr was bent on action, without being considered rash.[50]

The Americans' blundering did not end in New York. Putnam's men achieved a temporary victory in a brief skirmish at Harlem Heights, while Washington waited for Howe to make his next move. As October arrived, Washington's war council agreed to forsake lower Manhattan, but not Fort Washington, which was north of the city. Indecision again plagued the commander. When Howe toppled the fort, Generals Washington, Putnam, and Nathanael Greene—and most likely Burr—watched from Fort Lee, just across the Hudson in New Jersey. Fort Washington was perhaps the worst defeat in the contest for New York: 2,818 officers and men were taken prisoner, and valuable artillery and equipment were lost to the enemy.[51]

The debacle at Fort Washington proved quite damaging to General Washington's reputation. He peevishly blamed others and refused to take personal responsibility. While no one in Congress openly questioned the general, private criticism flowed freely, and many began to look to General Charles Lee as the army's savior. Even Washington's closest aide, Joseph Reed, joined the chorus of Lee's supporters. Fears of conspiracy in his own midst put Washington on his guard. If the men around him ridiculed his indecision, then perhaps Congress would replace him. This was the start of an obsession among Washington's staff, talk of "cabals" or secret plots, which in turn fueled the "party business" that Burr assiduously wished to avoid. In his yearlong tenure as Putnam's aide, Burr clearly saw the worst side of Washington, yet the historical record gives no evidence that he ever reproached the embattled commander.[52]

Rather, Burr vociferously defended the evacuation of New York. In letters to his aunt and uncle, he called it "a *necessary consequence*." He went on to claim that defeat had made the patriot force "more united, theirs more divided," and that it had aroused "our leading men . . . from their lethargy," insofar as Congress was "now levying a new army." In this surprisingly optimistic account, Burr is interested in assuaging his aunt's fears, dismissing accounts of "barbarities" by the Hessians as "incredible and false." He voices an unshaken commitment to the war, embracing America's cause as "the most important revolution that ever took place." He wrote with rhapsodic confidence: "We may be truly called a favoured people." The only criticism he expressed was directed at the British. He scoffed at an enemy that held the Americans "in the utmost contempt," and who felt they could "force all our lines without firing a gun." With grit and national pride, Burr taunted: "They have forgot Bunker's Hill."[53]

Bunker Hill was the glorious highlight of his good old general's career. As Putnam's aide, Burr had to think like Putnam in order to translate his commands. As the general's secretary, he often wrote letters for him, especially because Putnam had little formal education. Nor was he known as an administrator. Thus he relied heavily on Burr's advice in coordinating military operations. After leaving New York, Putnam and Burr were sent to Philadelphia to shore up its defenses in preparation for a British attack. After a short time, they had safely stored the city's available ammunitions, procured necessary supplies, imposed price controls to curtail the spiraling inflation, established a curfew, and advised Congress to leave the city, which it did. Putnam and Burr had maintained civil order. Now Burr helped Putnam devise administrative solutions to forestall the political collapse of Philadelphia, as many residents began to switch sides in anticipation of the British army's arrival.[54]

Burr enjoyed his post at the side of Israel Putnam, to whom he never showed any disloyalty. As he wrote to his college mentor, William Paterson, his position left him at a distance from military gossip; he was "no epistolary politician or newsmonger." As Putnam's aide, he became a kind of omnibus man, wearing many hats—clerk, adviser, and bureaucrat—assuming whatever role was needed to get the job done. Many of Burr's activities were logistical: he collected intelligence and kept track of the enemy's progress. He displayed a knack for overseeing military operations, developing some of the key organizational skills that would later serve him in his political career.[55]

His desire to prove himself a competent officer made him less likely to speculate on the failings of his commanders. Indeed, in the letter to his aunt, Burr criticized politicians who relied on "grand designs," and felt more comfortable with an approach to the war that stayed focused on the present. He seemed to be acquiring a style of problem solving that required realistic assessments, strategic planning, and an ability to find utilitarian rather than utopian answers. He retained his earlier patriotic zeal, though he tempered that zeal with a growing pragmatism. He saw himself as an able and loyal administrator, and by the spring of 1777, he felt confident that he was ready for his own command.[56]

TO DO "JUSTICE TO THE VIGILANT MEN"

On June 27, 1777, Burr finally received the promotion he felt he deserved. General Washington notified him of his appointment as lieutenant colonel in the Continental Army and of his attachment to Colonel William Malcolm's regiment. Malcolm's "Additional Continental Regiment" was brand new, consisting of 260 men, and all six companies were recruited from southern New York. Struggling to find the money to support new troops, Congress adopted a practice of allowing wealthy patrons to raise their own regiments. Malcolm acquired his command in this fashion. As a fabulously rich shipping merchant of New York City, he literally purchased his commission as colonel. By September, Burr headed off to the Clove, in the Ramapo Mountains in New York, to join his new regiment.[57]

There were no strict rules for promotion in the Continental Army. Burr understood this. Congress used what was later satirized as a "mysterious trinity of *Seniority Merit and Quota*," a system so flexible (if not arbitrary) that officers constantly bickered over rank. Ambitious subalterns who lobbied Congress, or appealed to state legislators, or who succeeded in catching the eye of senior officers, moved easily through the ranks. By the time Burr received his promotion, his good friend Matthias Ogden was already a full colonel in a New Jersey regiment, owing to these conditions; he would advance to the rank of brigadier general by the end of the war. But Burr's promotion from Washington would be his one and only: he remained a lieutenant colonel until he left the service in March 1779.[58]

When he learned of his promotion, Burr sent Washington a perfunctory response. He begins his letter by acknowledging the "honour done me," and goes on to assure Washington that he will be "studious that my Deportment in that Station be such as will insure your future esteem." He then observes, pointedly, that the "late date of my Appointment subjects me to the Command of many who are younger in the Service and junior officers the last Campaign," and he wonders whether it was "any Misconduct in me or extraordinary service in them, which entitled the Gentlemen lately put over me, to that Preference." Closing his letter with the accustomed nod to a sense of honor and order, Burr says he wishes "to avoid the Character of turbulent or passive," desiring only "a decent Attention to Rank."[59]

Burr's letter is relatively tame compared to the complaints Washington commonly received from disgruntled officers. After another officer was given seniority over him, Colonel John Lamb wrote the general that the action had "degraded" him. Lamb felt that his honor—the "only jewel worth contending for"—had been stripped from him. His "just right" had been given to another. He found it impossible to remain silent, because his "sensibilities" were so "deeply wounded." In 1777, the same year as Burr's complaint, the artist John Trumbull refused a commission from Congress. He protested that a manipulation of dates of service placed him under the command of those he had previously outranked. This kind of demotion, Trumbull concluded, "tasted indeed too loathsome of degradation."[60]

Unlike Lamb and Trumbull, Burr avoids all the hyperbole of outraged honor and personal degradation. His word choices are deferential: he asks his question "with submission"; he begs not "to have troubled his Excellency"; and signs his letter: "I have the Honour to be with the greatest Respect Your Excellencys very hum[ble] servt." He blames no one, presuming that his late appointment happened rather "thro Accident than Design." Nor was it odd that Washington did not reply. Both men knew the value of

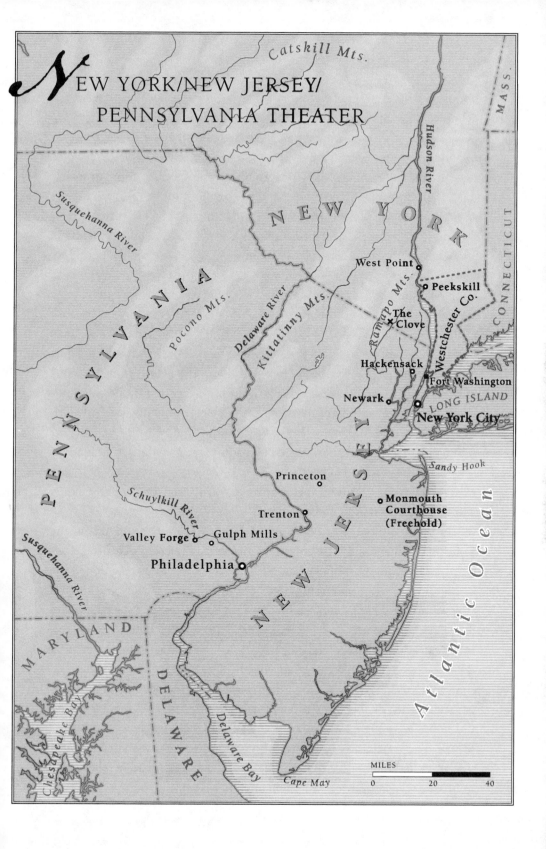

NEW YORK/NEW JERSEY/ PENNSYLVANIA THEATER

Catskill Mts.

MASS.

Hudson River

Susquehanna River

NEW YORK

CONNECTICUT

West Point

Peekskill

Pocono Mts.

Delaware River

Kittatinny Mts.

Ramapo Mts.

The Clove

Westchester Co.

PENNSYLVANIA

Hackensack

Fort Washington

Newark

LONG ISLAND

New York City

Princeton

Sandy Hook

Schuylkill River

Trenton

Monmouth Courthouse (Freehold)

Valley Forge

Gulph Mills

Philadelphia

Susquehanna River

NEW JERSEY

MARYLAND

DELAWARE

Atlantic Ocean

Chesapeake Bay

Delaware Bay

Cape May

MILES

0   20   40

honor and ritual. There is a highly ritualized tone to Burr's complaint: he acknowledges his displeasure (something Washington would have expected from a man of honor), and yet he makes clear his desire not to offend the commander in chief. Burr's prosaic and predictable letter complied with the unwritten rules concerning honor—nothing more or less.[61]

When Burr joined Malcolm's regiment in the summer of 1777, he was stationed at Smith's Clove, in the Ramapo Mountains of New York State. At this time, General Putnam had authority over the Hudson Highlands, a sprawling command that extended from Fishkill to its southern boundary in Westchester County, and stretched west from the Hudson Valley to the Ramapo Mountains and the narrow valley within, known as the Clove. Washington recognized the importance of controlling this region because of the vital artery of the Hudson River; the Hudson bisected the Highlands and provided direct access to the Atlantic Ocean. Protecting the Highlands meant guarding the river. It was believed that if the British gained control of the river, they could cut off New England from the rest of the colonies.

Along the Hudson were five garrisons. In close proximity sat Fort Clinton and Fort Montgomery on the western bluffs of the river; Fort Independence was to the southeast (near Putnam's headquarters at Peekskill). Farther up the Hudson was Fort Constitution, an island garrison; then West Point, destined to become key to the region's defense. Burr would briefly be stationed there in 1778.[62]

In the first months of Burr's appointment to Malcolm's regiment, the Continental Army suffered another series of humiliating defeats. Ticonderoga fell on July 5, 1777, when General Arthur St. Clair abandoned the fort without a fight, to Washington's chagrin. Next, in what Washington considered an embarrassing failure prompted by "vanity," General John Sullivan launched a futile raid on Staten Island in mid-August that left 150 Americans dead. On September 11, Washington himself suffered a devastating defeat at Brandywine, Pennsylvania. The battle at Brandywine bore similarities to the Battle of Long Island, demonstrating once again the tactical superiority of the British in outmaneuvering the Continental forces. Casualties were high: the Americans lost 1,000 men, twice as many as the British. The marquis de Lafayette, who had just joined Washington's staff, was wounded there. At the end of the day, Washington had no alternative but to escape, and salvage what remained of his army.[63]

Minor victories were all that Washington's Continentals could celebrate in these bleak months. Burr obtained laurels when a party under his command captured an advance guard during the British invasion of New Jersey, on September 14. While Putnam sent off Brigadier General Alexander McDougall to New Jersey with around 700 Continentals and 200 militiamen, Burr's men were already within reach of the enemy. Before McDougall arrived, Burr led a successful sortie against the British picket near Hackensack. Leading a small party, and carefully scouting the area, he surprised the sleeping enemy at night. They had little time for resistance, waking when Burr's men were within yards of their camp. According to Private Alexander Dow, a few "brave and obstinat[e]" men in the enemy's ranks received bayonet wounds, leaving at least sixteen dead. Burr's party secured the guardhouse and took several prisoners. His timing and daring gained the attention of other officers, demonstrating that the new lieutenant colonel had been worthy of his promotion.[64]

The Highlands command was politically risky. Despite the river forts, the vastness of the territory made it vulnerable to British and Tory raids. Troop strength was constantly depleted, because Washington regularly drew additional regiments from the area to reinforce the main army. Putnam was expected to fortify his defenses with militia, but as he and other Continental officers knew, the "militia intractables," as Colonel Malcolm labeled them, were notoriously unreliable; they often failed to show up when called and refused to stay and fight when needed. Burr discovered the seriousness of this problem on the morning of his successful surprise attack. "Not a man of Militia be with me," he angrily informed Malcom, despite the fact that "some Join'd us Last Night but are Gone."[65]

Putnam's tenure in the Highlands proved disastrous to his reputation. In addition to troop shortages and questionable militiamen, he had to put down a mutiny of disgruntled soldiers clamoring for their pay, in November 1777. A month earlier, he had watched Forts Clinton and Montgomery fall into British hands, losses that permanently stained his record. Two of New York's most powerful figures, Colonel George Clinton, who was also governor of the state, and his brother Colonel James Clinton, were commanding the garrisons; they, along with Washington and most of the members of Congress, blamed Putnam for this fiasco.

By February 1778, Malcolm wrote to Burr that the Highlands were in a state of "chaos," and that the "old general is gone to Boston." Malcolm had no idea whether Putnam would return to his post, observing that "he is very unpopular and the militia declare they will not serve under him." In late March, Washington relieved Putnam of his command, while Congress demanded a full investigation into the events that resulted in the loss of the two forts. Congress wanted a scapegoat, and Putnam's political enemies in New York easily obliged. Although he was eventually vindicated, "old Put" never again was entrusted with a major independent command.[66]

Burr was nowhere near the river forts when they were captured. Soon afterwards, he was sent with Malcolm's regiment to join the main army at White Marsh in Pennsylvania. He then settled in the winter camp at Valley Forge with the rest of the Continentals. The British took and occupied Philadelphia at the end of September 1777, and Washington shifted his focus to regaining the key city. He surrounded Philadelphia and cut off the British supply line. This tactic worked for a time, until the two Delaware River forts finally fell to the British commander, General Howe.[67]

During these months, the complexion of the war changed for Burr. The new lieutenant colonel found himself fighting with his own men over issues of discipline, and fighting the "rascally inhabitants" of southeastern Pennsylvania who were smuggling goods into the occupied city of brotherly love. He was not, however, fighting the British army. Adapting, Burr learned to use his military authority to police his men and local residents. He was finding that the war had less to do with grand battles than with finding a "system" (his word) for solving day-to-day problems: low morale, mutiny, petty crime, and plundering.[68]

American soldiers embraced discipline slowly and grudgingly. Men in the camps randomly fired off their muskets for entertainment; few companies ever truly mastered the drills and maneuvers meant to prepare them for battlefield conditions. Many soldiers got drunk, stole, and rioted, and some even threatened to kill their company commander. The British system allowed up to 1,000 lashes for such crimes, but that seemed too harsh to Americans. So the Continentals adopted the Mosaic rule of 39 lashes; this number increased to 100 in 1776, and remained the standard punishment until the end of the war. Military guidebooks of the time advised young officers to make themselves "both beloved and feared." Severity was to be "accompanied with great tenderness and moderation." In this way,

Americans never matched the rigors of the British army, though officers did rely on different kinds of social coercion. Shaming was a common method. In mock executions, condemned soldiers were pardoned at the gallows. Courts-martial occurred with great frequency.[69]

As with every story about Burr, his image as a disciplinarian is riddled with contradictions. He was, on the one hand, praised for his unparalleled leniency; one soldier in Malcom's regiment claimed many years later: "He never, in a single instance, permitted any corporal punishment." On the other hand, his supposedly authoritative biographer Matthew Davis paints him as a rigid taskmaster: in one vignette, Burr single-handedly puts down a mutiny at the Gulph, a post just a few miles from Valley Forge. In this episode, Burr learns that the leaders of the mutiny planned to kill him in response to his "rigid system" of policing, drilling, and discipline. Emptying their muskets of cartridges, Burr cleverly thwarts the plot. When the men assemble one night, the ringleader of the mutineers levels his gun at Burr and orders his comrades to shoot. At that instant, Burr draws his sword and "smote the mutineer above the elbow," foiling the mutiny with a dramatic display of intimidation. He was, we are to understand, not afraid to employ brute violence.[70]

Was he an angel of mercy or of vengeance? Neither portrait rings true, and there is no record of the Gulph incident in Burr's orderly books. It would have been virtually impossible for him to nearly chop off a soldier's arm without some kind of military report or court-martial proceeding. Enraged officers did have outbursts, and they hit unruly soldiers, but such behavior was frowned upon.[71]

Though every Burr biographer has repeated this story, the Gulph mutiny probably never happened—at least not the way it has been told. It is more likely a composite of more than one event as recorded in Burr's orderly books. At Valley Forge, in February 1778, a Corporal Robert Haddock was tried by court-martial for "m[alevo]lent and threatening behavior to Col. Burr," receiving only forty lashes for his death threats. Later that year, several disturbances (that did not involve Burr) resembled aspects of the Gulph incident: A private pointed a loaded musket at an officer; another officer manhandled a captain, in suppressing a riot; two lieutenants were charged with "riotous and mutinous behavior" for entering a colonel's house with drawn swords at midnight. If Burr had been a sword-wielding colonel, slicing up a mutinous soldier, his actions would hardly have gone unnoticed.[72]

A very different picture emerges in Burr's orderly books. It is clear that he had extensive authority over the regiment, primarily because Malcolm spent so little time in camp and left most of the responsibility for discipline in Burr's hands. The lieutenant colonel was neither especially liberal nor especially punitive. He had little difficulty, however, meting out the maximum penalty of 100 lashes to soldiers who plundered townspeople, neglected their duty, or deserted. He also knew when to show mercy. After the teenager Michael Brannon stole a shirt from Burr's room and was sentenced to fifty lashes, the offender was ultimately spared by his commander, owing to his youth.[73]

Brannon was young enough to learn from his mistake, and Burr was generally in a forgiving mood when he handled such disciplinary cases. In March 1778, at a court-martial where Burr was president, he excused the two men for wasting ammunition, but promised to "shew no lenity to any who are guilty of the same offence in the future." Here the lesson took precedent over the lash, which is not surprising given Burr's college and ministerial training.[74]

A decidedly moralistic streak ran through Burr's command style. He particularly appreciated the effect of public shaming, and he was not alone in this. According to the Articles of War, men found guilty of cowardly behavior could be cashiered and then publicly humiliated by having their names published in the local newspapers of their home state. Burr used shaming more than once, and always with creative results. The most humiliating punishment he ordered was for two soldiers found guilty of plundering a local family. Whipped at the injured party's house, the men then had to ask the victim for forgiveness. A scarlet letter "P" for plunderers? Burr might actually have liked the idea.[75]

He demanded honesty from his men. He had one sergeant court-martialed for lying to his face. In another instance, he promised to "particularize" those men deserving censure for poor performance rather than punish the entire unit. In his words, he wanted to do "justice to the vigilant men." Thus, Burr as commander was a far more complicated person than the empty platitudes and exaggerated stories about him suggest. He relied on mercy as much as on punishment, and he often used didactic

methods. As one soldier under his command later remarked, "every day afforded some lesson of instruction."[76]

Why is it so important to emphasize moral considerations? He was not
an arrogant upstart, as many later portrayed Burr in his relationship with
George Washington. Indeed, his "system" (of rewards and punishments)
tends to make him appear almost as a schoolmaster, prim and priggish, as
much as it might make him look honorable. Nor was he that other cliché,
a flamboyant, often ruthless commander who put errant soldiers in their
place. He demanded discipline, yes, but he readily accorded mercy to those
he felt might learn from his generosity. Burr was a minister's son, who was
learning to lead by adhering to a system that was practical and efficient.

"DIRTY EARWIGS"

After occupying Philadelphia for nine months, the British left the city on
June 18, 1778. By then, General Henry Clinton had replaced General Howe
as commander of the British army in America. France's entry into the war
had prompted the British to yield up the city without a fight. In April, the
French had recognized the independence of the United States, and the British realized they were no longer simply suppressing a colonial rebellion.
To the British, a treaty between France and the United States was a declaration of war, and so they launched an attack against the French in the
Caribbean. This left Clinton with a much smaller army of around 10,000
soldiers, forcing him to abandon Philadelphia for the more vital position of
New York City.[77]

As the British army made its overland trek through New Jersey, Washington's army remained in close pursuit. The British moved slowly, bogged
down by unseasonably hot weather. At Monmouth Court House, Clinton
decided to halt. At Washington's council of war, several of the officers
around him, especially Nathanael Greene, Anthony Wayne, and Alexander
Hamilton, urged the commander to provoke a general engagement. To
Greene, it was needed to "preserve our reputation," and others around
Washington agreed that to allow the British to pass through the Jerseys "in
tranquility" would be "humiliating." Yet General Charles Lee and others
took a more cautious approach, fearing that another defeat would do the
Continental Army lasting harm.[78]

Burr was part of this mass military migration, and when the two armies collided on June 28 at Monmouth, he faced his last major battle in the Revolutionary War. Suffering heatstroke, he decided afterward to retire his commission. His illness was serious, but it explains only part of Burr's reasoning. More important, he witnessed a political inquisition that enhanced his disdain for military life. Burr watched as Lee was stripped of his command in what became the most scandalous court-martial of the war. The charges were disobeying orders, making a shameful retreat, and disrespecting his commander. With Lee gone, Washington's leadership position was finally secure. But it was Washington's aides, especially Hamilton and his close friend John Laurens, whom Lee called "dirty earwigs," spreading the gossip that exacerbated this situation. Although Burr's health was a major factor, his letters written at this time suggest it was at least as much his dislike for such machinations—what Lee termed "party business"—that hastened his departure from the army in 1779.[79]

Burr was not present during the prolonged court-martial proceedings in July and August. He did, significantly, write a letter of support to Lee, a letter that unfortunately no longer exists; all we possess is Lee's reply. After his unsuccessful appeal to Congress to overturn his conviction, Lee wrote Burr that he was "convinced the Congress would unanimously have rescinded the absurd, shameful sentence" if it had come to a vote. Realizing that the decision was made "entirely on the strength of party," Lee saw the whole partisan proceeding as a disgrace to "national dignity." He promised to send Burr a transcript of the trial. Interestingly, Burr kept his notes on troop preparations leading up to the Monmouth battle tucked inside one of his orderly books—notes he probably intended to use if called to testify at the court-martial.[80]

Lee was not an easy man to like. He had a wagging tongue, an acerbic tone, and went on the attack with his famous wit. In his letter to Burr, he included a ribald slur on Washington. The officially chastised Lee claimed that he now planned to retire to Virginia, the home state as well of Washington, and there he would "learn to hoe tobacco." Adding sardonically that tobacco cultivation was "the best school to form a consummate *general,*" Lee meant that America's "great" George Washington was in fact nothing more than a farmer. How did farming, he snidely implied, give birth to military genius? Evidently, Washington was not always "first in war"—as he was later eulogized by another Lee—in the minds of those who served.[81]

Satire was a dangerous weapon. And Lee was not the first officer to fall because of his poison-tipped pen. While at Valley Forge, Washington expressed fears of conspiracies that crested at the time of the supposed "Conway cabal." Letters between two generals, Horatio Gates and Thomas Conway, seemingly critical of Washington, were made public, and Washington dismissed Conway with coldness and contempt. This caused the Irishman, a former French officer, to let loose, sabotaging his own reputation with the dispatch of one sarcastic letter, foolishly addressed to Washington in a moment of frustration. Conway's correspondence ended up before Congress, and Washington's devoted subordinates took full advantage. Hamilton labeled Conway "vermin," and others called him "cunning" and "dangerous." Washington referred to the indiscreet general as "a secret enemy."[82]

Lee made the same mistake as Conway. It was his harsh letter to Washington after the battle that provoked his court-martial. Of the three charges against him (disobeying orders, "making an unnecessary, disorderly and shameful retreat," and showing disrespect toward the commander in chief), Lee was correct in claiming that the first two charges were "absurd." But the truth was irrelevant. He had crossed the line when he insulted Washington.[83]

Lee did not accept his demotion quietly, as Putnam had done just a few months earlier. In December 1778, he published his self-defense in a prominent newspaper, and for the first time openly called into question Washington's abilities. Perhaps the strangest twist was what came next: Washington's aide John Laurens challenged General Lee to a duel. The unwritten, symbol-rich *code duello* described a protocol well known to the troops; under the *code duello,* Laurens had no grounds to challenge Lee. His own honor and reputation had not been questioned, but he insisted that as a member of Washington's military family he had a right to defend his chief, in essence claiming Washington as a surrogate father. This military operetta was the height of absurdity, revealing the lengths to which the code of honor could be exploited in wartime. Burr wrote a telling letter to his sister and brother-in-law about the affair. He observed that Laurens's challenge would not be the last, and that Lee "will probably have more of that Work to do." He then listed several other incidents concerning honor and reputation in which "Common sense is abused" and "kicked." Burr injected wit into the politically charged leadership squabbles when he referred ironically to "the prevailing Good Nature, Candour and Benevolence" that defined such political feuds.[84]

But Burr must have smiled when a fellow officer sent him a letter Lee had written, which was then published in the newspaper. In Lee's satirical letter, addressed to a Miss Franks, he mocked the meaning of dueling, threatening to challenge the young lady to a duel for insulting his green breeches. He was really taunting Laurens, comparing his challenge to a silly squabble over a fashion faux pas. Burr's friend wrote that the letter "has given me a hearty laugh," and it is a good guess that Burr found it funny, too.[85]

The Lee scandal was a harbinger of things to come, though Burr, of course, could not have imagined that his own career would eventually be ruined by a gossip campaign similar in nature, and perhaps greater in force. Lee would be compared to the "famous villain of antiquity, Cataline," a man "profligate in his morals and a parricide of his country." Burr had early on learned how petty the gossip of ambitious men could be. At Valley Forge, he saw adult soldiers convening courts-martial over such childish grievances as a stolen pair of mittens. Burr probably aligned himself with Lee's cause because he recognized that the general's fall from grace resembled that of Putnam. Burr's good friend Robert Troup aptly categorized the plight of the two generals when he coined "Putnamized" to describe an officer who foolishly invited his own disfavor and downfall.[86]

After the draw at Monmouth, Burr did some reconnaissance work for Washington. He then was ordered to West Point, but before assuming his post took a furlough for illness. He cut short his leave, worrying that other officers, jealous of his cozy retreat from camp life, might gossip about him. When he assumed his new assignment at West Point, once again a squabble broke out, this time between Colonel Malcolm and General Alexander McDougall over control of the garrison, but there is no record of Burr's position in this dispute. McDougall already had tussled with Colonel Henry Beekman Livingston in a heated court-martial that involved namecalling. At West Point, though, Burr had little time for political scandals. He found himself saddled with new duties, presiding over a series of courts-martial concerning forged passes, breaches of discipline, and insolent and riotous behavior. He enforced an order to stop his men from obtaining enlistments by getting recruits drunk in their tents. A general malaise swept through the camp, blamed on a "spirit of discord."[87]

Life at West Point had its lighter moments. Now twenty-two, Burr was frequently reminded of his boyish appearance at the garrison. One New York farmer refused to believe he was an officer. When he asked to see the lieutenant colonel, Burr identified himself. The man then assumed he had to be the colonel's son. After the story became scuttlebutt in the garrison, Burr was jocularly dubbed "Colonel Burr's son."[88]

Burr was hardly the only boyish officer in the Continental Army. Hamilton, and especially the marquis de Lafayette, were youthful, too, which seemed to belie their positions of authority. Yet Burr had another liability: he was not associated with a powerful general like Washington. Montgomery was dead, Putnam retired in disgrace, and Malcolm was not a leading military figure. Burr was a boy commander on his own, and that set him apart.

His last major assignment came in January 1779, when he was transferred to New York's Westchester County. He was now reporting to General McDougall, a New Yorker, who was similar in personality to Putnam, honest, blunt, and scrappy. McDougall may have lacked the polish of a gentleman but he had learned how to maneuver in the contentious ranks of the Continental Army. Burr respected him.

Since the fall of 1776, Westchester had been a major theater of war. It was one of the worst areas for civilians, a "no-man's-land" between the two major armies. War had crushed the spirit of its inhabitants; constant, unnerving activities made normal life impossible. Soldiers marched through towns, trampled fields, burned buildings, while marauding parties from both sides plundered the people without regard to their political allegiance. Loyalist troops known as the Queen's Rangers made regular incursions, captured Whigs, pillaged houses, and depleted families of food and livestock. General McDougall realized that he lacked the resources to protect the people. Other generals refused even to try to secure the region, claiming the civilians were not worth protecting.[89]

The Whig "skinners" were just as ruthless as Loyalist rangers or cowboys. Both were motivated more by greed than a desire to win the war. The skinners routinely used physical intimidation and violence to extort hidden treasures from frightened families. As one historian aptly describes these wartime bandits, "they 'skinned' their victims first and asked about their political affiliation later." Yet the problem of plunder was not limited to irregular forces. Militia units were often just as ready and willing to collect as much booty as they could at the expense of the locals. Burr's distinct loathing of all plunderers was most apparent during his duty in Westchester, when he ordered two soldiers whipped in the presence of their victim.[90]

Burr was at first unaware of how corruption flourished in Westchester. During the first days of his command, he wrote to McDougall of a scouting expedition: "I blush to tell you that the party returned loaded with plunder." He was outraged by his own men: "Sir, till now, I never wished for arbitrary power. I could gibbet half a dozen *good whigs,* with all the venom of an inveterate tory." He found it unbelievable that so-called *"good whigs"* would plunder some of "the most friendly families." His anger seemed directed mostly at the officers, whom he felt had planned and led the adventure. As gentlemen, they should have known better. As for the "petty rascals" caught with possessions, they deserved "pity more than indignation," because they were "honest men till debauched by this expedition."[91]

Burr felt he had been dropped into a pirate's lair. Taking command under such circumstances was, he remarked, a "truly ominous commencement." He let McDougall know that he would not tolerate any such hypocrisy, asking the general: "Is this the promised protection?" He voiced his sympathy for the victims, reading sorrow "in the face of every child I pass." He could not but feel personally responsible, "for the whole *honour* of the expedition redounds to me."[92]

Most revealing of all, Burr felt that his officers had hoodwinked him. The day before the above-noted expedition, he had written McDougall that the men were clamoring to go on a scouting party. He felt it was entirely "premature" to do so, and listed all the military reasons for postponement. By the next day, however, he learned "from whence arose the ardour for scouting." His reaction here is important: Burr felt betrayed by his men, but he just as quickly recognized his own failure to accurately read their motives. At this point in his career, far from being a schemer, Burr was highly sensitive to those who schemed.[93]

He faced problems other than plundering. He found he had to plead for shoes for his men, complaining early in winter that "many already are worn out." On January 17, 1779, he had to resort to begging for flour or wheat, urging that if grain was not sent soon, "we shall be starving." He also got a taste of espionage. McDougall added to Burr's worries by warning him against a mysterious interloper in his region. Make "noise," Burr was instructed. Call him "the vilest of Horse thieves," and "a great spy for the Enemy, but send no party after him." Perhaps it was all a ruse, to cover for a double agent, or a spy for the Continental Army. Burr was not immediately told. Washington had authorized a spy network in the Hudson Highlands, and Burr himself had done intelligence work for the commander in chief.[94]

Burr returned to his "system" for managing an army of disparate elements, but now on a much larger scale. He instituted a register of names and character types, distinguishing civilians according to their level of allegiance: Whig, timid Whig, horse thief, spy. He mapped the countryside, identifying roads and byways most often used by skinners or cowboys, pointing out possible hiding places. He was careful in monitoring the flow of the traffic in areas bordering British-controlled territory. Burr was especially concerned about prostitutes who acted as emissaries for the enemy. McDougall advised that such women were to be sent to headquarters to be searched by matrons for any hidden papers. Burr preferred a harsher punishment: "If they were men," he informed Colonel Malcolm, "I should flog them without mercy."[95]

One of his most interesting innovations involved recruiting young men of the county to serve as an informal intelligence corps. They were selected for their "patriotism, fidelity, and courage," but mostly because they showed a devotion to the lieutenant colonel beyond that which he could expect from regular soldiers. They were volunteers, who, according to the testimony of one of these recruits, Samuel Young, admired Burr for his deportment and his meticulous habits of duty and discipline. He organized activities for the young men, and his system succeeded in advancing *esprit de corps*.[96]

Nevertheless, Burr was impatient for results. His system demanded that he keep up a frenetic routine. He knew that he was the linchpin that held his system together. A good friend, Richard Platt, who by now was McDougall's aide-de-camp, warned Burr to slow down. His persistence was at times irksome. Platt advised moderation: "a little more Patience Burr and you'll have the most respectable Command of any officer in your rank in the army."[97]

His system was physically taxing and emotionally draining. Burr wrote another friend, Peter Colt, that the Westchester command was "the most fatiguing and most difficult and most troublesome that could have been contrived." On the same day he wrote to Major John Bigelow, wishing for a few "trifles" to make his life less depressing. Without elaborating, he told Colt: "My Life here is very foreign to my nature. I cannot account for my own conduct." What was making him so uncomfortable? Was he simply overwhelmed by his depressing surroundings? Clearly, he was growing more and more frustrated with military life.[98]

By February 18, 1779, Burr had had enough. In a lengthy letter to General McDougall, he detailed all the successes of his system. He asserted that the region was now protected from "internal enemies," plunder had been suppressed, a civil government, though still weak, was gaining respect; sufficient forage had been undertaken, and a list of friends and foes, designated by "character and history," was compiled. He assured the general that his system would work without him, for "the evils which still appear to exist will be removed by the mechanical operation of plans already in place." He then repeated his intention of retiring from the army.[99]

On March 25, Burr sent off his official letter to General Washington, adopting a formal, even obsequious tone. After explaining that his physical constitution was "no longer equal to the severities of active Service," he carefully pledged his devotion to the commander in chief, assuring that his "Attachment to the Service and his Excellency's Person are unabated." He further promised that he would "obey every summons to defend and secure." He would contribute in the future whenever needed, promising that his allegiance to the general was "not mere Words." It hardly read like a letter of resignation.[100]

Of course, no real candor went into Burr's letter to Washington. He reserved that for McDougall, hinting several times at the distasteful and destructive jealousy at work within the ranks: "I disdain the day of being moved by embarrassment, or I might urge the jealousy of the officers of your division as a distinct reason for resigning my present command." Knowing that he had merited McDougall's confidence, Burr concluded that he stood to "defy the malice of the world."[101]

The language he uses here is potent. He is clearly perturbed. It seems he felt that some dirty earwigs had insinuated themselves into McDougall's favor, and he was anticipating that he had enemies who would slander him after he left. His words state that other people's jealousy was not a motive for his departure, but it certainly seemed otherwise. He disdained petty gossip. No matter how successful his system was, not all "internal enemies" had been eliminated. He had had enough.

On February 17, Burr wrote to the son of General Israel Putnam, Rufus Putnam, who was himself a colonel assigned to the Highlands. On the face of it, Burr's letter was an answer to a request from the younger Putnam to forage in Burr's region, a request he happily granted. But as the tone of the letter changes, Burr exposes what was missing from his experience in command of Westchester forces: "It ever affords me the highest Pleasure, to concert with my Brother officers—Measures for mutual Convenience. Be assured Sir, within the Sphere of my Command, you shall find no Trace of that narrow Selfishness which is the bane of Society, and mutilates the Service." This was military life—comradeship, measures for mutual convenience—as Burr imagined it might be, not as it was.[102]

It was, as well, a commentary on Rufus Putnam's father, the "good old general," whose career Burr believed had been ruined by "narrow Selfishness." So, it would seem no coincidence that Burr penned these words the day before he sent off his letter of resignation to McDougall. He wanted to recall for Putnam those occasional moments in his career as an army officer when brother officers put cooperation before ambition.[103]

Burr's choice of metaphors is telling. He held that selfishness was not just "narrow" but a disease that "mutilates." The gossip that accompanied men's ambition caused him real consternation, and had finally sapped his will. Despite the promise to Washington to return when needed, Burr knew he was done with military life. As he confessed to his sister in April 1779: "I have no Intention to rejoin the Army or any Branch of it."[104]

Only known painting of Theodosia Prevost Burr (Aaron's wife), at age forty-four, on left; their daughter, Theodosia, at age seven, on the face of Burr's pocket watch.

Chapter Three

SUCH ARE THE LETTERS I LOVE

'Tis impossible for me to disguise a single thought or feeling
when writing or conversing with the friend of my heart.
—Theodosia Prevost Burr to Aaron Burr, 1785

The war years changed Burr's life in another way: he met his future
wife, Theodosia Prevost, a married woman of experience and learning, who was ten years his senior. During the war, Burr did more than learn
the ways of soldiering. He flirted with women openly, read and wrote about
sexual mores, and had occasion to discipline officers for sexual indiscretions that violated the military code of genteel behavior. In the end, he
emerged as a feminist—every bit a feminist, in the modern sense of the
word. His wife Theodosia was herself a remarkable woman, publicly savvy
and sophisticated.

Though Burr has been portrayed generally as a gallant, a seducer whose
principal playground was the parlor sofa, his early years as a bachelor, fi-
ancé, and husband paint a far more nuanced picture. As a man of the
Enlightenment, steeped in the polite manners of the eighteenth century,
Burr knowingly fashioned his behavior as he sought a higher station by
earning the respect of the Revolutionary elite. He was navigating a society
in which young men's actions were closely watched; he kept a journal before he went off to war, written for his sister, which reveals his earliest

sexual views, as well as his sense of humor about courtship. It is here that we begin to uncover the world of sexuality in the eighteenth century—rarely glimpsed.

"UNHAPPY NYMPH!"

Sexuality among elite men often began with the pen. Recall that Burr's college mentor William Paterson compared writing to masturbation. In 1774, a year before Burr volunteered for the march to Quebec, he learned that another classmate, Thaddeus Dod (called "old monk" because he was the oldest member of the Princeton student body), had "put the cart before the horse," becoming a father before he was a husband. Burr's friend Robert Stewart confided that he had laughed in amazement at the "improbable" thought of Dod sleeping with a woman. James Madison, William Bradford, and Aaron Burr all snickered about the "old monk." His story mimicked the bawdy tales of lusty old men found in colonial almanacs; besides, the young Princetonians may well have caught a glimpse of imported French erotica, which routinely poked fun at the promiscuity of Catholic priests. No wonder that Burr's cohort found it amusing that among them was a secular monk who was living a secret life chasing skirts.[1]

At the time Burr received the news about Dod, he was at some distance, studying theology in Bethlehem, Connecticut—living in the household of a professor of divinity, the Reverend Joseph Bellamy, and under the watchful eye of Bellamy's alert wife. Without much privacy, then, Burr took refuge in his private journal. It was a practice he would continue for the rest of his life.[2]

When he wrote, Burr invariably addressed himself to a female reader. His first journal, begun in 1774, was written for the benefit of his sister Sally. Later, as a married man, he would use the same technique in letters to his wife, urging her, too, to maintain a "memorandum" for him to read. Decades later, during his exile in Europe, he would commit shockingly candid words to a lengthy journal directed to his daughter.

In the opening entry of his first journal, Burr describes a humorous incident he has observed on the road, in which a gentleman and a lady, riding together, have fallen off their horse, and tumbled into a deep, snow-filled gully:

The young gentleman had the good fortune to light on his feet—not so the unhappy nymph! For falling backwards she was unable to help herself. Her head struck first, and she sunk in, up to her waist! O! miserable visu!

The sight was, in fact, amusing and erotically charged. A young woman upside down—her undergarments, if not more, exposed. The befuddled young man in Burr's account tries to rescue the maid from her "downy bed." At first, he is unable to move, hesitating over whether he should save her or keep his distance, owing to her indelicate position. Burr relishes the moment, laughing to himself at the genuine inconsistency between the rules of politeness and simple common sense.[3]

A few days later he offers up a similar story, but this time the sexual reference is even less guarded. He observes a company of "Bucks & Bell[e]s" drinking cherry rum at the local tavern. Eyeing the women, he concludes that they "looked too immensely good-natured to say no to anything." For dramatic effect, he adds: "And I doubt not the effects of this frolic will be very visible a few months hence." Burr seems to being saying: sex is natural. We all feel desire and shame—it is a part of the human condition.[4]

Adventures or "frolics" were the stuff of many men's diaries and journals. It is perhaps notable that Burr would be voicing such opinions while under the supervision of Dr. Bellamy, a "New Light" theologian, deeply committed to orthodox Calvinism. The Calvinist ideas of original sin and the corruption of the flesh were no part of Burr's thinking—of this there can be little doubt.[5]

Burr's attitudes may not have been out of place in the minister's home, after all. The entire Bellamy family teased him about his love life. For this clan, Calvinism may have been more about predestination than mundane sexual conduct. Jonathan Bellamy, the reverend's son, captured the tension between traditional and newer forms of sexuality. In a letter to Burr, he described the trial of a young woman indicted for murdering her bastard child. Bellamy does not condemn the woman for her sin, but seems rather more fascinated by the ladies who attended the trial, who were obviously curious to hear everything that was said. "Hang me if I ever again, am in pain for a *Ladies'* [sic] *delicacy!*" Bellamy wrote to Burr. It was clear to him that women had as much interest in sex as men—and it was foolish to pretend otherwise.[6]

In his journal, Burr displayed a considerable talent for painting a scene. Sitting down to record his experiences, he literally wrote himself into the story, adding conversation, interposing his own inner thoughts. His writing style has the feel of a Henry Fielding novel. He told one clever story about being "mauled" for over an hour by the entire Bellamy family about a "Miss D—— of Litchfield." Bombarded with accusatory looks and probing questions, Burr was unable to utter a word. He described his embarrassment: "'Ay silence gives consent, silence gives consent,' was the universal cry; 'a guilty conscience needs no accuser'—see how he blushes." Flustered and unable to defend himself, Burr disclosed to his journal that he considered biting his tongue off at that moment, since it was of "so little use."[7]

Eighteenth-century novelists loved the tongue-tied character—and so did Burr. At this moment, his literary self lacked the conceit he had displayed in leering at the "unhappy nymph" in the snow, or when he gleefully anticipated a roll in the hay for the tavern lads and lasses. It is interesting that Burr could at times enact a gender role reversal, depicting himself as overwrought, possessing too much feeling; he cannot help but blush, and, almost biting his tongue, he nervously loses control of himself. It is not going too far to say that Burr had a talent for writing like a woman, which explains why he wrote his journals with female readers in mind.[8]

Burr was not just writing to entertain his sister. He was preparing himself for the risky business of courtship. As one of the great journalists of the century, the Scotsman Samuel Boswell, noted, a "lady adjusts her dress before a mirror," while a "man adjusts his character by looking at his journal." It was commonly believed that the road to marriage was filled with harrowing twists and turns for the inexperienced traveler. Conduct books told women to be constantly on their guard for disreputable young men, while male suitors were warned to be modest when addressing young maids, lest they frighten them by their rude behavior.[9]

Even at eighteen, Burr was part of the marriage market, whether he wanted to be or not. He was an eligible bachelor, and eighteenth-century Americans were deeply suspicious of bachelors. Caught between two worlds, childlike dependence and adulthood, bachelors seemed dangerously unshackled from social supervision. Governor William Livingston of New Jersey, a close friend of Burr's father, wrote a scathing satire in which he compared bachelors to "free-booters," foraging "in the regions of corrupted female innocence." They were "rocks and statues" when deprived of the refining influence of wives—they were incomplete, social misfits. They were, as another contemporary remarked, the "rogue elephants" of colonial society.[10]

Before he joined the army, Burr was wary about rushing to the altar. His friends shared his hesitation. Jonathan Bellamy wrote a playful letter to Burr, defending their common resistance to marriage. Bellamy referred to the "spot where our castle is to stand," a castle "where we are to convince mankind that the only happy life is that of a bachelor."[11]

But social pressures to marry continued to harass Burr. Once again he resorted to a novelistic prose when he related to his sister a most remarkable rumor. Writing from Elizabethtown in the summer of 1775, he began: "none of our acquaintances dead or married lately," except "your brother *Aaron.*" Then, he explained:

> *I have it from several persons of undoubted authority that he was tied some months ago to a lady of exquisite beauty, immense fortune, &c. &c. This I assure you, my dear sister, is absolutely matter of fact—I have been very frequently wished joy on the occasion, and "pray sir, how did you leave Mrs. Burr?" As seriously as you would ask after Mrs. Pollock—No small trouble have I been at to retrieve the character of a batchelor.*

His imaginary wife was so "real" that in Elizabethtown society one would-be gallant threatened to duel with Burr, in an effort to protect the lady's reputation from Burr's repeated denials. His secret marriage was apparently so secret that the groom had not been invited to the wedding![12]

Meanwhile, his cousin Thaddeus Burr, a wealthy landowner in Fairfield, Connecticut, was actively nudging Burr toward marriage. A few months earlier, while Burr was living in Litchfield, forsaking theology to study law with his brother-in-law Tapping Reeve, his cousin Thaddeus claimed to have found the perfect match. He was pressing the young man to seriously consider a young lady of considerable fortune. But Burr refused to be pushed into marriage, writing to his good friend Matthias Ogden that only he could choose his future companion—no one else could do it for him.[13]

Of course, women were neither entirely coy nor passive in courtship. This was another lesson Burr was to learn. Even before the rumor of the secret marriage, Burr again wrote to Ogden that one (unnamed) woman "had absolutely professed love for me." He was concerned about it. He did not wish to be forced to the altar either by relatives or rumors.[14]

Young men of Burr's social class could rarely escape the watchful eyes of the women in their communities. Good breeding was often not enough to ensure a positive reception in society. Unfavorable rumors might circulate, demanding a chorus of denials. Young men regularly enlisted their friends to come to their defense against false or disparaging accounts. In a letter to Ogden, Burr dismissed what he called the "groundless" rumors of his romantic entanglements in Princeton, noting that the name of the woman changed depending on who told the story. Ogden knew him "too well," Burr assured, to think he was "in love with every new or pretty face" he saw.[15]

Yet men were just as willing as women to ostracize other men for unrefined and ill-tempered displays. Burr also confessed to Ogden that he was glad to hear of another man's downfall—one of those "narrow-hearted scoundrels," who will "pass through life respected by many." He disliked men who conveyed a pleasing deportment, but who concealed "malice" in their hearts. Here is Burr dismissing everything Lord Chesterfield stood for—everything he would later be accused of mastering in his social conduct.[16]

Burr did enjoy a little intrigue in his social life. He told Ogden that he had taken on the role of matchmaker. Like the romanticized story of Cyrano de Bergerac, Burr was secretly crafting love letters for a friend, who was "very little versed in letter-writing." He confessed that he had "now and then an affair of petty gallantry," but the details were too "insipid" to share. Though interested in romance, Burr was hardly living in the fast lane in Litchfield.[17]

A particularly tempting flirtation is revealed, once again through his cousin Thaddeus. In May 1775, Burr visited Thaddeus in Fairfield, and was there introduced to Dorothy Quincy. She was, at this time, the fiancée of John Hancock, and the couple would later be wed in Thaddeus Burr's mansion. While Dolly, as she was known, was a "catch," entertaining many eligible male callers at her home in Boston, she probably caught Burr's eye for another reason: she was nine years his senior. Dolly claimed that the attraction was mutual. His busybody cousin Thaddeus felt certain that, if Hancock was out of the way, Dolly would not wait a day to chase after Burr.[18]

Burr, then, was not a Chesterfieldian cad and flatterer, who indulged women's pride in order to seduce them. The Earl of Chesterfield's *Letters to his Son,* a popular guide to manners, advanced the idea that a man could nurture disdain or malice, but he must never reveal his disregard for a woman's feelings. Such rakish behavior does not comport with Burr's presentation to his friends, nor is it reflected in their perceptions of him. In Burr's actual social circle, if he had been seducing young women with abandon, as later claimed, he surely would have found himself forced to the altar (as Dod was), or, at the very least, he would have been rebuked for his behavior. But he never was.[19]

Burr was thinking and writing about sex in the same way as his peers thought and wrote. Young Burr could not have escaped the prying eyes of Mrs. Bellamy, or his cousin Thaddeus Burr, or his sister Sally, or her husband Tapping Reeve. And at this early stage, Burr cared deeply about what people were saying about him. He was still Reverend Burr's son.

THE "MISTRESS OF YOUR AFFECTIONS"

By July 1775, as he and Ogden headed north for the encampment in Cambridge, Burr was, probably for the first time, beyond the watchful eyes of his elders. Thrust into the ad hoc community of soldiers, officers, women, and wagoners who made up a military camp, he assured his sister that she had nothing to fear from his new life style. Bullets, he joked, were infinitely less dangerous than the "darts shot from the eyes of regiments of female angels" that had surrounded him at home.[20]

War would replace romance—or would it? Amid the divided loyalties of war, Aaron Burr found love across enemy lines. When he met his future wife, Theodosia Prevost, she was not only married but the wife of a British officer. Lieutenant Colonel James Marcus Prevost served in the southern campaigns and in the West Indies, dying from yellow fever in Jamaica in the fall of 1781.[21]

The Revolution created a unique social as well as sexual landscape. Regulating sexual behavior became a regular part of the business of the Continental Army, and officers judged each other, in part, based on their sexual conduct. Burr may have left communal standards of morality behind, but the army enforced its own rules for officers and gentlemen.

Expectations of politeness became a crucial feature of the symbolic battle between the American and English armies: the chivalrous treatment of ladies was one means of measuring which army was the more civilized, and thus more deserving of public support.

Burr's relationship with Theodosia must be examined in this odd cultural contest of civility. Theodosia herself was in no simple position: she had to navigate carefully between two worlds. Though married to a loyal British officer, she was a closet patriot; she forged strong alliances with George Washington himself, as well as other prominent officials in Revolutionary New Jersey. Governor William Livingston and Attorney General William Paterson ranked among her friends and supporters. Theodosia combined a unique blend of female heroism and social grace; executing skills of politeness was absolutely essential to her political survival. It was, undoubtedly, her political and social acumen that first caused Burr to admire her, and provided the basis for a deeper affection.

Burr's war was a series of contrasts. Refined circumstances might be followed by sordid ones—all were part of his daily routine. During the march to Quebec in 1775, he enjoyed the hospitality of polite society in the Maine wilderness when an obliging family gave him a feather bed and a warm meal. Not long after, during his prolonged encampment outside the Canadian city, he described himself as "dirty" and "ragged." This was merely preparation for Valley Forge, where soldiers drank to excess, cursed, and whored.[22]

Throughout the war, camp life was mean and dirty. Noxious smells filled the air; open latrines, poor hygiene, and crude quarters fed masculine vices, which officers were meant to temper. But officers did not always set the best example. A typical incident Burr recorded in his orderly book in 1778 told of one who was rumored to have had tea in his tent with his "whore" and her mother. This charade—a strumpet pretending to be a lady—offended enough other officers to elicit a court-martial.[23]

Though conditions at camp were often disagreeable, Burr quickly learned that one of the privileges granted to officers was the pleasure of polite female companionship. Washington had a lively inner circle at Valley Forge. Martha Washington, described by a French officer as a "Roman matron," gathered around her an intimate group of generals, their wives, and occasionally a distinguished belle or two. Holding dinners, dances, and teas, the ladies entertained select junior officers. Lord Stirling and his family were particularly known for their conviviality. Burr attended many of their gatherings at Valley Forge, and drolly remarked that the primary duty of James Monroe, Stirling's aide-de-camp, was to "fill his lordship's tankard."[24]

At more elaborate celebrations, the presence of ladies had a decidedly political purpose. When France recognized the independence of the United States in 1778, Washington selected May 6 for a *feu de joie,* a day of national rejoicing. Cannons roared, and muskets fired off rounds, as the commander in chief reviewed the troops. Colonel Burr was there, and marched off, arm-in-arm, with his fellow officers to a sumptuous buffet, joined by a group of fawning females. Less than three weeks later and just forty miles away in Philadelphia, the British rivaled the Americans by hosting a Mischianza. This was a grandiose affair, capped by an extravagant masquerade, in which British officers competed for the hand of one fair lady in a mock medieval tournament.[25]

Such public spectacles as these reflected the common belief among gentlemen that women's loyalty was measured by their *affections,* and that conquering the hearts of women ensured popular support more generally and foretold victory in war. It is essential to bear in mind that the Revolution was a civil war: there were deep pockets of pro-British sentiment in every state, city, and hamlet, and by winning the favor of the fairer sex, the smartly attired redcoats stood to sway public opinion as they demoralized the rebels.

Civilized warfare demanded that ladies—even Tory ladies—receive a show of respect, but this was not always the case. After states passed legislation authorizing confiscation of the property of known Loyalists, women and children were thrown out of their homes. The artist Charles Willson Peale, head of the Confiscation Committee in Philadelphia, literally dragged the wife of Joseph Galloway from her doorway, telling her bluntly that "it was not the first time he had taken a Lady by the hand."[26]

But the issue went even deeper. Loyalist women were caught in an impossible situation: their husbands, not they, owned their property, so that their voices, in a legal sense, did not matter. Indecision, or neutrality, was not permitted them. With the call to independence, all Americans were forced to choose sides—and yet, could wives oppose their husbands? Could they freely make a choice? When Burr first heard of the new confiscation policy in early 1776, he heartily endorsed the idea. But by the time he had met Theodosia Prevost, his opinion had already changed. He understood the difficulties she faced.[27]

It was within this combustible political climate that Aaron Burr and Theodosia Prevost grew to appreciate one another and eventually settled on marriage. She had achieved what few other women could, garnering the support of prominent patriots (military and civilian alike), knowing she was supportive of their cause, while convincing her husband and the British military that she remained a devoted wife of a British officer. Theodosia was adept at keeping up appearances, and keeping her family together; while raising her five children and maintaining connections with a large extended family, she entered into an unfeigned friendship with Aaron Burr that led to a secret romance. To be sure, this was no easy road for a woman in her situation to take. Theodosia's delicate and daring balancing act signals a complicated and fascinating woman.

It is difficult to put a precise date on the first meeting between Burr and his future wife, though he may have appeared at the Hermitage, in Bergen County, New Jersey, as early as September 1777. The introduction may have been made by her cousin John Watkins, who served in Burr's regiment. By the following summer, Burr was certainly a regular visitor. Her husband was off fighting in the southern colonies, while Theodosia and her mother ran the household.[28]

Burr would have been drawn to the Hermitage for the same reason other officers flocked there—it offered a taste of polite society. The property encompassed 98 acres, supporting two elegant homes, each of which enjoyed a constant flow of guests, and made it the perfect location for Washington's headquarters in July 1778, just after the fierce but ultimately indecisive Battle of Monmouth. Theodosia had presented the general with a gracious invitation that he found impossible to refuse. Theodosia's home, named after Jean-Jacques Rousseau's famous cottage, was a pastoral retreat. During his stay there, James McHenry, one of Washington's aide-de-camps, described the delightful company of "fair refugees" from British-held New York. McHenry claimed that he completely forgot the war, spending his days talking, walking, dancing, and laughing with Theodosia's relatives.[29]

It may seem odd that Washington would put his headquarters on the property of a Loyalist family. But Theodosia, for one, was not unsympathetic to Washington's aims. In addition, conditions under which armies and civilians coexisted—indeed, the very rules of warfare during the American Revolution—were different from modern times. Among elites a code of honor made it possible for those on opposite sides to interact with a kind of civility that would be impossible in today's political world. When General Charles Lee was captured by the British, for example, he was treated as a gentleman, despite being a prisoner of war, and was allowed to move freely around New York City, which was then under British occupation. Theodosia clearly adhered to the same code when she opened her home to Washington and his military family.[30]

At the Hermitage, Rousseau's influence could also be felt in the atmosphere. Theodosia's manner was decidedly French: she spoke the language fluently, while cultivating the smart conversational style that distinguished the French salons. She composed entertaining letters to Burr in French, and later, because her French was superior to his, translated political treatises for him. Her stepfather, Philip De Visme, and her husband's family, the Prevosts (pronounced "PRE-vo," more or less in the French manner), were Swiss émigrés. Tutored at home, she had been exposed to a cosmopolitan education that was unusual among colonial Americans.[31]

We receive a rare glimpse of her talents in an anecdote from this period, the source of which is probably Burr himself. One evening, after a boorish guest had unknowingly slighted the hostess, she decided to seek revenge. In a matter of moments, she dashed off a poem mocking the man, and passed it around the room, prompting general laughter. This display of mental agility suggests that she was a practitioner of the competitive game crambo, a test in which visitors to the European salons were obliged to perform spontaneous poetry writing—crambo was the height of fashion and a determinant of a person's verbal skill. Theodosia's impromptu wit eclipsed many of lesser talents.[32]

But Theodosia was an appealing companion in the midst of war for another important reason: she intimately understood how British and American military officers looked at the world. As a child and as a young woman, the British military community in New York City had been her primary social circle. Her stepfather was a captain in the Royal American Regiment, as was her husband when she first met him, and two of her aunts married military officers. That she wed Captain Prevost at the tender age of seventeen was not at all surprising for a young woman with her family background.[33]

Steeped in military tradition and custom, Theodosia moved easily within male military culture. She naturally made an impact on an older, more reserved commander like Washington, and seemed not to miss a step when endeavoring to please impressionable young men like Burr and McHenry. James Monroe, another of her youthful admirers, best conveyed why so many Continental officers had become enamored with this wife of a British officer. In a revealing letter he wrote to Theodosia, Monroe praised her "fortitude under distress" and "gaiety in the midst of affliction," despite the long separation from her husband. In Monroe's eyes, she was Odysseus' long-suffering wife Penelope. With his wartime sense of chivalry, Monroe could romantically imagine her as a chaste republican matron—better than to see her as a Loyalist woman married to the enemy.[34]

But her skill in dealing with officers was not limited to the Continentals. Theodosia also cultivated a congenial arrangement with the British officers who passed through her neighborhood. Their torches never touched her home. They even extended the military courtesy of allowing an American prisoner of war, a relative of hers, to be placed on parole in her household. Her home was a kind of war-free zone and sanctuary. Several times during the fighting, as the British army threatened, the families of Governor William Livingston and Lord Stirling wisely sought shelter at the Hermitage.[35]

Theodosia attracted a powerful circle of male patrons. And within this circle of prominent Whigs, she presented herself as a patriot. Governor Livingston and Robert Morris, a member of the Supreme Court of New Jersey, were some of her closest allies. Robert Troup, another young officer turned civil servant, and a friend of Morris, described her in the most glowing terms. "During the whole of the war," Troup wrote to a fellow officer, "she has conducted herself in such a manner as proves her to possess an excellent understanding as well as a strong attachment to our righteous cause." Like Monroe, he saw her as a lady in distress, but underscored her fidelity to the movement for independence. Troup gleaned his opinion from the "most respectable Whigs in the State." Theodosia could hardly have asked for a better recommendation. An unabashed patriot, she had to be rather shrewd to thrive in this highly volatile environment.[36]

As Burr became a part of Theodosia's political orbit, he became her patron, and she, in turn, became his. It all began in August 1778, when the colonel was assigned as military escort for three prominent Loyalists: William Smith, Cadwallader Colden, and Roeliff Eltinge. These men had all been members of the provincial government of prewar New York and were prisoners of war. For reasons unknown, Theodosia and her sister Catherine De Visme accompanied this party on a five-day journey from New Jersey to Fishkill, above West Point, and down the Hudson River to British-held New York City. Since Burr received the assignment only a month after General Washington had visited the Hermitage, it appears likely that Theodosia's good word probably swayed the commander to choose Burr for the job.[37]

Adding women to the escort was probably more than an afterthought. Theodosia and her female relatives had proven that they could be extremely helpful in gathering intelligence in the British-occupied city. One tantalizing piece of news they shared with the American commander was that an elegant gift sent to Martha Washington by the queen of France had been seized by the British. Behind enemy lines, small talk itself was a form of espionage. As witty traveling companions, Theodosia and her sister stood to uncover secrets from unsuspecting Loyalists.[38]

Perhaps the most crucial assistance Burr offered was in helping Theodosia protect her estate. As early as 1777, she was laboring on her own behalf, penning appeals to prominent officials. She sent petitions to the New Jersey Assembly, and enlisted the aid of Governor Livingston. Because of Burr, Attorney General William Paterson was in her corner. "Her situation demands a tear," Paterson warmly confessed to his friend. He kept Burr informed of his efforts, using his considerable clout and sharp legal mind to find a solution. He had already worked miracles for his wife's Loyalist brother, finding a loophole to save his personal property.[39]

Paterson was no different from Theodosia's other patrons. Though an avid Whig and strong-minded attorney general who insisted on enforcing the letter of the law, he still made occasional exceptions for friends and relatives. Patronage and persistence (such as Burr's letters) ultimately yielded results: prior to 1782, confiscation proceedings were undertaken against Theodosia's property until, all of a sudden, the prosecution of her case ceased—powerful friends had finally succeeded in making her case disappear. With the governor, attorney general, and Supreme Court Justice Robert Morris all on her side, she found a way to subvert the legal process from within.[40]

At first, Burr's feelings for Theodosia resembled those of her other young male acquaintances. In a tone identical to Monroe's, echoed by Troup, Burr fantasized rescuing her from the calamities of war. In 1779, he sped off to Boston on a knight's errand. There, Theodosia's poor Loyalist brother was held prisoner. Exuberantly, Burr told his sister, "How happy if I am his Deliverer!"[41]

Reinventing chivalry, Continental officers fostered what can best be described as a romantic cult of republican matrons. The language they used derived from the medieval model of courtly love, and encouraged devotion to mature women. The difference in age and status implied a relationship that existed on a higher, more spiritual plane, and which made the younger man's admiration appear noble and altruistic. Whether they realized it or not, the language of chivalry was highly sexualized: age differences aside, desire was sparked by the unlikely quest of winning the lady's hand. Seeking the unobtainable enhanced the desire, stirring that old-fashioned mixture of unrequited love and repressed passion. For Whigs Monroe, Troup, and Burr, chastened lust rose from beneath the surface of this new, revivified version of courtly love.

It is telling that the men in this chivalric trio were so close in age in 1778: Burr was the oldest at twenty-two, Troup one year younger, and Monroe two years. All three had been aides to prominent generals—Burr in the service of Montgomery and Putnam, Troup with Horatio Gates, and Monroe with Lord Stirling. All sported the laurels of battle and carried real battle scars. Troup had been incarcerated on the British prison ship *Mentor* in 1776, and Monroe received a severe wound during Washington's heralded raid on Trenton on Christmas Day. Burr's health had suffered when he succumbed to heat prostration at the Battle of Monmouth; many died and many more fell ill amid fighting in temperatures above 100 degrees F.[42]

Glory and gallantry was pursued on the battlefield, of course. But for these three, there was glory of a different kind—perhaps no less important to them—within the halls of the Hermitage. At Theodosia's side, they received mature advice, consolatory comfort, cheering company, and in Burr's case especially, a retreat where he might convalesce and overcome his headaches. Each man, in return, proved his honorable intentions by acting selflessly as her patron. More than anything else, this culture of chivalry explains how she acquired a following of young devotees. Burr, at least in the beginning, was no different than the others who were drawn to her as they were drawn to a courtly game of honor.

He began to imagine Theodosia as a member of his family. That is what eventually distinguished his affections from the others. Writing once again to Sally, he gave Mrs. Prevost the pet name "sister P.," describing her as "our lovely sister." This term of endearment was a telling departure from his previous flirtations. Burr's relationship with his older sister was extremely close; she had been his one female confidante, the trusted recipient of his journalistic musings on sex and polite society as he was coming of age. To Sally, he confessed in an emotional moment how his "pen and heart" were always entwined. He was gradually transferring his primary affections from Sally to Theodosia, while bringing "sister P." into the family fold. He explained in November 1778: "Believe me, Sally, she has an honest and affectionate heart. We talk of you very often, her highest happiness will be to see you and love you." By making Theodosia his surrogate sister, Burr could channel his growing desires into intimate terms that were acceptable. A chaste matron, the British officer's wife was increasingly a woman he could *love as a sister*.[43]

All this talk of sisterly affection failed to conceal his deeper feelings. His constant visits to the Hermitage provoked gossip. Two of William Livingston's daughters asked Troup if Burr was courting Theodosia's unmarried sister, Catherine De Visme. By 1780, Burr's questioning cousin Thaddeus finally agreed that he wouldn't "joke any more about a certain lady." By far the most amazing letter came from Paterson, following his own marriage in February 1779. Unguardedly referring to Theodosia as the "Mistress of your Affections," he strongly urged Burr to marry as soon as possible. "May I congratulate you both in the Course of the next moon for being in my Line, I mean, the married." What Paterson called his "strange unconnected Scroll [scrawl]," actually sounded the way he did when he was Burr's college mentor: the letter-writing Paterson was known for his intrusive commentary about students' love lives. Burr's desires could not remain hidden for long from Paterson—as this letter clearly shows.[44]

Paterson's congratulations were premature, to say the least. Theodosia was still married, and only a few months later her husband begged her to

join him. In the early fall of 1779, Lieutenant Colonel Prevost was appointed lieutenant governor of the royal administration in Georgia. That
November, another of Theodosia's sisters, Elizabeth Duval, who was also
married to a British officer, urged her to follow her husband "to Georgia, Jamaica, or wherever he may settle for a time." She could not understand why
Theodosia ignored his request, pointedly asking her: "What can be your
motive for not complying with it?" Theodosia made excuses—but her real
motive may well have been Burr, who was spending a great deal of time at
the Hermitage recovering from his illness. We can only speculate on what
their extended intimacy provoked. Yet Theodosia gives the appearance she
was not ready to break her marriage vows—at least symbolically keeping
that love alive. After telling her husband she could not join him, she sent
along a lock of her hair, the most remarked upon love token of the time.[45]

Theodosia's marriage would not formally end until December 1781,
when she learned of her husband's death by yellow fever in Jamaica. Her
two teenage sons, John Bartow and Augustine James Frederick, had joined
their father's regiment as ensigns; in 1780, they returned to New Jersey to
avoid contracting the deadly contagion. On the last day of 1781, Catherine
De Visme sent word to Burr. "If you have not seen the York Gazette," she
noted, "the following account will be news to you." The "news" was of Prevost's death. Her message was undisguised: the last obstacle to marriage
was now removed.[46]

All evidence suggests that Theodosia and Burr were by now openly
lovers. In a July 1780 letter to his sister, Burr described Theodosia as one
would a playful lover, sitting at "his elbow [and] is this moment pinching
my ear, because I will not say any thing about her to you." In Paterson's
1779 letter, which appeared long before Prevost's illness, he talked about
Aaron and Theodosia's marriage, and in the same breath refers to Theodosia as "Mrs. Prevost." There is only one inescapable conclusion: Paterson
knew that Burr and Theodosia were contemplating marriage long before
she had any idea that she might become a widow.[47]

Theodosia demonstrated finesse in negotiating between competing desires and ambitions. She saw herself as devoted, keeping her family intact
while changing her own life by becoming the not-so-secret mistress of
Burr's affections. War had decisively transformed her marriage. The decision not to join her husband in 1779 meant that she would remain

physically apart from him, and would remake herself as an independent supporter of the American patriot movement.

Her sister Elizabeth Duval saw her decision to remain apart as a highly improper one, damaging to her marriage. It is important to remember that in the eighteenth century, wives did informally end their marriages by living apart from their husbands. Whether or not she imagined her decision as an informal separation, Theodosia made a choice: not to continue her marriage on terms she found unacceptable.

Another possibility is that Paterson was hinting at divorce. Given her political influence, Theodosia may have been able to bring a divorce petition to the attention of the state legislature. Her husband was a Loyalist, an enemy of the state, and thus no longer recognized as a citizen of New Jersey. She could have presented herself as a patriotic matron who wished to cut the ties that bound her to a Loyalist husband, just as the new American nation had abandoned the British Empire. What could be more appealing to a Revolutionary legislature than this script—one that Theodosia already had successfully rehearsed before her prominent Whig friends? Yet divorce required many years of litigation, delays that neither Burr nor Theodosia would have wished to endure. If Colonel Prevost had survived, it might have been their only chance for happiness together.

It is apparent, then, that neither Aaron Burr nor Theodosia Prevost was prim or puritanical. They projected marriage, with the support of friends and family. As patriots, as lovers, they were undeterred by the challenges before them.

"A PLACE SACRED TO LOVE, REFLECTION, AND BOOKS"

In December 1781, the same month he learned of Colonel Prevost's death, Burr kept a journal for Theodosia. Recording his every feeling, Burr dwelled longest on the agony of separation; he was impatient for the day they would be "formally united." And so he begged her, "Visit me in my slumbers." A few days after this, lying prostrate with a severe headache, he longed for her company, and spent the entire day stretched out on a blanket before the fire. He fantasized feeling her "little hand" gently stroking his head.[48]

Eighteenth-century marriages pretended to be built on friendship and affection, but few actually were. The union of Aaron Burr and the previously married Theodosia, however, would be. "'Tis impossible for me," she wrote, unforced, using the same lover's vocabulary, "to disguise a single thought or feeling when writing or conversing with the friend of my heart." Their letters brimmed with need. They were earnest and resolute, as much as they were affectionate. To his future wife, and to her alone, perhaps, his life was an open book.[49]

Burr distinctly pursued a marriage based on a very modern idea of friendship between the sexes. He found such advocacy in the writings of John Witherspoon, president of his alma mater, Princeton; and as well in the more respectable courtship novels of his day, and in Mary Wollstonecraft's *Vindication of the Rights of Woman*. That ultra-liberal 1792 work rocked British and American society; but Burr had already begun practicing its egalitarian marital principles ten years before its publication.[50]

Burr's impending marriage—with its intimations of illicit love—was complicated by the ongoing war, and intensified by serious illness. Both he and Theodosia were suffering from real physical ailments. He routinely called himself an "invalid," and spent much of his time in the year or so leading up to his marriage seeking relief at mineral springs located near the Hermitage. His symptoms—migraine headaches, "eye trouble," and spells of depression—suggest some kind of nervous disorder. His sister suffered from similar ailments, though in her case temporary blindness may have been a sign of multiple sclerosis.[51]

Friends constantly worried about his delicate constitution. In the fall of 1780, Troup and Paterson felt he was, in Troup's words, "on the brink of eternity," ready to take his "final farewell of this wrangling world." Burr experienced uncontrollable mood swings. He confessed to Theodosia that many days were sacrificed to an all-consuming "ill humour." Noting that he was becoming something of a recluse, Burr felt "unlike himself"—"a little *hypo*," as he admitted to Paterson. He needed to be "remote from the noise of war," he said, dejectedly. Was this, perhaps, the eighteenth-century version of post-traumatic stress disorder?[52]

Illness was never far from his thoughts. Theodosia's condition was an "incurable disorder of the uterus," which possibly developed into cancer. She eventually succumbed to it at the age of forty-eight. As early as 1781, if not earlier, Burr was fully aware she was ill, and "dangerously so." Enduring periods of excruciating pain during their marriage, she increasingly relied on laudanum to ease her suffering. Laudanum was an opium-based drug, unregulated and freely administered, that could bring about periods of melancholy. Theodosia took solace in his "friendly sympathy," his willingness to let her "speak without reserve," while Burr hounded physicians for a magic cure. Occasionally he aired his frustration, complaining of false friends who asked about her health but did not adequately invest in Theodosia's recovery; theirs were merely "cold, uninterested inquiries." Pity had no appeal for him—it was a weakness he refused to indulge.[53]

The year 1781 brought stress for other reasons. In December, Burr was living in Albany, trying to get a license to practice law. He had studied with his brother-in-law Tapping Reeve before the war; afterwards, he worked his way through three apprenticeships, starting with Titus Hosmer of Middletown, Connecticut, followed by his good friend Paterson, and finally settling down to a rigorous routine with Thomas Smith of Haverstraw, New York, on the west bank of the Hudson. Under Smith's tutelage, Burr returned to his intensive habits of study, devoting an incredible sixteen hours a day to reading and compiling notes. There was little time to waste; he needed a career if he intended to marry and support Theodosia's family, and Smith promised to prepare him for the New York bar with dispatch.[54]

Friendship sustained Burr in this hectic period. Theodosia had left the Hermitage for the placid hamlet of Sharon, Connecticut, not far from his sister's home in Litchfield. By leaving New Jersey, she sought to undermine efforts by state commissioners to confiscate her husband's property. Burr, with his routine of racing back and forth from New York to Connecticut, was making a lawyer out of himself. Robert Troup, whom Burr described as "a worthy, sensible young fellow, and a particular friend of mine," became his constant companion in 1780. Mainly through Troup's persistence, they became inseparable, studying and living together, and promoting each other's ambition of joining the New York bar.[55]

Adding to their troubles, Burr and Theodosia were constantly hounded by gossip and "calumny"—as insult and invective was commonly called. Her decision to flee to Sharon failed to stifle the angry attacks back in New Jersey. As Burr astutely observed, many people thought it would be to their advantage—prove their patriotism—if they assailed her reputation. A particularly offensive "canting Reverend Doctor" used the art of the insult to puff up his less than sterling credentials as a Whig. Burr considered the reverend's moral hypocrisy plain as day, exclaiming: "What an amiable imitation of the meek philanthropy of the Savior whom he pretends to imitate!"[56]

Burr's regular visits to the Hermitage had caused tongues to wag. Theodosia had no intention of starting their marriage from a position of desperation. This is abundantly clear from a letter she wrote to Burr in May 1781. Advising him to study the law in order to guarantee his professional life—for "respect and independence," as she put it—she demanded at the same time respect and independence for herself. Theodosia understood that dependence generated resentment; she did not wish to live inconsequentially relative to Burr's rising career. She knew that dependence led to self-loathing, to a loss of pride no less likely to destroy what began as genuine affection. "Pride," she pointedly declared, was "inseparable from true love." Not wishing to be beholden to him, she explained that if she could not regain her "own happiness," she could never agree to marry for either "pecuniary motives" or out of emotional desperation.[57]

It was their passion for books, and the cultivation of a mature affection, that seems to have allowed them to weather the storm as they contemplated marriage. In December 1781, Burr advised Theodosia to install a Franklin stove in her rustic cottage in Sharon, and suggested placing it in the back room, for there she could have "a place sacred to love, reflection, and books." One of the books they read and discussed was *Emile,* Jean-Jacques Rousseau's groundbreaking treatise on education. It was one of Theodosia's favorite works.[58]

Just a few months before she wrote asserting her sense of independence, she had explored personal freedom as an intellectual problem. Writing with a sense of passion and purpose, she argued specifically that Rousseau's model of education was superior to that of Lord Chesterfield. The controversial French *philosophe* called for educating a child to be independent, responsible, and in Theodosia's words, "a happy, respectable member of society." In contrast, Chesterfield visualized a world of courtiers and envoys—as useless and parasitical as "ten thousand modern beaux."[59]

Her comments suggest why she and Burr later came to admire the writings of Mary Wollstonecraft. The connection between Rousseau and Wollstonecraft matters to us because it helps to explain what it was that drew this enlightened American couple together. Though *A Vindication of* the *Rights of Woman* was not published until 1792, Wollstonecraft's ruling concept derived from Rousseau: "liberty was the mother of virtue." In other words, every child must be given enough freedom to learn to exercise the faculty of reason, to cultivate understanding, and thus to be truly independent. Theodosia and Burr would have been familiar with this notion in 1781. Though the author of *Vindication* became one of Rousseau's greatest critics—because his radical plan excluded women—Wollstonecraft did not reject his ideas; she only challenged how they should be applied. Her solution was deceptively simple: extend Rousseau's plan of education in *Emile* to girls as well as boys.[60]

That Theodosia loved Rousseau's ideal of moral independence and utterly despised Chesterfield also made perfect sense. Wollstonecraft, too, railed against Chesterfield's model pupil—the courtier—calling him an "indolent puppet," devoid of reason and moral agency, whose only goal in life was to please others. Groveling was precisely what Theodosia found so unappealing in "ten thousand modern beaux."[61]

Burr and Theodosia modeled their relationship on the eighteenth century's ideal of an intellectual friendship. The heart and mind were meant to bind two kindred souls together into a noble communion based on mutual esteem and generosity. Sublime friendship required what Burr called the "impulse of feeling"—to speak without formality or artificial restraint. This kind of intimacy and openness allowed for an instructive exchange of ideas; one's "whole soul" was subject to examination.

Theodosia reflected this ideal when she admitted to Burr: "In writing without form or reflection your ideas and feelings of the moment, trusting to the partiality of your friend every imperfect thought, and to his candour every ill-turned phrase. Such are the letters I love, and such I request of those I love." Burr responded in kind, begging Theodosia to record any ideas she had while reading, praising her comments on Voltaire as containing "more good sense than all the strictures I have seen upon his works put together." What made this kind of exchange unusual is that this model of intellectual friendship was designed for two men—not husband and wife. This pattern of intellectual honesty set them apart and made their relationship distinctive.[62]

Theodosia and Aaron Burr were married on July 2, 1782, just a few months after he had been licensed as an attorney and approved as a counselor-at-law—the latter title allowed him to handle cases on his own in the courtroom. In April of that year, Burr had opened a law office in Albany. Perhaps another reason why the marriage occurred that summer is the fact that Theodosia's favorite sister, Catherine De Visme, had decided to marry Dr. Joseph Browne, a British-born physician turned rebel officer. Catherine was the sister who had informed Burr that Colonel Prevost was dead.[63]

Catherine offered to make the nuptials a joint affair at the Hermitage. The doctor and his bride had more money at their disposal, and as Theodosia joked in a letter to Sally Reeve, Burr used his last "half Joe" for the parson's fees. The wedding itself, she added, cost them "nothing." Nor did they have to do much to prepare for the occasion: Burr was dressed in his "old coat," and Theodosia's gown and gloves were "favors from Cathy." They even had Governor Livingston issue a special license, to dispense with the normal banns of marriage—a formal recognition of betrothal. Sending his congratulations, the governor hoped they would be blessed with love, happiness, and social acceptance. Livingston expected that marriage would bring an end to the malevolence the pair had experienced: "the tongue of malice," he said, "dare not I think calumniate it."[64]

Theodosia gave birth to a daughter a year later, on June 21, 1783. On Burr's insistence, the little girl was named after her mother. The new father took all of his parental responsibilities seriously, beyond just caring for the young Theodosia. He found a tutor for his wife's two teenage sons, Frederick and Bartow, giving them clerkships in his law office. On June 20, 1785, Theodosia bore another daughter, Sally, who "passed gently" at the age of three. She also endured two other difficult pregnancies that ended in stillbirths. Illness and death hovered over their union. Theodosia would be the Burrs' only child to survive to adulthood.[65]

Burr's new career placed demands on the marriage. With the official end of war, the British army had evacuated from Manhattan in November. American merchants and local politicians resumed control of the city. In 1783, Burr moved his law practice to New York City, hoping to attract commercial cases in the bustling seaport town. Uncle Timothy warned Burr that the city suffered from "both natural and moral pollution" in the wake of the British occupation. Burr, nevertheless, felt certain that it was the perfect location for an enterprising young lawyer. He settled his family on Wall Street, near City Hall, and the following year moved into a more spacious home on Little Queen Street. In 1790, they moved again, this time to No. 4 Broadway, occupying an even grander house.[66]

As Burr moved his family into bigger and bigger homes, he handled more and more cases, and made regular appearances in court in Albany. Traveling by stage and aboard ship, Burr often found himself "packed with the rabble" for long hours, as he wrote Theodosia, ending these days "chilled, fatigued, and with a surly headache." His wife worried about his "tender frame," questioning whether his health could endure the hectic pace of travel, the tedious paperwork, and ever-increasing bouts of ill-humor.[67] At least the Burrs' intellectual partnership did not suffer. As their third year of marriage began, he was reading her memoranda "as religiously as ever monk did his devotion."[68]

They relied on humor to expose each other's flaws (and, at times, to engage in self-criticism). In a marvelous letter to Tapping Reeve, Theodosia added a postscript, mocking one of Burr's letters for its unnecessary formality, noting: "he mistook you for a client," by signing off as "your most humble servant." At other times, she ironically referred to Burr as "your lordship." In general, Burr said what he meant, loath to retreat from what he identified as his "natural bluntness." In his letters, he readily bestowed both praise and criticism on his wife, in a tone no different than that he used in addressing male friends. He never flattered or patronized her, but reveled in candor. In this way, no one could be further from the Chesterfieldian beau in conversing with women. For her part, Theodosia openly disagreed with her husband's views, never shy to point out his flaws.[69]

Their relationship was unique in another crucial sense: they both believed that intelligent women could participate in politics. Burr routinely sent his wife political newspapers to read, and assumed she would pass them along to his male friends and colleagues in New York City. After forwarding to her a book about two "eminent characters" on the American political scene, he was so pleased with her portraits of the men that he showed her comments to a "friend of *one of the authors.*" Yet he sensed how important it was to show discretion—especially because he confided political secrets in her. Anything she might say while traveling in a public carriage could have an impact on his career, and so Burr advised her in 1792— the year of his election to the U.S. Senate—to remain aloof from other political men.[70]

Theodosia readily engaged in political patronage. In one instance, she asked Burr to consider a friend for an appointment. Activity of this kind became common among elite women in Washington City after 1800, and it was just as true when New York City was the federal capital in 1789–90. George Washington's administration established the first "republican court," setting a precedent that would stand for decades. Informal, behind-the-scenes, female influence over politicians' decisions was all in a day's business. What makes Theodosia special is the radical tone of her ideas about women's role in the enlightened nation state. These views crystallized in her admiration for Catherine the Great of Russia. In 1791, Theodosia wrote Burr of the empress: "The ladies should deify her, and consecrate a temple to her praise. It is a diverting thought that the mighty Emperor of the Turks should be subdued by a woman. How enviable that she alone should be the avenger of her sex's wrongs for so many years past. She seems to have awakened Justice, who appears to be a sleepy dame in the cause of injured innocence." Such language would be dramatic in any age, but was particularly dramatic in this one.[71]

Considered by Voltaire to be an "enlightened despot," the empress of Russia came to symbolize the Enlightenment's potential to transform the world. For Theodosia, as an American political observer, Catherine demonstrated that educated women could be innovative political leaders; and as a "glorious figure" on the "historical page," she could revolutionize women's place in politics. Writing at a time when the U.S. government was still young and untried suggests that she believed American women ought to be politicians.[72]

Politics, wit, esteem, and friendship—the Burrs' marriage no doubt supplied ample sexual satisfaction, too. While Burr wished for a marriage based on sense (rather than empty compliments and sentiments), he responded to Theodosia's sensual prose. In 1781, for instance, he picked up on her allusion to the caress of water, replying: "it kept me awake a whole night, and led to a train of thoughts and sensations which cannot be described." Theodosia countered with her own brand of pillow talk. She described how "every tender sensation is awake to thee," and in another letter pictured her "kindred spirit" lying next to her. Like Madame de Staël, and other French writers of the time, Theodosia compared her sexual desires to the euphoric sensations of an exotic opium den. Once, in 1784, she passionately wrote: "Love in all its delirium hovers about me; like opium, it lulls me to soft repose!" Openness was the bedrock of their love, if this rich correspondence tells the whole story of Aaron and Theodosia Burr.[73]

"WOMEN HAVE SOULS!"

The Burrs shared a passionate commitment to education. During the first ten years of their daughter's life (1783–93), her mother's role as educator was crucial, especially because her father was often away. Childrearing was a serious intellectual pursuit for this family. The elder Theodosia had read Plutarch and Herodotus; she devoured all four volumes of Edward Gibbon's *History of the Decline and Fall of the Roman Empire,* and had little trouble mastering the moral philosophy of the English theologian William Paley. As Burr's wife showed she could handle the standard eighteenth-century college curriculum, she applied this knowledge (with the aid of tutors) to the rigorous training of her daughter and namesake.[74]

Theodosia's beloved Rousseau's view of childhood also tapped into her husband's Presbyterian past. The French thinker may have rejected the innate sinfulness of children, but he retained a religious sense of the urgency of saving children from worldly corruption. Rousseau advised parents to "form an enclosure around your child's soul" and he believed that education represented the sum total of a person's adult potential: "All that we lack at birth and that we need when we are grown is given by education." Education was still about saving children's souls, something that Burr's ancestors—from Jonathan Edwards to his mother Esther Burr—strongly endorsed. Burr and his wife shared a philosophy of education: learning required self-knowledge and constant introspection.[75]

Theodosia also felt that education demanded a consciousness of virtue. Children must learn to identify character flaws in others and themselves. They must learn from the good example of their parents, and reject those adults who failed to live up to specific moral standards. Theodosia told her husband, in one instance, that she was delighted by her children's reaction to a particularly rude guest, who greedily consumed an excessive amount of wine during his visit: "Few parents can boast of children whose minds are so prone to virtue." She was proud that her children had viewed the guest with "utter contempt." Why was she so pleased? The children had reacted naturally, without any parental prompting; they were following their own inner monitor. This was the essence of Rousseau's prescription for raising independent children to become responsible adults.[76]

Indulgent parents, in this construct, posed a great danger to children. According to Mary Wollstonecraft, sentimentalization was a major defect in the education of daughters, who were, then, only being taught to be superficial—often their mothers were to blame. Petted and pampered, told to be amusing, attractive, and pleasing to men, young girls lacked the self-control that came from the "sober, steady eye of reason."[77]

Burr voiced these very sentiments when he wrote to his wife in 1793, after reading Wollstonecraft's *Vindication of the Rights of Woman*. He cursed the "effects of fashionable education," of which women were the greater "victims," and which he found so prevalent in Philadelphia high society. He wrote bluntly: "If I could foresee that Theo[dosia] would become a *mere* fashionable woman, with all the attentive frivolity and vacuity of mind, adorned with whatever grace and allurement, I would earnestly pray God to take her forthwith hence." His daughter would be spiritually dead. So what was the point of living?[78]

The Burrs introduced their daughter to a rigorous curriculum early in life. She could read and write by the age of three. She studied mathematics, geography, Latin, Greek, French, and excelled at a pace that was well beyond her years. A typical day for the eight-year-old prodigy was to practice her writing from 5:00 to 8:00 in the morning and for three more hours in the evening. She received demanding lessons from her tutor, devoted three hours to math and French, followed by some kind of exercise: riding, skating, or dancing. She had to be hearty and resilient. Skating was good for her, Burr teased his daughter: "falling twenty times" would teach her the "advantage of a hard head." He insisted that his children were constantly employed, "that no time is absolutely wasted," for he believed that busy children excelled and that a regular routine provided discipline. There was a Calvinist ring to his emphasis on industry and dutifulness. Young Theodosia was raised in accordance with (if not surpassing) the educational standards of most men. Few women learned Latin and Greek; she did. By the age of ten, she was reading and translating Horace and Terence, and she mastered Gibbon's *Decline and Fall of the Roman Empire*.[79]

The Burrs also adopted the conventional emphasis on "good breeding" and refinement. Lord Chesterfield's *Letters to his Son,* and others in this genre, gave direction to a young man's self-fashioning. While Burr rejected Chesterfield's unsound advice, he approved Chesterfield's method—letter writing—as an educational tool. Chesterfield had maintained a regular correspondence with his illegitimate son, giving instruction and advice. Theodosia began writing letters to her father by the age of five, which grew into a regular dialogue. He told her to keep a journal, which she sent to him every week. His early letters offered encouragement and criticism in equal amounts—spelling corrrections, vocabulary hints, and ideas to enable Theodosia to refine her writing style. She approached her studies no differently than a boy the same age would.[80]

Burr's devotion to his daughter's education deepened as his wife's illness worsened. He discovered Wollstonecraft the year before Theodosia's death. He confirmed for his wife what she no doubt suspected, that "it was the knowledge of your mind which first impressed me with respect for that of your sex." At the same time, he qualified that female genius was neither automatic nor universal; he had seen little evidence of "female intellectual powers," he said, "except in you."

It seems clear that Burr wished his daughter to grow to be capable and intelligent, as a tribute to his wife. In her mother's time of trial, he felt the mission to raise an accomplished daughter grew stronger in him. Through her, he would amend the "errors of education, of prejudice, or habit" that traditionally made women appear intellectually inferior to men. He said directly that he would make her his "fair experiment," his personal project for correcting the causes of the apparent "*rare* display of genius in women." She would possess ease and grace, showing none of the pomposity of the pedant or the insipid chatter of an untrained mind. Reason would reign. In echoing Wollstonecraft's words, he emphatically wrote to his wife in 1793: "But I hope yet by her, to convince the world what neither sex appear to believe—that women have souls!"[81]

Burr was unique in treating his daughter as his apprentice. He conceived of her enlightenment as a professional calling, more or less. By prodding Theodosia to become a scholar, he encouraged her to be more than conventionally ambitious: she had to be socially adept, and self-assured, as well as gifted. He explained to his daughter that he wished her to acquire an inner "serenity" that would enable her to rise above petty insults. From this foundation, she would develop mental "firmness," a kind of stoic confidence, giving her the tools to surmount life's inevitable problems. Above all, he said, she must inspire "respect," a quality Burr himself had conscientiously striven for as a young man.[82]

These were not *feminine* virtues. These were the ideals ordinarily associated with "good breeding" in the gentleman, as popularized by conduct books. Judgment, conversational skills, and confident ease, without signs of artificiality or insincerity—these were demands placed on young men, but only on the most promising ones. Thus, Burr expected Theodosia to transcend social convention, and he felt perfectly comfortable instilling in her male ambition. "Resolve to succeed, and you cannot fail," he urged. She had to walk a fine line: to gain knowledge of the world, to be capable of winning arguments, and to do so without offending a male adversary.[83]

His ideal vision for Theodosia was that she could transcend the supposed defects of her sex. Wollstonecraft had argued that it was the consciousness of "always being a woman" that inhibited women from becoming fully human. Burr's daughter was not simply meant to be a female version of himself; she was meant to exercise her reason as naturally as any man, and yet no one would doubt that she had the dignity and grace of a woman.[84]

Remarkably, Theodosia did live up to her father's expectations. In 1798, an English visitor gave the following description of her when she was fifteen: "Mr. Burr has introduced me to his daughter, whom he has educated with uncommon care; for she is elegant without ostentation, and learned without pedantry. At the same time that she dances with more grace than any young lady of New York, Miss Theodosia Burr speaks French and Italian with facility, is perfectly conversant with the writers of the Augustan age, and not unacquainted with the language of the father of poetry [i.e., Greek]." The significance of this characterization cannot be minimized.[85]

Lest we forget, Burr was not only a taskmaster, but an emotionally demanding one. He never withheld sharp criticism when he felt Theodosia needed to hear it. Her every mannerism was subject to inspection and reproof. In 1795, for instance, he rebuked her for the "habit of stooping," calling it "vile," for it would "disfigure" her body and destroy her health. How so? Burr hyperventilated: stooping would "produce consumption."

And then? "Then farewell papa; farewell pleasure; farewell life!" Burr apparently had a flair for drama when it came to his daughter's conduct. He refused to listen to any excuses for laziness in her studies, and he made it clear to her that to abandon the effort would indicate "a feebleness of character" that would seriously disappoint him.[86]

It is fairly clear why Burr felt this way. His own education had involved long hours of study. In his first year at Princeton, at thirteen the youngest in the class, he had buried himself in books for a seemingly impossible sixteen to eighteen hours. He had followed the same regime when he studied theology with the Reverend Joseph Bellamy, and accomplished all this before he was twenty. After the war, he condensed a three-year apprenticeship in the law into one year of rigorous study. Theodosia was seventeen when he pleaded with her: "The happiness of my life depends on your exertions, for what else, for whom else do I live?"[87]

Her apprenticeship had its limits, of course. Theodosia could not follow in her father's footsteps. She could not become a lawyer or politician, though she could educate her own children and serve as a model for other women. She could, in that sense, follow in her mother's footsteps and become the perfect companion, "maturing for solid friendship." Burr never imagined that she would enter the male world of politics. Yet he would have felt perfectly comfortable with her voting, or holding political office. He was, by any definition, a feminist.[88]

In 1793, when Burr had first discovered the *Vindication of the Rights of Woman,* he called it a "work of genius." None of his male peers, or the women he occasioned to meet, agreed. He revealed to his wife his frustration with these people: "Is it owing to ignorance or prejudice that I have not yet met a single person who had discovered or would allow the merit of this work?" As Burr conceived the nature of the world around him, unenlightened opinions ultimately did not matter. He knew, and harbored no doubt, that women could contribute to the growth of knowledge—to the spread of liberty—which was essential in a modern republic. This was Burr at his most idealistic and his most progressive: The Enlightenment encompassed a radical transformation of women's minds. His daughter's special calling was to prove that Wollstonecraft was right and that women were as capable as men of genius and reflection—that, indeed, "women have souls."[89]

A View of Broad Street, Wall Street, and City Hall in New York City (1797)

Chapter Four

AN UNPREJUDICED MIND

I do not see how any unbiased mind can doubt [reasoned arguments], but still do not pretend to control the opinion of others, much less take offense at any man for differing with me.

—Aaron Burr to Jacob Delamater, 1792

The political career of Aaron Burr began with little fanfare and no notoriety. Long before Burr decided, in his wife's words, to "*commence politician*," three dominant factions vied for power in the Empire State. The faction that loomed largest, and for the longest time, was that of George Clinton. Clinton, who held the governorship from 1777 until 1795, gathered around him a patriotic coalition of radical Whigs turned Anti-Federalists (men who opposed the adoption of the federal Constitution). Many of these men, like Clinton himself, had risen from humbler ranks, acquiring wealth and reputation as a result of the Revolutionary War. These men did not have ties to the colonial ruling elite, and saw themselves as defenders of the "middling" class. They were reluctant to cede authority to a strong national government, preferring instead to keep power closer to home in the state, where men of less stature had a voice in politics.[1]

Robert R. Livingston headed a second major faction. His family's vast manorial landholdings had given it dominance over several generations. After 1789, he relied on his own pen, and those of his energetic younger relatives, to simultaneously support the Constitution and promote his family's interests. Appointed chancellor, a position that entailed presiding over the Chancery Court, Livingston also exercised sway over the Council of Revision, which in turn had veto power over all state laws. Thus, from 1777 to 1804, his was the only state office to rival the governor.[2]

A third faction was that of Philip Schuyler and his son-in-law Alexander Hamilton. The Schuylers were wealthy, and like the Livingstons were members of New York's landed aristocracy. Before the federal Constitution was ratified, they were conservative Whigs, and as such, they were frustrated by their loss of power to the Clintons, whom they dismissed as men lacking in education, refinement, and elite family connections. Theirs was an aggressively nationalistic faction—and they used their ties to the federal government to challenge Clinton's dominance over the state. As Washington's secretary of the treasury, Hamilton was perhaps the most influential figure in American politics in the years after 1789. Through sheer force of personality, he brought the Schuyler faction its prominence in New York. At the same time, his contentious style of partisan warfare provoked unceasing controversy.

The three rival groups occasionally allied. When they fought, however, it was of a highly personal nature, marked by intentional snubs and brash maneuvers. The nineteenth-century biographer James Parton cleverly described the factions this way: "The Clintons had *power,* the Livingstons had *numbers,* and the Schuylers had *Hamilton.*" This was the volatile world that Burr learned to navigate—and he did so successfully up through the election of 1800.[3]

State politics did not always follow national trends. As the Revolutionary War ended, two groups—conservative and radical Whigs—vied for control in New York. When debate arose over whether to form a stronger national government, two new coalitions emerged: the Federalists and the Anti-Federalists. They began as loose coalitions, and only the victors, the Federalists, went on to organize as an official party. Conservative Whigs most easily moved into the ranks of the Federalists, drawing mainly from the Schuyler and Livingston factions, and from former Loyalists, who had supported the British during the war. After the Constitution was ratified, Anti-Federalists abandoned their opposition to the new national government, but they did not lose their critical perspective. In the 1790s, as opposition to the Washington administration grew, a new party formed, the Democratic-Republicans—or Republicans, which attracted both former Anti-Federalists and disgruntled nationalists. In New York, this led to an uneasy alliance between the Livingstons and the Clintons, and gave rise to a new state democratic faction headed by Aaron Burr.

Burr's support came from a diverse group. His inner circle included former Anti-Federalists who believed in commercial growth. (They were not Jeffersonians, except when it meant thwarting Hamilton's centralizing policies.) Burr's men tended to be military veterans who had become land speculators; they were willing to promote him, because he advanced their financial interests. Additionally, Burr was perceived as an intellectual, a man of the Enlightenment, who endorsed liberal legal reforms; this set him apart from other New Yorkers who were scrambling for positions of power.

Four men, older and more experienced than Burr in New York State politics, proved most essential to him. All four were Anti-Federalist merchant speculators, three of them Clinton supporters before coming to recognize Burr as the future of the Republican interest. Former militia captain Melancton Smith headed this intimate circle. He was known as the "Patrick Henry" of the 1788 New York constitutional ratifying convention, because of his plain yet compelling oratory, and because he broke with Clinton and endorsed the Constitution. Second was Marinus Willett, a humble cabinetmaker who had become a wealthy land speculator. As the "Hero of Stanwix" during the Revolution, Willett had played a pivotal role in defending New York's western frontier. The third man, David Gelston, was a prosperous New York City merchant, who had earned his reputation as a dealmaker in the state assembly and senate. Distinct from the other three, Dutchman Peter Van Gaasbeek hailed from central New York State, not New York City. Though he attended the ratifying convention as an Anti-Federalist delegate, he went on to embrace the Federalists. He proudly hung a portrait of Burr on his mantelpiece.[4]

ANOTHER "LABORIOUS PIECE OF BUSINESS"

Burr devoted the decade of the 1780s to the practice of law. Then as now, law was a steppingstone into politics, providing a decisive young man with financial independence and a professional reputation. At this moment especially, the legal profession was wide open. Before the Revolution, Loyalists (also known as Tories) had been dominant at the bar, until legislation of 1781 prohibited Tory lawyers from pursuing their trade anymore. When Burr set up his practice in New York City, in 1783, he discovered that only a handful of attorneys were left. Men with little or no experience in the courtroom—Hamilton, Robert Troup, and Burr—quickly came to prominence.[5]

New York City was in turmoil when Burr set up his office on Wall Street. The British army had occupied the city for seven years, and two devastating fires had reduced sections to rubble. Buildings that had been used by the British were in desperate need of major repair, and wharves and warehouses essential to commerce were falling apart. In 1783, Burr was part of a mass migration into the city, which doubled the population from 12,000 to 24,000 in two years. Many were former residents, others ambitious newcomers, battling to reestablish New York as a prosperous mercantile city in the new republic.[6]

New Yorkers were also fighting over the political soul of their city. Hostility toward former Tories was high in the wake of the British evacuation. Encouraged by Governor George Clinton, the so-called "violent" or "radical" Whigs took over the state assembly, and passed legislation that effectively removed Tories' political and property rights. The wartime measure of the 1779 Confiscation Act had allowed the state to take possession of the estates of known Tories; a subsequent law enabled the land to be sold at auction, creating a windfall for ambitious patriots looking for a sure and profitable investment. The Citation Act of 1782 permitted patriots to delay payment of debts to Loyalists—or to repay them in worthless, depreciated Continental dollars. In the following year, the Trespass Act gave patriot refugees the right to sue Loyalists who had occupied and damaged their property.[7]

The anti-Tory legislation created what Alexander Hamilton described as a "harvest" for lawyers in settling civil suits. Burr spent much of his time handling cases before the Mayor's Court, which was located at City Hall, on Wall Street, just two doors down from his law office. From 1784 to 1789, Mayor James Duane presided over the court, a man known as a sound and conservative jurist. Burr must have found it somewhat comical to argue cases before Duane, who had a "sly, surveying eye, a little squint eyed," which made him look a bit crazy.[8]

At this early date, before they knew one another very well, Burr and Hamilton looked at the anti-Loyalist climate differently. When Burr appeared before the Mayor's Court in the politically charged trespass cases, he generally represented patriots, whereas Hamilton almost always took on Tory clients. Though it would be unfair to say that Burr was any less ambitious, his cases involved smaller sums than the £8,000 that was in dispute when Hamilton argued on behalf of a Loyalist in the high-profile 1784 case of *Rutgers v. Waddington*. Hamilton became, almost immediately, the foremost critic of the Trespass Act, calling it "legislative folly" and the work of "levellers"—he saw control of the city in decidedly class terms. Privately, he lamented the sale of Loyalist lands, which had caused as many as 29,000 Tories (whom Hamilton called New York's most "valuable citizens") to sail from Manhattan in 1783 alone. Burr, and many other Whigs, however, viewed the Trespass Act as disaster relief; his clients used the money they recovered to fix up storefronts, replenish merchant stock, and repair homes that had been devastated by the British occupation. In Burr's mind, trespass suits had less to do with revenge, and more to do with rebuilding a battered city.[9]

Burr's client list was diverse, to say the least. The Mayor's Court was primarily a debtor's court—and debt touched those of all political persuasions. Burr was hired by one of his wife's Tory relatives to hunt down a delinquent debtor for unpaid rent. The up-and-coming John Jay hired Burr to sue a man who owed him £30, insisting on twice that amount for damages. One desperate client sent him a heart-wrenching letter from debtor's prison, claiming that if he stayed in jail much longer he would "starve to death." As prisons provided no food for debtors at this time, the man was probably telling the truth. By far his most steady client was his former commander, New York merchant and radical Whig William Malcolm, who sued several times for trespass and debt recovery.[10]

Burr's political instincts were being shaped by this experience. He was positioning himself as a moderate Whig, who looked at the anti-Tory legislation as a necessary but temporary remedy. His moderation is evident in his response to the Citation Act. It was a law that he opposed because it disrupted the repayment of debts across party lines, hurting Loyalists and patriots alike, and creating havoc for the entire New York economy. The Trespass Act only penalized individuals, and he believed was a just response to the economic hardships of war.[11]

Burr could see the value of some leveling—unlike Hamilton, who disagreed with all anti-Loyalist legislation. Indeed, Burr felt that the moderate transfer of power away from wealthy Tories was not only the price of war but a commercial boon in peacetime. As someone who saw the worst side of Loyalists in Westchester County during the war, Burr fully appreciated the anger of ardent Whigs. Many of his close friends were radical Whigs—William Malcolm, Marinus Willett, and John Lamb were all former Revolutionary officers and now ambitious merchants looking to speculate in Tory property and move up the social ladder. In 1783, Burr himself was one of those ambitious Whigs, consulting with Malcolm about purchasing a confiscated estate in the southern district of New York. He was practical and sure-footed.[12]

There was little doubt about Burr's Whig credentials. Several of his cases in the Mayor's Court exposed the seamier side of New York during the occupation, including a handful of suits for assault and battery that fell his way in 1784. One of the stranger cases involved a civilian who had been beaten and imprisoned by a Loyalist officer for five months in 1781. He hired Burr to sue his tormentor for £1,000.[13] Slave cases were also part of Burr's diverse legal trade. By 1790, New York City had over 2,000 slaves as well as a considerable free black population. As one British visitor observed, the streets of the city were filled with blacks of "all shades." In 1784, one of Burr's clients brought suit against a man for luring away his female slave and, presumably, having sex with her. The damages sought, then, were for both her labor and sexual favors. Burr showed no qualms when he took on this case—and others—that treated slaves as property.[14]

Yet Burr's views on slavery were not simple. He represented two manumitted slaves before the New York Court of Chancery in what must have been considered a controversial case: The freedmen were suing for the rightful portion of an estate bequeathed to them by their white slaveholder father. During his short term in the state assembly in the 1780s, Burr went so far as to propose a radical revision of a bill to abolish slavery, calling for the immediate emancipation of all slaves. He opposed three different amendments that restricted the right of free blacks to vote, to serve on juries, or to testify against whites—and he fought a statute that penalized a black £100 for marrying a white. His position seems all the more improbable because Burr himself was a slaveowner.[15]

There were gradations of support for or protest against slavery at this early date, and so Burr's views on slavery are hard to put into a single category. One telling vignette involves Burr's own slave Carlos, a young boy and his body servant. In a letter to Theodosia in 1781, Burr expressed his disappointment with a friend who mocked the idea that Carlos might learn to play the violin. The "insult," as he termed it, shocked him. He found it hard to believe that someone he knew so well could be so insensitive and so unenlightened. Burr made sure that his slaves were well educated. He insisted that Tom, another house slave, apply himself diligently to his reading and writing lessons.[16]

How unusual was this? Not very, among the enlightened thinkers of New York's ruling elite. Burr defended the rights of both masters and manumitted slaves. He appears to have viewed slavery as a temporary condition of servitude rather than a status based on racial inferiority. Many prominent members of the New York Manumission Society owned slaves. Slaveholding was not a partisan issue either: future Republican George Clinton and staunch Federalists John Jay and Alexander Hamilton were both slaveholding members of the society. Nor is any of this surprising if we recall that Burr was deeply influenced by the philosophy of Jean-Jacques Rousseau, whose revolutionary theories assumed that children everywhere had the ability to learn. In Burr's eyes, teaching Carlos the violin was no more daring an experiment than encouraging his own daughter to master the Greek and Roman classics (which, for many men, would have seemed no less radical).[17]

This was Burr's workaday world in the 1780s. An ever-expanding caseload covering the gamut of civil suits, some of it extremely complicated, committed him to years of litigation. He went on long trips to Albany, mainly to attend to business before the Supreme Court. His client Alexander Macomb was one who observed at this time—as many others would echo as the years passed—that Burr never gave up on a case and never shirked his responsibility. He constantly reminded clients to hunt down potential witnesses and to forward any documents that could aid their cause. In preparing for a case, he devoted long hours to a review of the paperwork, and then meticulously condensed his argument so that it could fit on a single sheet of paper.[18]

Burr's diligence is noteworthy, given that he derived little pleasure from his legal practice. In 1791, he confessed to his wife that he was under-taking yet another "laborious piece of business" simply for money. Tedious legal work was, he felt, a complete waste of his intellectual talents. Only his love of family could induce him, in his words, "to spend another day of my life in objects in themselves uninteresting, and which afford neither in-struction nor amusement." While such testaments were common, there is every reason to believe in Burr's case that they were sincere.[19]

His contemporaries reported that Burr spoke with great precision be-fore the court, and would judiciously employ a pointed remark to dismiss opposing counsel's ponderous arguments. One later colleague at the bar claimed that Burr's legal style was *persuasive* and *imaginative* rather than strictly argumentative. The same literary flair that he brought to his jour-nals was displayed in the court of law. Those who bore witness to Burr's courtroom performances voiced the widespread opinion that his style was "peculiarly his own."[20]

"LAND MATTERS"

In spite of his dissatisfaction with the law, Aaron Burr recognized that his profession afforded other opportunities. "Land matters," as he called them, drew him into the risky realm of speculation—which, lest anyone doubt, was the principal pastime of *all* ambitious men in the early years of the republic. Beginning in the 1780s, the obsession for land speculation was triggered when the states of New York, Virginia, Connecticut, and Massa-chusetts ceded their western territories to the national government. Land companies quickly multiplied, each promoting grandiose schemes. Both English and French visitors (who rarely agreed on anything) observed that a more suitable name for the United States would be "the land of speculation."[21]

Many have underscored Burr's unquenchable ambition and extrava-gant lifestyle—his distressed finances have been reduced to a character flaw. But in truth, his various enterprises actually place him in the minor league of speculators, a secondary player compared to the high rollers of his day. Fated figures such as the once notable Assistant Treasury Secretary William Duer; the so-called financier of the American Revolution Robert Morris; Comptroller-General John Nicholson of Pennsylvania; and Bostonian James Greenleaf devised many of the grand schemes of the 1780s and 1790s, and they lured trusting men like Burr into their web of speculation with promises of easy profits and tremendous wealth.

This is not to say that Burr was a naive and hapless stooge. His behavior makes sense only if we acknowledge the pervasiveness of speculation among his peers. The "peerless" George Washington became an extremely wealthy man from land-jobbing, acquiring much of present-day West Virginia, and vast tracts of land in Pennsylvania, Ohio, and Kentucky. As secretary of the treasury, Alexander Hamilton adopted fiscal policies that gained him a dubious title from Chancellor Livingston: "Magnus Apollo of the Speculators." His 1790 federal plan of assumption (paying 6 percent interest on state debts) set off a speculative frenzy in state debt certificates. The policy provoked vigorous criticism, mainly because so many of Hamilton's political allies were grabbing up certificates even before the official policy was announced.[22]

The staunch Virginia Republican James Monroe speculated in land, buying up property in Paris in the wake of the bloody Revolution there. And among Burr's circle of New York legal associates, attorneys Robert Troup and Brockholst Livingston "plunged head and ears"—as one of Burr's contemporaries referred to speculation—into various projects. One of the more sordid deals they backed was the "Million Dollar Bank," less a legitimate bank than a thinly disguised stock-jobbing scam that fooled no one.[23]

Burr's opportunity to speculate arose from three predictable sources: family, military friends, and clients. During the war, his friend from Litchfield, Peter Colt, dragged Burr into what appears to be his first minor venture. Later, Burr turned to him for investment tips. In 1787, when Burr asked Colt about the exchange rate on Continental Loan Office certificates in Connecticut, his friend lightheartedly admitted that they were of little value except, he tempted, for "speculating on Western Lands." The redoubtable William Malcolm not only gave Burr advice on confiscated estates; in 1785, the two men jointly invested in a tract of land in Manhattan.[24]

Most of Burr's early land ventures came through family connections. One of Theodosia's relatives stood out among the rest: Major Augustine Prevost. He was the illegitimate son of General Augustine Prevost (the older brother of Theodosia's first husband). Like both his father and uncle, Major Prevost served in the Royal American Regiment, remaining a loyal British officer throughout the Revolution. Most of his later legal troubles stemmed from his marriage to Susannah Croghan, the only heir to George Croghan, the legendary Indian agent to the crown. Croghan owned approximately 8 million acres in New York, Pennsylvania, and western Virginia. Susannah may have been the sole legitimate heir, but her father also had an Indian mistress. In this roundabout way, Burr's marriage connected him with Joseph Brant, the renowned Mohawk chief, educated in London, who married another of George Croghan's daughters.[25]

By the time of his death in 1782, Croghan's wealth was indefinable. Forced to mortgage much of what he owned because of mounting debts, he left his daughter and son-in-law with a legal nightmare of contested land claims. Hired as Prevost's attorney, Burr channeled his main energies into protecting Prevost's interest in the Otsego Patent in New York's Mohawk Valley. Burr and Hamilton were retained by the contending parties, and, in 1785, two very powerful speculators entered the fray: William Cooper (of Cooperstown renown) and Andrew Craig, who urged Hamilton to find a way for the land to be sold. Burr tried to stop the sale by getting an injunction. Serious accusations were hurled at the sheriff for blatantly ignoring the injunction (that prohibited the sale), and then rigging the auction so that Cooper acquired the land—without his having made the highest bid.[26]

Despite Burr's failure to protect Prevost's claim, in ensuing years Burr and Prevost grew even closer. Twelve years Burr's senior, the generous and good-natured major relied on his younger relative for advice on his business enterprises. And Burr no doubt admired his friend's genteel lifestyle. Surrounded by a large and loving family, Prevost resided at Mill Grove, an estate outside Philadelphia. Burr even professed to Prevost that he had "serious thoughts of moving into the country . . . with the hope of being your neighbor."[27]

Augustine Prevost embodied another species of ambition that Burr found irresistible: He pictured himself owning a vast estate on western land. After his first wife died in 1790, Prevost sold Mill Grove, building a country estate in upstate New York. Burr was actively involved in surveying and overseeing (and possibly speculating in) these "Katskills lands," near the banks of the Hudson west of Albany. But Prevost's vision did not stop there. He had inherited from his father some 10,000 acres in Missis-

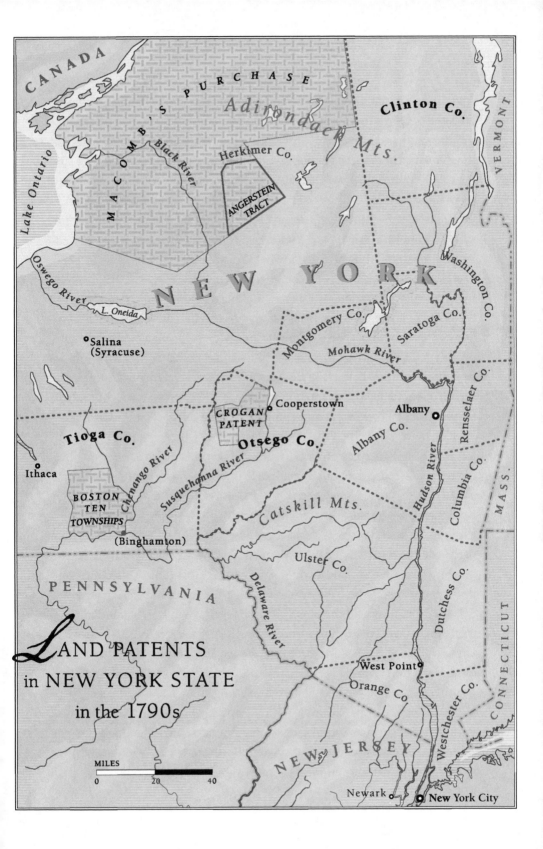

CANADA

MACOMB'S PURCHASE

Adirondack Mts.

Clinton Co.

VERMONT

Black River

Herkimer Co.

ANGERSTEIN TRACT

NEW YORK

Lake Ontario

Oswego River

L. Oneida

Salina (Syracuse)

Washington Co.

Montgomery Co.

Mohawk River

Saratoga Co.

Rensselaer Co.

CROGAN PATENT

Cooperstown

Albany

Tioga Co.

Otsego Co.

Albany Co.

Ithaca

Chenango River

Susquehanna River

Columbia Co.

MASS.

BOSTON TEN TOWNSHIPS

Catskill Mts.

Hudson River

(Binghamton)

Delaware River

Ulster Co.

PENNSYLVANIA

Dutchess Co.

CONNECTICUT

𝓛AND PATENTS
in NEW YORK STATE
in the 1790s

West Point

Orange Co.

Westchester Co.

MILES

0   20   40

NEW JERSEY

Newark

New York City

sippi and Louisiana, lying close to Natchez. This is the land Burr would revisit in 1805 to much lasting notoriety.[28]

Burr's own family had their sights set on land in New York State. His three maternal uncles—Timothy Edwards, Jonathan Edwards, Jr., and Pierpont Edwards—drew their nephew into various ventures. One of the most important was the Boston Ten Townships in New York's "Southern Tier," just north of the Susquehanna River, along the boundary with Pennsylvania. This portion of New York was a contested domain: Massachusetts had claims to millions of acres in what is now western New York. In 1786, a two-state commission (on which Uncle Timothy sat) reached an agreement by which Massachusetts gained full preemption rights to land between the Oswego and Chanango Rivers, and west of a line drawn from Lake Ontario to the boundary with Pennsylvania. New York retained sovereignty over the vast territory, but Massachusetts could make treaties with Indians to purchase lands. Before the ink was dry on the agreement, Timothy and Jonathan Junior began negotiating to buy 230,400 acres from the Indians on the Chanango, using a land company known as the Ten Townships.[29]

Controversy plagued the venture, especially when it came to partitioning land among the investors. The Edwards brothers owned over one fifth of the tract—more than any other single investor—and wanted their share as one large parcel. When the other major associates reneged on this arrangement, the Edwardses turned to their nephew, hoping for a favorable ruling from the New York legislature or courts. After a long, drawn out battle, Burr could not get them what they wanted, but he did his best to protect their interests. Meanwhile, Burr himself invested in a smaller land venture north of Troy, New York, another pet project of Uncle Timothy.[30]

Speculation was in the blood of the Edwards line: Burr's grandfather—the great Jonathan Edwards—had been a missionary to the Indians in western Massachusetts, and he paved the way for land profiteering among his less religious sons. Like so many other speculators, Timothy Edwards prepared for a career in speculation by serving as an agent for an army supply contractor during the war. Thus, Timothy hardly appears the stern Puritan guardian that most of Burr's biographers have identified. On the contrary, he was an adventurer, an ambitious merchant, who gave up his ministry to cash in on the western land grab. Burr was merely carrying on a family tradition.[31]

Burr's youngest uncle, Pierpont Edwards, was only six years Burr's senior, and he lived just as precariously as his older siblings. In 1785, he sent
Burr a desperate letter, begging for a loan of $500. He claimed that he
would sell his house if necessary to cover his debts, because his "honor"
was at stake. Pleading for assurances, he added urgently, "Pray don't fail me
in this matter." But his money woes were only one part of his predicament.
In the very next letter to his nephew, Pierpont had another, even more delicate assignment. The man hired to care for his mistress's child was
threatening to return the "bantling," or bastard, to his doorstep, if he was
not paid immediately. Edwards needed Burr to shell out money to the ex-
tortionist, and to find a new place for the baby and free Pierpont from this
"damned rascally wretch."[32]

Edwards's sexual escapades put him in a distinct class. The child Burr
was sent to rescue was actually Pierpont's second child with his mistress
(and sister-in-law) Mary, who was the much younger sibling of his wife,
Frances Ogden Edwards, and still in her teens when she first became pregnant. Everyone in the Edwards family appears to have known about the
unusual arrangement. Burr, Theodosia, and another cousin, Timothy
Dwight (the future High Federalist theologian and president of Yale), were
all involved in finding Pierpont's "bantling" a new home.[33]

Land deals, debt, and illegitimacy were the invisible threads binding
Burr's extended family. Bastardy was clearly not a barrier to social climbing
in America, as evidenced by the success of Augustine Prevost. John Adams
could call Alexander Hamilton the "bastard brat of a Scotch pedlar," and yet
Hamilton's obscure family heritage did nothing to undermine his career—
his marriage to Elizabeth Schuyler gave him the aristocratic stature he
longed for, which enabled him to become one of the most powerful political figures in New York, and President Washington's top aide. Pierpont
Edwards's career never suffered as a result of his scandalous affair.[34]

Land and the acquisition of property through marriage remained the
major sources of wealth in the post-Revolutionary era. What changed in
the 1780s was an unprecedentedly volatile mixture of speculation and family investment schemes. This made Burr, in a sense, an "ordinary" investor
of his time, as we shall soon see in untangling the larger web of government
officials and their shady land deals. Burr's marriage drew him into the adventurous world of Augustine Prevost—a gambler whose own marriage

linked him to one of the greatest speculators of the century, George Croghan. Burr's boyhood guardian, Uncle Timothy, whose speculating ventures derived from his days as an army supply contractor, lured Burr into the game of New York real estate. Pierpont Edwards continually involved Burr in his various land schemes throughout the decade of the 1790s, which only sank his nephew deeper into debt. Yet Pierpont cannot be painted in black and white, as a scoundrel. He followed Burr into the Republican Party, remaining loyal to him even after Burr's notorious treason trial; years later, one of Pierpont's sons would care for an aging Burr, and make the payment on his tombstone. Despite the taint of illegitimacy and financial ruin within Burr's family circle, blood was thicker than water.[35]

FOR "THE PEACE, LIBERTY, AND HONOR OF THE STATE"

Burr did not rush into politics. In fact, he entered the fray with little genuine enthusiasm. In May 1784, he was elected to the New York Assembly, but when the first session opened in October, Burr was not there. He did not appear until three weeks later, and even then, he failed to propose a single bill, engage in debates, or make any impression whatsoever.[36]

He had been voted in on a ticket headed by Alexander McDougall, his old military commander, under whom he had served when assigned the tricky task of restoring order to the volatile "Neutral Ground" in Westchester County. As a political candidate, McDougall was attractive as a onetime rabble-rousing "Liberty boy" turned nationalist. At war's end, he led an important military delegation that demanded from Congress overdue compensation for Continental officers and soldiers. He then became the first president of the Bank of New York, which opened for business in June 1784, and this made him the friend of merchants and future Federalists alike. As a state senator, he vociferously defended poor debtors and veterans, continuing to see himself as a protector of destitute soldiers. His constituency was all-encompassing.[37]

McDougall's appeal was simple enough: he was one of the heroes of '76. When New Yorkers reclaimed their city from the British on November 25, 1783, he proudly paraded down Broadway behind Governor George Clinton and General George Washington. Burr had the advantage of riding on the coattails of the old warhorse. Besides, Burr had proven himself to be a loyal New Yorker, with his long list of patriotic clients seeking redress under the Trespass Act.[38]

During the second session of the state legislature, Burr was more active. He served as chairman of a joint committee to revise the laws of the state—an assignment suited to the young attorney's skills and rising reputation. He defended the rights of free blacks at this time, and called for the immediate emancipation of slaves in New York. And yet, after a fairly routine session, he found himself under attack for his opposition to the Mechanics' Bill, a piece of legislation designed to incorporate a group of tradesmen and skilled laborers. Burr's political motives are unclear, but he most likely opposed the bill because it granted excessive power to the mayor and alderman of the City of New York, making the mechanics beholden to the city fathers and thus vulnerable to political manipulation.[39]

Politics in New York became increasingly fractious over the ensuing years. Though the three ruling families, the Clintons, Livingstons, and Schuylers, maintained their grip over the state, new tensions emerged as a movement grew to increase the strength of the national government. In 1787, the confederated states did not as yet constitute an effective national authority. That was the reason why the Constitutional Convention was called in Philadelphia. Issues before the delegates included the new republic's structure and balance, the basic question of how to define common problems, agreement on how much power the states would cede to the national entity, and the theoretical challenge of understanding how popular sovereignty could be at the heart of an electoral system when it was to be headed by a single executive. Federalists were comfortable with a strong central authority; the equally patriotic Anti-Federalists dissented, believing that the federal authority would grant too much power to a new elite, and effectively disenfranchise the "middling classes," as they were called. Questions loomed: Could there be too much democracy? Would all interests be heard? The future was impossible to predict, as each state met in convention to decide whether or not to ratify the Constitution, and sign up for membership in the new federal government. New Yorkers met in Poughkeepsie for this purpose in June 1788.

At the ratifying convention, New York's Anti-Federalists had more delegates than their Federalist colleagues, but they had fewer skilled orators.

Silver-tongued Federalists Alexander Hamilton, John Jay, and Chancellor Robert Livingston dominated the Poughkeepsie forum, while Melancton Smith took the stage as the most articulate critic of the Constitution. In New York, as elsewhere, Federalists supported a more energetic national administration with clear authority to tax, enforce treaties, and raise armies. Their opponents felt more comfortable with strong state governments, and local institutions that were more likely to remain responsive to the people's will. Yet New York Anti-Federalists also reflected the unique conditions of their state: they favored commercial growth while opposing unfair "concentrations" of wealth and political power. Thus, they cannot be dismissed as backward-looking agrarians, nor did they subscribe to an unrealistic vision of republican virtue—the belief that men in power could be trusted to act disinterestedly for the public good.[40]

By the end of the convention's second week, Anti-Federalist delegates were forced to concede when they saw that New York and Rhode Island were the only two states that had yet to ratify the Constitution. Even so, the delegates endorsed the Constitution by a narrow margin of 30 to 27 votes, and Anti-Federalists insisted that amendments be added—amendments that later became the Bill of Rights. The new ship of state was launched; but not without some New Yorkers still wondering if they had actually formed a "more perfect" union.[41]

Where was Burr during this decisive turn of events? He did not attend the Poughkeepsie ratifying convention; so there are no speeches, debates, or notes on the proceedings to tell us his full opinion of the federal Constitution. While he was clearly an opponent of ratification, he quickly aligned himself with men like Judge Robert Yates, an Anti-Federalist leader who wholeheartedly supported the new government once the Constitution became the law of the land. Burr's only relevant comment appears in a letter to his friend and client Richard Oliver in July 1788: "after the adoption by ten States"—a phrase Burr underlined—"I think it became both politic and necessary that we [New York] should also adopt it."[42]

At least publicly, Burr remained mute. In 1788, he was considered both for the assembly and as a delegate to the Poughkeepsie convention, but he declined to serve in either body. A week before the polls opened, he notified the *New-York Journal* that "his Name has been given out without his Knowledge or Consent."[43]

Privately, however, Burr must have shown his hand. Otherwise, how could his name have appeared on a handbill with several prominent Anti-Federalists—Melancton Smith, Marinus Willett, and William Denning—all of whom were later identifiable as Burrites? In New York City, not a single Anti-Federalist came close to winning a seat at the convention. "Antis" George Clinton, Denning, and Willett barely received 100 votes each, while well-known Federalists like John Jay received 2,735 votes. Melancton Smith was elected from Dutchess County, not New York City. If Burr had been known as a supporter of ratification, even a mild one, his candidacy would have been assured. Whoever had, without Burr's knowledge, put forward his name in the papers, and on handbills and broadsides, as a spokesman for "the peace, liberty, and honor of the state," saw him as a useful Anti-Federalist ally.[44]

There is one more tantalizing incident that suggests Burr's early affinity for the Anti-Federalists. Upon its adoption in July 1788, the U.S. Constitution received a surge of popular support across New York State. In cities and rural areas alike, local militia marched triumphantly, and local officials raised toasts to the reconciliation of political differences. (The Anti-Federalists and Federalists, though not official parties, had provoked intense passions and revealed wide ideological divisions.) Yet violent clashes marred the festivities in both Albany and New York City. As late as October, Burr wrote from Albany to Theodore Sedgwick (soon to become Hamilton's principal champion in Congress) that "political Strife is still high in this City, the only part of the State where the Spirit of Party is kept thoroughly alive." By "Spirit of Party," he meant intense partisanship.[45]

Burr disapproved of all political excess. Along with fellow attorney Nathaniel Lawrence, he took on the civil suit of Thomas Greenleaf of New York City, a prominent victim of party spirit. Greenleaf was editor of the Anti-Federalist New-York Journal, and his print shop was ransacked in August 1788 by a mob of ratification revelers. Greenleaf became a convenient target after publishing a satire mocking the "pompous appearance" of the Federalists in their "Grand Procession." With ax in hand, Colonel William Smith Livingston, the parade's grand marshal himself, broke down the door to Greenleaf's shop, and joined his drunken cronies in destroying the printer's equipment. They then made their way to the house of General John Lamb, another Anti-Federalist and future Burrite, but dispersed when they thought his home was empty.[46]

That Burr took Greenleaf's case is instructive—it speaks to his political instincts. A trial would redeem Greenleaf's reputation, while placing the Federalist rioters in an unfavorable light. It was the redemption Greenleaf needed. He had become a local pariah, and a significant number of New Yorkers had already canceled their subscriptions, probably thinking he had gotten what he deserved. As a younger and less experienced lawyer, Nathaniel Lawrence served as Burr's co-counsel. Lawrence numbered among the Anti-Federalists at Poughkeepsie, yet was one of the pivotal swing votes in favor of ratification. Looking up to Burr "with Veneration," in the words of one knowing observer, Lawrence must have figured he and Burr were of one mind on the larger subject of ratification when he agreed to join in Greenleaf's defense. And Burr? He just as easily could have represented Livingston, a friend from his college days, but instead he sided with Greenleaf. Taking everything in stride, he watched over the vulnerable Anti-Federalist printer—though, since ratification, "Anti-Federalism" had become a dirty word.[47]

"TWISTINGS, COMBINATIONS AND MANEUVERS"

Over the next three years, the entire complexion of politics in New York changed dramatically, and Burr was at the center of this radical reorganization. With the adoption of the federal Constitution, and the election of George Washington as president, the Schuyler faction, headed by Hamilton, felt that it finally had a chance to recover control of the state from Governor George Clinton. Clinton, the radical Whig turned Anti-Federalist, had been behaving for years as though he were unchallengeable.

At the time of Washington's inauguration, which took place on April 30, 1789, Federalists and Anti-Federalists reached a truce of sorts. A week earlier, Washington had arrived in grand style: crossing the Hudson by barge, he landed in New York City to the sound of thirteen guns, and according to one witness, "the whole city rung with repeated huzzas." Meeting the "First of Men" when his boat docked at the wharf, Governor Clinton was sure to give Washington a warm reception, escorting his former commander through the streets of the city, and then bringing him home to dine. Many opponents of the Constitution became caught up in the excitement. Burr's former commander, the ardent Whig (and now Anti-Federalist)

William Malcolm, proudly strode in the procession that celebrated Washington's arrival. Clinton supporter David Gelston, another Anti-Federalist friend of Burr's, confessed: "I never felt such strong emotions upon any public occasion."[48]

On the day of the inauguration, a more formal ceremony and procession were arranged. Whereas Washington had walked among the citizens on the day he arrived, now, as befitting a new head of state, he rode in an elegant coach drawn by four horses. The paraders who accompanied him marched up Broad Street to Federal Hall, at the corner of Wall Street, where Washington took the oath of office. Burr, too, prepared to celebrate in high style, telling his stepson to hurry home. "Unless you are here to partake," he wrote Frederick, "we shall but half enjoy the Glee of the day."[49]

Yet the feeling for Washington could not heal the political divisions, especially as Washington's wartime aide, treasury secretary-designate Alexander Hamilton, was rubbing salt in the Anti-Federalists' wounds. Two months earlier, he had recruited a former Anti-Federalist judge, Robert Yates, now a nationalist, to run for governor against Clinton. The point was to portray Yates as a moderate, in order to paint the incumbent Clinton as one who might subvert the Constitution. Yates, said Hamilton, was "better calculated to heal the present divisions." On a nominating committee stacked with Federalists, there was one lonely (and somewhat closeted) Anti-Federalist standing up for Yates, a personal friend of his since 1783, and a closer friend to Yates than Hamilton ever was or would be. He was Aaron Burr, of course, who was now under consideration as a possible candidate for Congress.[50]

Hamilton ran Yates's campaign. He wrote a series of letters to the newspapers, attacking Clinton's "obstinate" opposition to the Constitution, as he put it, while dismissing Clinton's military reputation as nothing more than "mere rant and romance." He observed acidly, "I have not been able to learn that he was ever more than once in actual combat." He also accused Clinton of stealing the 1777 governor's race from his father-in-law, Philip Schuyler. Hamilton went on to call Clinton "a very *artful* man," known for his "CUN-NING"—favorite insults that he would later use against Burr.[51]

But the thrust of Hamilton's attack was to insist that Clinton was a man out of his sphere. Clinton lacked "decorum." He lacked the class background, the genteel standard, necessary to claim high office. Clinton's humble origins had always rankled the aristocratic Schuyler, but this class baiting was something new. Even Clinton's wife came under attack for failing to keep her "pantry . . . in order" and for refusing to hire cooks "capable of suiting the palate of everybody." It sounds petty, but President and Mrs. Washington would shortly convene what became known as the "Republican Court," holding weekly formal receptions, or levees—part of a calendar of teas, gala balls, and presidential dinners in the new federal capital of New York City. Even before these began, Hamilton was advancing a new federal standard: he wished to make social appearances matter on the political stage; he expected national and state figures who had previously shown their leadership skills on the battlefield to demonstrate a comparable facility in the parlor. A new style of manhood would measure political merit by a gentleman's display of gentility and his wife's display of social grace.[52]

Yates lost the gubernatorial election. But the scurrilous nature of the campaign set the tone for all subsequent New York elections. The family factions were jockeying for position, as they watched this attempt to find a moderate to fill the governor's seat. This occurred at a moment when Burr and Hamilton were ostensibly working side by side on behalf of the same candidate. Because the election was close, Clinton realized that he would need new allies. Burr was one of those "talents," as one Federalist at this time described him, whom Clinton tried unsuccessfully to bring into his fold. The ascendant Hamilton probably still thought that Burr was "his" man, but he would soon learn otherwise.[53]

By September 1789, a half-year after the election, Clinton had made an opening gesture to Burr, offering him the post of state attorney general. It was a thankless job that paid relatively little (£400 per year), but it was a position that gave Burr wider visibility. Recognition came at a price: the attorney generalship demanded endless hours in court, time sitting on commissions, and more than enough paperwork. In his two years in the position, Burr would prosecute as many as 158 cases before the Supreme Court. Within his heavy caseload were many dramatic criminal cases: murder, theft, forgery, counterfeiting, and what Burr himself called "charges of a heinous nature"—rape.[54]

His experience as attorney general gave Burr an exceptional opportunity to present himself as a legal reformer. In 1791, he prepared a report of "Observations," which Clinton promptly brought to the attention of the

New York legislature. Here we are able to see Burr's Utilitarian philosophy put into practice, a philosophy based on the ideas of the Italian Cesare Beccaria, a leading Enlightenment rationalist.[55]

Beccaria's principle was a straightforward one: a punishment had to be proportional to the actual harm caused by the crime. In New York at this time, forgery and counterfeiting were capital crimes. In his "Observations," Burr used Beccaria to oppose this law. Not all counterfeiters or forgers were equal, he said. Those who caused the greatest harm were the most ingenious men, who typically eluded detection. Then why go after the little guy, who was just a petty thief? Burr put forward his logic, using one of his favorite phrases: "An unprejudiced mind will not readily admit the justice or policy of sentencing to death him who forges an order for three crowns or for a pair of boots, when he who steals a thousand pounds is sentenced to be whipped." Such inconsistencies had no place in New York's criminal code. Despite his liberal plea, Burr's fellow legislators ignored his reform agenda, suggesting that his view was perhaps too "unprejudiced"—or, one might say, ahead of its time.[56]

Still, Burr was rewarded for his service. Clinton decided to make him the next U.S. senator from New York. But the embattled governor could not succeed in this without help. In promoting Burr, he would inevitably be demoting Hamilton's father-in-law, the incumbent Philip Schuyler, at the same time; and so it had to be done discreetly. Because the New York State Assembly and State Senate selected U.S. senators (there would be no popular vote for senators until the twentieth century), Clinton worked a backroom deal. Robert Troup, previously a loyal friend to Burr who had by this time joined Hamilton's inner circle, described the situation as "twistings, combinations and maneuvers." Burr was to squeak by with a 32-to-27 vote in the state assembly, and then a more comfortable 14-to-4 vote in the state senate. His friend David Gelston led the charge in the senate. Burr was doing his part, meanwhile, by wining and dining the men who subsequently elected him.[57]

This unexpected turn of events had as much to do with Hamilton's bungling of federal patronage as it did with anyone's conscious desire to reward Burr. Hamilton's mistake turned into his greatest political headache, when out of jealousy or distrust he prevented Chancellor Robert Livingston from receiving spoils from the Washington administration. Livingston was a proud man and formidable intellect; ten years older than Hamilton, he was not likely to humble himself and do the new treasury secretary's bidding. Even so, Livingston had been an unwavering supporter of General Washington during the Revolution, and an outspoken defender of the Constitution at Poughkeepsie. Practically begging for an appointment (even sending his sister Janet Livingston Montgomery to appeal to Washington directly), he expected some post equal to his stature in the new republic. He received nothing. Rebuffed and humiliated, Livingston broke with the Hamiltonian Federalists and turned to Clinton.

There can be no doubt that the alliance between these two New York power brokers proved crucial to Burr's career. Clinton and Livingston backed Burr so as to punish Hamilton, sending a powerful message that the Hamilton-Schuyler faction would face a vigorous opposition in New York. Thus Hamilton's miscalculation—his desire to keep Livingston outside Washington's inner circle—ended up giving Burr a chance he might never have had otherwise. It was Hamilton who inadvertently sent Burr to the U.S. Senate.[58]

In Hamilton's model for effective politicking, whether at election time or simply promoting legislation, successful campaigns required a well-tuned army, and allowed for only one party commander. Within the new federal administration, Hamilton was positioning himself as Washington's unofficial minister of finance, based on the English model, using patronage to shore up the ranks and build a loyal following. Concerned at the same time about protecting his political command in New York, he demonstrated intolerance for any—a Livingston or a Burr—who might challenge him. Hamilton was known for surrounding himself with loyal subordinates; even his father-in-law had earned the nickname "supple Jack," indicating that he left the policy making to Hamilton. Burr was too independent to play by Hamilton's rules. He could never belong to a Hamiltonian network, and so Hamilton was bound to see him as a deterrent, a detractor, a potentially dangerous interloper.[59]

In 1791, Hamilton arrived at a new level of concern. The quintessential Federalist of 1787, Congressman James Madison, was by now adopting the perspective of his Virginia neighbor and less certain Federalist, Thomas Jefferson, who together were soon to more visibly symbolize a formal opposition to the Washington administration—and the inauguration of the two-party system as Republicans. Secretary of State Jefferson was presently vying with

Hamilton for the president's attention, while exhibiting his suspicion that Hamilton's policies were undermining the independence of the legislative branch of government and the balance of power between that branch and the executive. So, in the spring of 1791, when Jefferson and Madison came by carriage to the heart of New York State, Hamilton took note. The two Virginians met privately with Chancellor Livingston and newly elected Senator Burr. Though the stated rationale for their upstate visit was a botanical excursion—literally to collect floral specimens—canny Hamiltonians assumed that their real intent was to collect political allies. Robert Troup, one of Hamilton's most active snoops, wrote breathlessly in June: "There was every appearance of a passionate courtship between the Chancellor, Burr, Jefferson and Madison." And with a spectacular flourish, he added: "*Delenda est Carthago* [Carthage must be destroyed] I suppose is the maxim adopted with respect to you." It is equally clear that Burr saw the meeting as the opening of a friendship that could lead to a stronger political alliance. When asked later that year by Nathaniel Hazard, another devoted Hamilton supporter, what his role would be in the Senate, Burr did nothing to ease his fears: "I shall not renounce my acquaintance with M[adison] and J[efferson] as Men of Science," Hazard quoted Burr back to Hamilton.[60]

The buzz among New York Federalists was that Hamilton's enemies appeared to be lining up against him. Yet Burr somehow still wanted to consider Hamilton his friend, not his foe. Beginning at this time, and for the next thirteen years, until he killed Hamilton in their famous duel, Burr would be the object of Hamilton's relentless political and personal attacks. Losing Schuyler's Senate seat was the first major setback for Hamilton's New York faction; it was a personal blow to Hamilton as well as his humiliated father-in-law. If Hamilton's motive was not simply a matter of revenge, it might be more accurately called politics as usual. It was generally known, by 1791, that Burr's star was on the rise—and Hamilton would be there every step along the way to nervously monitor its trajectory.[61]

"I DO NOT PRETEND TO CONTROL THE OPINIONS OF OTHERS"

Burr was not overly concerned about Hamilton's opposition to his election, though he did confide to Massachusetts congressman (and Federalist) Theodore Sedgwick, "my election will be unpleasing to several Persons now in Phila." Less than a month later, Burr wrote to Sedgwick again, with "unreserved confidence," on the subject of the national bank devised by Hamilton that still lacked a charter: A "Charter granted cannot be revoked, and this appears to me to be one of those Cases in which Delay can be productive of no Evil." This seems a repeat of Burr's Anti-Federalist distrust of concentrations of power; but his somewhat cautious response to Hamilton's pet project reveals something even more important: he was not going to let Hamilton, at any point, pressure him.[62]

Burr was an active senator from the start: he served on roughly sixty committees between 1791 and 1797, many of which dealt with military issues, public lands on the frontier, and veterans' pensions. It was probably in early 1792 that his New York constituents first learned of Senator Burr's duties, when he chaired a special committee and drafted its report on an act "for the relief of Widows, Orphans, and Invalids." He made few political waves in this philanthropic endeavor.[63]

His support for increasing the size of the military on the frontier proved to be more controversial. He heard it rumored that the administration had resorted to bribes in order to change legislators' views, and that someone had dangled before him the prospect of a prestigious command appointment. Burr warned Theodosia: "You may expect a host of such falsehoods." The rumors began to circulate in February 1792, after Burr had joined Hamiltonian Federalist Rufus King (New York's other senator) in support of raising five additional regiments for the "Indian wars." The United States Army was not faring well against the western tribes; during the previous fall, General Arthur St. Clair had suffered a devastating defeat in the Ohio Country, 600 of his men killed by the Miami. With his strong stand on defense, Burr did not follow the lead of the Virginian wing of the Republican Party, which would come to stand for small government and feared the growth of a standing army. Many New Yorkers agreed with Burr. He remained confident that he had reached a wise decision, telling his wife, "when the part I take in the bill on that subject is fully known, I am sure it will give entire satisfaction to my friends."[64]

Burr still kept his eye on the New York political scene, becoming a player in the 1792 New York gubernatorial campaign. When the *Albany Register* reported in early February that Judge Yates had declined to run again, prominent Federalists *within Hamilton's faction* proposed Burr for the job. Then Yates himself came out in favor of Burr. Hamilton and Schuyler panicked. They began pulling strings to stifle the growing movement: "Col. Burr is not the man," Schuyler or one of his supporters wrote, pseudony-mously, in the *Register*. Within days, Hamilton persuaded Supreme Court Chief Justice John Jay to run for the office. Suddenly, it was a three-man race for governor: John Jay, George Clinton, and Aaron Burr.[65]

Schuyler and Hamilton had every reason to worry. Burr had appeal be-cause, according to the New York *Daily Advertiser,* he stood "clear of party attachment" and was "aloof from party aspersion." Just like Yates, Burr pre-sented himself as a moderate, without direct ties to any of the ruling family factions. His military credentials, including, now, his support of the army on the frontier, helped him immensely. The *Daily Advertiser* further proph-esied: "If any unusual concern of the state should require the abilities of a prompt and active governor, it will probably be a threatened frontier. For war and negotiation this candidate is known to be happily qualified."[66]

Federalists pressured Yates to withdraw his support from Burr, with warnings that his chances would be hurt if he planned to run for office in the future. Neither Burr's land speculation, which was all too common among this crowd, nor his supposed political instability caused any alarm. Instead, as one New Yorker confided to Yates, the principal objections to Burr were his youth, and more important, his lack of "ties of birth or family connection to this state." Family connection mattered in New York. One could rise to political prominence by choosing the right wife: Massachusetts-born Rufus King, who was merely a year older than Burr, married into the wealthy Alsop family of New York City, and this allowed him, in 1789, to become one of the first U.S. senators from the Empire State. Hamilton overcame much more: he surmounted his illegitimate birth and alien status (born on Nevis, an island in the West Indies), when he wed Elizabeth Schuyler, the daughter of Dutch-American patroon Philip Schuyler.[67]

In the end, Hamilton convinced key political operatives not to back Burr. National party divisions were not yet firmly entrenched in New York, and like Yates, Burr had been proposed as a moderate who would attract men of all political persuasions. One of them, former Anti-Federalist turned Federalist Peter Van Gaasbeek, wrote to his friend Burr at the end of March that it was "with the greatest reluctance we agreed to relinquish You as our

Candidate for Governor." Burr withdrew and, curiously enough, took no part in electioneering—preferring, at least for the moment, to attach himself to no candidate.[68]

The 1792 election was acrimonious, even more fiercely waged than the last. The Hamiltonians charged the Clinton administration with corruption. Accusations were hurled at the Land Office Commission for "lavishly" rewarding friends of the governor in the form of large land grants. The most conspicuous of these sales—3.6 million acres—was to Alexander Macomb, a "merchant prince" Federalist, who hardly fit the profile of a Clinton crony. Yet the Federalists charged that Macomb had secret partners in the fabulous deal; they clearly intended to point the finger at Governor Clinton or, minimally, his closest friends. Given that Burr (as attorney general) had served as an ex officio member of the commission, it is surprising that he was not lumped together with the other purported villains. But he was not. He was not present at the meeting when Macomb's purchase was approved, but he was fully aware that Clinton and his fellow commissioners had played the patronage game. On a much smaller scale, Burr had used his clout on the same commission to ensure that a system of roads was built in southern New York—which unmistakably served the interests of Uncle Timothy, as well as his Federalist friend Van Gaasbeek.[69]

All sides were making sweetheart deals. Federalists wanted to stigmatize those outside a trusted inner circle, but they had a difficult time painting themselves as the virtuous party. In March, as the Hamilton faction applied its energies to reputation bashing in order to secure the governorship, Hamilton's close friend William Duer went bust. Until recently his assistant secretary at the Treasury Department, Duer had concocted a grandiose scheme for cornering the market on bank and government securities. The plan fell to pieces, sending shock waves through the national economy, while Duer and Macomb, two of the state's most spectacular speculators, were unceremoniously carted off to debtor's prison. Now it was Hamilton's turn to squirm; his cozy relationship with Duer came under scrutiny, suggesting to neutral observers that no one of any stature in New York politics seemed to be able to steer clear of speculators and scandals.[70]

Scandal pursued the 1792 New York gubernatorial election to its bitter end. By May, the votes had all been sent to the committee of canvassers, whose job was to inspect and count ballots. Rumors began circulating of apparent irregularities in three counties—this would necessitate discarding those votes altogether. Otsego, a Federalist stronghold under the control of Judge William Cooper, was one of the counties under scrutiny. In an extremely close race, many of the Federalists now feared that the canvassers, who were mostly Clinton men, planned to steal the election.[71]

Despite staying clear of electioneering, Burr found himself at the center of this growing controversy. The canvassers had turned to him, as well as to his fellow senator, Federalist Rufus King, to supply them with legal advice. Burr and King debated the matter for two days, but could not reach agreement. King wished all the votes counted, and insisted on publishing his opinion; and so Burr was left with no alternative but to do the same. He was convinced that there were sound reasons for discarding the ballots, and was loath to trim his view to please others. He explained to a friend, "I shall never yield up the right of expressing my opinions."[72]

The canvassers disqualified the votes from Otsego, Clinton, and Tioga Counties. Clinton achieved victory, but by the slimmest of margins: 108 votes. Pandemonium ensued. Burr came under attack for what Robert Troup fumed in a letter to John Jay was a "shameful prostitution of his legal talents." Outraged Jay-ites (as they were called in the press) filled the pages of New York's newspapers with sharply worded criticisms and thinly veiled threats of armed rebellion; they urged a public convention to override the election and alter the existing constitution. Federalist lawyers claimed that Burr and the canvassers ought to be impeached for usurping the will of the people. As one of the Federalists saw it, "we have *as it were,* two chief magistrates, *one,* the governor, by the voice of God, and the people, and another the governor of Mr. Burr and the canvassers."[73]

Why, we must ask, did Burr defend the canvassers who disqualified the three counties and elected Clinton? It was not for reasons of partisanship alone, as many charged at the time, and as historians have argued. Only Otsego was a clear Federalist district, and Clinton was by no means Burr's friend—he characterized Clinton's disregard for him as an expression of "jealousy and malevolence." On the surface, it may have looked different, insofar as Clinton had built up his political empire in New York by making alliances with potential enemies; this explains why he courted Burr after the 1789 gubernatorial election, offering him the post of attorney general. When Clinton helped to make Burr senator, it was out of self-interest only, that is, so as to curb Hamilton's growing influence, and to keep Burr from (as he imagined it) falling completely under the sway of the Federalist treasury secretary. Whatever else might be said, Burr was never in Clinton's pocket. Nor was he willing to "prostitute his legal talents," as Troup charged, to help the governor win the election by "legal chicanery."[74]

So the truth lies elsewhere. Burr personally liked John Jay, a moderate Federalist, much as he was personally wary of Clinton. He ultimately supported the canvassers because they had reason to believe that the Otsego election was not free, but had been corrupted by "mischiefs" and "unfair practices." Additionally, two members of the committee were his close friends Melancton Smith and David Gelston, and while they were Clintonians, he trusted in their judgment and their honesty. Anti-Federalists like Smith believed that only strict regulations insured free elections—it was a cherished principle of the New York Bill of Rights. And nothing up to this point in his career suggests that Burr would have been at ease grossly distorting the law for political gain.[75]

In fact, Burr saw the law being twisted, and it troubled him. In Otsego County, Sheriff Richard Smith continued to hold office and improperly delivered the votes to the canvassers even though his appointment had expired and he had taken a new job as town supervisor. Holding two posts at the same time was, in itself, a violation of the letter of the law. But the canvassers—and Burr—were not simply looking for a technicality in order to deny votes to the Federalist Jay. They grew even more suspicious when they learned that the new sheriff's commission was "in the hands of *William Cooper*," who was harassing poor but enfranchised farmers who had purchased land from him, in order to oblige them to support Jay. Cooper's antics were legendary: he threatened Clinton supporters, and even an election inspector, with jail time or the stocks if they refused to do his bidding. Burr already had sufficient reason to distrust Judge Cooper: in 1785, he had watched him bribe another sheriff to get his hands on Major Prevost's land. Once again, Cooper had colluded with a sheriff to get his own way, this time at the expense of the legitimate voters of Otsego.[76]

Burr was won over by facts that he considered beyond dispute, if he was also plainly influenced by Cooper's resort to strong-arm tactics. Confident in his legal opinion and concerned about the Federalists' relentless attacks on his personal integrity, Burr decided go public and defend his reputation. In midsummer, he began soliciting lawyers who he felt would concur with his argument. He first approached two members of his own family, Pierpont Edwards and Tapping Reeve, both of whom were respected members of the Connecticut bar. Edwards would pen the most convincing defense of Burr's opinion. He next rounded up support from Pennsylvania's former attorney general, Jonathan Dickinson Sergeant; but his biggest coup was the endorsement he received from Edmund Randolph—Washington's attorney general.[77]

As he explained in a letter to James Monroe, whom he also solicited, Burr said that he needed the "authority of great names" because he felt the public at large needed to know that the "Canvassers did honestly pursue the direction of the law." Eventually, he published a 46-page pamphlet, a concise legal brief, entitled *An Impartial Statement of the Controversy, Respecting the Decision of the Late Committee of Canvassers.* Issued in November 1792, the brief attracted positive notice among Republicans outside the state, who were hoping to see the mess in New York cleaned up.[78]

His handling of the 1792 election controversy is a demonstration of Burr's politics. He adhered to republican ideals, dispassionately sought out facts, and espoused a distinctive ideology—an ideology founded on the pursuit of justice and delivered with a candor that later detractors chose to overlook. These are hardly the actions of a man without principles, a man "for or against nothing, but as it suits his interest or ambition," as Hamilton would characterize Burr in a private letter.[79]

The evidence shows the opposite to be true. Burr displayed time and again, during the years of his rise in New York political circles, that he did not automatically take one side over another; he did not jump thoughtlessly to every Republican viewpoint, nor immediately discard every Federalist one. These were his principles. He relied first and foremost on evidence, and, as an above-board republican, aimed to root out flagrant election fraud. But he was an optimist as well as a moralist, for he believed that men should be able to disagree and remain friends. He respected many a Federalist. He also believed that no man should be bullied into reversing himself, but should change an opinion only when reason persuaded him to do so. Writing to a friend, Jacob Delamater, whom he knew would dispute his opinion on the election, he confided: "I do not see how any unbiased man can doubt [reasoned arguments], but still I do not pretend to control the

opinions of others, much less take offense at any man for differing with me."
This was the political style of Aaron Burr that history has misplaced.[80]

So determined was Burr to prove the validity of his legal argument that
he sought out two friends among the Federalists, Theodore Sedgwick and
Jonathan Trumbull, and asked them whether they might draft opinions in
support of his views on the canvassers. He did this because he thought he
could find objectivity and fair-mindedness even among highly ideological
men who desired a particular outcome and were disappointed when Clinton emerged victorious. Was Burr naive or simply straightforward? Neither
Sedgwick nor Trumbull agreed with his perspective on the election controversy—indeed, they did just the reverse of what Burr hoped for, and wrote
strongly against him. In the case of Sedgwick, the relationship suffered. By
the end of 1792, the Massachusetts congressman began to exhibit signs of
the scorn he would display with increasing regularity as Burr became a
more powerful figure in the Republican Party.[81]

But in October of that year, Burr had not ceased to feel that he and
Sedgwick could remain close friends. Acknowledging how their opinions
had diverged, Burr ventured, "It is at all times painful to differ in Opinion
with one we love." Convinced that they would never see politics the same
way, he had no intention of soft-pedaling his beliefs. Burr was one of the
last holdouts in an increasingly spite-filled young republic, who maintained
the belief that it was possible to rise above partisan bitterness and retain
friendship with an opponent. As he came to feel uncertain about his Federalist friend, he gamely, good-naturedly chided Sedgwick: "if you have been
in your sober senses, you are now far beyond the reach of reason—You
have my prayers for your speedy recovery." It might be argued that Burr allowed his own partisanship to sway his legal opinion in this instance; but
if that were the case, he would have had to be either cocky or insensitive to
approach men like Sedgwick and Trumbull and expect to persuade them
of anything. And that seems unlikely.[82]

Burr was far more sincere, and far more enlightened, than he has been
given credit for—and yet he may have been stubborn, even foolish, to per-
sist in conducting open and free discussions with those of dissenting
political principles. When he published his *Impartial Statement of the Controversy*, he faithfully included opposing opinions—King's, those canvassers
who disagreed with the majority decision, and a joint statement of New

York City attorneys, including Troup, who rejected Burr's stand on the case. He did not publish Sedgwick or Trumbull's negative opinions, and his enemies did see fit to print Trumbull's a mere eight days after his pamphlet appeared. Even Burr's idea of impartiality had its limits.[83]

"YOUR FRIENDS EVERY WHERE LOOK TO YOU"

Burr was not campaigning for any office after his name was withdrawn from contention in the recent governor's race. Nevertheless, his handling of the election controversy drew attention from Republicans elsewhere. He had been forced into the limelight and had taken a leadership role, in the process of attempting to rise above partisan bitterness. Yet, at the same time, he saw that party lines were now more sharply drawn. And his sympathies clearly rested with the Republican interest.

As of 1792, national parties were still undeveloped—there were no party platforms, no coordinated campaigns. Presidential and vice-presidential candidates did not run as a joint ticket, but as individuals. In fact, until the vice-presidential race of that year, it was not yet routine for opposing candidates to compete directly for high office. Washington had agreed to serve a second term, and fledging Republicans did not even consider challenging the unassailable incumbent. But the same shield did not protect the crusty New Englander John Adams. By publicly praising the English Constitution as the best in the world, Adams had become a target of attack, and was painted by his critics as a secret admirer of monarchy. He was vulnerable, and so Republicans decided to try to unseat him, in effect testing the waters as a prelude to the more important presidential contest four years down the road.

Philadelphia physician Benjamin Rush, a signer of the Declaration of Independence, was an admirer of Aaron Burr, Sr., and had known the son and namesake at least since 1772, when he attended the Princeton graduation at which Burr gave his well-received commencement speech. In September 1792, Rush sent Burr an impulsive letter of introduction on behalf of a former indentured servant turned political organizer, Virginian John Beckley. As the first clerk of the House of Representatives, the upwardly mobile Beckley was an ardent Republican who was proving to be a most valuable resource for the newly formed, anti-administration party.

The historian Noble Cunningham has described him as the Republicans' "political intelligence agent." He was the eyes and ears of Jefferson, Madison, and Monroe throughout the 1790s. In his letter to Burr, Rush confirmed that view, confiding that Beckley "possesses a fund of information about men & things."[84]

Beckley's visit to Burr was meant to serve a special purpose: to enlist the New Yorker in the Virginia-Pennsylvania campaign to remove Adams from office. Washington was a southerner; therefore, a northern vice president had to be found to replace the northerner Adams. Most remarkable in Rush's letter to Burr was its strident, almost incendiary tone: "Your friends every where look to you to take an active part in removing the monarchical rubbish of our government. It is time to *speak* out—or we are undone." The appeal was more than a call to arms; it was a bold invitation to Burr to personally lead the campaign against the Federalists in New York and beyond.[85]

It is impossible to know exactly what Burr thought of this letter. Yet within a week, his friends were zealously promoting him as the candidate to replace Adams. Three of Burr's friends took charge of the negotiations: Melancton Smith, Marinus Willett, and Pennsylvania's high-flying speculator, John Nicholson. The negotiations had to be handled delicately, because Burr's name was being floated alongside that of Governor Clinton, who was the Virginians' first choice for vice president. Pennsylvania Republicans liked Burr, and were unimpressed with Clinton. Nicholson explained in an October 3 letter to James Madison that the New York election controversy had harmed Clinton's reputation—the governor himself felt it might be wisest not to abandon his post in the aftermath of the canvassers' scandal. To Nicholson, Burr had a better chance of gaining support from "middle and Eastern States which would not be given to Clinton." Unless Burr was the Republican candidate, he warned Madison, Pennsylvania could not be counted on for support.[86]

Jointly writing to Madison and Monroe a few days earlier, Smith and Willett had made a similar case. Smith then traveled from New York to Philadelphia, carrying a letter of introduction from Burr to Nicholson. Designating Smith as "the representative of the republicans in this State," Burr empowered him as a party agent, a manager "as to men and measures." Curiously, just five days earlier Clinton had voted to appoint Burr to the state Supreme Court, which would have put Burr out of the running. But Burr did not care to don the judicial robe.[87]

The governor was not ready to concede the vice-presidential nomination to Burr. But Melancton Smith was. Smith and Willett were Clinton men, now inching toward the Burr camp. Neither man wanted to abandon Clinton so much as they wished to strengthen the ties between Burr and Clinton's camp. But both felt the younger politician represented the future of New York Republicans. As his "confidential friends," Smith and Willett regularly loaned Burr money, and constituted the first informal band of Burrites, a collection of men of who backed his political ambitions. At this time, Burr's stable of supporters included a few stray Federalists like Peter Van Gaasbeek (formerly an Anti-Federalist), as well as New York City Clintonians of the "middling" sort. Burr attracted men without elite family connections such as Smith and Willett—former soldiers and Anti-Federalists whose liberal principles matched Burr's own.

Yet the role of the Pennsylvanian, Nicholson, was just as significant, because his word carried weight with James Monroe. Nicholson had relied on Monroe in his land deals, and had recently enticed Burr into his Pennsylvania Population Company—Burr ended up as one of its largest shareholders. Nicholson was part of the entrepreneurial-speculator wing of the Republican Party, and he shared the commercial vision of Burr and Smith. Monroe is important here because he apparently did not share Jefferson's pronounced distaste for "speculating scoundrels"; he had purchased 100,000 acres in the Kentucky Territory and, along with Madison, had pursued an investment scheme in New York land patents. At this time, the two younger Virginians (though not Jefferson) were actively coordinating the campaign against Adams.[88]

The behind-the-scenes negotiation engineered by Smith, Willett, and Nicholson revealed an unspoken sectional division among Republicans, one that would continue to thwart Burr's rise in the party. The Virginians had every intention of running the show themselves; perhaps because their state possessed more electoral votes than either New York or Pennsylvania, neither Madison nor Monroe was ready to relinquish control of the candidate selection process to their northern brethren. (Of course, if New York and Pennsylvania worked together, their combined vote would exceed Virginia's.) At any rate, the two Virginians drafted a carefully worded response to Smith and Willett, arguing that any change in strategy might upset the existing understanding as to the most promising means of unseating Adams—and so they continued to insist on Clinton's candidacy. Monroe cautiously added that Burr's "youth" was their rationale for not selecting him.[89]

Reading between the lines of this letter, we can detect the Virginians' belief that the less dynamic Clinton posed little threat to a Jeffersonian-led party. In a June letter to Jefferson (written after the election controversy and before Burr's candidacy was raised), Monroe admitted that he found Clinton's "extreme parsimony" and ungenteel manners appalling and "vicious," but he felt confident that the governor's lack of sophistication made him manageable. In the end, though he favored Clinton, Monroe still considered Burr an attractive possibility, adding as a postscript in his letter to Madison: "I sho[ul]d not hesitate to aid Burr in opposition to Adams. If he co[ul]d succeed, it might have its good effects and co[ul]d not possibly do any mischief."[90]

The 1792 national election results proved that the Virginians would have to make more concessions than they had originally intended. President Washington, of course, stood unopposed. In the contest for vice president, Clinton won the votes of Virginia (21), New York (12), North Carolina (12), and Georgia (4), but among the eleven other states he received only 1 vote. Pennsylvania (with 14 of its 15 votes going to Adams) decided the election: the final tally was Adams 77 and Clinton 50. If Clinton had swept Pennsylvania, he would have won by 1 vote, 64 to 63. Nicholson's prediction that the Republicans in his state "prefer *Burr* to *Clinton*" proved to be the difference in this election, a fact that neither Madison nor Monroe could ignore. Clinton may have been a "safer" candidate for the Virginians, but Burr alone could have given the Republicans their victory. Burr, in fact, received one electoral vote—from South Carolina.[91]

In the election of 1792, as he would in 1796, and again with even more false righteousness in 1800–1801, Hamilton unleashed a letter campaign aimed at sinking Burr's chances. There was nothing subtle about Hamilton's intentions—there never was. In 1801, when he actively solicited his friends to break the electoral tie in Jefferson's favor, he would call Burr "desperate and profligate," a man who "has not principle, public or private." Here in 1792, writing to an anonymous ally, he made the very same case, favoring Clinton, a man he thoroughly detested (and had mocked for his parsimony) but now praised for his "probity."[92]

Over the years, Hamilton's personal attacks against Burr were consistent, and they all began with his three characterizations in the early 1790s: devoid of principles ("for or against nothing"); privately reckless (financially "embarrassed"); yet personally powerful (capable of becoming "head of a popular party" because he was "bold enterprising and intriguing"). Willing to resort to any ploy if it would convince his reader, Hamilton justified his vilification of Burr by reinforcing it with an ostensible moral impulse: In the fall of 1792, he claimed he had "a religious duty to oppose [Burr's] career."[93]

Religion, of course, had nothing to do with it. As to the charge of fiscal irresponsibility, there were men in Hamilton's party whose finances were far more desperate than Burr's. While Hamilton railed against Burr's "embarrassed . . . circumstances" and "extravagant family" in 1792, Hamilton's chum William Duer languished in debtor's prison. No man at this time was better known for his wild speculative schemes, yet Hamilton had seen fit to appoint Duer to the second highest office in the Treasury Department! Though himself the beneficiary of a prudent marriage, nothing would prevent Hamilton from dying in debt.[94]

All political campaigning, then as now, relies in some way on distortion, on portraying the opposition as a caricature of a negative behavior. That certainly was the case in the 1790s, when Burr and Hamilton competed for favor among New Yorkers, and when Hamilton, a powerful national executive, fearfully envisioned the rise of an anti-administration party. Therefore, his personal feelings toward Aaron Burr could not but be fused with his larger concern about the preservation of Federalist rule.

The *personal* dynamic between Burr and Hamilton has inspired virtually all of the accounts of the circumstances that ultimately led to their 1804 duel. But Hamilton's real reason for wanting to destroy Burr's career, at least in the early 1790s, was political: Burr's growing support in New York. Hamilton's lieutenants, such as Nathaniel Hazard and Robert Troup, had been watching Burr, and observing his increasing popularity. Burr had acquired a political base. He had been assembling a team of influential men, such as Melancton Smith, who could help him organize his own "popular party." And despite what Hamilton claimed, the men around Burr were attracted to his principles: his belief in promoting commercial opportunities for the middling sort, his advocacy for liberal legal reform, fair elections, and freedom of speech—the last evidenced by his moral stand to defend the silenced and censured printer Thomas Greenleaf.[95]

In letters to close friends, Hamilton held nothing back in condemning Burr, but in correspondence with casual acquaintances he cleverly pretended that he had only heard rumors disparaging Burr's behavior. Less than three weeks after Hamilton had written in one letter that Burr was "unprincipled, both as a public and private man," and in another letter that he was an "embryo Caesar," he disingenuously wrote to Congressman John Steele, a moderate Federalist, that his "opinion of Mr. Burr is yet to form. . . . Imputations, not favorable to his integrity as a man, rest upon him, but I do not vouch for their authenticity." Here is clear evidence of Hamilton's political gamesmanship. He wanted to undermine Burr and to pretend that he had had nothing to do with it.[96]

It is rather ironic that Hamilton vilified Burr as "unprincipled" in the fall of 1792. For in December of that year, he was forced to defend his own reputation against charges emanating from his private behavior—charges that would certainly drive any modern politician from office.

Gathering intelligence on behalf of the Republican interest, John Beckley brought the sordid details of the "Reynolds Affair" to light. Beckley had heard rumors, which he conveyed to Senator James Monroe, that Treasury Secretary Hamilton had used privileged information in a possible speculation scheme that involved one James Reynolds as his agent. In prison at the time for suborning perjury in another case related to the Treasury Department, Reynolds released the story about Hamilton in the hope that the secretary would drop the charges against him.[97]

To strengthen Reynolds's hand, and prove Hamilton's wrongdoing, Reynolds's wife, Maria, provided letters indicating that money had changed hands between Hamilton and her husband. Monroe, along with Congressmen Frederick Muhlenberg of Pennsylvania and Abraham Venable of Virginia, investigated the charges. On December 15, 1792, they presented the evidence to the treasury secretary. That evening, when Hamilton met with the Republicans, he confessed—but not to any financial impropriety. He had been having an affair with Maria Reynolds, he said, and paying her husband hush money. The Republican delegation agreed to keep the matter confidential. Hamilton's secret would be not be publicly revealed until 1797, well after he had left the Treasury Department.[98]

So in 1792, Hamilton was hardly in a position to censure Burr's moral character. It was Hamilton who was engaged in a low intrigue, making desperate, clandestine payments to protect his reputation. But as Hamilton saw the situation, extramarital sex could be separated easily from financial impropriety. As long as he did not violate the public trust by misusing his office, he could continue to insist that he was an honest man. He did not extend the same courtesy to Burr, exaggerating the significance of his being financially overextended while ignoring the fact that so many of their colleagues were routinely on the verge of debt. Hamilton's political maneuverings and political motives reveal a man whose objectivity could not be trusted—especially with regard to Burr's personal character. To be perfectly clear, outside of Hamilton and his cronies, no one was criticizing Burr's character in 1792.

"THE WITS, THE SALT, THE BRILLIANCY OF SOCIETY"

Hamilton's affair with Maria Reynolds had begun in 1791, the same year Burr arrived in Philadelphia, the new federal capital. In a strange twist, Burr was drawn into the scandal in 1793, when he agreed to serve as Mrs. Reynolds's divorce attorney. Later, he would act as ward for her daughter, whom he placed in the home of Congressman William Eustis of Boston so that she might avoid the shame associated with her mother. The legal careers of Burr and Hamilton intersected often, so the connection is not as unusual as it might seem. Of course, it is hard to imagine that Burr could have remained unaware of his client's liaison with Hamilton (gossip concerning this matter had circulated among the elite after 1792, five long years before the public learned of the affair). Yet Burr's reasons for taking the case are still unknown. Did he feel pity for an abused wife? Or was he actually protecting Hamilton by freeing Maria from the clutches of her manipulative husband? Burr had already acquired a reputation for handling divorce cases, and throughout his life would assist a long list of orphans and wards just like Maria's daughter. So his relationship to Hamilton did not have to be the reason why Maria Reynolds approached him. Still, whether they liked it or not, Hamilton and Burr were often privy to each other's private confidences.[99]

Little went unnoticed in the close-knit community that formed among federal officials and their families in Philadelphia. Residing in the home of two elderly widows on High Street when he first arrived in the city, Burr was just down the street from President Washington and Secretary of State Jefferson; his other neighbors were fellow senators John Langdon of New Hampshire and Pierce Butler of South Carolina. "The city of brotherly love" was the largest in the nation, with 43,000 residents (10,000 more than New York at this time). As a planned city, it was composed of rectangular blocks fanning out from the Delaware to the Schuykill River.[100]

Philadelphians were proud of their city, the imposing brick buildings, tree-lined streets, and cultural attractions. In 1790, Congress moved into the courthouse—adjacent to the State House—that was renamed Congress Hall. The serpentine promenade behind the two buildings became a prominent social spot, where men and women conversed and displayed the latest fashions. A national elite was emerging: power was not only being exercised in the halls of Congress but outside government as well—at dinner parties and in great mansions. A new class was forming, aligned with the federal government and the Federalist Party, and it linked politics to the display of cultural authority.[101]

Though Martha Washington continued holding her weekly levees in Philadelphia, she was quickly outclassed by the newly anointed social hostesses of the federal elite: Anne Willing Bingham and Mary White Morris. According to Abigail Adams, Bingham and Morris hosted "one continued scene of parties upon parties." Mary was the wife of Pennsylvania senator Robert Morris, so-called "financier of the Revolution," whose grand home became the official residence of President Washington. Bingham hailed from one of the wealthiest families in Philadelphia, and her father and Robert Morris had been business partners in a highly successful trading firm. While touring the European courts in the 1780s, Anne's husband, the merchant turned speculator William Bingham, had actively, transparently sought a diplomatic post. Anne, known for her beauty, became a sensation, charming nobles and diplomats in London and Paris alike.[102]

On their return to Philadelphia, the Binghams built an extravagant mansion (modeled after the Duke of Manchester's London home), which served as a stage for political entertainment. Anne Bingham threw lavish dinners in the style of the English aristocracy, including the opulent practice of announcing the arrival of guests. She even had a retinue of female friends and family present at her parties, who accompanied her as she made her weekly rounds of social calls. Anne Bingham purposefully created a code of behavior for the Federalist elite. She provided a social arena in which diplomats, prominent government officials, and ambitious office seekers like her husband vied for distinction and patronage.[103]

Though Burr has been refashioned into the very type who would have flourished in this environment, he did not, at least not comfortably. After arriving in Philadelphia to attend the Second Congress in October 1791, he admitted to Theodosia that he had received "many attentions and civilities" and "invitations to dine," but had declined such offers. Ill equipped for social visits, he lacked "decent clothes," as he put it, begging his wife to send him a suitable waistcoat. Resenting what he called "this absurd and irrational mode of life," he pleaded with her to visit him as soon as possible.[104]

When Theodosia finally joined him the following March for a short stay, she discovered a city that was "uninhabitable," for all its "boasted refinement." In a devilishly witty letter to her son, John Bartow Prevost, she not only ridiculed the "beauties and attractions of Philadelphia" but mocked the pretentious manners of the reigning Federalists, putting particular emphasis on their peculiar obsession with social display:

> All our disdained and slighted beaux here are esteemed the wits, the salt, the brilliancy of society. The parties resemble a playhouse before the curtain is drawn up. The ostentatious part is a footman with a silver breadbasket, and the hospitality is proffering a cup of cold tea to a mob—while the lady is fluttering around in utmost apparent dizziness, lest the number of female attendants should not exceed all the household chairs—Should one remain, in the use of a single gentleman, god knows what might be the consequence— sacrilege would not be half so horrid.[105]

Burr echoed his wife's complaint, attacking the "frivolity and vacuity" of the fashionable men and women he observed in the homes of Philadelphia high society. Theodosia's remarks remind us that Burr could never have played the Chesterfield beau—she would not have tolerated it. Rather than revel in the swirl of high society, the Burrs, as self-appointed social critics, seemed more comfortable disparaging it.[106]

What we know of Burr's personal interactions followed a very different pattern. He seems to have enjoyed more informal, salonlike gatherings, with his close friends, where he could engage in wide-ranging conversations (as he confided to his uncle Pierpont Edwards) about "men and measures, Love, Religion, and politics." He made a point of befriending James Monroe, his fellow Republican senator. During the Revolution, Monroe had been a great admirer of Theodosia, and his respect for her must have influenced his opinion of her husband. In 1791, Burr encouraged Theodosia to travel from New York to Philadelphia with Monroe, who like Burr, had to commute if he was going to see his wife (Elizabeth Monroe lived there with her family). Burr, in turn, did favors for the Virginian. After Elizabeth's father died, Burr represented Monroe and his wife in a case before the New York Chancery that concerned her father's estate.[107]

At the same time, Burr cultivated the distinguished legislator and constitutional thinker (and fellow Princetonian) James Madison. In the spring of 1794, he introduced Madison, then a forty-three-year-old bachelor, to Dolley Payne Todd. At one point, probably the year before he played matchmaker, Burr had boarded with Dolley's mother, Mary, and he remained close to the Payne family. When Dolley's first husband died during the yellow fever epidemic of 1793, Burr agreed to serve as her son's guardian. Dolley chose Burr to be her son's sole guardian because, as she expressed it in her will, "the education of my son is to him and to me the most interesting of all earthly concerns." Burr and the widow shared views on children's education: his unusual devotion to his daughter's training reaffirmed Dolley's trust in his abilities.[108]

Whether she knew it or not, in her observations about High Federalism Theodosia had drawn an acute picture of the partisan landscape. Increasingly, Anne Bingham and her London style showcased the cultural values of those in power in the decade of the 1790s. Federalists liked opulent display; Republicans preferred things simpler. Theodosia's comments to her son suggest how central social performance was becoming to the conduct of politics: the "parties resemble," as she put it, "a playhouse before the curtain is drawn up." She meant, of course, social gatherings, but one could as easily be referring to political parties.

"English" and "French" principles set the emerging political parties apart. Just as the Federalists aped the English aristocracy, the Republicans were drawn to all things French. In 1793, as the French Revolution progressed, 400 members of the New York Republican Tammany Society went on parade carrying the American flag and a French liberty cap. The following year, young Republicans donned French fashions, while one New York woman requested that Republican bachelors wear French cockades "to distinguish between *Friends* and *Enemies* of the RIGHTS OF MAN."[109]

Hoping to curb mounting sympathy for America's "sister" republic, President Washington issued a Proclamation of Neutrality to avoid dragging the United States into the war between England and France. But the new French minister, Citizen Edmond-Charles Genet, came close to provoking an international incident when he appeared to challenge Washington's will on the streets of America. Touring the nation from Charleston, South Carolina, to New York City in May 1793, Genet was warmly greeted by adoring crowds. Soon, rumors surfaced that he refused to acknowledge Washington's proclamation and planned to appeal directly to the American people to reject the administration's policy of neutrality. Prominent Federalist leaders such as Hamilton, John Jay, and Senator Rufus King played key roles in spreading gossip about Genet. After a time, even Jefferson came to feel that the French minister had become a liability for Republicans, and he urged his party's supporters to distance themselves from him.[110]

Sensitive to the growing problem, Burr asked Pennsylvania Republican John Nicholson to confirm the stories about Genet, whether he "goes about Visiting the Mechanics, and the lower orders of people, leaving Cards at their houses when they are not home!" To Burr, it all sounded nonsensical, but his inquiry demonstrates how fears of Genet's Revolutionary etiquette (leaving cards at the homes of the lower class) put manners at the center of the controversy. Federalist congressman John Steele offered a similar observation, musing, with more than a little irony, that Genet was so affable that he might "laugh us into the war if he can." *L'affaire Genet* was not simply a partisan dispute about foreign policy, but the first culture war in America, in which political differences were understood in terms of social etiquette and cultural identification.[111]

Burr was already identified with the French Enlightenment. He gave Rousseau's *Confessions* as a gift to a friend, and he voiced his admiration for the new French Constitution. He generously agreed to sponsor Madame de Senat, the governess of a young French exile, Nathalie de Lage de Volunde, who was herself the daughter of a French admiral and former maid of honor of Marie Antoinette. Through his patronage, Madame de Senat opened a school in Burr's Manhattan town house on Partition Street, just blocks from Federal Hall. While his daughter was immersed in the French language and acquiring French manners, he himself established ties to the French refugee community in New York.[112]

His close friends were no less enthusiastic in their support of the French Revolution. Melancton Smith helped organize a gala reception for Genet when he arrived in New York City. The New York Democratic Society, modeled on the French Jacobin societies, made its debut in 1793; and Burr's supporters—Smith, David Gelston, and others in his camp—filled the leadership ranks. As a fraternal club, French salon, and protest group all at once, the democratic societies in New York and elsewhere became an organ of the Republican Party; as ardent defenders of the "rights of man," they were culturally and politically pro-French. Among New York Republicans, Burr's overt sympathy for France made him even more attractive as a political manager.[113]

As political tensions over France grew, Burr assumed a prominent role in the Senate. Imbued with the Enlightenment's emphasis on research and discovery, Burr set out to master foreign policy, requesting permission from Secretary of State Jefferson, in 1793, to review the correspondence of America's ministers abroad. Putting his research to immediate use, Burr led the charge in criticizing Gouverneur Morris, the plenipotentiary in Paris and lately a prominent target of Republicans. Morris had shown little sympathy for the aims of the French Revolution. In April 1794, Burr drafted a Senate resolution congratulating the French Republic on its recent military victories over England. The senator from New York was now under consideration for a possible appointment as the next minister to France. His Republican allies Madison and Monroe proposed him for the job, though Monroe voiced some concern when he learned that Burr's old Princeton confidant, Federalist William Paterson, had expressed support for Burr in this instance.[114]

In the end, Washington selected Monroe. Trying to appease Republicans by selecting one of their own, Washington preferred the Virginian, Monroe, a man whose personality and breeding was much like his own. Appalled by his replacement, Gouverneur Morris called Monroe "a person of mediocrity in every respect." Two years later, Federalists claimed that "Republican machinations" had kept Burr from the diplomatic assignment. Yet Hamilton's influence over Washington probably mattered more, and he certainly would not have endorsed Burr's appointment.[115]

"POOR COLN BUR HAS LOST HIS WIFE"

Foreign policy was a preoccupation during the Genet affair. But then, Burr's life changed forever. On May 18, 1794, Theodosia died. Learning in Philadelphia of the "fateful event," he rushed to New York. Though her illness had grown progressively worse over the past two years, Burr was unprepared; more than that, he was disbelieving. "So sudden & unexpected was her death," he wrote to Pierpont Edwards, "that no immediate Danger was apprehended until the Morning that she was relieved from all earthly cares." Her death, he recalled years later, "dealt me more pain than all sorrows combined."[116]

Theodosia had been reconciled to her fate. She had even joked about it to her son John Bartow two years before. Anything was "preferable to dying on the road," she wrote, and then, with comic timing, "indeed to dying anywhere." But she did die—and not just anywhere: she died at home without her husband. We do not know what her last moments were like, nor is it possible to predict what might have happened if Theodosia had not been lost so soon after Aaron's career had begun. She was forty-eight, ten years older than he, and their twelve years of marriage were, by all accounts, loving. Of course, death has momentous consequences for the living, always. Now, Burr would have to go on without his most trusted political aide. She had been a keen observer, adept at judging his peers on the national scene. Had she lived, she might have more quickly unmasked his enemies—a skill Burr certainly was to need during the turbulent years ahead. Federalists and Republicans were stepping up their attacks on one another. "Poor Coln Bur has Lost his Wife," the soon-to-be Mrs. Madison heard from a relative. He had not only lost his wife; he had lost his best ally in the political wars to come.[117]

Satirical print: *A Peep into the Antifederal Club* (1793)

Chapter Five

A CERTAIN LITTLE SENATOR

Next in the train, the courtly Burr is seen.
With piercing look, and ever varying mien;
Tho' small his stature, yet his well known name,
Shines with full splendor on the rolls of fame;
Go search the records of intrigue, and find,
To what debasement sinks the human mind,
How far 'tis possible for man to go,
Where interest sways and passions urge the blow;
While pride and pleasure; haughtiness and scorn,
And mad ambition in his bosom burn.
                —Unknown author, *The Democratiad* (1795)

The powerful caricature shown at left symbolizes the fears of Federalists as they witnessed the success of the new Republican Party. City- and county-level democratic clubs were the Republicans' radical auxiliary, hammering out texts and convening public meetings in support of more popular government. In the 1793 cartoon, our eyes move directly to one image in particular, a rabble-rousing speaker who stands before the undistinguished, if not shabby, club members. He disguises his crass private ambition behind his loudly trumpeted democratic ideals. Some have suspected that the fiery radical in this political cartoon is Burr. But, in fact, it is a democrat who has been lost to history. While we cannot know with 100 percent certainty, it appears to be a man named John Swanwick.[1]

Swanwick became a Pennsylvania congressman in 1794, serving along-side Burr's good friend Albert Gallatin (later Jefferson's secretary of the treasury). He had a lavish lifestyle and pronounced literary tastes (he is quot-ing a Hamlet soliloquy in the cartoon). As "merchant-poet," he championed female education and, it was said, vainly sought to impress the ladies at the theater. Like Burr, he had a small build (he was five foot four, Burr five six), and was mockingly designated a "Great Man" as often as he was called "Lit-tle Man." Driven, according to his critics, by his "passion for superiority," Swanwick was referred to as a "puffing orator," which is, indeed, how he is portrayed in "A Peep into the Antifederal Club."[2]

There was another striking parallel between the two men. Swanwick was a self-made man, "the son of [a] British Waggon Master," whose sud-den wealth and reputation posed a threat to some among the established Federalist elite in Philadelphia. Though Burr had a proud family heritage, he was attacked for his premature expectation of political honors. As a self-made politician, Burr was rebuked for leaping ahead—stealing the Senate seat from Philip Schuyler in 1791—and for seducing voters.[3]

Nothing fed Federalist anxieties quite so much as the democratic clubs. Burr's friends across New York and Pennsylvania came out of the demo-cratic clubs in those states; he stood up in the U.S. Senate and boldly defended the clubs' activities, and he was listed as a member of the New York Democratic Society in 1798. Swanwick, in another sense, resembled Burr's closest supporters—Melancton Smith, Marinus Willett, David Gelston, and John Lamb—all of whom lacked social position but who had thrived economically since the Revolutionary War, and were ambitious merchants and speculators. All such men were satirized in the caricature, as in the telling line at the end of the orator's speech: "Glorious thought thus to emerge from dirt to Gold."[4]

The political ambitions of the modestly formed Swanwick extended only as far as Congress. But the rising star Aaron Burr was destined for even higher office. This made him a target of Federalist rancor and wild words—fearful accusations that his affiliations brought him in contact with those guilty of sedition and treason, and made him no less guilty of disloyalty. The charge of ambition against Burr represented a smoke screen, hiding a discomfort increasingly common among those in power. As a new style of politician who possessed the talent to court voters outside the ruling elite, Burr was primed to take advantage of electioneering opportunities. This would bring him new enemies.

THE "PATRIOTIC TEN"

By 1794, the Federalist mind—and President Washington's governing principle—centered on maintaining social stability and building credit abroad. As the party in power, the Federalists began to exhibit outlandish fears of conspirators. They associated Senator Burr with the French threat, the larger fear of aliens, and their distaste for democratic "disorganizers." They linked him to Citizen Genet, whose specter continued to haunt long after he had disappeared from the political scene. Genet, not surprisingly, is a figure in "A Peep into the Antifederal Club." He is the doll-like puppet (of the French), tossing coins into the hand of the man seated on the floor.[5]

Appealing directly to the people to decide foreign policy instead of bowing to the will of the executive, Genet had done more than insult the president; he became a symbol of foreign disorder, of social chaos spilling onto America's shores. His warm reception at the democratic clubs in Philadelphia and New York gave the Federalists further cause for alarm. Jacobin ideas of sedition appeared to be spreading through "self-created societies," as Washington called the unelected and unrepresentative political clubs that openly criticized his administration. For proof of their charges, Federalists pointed to the 1794 Whiskey Rebellion, an uprising against the federal excise tax on whiskey, centered in western Pennsylvania. While Washington dispatched 15,000 soldiers to suppress the so-called "western conspiracy," he blamed the "diabolical" Genet and democratic societies for the turmoil.[6]

Months before the Whiskey Rebellion came to the public attention, the Senate met to determine whether western Pennsylvania's Albert Gallatin should retain his newly won seat. Sworn in on December 2, 1793, Gallatin, a Republican, had little time to enjoy his office, for on the same day a petition was submitted challenging his credentials. Federalists, hoping to maintain their slim majority in the upper House, insisted that Gallatin, Swiss by birth, had not been an American citizen long enough to hold such a high office. The exact date of his American naturalization was at issue: he needed nine years of citizenship to serve in the Senate, and the petitioners claimed he was one year shy of meeting that requirement.[7]

The French-speaking Gallatin sparked the animosity of Federalists because, in their minds, he threatened political order. As early as 1791, when the excise on whiskey was first passed, Gallatin was its leading critic. As a member of the Pennsylvania state legislature, he drafted resolutions against the tax, calling for his fellow citizens to treat all tax collectors with contempt and to resist paying them. Gallatin himself later admitted that the resolutions were "perhaps too violent, and undoubtedly highly impolitic," but they were still well within the law. When, in 1793, Gallatin was elected to the Senate, many Federalists were, he said, "exceedingly mortified."[8]

Gallatin's right to hold his Senate seat came under attack. With his reputation as a talented lawyer, Burr assumed a prominent role in Gallatin's defense. The Senate proceedings, begun in mid-February 1794, were handled like a trial. For the first time, the Senate chamber was open to the public; the debates were closely covered in the newspapers, and large crowds were in attendance, giving the Senate forum the atmosphere of a courtroom. Virginia Republican John Taylor of Caroline felt that Burr's role was crucial. Burr would have to reprise his role in the 1792 election controversy in New York, when he crossed legal swords with Federalist senator Rufus King. During Gallatin's defense, Taylor dashed off an encouraging note to Burr: "We shall leave you to reply to King: *first,* because you desired it; *second,* all depends on it; no one else *can* do it; and the audience will expect it." Burr was the only Republican in the Senate with the legal expertise—and oratorical skills—to win this forensic contest.[9]

A Philadelphia attorney, ultra-Federalist William Lewis, represented the petitioners—Gallatin's critics—and several people were brought in to testify. He and Rufus King led the charge against Gallatin. Lewis was particularly driven. He took the case far beyond simply contesting the date of Gallatin's naturalization: he questioned whether Gallatin was worthy of holding office. The Philadelphia lawyer identified Gallatin as an interfering foreigner who had no business running for the Senate. Though the Senate was weighing whether to invalidate an election, Lewis hinted that failing to remove Gallatin would have "mischievous consequences," noting that "ancient Republics made it death for an alien to intermeddle in their policies." More than once he mocked Gallatin's "novel and absurd" ideas about citizenship, suggesting that this new American was clueless about American legal traditions and, in this sense, would always be an alien.[10]

It is just as clear that the Republicans intended to make use of the showcase trial as a means to dramatize Gallatin's victimization. This way, even if the Federalists voted to oust Gallatin, the administration's critics might still win over the general public. In any event, Aaron Burr was expected to steal the stage, and at the same time be the voice that rang out for a new and broader conception of political participation; he was, consciously, it seems, speaking for more than one man's right to a Senate seat.[11]

The main thrust of Burr's argument was that citizenship came from consent. Drawing on his favorite writer, Jean-Jacques Rousseau, Burr defended the basic premise of the social contract: citizens were not born, but made, through their participation in civil society. Gallatin had arrived in America in 1780, and during the next three years, while a resident of Massachusetts, he had owned property, taken up arms, and voted. These actions, as Burr saw things, revealed an "intention," Gallatin's "tacit consent" to act, as well as to be recognized, as a member of the social compact.[12]

Burr's theory was genuinely radical and enlightened: referencing the time of the Revolution, he removed the distinction between British and non-British. Gallatin was just like any British subject (whether born in the colonies or elsewhere) whose residence and support of the patriotic cause qualified him for American citizenship. Anglo-American heritage, prized by Federalists as a crucial apprenticeship to full citizenship, Burr dismissed as irrelevant. It was consent—not descent—that made citizens, a phenomenon never more true than at the moment of America's creation.[13]

In 1800, Burr would again make this argument, when Gallatin's appointment to Jefferson's cabinet was opposed because of his alien birth. The objection was "frivolous and absurd," he would write Maryland Republican Samuel Smith at that time, adding: "Why was it not made against Hamilton . . . and a score of others." Burr's point was obvious: If Hamilton, born in the British West Indies, held high office, then so could Gallatin; they were equally aliens—Hamilton's British heritage did not change that fact.[14]

So, in February 1794, senators voted along strict party lines, and by 14 to 12 declared Gallatin's election void. Without undue pleasure at the results, Vice President John Adams praised the hearings for the "learning, eloquence, and reasoning of some of the senators." He undoubtedly had Burr in mind as much as his fellow Federalists. Still, some Republicans wanted revenge. A month later, James Monroe contested the appointment of Delaware senator Kensey Johns. By a 1-vote margin, Johns lost his seat, and the Federalists were denied the company of one of their own.[15]

As always, personal ties raised the political stakes. Burr had both personal and political reasons for supporting Gallatin. In the months leading up to the Senate hearings, the Pennsylvanian had courted and married Hannah Nicholson, daughter of Commodore James Nicholson, a close friend of Burr's who was influential in Republican circles. Nicholson was a founder of the New York Democratic Society, and Hannah, as Gallatin described his wife, was a "pretty good Democrat."[16]

A genuine affinity had developed between Burr and Gallatin, based in part on their common search for balance between the life of the mind and financial security. Gallatin had spent much of his early life as a western adventurer, traveling along the Virginia and Pennsylvania frontiers, buying up land and speculating freely. But he was no less an accomplished scholar, having received his early training in the elite schools of Geneva. Burr later described Gallatin as the "best head" in the United States, a compliment that meant a great deal given the many, more memorable founders associated with thought. It may well have been Gallatin who introduced Burr to the work of the British philosopher Jeremy Bentham. Impressed with the precepts of Utilitarianism, Burr regarded Bentham as "second to no one, ancient or modern, in profound thinking, in logical and analytical reasoning." After meeting Burr in 1808, Bentham would return the compliment, describing him as an expert in military matters and the management of parties, and "better qualified to pursue my ideas, as well as better disposed for it than any man I have yet met with, or ever expect to meet with." It is well worth adding that Gallatin, like Burr, admired women for their intellectual attainments.[17]

Gallatin matters greatly. It is nearly impossible to describe the practical progress of liberal republicanism in early America without focusing on Albert Gallatin, yet in virtually all narratives involving the founders, he never seems to be more than a supporting player. He would become, under Jefferson and Madison, the longest serving treasury secretary in American history. His relationship with Burr in the 1790s tells us much about the coalescence of the northern Republican element: both Burr and Gallatin favored an independent economy (free from foreign, especially British, dependence), supporting commercial growth and western expansion. Influenced by the Enlightenment, they fashioned themselves as rational Republicans, social liberals, independent thinkers. They saw politics as a thinking person's game, in which rational planning was essential to partisan victory. His greatest political strength, as Gallatin said about himself, was the intensive research he conducted into political-constitutional issues—such as he and Burr displayed when they defended his right to be in the Senate. Cut from the same intellectual cloth, Burr and Gallatin were natural allies.[18]

Despite his removal from the Senate, Gallatin was immediately chosen to serve in the House in 1795. There he joined forces with James Madison and Edward Livingston; known familiarly as "beau Ned," Livingston was the younger brother of the chancellor; but it was his radical credentials as a member of the New York Democratic Society—not his family name—that got him elected as a Republican congressman from New York City. As a friend of Burr's, Livingston would later find himself in position to play a pivotal role in the 1800 election.[19]

At the time Burr was defending Gallatin's seat in the Senate, the British were assaulting American commercial vessels. In an effort to keep the French from capitalizing on American neutrality, the British had seized perhaps 150 American ships. In the House, Madison had introduced a series of retaliatory measures against the old enemy. While talk of war filled the air, Federalists searched for a way to outmaneuver their opposition, and proposed that a special envoy be dispatched immediately to England to smooth over problems. President Washington selected John Jay of New York for the delicate mission, submitting his name to the Senate for approval in April 1794.[20]

Burr continued to frustrate the Federalists in the Senate. In concert with Virginians James Monroe and John Taylor of Caroline, he led the charge against Jay's nomination. In the minds of many Republicans, Jay was far too friendly to the British, and hardly the best choice to negotiate a treaty that would protect American interests or honor. But Burr did not seethe with partisan rage; rather, he framed his criticism broadly, on constitutional grounds. In a resolution he drafted, Burr argued that Jay, as a Supreme Court justice, should not hold "any other office or employment . . . at the pleasure of the Executive." To do so was "contrary to the spirit of the Constitution," exposing him "to the influence of the Executive," which was "mischievous and impolitic." Simply put: having a justice at the beck-and-call of the president undercut the balance of power between the executive and the judiciary branches. Jay's appointment improperly augmented the power of the presidency. Instead of entrusting Congress to determine an appropriate response to British harassment, it would be a sitting judge who shaped foreign policy, in Burr's words, "at the pleasure of the Executive."[21]

Burr's resolution was shot down, and Jay left for London in May. On the other hand, James Monroe had just received his appointment from President Washington as minister to France, and sailed in June. With Monroe abroad, Burr assumed a more visible leadership role among Republicans in the Senate. In constant communication with Monroe, he forwarded newspapers and gossip, keeping the Virginian abreast of the latest developments on the national political scene. As he had with Gallatin, Burr strengthened his personal ties to Monroe when he offered the services of his stepson, John Bartow Prevost, to act as Monroe's personal secretary in France. Perhaps Burr's most important duty, though, was shoring up the Republican ranks in the Senate. In 1794, after the departure of the Virginians Monroe and Taylor, Henry Tazewell and Stevens Thomson Mason became the new pairing from that state. Though both were devoted to the Republican Party, they were not party leaders. Burr worked closely with the newcomers, especially Tazewell, who was Monroe's personal friend. Thus Burr consolidated the ranks, and took charge of managing the anti-administration wing of the Senate.[22]

Negotiations with the British Ministry were completed in November 1794, but both the Senate and the general public remained in the dark about Jay's activities for seven more months. By that time, Republicans were absolutely furious at the Federalists' repeated attempts to shroud the treaty's provisions in secrecy. Through procedural technicalities at the time of Jay's confirmation, Federalists made it impossible for Republicans to have any say in the negotiations. With instructions crafted by Hamilton, Jay was given full discretionary power to carry out his mission; he neither had to inform the Senate of his progress nor submit his instructions for their advice or judgment. When Jay finally sent the treaty to President Washington in March 1795, the cagey chief executive refused to disclose its contents until he had called a special session of the Senate on June 8. Even then, Federalists took the unusual step of placing an injunction of secrecy on the senators, insisting that the treaty could not be discussed outside its closed chambers.[23]

When the senators finally were permitted to review the terms of the treaty, Republicans were appalled, and even a number of Federalists privately confessed their dissatisfaction. The treaty read like a list of humiliating concessions. The only privilege Jay secured for American commerce was permission to resume trade with the West Indies; and even here, the tonnage restrictions were so severe that, as Madison mockingly noted, it was like having the right to trade in canoes. Southerners were doubly angry because Jay had ignored instructions to secure compensation for their loss of slaves, lured away or captured by the British during the Revolution. The treaty was a retreat from the policy of neutrality, insulting to America's French allies, and there was no provision protecting American seamen from impressment into the British navy either. Americans were denied use of several waterways and ports within Canada, while British ships were given few restrictions, plying the Mississippi alongside American vessels. Significantly, too, the British refused to pay the United States monetary damages stemming from their failure to abandon frontier posts in the Northwest for thirteen years, though they were meant to have done so immediately after signing the 1783 Treaty of Paris. The list of embarrassments went on. Jay's Treaty seemed like a complete capitulation.[24]

A two-thirds majority was needed in the Senate to ratify the treaty, and there were just enough Federalists to clinch the vote, if all sided with the administration. The only chance Burr and the other Republicans had to defeat Jay's Treaty was to lure away a few Federalists who might be wavering. So the Republicans tried a few tactics, such as lifting the secrecy injunction in the hope of generating a public outcry sufficient to exert pressure on a few Federalists. But even the motion to take the debate beyond the walls of the Senate failed, and vigorous debate continued—away from the public eye. At this tense moment, Burr made a direct appeal to President Washington, writing for an audience, so that they could "converse"—amicably—and come to some terms. There is no indication that Washington even replied.

Burr returned to the Senate. According to Gallatin, "Burr made a most excellent speech," summarizing the treaty's most glaring flaws. He proposed that ratification be postponed until several offending articles were renegotiated—it was Burr's intention to send the treaty back to the drawing table. But again the motion failed, by the same predictable 20-to-10 vote that a few days later would officially convey Senate approval of the treaty.[25]

In spite of their defeat in the Senate, the Republicans carried the fight into the streets. Newspapers were already railing against the veil of secrecy: "If the people have the right and capacity to govern themselves," a writer in the New York *Argus* contended, then "they are certainly entitled to a knowledge of their own affairs." One correspondent sarcastically regretted "that the Treaty cannot be kept secret after as well as before it was ratified." Another angry critic charged that the senators' behavior was unconstitutional as well as unrepublican, by comparing the rule of secrecy to the debauched and despotic "darkness of a conclave or a seraglio."[26]

Loath to keep the treaty a secret any longer, Senator Stevens Thomson Mason of Virginia sent a copy to the Philadelphia *Aurora,* probably the most radically Republican of all American presses. As he set it in type, editor Benjamin Bache (grandson of Benjamin Franklin) forwarded the text to sister papers across the country. Thomas Greenleaf published it in the *Argus* on July 4, and it appears that Burr had already circulated his copy among his constituents. Heralding Burr for his critical stand against Jay's treaty, Greenleaf published the treaty alongside "two IMPORTANT MOTIONS, one by MR. BURR and the other by MR. TAZEWELL."[27]

For Republicans in New York, Burr was a voice of reason against the treaty, and a galvanizing force. At this critical moment, three prominent civic groups—the Democratic Society, Tammany Society, and Mechanic Society—all drank toasts to the "ten virtuous, wise, and independent Senators," the *"Patriotic Ten,"* who had "refused to sacrifice their country's commerce, rights, and honor."[28]

"MAD AMBITION IN HIS BOSOM BURN"

A momentous development occurred at this time—momentous, at least, in Burr's political career. In 1795, he found himself the object of two devastating satires published in the nation's capital of Philadelphia. For the first time, and in what would become a constant refrain in later years, Burr was depicted as an intriguer. The attacks were highly personal, criticizing his private life, his manners, and his physical appearance. The first poem, the anonymous *Democratiad* (1795), devoted one long section to the "courtly Burr." It made light of the senator's "piercing look, and ever varying mien," mocking, too, his small stature, and belittling his "well known name." Burr did not deserve the fame that his worthy ancestry afforded him. Echoing what Hamilton had already whispered in private, the satirist painted him as a creature of intrigue and disguise, a man of overblown pride and irregular passions. He displayed "haughtiness and scorn"; and beneath his courtly veneer, the poet claimed, did "mad ambition in his bosom burn."[29]

The unknown author of the second satire, a poem entitled *Aristocracy,* displayed an intimate knowledge of his subject's life. Though not mentioned by name, Burr was identified through clues that closely paralleled his personal history. There was his rejection of his family's religious faith, his absence from the Constitutional Convention, and his daring experiment in training his daughter according to the precepts of Mary Wollstonecraft. Recognized as a prominent leader of the Republican Party, second only to Jefferson at this juncture (according to the poem), Burr was a target. Even his talents as a party manager were chided: as the consummate political manipulator, he employed "art superior," that is, a creative yet disruptive knowledge, and he capitalized crudely on partisan alliances to advance his ignoble career.[30]

The Federalists were on the warpath. *Aristocracy* associated Burr with treason in the form of a secret pact with the pushy, power-hungry Citizen Genet. Wining and dining the French envoy at his home, Burr appears unctuous, a scheming courtier, teaming up with the dangerous Jacobin foreign minister. In a long "confession," Burr is made to admit that his relentless ambition stems from jealousy of Hamilton. Only by winning the presidency could he ostensibly eclipse Hamilton's undiminished fame. This mock-Burr explains:

> *Then might I hope the Empire's highest seat;*
> *Then see my rival humbled at my feet;*
> *The utmost object of my vows be found;*
> *And pride, ambition, and revenge, be crown'd.*[31]

Both of these satires underscored Federalists' growing concern with Republican success in attracting a popular following. In 1795, Burr was increasing in stature just as Hamilton had decided to step down as Washington's influential secretary of the treasury. To most Federalists, the Genet Affair, the Whiskey Rebellion, and the Jay Treaty all pointed to treasonous behavior. They were the poisonous fruit of one tree: the democratic societies. Hamilton's successor at the treasury, Federalist Oliver Wolcott, received a telling letter from his father, who confidently wrote in February 1795 that the "democratical, or as some call them, demoniacal societies," were "nurseries of sedition." In *Aristocracy,* as Burr plotted with Genet, the democratic interest attracted an adoring "throng." With satanic glee, the conniving Burr promoted disorder throughout the land.[32]

Continuing protests against the Jay Treaty added to these fears. Town meetings took place not only in the South but in Federalist strongholds in the Northeast as well. In Boston, Jay's portrait was burned in effigy; and a copy of the treaty was set afire on the streets of New York. At a meeting organized by that city's Democratic Society on the Fourth of July, Hamilton himself was pelted with stones while he tried to defend the treaty. Later that day, after he had impulsively challenged the fifty-nine-year-old Commodore James Nicholson to a duel, Hamilton turned and invited a group of democrats to engage in a bare knuckle fistfight, claiming he was ready to fight the "whole detestable faction" one at a time. The "self-created societies," which Washington had blamed for the Whiskey Rebellion, were now accused of inciting mob violence over the treaty.[33]

The democratic societies did oppose the Jay Treaty. Recall that the New York Democratic Society had toasted Burr as one of the "*Patriotic Ten*" who opposed the treaty in the Senate. Although we do not know if he was a member of the society in 1795 (he definitely was in 1798), some of his closest allies, such as Commodore Nicholson, David Gelston, and Melancton Smith, were. And Burr had gone on record defending them. He had opposed the Senate's censure of the New York Democratic Society in November 1794. And when drafting the Senate's response to the president's address before Congress, Burr had tried to excise the passage in which the Senate endorsed Washington's harangue against "self-created societies."[34]

Burr was fully sympathetic to the goals of the democratic societies, believing that they had every right to shape public opinion. Throughout the summer and fall of 1795, as public outcry over the Jay Treaty peaked, Burr felt perfectly comfortable praising all such popular protests. In a letter to Henry Tazewell, a letter signed "health & fraternity," Burr embraced the trademark greeting of the French-inspired democratic societies.[35]

Interestingly, the two satires of 1795 played with an image of Burr as a faux democrat. He was alleged to be an aristocrat slumming with democrats, using the "people" to promote his private ambition. Known in Federalist circles for his shifting alliances (his "ever varying mien"), Burr was a demagogue waiting to be crowned. Likened to Genet, he was a political alien, an outsider in his native land. His glaring absence from the Constitutional Convention ("silent, at home, neglected") was meant to demonstrate his lack of commitment to the federal government, insofar as he had no hand in its creation.[36]

But the added fear for Federalists was that Burr was dangerous—more so even than Jefferson—as the author of *Aristocracy* claimed because, unlike the heralded Virginian, he could mobilize support for the Republicans in the North. Burr's rivalry with Hamilton presented a cruel irony. The Federalists' talented, charismatic leader was not the heir apparent to Washington in 1795, because the ornery, yet statesmanlike, John Adams was. Hamilton would never be elected senator or governor, let alone president of the United States. Universally regarded as the most ambitious among ambitious men, he would never claim "the Empire's highest seat." Burr, on the other hand, though he was roundly attacked for his ambition by Hamiltonians, was both electable and, at this moment, a seeming successor to Jefferson. The Virginia Republicans may not have been gazing so far into the future, but it would appear that some fearful Federalists were. By 1795, Burr was already a "dangerous" Republican who had to be tarred as a faux founder. Standing in the shadow of Jefferson, he was, as importantly, hovering in the path of Hamilton, threatening to eclipse his glorious career.

"MR. NOBODY"

This fear was manifest on a regional as well as national level. Federalists were troubled by Burr's political ambition within New York State. In December 1794, Hamilton's father-in-law, Philip Schuyler, fretted in a letter to Rufus King that Burr might be scheming to steal the governor's seat in the upcoming election. Schuyler assumed that Clinton and Burr had made a secret pact: the old governor would back Burr, while Clinton ran for the U.S. Senate, positioning himself to be Jefferson's running mate in 1796. Schuyler was mistaken about Clinton, but right about Burr, who did set his sights on the state's highest office.[37]

Yet Burr had competition. While Clinton's plans were uncertain—except that it did seem likely he would step aside—two other familiar figures had joined the race: Chancellor Robert Livingston and New York State Supreme Court Chief Justice Robert Yates. None of the above candidates pleased the Schuyler faction. John Jay—a gracious loser in the last contest—was their best hope, even though his diplomatic mission to England had taken him out of the country. They would run Jay *in absentia,* a move that makes little sense to modern observers but did nothing to hurt his chances then. Indeed, landing in New York a full month after the polls closed, the victorious Jay was inaugurated on July 1, 1795.[38]

This bizarre gubernatorial election reveals some of the odd twists and turns of early New York politics. Outside the state, Republicans like James Madison speculated that Burr would run against Hamilton. They were wrong. The former treasury secretary refused to stand for elective office. Parties, in fact, had little impact on the 1795 governor's race—the candidates presented themselves as moderates, independent of national alliances. To put it best, they *straddled* parties. Yates, not Burr, became the favorite among Clintonians after Clinton announced he would not seek reelection. Though he received support from Republicans in the state, Yates was also courted by prominent Federalists.[39]

Yates's career was indicative of the difference between state and national politics. Looking back, during the volatile election of 1792, Yates had first endorsed Burr before supporting Jay. In 1789, he had run against Clinton, and received Hamilton's backing. The picture might seem blurred, but really is not. Yates was not a Clinton man. He was a bipartisan candidate, an Anti-Federalist embraced by the Federalists, who would find himself "repackaged" to satisfy the Clinton wing of the Republicans. The national parties had hardened by 1793, but state conditions did not mirror the national scene—and we must be careful not to equate political identities and individual actions in the 1790s with the way today's system functions.[40]

We must understand Burr's political personality in a similar way. His campaign followed a strategy of non-partisanship, much like that of Yates. What made him attractive as a candidate was his independence from the dominant family-based factions—the Clintons, Livingstons, and Schuylers. In the *Albany Gazette,* he gained the support of one adherent "not because I know him to belong to either one faction or another but because I believe him to belong to none." His integrity resided in the liberality of his views. Incongruously, Hamilton would turn Burr's moderation on its head and equate it with lack of principle (and in saying so, mean moral principle) when he knew full well, if he could have admitted it to himself, that Burr was acting in a predictable fashion for a New York office seeker. Hamilton's peevish characterization of Burr as a man devoid of principle obscures the fact that straddling parties was the way New York governors were elected at this time. A less judgmental Federalist at the same time praised Burr for "his abilities as a statesman, Philosopher, and soldier," a suitable candidate for "every enlightened citizen."[41]

Federalist-friendly Peter Van Gaasbeek, who proudly hung a portrait of Burr in his home, ran the unsuccessful campaign. Most, if not all, of Burr's Federalist support came from Van Gaasbeek's bailiwick of Ulster County. Writing to Stephen Van Rensselaer (one of the landed gentry in the state and Schuyler's son-in-law), Van Gaasbeek readily admitted that Burr was not a Hamiltonian Federalist: "As to politicks, he and I often differ in our Votes on particular measures." And yet the political strategist defended Burr as "an upright Man and as good a friend to the Constitution & to good Government as you or I."[42]

Adding to the oddity of the campaign, Van Rensselaer toyed with the idea of running as Burr's lieutenant governor, and secretly kept Schuyler informed of Burr's plans. Schuyler had no sense of irony. He simply reacted, preferring anyone to the "obnoxious" Burr—even if it meant another term under Clinton, whom he considered "the least of two evils." Meanwhile, Burr's Republican stalwarts in New York City—men like Marinus Willett, Melancton Smith, and John Lamb—also failed to drum up meaningful support. By the end of March, Burr and Livingston had folded, and though Yates remained in the race, the absent Jay cruised to the governorship.[43]

But Burr was attracting attention for his campaign style. And he was doing something quite different from the other candidates, which his enemies were quick to point out. Chancellor Livingston observed that Burr had rented a house in Albany, setting up shop in the capital to secure the votes from the northern part of the state. This was the most striking feature of Burr's activities: his willingness to openly engage in campaigning. It was a practice that virtually all eighteenth-century candidates avoided. Candidates were not to behave as "candidates"; they strenuously sought to appear aloof and disinterested. By 1795, however, indifference to electioneering had become simply a pose. Burr refused to play the game of appearances, and in doing so anticipated the modern democratic campaign style.[44]

Seeking the governorship, he traveled across the state personally, using his court appearances in various districts as a means of shoring up support. He did not rely just on Van Gaasbeek or other emissaries to promote his candidacy, nor did he depend heavily on letter campaigns or newspapers to shape the opinion of the electorate. Burr, prompted by an emerging but still unspoken democratic impulse, felt that the candidate himself had to hit the campaign trail.[45]

High Federalists, married to traditional definitions of political decorum, took this opportunity to mock Burr's ambition. Pedantic Noah Webster, editor of the New York Federalist newspaper *American Minerva,* decried a "certain *little Senator,* running about the streets, whispering soft things in people's ears, and making large entertainments." It helps to qualify what Burr did by seeing it as his eagerness to be both the candidate and the party manager. He preferred to undertake tasks rather than to delegate them. He differed from Jefferson, who relied on men like John Beckley, Republican clerk of the House of Representatives, to serve as his intelligence agent and campaign coordinator. Similarly, Jay allowed Schuyler and Hamilton to control his campaign from behind the scenes. Burr was willing to canvass the voters, collect useful information, and win over voters in person. He did so primarily because he enjoyed being a strategist, a hands-on organizer—a political general. He was drawn to the political battlefield. While Federalists unsparingly satirized Burr's "*modest, unaspiring disposition, his aversion to office, and his abhorrence of every species of intrigue to obtain political preferment,*" the truth they refused to acknowledge was that Burr was naturally honest about campaigning, and his opponents dared not be as open.[46]

Burr struck a nerve among New York Federalists, who uncomfortably perceived the beginnings of political change. Self-created democratic societies were calling novel kinds of public forums, fostering newer, more intimate alliances among private citizens. Self-created candidates provoked the same underlying anxiety. In 1794, Noah Webster had published another parody of democratic electioneering, which anticipated the complaint he would make against Burr. His generic candidate avidly pursued office: "I can do all the rest myself—I will run about the streets, take every body by the hand, squeeze it hard, smile and look sweet." What most annoyed Webster was that the new style of campaigning could make a "SOMEBODY" out of a "MR. NOBODY." Politics was a crude avenue for social climbing, a means of gaining fame without possessing an earned reputation.[47]

Burr's innovation (or transgression, to his enemies) was his willingness to cross certain social boundaries. By campaigning openly, he exposed the hidden side of politics, revealing the mechanics of electioneering that most eighteenth-century politicians concealed behind the mask of virtuous disinterestedness. He was not the only candidate to behave in this manner, though perhaps at this time none made his opposition feel quite so uneasy.

Though Jay won the governor's race, Burr continued to make campaign excursions that year, leaving his home state to get a feel for the broader political climate, with his eye on the upcoming presidential election. In August 1795, he headed north to Boston and Portsmouth, New Hampshire, gleaning the sentiments of New Englanders with respect to the Jay Treaty. He assured a fellow Republican that the general hostility exhibited toward the treaty would "produce some effect" in New England's next elections. Almost immediately after he returned to New York, in September, he took the stage south, spending over three months in Virginia, the embryonic District of Columbia, and Philadelphia. While in Richmond, he met with Governor Robert Brooke, and several other state power brokers, including former Senator (and friend) John Taylor of Caroline. Warmly received in Virginia, Burr acknowledged the "Civilities which are lavished upon me" by its Republican leaders.[48]

He spent only one day at Monticello. There is no record of what Jefferson and Burr discussed during this brief visit. Later, in the heat of 1796 presidential campaign, rumors flew that they had mapped out "rash and violent measures" against the Jay Treaty, with one nefarious design in mind: "to change our government," Federalist Chauncey Goodrich claimed, "and make Jefferson President, and Burr Vice President." The two men had little time to plan, and it is highly unlikely that they accomplished anything so momentous as cementing the Republican ticket. Still, Burr *was* actively campaigning. He had made the long trip not just to consult with Jefferson but to show *in the flesh* his commitment to the Virginia Republicans.[49]

Though the national election of 1796 was technically the first contested presidential race, it is best described as a transitional moment separating the ostensibly non-partisan era of Washington from the fiercely partisan struggle to take place in 1800. The only state with an effective (Republican) party machine was Pennsylvania. It appears also to have been the only state to clearly identify candidates for president and vice president. Why is this significant? The Electoral College did not yet distinguish between the two top national offices, and so every elector in every state cast 2 votes, each vote bearing equal weight. The presidency was to be awarded to the person receiving the most electoral votes; the second-place finisher would become vice president. Except in Pennsylvania, where a "ticket" was introduced into voters' minds, presidential electors were left, more or less, to their own devices when it came to voting for the number two spot. Although the two emerging parties, Federalists and Republicans, did present tickets, pairing Adams and Thomas Pinckney of South Carolina, and Jefferson and Burr, the state electors did not necessarily follow suit. In the end, over a dozen candidates received votes.[50]

Following Hamilton's advice, President Washington delayed announcing his retirement until September 1796. The campaign officially opened, in that sense, in September. But even before Washington made his intentions known, the two parties were devising their campaign strategies in private. By May of that year, the leaders on both sides had already prepared for a contest between Jefferson and Adams. They did not anticipate what actually happened, however: that a seemingly peripheral candidate—Pinckney—would complicate the electoral vote tally and cause confusion among partisans.[51]

The election of 1796 eventually became a three-way competition marked by sectional distrust and internal party division. Pinckney had been selected by mainstream Federalists to be, in effect, Adams's running mate; but Hamilton, taking advantage of the fact that there were no rules as yet, surreptitiously promoted Pinckney as the dark horse candidate for president. Remarkable as it must seem to us, none of the key political play-ers expressed interest in the selection of a vice president, save for a few Federalists who recognized the very real (and alarming) possibility that Jef-ferson might fill the second spot. The presidential vote of 1796 is on close inspection a revealing study in the fitful process by which national election standards came into being.[52]

Because the party system was new, there was an unusual lack of leader-ship or party discipline. Jefferson, living in retirement since 1793, was a genuinely reluctant candidate. Madison, fearful of the alternative, took on the responsibility of convincing his friend to stay in the race, but even Madison abandoned Philadelphia after the adjournment of Congress in June. The historian Stephen Kurtz observed that "no Republican of [Madi-son's] stature took over the direction of the campaign in the decisive last three months." This disorganized state of affairs allowed sectional concerns to take precedence over national ones. Party manager John Beckley, a Vir-ginian, orchestrated a surprising victory for the Republicans in Pennsylvania, but in the course of doing so he sparked tensions with local Republican leader Alexander Dallas. It was provincialism that contributed most to Burr's weak showing in the election; the candidate's personal qualities were, at best, a secondary factor.[53]

We need to examine the sectional problem more closely. Before he left Philadelphia, Madison called a caucus meeting of Senate Republicans in May to select a running mate for Jefferson. Unfortunately, evidence of what happened at the meeting is fragmentary, the only "records" emerging from gossip circulated by Federalists, who were, as always, quick to find fault with their opponents. The vice-presidential possibilities were Burr, New York's Chancellor Robert Livingston, New Hampshire senator John Lang-don, and South Carolina senator Pierce Butler. It was not a friendly gathering: tempers flared, and when Butler failed to garner support, he stormed out. It appears that Butler opposed Burr's candidacy on strictly sectional grounds, claiming he (Butler) could guarantee the votes of South Carolina, whereas Burr, a northerner, could only lose valuable southern support for the Republican ticket. His point, whether he intended it or not, was obvious: the Republican Party, as constituted in 1796, remained a re-gional party, and could only win by solidifying its southern base, and hoping for a few northern defectors.[54]

Sectional distrust punctuated the Philadelphia meeting. Langdon and Livingston were northerners, neither of whom had much national influence. Like George Clinton, they were "safe" candidates, who posed no threat to the southern Republican interest. On the other hand, the more prominent Burr was hard for his southern colleagues to trust: he was an active and mobile politician, the kind who generated impatient rumors. One Federalist congressman and confidant of Hamilton, William Loughton Smith, reported of the caucus meeting that many southerners felt Burr was "unsettled in his politics and are afraid he will go over to the other side." The other side? There is no real evidence of this. A modern study of Burr's voting record in the U.S. Senate demonstrates that he ranked high in party loyalty. Everyone at the Philadelphia meeting knew Burr's voting record, which suggests that their fears were rather a function of sectional distrust. Did the southerners really want their party to be a national party? In 1796, the answer was not at all clear.[55]

Federalist Oliver Wolcott of Connecticut recorded an interview he had with a prominent (unnamed) Virginian in 1794, in which this southern hostility toward Burr comes across. Wolcott's source compared Burr to Hamilton, and said he wished that Burr was a Federalist so that Virginians could sink the popularity of both men at once. Burr was dangerous because "he is determined the play the first part" (i.e., win the presidency), and could easily become a "leader of a popular party in the northern states," which threatened to "subvert the influence of the southern states." This seems a more likely explanation for Burr's lack of acceptance in the South than the imagined prospect of his defecting to the Federalist side. We must bear in mind, too, that Jefferson himself viewed the election of 1796 as a sectional contest. In a letter to Madison the previous year, he described the Republican Party, in no uncertain terms, as that party which embodied the "Southern interest." The idea that Burr might stray had less to do with his avowed principles than with his regional identity. Political parties had arisen in the 1790s largely in order to protect group self-interest and broader sectional interests, making it unlikely that Virginians—the party of established planters—would ever really trust Burr.[56]

Senate Republicans finally agreed that a Jefferson-Burr ticket was the best answer to Federalism. And in spite of southern resistance, Burr had already mustered considerable support for his candidacy. In June, Beckley confidently wrote Madison that in Pennsylvania "the whole body of Republicans are decidedly in favor of Burr." Burr's friend Albert Gallatin, the scientist David Rittenhouse (a prominent member of the Democratic Society of Philadelphia), and Chief Justice Thomas McKean of the Pennsylvania Supreme Court were all listed by Beckley as firmly in Burr's camp. That support would never wane: Burr received 13 electoral votes (just 1 shy of Jefferson) in the Keystone State.[57]

At the same time, Beckley assured Madison that Burr could count on the votes of the new states in the West, Kentucky and Tennessee. Why did these states not share the sectional bias of the Virginians? Because, as in Pennsylvania, Burr had friends and allies actively promoting his cause there. Republican senator John Brown urged Burr's candidacy in Kentucky, and knew firsthand of Burr's decisive role as a partisan leader in the Senate. Though born in Virginia, Brown was raised by a Presbyterian minister (recall that Reverend Aaron Burr was a Presbyterian). He joined the freshman class at Princeton just two years after Burr graduated. Later, as their friendship deepened, he would accompany Burr on his notorious western journey in 1805. Tennessee presented an equally favorable political climate. William Blount and William Cocke were that state's first U.S. senators, and also active party managers. Burr had led the charge for Tennessee statehood in the Senate early in 1796, winning friends in Knoxville and Nashville. During the campaign, Blount wrote to Tennessee's governor, Revolutionary War hero John Sevier, that Burr "may be ranked among [Tennessee's] very warmest friends."[58]

Federalists, too, noted that Burr and his associates in the Senate were "quite zealous" in securing Tennessee statehood. New Englander Chauncey Goodrich tartly observed that Burr's efforts were simply "one twig of the electioneering cabal for Mr. Jefferson." Burr genuinely favored western expansion, which made him unusual for a New Yorker. Yet Westerners had good reason to be wary of the northeastern states. In 1786, another New Yorker, John Jay, attempted to negotiate a treaty with Spain that restricted Americans' right to freely navigate on the Mississippi for the next thirty years. The West could not expand without the Mississippi—it was the economic artery of the region. Two years later, in 1788, men like John Brown felt that the northeastern states were intentionally trying to stall western expansion by delaying Kentucky's admission as a state. Regional distrust was reignited once more, in 1796, over Tennessee statehood, as Federalists blatantly blocked admission.[59]

Western expansion and western conspiracy conjoined the careers of Blount and Brown. Blount would be expelled from the Senate in 1797, when he was placed at the center of an intricate plot, involving Americans, Britons, Canadians, and Indians, to invade Spain's North American colonies. Blount's design was to proclaim New Orleans a free port and to ensure the unrestricted use of the Mississippi for Americans. Brown had even earlier been associated with the "Spanish Conspiracy" of 1788, an abortive scheme to separate Kentucky from the union and establish friendly relations with Spain. The issue, again, was control over the Mississippi River. Unlike Blount, Brown's rumored conspiratorial activities did him no harm. Kentucky voters never deserted him. He was elected to the first two U.S. Congresses, and served in the Senate from 1792 to 1805.[60]

During the 1796 presidential election, the Mississippi again became a campaign issue. Federalists hoped to capitalize on a recent diplomatic success. Thomas Pinckney emerged as the Hamiltonians' candidate after he negotiated a popular treaty that gave the United States free navigation of the essential river. Unlike the Jay Treaty, the Pinckney Treaty was warmly received by Federalists and Republicans alike. It was New York senator Rufus King who suggested to Hamilton that he consider the South Carolinian. "Should we concur in [Pinckney,] will he not receive as great, if not greater, southern and western support than any other man?" King observed. The senator, of course, was unduly optimistic: the western vote went to Jefferson and Burr. Perhaps more than Jefferson and Madison's quiet efforts, it was Burr's skill at forging meaningful political alliances in the Senate that best explains the Republicans' success in the West.[61]

Yet in Burr's home state of New York, there was little hope of success. Beckley saw that the state assembly, which named the presidential electors, was "wholly Jayite," that is, under Federalist control. New England, though another Federalist stronghold, held out greater promise, because the electors there were chosen in a general election. Beckley's agent in Massachusetts was James Swan, a Boston merchant who had met Monroe in Paris and whom Monroe had subsequently introduced to Burr. Swan wholeheartedly backed Jefferson, and was "strongly in favor of Burr[']s election."[62]

Burr preferred to remain optimistic about New England. He relied in part on his own observations; the scouting trip he had taken the year before remained fresh in his mind. His contact in New Haven, Pierpont Edwards—the only one of his close relatives to follow him into the Republican Party—gave added encouragement. By May, hardened Connecticut Federalists were being warned to respond vigorously to signs of support in their state for Jefferson and Burr. Yet Burr, as he had done in the New York governor's race, refused to leave the campaigning for Jefferson or himself in the hands of others. In September, he headed north again, spending six full weeks electioneering in Connecticut, Massachusetts, Rhode Island, and Vermont.[63]

But the campaign soon devolved into fears of schisms and intrigues. Before Hamilton had settled on Pinckney, he toyed with the idea of persuading Virginia's Revolutionary hero and former governor Patrick Henry to run with Adams. When Jefferson caught wind of the scheme, he felt certain that Henry would never accept. As Henry's name circulated, however, Jefferson still worried that the orator might split votes in Virginia. Other Republicans meanwhile tried similar tactics in the North, hoping to divide the Federalist ticket. Though he preferred Burr, Bostonian James Swan still suggested to Beckley that Republicans might circulate Robert Livingston's name as a vice-presidential candidate in New Jersey and New York; this might result, he said, in "a successful diversion" of votes away from Adams, in favor of Jefferson.[64]

By fall, Federalists and Republicans were imagining all kinds of possible combinations. In November, weeks before election day* but after the selection of electors had ensured a Republican victory in Pennsylvania, Burr's boyhood friend, the New Jersey *Federalist* leader Jonathan Dayton, proposed backing him for president. Having failed in Pennsylvania, Adams seemed to Dayton (writing to Theodore Sedgwick) doomed to defeat. He pondered whether the Federalists might not be better off promoting Burr than swallowing Jefferson. "Is it not desirable," he asked, "to have at the helm a man who is personally known to, as well as esteemed and respected by us both?" In a letter to Tennessee governor John Sevier, William Blount also assessed Burr's prospects. He predicted that in the South and West, Pinckney would only get the votes of South Carolina, and that few north-

---

* Election day in 1796 was December 7.

ern states would be willing to back either Jefferson or Pinckney. Blount concluded that Burr stood a good chance of winning the vice presidency—not with Jefferson but with Adams. And not because Burr was Federalist in his political tastes, but because his balance and moderation simply made him less objectionable. Burr was the one man in this contest who could potentially transcend sectionalism.[65]

As late as December, before definite results were reported, Adams admitted to his wife that he would "rather hazard my little Venture in the ship to the Pilotage of Jefferson, than that of Pinckney, or Burr." If he was going to face defeat, and be saddled with another term as vice president, he preferred losing to Jefferson, his friend of many years, who was older and more experienced than the others. Note, though, that he voiced no particular fear that Burr might win and drive the ship of state aground: Burr was no more undeserving than Pinckney.[66]

What had occurred? In a climate of uncertainty and anxiety, fueled largely by Hamilton's plot to sneak Pinckney past Adams, party loyalty collapsed. In its wake, sectional jealousy returned, and now prevailed. Burr's decision to campaign in New England suddenly caused Beckley, the Virginia Republicans' watchdog, to view the New Yorker through the eyes of his fellow Virginians. Given that Jefferson was left with little hope of capturing any votes north of Pennsylvania, Beckley retreated from his enthusiastic support of Burr and complained to Madison that Burr's efforts "are more directed to himself than any body else." Should Burr succeed, Beckley suggested that Virginia's electors ought to throw away half their votes on Clinton. Burr's natural detractors saw his activities differently: Hamilton snoop Stephen Higginson of Massachusetts reported that Burr was doing his best to promote Jefferson. According to Higginson, Burr's trusted friend Melancton Smith had "sent letters to some of our electors, & I believe to New Hampshire, soliciting Votes for Burr very strongly, & rather pressing for Jefferson." But for Beckley, a vote for Burr in New England was a vote against Jefferson *and* Virginia. As Burr made inroads, the threat of a decidedly northern-biased government increased.[67]

Local Virginia Republicans, even without Beckley's prodding, had already decided to make the election about Virginia, and to put all their efforts behind electing Jefferson, and Jefferson alone. The vice presidency became irrelevant. In a revealing article published in the Richmond *Argus* in October, the writer insisted that Virginia, because of its extensive territory, wealth, and population, had a superior claim to determine the election. (It was already understood that Virginia held the largest number of electoral votes.) Such displays of arrogance show how little the Virginia Republicans actually cared about winning with a national party ticket. Just as Beckley had advocated, the *Argus* writer urged that the electors' second vote should be wasted on unlikely candidates Samuel Adams or George Clinton.[68]

And that is exactly what happened in Virginia. Jefferson received 20 out of a possible 22 of the state's electoral votes; Samuel Adams received 15; Clinton 3. John Adams, Burr, Pinckney, and non-candidate George Washington each got 1 vote. The Pinckney plot had caused this confusion, more than any suspicion aroused by Burr's campaigning. The real fear among Virginia partisans was of Pinckney squeaking past Jefferson (and Adams) in electoral votes. Pinckney had talents, one confidant of Madison's admitted, but he was plainly a Hamiltonian puppet, who remained vulnerable to "being misled by artful[l] and designing men." On election day, Jefferson was the only candidate in the eyes of Virginia voters, and he was not, as yet, the head of a national party.[69]

The breakdown of electoral votes in the 1796 presidential election was as follows:

Candidate	State	Party Affiliation	Votes
John Adams	Massachusetts	Federalist	71
Thomas Jefferson	Virginia	Republican	68
Thomas Pinckney	South Carolina	Federalist	59
Aaron Burr	New York	Republican	30
Samuel Adams	Massachusetts	Federalist	15
Oliver Ellsworth	Connecticut	Federalist	11
George Clinton	New York	Republican	7
John Jay	New York	Federalist	5
James Iredell	North Carolina	Federalist	3
John Henry	Maryland	Republican	2
Samuel Johnston	North Carolina	Federalist	2
George Washington	Virginia	Federalist	2
Charles C. Pinckney	South Carolina	Federalist	1

This meant that Adams would be president, and his Republican rival, Jefferson, his vice president. No one got what they wanted in the end.

We do not know how Burr felt when he learned of the election results. He certainly knew what Hamilton and his allies were up to when he warned a Massachusetts elector about Adams's "pretended friends" in New York. But he was most likely unprepared for the news that his own party had deceived him. Four years later, he would finally admit that he had "no confidence in the Virginians . . . and they are not to be trusted." But Burr had no chance of winning the vice presidency in 1796, regardless, unless he secured a good number of votes in New England: indeed, he did not persuade a single elector there. This simple fact explains why he devoted his energies to the New England states. In the South, he lost 28 Republican votes to other candidates; but with that southern support, he would have only reached a total of 58 electoral votes, still 1 less than Pinckney.[70]

Hamilton's reaction was predictable. Ignoring his political blunder in making the incoming president his confirmed enemy, he expressed satisfaction that Burr had been soundly beaten. "The event will not a little mortify *Burr*," he wrote Rufus King. "Virginia has given him only one vote." Other Federalists were shocked by what they had not foreseen: "Virginia has treated Burr scurvily in the election," Chauncey Goodrich observed, "and North Carolina not much better." Virginia's desertion embarrassed (but did not surprise) northern Republicans who respected Burr. John Langdon, according to Goodrich, was "simple enough to say he might have known they would lurch him." Even Abigail Adams was surprised, writing her husband that she was "at a loss for the politics of Virginia," assuming that those who voted for Jefferson would naturally support Burr.[71]

On the other hand, there were some southerners who expressed sincere regret for the way things turned out. John Taylor of Caroline, a Virginia elector, wrote Henry Tazewell that he had been "compelled to reluctantly sacrifice Burr." Whether Taylor took his the orders from Madison or acquiesced to a quiet consensus of provincials, there were signs, at least among Burr's Senate colleagues, that Virginia had been wrong to disavow him. If the election of 1796 did not make the Virginians appear self-defeating, and their rhetoric of unity hollow, still it was clear that their methods would have to change dramatically, or else the Republicans would never truly be a national party.[72]

"THE MOST HUMILIATING EVENT OF MY LIFE"

In March 1797, as Burr's term in the Senate expired, he returned to New York without immediate political prospects. As his onetime friend turned gossipy critic, Robert Troup, observed, the presidential election had left Burr "very much in the background." His enemies figured that his political career was over, for if his humiliating defeat in the national election did not push him from the national stage, then, as Troup and others believed, "embarrassing" financial engagements would keep him from the public eye.[73]

Burr's finances had indeed spiraled out of control, but it was not simply a matter of personal extravagance. The 1790s witnessed two major financial crises: the first, in 1792, was triggered by New Yorker William Duer's aggressive speculation in bank stock and government securities; and the second, in 1797, was the result of failures in land speculation. "The Bubble of speculation is burst," Theodore Sedgwick wrote Rufus King, and Burr was rumored to be among the vast numbers "irretrievably ruined."[74]

Sedgwick had been a witness to Burr's misfortunes, though he might not have known it at the time. Burr had not let the fact that Sedgwick was in Hamilton's pocket deter them from maintaining social relations. Clearly, the friendship had cooled somewhat with the heightened partisan rancor, but some of the trust of old times remained. Sedgwick visited Burr in early 1797, and Burr wrote him a friendly note a short while later alluding to the "chaos" in his household. Indeed, his domestic life was soon to be turned upside down as he was forced to mortgage his house and sell his furnishings in a desperate attempt to pay back his creditor-friends and preserve his own reputation.[75]

Like everyone else in his cohort, Burr borrowed. His real problem began, however, when he agreed to enter into a partnership with James Greenleaf, one of the most notorious speculators of this frenzied decade. Greenleaf (no relation to the controversial journalist Thomas Greenleaf) was still in his twenties when he found himself at the center of a speculation craze. Born in Boston, he lived for a time in Philadelphia and then New York, before traveling to Europe in 1788, where he established valuable contacts by selling U.S. securities, gaining additional prestige as a U.S. consul in Holland. He returned to the United States in 1793, and established a company to purchase land in Washington City (the future national capital). His initial partners were two prominent Philadelphia speculators, Pennsylvania senator Robert Morris and the state's comptroller-general John Nicholson. Burr became involved after he purchased the "Angerstein tract" (north of the Mohawk River and east of Lake Ontario) in north-central New York State in 1796. When he signed the contract, he was forced to take on Greenleaf as a partner. (See map, p. 95.)

Taking what he thought was only a moderate risk, Burr found himself in the same predicament as the more experienced speculators Morris and Nicholson. Young Greenleaf had betrayed them all. He misappropriated funds and deceived Burr by mortgaging the entire Angerstein tract in order to pay off his own debts. For Burr, this meant that he not only had to pay his share of the tract (£12,000) but Greenleaf's equal share as well; he had countersigned Greenleaf's bond for £12,000, which carried a non-payment penalty of £24,000. He suddenly could owe a total of £36,000. Adding insult to financial injury, the original owner of the tract, London merchant John Julius Angerstein, had hired Burr's nemesis, Alexander Hamilton, to press his claim in court. When a judgment was finally reached in the Court of Chancery on June 4, 1799, Burr was expected to pay £24,000 (approximately $80,000), the amount of the penalty.[76]

To make matters still worse, Burr's friend General John Lamb, collector of customs for the port of New York, faced prosecution, when it was discovered that he was short of funds in 1796. While Lamb was not charged with embezzlement (because it was one of his subordinates who had taken the money), he was still liable to the U.S. government for $150,000 in losses; and his sureties, who had signed a $50,000 bond in order that Lamb could assume his post, were liable as well. These sureties were Burr's confidential friends Melancton Smith and Marinus Willett. Burr could not but feel for his friends in this situation; Lamb had generously lent Burr $20,000 over several years, and was one of his principal sureties in the Angerstein fiasco. Lamb had been at Burr's side in the harrowing days of 1775, manning the artillery during the invasion of Quebec. Burr could not ignore his old friend now, regardless of his own troubles.[77]

Meanwhile, he watched John Nicholson's life and reputation crumble. Though he had survived an attempted impeachment as comptroller-general in 1794, Nicholson was constantly hounded by a hornet's nest of creditors who repeatedly dragged him into court. By May 1797, 125 suits had been brought against him, and several costly judgments left him owing over $300,000. In 1799, Nicholson, once the most powerful speculator in America, joined James Greenleaf and Robert Morris in the Prune Street Prison, in Philadelphia. He died there in December 1800, just as Burr was tied with Jefferson in votes for the presidency.[78]

No matter how one looks at it, these were tumultuous times for the unbalanced republic. Investment schemes intertwined the finances of many prominent men, and if one investor suffered major losses, then everyone involved felt the repercussions. In the case of Greenleaf, Burr refused to admit to himself that he had been betrayed. In January 1796, he reassured his erstwhile partner that he had never once doubted his "integrity and honor," and he made sure that Greenleaf knew that he would "cheerfully seize every opportunity to repeat this." Burr was more concerned with finding a way to extricate himself from debt than seeking revenge from his less than honest partner. Nicholson's problems were so complicated that Burr had no chance whatsoever to provide assistance; he did what he could, which was to offer Nicholson legal advice during his impeachment trial. Commiserating, he wrote: "my sympathy with your misfortunes is too sincere to allow me, from any personal considerations, to add a particle to their weight."[79]

He was able to do more for John Lamb. Burr convinced Richard Harison, the attorney for New York City, to reduce the amount of security Lamb would have to pay to cover the embezzled funds. By making personal appeals, he was able to delay legal action by the U.S. government, which he hoped would give Lamb enough time to recover the losses from his accounts. In January 1798, he wrote Lamb nobly that he would "superintend the Sales of my own property, until you shall be exonerated." Burr kept his word. He placed a mortgage on his Richmond Hill estate, and sold other city property he owned, along with his household furnishings. To bolster his modest income, he leased the farmland on his estate.[80]

These frantic efforts to rescue Lamb were certainly genuine. Like so many ambitious men in the early republic, Burr and Lamb understood that co-signing a promissory note (a loan agreement) constituted an almost ritualistic bond of friendship. Lamb had been Burr's major surety, and his decision to endorse Burr's notes had nothing at all to do with profit and everything to do with honor and friendship. "That your peace of mind should be distressed or personal safety endangered by an act of friendship and generosity to me," Burr confessed to Lamb, "is the most humiliating event of my life." Friends' finances were interconnected; sometimes the tension, in letters, between a lender's willing sacrifice and his anticipation of trouble was thinly veiled (and powerfully felt by both parties). If Burr had done nothing to help Lamb out of his difficulties, he might have become a man without friends, and this, most certainly, would have doomed his career. In Burr's world, confidential friends were his society, the very core of his political support. The circle of intimate acquaintances was what made the wheels of politics turn—much more so than any achievement by any singular "great" man.[81]

But Burr's financial difficulties forced him to drastically change his lifestyle. Since 1793, he had occupied the Richmond Hill estate in what later became Greenwich Village, a sprawling property of 160 acres, boasting English-style gardens, meadows extending to the Hudson River, and a man-made pond graced the gateway to the grounds. Richmond Hill mansion was a two-story house with neoclassical features, a portico and Ionic columns, and Chinese Chippendale porch railings. Like other prominent men of his time (think of Jefferson's Monticello, Washington's Mount Vernon, or Hamilton's The Grange), Burr had personally supervised the transformation of his home into a political statement that reflected his rise in New York and the young nation. Like Jefferson, like Hamilton, Burr conceived of his home as an extension of the man, a theatrical space in which he displayed his refinement and social status. Consequently, he took great care to fill his home with the finest furnishings: he had purchased numerous large looking glasses, chintz window curtains, an elegant china tea service, a Dutch liquor case, Brussels carpet, inlaid card tables, pianoforte, and a large bathing tub. For several years, he lived in grand style at the center of New York society.[82]

Burr probably moved into the Richmond Hill mansion a year before the death of his wife. Theodosia spent her last days there, and the ambiance resembled her former home in New Jersey, the Hermitage. Burr's home was designed almost as a French salon, with gracious surroundings meant for entertaining (usually small dinner parties); above all, his goal was to create an enlightened atmosphere of taste and learning. He became the patron of John Vanderlyn, a young American artist destined for celebrity, who joined his household in 1796. With his own artist in residence, Burr commissioned portraits of himself and his daughter, and obliged Vanderlyn to paint close friends like Albert Gallatin. Richmond Hill had a window-lined gallery to display Burr's art collection, and an extensive library filled with books on various subjects, imported from a London bookseller.[83]

Vanderlyn was not Burr's only project. He readily opened his home to other struggling young artists, offering the Englishman John Davis a room in which to write his engaging travel narrative of the United States, which featured Burr prominently in its pages. Fascinating guests came to dinner, including the chief of the Mohawks, London-educated Joseph Brant. The famed French philosopher-historian Constantin-François Chasseboeuf, comte de Volney, was a regular guest. It was during this period, too, that Burr took in the young French refugee Nathalie de Lage de Volunde as a companion and "foster sister" for Theodosia. His home was more than a status symbol; it was a cosmopolitan entrepôt, a way station for foreign travelers, literati, French exiles, friends, and family. To lose Richmond Hill was to give up far more than a house.[84]

He sold his belongings on June 27, 1797, and from that moment on, the estate was used to raise collateral for loans to cover his debts. If he could have seen into the future, he would have regretted his decision. The next owner of the Richmond Hill property was John Jacob Astor, who purchased it for $32,000. Astor would reap millions after dividing the land into smaller lots in what would become the real estate gold mine of Greenwich Village.[85]

Burr's financial misadventures had lasting consequences. Nothing in his life was left untouched by the hovering threat of financial ruin. His step-son Frederick Prevost was forced to sell his house and farm to cover a bond he signed for his stepfather. In 1799, sixteen-year-old Theodosia was horrified. Writing her other stepbrother, John Bartow, she wondered "whether it is determined that some misery should constantly attend us." Acknowledging her father's responsibility, she added, "how little [Frederick] deserves such a fate."[86]

Only two months earlier, she had urgently asked John Bartow if he had the means to repay his debts. She wished she could rescue him: "Oh dear brother; that I had a large fortune it should be yours to pay what you owe." Theodosia's desire to have a "large fortune" even suggests why she might consider a less than ideal marriage. Her friends in New York would repeat less than flattering descriptions of Theodosia's future husband, Joseph

Alston, a South Carolinian due to inherit over 6,000 acres and 253 slaves, and to become an exceedingly wealthy rice plantation owner. Maria Nicholson blamed Burr outright. After learning of the 1801 marriage she asked her sister Hannah Gallatin: "Can it be that the father has sacrificed a daughter to affluence and influential connections?" Theodosia's constant concern over her family's debts offers the best explanation for why a gifted, independent-minded woman would, at the age of seventeen, marry a man she barely knew. The only available means for any female to acquire a "large fortune" at this time was by marriage or inheritance. By tying the knot with Alston, Theodosia could realistically assist her financially troubled family.[87]

Burr was well aware of all he stood to lose politically. Writing John Lamb, he begged "that the scraps which I write you may not go out of your hands." And to Pierpont Edwards: "I beg you to make no unnecessary confidences about our Concerns. It will only give pleasure to those who wish well to neither of us." Any hint of scandal would circulate quickly.[88]

During the presidential election of 1796, Burr had already been taken to task for his involvement with Greenleaf and Nicholson. Hamilton could not resist blabbing to his fellow Federalists about the Angerstein suit. Federalist William Smith wrote to a friend, at Burr's expense: what "a charming character to be sure for V. President! . . . sued here [Philadelphia] for 5,000 at the Bank and in N.Y. for £12,000 Sterl[ing] for land speculation." In the election of 1800, Hamilton would again make capital use of the Angerstein suit, arguing that this was indisputable proof that Burr was a dangerous man. It bears repeating: Four years later, at the time of his death, Hamilton would be deeply in debt, owing close to the amount that Burr had to pay for the Angerstein debacle.[89]

Burr's political notoriety aroused suspicion in this suspicious decade, so that Burr did not even have to undertake questionable actions to get into trouble. In the most bizarre of his speculative ventures in the 1790s, he became inadvertently linked to a group of disaffected Germans in western New York who were negotiating to leave the United States and resettle in Upper Canada. By the time Canadian authorities smelled a takeover of a portion of their territory by American interests, the name of Aaron Burr was invoked as the force behind the proposed action, a proposition that, at least in his mind, never even existed.

The German Company, so-called, was formed in 1794 and involved his friend Melancton Smith and the land agent Timothy Green, in addition to Burr. The German settlers who first set things in motion believed that the Canadian government would be willing to grant them 2 million acres—much more than they needed. So they hoped to sell the excess land to European investors and reap tremendous profits. John Graves Simcoe, the lieutenant governor of Upper Canada, at first eager to attract settlers, balked after he began to fear American designs. Simcoe revoked the patents when he saw his colony becoming "the Prey of Land Jobbers" and "Insurgents." The British minister in the United States, Robert Liston, agreed, nervously writing that if men with "High-flying democratick sentiments" such as Aaron Burr were involved, then it was only a matter of time before they would try to establish an "independent Republick" in Canada.[90]

Eventually, a small group of American investors in Canada (who did not include Burr) did what Liston predicted: they plotted to recover the townships that Simcoe had arbitrarily taken away. They met with Burr and Green in 1801, and appealed for their help. It appears that the plotters never really planned anything more than to scare the Canadian government into returning the land earlier offered. One of the organizers claimed that Burr had given him and others encouragement. But that was all. Burr was merely a prop in a staged faux conspiracy. His only interest in Upper Canada was as an economic investment.[91]

Still, as we attempt to understand the widespread opportunity, ordinary flexibility, ambiguity, and extralegal temptations associated with land speculation in early America, it is significant how readily speculators turned to filibustering as an "easy," if not legitimate, form of political expression. The faux rebels were entirely comfortable approaching Burr when he was the sitting vice president with their ploy to pressure the Canadian government to play fair with American speculators in their country. In fact, in the minds of most Americans of this era, filibustering hailed back to the American Revolution and the invasion of Canada—a quest fueled by patriotic and religious ardor. Many Americans believed the same colonial discontent could be kindled elsewhere in North America. Burr was hardly the architect of this rebellion. He was, at best, a curious spectator, though he may well have used the faux rebellion of Upper Canada as a blueprint for his own later filibustering scheme in the American Southwest that would end in a trial for treason.

"RESENTMENT IS MORE DIGNIFIED WHEN JUSTICE IS RENDERED"

Despite his financial troubles, Burr did not retreat from the political scene as the Hamiltonian Robert Troup had gleefully predicted. In April 1797, the former senator helped select a slate of Republican candidates from New York City to run for the state legislature. Moreover, he willingly put himself forward for a "lowly" assembly seat. His demotion from the lofty heights of the U.S. Senate to the minor league of state politics did not seem to matter to him. On the contrary, Burr saw an opportunity; in the assembly, he could achieve something that had previously eluded him: a genuine grass-roots base of support. By a two-to-one margin, Burr and his Republican ticket won the election handily.[92]

Meanwhile, he solidified his Republican contacts outside the state. His relationship with the Virginians grew stronger. In June, when James Monroe returned from his diplomatic mission in France, Burr, in the company of Jefferson and Gallatin, came aboard ship to welcome him home. Even before this reunion, Jefferson sent him an urgent news brief about disturbing events in Congress; he also solicited Burr's opinion about the prospects for republicanism in the northern states. In a world of personal and political favors, Jefferson made one more important gesture toward friendship: He asked Burr to take on a legal suit, for a close friend, in the New York courts. And the two men agreed to meet discreetly in Philadelphia, as Burr put it, to discuss "ideas."[93]

Republicans needed to stick together. For the next two years, they were the embattled party. War fever permeated the air. From Philadelphia, Burr received reports about the "present infatuation" for war with France, and he shook his head at the bellicose posturing of the Adams administration. To his friend Dr. William Eustis of Boston, an ardent Anti-Federalist turned Republican, whom Burr had served with during the Revolution, he drolly observed: "Perhaps however the *bold* Language of the President, and the fierce speeches of [Federalist senators] Harper and Smith may intimidate the French directory." How, Burr asked, could the United States, a country without a navy or army, scare what was perhaps at this moment the greatest military power in the world? Burr was not opposed to strengthening America's defenses; he was, however, against a reckless confrontation.[94]

James Monroe's embarrassing dismissal from his post as minister to

France served to rally the Republicans. Accused of being too cozy with the French Directory (Washington privately called him a "mere tool in the hands of the French government"), he had been unceremoniously recalled. Monroe was livid over his public humiliation. Adding to his grievances, Secretary of State Timothy Pickering refused to give an "official" reason for his dismissal. Burr sympathized, calling Pickering's "tergiversation, hypocrisy & equivocation . . . disgraceful." Showing their approval of Monroe's conduct, Republicans held two public dinners in his honor in Philadelphia and New York City. Burr was present at both, and at the New York gathering in July, he gave the most rousing toast: "success to the efforts of Republicanism throughout the world."[95]

In July, as Monroe visited his wife's family and dined with fellow Republicans in New York, he was confronted by Hamilton. He had sent Monroe a letter, demanding a formal statement that would clear the ex-treasury secretary of all charges of public corruption and speculation stemming from the Reynolds Affair. Why now? Because a Scottish journalist and hack writer, James Thomson Callender, known for his scathing political attacks, had just published a series of pamphlets that revealed the sordid details of the affair. Callender had reprinted many of the papers that Hamilton had given to Monroe, Pennsylvanian Frederick Muhlenberg, and Virginian Abraham Venable—the committee that investigated the charges in 1792. Hamilton blamed Monroe.

Hamilton arrived at Monroe's lodgings in an agitated state. He abruptly accused Monroe of releasing the documents to Callender, which the Virginian quickly denied, confessing he had left the papers with a friend. Unable to contain his anger any longer, Hamilton retorted that Monroe's statement was "totally false." He had called Monroe a liar. Burr's friend David Gelston observed the exchange, and he reported that Monroe rose from his seat, called Hamilton a "scoundrel," and then challenged him to a duel, with the words, "I am ready get your pistols." Gelston, along with Hamilton's brother-in-law, the Englishman John Barker Church, intervened. They momentarily persuaded the two men to back off, and to forget their hasty remarks. Neither, however, was ready to forgive: the quick-tempered pair prolonged the affair of honor for five long months. Burr, as an old acquaintance of both, found himself at the center of the imbroglio, after Monroe asked him to serve as his intermediary.[96]

Hamilton had a habit of engaging in affairs of honor. Over the course of his lifetime, he was a "principal" in eleven affairs, which meant that he either challenged or received challenges from nearly a dozen different men between 1779 and 1804. In stark contrast, Burr never even came close to dueling until 1799, and he invoked the *code duello* with just two men: Hamilton and John Barker Church. Burr's duel with Church was, not surprisingly, a family affair. Hamilton had triggered the incident by supplying his brother-in-law with the inflammatory gossip (concerning a land syndicate purportedly offering a bribe) that caused Burr to issue his challenge in the first place. During his duel with Church in the fall of 1799, Burr survived a near miss when a bullet passed through his coat after the first fire. For whatever reason, while preparing for the second round, Church apologized, abruptly ending the duel.[97]

The meaning of dueling itself was in flux. Hamilton and Burr handled their affairs quite differently. Hamilton's brashness invited confrontation, whereas Burr went out of his way to avoid it. For Burr, a true gentleman resisted raw provocation. After the unproductive Church affair, he explained his policy to a concerned party (whose identity has been obscured in the historical record): "This, sir, is the first time in my life that I have condescended (pardon the expression) to refute calumny." In eighteenth-century English, "to condescend" meant to depart from one's habitual conduct; it did not ordinarily connote, as it does today, perceiving oneself as superior. Yet Burr's "pardon the expression" also suggests his sensitivity to the emerging modern meaning of the word.[98]

He continued: "I leave to my actions to speak for themselves, and to my character to confound the fictions of slander. And on this very subject I have not up to this hour given one word of explanation to any human being." This statement is quite remarkable. He was speaking to his preference for allowing his known good character to silently sustain him—there was no value for him in a violent encounter. Burr's main point was that he did not, as a rule, push or prod or bombard his friends with self-defensive language. This is his outright rejection of Hamilton's way.[99]

For Burr, dueling was never simply about honor. In his 1804 exchange of dueling letters with Hamilton, he would declare that "political opposition can never absolve gentlemen from the necessity of rigid adherence to the laws of honour, and the rules of decorum." In the vocabulary of this age, "decorum" meant dignified conduct, or what Burr described as a serene and stoic graciousness—a style of behavior suited not only to the field of honor but all other social performances. Getting to the field of honor, firing one's pistols, was only half as important as the manner in which a combatant treated his opponent. This was not Arthurian chivalry, but the Enlightenment value of heartfelt sincerity, a mark of educated sociability.[100]

Whether advising his daughter or his combustible friend James Monroe, Burr employed the same rules of decorum. To Theodosia, when she was just thirteen, he instructed: "Receive with calmness every reproof, whether made kindly or unkindly; whether just or unjust. Consider within yourself whether there has been no cause for it. If it has been groundless and unjust, nevertheless bear it with composure, and even with complacency." Using similar logic not long after, Burr urged Monroe to follow the same course with Hamilton in 1797: "If you and Mulenburgh really believe, as I do, and think you must, that H. is innocent of the charge of any concern in speculation with Reynolds, It is my opinion that it will be an act of magnanimity & Justice to say so in a joint certificate." This is a crucial commentary: despite Hamilton's offensive attitude, Burr regarded Hamilton generously, refusing in the Reynolds Affair to take political advantage of him; this is something Hamilton would never do, something wholly impossible for one of Hamilton's constitution. To this Burr added, for Monroe's consideration: "Resentment is more dignified when Justice is rendered."[101]

Celebrating reasonableness and generosity, Burr expressed an enlightened (arguably a literary) sensibility. For him, if honor was not backed by the ennobling quality of sincerity, then honor meant nothing at all. A gentleman had to be willing to admit publicly when he had wronged someone else. This was something Monroe and Hamilton alike refused to do. The same disregard for sincerity would mar Hamilton's purposes and make it impossible for him to retract—before the public—his "despicable opinion" about Burr in 1804, when he resorted to equivocation instead of regretting his choice of words. "Having considered [your letter] attentively," Burr would write Hamilton less than a month before they met at Weehawken, "I regret to find in it nothing of that sincerity and delicacy that you profess to value."[102]

The key here is the word "public." On two occasions prior to 1804, Hamilton had privately made amends with Burr after publicly insulting him. But he would not go beyond that. What is the good of a private apology if one is not willing to repeat it in public? Burr's repeated acceptance of halfhearted apologies points to his tolerance and generosity toward Hamilton.[103]

All Burr asked for in the buildup to their famous duel was that Hamilton admit that his insulting language was that—insulting—and the two men could have carried on as before, resuming their public business. But Hamilton refused to make a public retreat. In that sense, as familiar as each had become over the years with the other's methods, the seeds of tragedy were sown well before their final collision in their incompatible definitions of honor: what was for Burr the greatest embarrassment (letting insincerity stand) conflicted with what was for Hamilton the greatest embarrassment (acknowledging a misstep before the world).

The Hamilton-Monroe affair died a rather undignified death. From July 1797, when Hamilton appeared on Monroe's doorstep, until December of that year, letters changed hands. Burr refused to deliver several of Monroe's angry letters, trying to keep the rhetoric from escalating. By winter, Burr was appalled by what he described as the "childish" behavior of both men. Monroe's biographer Harry Ammon admits that the affair took a "comic" turn when neither man would assume the role of aggressor, and instead pretended to be waiting for the official challenge from the other. This way, both convinced themselves they had not backed down; but it was a ruse, and everyone knew it.[104]

Even so, the odd affair took on a significance beyond the stubborn pride of two men angling to preserve reputation. Monroe saw fit to drag all his friends into the dispute, making a private quarrel into a partisan battle. In August 1797, Hamilton published a tortured explanation for his amorous adventure with Maria Reynolds back in 1792. Monroe begged Madison to carefully examine Hamilton's 95-page "defense pamphlet" and make sure there was nothing insulting about him in it. Madison did so, though he had grown weary of Monroe's controversy with Hamilton. In November, Jefferson and Madison organized a meeting of Republicans in Philadelphia to discuss what could be done. They consulted Burr, who concurred with the party consensus that the Hamilton-Monroe affair should end as quickly and quietly as possible.[105]

The two men never dueled. Hamilton, however, had made his situation worse by writing his pamphlet. He unleashed a barrage of principled words attempting to portray James Reynolds (Maria's blackmailing husband) as a rogue, while he described himself as the righteous defender of the nation. It all fell on deaf ears. Admitting to his adulterous relationship with Maria Reynolds in an effort to defend himself against what he felt was the more serious charge of public (financial) misconduct, Hamilton misjudged his audience. The Reynolds pamphlet, Madison concluded, was a work of "ingenious folly"; as he saw it, Hamilton did not understand that "simplicity and candor are the only dress that prudence would put on innocence." He meant that Hamilton's characteristic imprudence had done him in.[106]

Sleight of hand was a poor tactic. In believing he could verbally outmaneuver his critics, and by treating his adultery as a lesser crime than an illegal speculation scheme, Hamilton failed to portray himself as an innocent man. Instead, he appeared arrogant and unrepentant. He saw himself as the victim in a nefarious plot, in which Maria Reynolds, at the behest of her husband, had seduced him. Using the literary conventions of the day (while reversing the gender roles), Hamilton likened himself to the English novelist Samuel Richardson's pitied heroine, the poor, innocent, seduced Clarissa, protesting in the same breath that he was *not* the randy and rakish Lovelace.[107]

The newspapers had a field day with his pamphlet. Republican journalists chastised Hamilton for assuming that his private indiscretion had no bearing on his public character. As one female poet cleverly reminded her readers, "only fools do kiss and tell." Hamilton had made a phenomenal blunder: trying to sell himself as a man of candor only served to open him up to further criticism and ridicule. For most observers who read the pamphlet, the once imperial secretary of the treasury had no clothes. One member of Hamilton's New York crowd did not hold back when he said, almost with a leer, that the pamphleteer was aiming "to creep under Mrs. R's petticoats. A pretty hiding place for a national leader!" Even Hamilton's most devoted admirer, Robert Troup, acknowledged that the "ill-judged pamphlet has done him incomparable injury."[108]

"WAS ARNOLD A FOREIGNER . . . ?"

The Hamilton-Monroe episode was not the only time that Burr found himself involved in Hamilton's concerns. In 1798–99, the two erstwhile adversaries worked side by side to improve New York City's defenses, as the United States edged closer to a full-scale war with France. In spite of a Federalist-generated war frenzy, however, no real fighting occurred. The anomalous Franco-American conflict of the Adams years ultimately amounted to the seizure of a few ships, but consisted mainly of angry editorials and diplomatic posturing. It is known to history as the "Quasi-War." Although Burr was a Republican, and a Francophile, he believed in shoring up American military defenses against any possible foreign threat. Of course, that does not tell the whole story: at this especially tense moment in American politics, Burr vigorously opposed other administration measures that were put in place to keep French influence out.

The hysteria commenced in June 1798, as Americans learned that three special envoys sent by the president to Paris had been rudely mistreated by their hosts. In the "XYZ Affair," the French Directory's minister of foreign relations, Charles-Maurice de Talleyrand-Périgord, informed the U.S. envoys that they needed to pay a bribe before enjoying an audience with the new Revolutionary leadership. For Federalists, this was evidence enough that the French government was corrupt. Like the Reynolds Affair, the XYZ Affair quickly acquired a tabloid quality. One of Talleyrand's agents, Madame de Villette, the niece, adopted daughter, and mistress of Voltaire, was rumored to have tried to seduce the youngest member of the diplomatic team, the future chief justice of the Supreme Court, John Marshall.[109]

President Adams called George Washington out of retirement to serve as commander in chief of the armed forces in preparation for war with France. Washington promptly named Hamilton his inspector general, and second-in-command, at the rank of major general. The nomination sparked controversy, not the least of which was due to Hamilton's elevation over his wartime superior, Brigadier General Henry Knox. Insulted, Knox (lately Washington's secretary of war) refused to serve. Hamilton's allies had already spread rumors about Knox's "pecuniary affairs," using the same brand of defamatory gossip that the Federalist side had circulated about Burr during the 1796 presidential race. Although Adams preferred Knox, and had been distrustful of Hamilton ever since the New Yorker had betrayed him in the presidential election, the president finally conceded to his predecessor's wishes, and supported Hamilton's appointment.[110]

In June, Burr was named to a "Military Committee," serving with Hamilton and Ebenezer Stevens, a War Department agent in charge of New

York's fortifications. Acting as liaison with the state assembly, Burr collected facts and figures from Stevens in order to convince the legislature of the need to rebuild harbor defenses. Burr was in his element, working on a project that drew upon the skills of surveying and strategic planning that he had used during his days as a Revolutionary officer. He mobilized a fragile coalition that reached agreement on a bill worth over $1 million, a massive appropriation for its time. But his success was short-lived: the assembly reconvened and whittled down the amount to $200,000, before the senate entered the picture and reduced it once again, until it was only worth $150,000. The city would get new fortifications, but hardly on the scale envisioned by Burr and his unlikely ally Hamilton.[111]

Whether impressed by Burr's commitment or competence, the new inspector general suddenly viewed his former foe in a different light. In June 1798, Hamilton wrote a remarkable letter to Secretary of the Treasury Oliver Wolcott, entreating his Federalist allies to support Burr: "Col. Burr sets out today for Philadelphia. I have some reasons for wishing that the administration may manifest a cordiality to him. It is not impossible he will be found a useful cooperator. I am aware there are different sides but the case is worth an experiment." Hamilton's "I have some reasons" leaves us wondering. Rumors circulated among Adams's cabinet that Burr was being considered for the position of U.S. quartermaster general, in which case he would be responsible for the finances and supplies of the new national army. It was a most unlikely moment in the young republic's political development for Hamilton to be lending his support to Burr's appointment. Nothing would seem more improbable after years of attacking Burr as a "dangerous man" incapable of managing his own finances; yet Hamilton may have been prepared to elevate his enemy to a post of tremendous power.[112]

What explains this change of heart? Hamilton must have believed that Burr saw eye-to-eye with him on military matters. He had already recommended Burr to Governor John Jay as the most "competent character" to serve as superintendent of the newly fortified port in New York City. Hamilton's ability to switch gears reconfirms a simple fact: his vicious criticism of Burr was motivated by simple politics—his fear of Burr as an opposition leader—and not by distaste for Burr's personal character.[113]

Hamilton's indirect method of advancing Burr is equally revealing. He did not discuss the matter with Washington. Instead, he worked behind the scenes through his loyal followers in Adams's cabinet. Washington did not hear of Burr's possible appointment until President Adams presented the idea to him.

Many years later, Adams recalled having suggested Burr for the position of brigadier general. Washington's response was damning: "By all that I have known and heard, Colonel Burr is a brave and able officer; but the question is, whether he has not equal talents at intrigue?" The first president's remarks, if we can trust the second president's memory, echo Hamilton's long-standing criticism of Burr. Doubtless Washington did not arrive at this view on his own. During the volatile second term of his presidency, Washington had absorbed his treasury secretary's recurrent insinuations that Burr was an "intriguer"—and so he formed the opinion Adams recounted. For Hamilton to tell Washington otherwise in 1798 would have been an admission that he had earlier overreacted when he repeatedly bad-mouthed Burr. And so Hamilton resolved he would promote Burr behind Washington's back.[114]

Nevertheless, Burr's cordial interlude with Hamilton did not last long. His generalship evaporated, perhaps because he continued to confound the Federalists. Surveying his activities over the past few months, Robert Troup observed that Burr had been "zealous" in promoting measures for defense of the harbor, and "particularly courteous to Hamilton" in the hope of gaining an appointment in the army. And yet, Troup found it baffling that "before the appointment of General Officers took place, and in the midst of conciliatory appearance," Burr openly opposed the administration. He raised bail for the notorious John Burk, a young Irish émigré and New York printer arrested, in Troup's words, "for a most infamous libel on the President."[115]

Troup's confusion stemmed from his black-and-white view of partisan politics. In his mind, Burr's conduct on defense "showed strong symptoms of a wish to change his ground." He meant a wish to change party affiliation. But Burr's record in the Senate suggests otherwise. He had strongly backed the military before; in 1792, he sided with Federalist Rufus King, supporting the expansion of the army for the Indian Wars in the western territories. And for six years he ably served on numerous military and veteran committees.[116]

His position had not changed. When working for the tax bill to pay for the new fortifications, Burr never came close to endorsing the Federalist agenda. In the final wording of the bill, he eliminated references to a war with France, stating that the defensive measures were for the possibility of war with any foreign nation. He saw the threat from the British to be equal to, if not greater than, that from France. In June 1798, as a member of the Democratic Society of New York, he drafted a message to Congress urging action against British attacks on American shipping. He had no "wish to change his ground," displaying instead his consistency on military matters and foreign policy.[117]

It is amazing how poorly Burr's former friend knew him. That he supported John Burk was not at all uncharacteristic. He had avidly defended the democratic clubs, and pushed the Senate to lift the veil of secrecy surrounding the Jay Treaty; he was calling again for greater transparency in government. Burr had also come to understand that the Republican Party required printers with pointed pens, those willing to provoke debate.

Burk had replaced Princetonian Philip Freneau as editor of *The Time Piece,* a literary paper which Burr had helped his former classmate to set up in 1798. Under the leadership of Burk, a Burr protégé, the paper took a decidedly radical turn. Burr had just helped Burk prepare and publish his play *Bunker-Hill,* which the Irishman had dedicated to his generous sponsor. Later, in a letter to Jefferson in 1801, Burk enthusiastically noted that Burr was "a friend and father" to him. Burr did more than rescue Burk from jail at the end of 1798, for the release was made contingent on Burk's leaving the country; and yet, instead of sailing for Europe, he headed for Virginia. It was, in fact, Burr who made Burk's escape and asylum possible. In a letter to James Monroe, Burr praised the young man's "enthusiasm in the cause of liberty," asking the Virginian to take Burk under his wing and protect him from further prosecution.[118]

The Burk case was a sign of the times. As anti-French sentiment intensified in response to the "XYZ Affair," the effective Federalists pushed legislation through Congress. The Alien and Sedition Acts were designed to counteract the imagined French Revolutionary influence over American minds by physically removing French and other foreign, socially disruptive troublemakers from American shores; and, more generally, to severely restrict American citizens' right to dissent from administration policies. Inappropriate speaking, as well as writing, was punishable by jail terms.

Though he was prosecuted for sedition for criticizing the president in print, John Burk's status as a foreigner subjected him to deportation. This was the penalty for "dangerous aliens" under the Alien Act. There were in fact three anti-alien acts: the Naturalization Act, the Alien Enemies Act, and the Act Concerning Aliens. The first increased the length of residence needed for aliens to become citizens; the second forced enemy aliens to leave the country in time of war; and the third gave the president broad powers to deport and imprison any aliens considered dangerous to public safety. The Sedition Act had even more far-reaching consequences, in prohibiting "false, scandalous and malicious writing" against the government. Those convicted faced up to $5,000 in fines and prison sentences of up to five years.[119]

Madison and Jefferson agreed that the legislation was detestable, for it was aimed at nothing less than crushing the Republican Party. Burr's once-embattled friend, foreign-born Albert Gallatin, and fellow New Yorker Edward Livingston were the most articulate opponents in Congress, when they took the lead in battling the partisan acts. Meanwhile, still angry over his dismissal, the recent minister to France, James Monroe, predicted that the Federalists' aggressiveness would backfire on them. In the short term, however, the repressive Alien and Sedition Acts were quite successful, because they shut down Republican presses. The most outspoken critics, those considered provocateurs, were arrested.[120]

No one was spared. Thomas Greenleaf's widow, Ann, who had inherited New York City's Republican *Argus* after her husband's death in 1798, found herself, at Hamilton's urging, prosecuted and put out of business. Similarly, Margaret Bache, the widow of Benjamin Franklin's grandson Benjamin Bache, was viciously slandered with crude sexual slurs in the Federalist press, while her husband's successor, William Duane, was harassed by libel suits, and beaten up by a group of Federalist soldiers. Her Philadelphia newspaper, the *Aurora*, headed the Adams administration's enemies list. For aiding Burk, Burr was accused of not only harboring a traitor, but being one himself—since the "seditious foreigner," his critics claimed, was merely a "mouthpiece" of a larger infestation of conspirators lurking in the United States.[121]

Elected politicians were dragged into court and tempers produced ugly personal encounters. In 1798, for some harsh remarks published about

President Adams, Congressman Matthew Lyon of Vermont was sent to jail. The Irish-born Republican radical was the perfect target. On the House floor earlier that year, Lyon spat in the face of Connecticut Federalist Roger Griswold after an exchange of insults. Several days later, Griswold armed himself with a cane and beat Lyon twenty times about the head; Lyon famously fended off the attack with fireplace tongs. Imprisoned for four months after his sedition conviction, Lyon still had defenders, prominent among them Burr and Gallatin, both of whom sent Lyon the money he needed to cover his $1,000 fine. Defiantly, the voters rallied to his cause, reelecting Lyon to Congress while he sat in prison.[122]

Burr became a voluble opponent of alien laws in his own state. In early 1799, the legislature weighed a constitutional amendment to bar naturalized foreigners from elected offices: the presidency and Congress. Once passed in Massachusetts and several other New England states, it eventually made its way to New York. There, in the assembly, a debate ensued, and as the *Albany Register* reported, Burr gave a speech "of considerable length, and with peculiar eloquence."[123]

The main thrust of Burr's argument was this: The amendment was illogical and illiberal because fear of foreign influence had no basis in fact. In that the existing laws made sure that no one could be elected who was not "of approved talents and virtue," the current system demanded no radical changes. With a sense of the dramatic, Burr proceeded to offer evidence to the contrary: Many foreigners held important posts in the military or sat on the Supreme Court, justifying the "confidence" that the government had already placed in those not of native birth. He asked the members of the assembly if there had yet been "any instance of conspiracy or treason" *not* instigated by natives. In what must have been a moment of breathless anticipation and indeed supreme irony, given Aaron Burr's ultimate political fate, the accomplished politician contended: "Was Arnold a foreigner, is not Blount an American?"[124]

Arnold, of course, was the traitorous Benedict Arnold, whose name remains infamous to this day. Blount was the Tennessee favorite who had lost his Senate seat only a short time before, because he had dreamt out loud and plotted a land grab in Spanish America, conducting his own foreign policy. Conspiratorial schemes were often enough homegrown.

Burr's poignant remarks emphasized a recurrent theme for him since the debate over the Jay Treaty: greater transparency in government. If treason was to occur anywhere, he reasoned, it would be in the military and in the Supreme Court—two powerful institutions whose activities tended to be hidden, and resistant to public oversight. As to the Supreme Court, he noted that it was "completely screened from [congressional] observation." The elective national legislature, in contrast, carried out its deliberations in the open, in the public's view: "every word and action are open to the inspection, censure, or approval" of the people. This was the central tenet of republican governance.[125]

The *Albany Register* heralded Burr's expressiveness, paraphrasing his language:

> *America stood with open arms and presented an assylum [sic] to the oppressed of every nation; we invited them with the promise of enjoying equal rights with ourselves, and presented them with the flattering prospect of presiding in our councils and arriving at honour and trust; shall we deprive these persons of an important right derived from so sacred a source as our constitution [?]*[126]

To pass the amendment would be to betray the Revolution and the Constitution.

Revisiting the role he had decisively assumed in the Senate in 1794, Burr again took the position of defending his Swiss-born friend Albert Gallatin. Many Republicans believed that the federal Alien Act had been directed at Gallatin; it was the Federalists' second attempt to remove him from office, this time from his seat in the House of Representatives. And so, in his speech before the New York Assembly, Burr rebuked his colleagues for their slander of Gallatin, a man who was, he insisted, "most eminently distinguished for virtue and talents." More philosophically, Burr contended that place of birth was no guarantee of virtuous conduct, for that depended "solely on the character of the person. . . . A man of innate virtue and honour, whether born in Paris or at London, is a man of virtue and honour in every part of the world." Burr subtly exposed the faulty logic of the Anglophilic/Francophobic party. London and Paris were not as different as the Federalists imagined. England (and its former colonies) were not the only countries that produced virtuous citizens: character could as well be found across the Channel in France.[127]

Burr's activism drew attention both inside and outside New York. Always the watchdog, Troup took careful note of his remarks, concerned about Burr's contention that the "only instances of corruption we have had are a corruption in our own countrymen." It was a jab at the party in power. The mouthpiece of the Republican cause, Philadelphia's *Aurora,* published Burr's speech, proving that even though he no longer held national office, Burr could still reach a national constituency. His standing among Republicans was high, as the critical election of 1800 approached.[128]

NEWPORT, (R. I.) Dec. 27.

On Saturday morning laſt, about the time the news was announced to us of the election of Mr. Jefferſon and Mr. Burr, to the Preſidency and Vice Preſidency, one of our citizens was preſented, under the benediction of divine Providence, with a pair of twin ſons of the ſame hour. To perpetuate "the glad tidings of great joy," they were on Chriſtmas Day chriſtened, the eldeſt *Thomas Jefferſon*, the younger *Aaron Burr*, upon which they were each preſented with an elegant Medal with their names inſcribed, the times of their birth, and this inſcription—" Rebellion to tyrants is obedience to God ;" an inſcription which graced the ſeal of Mr. Jefferſon in 1775. They diſcover to each other ſymptoms of an involuntary attachment, as if they were aſſociated by an irreocable decree, in the cauſe of their country— maſculine and healthy, they afford the ſtrongeſt indications that they will one day prove themſelves according to the names that have been given them. May they live and proſper with the proſperty of their country.

"Twin sons." Premature newspaper commentary, announcing the success of the presumed Jefferson-Burr ticket

Chapter Six

THE STATESMAN AND THE SOLDIER

I shall conclude by recommending [Burr] as a General far
Superior to your Hamiltons, as much so, as a Man is to a Boy
& I have but little doubt this State through his means &
planning will be as Republican in the appointment of Electors as the State of Virginia.

      —James Nicholson to Albert Gallatin, 1800

Mr. Jefferson is President. Our opposition was continued till
it was demonstrated that Burr could not be brought in and
even if he could, he meant to come in as a Democrat.

      —James Bayard to Allen McClane, 1801

The election of 1800 is arguably the most controversial presidential
contest in American history. It played a crucial role in the shaping
of political parties. Like the election of 2000, it could not be resolved for
weeks after the national vote was taken, and it was marked by invective,
charges, and countercharges. Historians and political scientists continue to
debate its significance, some emphasizing its revolutionary character, others seeing it as the first peaceful transition of power from a ruling party
(Federalist) to the opposition party (Democratic Republican). On one issue, however, there is general agreement: Burr's maneuvering behind the
scenes, his apparent willingness to steal the election from Jefferson, made

him the closest thing to a villain in the common narrative of events over the period of November 1800–February 1801.

Burr has had his defenders. Writing about the charges of intrigue against him, the popular nineteenth-century biographer James Parton remarked that "no accusation made against a politician was ever so slenderly supported by evidence, or refuted by evidence so various, so unequivocal, so lavishly superfluous in quantity." But the problem goes deeper. Burr serves as a convenient scapegoat, allowing historians to simplify, or explain away, the division, disorder, and mayhem of the election crisis.[1]

Unraveling the crisis must begin with Burr's activities leading up to the controversial election. His prominence in New York—as a member of the state assembly and as a member of the bar—gave him the edge he needed to sustain his national reputation after having lost his Senate seat. How he became Jefferson's running mate had to do with his ability to effectively maneuver within the fractious political environment of his home state. As with everything in Burr's career, the partisan battles waged in Washington had their roots in local politics, and this was never more true than in the bitter contest for the presidency waged in 1800–01.

HE "HAS DONE A GREAT DEAL TOWARD REVOLUTIONIZING THE STATE"

Burr served two terms in the state assembly leading up to the election of 1800, and it was here that he acquired the influence that made him a leader of the New York Republicans. In January 1798, he arrived in the state capital of Albany, where he resided while the assembly was in session. He was joined there by his daughter, Theodosia, who drolly observed: "Albany is not as much like purgatory as I had expected to find it." Her father continued to pursue his legal career, while making local politics his life: hobnobbing with colleagues and carefully maneuvering behind the scenes to ensure successful passage of important bills, he steered the course of several crucial debates on the floor, and drafted key pieces of legislation. He became an indispensable power broker.[2]

Almost immediately, his Federalist enemies grew alarmed. By the time Burr was voted out of office in 1799, Robert Troup reported that if he had stayed much longer he would have turned the entire state Republican. "By his arts and intrigues," Troup angrily acknowledged, Burr "has done a great deal toward revolutionizing the state."[3] Still he faced a formidable challenge. In spite of Governor Clinton's long tenure in office, the legislature remained firmly in Federalist hands. When Burr was elected to the assembly in 1797, John Jay was governor; of New York's ten congressmen, six were Federalist. At this point, the real political battleground was Burr's home turf of New York City. Here Federalists held the reins of power over municipal politics. The mayor's office, Chamber of Commerce, and Common Council were all Federalist-dominated institutions. Not until the year Burr won his seat did Republicans begin to make their presence felt by capturing the city slate for the assembly.[4]

The Republicans understood that they were being tested. To reap significant gains in the assembly elections, they had to improve their commercial image. Unlike their southern Republican allies, the New Yorkers had to stop appearing to represent only the yeoman farmer if they were to retain power. This was easier for Burr to do than Governor Clinton, who had risen to power by relying on rural voters. The party was now obliged to reach out to those with decidedly commercial interests, a constituency that had gravitated toward Burr as early as 1792. Former Clintonians Melancton Smith, Marinus Willett, and David Gelston (all New York City merchants and speculators) had been part of Burr's inner circle since that time.

But wooing merchants was not enough. To control the assembly, it was just as crucial to secure support from the mechanics (the equivalent of today's blue-collar workers). To this point, the powerful urban constituency of master craftsmen, who worked in the building, manufacturing, and maritime trades, had overwhelmingly supported the growth-oriented Federalists; so had even the poorer mechanics, journeymen, and petty tradesmen. Master craftsmen and mechanics fell into two categories of voters: the £100 freeholders who could vote for state senators and the governor, and the 40 shilling renters allowed to vote for assemblymen. In 1800, two thirds of Republican voters in the city came from the lower classes, including the lowly cartmen who made their living by hauling goods through the streets. It was this group, the mechanics, who tipped the scales in favor of the Republicans in 1800.[5]

How did Burr win them over? As a leader of the assembly, he shaped a progressive commercial agenda that promoted internal improvements, a fairer tax system, liberal banking practices, lower municipal taxes, and debtor relief. The philosophy behind this legislation was utilitarian and liberal, aimed at encouraging commercial growth and extending material benefits to ambitious Republicans as well as moderate Federalists, while reducing the tax burden on those in the poorer wards of the city. Burr introduced bills for bridges, roads, waterworks, and fortifications that appealed widely to these groups. He promoted lower and fairer taxes in the assembly in 1799; this gained him support from struggling laborers, especially because municipal taxes at this time were flat taxes by which rich and poor paid the same amount.[6]

Robert Swartwout became an important ally of Burr's during his time in the assembly. He was an ambitious merchant and a relative of Melancton Smith's, who had moved from Poughkeepsie to New York City. When Smith died during the yellow fever epidemic of 1798, Swartwout took his place as Burr's right-hand man. He had been elected to the assembly on a ticket with Burr, and shared his commercial interests and larger political vision. Together, in 1799, they secured a charter from the state legislature for the Cayuga Bridge Company, and Swartwout owned much of the stock. When the bridge was completed the following year, the 132-foot-wide structure across one of the Finger Lakes was the longest bridge in the world and considered a modern marvel of engineering. It was not just ingenious but also quite profitable.[7]

Burr also found an ally in Dr. Joseph Browne, his brother-in-law. When, in 1783, Aaron Burr and Theodosia Prevost had married at the Hermitage, Browne and Theodosia's half sister, Catherine De Visme, stood beside them under the low ceiling, taking their vows too. Early in the 1790s, Burr and Browne had encouraged construction of the Boston Post Road, to provide an easily accessible route from New York City to New England. They again joined forces in 1798, when Browne presented a proposal to the New York City Common Council for a new waterworks: the Manhattan Company, which would soon be associated primarily with the efforts and strategic manipulation of Aaron Burr, received one of the most favorable charters ever granted by the state legislature. Its board of directors would include the man who held a sixty-year charter on the Boston Post Road, and John Swartwout would be one of its major stockholders. In the early republic, big business nearly always involved the extension of patronage, and so it should not seem odd that Burr sought advantages in this way. To get things done, one made deals.[8]

Moreover, state charters followed certain patterns. They allowed private corporations to fund internal improvements. In doing so, they cemented alliances: the merchant-speculators who ran these projects were supported by the mechanics who built them. But even public projects relied on the same kind of cooperation. The military fortifications of New York Harbor were no exception: The New York City Chamber of Commerce, dominated by merchants, organized the Military Committee on which Burr served. Burr made certain that the mechanics got paid, and stood as a key protector of the city's commercial center. He made political capital.[9]

Burr was pro-growth in the western and unsettled counties, too. Some deals, however, created more problems than political gains. For instance, he assisted the Holland Land Company, a Dutch-owned venture that had purchased 3.3 million acres in western New York State. Since 1793, Théophile Cazenove, the company's land agent, had been attempting to get a law passed that would allow non-Americans to own New York land outright. It was typical, at this time, for foreign investors to hire Americans to act as trustees, holding temporary title to the land. But the Holland Company could not rely on this strategy. A 1796 statute had stipulated that if the land was not in American hands at the end of seven years, the title reverted to the state. The writing was on the wall, and Cazenove was urgently shopping for new law.[10]

He approached Hamilton for help. Through his Federalist friends in the legislature, the former treasury secretary arranged a sweetheart deal in 1797. The Dutch firm would get an extension on its grace period to 1816, but only if it agreed to pay the Western Inland Lock Navigation Company $250,000. Why the Lock Company? By no coincidence, Hamilton's father-in-law, Philip Schuyler, was its president, and in desperate need of a fresh infusion of capital to keep his canal company afloat.[11]

This was business as usual. It is hard to imagine that Hamilton or Schuyler lost any sleep over the decision to bribe Cazenove. Nevertheless, the deal fell through. A year later, Burr got around to shepherding a similar bill through the state legislature, a bill Cazenove liked, which caused Hamilton and Schuyler to blame Burr for *their* failure to secure support for the Lock Company.

Burr was as much of a realist as Hamilton and Schuyler were. He understood that a foreign landholders bill would not pass until key assemblymen and senators were paid off. Cazenove distributed legal fees to several prominent Federalists: Josiah Ogden Hoffman, the state's attorney general ($3,000); Thomas Morris, the state senator who steered the bill through the upper house ($1,000); and a "Mr. L," whose identity remained secret. Burr secured a $5,500 loan from Cazenove, hardly odd for a man who routinely borrowed money from his clients—it was a small sum compared to what he borrowed from others. Burr, along with Hamilton, Richard Harison, and David A. Ogden, had already been hired by Cazenove for $400 to issue an opinion on the new Alien Landowners Act.[12]

Federalist David Ogden, an attorney for the Holland Land Company, was perhaps even more important than Burr in buying political support for the bill. Hoffman was his cousin, and the mysterious "Mr. L" was most likely his brother, who was in the assembly. Though a relative of Burr's (Timothy Edwards had married into the Ogden clan), Ogden was extremely close to Hamilton, who no doubt was aware of the payoffs.[13]

Hamilton never missed a chance to use gossip for political advantage. He engaged in a whispering campaign, insisting that Burr had accepted a bribe while ignoring or rationalizing his own attempt to extort money from the Holland Company. The rumors did not begin to circulate, however, until at least a year after the fact, in September 1799. It was this nasty piece of gossip that led Burr to challenge Hamilton's brother-in-law, John Barker Church, to a duel, in which Burr barely missed being hit when a bullet passed through his coat, and Church ultimately offered his opponent an apology.[14]

By today's standards, neither Burr nor Hamilton could claim incorruptibility with respect to Cazenove. And though the Holland Land Company deal has often been used as evidence of Burr's venality, it just as easily underscores Hamilton's inability to admit that he was no different from Burr in orchestrating backroom deals. Moreover, Hamilton and Schuyler's greed exceeded Burr's, for they had demanded a much bigger payoff: $250,000, compared with Burr's meager $5,500 loan.

This was not the end of Burr's dealings with Cazenove. He purchased a large tract of land from the Holland Company, expecting to sell his portion to European buyers. But like most speculative ventures he became involved in, this one proved disastrous for Burr. He was unable to sell the land, and was forced to return his holdings to the company to cover his debts; he had to hand over 20,000 acres as a penalty for breaking the contract.[15]

Burr's culpability is undeniable, but his erstwhile Federalist allies were just as guilty, and Hamilton's scheming was no less unattractive than Burr's. Suffice it to say that the actions taken cannot be reduced to flawed moral character; all of the men involved knew only too well how the patronage game was played. Burr played it well—up to a point. In the case of the Holland Company, he proved himself a bit cleverer than Hamilton, without looking much better in the eyes of history.

THE "MONSTER IN OUR CITY"

The rumors about Burr's so-called "bribery" in the Holland Land Company deal came in the wake of yet another contentious election. The previous spring, Federalists had ridiculed every major piece of legislation Burr supported, claiming that, as one man, he had "half disorganize[d] the state in a single winter." Both parties knew that the 1799 assembly election was crucial for New York City; it would determine which party had control over the city's electorate.

Though Burr's pet project, the Manhattan Company, gave Federalists a ready target, there were other, equally profound activities on Burr's part that roiled his New York antagonists. For them, a larger political issue was at stake: they saw Burr as the driving force in a social upheaval that they greatly feared: the empowerment of the "middling sorts." The Manhattan Company became merely a symbol (albeit a poignant symbol) of class warfare, pitting elite merchants against lowly mechanics. The former needed protection from the "monster in our city," as one newspaper column projected, a monstrous set of liberal financial policies that threatened to elevate upwardly mobile Republicans and weaken the traditional power brokers. Federalists won the 1799 assembly election, but victory came at a cost: They were no longer able to bridge class divisions in the city with their old rhetoric. Instead, they were seen from this point forward strictly as the party of the commercial elite.[16]

The Manhattan Company began innocently enough as an effort to provide fresh water to the city. In July 1798, Dr. Joseph Browne presented a proposal to the Common Council for establishing a state-chartered private company that would supply water from the Bronx River. Browne believed that a plentiful supply of fresh water would prevent yellow fever—a dread disease that killed New Yorkers every few years and was ravaging the city that very summer. The council agreed, but with significant reservations. It had no intention of surrendering the city's control of this valuable public utility to a private company.[17]

Burr had different plans. He wanted his water delivery corporation to function also as a bank. He had been studying bank charters for three years, and was aware that the Federalist-dominated legislature would never, under ordinary circumstances, endorse the creation of a new bank to rival their monopoly. In 1799, a branch of the Bank of United States and the Bank of New York jointly ruled the city's finances; both were run by the same circle of Federalist merchants. Burr intended to establish a different kind of financial institution, one that would involve "middling sorts" of citizens who were excluded from the Federalist monopoly.[18]

To defeat the council members' proposal, he had to outmaneuver them. He knew that without compelling reasons, his fellow assemblymen would be unwilling to dismiss the council members' request for a city-owned waterworks. It took him a mere ten days in February 1799 to effect his plan. Leaving Albany for Manhattan, he recruited a six-person committee made up of prominent city officials to convince the council to change its position. The gist of Burr's argument was one of fiscal responsibility; the city lacked funds. Unaware of the full scope of Burr's intent, Hamilton joined him in this endeavor, drafting the counterproposal that ultimately won over the council. Mayor Richard Varick, a die-hard Federalist and presiding member of the council, grudgingly conceded defeat. In an angry letter to Governor Jay, he grumbled that Burr had flattered Hamilton so as to secure his support.[19]

Why did Hamilton come to Burr's aid? It was primarily a matter of money. The city simply could not raise the cash to pay for the waterworks; it was already committed to funding harbor fortifications, and the state assembly had already refused to burden the city's residents with any additional taxes. Private companies were the accepted means, at this time, for providing public services.

As always, Hamilton had personal reasons besides. He was sure to guarantee a spot for his British brother-in-law, John Barker Church, on the board of directors. This meant that Hamilton's family would benefit from the company's stock sales. (Hamilton often acted as an agent for his family's business interests.) His role here was, in fact, no different than his wrangling to get the Holland Company to subsidize his father-in-law's failing canal venture two years before. With Church on the board, Hamilton could keep his eye on the Manhattan Company. Of course, Burr had personal motives, too; the bank would keep his finances afloat for several years, granting him loans to cover his debts.[20]

Hamilton estimated a higher capitalization of the corporation ($1 million rather than Dr. Browne's original $200,000), and he suggested that the city (or the council) retain its authority over the waterworks by owning one third of the stock. In the final version of the state charter, however, Burr removed this last privilege, reducing the number of shares held by the city so as to diminish the power that the Federalist-controlled council could wield.[21]

Even before the ink was dry on Hamilton's proposal, Burr was making other changes as well. Before he returned to Albany, he expanded the number of directors from seven (as Hamilton had suggested) to twelve. While in Manhattan, Burr also collected a list of subscribers to the company, and circulated a series of petitions so that the assembly would favor his plan. His most clever move was to depoliticize the board, curbing partisan jealousies by including representatives of the four principal factions in the state: Schuyler-Hamiltonians, Clintonians, Livingstons, and Burrites all found places as directors. Suddenly, the private water company had everyone's endorsement.[22]

Burr distanced himself just enough, obliging a friendly city assemblyman, James Fairlie, to introduce a bill of incorporation for the Manhattan Company. It easily made its way through the assembly and senate in late March, facing no opposition until Judge John Lansing of the Council of Revision raised objections. But he was outvoted.[23]

As to Burr's unannounced purpose—creating a bank—a clause he inserted in the charter permitted the company to use its "surplus capital" for other unnamed enterprises solely for its own benefit. The charter was not bound by time; it did not have to be renewed at any future date; it existed in perpetuity for as long as the company provided water to the city. Shielded from state interference, the Manhattan Company could never be dismantled.[24]

Burr did something rather remarkable at this point. He set the cost of a public share at $50, a fraction of what other banks typically charged for their stock. This created a new class of investors: ambitious Republicans of the "middling sort" and entrepreneurial mechanics. New Yorkers were keenly aware of this innovation. There was nothing so Republican, so inclusive— so non-Federalist—as to put in place a means by which lowly cartmen, as stockholders, could potentially receive discounts on credit.[25]

The election season began just as the stock for the Manhattan Company went on sale, and with the Federalists staking everything on discrediting Burr. The *Commercial Advertiser* led the attack in a series of spiteful harangues which began on April 26, 1799. The election rested on "the gilded name of Aaron Burr," one anonymous writer claimed, and it was his "services of the past year" that would determine the fate of his party. All of Burr's legislative measures came under scrutiny: his opposition to the Massachusetts Resolutions (to disenfranchise naturalized citizens), his support of debtor relief, the role he played in election reform, and his orchestration of the Manhattan Company.[26]

What did these actions have in common? They all made it possible to paint Burr as a fanatic, a "radical," whose policies threatened to turn America into a colony of Revolutionary France by overturning the existing social order. In failing to keep seditious foreigners under control, Burr had opened the flood gates for a French invasion. Already, Federalist stalwarts were nervously projecting Jefferson's election as president, which they claimed Burr had now put in motion. If their worst fears came to pass, Gallic troops would occupy the country, honest industry and religion would disappear, and Americans would quickly be reduced to enslavement under the unprincipled French. This kind of hysterical rhetoric was not new in American politics: Federalists had raised the specter of French domination before and during the Quasi-War. Yet now the same language was invoked to warn of a coup, naming Burr as the arch villain stirring up the underclass.[27]

In the *Commercial Advertiser* on April 27, "The Anti-Revolutionist" spoke out against a new political class in the making. He rebuked Burr's efforts in the assembly (through the mouthpiece of his good friend Robert Swartwout) to democratize the election of state senators by dividing the state into as many districts as there were electors, giving preference to local favorites over the state's best known names. "The Anti-Revolutionist" contended that this would bring into office "many a man . . . who would never acquire respectability enough to be elected by a large number of his fellow-citizens." Men outside the circle of ruling families would get a taste of power.[28]

The same article poked fun at "the slough of the Democratic Society." The Federalist ticket was distinguished by "respectable and confidential names . . . men of personal worth, reputable in their several professions." Burr's ticket, in contrast, was a register of "dupes" and "knaves," which was another way of saying that Burr's followers lacked the independence that derived, almost as a right, from class position. This made Burr, most significantly, a "master magician." He held the strings that controlled his puppets; indeed, he was a "Lyon among the beasts," lifting up a new class of followers from the dregs of society.[29]

Burr's underhanded plan required a bank, in the minds of his reanimated detractors. The Manhattan Company had become an Anti-Federalist plot, and "three quarters of its directors" were "Democrats," supporting an "anti-federal monied interest." Its *Politico-Commercial-Financial-Bronx-Operation* would monopolize trade, oppress industry, and upset the value of credit in the city. The clause that Burr had added to the charter was nothing more than a trick, which he "surreptitiously" slipped by his colleagues in the assembly, through "cunning, intrigue, artifice, and falsehood." "Preying upon fellow laborers and dupes," Burr plotted to lure his unsuspecting pawns into the unstable world of "banking, stockjobbing," and "jewing."[30]

One merchant, writing in the *Commercial Advertiser,* claimed that Burr's bank would increase the flow of "fictitious capital." When men of questionable worth could borrow money as easily as the acknowledged elite, they would destabilize the world of finance, exaggerating their actual credit worthiness. The real problem, of course, was that this new prosperous class would vote Republican.[31]

Federalist predictions about the bank, if frenzied, were quite accurate. When the Manhattan Company opened in September, it did as promised, extending services beyond the usual client base of merchants and lawyers. It was the Federalists who had first used their banks for purely political retaliation, refusing discounts to Republicans during state elections, and they now attempted to boycott the Manhattan Company by refusing to accept its bank notes. Yet many Federalists kept their stock, such as Robert Troup, one of the loudest of Burr's critics, while a concurrent effort was being made (at the instigation of Hamilton and followers) to take over the bank. Here was another reason John Barker Church's position on the board mattered. The Federalists were leaving mixed messages, divided over whether to slay the monster or to steal it.[32]

One of the stranger incidents sparked by the Manhattan Company involved Nicholas Low. A prominent merchant, bank director, and president of an insurance company, Low was a friend of Hamilton's, and Burr's most vocal opponent. In this little known episode of 1799, Low received a letter from someone pretending to be Aaron Burr. The imposter hinted that he might challenge Low to a duel. Charging that Low had "taken unwarrantable Liberty with my name and character," the troublemaker (the supposed Burr) requested that the two men meet as "gentlemen" to establish the operative rules for their affair of honor. When he learned of the letter, Burr wrote Low immediately, denouncing the fake letter, and that was the end of it. Yet the ruse reveals the nastiness of New York politics at this time. Nothing was off limits, even the possibility that two men might shoot at each other for no reason whatsoever. The letter to Low appeared the same month as Burr's duel with Church, strongly suggesting that one of Hamilton's cronies had something to do with it.[33]

The Federalists were able to claim a victory in the assembly elections. The ticket headed by Burr lost, though not by the margin predicted. The Republicans won the Sixth Ward, known for its large number of mechanics, Irish and French immigrants; the Federalists registered their largest gains in the Second and Third Wards, the conservative and merchant base of the city. All went as expected, except that the Manhattan Company did not remain a permanent liability for the Republicans, as many Federalists hoped. Its liberal banking policies gained it partisans, whereas the Federalists who opposed it appeared reactionary and elitist. Burr had established a Republican-friendly financial system without excluding Federalists from its daily operations. By 1800, the bank was a commercial success, and even Virginians were bragging that the bank would make Jefferson president.[34]

"THE THOUSAND TONGUES OF RUMOUR"

Burr may have lost his platform in the assembly, but he did not depart the limelight. Two court cases commanded unprecedented attention, in both instances placing him side by side with his old nemesis, Alexander Hamilton. The first case, *Le Guen v. Gouverneur and Kemble,* was the culmination of several proceedings making their way through the labyrinth of the New York court system. It entailed eight different suits and five years of litigation. The final appeal was heard before the Court of Errors, the eighteenth-century equivalent to a modern court of appeals. This battle between two prominent New York merchants and one French trader—Louis Le Guen—came to a close in Albany during the winter of 1799–1800.

Le Guen was a French citizen who came to New York in 1794, looking for buyers to purchase his large cargo of cotton and indigo. He made an arrangement with Isaac Gouverneur and Peter Kemble to store his goods, and eventually the two New Yorkers signed an agreement to become Le Guen's partners in a venture to sell the goods overseas. It was this contract that triggered the dispute. To represent his interest, Le Guen settled on three of the best attorneys in town: Burr, Hamilton, and Richard Harison, all of whom remained on retainer from 1795 until 1800.[35]

The legal maneuvering in the *Le Guen* case reflected the high stakes involved, as the French trader demanded an unparalleled $119,915 in damages. The case gained added notoriety once the sparring became public, spilling over into the press. Courtroom antics centered on Hamilton's unpoliceable mouth. He attacked the defendants, witnesses, and opposing counsel with a peculiar viciousness, causing even his devoted admirer Robert Troup (in this instance, one of the opposing counsel) to remark upon his "utmost animosity & cruelty."[36]

Gouverneur and Kemble retaliated, speculating about Hamilton's purposes. They argued that the suit was specious to begin with, benefiting the lawyers more than Le Guen. But their tactic backfired. It fueled Hamilton's ire, and the case became a war of words they were unlikely to win. The astute Brockholst Livingston, counsel for the New York merchants, warned his client Gouverneur: "I much fear you are marked out as a victim to the reputation of Mr. Hamilton." He meant that the case had become more about Hamilton than Le Guen, and that Hamilton was intent on winning at all costs, even if he had to trample on his friends along the way.[37]

Eventually, Gouverneur aired his complaints in print. While the case was before the state supreme court in early 1798, he published in the New York newspapers the opinions of three Pennsylvania attorneys who refuted Hamilton's argument. He also attacked Hamilton for having compared him to the "odious character of Shylock." At the same time, Gouverneur tried to find something negative to say about Burr, but he could find nothing to criticize in Burr's conduct during the *Le Guen* hearings. Instead, he made reference to an earlier case. Burr had insulted the principals of an insurance company, comparing the president and its directors to "the Pope and 39 Cardinals." The president had whispered, "What a blackguard." Burr overheard him, and responded coyly, "Not so loud." Both Hamilton and Burr were adept at sarcasm, but their styles were noticeably different. Burr had a lighter touch, and he never let his emotions get the best of him.[38]

By the time the case came before the Court of Errors, in February 1800, Robert Troup, long Hamilton's toady, was now Hamilton's punching bag. Writing to a friend, the abused Federalist observed of Hamilton that he had never been "on any occasion so heated and wound up with passion." Troup pathetically hoped he might survive his barbs, and "escape the General's pistols as well as his sword." When the trial ended, however, Troup could not so easily turn the other cheek. "I ought to forgive," he admitted to Rufus King, but "my friends will not permit me as yet to bury [his insults] in oblivion." For his part, Hamilton recorded notes that he probably never expected would see the light of day: "Robert Troup—a creature it is *almost a vice to name*—"[39]

The Albany hearing lasted over a week, and involved eight lawyers: Hamilton, Burr, Harison, Troup, and Brockholst Livingston were all there. Gouverneur Morris's diary offers insight into the forensic arts on display that week. Morris was a relative of Isaac Gouverneur's, and at the final hearing before the Court of Errors, he was added to the team of lawyers in a desperate attempt to salvage the case for his kinsman. Morris (America's minister to France under Washington) had not been in a courtroom for a dozen years. Still, his talents were considerable; in Troup's words, he supplied "bursts of sublime eloquence."[40]

Though Morris was Hamilton's good friend, he too found his behavior appalling. "Hamilton is desirous of being witty," he confided to his diary, "but goes beyond the Bounds and is open to a severe Dressing." That "Dressing" was, in Federalist-era parlance, a good beating—the treatment due a social inferior. Had Hamilton's insults risen to the notice of a proper gentleman, their recourse would have been to the dueling field. Rather contemptuously, then, Morris dismissed Hamilton's antics as evidence of his lowly origins.[41]

Though Burr, as U.S. senator, had attacked him, demanding Morris's recall from France in 1794, the New York Federalist recorded: "Col. Burr is very able & has I see made considerable Impression." Burr was not the principal presenter at the hearing, but his influence was decisive, and Morris was not too peevish to acknowledge this. Both Burr and Hamilton gave closing arguments, yet it was Burr's summary that most impressed Morris.[42]

Burr was not a lightning rod in the *Le Guen* case. He was, rather, the voice of reason amid a public spectacle. It was Hamilton who made himself the butt of gossip—and, significantly, not among his political enemies, but among his close friends and allies. Gouverneur and Kemble felt that Hamilton had thoroughly abused them. Gouverneur died less than a month after the final verdict was handed down. His "unfortunate exit," to use Burr's words, moved the public, and colors on the commercial vessels sitting in New York Harbor were lowered to half-mast. As pillars of the merchant community, and friends to the mechanics, Gouverneur and Kemble were just the sort of men that Hamilton needed to rally to the polls at election time. Unwisely, Hamilton had undermined his influence as a party leader in his own state, and alienated many of his key supporters—men he would need in the upcoming assembly election.[43]

While the *Le Guen* hearing captivated the merchants in the city, another trial, involving a crime "of so atrocious a nature," became the talk of the town. Levi Weeks, a young man of twenty-three, was accused of murdering Gulielma Sands, a young Quaker woman. She was found dead at the bottom of a Manhattan Company well, in Lispenard Meadows.[44]

Gulielma had gone missing on December 22, 1799, and her relatives were certain that she had last been seen in the company of Weeks. Suspicion fell on him because the two lived at the same Greenwich Street boardinghouse, and Weeks and the victim were thought to be on intimate terms. On the night of her disappearance, Gulielma had confided to her cousin that she and Levi planned to be secretly wed that evening. On January 4, 1800, two days after the body was found in the well, a local newspaper printed an accusatory story, intimating that her lover was the last person to see Gulielma alive: "Strong suspicions are entertained that she has been willfully murdered."[45]

Though he was described as a laborer in the indictment, Levi Weeks had powerful friends. His brother, Ezra, was a prominent builder in New York who quickly assembled a first-class defense team consisting of Burr, Hamilton, and Brockholst Livingston. At the time of the trial, Ezra had been commissioned to build Hamilton's country mansion, and Burr had business dealings with him as well: it was Ezra Weeks who had supplied the wood for the pipes laid by the Manhattan Company. Levi (a carpenter) and his brother were technically "mechanics," but they were also prosperous, well-educated men.[46]

Before the trial began, Gulielma's relatives worked assiduously to persuade the public of the young man's guilt. Handbills about the crime were distributed around the city to stir up public outrage, and the mangled corpse was displayed on the street before thousands of curious onlookers. Speculation and gossip circulated among the *beau monde* and lowly cartmen alike. On the first day of the trial, a large crowd gathered at Federal Hall; citizen-volunteers guarded the defendant as he entered the packed courtroom, and angry spectators shouted: "Crucify him, Crucify him!"[47]

In the absence of eyewitnesses, the case rested on the reputation of Levi Weeks. Aware of the mounting hostility against him, his defense attorneys issued their own press release. The defense published what amounted to a preview of its case in the *Daily Advertiser*. This piece may in fact have been written by Burr, anticipating what he would say during the trial. Weeks hardly fit the profile of a murderer. The article described him as a "moral, sober, industrious, amiable man." The secret marriage was dismissed as unsubstantiated hearsay; the autopsy proved that the victim was not pregnant. Given that the evidence was circumstantial, why, then, was the public jumping to conclusions? Only the "unprejudiced voice of an impartial jury" should decide the defendant's fate.[48]

The trial opened on March 31, and went on for over forty hours, considerably longer than the average criminal trial of this era. It would be at three o'clock in the morning two days later that the jury rendered its verdict. Supreme Court Justice John Lansing presided, and Assistant Attorney General Cadwalader David Colden served as prosecutor. Colden, only thirty-one, bore sole responsibility for the case. In opening remarks, he deferred to his distinguished opposing counsel, describing the defense team as "so vastly my superiors in learning, experience and professional rank."[49]

Before Aaron Burr was even able to deliver his opening statement, Colden paraded twenty-four witnesses before the court. He staked his case on two arguments. First, that the defendant had seduced the young woman, and then murdered her to avoid marriage. Second, that the couple surreptitiously left the boardinghouse together on the night Gulielma disappeared. The victim's two female cousins gave strong testimony that they knew about the secret romance. When Gulielma did not return home, they noticed that Levi was behaving uncomfortably, which they interpreted as a sign of his guilt.[50]

The prosecution suffered as a result of credibility issues. Colden's witnesses tended to obscure rather than focus: one woman, "aged and very infirm," was so confused that her testimony made his case look uneven, his evidence unreliable. Another witness, a man who took his meals at the boardinghouse, seemed all too eager to condemn the defendant. And his morose and sadistic appearance caused some jurors to suspect him of involvement in this—or at least some—crime. Finally, the ungainly co-owner of the boardinghouse, a Quaker, struck the jury as foolish. He wore baggy clothing and a broad-brimmed Quaker hat, and his unconvincing answers, under the aggressive questioning of the defense team, led jurors to think that he might have had sexual designs on Gulielma.[51]

Who was the jury to believe? The clownish Quaker? The dark and surly lodger whose "unfortunate physiognomy," according to Brockholst Livingston, helped to convince another jury, later that year, that he raped his own stepdaughter? Or would they settle on Levi Weeks? That young man had reputable connections, and (as one pamphleteer put it) a "face [that] appeared the index of a virtuous and benevolent heart." Appearance swayed the jury—then as it does now.[52]

On day two, Burr mesmerized the court with his brilliant presentation. "Mr. Burr opened the *defence* with such perspicacity and force," wrote the reporter from the *Daily Advertiser,* "as disentangled every circumstance of perplexity; tore away the suspicion that had obstinately hung in the public mind; and shed such luminous evidence on every part of the subject, as dispelled all the distraction of doubt." He made it perfectly clear that Levi Weeks was "an injured and innocent man."[53]

Fortunately, Burr's speech was recorded, allowing us to evaluate what the newspaper saw fit to acclaim. "Gentlemen of the jury," he began, thanking his hearers for their patience and perseverance in adopting an unprejudiced stance. Indeed, overcoming prejudice was a key to his purpose in defending Levi Weeks:

> You have relieved me from my greatest anxiety, for I know the unexampled industry that has been exerted to destroy the reputation of the accused, and to immolate him at the shrine of persecution without the solemnity of a candid and impartial trial. I know that hatred, revenge, and cruelty, all the vindictive and ferocious passions have assembled in terrible array and exerted every engine to gratify their malice.

As he proceeded, his oratory resembled nothing so much as a work of literature:

> The thousand tongues of rumour have been steadily employed in the fabrication and dissemination of falsehoods, and every method has been taken to render their slanders universal. We have witnessed the extraordinary means which have been adopted to enflame the public passions and to direct the fury of popular resentment against the prisoner. Why has the body been exposed for days in the public streets in a manner the most indecent and shocking?—to attract the curiosity and arouse the feelings of numberless spectators. Such dreadful scenes speak powerfully to the passions: they petrify the mind with horror—congeal the blood within our veins—and excite the human bosom with irresistible, but undefineable emotions. When such emotions are once created they are not easily subdued.[54]

These last lines bear an uncanny resemblance to Thomas Jefferson's much-lauded first inaugural address, delivered one year later. Jefferson, too, used violent imagery to characterize a society wrought by powerful passions: "the agonizing spasms of infuriated man, seeking through blood and slaughter his long-lost liberty." Jefferson was wishing to "restore to social intercourse that harmony and affection without which liberty and even life itself are but dreary things." Burr was appealing for impartiality toward an accused murderer; but the vocabulary was equally an effort to replace excitability with compassion.[55]

He cautioned the jury to be wary of circumstantial evidence: "all the fabric must hang together or the whole will tumble down." He claimed that the storyline in the prosecution's case was "broken, disconnected, and utterly impossible." There were too many holes in the fabric, especially, Burr claimed, when the jury was being asked to jump to conclusions in linking presumed sexual behavior to a motive for murder:

> *Notwithstanding there may be testimony of an intimacy having subsisted between the prisoner and the deceased, we shall show you that there was nothing like a real courtship, or such a course of conduct as ought to induce impartial people to entertain a belief that marriage was intended.*

Levi had a solid alibi—except for "15 minutes," too little time to commit the crime. He had been dining with his brother some distance from where the murder took place. Burr asked the jury to consider another possibility: that the "melancholy" young woman might have taken her own life. Until rumors had begun to circulate, the defendant's morals had been held to be irreproachable: "That such a character should be impelled," Burr stressed, "without motive, to the commission of so horrid a crime, cannot be believed." Burr gave several examples of mistaken verdicts, and then appealed to the jury: "What remorse of conscience must a juror feel for having convicted a man who afterwards appeared to be innocent." Levi Weeks, he insisted, was the wrong man.[56]

By the end of the trial, the defense team had grown so confident that it agreed to forego closing arguments. Judge Lansing gave his charge to the jury, largely echoing Burr's summary of the case. The jury returned in less than five minutes with a verdict of not guilty. The courtroom audience broke into applause.[57]

Reporters praised the verdict as a "Triumph of Innocence." Yet a cloud of suspicion still hung over Weeks, and two years later, unable to escape the stigma of the trial, he left town for good. Though it is impossible to know with any certainty, the jury's verdict could have been wrong. Gulielma Sands had been murdered, and Burr's alternative theory of suicide, in historical perspective, appears unpersuasive. Gulielma's lover, described in one pamphlet as "prudent, discreet and amiable," remains the only viable suspect. Burr no doubt believed his client, and he rallied to Weeks's cause, because he understood the deadly force of gossip, based on his own experience as a public man. Was he, perhaps, thinking of Hamilton, who sat next to him, when he righteously refuted the "unexampled industry that has been exerted to destroy the reputation of the accused"? The Weeks trial afforded Burr a rare opportunity to rebuke the powerful engine of slander. Never again would he have this chance, amid the onslaught of abuse he was fated to endure.[58]

"HE DESERVES ANY THING AND EVERY THING OF HIS COUNTRY"

At this time in American history, presidential races were most often decided in state legislatures—where the power to name electors resided. The federal Constitution intended that presidents should only be *indirectly* elected by the people. In contrast to 1800, the popular vote today directly determines each state's electoral vote, without having state legislators as middlemen.

In most discussions of the election of 1800, Burr often appears to have shown up suddenly, at just the right moment, to put together an unbeatable slate of candidates for the state assembly who, in turn, decided who among the party faithful would serve as presidential electors. We know now that he did not show up suddenly, but rose to a leadership position as an activist assemblyman to whom his Republican colleagues listened to on a host of legislative matters. What Burr did in 1800 was no minor feat, of course. By helping to change the composition of the New York State Assembly, he in effect secured the electors of the president: with Burr's helping hand, New York's 12 electoral votes ultimately put Jefferson ahead of Adams.

At first, nothing was at all certain. The tide began to turn for the Republicans at the end of April 1800; this was really when the presidential campaign entered high gear, when New York held state elections, the results of which would determine the composition of the slate of presidential electors for the national contest that autumn. The state legislature chose its electors by a simple majority: the state would put together either an all Federalist or all Republican slate. Burr had spent the entire year leading up to this preparing for the April election, learning from past mistakes and perfecting a system of party management.

He understood that everything boiled down to his being able to secure the greatest number possible of Manhattan assemblymen. These thirteen individuals would hold the balance of power—that was Burr's calculation, as he reported it directly to Jefferson. If Republicans regained control of the city delegation, they would be a majority in the lower house; the Federalists already maintained a slight margin in the state senate. But it was the combined vote of both houses that counted in determining the makeup of the slate of electors in November. It was winner take all.[59]

Long before the polls opened in April, Burr had developed a "system," adapted from his military experience. While patrolling the "Neutral Ground" in Westchester County in 1779, he had carefully classified residents into the categories of Tory or Patriot; he now dispatched his staff to collect data, and profiled the city's voters in terms of partisan allegiance. He knew which Republicans would contribute money, who would volunteer their time at the polls, and who could only be counted on to vote. What is now standard practice—basing campaign decisions on voter behavior—at this time in American history startled the Federalists, unaccustomed to such ingenuity. As the Federalist *Commercial Advertiser* lamented later, Republicans had "discriminated throughout this city, between their partisans, and those opposed to them, and they soon knew to a man the name of every doubtful character."[60]

In January 1800, as the lead tactician behind the effort, Burr had made a "flying trip" to Philadelphia to discuss his plans with Jefferson. Though we do not know precisely how impressed the Virginian was with Burr's maneuvering, Jefferson certainly understood, as he related to James Monroe, that "all depended on the city election." Success in New York became even more critical in March, when the Pennsylvania legislature appeared unable to agree on a method for choosing electors. This was dire news, for Jefferson had won 14 of that state's 15 electoral votes in the 1796 presidential contest, and it now appeared that the Keystone State might not even participate in the national election. New York remained the Republicans' best hope in the North. It was increasingly clear that Jefferson could not win without Burr's help.[61]

Burr next concentrated on organizing his party more efficiently. Each city ward had a Republican committee, which sent a representative to the General Republican Committee. Burr controlled the key subcommittee of the General Committee, which chose the city ticket. On this select committee he put his closest allies: David Gelston; John Swartwout; and an ambitious, twenty-seven-year-old Republican printer named Matthew Livingston Davis—his future biographer. Davis had first met Burr a couple of years before while working at Philip Freneau's radical newspaper, *The Time Piece*; in 1800, he fashioned himself as Burr's "lieutenant."[62]

Burr put together an unbeatable slate. It included men with sturdy national reputations. Former Governor George Clinton topped the list, along with the hero of Saratoga, General Horatio Gates. As both men were reluctant candidates, Burr needed his full talent to persuade them to run. In his seventies, Gates had never held any civil office. But he lent *gravitas* to the Republicans, as a symbol of Revolutionary glory. His stunning capture of the British army had made Gates Washington's only serious rival. Burr added two other "Republican veterans," so-called, to his slate: Colonel Henry Rutgers, and another war hero, John Broome. This ticket of "venerable patriots" attracted notice. As the Philadelphia *Aurora* proudly claimed, a heroic band of patriots had risen again to battle the "abandoned policy instigated by Hamilton."[63]

Burr saw that the ticket was rounded out with prominent merchants, mechanics, and trusted ex-assemblymen who had recently served with him in the lower house. At the same time, he sought to smooth over factional jealousies and traditional rivalries. Three of his candidates were Manhattan Company directors, including his co-counsel in the Levi Weeks case, Brockholst Livingston. Burr also made sure that all three Republican factions—Clintonians, Livingstons, and Burrites—were on the ticket. Though Burr himself was not on the ticket, his influence—and his recently established bank—were omnipresent.[64]

Stagecraft complemented his meticulous planning. He delayed announcing his ticket until the Federalists had first revealed their hand. According to Burr's lieutenant, Matthew Livingston Davis, the unimpressive opposition included a ship chandler, a baker, a bookseller, a shoemaker, two grocers, and a bankrupt. Assistant Attorney General Cadwalader David Colden, who had failed to win conviction in the Weeks trial, also made the list; but even he had little chance against the elder statesmen on the Republican ticket. The Federalists had shown too little zeal and rather hasty planning. Their troubles mounted, and as the weakening party argued, its squabbles spilled over into the press. To the delight of the rising Republicans in New York, a frustrated Hamilton angrily stormed out of one of their meetings. Federalist tempers were still flaring, as they formally announced their ticket.[65]

That same night, April 15, Republicans held their own "private Meeting" at the home of Brockholst Livingston, and a larger public meeting took place two days later. That is when and where Burr's subcommittee presented its list of candidates, which gained unanimous support. Davis reported that "joy & Enthusiasm" filled the room, as they anticipated doing battle with the Federalist slate. Burr had mobilized his troops, and had put together a winning ticket.[66]

But Burr's campaign efforts did not stop there. In the months leading up the election, he turned his Manhattan home into a command center. One New York merchant recorded in his diary at length that Burr "kept open house for nearly two months, and Committees were in session day and night during the whole time at his house. Refreshments were always on the table, and mattresses were set up for temporary repose in the rooms. Reports were hourly received from sub-committees—in short, no means left unemployed."

Burr had no intention of remaining in the background. As Matthew Livingston Davis reported to Albert Gallatin in late March, Burr had "pledged himself to come forward, and address the people in a firm & manly language on the importance of the election." Davis was aware that this kind of campaigning was new, and that Burr had "never done this at any former election." Thus, when the polls finally opened on April 29, Burr stationed himself as a sentinel outside the polling place for the critical Seventh Ward, "*Ten Hours,* without intermission."[67]

Burr was so certain that his disciplined management of the process had resulted in a "highly honorable" victory that he wrote to Jefferson: electoral success had occurred with "no indecency, no unfairness, no personal abuse." His associates, however, preferred to view the contest as a glorious

battle between two great generals, Hamilton and Burr—a battle of wits and
will. As Davis contended, using the loaded word "intrigue" to mean "tactical brilliance," the Republican campaign was "headed by a man whose
intrigue and management is most astonishing, and who is more dreaded by
his enemies than any other character in our cause." Both Burr and Hamilton felt completely at ease on the public stage, inspiring loyalty from those
around them by engaging in political theatrics. For his part, mounted on
his white steed, Hamilton rode from ward to ward, a general (which he
was) surveying his troops in the heat of political battle. Burr, fashioning
himself after Montgomery at Quebec, rushed forward at the head of his
forces, speaking in a "manly language," never accepting defeat. Those closest to Burr at this critical moment characterized his leadership style as
"astonishing."[68]

James Nicholson wrote to his son-in-law Albert Gallatin several days
after the election results became known: "I shall conclude by recommending [Burr] as a General far Superior to your Hamiltons, as much so, as a
Man is to a Boy. . . ." The contest appeared in many ways—and this is important to understand—as a quest for manly glory. Party men enlisted in a
boasting match, defending their generals while tossing off insults and broadly
taunting. The New York campaign of 1800 was a replay of Revolution-era
military zeal fueled by a fascination with masculine prowess.[69]

In the end, the Republicans carried all thirteen assembly seats. New
York's Federalists were stunned. On May 3, they called a meeting, and the
defeated partisans openly contemplated a coup. They wished to empower
Governor John Jay to choose the electors of president and vice president.
Aware that, in doing so, they might provoke a civil war, those in atten-
dance still agreed that war would be "preferable to having Jefferson for
President."[70]

Hamilton, amazingly, endorsed this idea. On May 7, he dashed off a
highly revealing letter, urging Jay to convene a lame duck special session of
the legislature immediately. This way, Federalists could institute a new
procedure for naming electors, taking the choice out of the hands of the
newly elected assembly. "It will not do to be overscrupulous . . . by a strict
adherence to ordinary laws," Hamilton prodded the governor. Drastic action could be justified, he said, as a matter of *public safety.*" Jefferson's
prospective election was, in Hamilton's mind (at least at this time), a na-

tional crisis that demanded a determined response: "Scruples of delicacy and propriety . . . ought not to hinder the taking of a *legal* and *constitutional* step, to prevent an *Atheist* in Religion and a *Fanatic* in politics from getting possession of the State." There was nothing "legal" or "constitutional" in what he was asking. In spite of his phraseology, Hamilton was authorizing a subversion of the political process.[71]

What could be clearer? Defeat loomed on the horizon, and Hamilton could not accept it. He did not care to imagine a peaceful transition of government. Burr's slate had won fairly; corruption had not tainted the election. But now, Hamilton was prepared to set a dangerous precedent by sacrificing the constitutional integrity of the election process. He failed to grasp the irony of the situation, having, in the words of one biographer, "never tired of accusing Burr of political chicanery and loose ethics." Jay, at least, understood the full implication of Hamilton's request, and noted to himself at the bottom of the letter: "Proposing a measure for party purposes which I think it would not become me to adopt." Jay refused to endorse Hamilton's proposal.[72]

The Republicans were to meet in Philadelphia on May 11 and decide on a national ticket. Of course, Jefferson would be their nominee. The highly respected congressman Albert Gallatin was asked to come up with an ideal running mate. It would have to be a New Yorker, for regional balance. The "serious question," as Gallatin put it to his politically astute wife, was: "Who is to be our Vice President—Clinton or Burr?" Matthew Livingston Davis already had urged Gallatin to favor Burr, for he was the most "eligible character," and more attractive to New York Republicans than either Chancellor Livingston or former Governor Clinton. While it was true that Burr had done all of the essential work to reconfigure the state assembly, Clinton could not be so easily dismissed, for he still had clout with southerners. Gallatin, in turn, deferred to his father-in-law, James Nicholson, asking him to talk to both men and decide which of them should be Jefferson's running mate.[73]

By now, Nicholson was already singing Burr's praises. He claimed that Burr's victory at the polls was nothing short of "miraculous," and imagined that the favorable result was owing to the "intervention of Supreme Power." On May 6, he wrote to Gallatin exuberantly that Burr's "generalship, perseverance, industry, & execution, exceeds all description, so that I think I can say he deserves any thing and every thing of his country." Gallatin had to have had some idea in advance that his father-in-law would ultimately go with Burr. When Nicholson finally reported back, he spelled out what had happened: "Geo. Clinton with whom I just spoke declined—His age, his infirmities & his habits & Attachment to retired Life in his opinion has exempted him from an active life. As Geo. Clinton thinks Col. Burr is the most Suitable person & perhaps the only Man. Such is also the opinion of all the Republicans in this quarter that I have conversed with, this confidence in AB is universal & unbounded." And so, Burr would run with Jefferson.[74]

"ET TU, BRUTE!"

As the presidential election of 1800 became a national preoccupation, the partisan environment guaranteed that deals (and double-dealing) would bring pen-wielding politicians and responsive newspaper editors to fever pitch. Excitement filled the air, as the Republican upsurge of 1799–1800 led the High Federalists to express their apocalyptic visions of what a Jeffersonian order would entail. Inflamed Hamiltonians and New England divines predicted public immoralities unknown since the fall of Rome, along with Bible-burning, incest, rape, and other outrages. Jefferson was called an atheist, demagogue, and Jacobin; he was compared to a "ravening wolf," prepared to "glut his deadly appetite on the vitals" of the country. Rumors of conspiratorial plots and an impending civil war began to spread.[75]

For the moment, Burr was the least of the Federalists' problems, though temptation struck in September, when he traveled through New England in the company of his uncle Pierpont Edwards. The *Connecticut Courant* wailed that "the pious Col. Burr, and the pious Mr. Edwards, are uniting their pious exertions to introduce the pious Mr. Jefferson to the presidential chair." Their motives are "of the truest benevolence and philanthropy," the editorial droned on, projecting Burr as a corrupt vice president and Edwards as a sycophant in search of "lucrative office" as soon as the "new order" commenced. Not every New England divine felt this way. One Republican reported to the *Aurora* that Reverend Timothy Dwight, president of Yale, "had taught his pupils, that there was not a Democrat fit to give a crust to a dog"—except Dwight's cousin, "col. Burr."[76]

Meanwhile, the energetic Hamilton engaged in a campaign within a campaign. The former treasury secretary was in an uphill battle, intent on defeating Jefferson and at the same time keeping Adams from retaining the presidential chair. As he had in 1796, but with far more vigor now, Hamilton worked behind the scenes to elevate a South Carolinian Pinckney—this time Charles Cotesworth Pinckney—over Adams. The ostensible ticket of Adams and Pinckney was put in place on May 3. Less than a week later, Hamilton made his intentions clear by telling his friend Theodore Sedgwick that he would do all he could to oppose Adams, whom he described as "unfit" for office. Hamilton went so far as to confess that he would rather let Jefferson win than publicly support Adams; either man, he believed, would "sink" the government.[77]

Adams was fully aware of Hamilton's efforts to undermine him. The second president was self-righteous and hard to love, but he was also uncomfortable resorting to political machinations. His well-earned hatred for Hamilton, however, compelled him to take some action. As news of the ticket was announced, Adams dismissed two of his disloyal cabinet officers, Secretary of State Timothy Pickering and Secretary of War James McHenry, both of whom were confidants of Hamilton. The Federalist Party was unraveling, as internal bickering and outright backstabbing divided its members.[78]

Long before the election of 1800 resulted in a tie between Jefferson and Burr, there were solid hints that the next president would be decided by a backroom deal. Even before the New York election returns were known, rumors circulated of an unexpected alliance being struck between Jefferson and Adams. In this improbable construction, Adams was to be kept in office by a group of moderates from both parties, with the understanding that Jefferson would succeed him after four years, fully supported by that same collection of moderates. In preparation for the transition, Adams would appoint to his cabinet men whom Jefferson approved. One such rumor put Burr in the middle, brokering the deal. No such thing was contemplated by either Adams or Jefferson, of course, but that did not stop Samuel Smith of Maryland from making believers out of some of Adams's allies.[79]

Smith was a Republican congressman, and he deeply desired to negotiate this kind of agreement. He met with Adams's secretary of war, Benjamin Stoddert, wondering out loud about the possibility of a secret alliance. An eager politician mostly unknown to history, the interloper Smith embraced his "fifteen minutes of fame" as a potential kingmaker. Though he made no headway with Stoddert, he would subsequently play a key role in resolving the tie between Jefferson and Burr.

Burr spent summer and fall electioneering. Not only did his uncle accompany him on his trip through New England; Theodosia joined him as well. He met with the governor of Rhode Island, Arthur Fenner, who convinced him that his state would give some of its electoral votes to Jefferson. This information proved wrong, but it revealed the infectious optimism shared by many Republicans after the successful campaign in New York. Early on, New Jersey appeared likely to vote Republican. In September, the chairman of the Jersey Republican meeting, Major General Joseph Bloomfield, gave a rousing address to supporters, published in the *Aurora,* that celebrated the ticket of Jefferson and Burr; this included praise for Burr's "great talents, his republican principles, and solicitude to preserve the independence of his county." He was to be considered "inferior to no man in America."[80]

Yet New Jersey, like Rhode Island, proved a disappointment. Burr was particularly troubled by the result in Rhode Island, and penned apologetic letters to Vice President Jefferson and John Taylor of Caroline, making sure his Virginia allies knew that he had not intentionally misled them.[81]

In fact, except for the rout of the Federalists in New York, most states followed predictable patterns. Jefferson and Burr swept the South and West; Maryland split its votes. New England went Federalist, and Pennsylvania gave 8 votes to the Republicans, 7 to the administration ticket. The whole process took until the end of November, at which point three candidates, Adams, Jefferson, and Burr had 65 votes each. Pinckney trailed them by just 1 vote. The entire election now fell on South Carolina, which did not convene its legislature until early December, and several of the electors still appeared undecided.[82]

Initially, Hamilton had hoped that the Carolinas would put Pinckney in the presidential chair: if the electors divided their votes between Jefferson and Pinckney in South Carolina, and Pinckney got a few votes from North Carolina, it might have happened that way. But by December, acting impetuously, Hamilton made any kind of Federalist victory impossible. (In the process, he destroyed his credibility within his own party.) The low point came in October, when he published a vicious pamphlet entitled *Letter from Alexander Hamilton, Concerning the Public Conduct and Character of John Adams, Esq., President of the United States*. It appears that he had originally intended to distribute his attack on Adams covertly in South Carolina, hoping to sway the state's electors at the last minute. But his plan backfired when knowledge of the pamphlet's existence escaped his immediate circle: an industrious Republican, most likely John Beckley, got his hands on a copy of the diatribe, and published extracts in several prominent Republican newspapers. Hamilton was then compelled to release it nationally.[83]

So South Carolina was just as crucial a contest as that which had taken place in New York earlier. Although the Republicans had won the assembly election there as well, signs pointed to new problems: some of the electors hinted that they would not vote a straight party ticket. It was rumored that these men had approached General Pinckney with a secret deal for a Jefferson-Pinckney ticket. Next, it was said, Pinckney weighed and rejected this proposition. Could the South Carolina Republicans hold together? At this moment, anyway, they seemed willing to break with their northern allies and put two southerners at the head of the federal government.[84]

Given these tensions, the local Charleston newspaper, edited by Peter Freneau, published a strong endorsement of Burr, urging electors not to simply vote for Pinckney because he "happens to belong to your own state!" This article provided a detailed and laudatory biography of Burr; it celebrated the "Manhattan company" for freeing the "long enslaved . . . poorer class of citizens," and praised Burr's qualifications for office. He was both a man of the Enlightenment and a man of action:

> *Endowed with a mind vast, liberal and comprehensive, America owes [owns] not a citizen more fitted than col. Burr, to be placed at the head of her government. With an energy and decision of character peculiar to himself, while other men are debating, he resolves; and while they resolve, he acts.*

The article was signed "A Rice Planter." It may have been the work of Joseph Alston, soon to be Burr's son-in-law—or maybe Joseph's father, William Alston, who was one of the most prominent planters in South Carolina. Whoever wrote the article knew Burr personally. But the article revealed something more: a conscious effort was underway to fashion Burr into a more attractive candidate and sell him to southern voters. It was his character—described here in more masculine words than were typically associated with Jefferson himself—that ostensibly raised Burr's stature and warranted trust. Personal style mattered nearly as much as party affiliation; both were being used to overcome sectional prejudices at this critical moment.[85]

In the middle of December, when the votes of South Carolina went to Jefferson and Burr, the final tally still could not be made. The results in Kentucky and Tennessee were not yet known. Conflicting news spread: one report said that Burr would gain 4 votes in Kentucky and Jefferson only 3; another source had it on "good authority" that Jefferson had won by 1 vote. Supposedly, Kentucky elector Major Scott held the election in his hands. Either he had voted for Jefferson and Pinckney because of a "personal dislike to Mr. Burr," or he was heard "to say, nay to swear, that he would not vote for Mr. Jefferson upon any account." The country waited and wondered.[86]

In the midst of all the confusion, Jefferson sent Burr a curious letter. He wrote from Washington—the center of the storm—informing his running mate that the Republicans had won. His information was incomplete: he had heard that three friendly states were expected to drop 1 vote for Burr, but that would still leave Burr with 4 or 5 more votes than Adams. Jefferson went on to repeat the recent rumor that some "highflying" Federalists planned to subvert the election, if it turned out that the two Republicans had an equal number of votes. If this were the case, the Federalists could put off the final decision (in the House of Representatives) past the scheduled March 4, 1801, inauguration date.[87]

Jefferson dreaded a tie. He wrote with hesitation. He flattered Burr, regretting the "chasm" in his plans if events made it such that Burr would not be able to serve in his cabinet. His cabinet? What was the presumptive president saying to his future vice president? Perhaps he was reflecting on the unimportance of the vice presidency, the position he himself still occupied. Or perhaps he was preparing Burr for electoral defeat, assuring him that he would not be overlooked if somehow Adams still ended up with more votes. It is also possible that Jefferson was simply trying to prod Burr into agreeing not to compete with him, if the election did in fact end in a tie.[88]

Jefferson was covering all possibilities. He did not wish to alienate Burr (or his New York supporters). He adroitly appealed to Burr's sense of decorum and propriety, insisting that he took no part in "dropping votes intentionally"—he stayed apart from this activity out of a sense of "decency." And he observed that, as vice president, Burr would be an integral part of his administration.[89]

A week later, Burr answered. There was no need to worry, he assured Jefferson, "if the Votes should come out alike for us." He spoke for himself as well as his "personal friends," who were "perfectly informed of my wishes on the subject and can never think of diverting a single vote from you." Significantly, he agreed to "cheerfully abandon the office of vice president if it shall be thought that I can be more useful in any active station." And he concluded his letter with a promise: "my whole time and attention shall be unceasingly employed to render your Administration grateful and honorable to our country and to yourself." Jefferson had his concession, and a solid declaration of loyalty.[90]

When the results were known, Jefferson had 73 electoral votes; Burr 73; Adams 65; Pinckney 64; Jay 1. The election would have to be decided in the House of Representatives. Many southerners were furious when they learned of the tie; one angry Republican wrote James Madison that the Virginians had erred in being "*too honest*" rather than ensuring victory to their favorite.[91]

The election tie created an unimaginable dilemma. Symbolizing the ironic conjoining of the two names, the *Aurora* reported that upon the news of the Republican victory, a woman in Newport, Rhode Island, gave birth to twins. To honor the occasion, the two infants were christened on Christmas Day, "the eldest Thomas Jefferson, the younger Aaron Burr." The tie made Jefferson and Burr political "twins," bound by fate. Unlike the Newport twins, they were not joined by any "involuntary attachment"; they could not read each other's minds. Jefferson and Burr responded to the crisis differently, receiving dissimilar reports (some accurate, some grossly distorted). Neither candidate had complete control over the outcome. Both had to depend on others to carry out their "wishes," as Burr confided to Jefferson. Yet even news entrusted to "personal friends" might be manipulated or misconstrued. So, in addition to the "highflying" Federalists, Republicans also had to battle what Burr called "phantoms," owing in large measure to sectional distrust that threatened to divide the party.[92]

Northern and southern Republicans had been held together by a tenuous compact since the beginning of the campaign. Burr had joined the Republican ticket with one clear stipulation. In agreeing to run for vice president in May, he had conveyed serious misgivings to James Nicholson. As Nicholson explained it, Burr was unwilling to seek national office without southern concurrence, recalling 1796, "in which he was certainly ill used by Virg[ini]a & no[rth] Carolina." Their wasted votes for George Clinton and Samuel Adams had only embarrassed Burr. He insisted on party loyalty this time, asking "if assurances can be given that the southern states will act fairly." On the same day, Hannah Gallatin echoed her father's warning: "Burr says he has no confidence in the Virginians; they once deceived him, and they are not to be trusted."[93]

Burr voiced his concerns directly in a letter to the Virginian John Taylor of Caroline on October 23. "After what happened in the last election (*et tu Brute!*)," he railed, "it is most obvious that I should not choose to be trifled with." Over and over, he had made plain what he expected from southerners; he refused to be humiliated a second time. He had spelled out his code of ethics and honor in writing to Jefferson on the success of the earlier New York elections, and expected the same rules to apply to the national campaign: there should be "no indecency, no unfairness, no personal abuse," he insisted at that time. That was Burr, in 1800.[94]

Nonetheless, the threat of betrayal loomed over the entire election. Over the next two months, Republicans confronted a variety of Federalist plots, some real, others imagined, and all requiring a response. It became impossible to know what the truth was, or whose word could be trusted. There were temptations to make backroom deals, and that dealmaking, unfortunately, was in the hands of middlemen like Samuel Smith—proxies for the candidates—whose motives were unclear.

"I SHALL ACT IN DEFIANCE OF ALL TIMID TEMPORIZING PROJECTS"

Even before the votes were officially counted on February 11, it was clear to everyone in Washington that Jefferson and Burr had tied for the presidency. And it was just as obvious that election guidelines no longer matched political practice. The Constitution made no allowances for a two-party system or for any party at all: it simply dictated that the person with the most electoral votes became president, and the second place finisher was awarded the vice presidency. If a tie occurred, the House was to "immediately" choose between the candidates, voting not as individuals, but as state delegations—each state had 1 vote. A majority (nine states at this time) was needed to confirm the House's choice.

Partisanship seriously compromised what should have been a straight-forward procedure. The election could not be resolved without Federalist cooperation, and this gave them the upper hand in any negotiations. Theodore Sedgwick reported as much to Hamilton, observing that the tie "rendered the Jacobins in the House more civil in their attentions than I have ever known them." Given the current composition of the legislature, Jefferson could muster at most eight states, one shy of the required majority.[95]

By voting for Burr, Federalists quickly realized that they could bar Jefferson from the presidency. If they failed to convince a few Republicans to switch sides, they could simply refuse to elect any president at all, opening the door for an interregnum (and Federalist) government to conduct the nation's business until another election was held. The Constitution was ambiguous; it did not list the precise steps to be followed if no one was elected. Rumors spread that the Federalists aimed to pass a law allowing for the president pro-tem of the Senate, secretary of state, or the chief justice of the Supreme Court to act as chief executive while the government was in limbo. New York senator Gouverneur Morris informed Hamilton that a serious effort was underway to "cast about" for a successor. The possibilities seemed endless. One writer to the *Washington Federalist* proposed that if neither Jefferson nor Burr was elected, then Adams and Jefferson should be left in charge as if the election had never taken place.[96]

The Republicans found themselves in an unenviable position. They could wait and see what the Federalists might do, or they could try to counteract, or even preempt, them. The first step was to try to persuade certain Federalists of the hopelessness of their scheme. In December 1800, when Burr wrote to Jefferson, he sent a similar letter to Samuel Smith, asking his "proxy" to declare his sentiments to others in Washington. He made it a strict point of honor: "every Man who knows me ought to know that I should utterly disclaim all competition," and to the conniving House members he was specific: "Be assured that the federal party can entertain no wish for such an exchange." Smith's publication of Burr's renunciation did little to curb Federalist machinations. Burr had no choice in the affair, some of them dared to argue, because he had a duty to comply with the will of the people (which was now embodied in the House vote). Others scoffed at his disavowal, dismissing it as a ploy that cleverly disguised his actual ambition.[97]

Second-guessing Burr was nothing new. Even before the election tie, cynical Federalists had convinced themselves that Burr was capable of changing sides. Some hoped that he would "see the light," realizing that the Virginians would never truly embrace him. Others thought he was "on the market," ready to sell his talents to whichever party had the best chance of winning.[98]

Many Federalists arrogantly assumed, as Robert Troup did, that they knew Burr's motives better than he did. Senator Robert Goodloe Harper of South Carolina took this kind of self-serving reasoning to a new level during the election crisis. To his colleagues in the House, he presented himself as "an intimate friend of Mr. Burr." He advised his fellow Federalists to support Burr fully, requiring no assurances as to the policies to be pursued in a Burr administration. On December 24, Harper sent Burr a curious letter, urging him to do nothing; he warned him not to acknowledge "overtures" from members of the House, and to "keep the game perfectly in [his] hand." He even told Burr not to answer his letter. Burr's actual intentions apparently mattered little to the overconfident Harper.[99]

While some Federalists pretended to know his views, and others thought Burr would feel obliged to work with them, many, like Massachusetts congressman Harrison Gray Otis, gloated over the chance to "sow" among the Republicans the "seeds of a mortal division." Voting for Burr would humiliate Jefferson. Initially, Hamilton agreed, confiding to Adams's secretary of the treasury, Oliver Wolcott, that it might prove useful to "lure" Burr into a compromising situation that would ultimately prove difficult for him, that is, to "lay the foundation of dissention between two chiefs." But for those Federalists who seriously considered putting Burr in the presidential chair, a darker plot emerged: that of converting the imposter president into a puppet prince. Federalists could lose the election and yet be the power behind the throne, taking advantage of the fact that Burr would be a weak leader without popular support. Theodore Sedgwick told his son that Burr "will not be able to administer the government without the aid of the federalists & this aid he cannot obtain unless his administration is federal." Between Sedgwick and Harper, there was no rational perspective as to what Burr himself might have thought.[100]

In defense of Burr, Federalists made two arguments. The first was simply that they should vote for him because he was *not* Jefferson; that is, he did not strike them as a deist, a theorist, or a democrat, and most important, he was not a Virginian. The second argument in favor of Burr was that he impressed many Federalists as a "vigorous practical man," who combined "courage" with "generosity," as Gouverneur Morris described the view of his House colleagues. Here again, Burr's appeal was his military record and his balance of masculine traits.[101] One article in the *Washington Federalist* celebrated him as a man of action, with a "strong and comprehensive mind," who was "neither timid nor wavering" but "firm, intrepid and energetic." As one who never "shrank from the post of danger," he was "equally fitted for service in the field, and in the public counsels." Burr's well-defined masculinity was preferred to Jefferson's effete pose as a draftsman:

> [Burr] *never penned a declaration of independence, I admit;—but he has done much more—he has* engraved that declaration in capitals *with the point of his sword: It is yet* legible *on the* walls of Quebeck. *He* fought *for that independency, for which Mr.* Jefferson *only* wrote. *He has gallantly exposed his life in support of that declaration and for the* protection *of its* penn-man; *He has been* liberal *of his* blood, *while Mr.* Jefferson *has only* hazarded *his* ink.

Burr had the guts to take the field in order to protect weaker men like Jefferson who sat scribbling at their desks. Burr was an officer and a gentleman who possessed "urbanity of manners," whereas the Virginian was but a "cool, dark, designing theorist." According to the Federalist definition of right to rule, Burr easily bested the Republican standard-bearer.[102]

When Hamilton realized that House Federalists were more than willing to elect Burr, he was startled and dashed off frantic letters to all the key congressional leaders. Horrified that Burr might become the head of his party, he pleaded with Theodore Sedgwick and others: "For heaven's sake let not the Federalist party be responsible for the elevation of this Man." His worst nightmare seemed to be unfolding. Burr's favorable press must have infuriated him. How could it not? He was being praised as an energetic statesman and a bona fide military hero, in terms that reflected Hamilton's image of *himself*.[103]

His repetitious letters were filled with outrageous, and occasionally, petty charges. He conjured all the Federalist demons, calling Burr an "American Cataline" and a revolutionary fanatic who "talked perfect Godwinism." Cataline was the greatest of Roman conspirators, a familiar figure to eighteenth-century readers, whose unspeakable crimes included incest and homicide—murdering his wife, sister, and son. William Godwin was married to the feminist Mary Wollstonecraft. He was a supporter of the French revolutionaries and a ready symbol of sexual equality and social leveling; his writings critiqued the established political and religious order with equal fervor. In these comparisons, Hamilton was accusing Burr of being unbalanced, of lacking moral values, of behaving as a political chameleon, and of despising democracy, while playing it for all it was worth.[104]

Hamilton went on to paint Burr as a man of "extreme & irregular ambition—that is selfish to a degree which excludes all social affections & that he is decidedly profligate." He wanted his traditional allies to view Burr as a man without love of country, family, or society, an unscrupulous despot in the making, whose main goal was nothing less than to "establish supreme Power in his own person." As the ultimate narcissist ("he loves nothing but himself"), Burr was unconstrained; as a "bankrupt" and "voluptuary," his unquenchable ambition had no limits. In predictably hysterical tones, Hamilton charged that Burr would rush to war with Great Britain, if it suited his whims, signing a "death warrant" for the nation. If members of the House believed they could tame Burr, he declared, they were sadly mistaken. Burr would surround himself with the "worst men of all parties," courting the "young and profligate," all the while "laughing in his sleeve" at those who imagined they could rein him in. Lest they doubt him, Hamilton reminded his colleagues that he was an authority on Burr; his wrathful words were meant, somehow, to be understood as a fair and balanced sketch of Burr's character. Amazingly, there are still chroniclers of the election of 1800 who rely on Hamilton's letters as authentic and reasoned artifacts.[105]

Nor could Hamilton resist a few callous cuts at Burr's touted abilities.

He dismissed his rival's military record as undeserved, claiming that Burr had resigned his commission "at a critical period of the war," feigning illness; afterwards he was "seen in his usual health." His "understanding was overrated," Hamilton went on. Burr was "far more cunning than wise," and he had never shown any "proofs of those solid abilities which characterize the statesman."[106]

A series of letters shows Hamilton's mind at work. He dispatched a letter to the New York patrician Gouverneur Morris (changing little in his formulaic harangue), forgetting that Morris knew Burr's character, and was not easily fooled. Morris had already sent one of his own to Hamilton, noting perceptively how odd it was that the Federalists seemed so willing "to support a man (unjustly perhaps) they consider as void of principle." The key words here are the parenthetical "unjustly perhaps." By saying that he doubted those who diminished Burr's character, Morris showed that he knew the difference between a fish story and the real Burr.[107]

Hamilton's response is revealing. He could hardly deny what the perceptive Morris reckoned to be true. So he wrote back: "If there was a man in the world I ought to hate it is Jefferson. With Burr I have always been personally well." This letter has often been quoted to prove that Hamilton's evaluation of Burr was unbiased, and that his preference for Jefferson was somehow based on a fair comparison of the two candidates. But what it actually demonstrates is Hamilton's willingness to use any ploy to persuade the skeptical Morris. Furthermore, Hamilton's fierce opposition to Burr was no different than his maneuvering behind the scenes to defeat Adams—and his almost identical statement (before the tie) that he actually wished Jefferson to win rather than having to lift a finger to help the sitting president get reelected. In both cases, Hamilton preferred to do battle with Jefferson, as head of the contending party, rather than to compete for the leadership role in his own party. If the Federalists elevated Burr, then Hamilton faced the prospect of losing control of the Federalists both nationally and locally. In Hamilton's mind, having a rival within his own party, and from his own state, was far more dangerous than a Jefferson presidency. It meant the end of his political career.[108]

Yet all of Hamilton's fussing had little impact. No one shared his dire outlook. John Marshall politely thanked him for his "impartial" account of Burr, but still refused to do anything to help Jefferson. James A. Bayard of

Maryland interpreted Hamilton's rant as nothing more than a concern with Burr's "want of probity," a defect (common to politicians at this time) hardly serious enough to disqualify him. Hamilton's overwrought conspiratorial portrait of Burr seemed ludicrous to the South Carolinian John Rutledge: If Burr attempted a coup, as Hamilton was predicting, the government would quickly stop him. And as for Jefferson, Rutledge reasoned, little could be done to curtail his "*subversion*" [i.e., undoing Federalist policies], as long as it remained within the law. Only Sedgwick's duplicity may have exceeded Hamilton's: perhaps Burr was "ambitious—selfish—profligate," yet character flaws were irrelevant. All that mattered, said the Massachusetts Federalist, was that Burr's election could be used to destroy the Republican Party. For Sedgwick, at least, sowing distrust and dissension among the enemy was worth the risk of making a profligate man president.[109]

Meanwhile, Republicans were angry and confused, uncertain what response would effectively avert an "usurpation." Jefferson was appalled that Federalists might refuse to name a president, leaving the government without a head and creating what he called an "abyss" that would undermine the nation's safety and survival. In the *National Intelligencer,* the Republican newspaper in Washington, one writer echoed this theme, contending that the Federalists had to make a choice and that Jefferson, embodying the true will of the people, could be the only valid victor; if they refused to abide by that will, the same writer warned, the federal government would dissolve on March 4, returning to its original form (pre-1787) as a confederation of independent states. Congressman Joseph H. Nicholson fumed that if the Federalists persisted, "Virginia would instantly proclaim herself out of the Union." Talk circulated that the Virginia and Pennsylvania militias were ready to march on Washington and forcibly remove any pretender whom the Federalists might put in the president's chair.[110]

Such were the scenarios that colored public discourse in the winter of 1800–01. Republicans at once brandished their swords and indulged in fantasies of their own victimization. The *Philadelphia Aurora* prophesied that the Federalists would soon have blood on their hands, for their real intent was to assassinate Jefferson, and then march on the poorly defended capital with 70,000 armed soldiers. After a mysterious fire broke out in the Treasury Department in January, only two months after a fire had damaged the War Department, some cried arson. Rumors quickly spread that valuable state papers had been torched to conceal some dark secret of the Adams administration.[111]

When Albert Gallatin arrived in Washington in early January 1801, he immediately perceived just how unhealthy and claustrophobic the city was. Nearly all the elected officials inhabited the same eight boardinghouses near the Capitol. Gallatin roomed at Conrad & McMunn's, as did Jefferson, Samuel Smith, and other Republicans. He wrote his wife, partly tongue-in-cheek, that "being all thrown together in a few boarding houses without hardly any other society then [sic] ourselves, we are not likely to be either very moderate politicians or to think of anything but politics. A few indeed drink and some gamble, but the majority drink nought but politics, and by not mixing with men of different or more moderate sentiments, they inflame one another." Whether or not they were naturally alarmist, Republicans were at this moment feeding on their own fears.[112]

Gallatin himself was caught up in the frenzy. He began to think that the Federalists might delay electing a president in order to force a new election— an election that would be rigged so that the Republicans could not possibly win. On January 22, he wondered in a letter to his wife: "Will they usurp at once the Presidential Powers?" Would they try the "overthrow of our constitution" and incite a civil war? Twelve days earlier, suspecting something of the kind, James Madison had decided that it was too dangerous to stand idly by and wait for the Federalists to act. On January 10, he proposed that Jefferson and Burr issue a joint proclamation, calling the new legislature into session for the purpose of selecting the president. This aggressive, extraconstitutional measure was endorsed by both Jefferson and Burr.[113]

Madison's plan may have been overreaching, but some Republicans were altogether too pliable. One Republican plan that made the rounds in Washington would have made Burr president and Jefferson vice president for one year, after which a new election would be held. Another plan called for Burr to resign before balloting began in the House, awarding Jefferson the presidency; but it would have made outgoing President Adams his successor's vice president, leaving Burr with no office at all. (Samuel Smith would make this proposal to Burr, which Burr flatly rejected.)[114]

Gallatin could support neither plan. Upon careful reflection, he concluded that the best course for Republicans was to remain firm, for he supposed the Federalists to be bluffing. Gallatin figured that the defeated party was hoping that the Republican strategists' "imbecility" would lead them to "yield . . . rather than run any risk." That is, if the Republicans' fear got the better of them, they might be willing to hand over the presidency or vice presidency, or make some other dangerous compromise, in order to avoid further turmoil or outright civil war, even though they had won the election.[115]

Throughout the election crisis, Burr stayed away from Washington. On February 2, 1801, Theodosia married Joseph Alston in Albany. The two had been courting for the past year, exchanging lively letters, even debating the rationale for marrying young. Alston, who was twenty-one, belonged to one of the wealthiest plantation families in South Carolina, and Theodosia may have seen this marriage as a way to rescue her father's desperate finances. But it was never simply about money. Alston had briefly attended Princeton, and then studied law. He had met Theodosia while traveling in the North. Alston struck some as arrogant, and as a young man in a position of social authority, he undoubtedly was. To the sister of one marital prospect whom he had rejected, he appeared the "most intolerable mortal I ever beheld." But by all accounts, he adored his eighteen-year-old wife and respected his father-in-law. His courtship letters, in which he mingled talk of mutual self-improvement with romantic imagery, show that he admired his wife's intelligence. Thus, Burr had more on his mind than the election, at least for part of the winter of 1800–01.[116]

But Burr never lost touch with his colleagues in Washington. He received reports from Jefferson, Gallatin, and Smith, and even agreed to spend a few days with Smith in Philadelphia in early January. On December 29, in advance of their meeting, he wrote Smith of his anger toward certain unnamed Republicans whose "jealousy and distrust" of him had caused them to query him about resigning should he be made president. Just two weeks earlier, he had told Smith in no uncertain terms that he "should utterly disclaim all competition" with Jefferson for the top spot on the ticket. Now, he was annoyed that it was not only necessary to repeat himself, but that he was expected to resign under *any* circumstance that threatened what Republicans were calling a Federalist "usurpation." House Federalists might still create a deadlock by refusing to give Jefferson a majority; in failing to elect a president, they could then appoint a temporary chief executive until the next election.[117]

Burr considered the unnamed Republicans' anxious appeal to him to resign as "unnecessary, unreasonable and impertinent," because he did not believe the Federalists could succeed in manipulating the process to any such degree as they feared. He made his feelings clear to a Republican confidant, William Eustis, when he noted that the Federalists had chosen to completely ignore even his most decisive disavowal. They had decided to do what they wanted, regardless of his wishes, so why issue a further disavowal? The Federalists were not united, Burr insisted, and "cannot probably unite" to achieve their aim of substituting him for Jefferson, the man who the Republicans uniformly intended for the presidency. Why, as he had said to Smith, should he have to put up with those who, after supporting him for vice president, now suddenly feared he might have loftier aspirations? He was insulted. And he was not in a forgiving mood.[118]

Burr was sick and tired of the southerners who were suddenly intent on impugning his motives. But it was Smith's obstructive behavior that troubled him even more than southerners' capriciousness. Burr now sensed that Smith wanted him to resign, just as much as some of the other panicky Republicans. No "democrat" should "for a Moment doubt about the line of Conduct I should pursue," he insisted, cautioning Smith against "phantoms" and urging him to show "firmness and Vigor." Smith's gullibility made him an easy mark for Federalist manipulators, prompting Burr finally to rail at him: "You seem to believe every lie you hear." Though he probably was unaware of Smith's earlier machinations, Burr should have been wary of his fellow Republican before this anyway. Recall that Smith had at one point recommended a Jefferson-Adams compromise ticket. At this crucial moment, there was a simple reason why Burr and Smith were at odds: Smith was willing to compromise Burr's future, and Burr was not.[119]

But Smith persisted. When they met on January 3, 1801, the Marylander still wanted Burr to issue a strong public statement declaring that he would resign to break any deadlock in the House, if a president was not in place by March 4, inauguration day. While Smith was advising Burr to sacrifice himself, no one of consequence was—not Jefferson, not Madison, not Gallatin. In fact, the Republican leadership was entirely pleased with Burr's response to these pressures. Gallatin wrote to his wife on January 15 that Burr had no intention whatsoever of satisfying the Federalists. He "*sincerely* opposed the design," said Gallatin, "and will go [to] *any lengths* to prevent its execution." Earlier in the month, Jefferson told his daughter that "the Federalists were confident at first they could debauch Col. B.," and then he reassuringly added: "His conduct has been honorable and decisive, and greatly embarrasses them." George Clinton, hardly inclined to trust his old rival, was convinced of Burr's honorable intentions after a personal conversation with him. On January 13, he wrote his nephew, DeWitt Clinton: "I have reason to believe from Burr's explicit declaration to me that he will not countenance a Competition for the Presidency with Mr. Jefferson."[120]

As the crisis escalated, rumors quickly spread that Burr had double agents in Washington, secretly promoting his presidency over Jefferson. Many historians have assumed that Burr and his agents were jockeying among Republicans and Federalists, open to a deal of some sort. But no reliable evidence of this exists. One New York congressman caught in the web of gossip was Edward Livingston. It is true that Burr trusted Livingston and bade him carry a message to Washington, but the message was the same one that Burr had made perfectly clear to Smith: Republicans must stand firm, and he would never comply with the "proposed Usurpation." So where did the idea of Livingston as Burr's double agent originate? Not surprisingly, it was Hamilton who concocted a story that Livingston was cornering the New York House delegation, and convincing them to vote for Burr.[121]

The same can be said for the other supposed double agents of Burr, and those such as James Linn of New Jersey, accused of becoming a turncoat. Linn, a Republican congressman, was said to have been easily tempted to sell out Jefferson, though he never cast a vote for Burr. Meanwhile, Samuel Smith and David Ogden of New York were meant to be haunting Congress and the boardinghouses, looking for a way to make Burr president. These were real people, but none of them in fact acted as a double agent of Burr. Most remarkable was the charge that Samuel Smith was one of these agents, given that every piece of evidence shows a growing distrust between them. Burr doubted Smith's ability to function as an honest intermediary, let alone his agent.[122]

It is just as far-fetched to suggest that Burr would abandon the Republican Party at this moment, given the decisive role he had undertaken in transforming New York into a Republican state. He would have lost his base, loyal supporters he had acquired over the years, especially through his labors in the state assembly. No politician could maintain his national stature without a strong local following in his own state. Does it really make sense that Burr would sacrifice everything he had worked for? He was still only forty-six, and in eight years he would be in line for the presidency.

After balloting in the House (to break the tie) began on Wednesday, February 11, 1801, Burr, in New York, wrote to Gallatin, who was in Washington: "I shall act in defiance of all timid temporizing projects." Livingston, meanwhile, wrote from Washington to Matthew Livingston Davis in New York: "Our city shall never be disgraced by any temporizing plan or acquiescence in usurpation." Burr's and Livingston's matching vocabulary was no accident. For Burr, it was a matter of honor that his position be rightly understood and that the Republicans make no compromises. And *that* was his loftiest ambition at this perilous moment in American politics.[123]

There were nineteen ballots read and recorded on Wednesday. Congress remained in session long past midnight. The *Aurora* reported: "It is ludicrous to see some of them running with anxiety from the committee rooms, with their nightcaps on." The deadlock remained unbroken: eight states for Jefferson, six for Burr, and two states with split delegations. Three more ballots were taken over the next two days, without any different result. Another observer described the character of these proceedings as "a pontifical enclave." Finally, on Saturday, excitement rocked the legislative chamber. That day, Federalist James Bayard of Delaware resolved to try to reach an understanding with the Republicans, approaching John Nicholas of Virginia: If Jefferson would agree to continue to strengthen the navy and, by the by, maintain a particular friend of Bayard's in his appointed office, Bayard—who had cast his vote for Burr since Wednesday, and was the sole representative from his tiny state—would withhold his vote on the next ballot, and other Federalists would follow, making Jefferson president.[124]

Nicholas told Bayard that he believed Jefferson would comply. But he qualified that he did not speak for Jefferson. Because Bayard did not receive the assurance he wanted, he turned next to Samuel Smith. Smith, the self-anointed middleman, said he would talk to Jefferson. He did, and then approached Bayard on Monday morning, February 16, with the following:

Jefferson had "authorized" him to agree to Bayard's terms. Later, Smith denied he had ever used the word "authorized." But Bayard came away from their conversation without any further doubts, and he delivered the presidency to Jefferson. He did not act alone, for after Bayard agreed to withhold his decisive vote, other delegations followed suit. Maryland and Vermont Federalists withheld their votes, which enabled their Republican members to vote in Jefferson. The South Carolina delegation, like Delaware's, abstained because it contained only Federalists. Thus, Jefferson carried ten of the sixteen state delegations, Burr four, with the two abstentions. After thirty-six ballots, on Tuesday, February 17, the long contest was over. In downtown Philadelphia, Republicans paraded in a sled, playing fifes and drums, and hoisting flags featuring mottos: "Jefferson the friend of the People" and "Jefferson and Burr."[125]

Four days after Jefferson was inaugurated, James Bayard wrote a letter to Alexander Hamilton, admitting why he had acted as he had: "The means existed of electing Burr, but they required his cooperation. . . . He might have secured a majority of the states. He will never have another chance of being President." Even more tellingly, to the collector of customs in Wilmington, Delaware, whose job he was trying to preserve, Bayard wrote: "Our opposition [to Jefferson] was continued till it was demonstrated that Burr could not be brought in and even if he could, he meant to come in as a Democrat." And to his father-in-law, Bayard had complained that Burr actually worked to stop the Federalists: "We have been counteracted in the whole business by letters he had written." So much for trying to influence the mind of Aaron Burr.[126]

Aaron Burr!

AT length this Cataline stands confessed in all his *villainy*—His *inveterate
hatred* of the Constitution of the United
States has long been displayed in one
steady, undeviating course of *hostility* to
every measure which the solid interests
of the Union demand—His *political per-
fidiousness and intrigues* are also now pretty generally known, and even his own
party have avowed their jealousy and
fear of a character, which, to great talents
adds the deepest dissimulation and an
entire devotion to self-interest, and self-
aggrandizement—But there is a new
TRAIT in this man's character, to be unfolded to the view of an *indignant public!*
—His *abandoned profligacy*, and the numerous unhappy wretches, who have fallen victims to this accomplished and but too successful *debauchee*, have indeed been long
known to those whom similar habits of
vice, or the amiable offices of humanity
have led to the wretched haunts of female
prostitution—But it is time to draw aside
the curtain in which he has thus far been
permitted to conceal himself by the for-
bearance of his enemies, by the anxious
interference of his friends, and much
more by his own crafty contrivances and
unbounded prodigality.

It is time to tear away the veil that
hides this monster, and lay open a scene
of misery, at which every heart must
shudder. Fellow Citizens, read a tale of
truth, which must harrow up your sensibility, and excite your keenest resentment.
It is, indeed, a tale of truth! and, but
for wounding, too deeply, the steady la-
cerated feelings of a parental heart, it could
be authenticated by all the formalities of
law.

I do not mean to tell you of the late
celebrated courtezan N——, nor U——,
nor S——, nor of half a dozen more
whom first his *intrigues* have *ruined*, and
his *satiated brutality* has afterwards thrown
on the town, the prey of disease, of infamy, and wretchedness—It is to a more
recent act, that I call your attention, and,
I hope it will create in every heart, the
same abhorrence with which mine is filled.

☞ When Mr. Burr last went to the
City of Washington about two months
ago, to take the oath of office, and his
seat in the august Senate of the U. S.—
he seduced the daughter of a respectable
tradesman there, and had the cruelty to
persuade her to forsake her native town,
her friends and family, and to follow him
to New York. She did so—and she is
now in keeping in Partition-st. Vice however, sooner or later meets its merited
punishment. Justice, though sometimes
slow, is sure. The villain has not long enjoyed this triumph over female weakness. The father of the girl has at length
after a laborious and painful search, found
out the author of his child's *ruin* and his
family's *dishonour*.—He is now in this city,
and vengeance will soon light on the guilty head——Fellow-Citizens, I leave you
to make your own comments on this complicated scene of misery and vice. I will
conclude with a single observation.—Is
that party at whose head is this monster,
who directs all their motions and originates all their nefarious schemes worthy
of your SUPPORT?

"Aaron Burr!" Widely distributed Federalist handbill that slanderously
attacks Burr for his sexual behavior in 1801

Chapter Seven

THE RUIN OF THE VICE PRESIDENT

I wish the Republicans throughout the Union would make up their mind. Do they eventually mean not to support Burr as your successor, when you shall think fit to retire? Do they mean not to support him at the next election for Vice-President?

—Albert Gallatin to Thomas Jefferson, 1801

In a Day or two will be published another pamphlet in which you . . . are to [be] proven part[y] to certain imaginary intrigues of mine. This knot of knaves cannot long hold together—they begin already to call each other lyars—the only truth they have uttered.

—Aaron Burr to Pierpont Edwards, 1802

Burr arrived in Washington on March 1, 1801, three days before Jefferson took the oath of office. On his trip to the Capitol, he met his daughter and new son-in-law in Baltimore. There, Burr was greeted by an adoring crowd and a discharge of sixteen cannon. A local committee addressed the incoming vice president, praising his patriotism for having disclaimed all competition with Jefferson. Burr graciously thanked the citizens of the city, and echoed what he had said during the election crisis: "No person could have supposed that I would have stepped in between the wishes of the people and the man whom they have looked up to."[1]

The inaugural was an informal affair. Jefferson, dressed in plain attire, had walked to the Capitol from his boardinghouse. There was no grand procession as there had been for Washington, and no fancy carriage as with Adams. Burr himself described the inauguration as "serene & temperate," with the large crowd displaying "great joy but no riot." His brief speech, which he described as "about three sentences," was ignored in the papers. In fact, the most telling gesture was that of Burr graciously offering his seat to the president-elect as Jefferson entered the Senate chamber. Few could have missed the symbolism: it marked a moment of closure to the election tie. The man intended for the vice presidency had saved the nation by honorably ceding the presidential chair to his Virginia running mate.[2]

Across the country, meanwhile, celebrations, some grand, some simple, took place on inauguration day. In a Philadelphia church, thankful parishioners sang a song written for the occasion, praising the "God of Life and Liberty" for helping to avert "a Nation's ruin." There, too, Republicans lifted their glasses to Burr, calling him the "enemy of Tories and traitors" and a "steadfast Republican." In one Pennsylvania oration, Burr was praised for his "capacious soul," his unparalleled role in winning the election, "whose active genius" made him "a suitable successor to the great and sagacious *Jefferson*." In New York City, festivities included a vibrant parade and accompanying band music; the backdrop of a nighttime pageant was lit by colored lamps, illuminating two hearts meant to symbolize the harmony that subsisted between Jefferson and Burr. Fireworks supplied the final entertainment, and one newspaper editor claimed that representations of Jefferson and Burr, "in colored fire," filled the sky.[3]

By the following year, however, everything had changed. New York Republicans joined the Federalists in a concerted campaign to destroy Burr's political reputation. His foremost critic was the English émigré James Cheetham, editor of the *American Citizen,* New York City's one Republican newspaper. But Cheetham did not act alone. His barrage of sleazy insinuations and crude insults was encouraged by DeWitt Clinton, a rising star among Republicans in the Empire State. To Burr's chagrin, he soon discovered that Jefferson condoned these attacks, refusing, when Burr asked him, to publicly defend his vice president. Why did Jefferson, secure in his office, decide to treat Burr as an outsider and exile him from the party leadership?

A "SLASHING WORK"

Washington City became the capital in 1800, just a year before Jefferson assumed the presidency. Barely a city at all, the rural, isolated town had few public buildings to boast of. The President's House (not yet known as the White House) was large and imposing, but it remained unfinished and sparsely furnished throughout Jefferson's two terms. It was flanked by two brick buildings, the Treasury Department to the east, and the offices for the State, War, and Navy Departments to the west. The Capitol stood half built; the foundation for its south wing had been laid, but inadequate funding stalled its construction. Congressmen grumbled over their cramped quarters, which only became worse as the House of Representatives increased in size in accordance with the 1800 census.[4]

The president was responsible for employing over 300 persons in 1802. Though Jefferson did not care for bureaucracy, nevertheless one of his first duties was to dole out federal patronage. Among the highly prized positions up for grabs were collectorships at the major ports, as a revenue collector's salary was often higher than that of the members of Jefferson's cabinet. The president adhered to two general principles in the first days of his administration: He would appoint his own cabinet (something Adams had failed to do by inheriting Washington's cabinet, and suffered for); and he would to set a new standard for federal appointments, by refusing to eliminate all but the most strident Federalists from the government rolls. As he powerfully phrased it in his inaugural address, "We are all Republicans; we are all Federalists."[5]

Jefferson aimed to accomplish the impossible—to heal the wounds caused by the intense and exceedingly malicious campaign just past, and to discourage the impulse for partisan revenge. Despite his fine words, however, a fierce battle over lucrative patronage posts sparked violent turf wars, and, not surprisingly, infighting among the Republicans themselves. Burr found himself in the middle of this wrangling for jobs. He did what he could to temper the situation he faced, endeavoring to uphold his stature as vice president while retaining his standing as New York's most powerful party leader.

At a special session of the Senate held on inauguration day, over which Burr presided, the Federalist-dominated body gave their blessing to James Madison as secretary of state, Henry Dearborn as secretary of war, Levi Lincoln as attorney general, and Chancellor Robert Livingston as minister to France. Dearborn and Lincoln were New England Republicans; they were chosen to demonstrate a tone of compromise, inclusiveness, and a distribution of power across sectional lines. Critics called them provincials with meager talents, proof that Jefferson was bent on surrounding himself with impressionable subordinates. Dearborn unquestionably knew Burr, insofar as both men had made the long, arduous expedition from Maine to Canada in 1775; yet we do not know whether they were at all close. Jefferson had a difficult time finding a suitable Republican to be secretary of the navy; Samuel Smith held the post temporarily until his brother, Robert, agreed to serve.[6]

Gallatin's appointment as secretary of the treasury was delayed until December. Given their past performance, Jefferson feared that the Federalists would reject his nomination. Once again, they attacked Gallatin as a dangerous foreigner. Angry newspaper editors called for the "jealous pride of Americans" to rise up against his appointment. To his wife, Gallatin wrote of his contentious nomination with a touch of humor, announcing that of the various cabinet nominees, the "most obnoxious to the other party, and the only one which I think will be rejected, is . . . a certain friend of yours." Any objection to Gallatin was, as Burr wrote to Samuel Smith, "absurd." With emphasis, Burr added: "No other man will ever have my Vote or influence." For him, it was Gallatin for Treasury, or no one.[7]

Rewarding the party faithful was a crucial concern of Burr's, and he considered it one of his most important duties as vice president. On March 17, he prepared a memorandum for Jefferson, listing his suggestions for appointments, not only for New York but for Connecticut and South Carolina as well. Noting that the New York posts had been approved by the Republicans of his state, he offered a short list of names, encompassing his trusted allies, David Gelston, John Swartwout, Matthew Livingston Davis, and Edward Livingston. Swartwout was made a U.S. marshal, and Livingston district attorney, that same month, while Gelston's more lucrative position as collector of customs was not made official until July.[8]

Burr watched over Connecticut as well. Jefferson's conciliatory approach would not work in this ultra-Federalist state. Pierpont Edwards played a leading role at this point, pleading with the president to take vigorous action to reshape the state's power structure. Removals were necessary, Edwards argued, to ensure the "confidence of the majority" of true Republicans who were disheartened by the administration's failure to reward them. Early on, Burr sent his uncle encouragement, feeling certain that he would be "satisfied with the Conduct of the administration." Jefferson must have listened to his vice president in this instance, for his uncle's dire warnings were taken seriously. The president agreed to drastic measures, conceding that in enemy territory, which Connecticut surely was, "a general sweep seems to be called for."[9]

New York was different. The Federalists were being voted out of office, and expected little in the way of patronage. Absent any Federalist challenge, conflict among the Clinton, Livingston, and Burrite Republicans renewed. Although he was the vice president of the United States, Burr could not permit himself to cede his interest in New York politics if he wanted to retain a power base there. His position in New York would be conditioned by his relationship with the president; that is, whether he possessed the power to deliver appointments, and his position within the administration would be decided, in some measure, by how well his faction bore up in the course of intrastate wrangling.

George Clinton was returned to the New York governor's chair in May 1801. This left state spoils in the hands of his self-satisfied and highly motivated nephew, DeWitt Clinton. The game was on. Jefferson took note of the Livingston and Burrite reaction to the Clintons' ascendancy, and knew that he could not remain neutral forever, or the Republicans would chew each other up. "We shall yield a little to their pressure," he wrote to a fellow Virginian, as he observed the New Yorkers in disarray, "but not more than appears absolutely necessary to keep them together." Jefferson may have sought to appease all factions, but given the small chance of success in securing harmony among them, he was an astute enough politician to realize that he would eventually have to play one faction off against the others, delicately trying to ensure that whatever happened, the majority of New York Republicans would remain in his camp.[10]

Burr, meanwhile, had made an uncharacteristic political mistake. In

February, he had thrown his support to Edward Livingston in the contest for mayor of New York City, thereby antagonizing DeWitt Clinton, who also wanted the job. Burr confidentially wrote to Livingston that he recognized he would never be forgiven for that decision. Thus, Burr soon found himself under attack by the Clintonians and a few stray Livingstons, who sought to undermine his relationship with Jefferson and ostracize his followers. Neither George Clinton nor Chancellor Livingston headed this assault, however; it was two of their ambitious underlings, DeWitt Clinton and John Armstrong, Livingston's brother-in-law, who joined forces to destroy Burr's career.[11]

Armstrong and DeWitt Clinton were an unlikely duo, but in many ways their united front reflected the unstable political climate in New York. Clinton, who was only thirty-two in 1801, made Burr look like an amateur when it came to intriguing for political power. He went from the influential council of appointment in Albany in 1801 (which decided all state patronage jobs) to the U.S. Senate in 1802; a year later, he would accept the coveted and highly lucrative post of mayor of New York after Edward Livingston's resignation. DeWitt Clinton applied the familiar tactic of divide and conquer: he kept the Livingstons at bay by gorging them with appointments, while he isolated the Burrites. Known as haughty and imperious, Clinton considered governing New York to be a family business—and he had no desire to share it with the sitting vice president. Burr was a major threat to Clinton: he was the only New Yorker with a truly national reputation.[12]

Armstrong's motives were less obvious. He had been a Federalist until 1798, and he acted like one. Diffident and aristocratic, and just two years younger than Burr, he inexplicably became a confidant of Jefferson's when he was sent to Washington in 1801 as senator from New York (Armstrong and Clinton were playing a kind of "musical chairs" with the Senate seat; Clinton replaced Armstrong in the Senate, then resigned to become mayor, and Armstrong resumed the seat in 1803). Living at the same boardinghouse as the incoming president, Armstrong was trusted enough that he was given the task of evaluating Vice President Burr's memoranda of suggested appointments. At first, Armstrong claimed that he liked Jefferson, but before long he was dismissing the new administration as one that lacked "vigor"—reflecting the "character of the man himself." Armstrong, it appeared, had no genuine loyalty to anyone. If Jefferson did indeed trust this fickle New Yorker, he made a thorough misjudgment.[13]

At best, Armstrong can be described as a spoiler, relishing the game of ruining Burr. This was not a new role for him: back in 1783, he had written the notorious "Newburgh Address," which severely criticized General Washington and aroused suspicions that a military coup was brewing in the Continental Army. It is also thought that Armstrong anonymously penned a series of satires against his brother-in-law, Chancellor Livingston, during the heated New York gubernatorial election of 1792. It is difficult to say whether sport or spite inspired him. At any rate, beginning in 1801, along with his erstwhile associate DeWitt Clinton, he spent his time in Washington trying, in his words, to "prostrate Burr and his ambition forever."[14]

Burr was not immediately abandoned by the Jefferson administration. It happened gradually over the first year of the president's first term. Burr found his position threatened in his home state in August, when the Council of Appointment, under DeWitt Clinton, doled out spoils to his followers and a select number of Livingston allies, conspicuously leaving the vice president's men high and dry. Even Robert Livingston, who had no reason to take Burr's side, found this treatment appalling, calling the younger Clinton's lopsided patronage gambit a "slashing work." At the same time, another controversy was brewing, when "secret Machinations," as Burr called them, were underway to deny Matthew Livingston Davis the post of naval officer, which was another highly sought after job, second-in-command behind collector of customs. Other New York Republicans were equally riled: James Nicholson sent his son-in-law Albert Gallatin a heated letter, insisting that he would not support Jefferson in the next election if Davis was not installed.[15]

In September, Matthew Livingston Davis took the unusual step of traveling to Monticello to appeal to the president in person. He arrived armed with recommendations from prominent New York Republicans. Burr admitted to Gallatin that Davis had been "goaded into this journey" by a "hundred friends," but he agreed that the matter was too important to be "left in suspense." Gallatin worried that the trip might antagonize Jefferson; nevertheless, he added his recommendation. Davis's effort was to no avail. The president gave him no encouragement, leaving the position empty until he finally appointed DeWitt Clinton's father-in-law, Samuel Osgood, in 1803.[16]

Burr still had his defenders. The most important was, unquestionably, Secretary Gallatin, who had grown alarmed by the machinations in New York and wrote Jefferson a provocative letter, in September 1801, in response to the controversy over Davis's appointment. What is striking about this letter is Gallatin's willingness to push and prod Jefferson about Burr, and the future of the party. Other than Madison, no one was quite so fearless (and uncensored) in voicing his concerns to Thomas Jefferson.

Wondering aloud, the trusted Gallatin asked the president point-blank: Do the Republicans "eventually mean not to support Burr as your successor, when you shall think fit to retire? Do they mean not to support him at the next election for Vice-President?" Anticipating Jefferson's response, he acknowledged that Madison was "the only one" who loomed as a desirable alternative; but being a Virginian, Madison could never run for vice president without inviting sectional jealousy. Gallatin understood Jefferson's plans for a succession. He simply wanted confirmation of the president's thought process, by which Burr had to be sacrificed—no matter what—if Secretary of State Madison was to have the way clear to move up the ranks to chief executive.[17]

Gallatin acknowledged that the election tie had hurt Burr. Not because he had tried to steal the election; it was rather the perception of "diffidence" toward him than anything more devious. The treasury secretary was baiting his president, saying that if the concerns raised in 1801 had been raised in 1800, "I would have been wise enough never to give my consent in favor of [Burr's] being supported last election as Vice-President." What Gallatin really wanted to know, and what the preceding statement neglected to ask, was whether the Virginians had merely concealed their distaste for Burr long enough to win the election. Or was their subsequent resentment toward Burr cooked up and exaggerated so as to prevent the New Yorker from wresting the presidency from Virginia? In either case, Gallatin made clear, any lingering uncertainty or indecision "will produce much embarrassment" for the Republican Party in the buildup to election year 1804. Gallatin was thinking ahead because he knew that Jefferson was thinking ahead.[18]

Gallatin was certain that Jefferson had not fully assessed the viciousness of New York state politics. His point was simply this: Vice President Burr was at this point the leader of a majority of New York Republicans, and the "selfish" and unrepresentative coalition of Clintonians and Living-stons, "who hate Burr," would sooner run the Republican Party into the ground than adhere to the principles that best represented Jefferson's de-mocracy. Gallatin trusted Burr's men far more than he trusted the circle of cronies swarming about Clinton or Armstrong. Furthermore, Chancellor Livingston, John Armstrong, and George Clinton all struck Gallatin as unremarkable—certainly when compared with Burr. The chancellor, Gall-atin wrote, "is in that State only a name, and there is something which will forever prevent [Armstrong] from having any direct influence with the people." These men were not real (or popular) democrats. Without men-tioning DeWitt Clinton, who had not yet achieved the stature he would later on, Gallatin observed that the aging Governor Clinton (four years older, and less healthy, than President Jefferson) was past his prime. Burr was the only genuine democratic leader in the fractious Empire State.[19]

Jefferson was thinking of a different brand of politics. He probably saw it as safer, for him, to risk schism in New York than to allow Burr to con-tinue as the Republican leader in that state, as he had been before 1801. Burr alone, among the party faithful, might mount a northern challenge to Virginia's preeminence among Republicans nationwide. By refusing to grant an appointment to Burr's close associate Matthew Livingston Davis, Jefferson was sending a powerful message. It would be seen by Burr, Gallatin con-cluded, as a "declaration of war"; it would be seen by Burr's enemies as proof of the vice president's shrinking role in the administration. "There is hardly a man who meddles with politics in New York," Gallatin certified, "who does not believe that Davis's rejection is owing to Burr's recommendation." Most revealing, perhaps, is the fact that Jefferson never answered Gallatin's questions, at least not in writing. The writing was on the wall, however, as to what his attitude toward Burr would be from this moment on.[20]

"AARON BURR!"

As the battle over patronage raged, Burr came under attack from a different quarter entirely. Early in May 1801, a handbill appeared entitled "Aaron Burr!" It not only called Burr a "Cataline . . . *confessed* in all his *villainy*," but added a "NEW TRAIT" that the public needed to be aware of—though not so new if one was a correspondent of Alexander Hamilton—and that was

Burr's *"abandoned profligacy."* As for proof, all one had to do was to travel about New York City to discover the numerous "wretches" whom the vice president had seduced; many of these had become celebrated courtesans, while others had allegedly fallen victim to disease, infamy, and death.[21]

The author of these charges was intending to mock Burr's pretensions to leadership: having taken a sacred oath of office, the lusty Burr had been unable to restrain himself from preying on the female population of the nation's capital as well. Jefferson had been critiqued as a dangerous atheist, and now his second-in-command was being labeled a deviant: "Is that party at whose head is this monster, who directs all their motions and originates all their nefarious schemes[,] worthy of your SUPPORT?" A public warning was now in order, so that citizens could see the new administration in its true light.[22]

Burr casually dismissed the handbill, writing offhandedly to his friend William Eustis of Boston that his political enemies had nothing better to do: "To vilify A.B. was deemed of so much Consequence, that packages of [handbills] were sent to various parts of the Country." His friends wished to issue a printed denial, but Burr felt that to do so would be "degrading." Honor needed no defending under such absurd conditions. With confidence, he turned to one of his favorite aphorisms: "I always presume that my friends will treat as false, every thing, said of me, which ought not to be true." Although Burr knew to expect Federalists of being behind this most recent slander, he was unmoved; to his way of thinking, such attacks always backfired: Republicans would only become more indignant and Federalists would end up retreating into "shame & confusion." All in all, he assured Eustis, "we extract good from evil."[23]

Burr's reaction was characteristic. He resisted bad-mouthing his political rivals, and under ordinary circumstances tried to deflect abuse that was directed at him. And at this moment, of course, he could not have foretold the damage his reputation would suffer in the not too distant future. From this point on, however, all depictions of Burr would in some way invoke his sexuality. This is not to say that his actual behavior was being monitored by those who saw fit to describe it sexually; rather, the sexualized image of Burr was principally a function of political rivalry. Just as Hamilton's embarrassing affair with Maria Reynolds came to light when he was most frustrating to Republicans, and the rumors concerning Jefferson's slave concubine, Sally Hemings, would shortly surface at the height of the president's popularity, Burr's sex life was easily used to tar him as a libertine at just that time when certain people were whispering that he might be in a position to succeed Jefferson.

Given how vicious early American politics was, we still have to ask: How did Burr's personal life—false rumors aside—contribute to the attacks on his character? Why has this image persisted and obscured the other important parts of his life? Why is Aaron Burr to this day still known principally as a rake? In the sexual world of elite men, was Burr, in fact, less unusual than he has been made to appear?

Men and women of the foundering generation were no more puritanical in their sexual tastes than their descendants. Prostitution was a common feature of cities. In 1794, the Frenchman Moreau de Saint-Méry was shocked to discover that New York, though a relatively new city compared to the ancient urban centers in Europe, already had "whole sections of streets given over to street-walkers for the plying of their profession" and "many houses of debauchery." Prominent people drew attention, but rarely moral censure, when they indulged their sexual appetites. In 1801, when William Wister, an extremely wealthy bachelor, died at the age of fifty-six, Dr. Benjamin Rush described the Philadelphia Quaker as "kind, charitable, generous, friendly," observing that his life was marred by only one vice: "an unlimited commerce with women." At death, he had not one but four mistresses. As a lawyer, while his wife was still alive, Burr took up the defense of Anne Livingston, who had accused her husband of having a mistress for three years and was now suing for divorce. Burr's longtime friend Marinus Willett had an illegitimate son during his first marriage, but this only became an issue when his name was put forward for a patronage post in Jefferson's first term.[24]

In Philadelphia, one could buy condoms at a local bookstore, which indicates that both reading and sex were genteel pastimes. That Burr himself rented, in 1798, what he described as a "bachelor's" retreat in Philadelphia, suggests that he pursued amours there. He encouraged his uncle Pierpont (who already had one mistress) to visit his new place, offering "a bed for you & bachelor's fare, with the certain advantage of freedom from restraint." It seems clear how the two men planned to spend their time at Burr's home away from home.[25]

Politicians were not shy about discussing sexual pleasure, even as a matter of state business. During Jefferson's second term, when the ambassador from Tunis arrived in Washington, he requested that the secretary of state make his stay complete by providing him and his entourage with concubines. Madison (generally portrayed as prim and proper) charged the ambassador's pleasure to the government, listing "Georgia a Greek," as one of the expenses among "appropriations for foreign intercourse." He made light of the incident in a letter to Jefferson, noting the double meaning of "foreign intercourse."[26]

Mature bachelors dotted the political landscape. Thomas Jefferson had been a widower for nineteen years when he became president; seven years had passed since Burr lost Theodosia. James Madison did not marry until he was over forty, and it is hard to imagine that he spent his entire early life in a state of celibacy. Only in satires such as "The Old Bachelor's Masterpiece," published in 1797, were such unmarried men portrayed as social misfits, requiring attentive wives to remind them of the social graces. More typical is the reputation of the New York Federalist congressman Egbert Benson, described as an "invincible bachelor" because he lived to the age of eighty-seven and never wed; no morose outcast, he was well known for his conviviality and Epicureanism. In fact, there is little evidence that unmarried older men suffered any stigma among the social elite.[27]

Eighteenth-century elites employed a series of euphemisms in describing sexual encounters outside of marriage, such as "gallantry," "intrigue," and "adventure." The first could encompass old-fashioned adultery; the latter two were more likely words for the more salacious act of seduction or a visit to a prostitute, of which America's cities had a considerable number. One of the Livingston clan came to own more than a dozen brothels. Thus, despite the fact that Chancellor Robert Livingston had been the highest legal authority in New York State, his younger brother John became (without apparent embarrassment) a noted whoremaster.[28]

The nation was simply not as virtue-bound as we would like to imagine. Philadelphia was a raucous city, in which many residents engaged in casual sexual encounters. Men and women had extramarital affairs in their homes, wives consorted with boarders, husbands with servants, and some couples even had dalliances on the ferries along the Delaware River. In 1797, when Sally McKean, daughter of Pennsylvania's governor, learned of a visiting diplomat's scandalous intrigue, she promptly conveyed the details to her best friend, Dolley Madison. The diplomat in question was well past his prime. He had been discovered, in the middle of the day, in the act of fornication with the wife of a servant; the husband had come home and "caught the old goat, with his wife, and in not the most decent situation—so the fellow very politely took him by the nose and saluted him with ki[c]ks till the corner of the street." The whole town was laughing at the diplomat's expense.[29]

Washington then was a town of no more than 3,000 inhabitants, where few politicians brought their wives to live. Most elected officials lodged in crowded boardinghouses; privacy was rare and rumors traveled fast. Congressmen regularly dined together, and slept just down the hall from their colleagues; indiscretions were hard to contain, and the humorous misadventures of politicians kept the city's populace buzzing. Charles Cotesworth Pinckney, the Federalists' vice-presidential candidate in 1800, was seventy-two in 1818 when he was "accidentally" arrested. As Massachusetts Federalist Harrison Gray Otis told the story to his wife, Pinckney, a widower, was in the wrong place at the wrong time. A local storeowner had been robbed, and in the course of the ensuing manhunt, the police spotted Pinckney sneaking out of an abandoned house where he had arranged to meet a prostitute. Everything was cleared up when the statesman was recognized; but even in the absence of a tabloid reporter, the septuagenarian Don Juan became the subject of gentle gossip in affectionate letters home. So, even New England Federalists were not particularly shocked by the sexual permissiveness of their colleagues.[30]

We can piece together Burr's relationships with women in the years after the death of his wife, although much of his correspondence with women was destroyed (protectively, we must assume) by Matthew Livingston Davis, who compiled these papers in the year of Burr's death. From what remains, a pattern emerges: the three people with whom Burr felt comfortable discussing his sexual affairs were his uncle Pierpont Edwards, his Revolutionary comrade William Eustis, and his married daughter, Theodosia. His choice of confidants made perfect sense. First of all, he seemed to unburden himself easily with Pierpont, whether the subject was speculative ventures, sexual intrigues, political ambitions, or personal sorrows. More like brothers than uncle and nephew, they had been raised in the same household; Pierpont was only six years older than Aaron, which helps to explain their fraternal bond.[31]

Burr cultivated a similar kind of relationship with Eustis. As middle-aged men, the two shared a similar nature as *bon vivants*. Three years his senior, Eustis had a reputation for urbanity and charm; he was a bachelor whose tastes matched the New Yorker's fascination with smart, accomplished women. A physician who graduated from Harvard, Eustis was an army surgeon in New York during the Revolution, when he met and befriended Lieutenant Colonel Burr. They renewed their friendship during the politically combustible 1790s, and his fellow Republican literally became an informal member of Burr's family. He was close to Theodosia, a kind of older, avuncular friend, whom Burr trusted enough to give the delicate assignment of sizing up her prospective husband. In 1800, Burr implored Eustis to "analyze and anatomize him Soul & heart & body," making sure the South Carolinian was a worthy companion for his beloved daughter. Eustis was one of the few friends to attend Theodosia and Joseph's small wedding—another sign of his intimate, almost familial, bond with Burr.[32]

It is true that Burr had an unusual relationship with his daughter, but this was mainly because he educated her to think like a man. There was nothing "unfeminine" in her being a formidable intellect, as her mother was, though the sometimes too glib Robert Troup scoffed at her, describing Theodosia's education as "wholly masculine," which supposedly rendered her "an utter stranger to the use of the needle, and quite unskilled in the different branches of domestic economy." Troup would have been horrified if he had known the full extent of Mary Wollstonecraft's authority in the Burr household. On the matter of sexual knowledge, the late eighteenth-century feminist believed that women should know as much as men; she despised the false delicacy that kept women ignorant of their own bodies, and proposed that men and women should "speak of the organs of generation as freely as we mention our eyes or our hands." Thus, Theodosia did not enter marriage blinded by convention; she probably knew as much about sex as her husband-to-be. After becoming a wife and, in 1802, a mother, Theodosia took on the unofficial role as her father's adviser; she freely expressed her opinions as to how he should conduct his courtships as well as less serious amours. Such intimate involvement in each other's lives apparently had no negative effect, insofar as Burr was just as open in his communications with Alston.[33]

Theodosia's marriage may have prompted Burr to search for a new wife. In his letters to her during his vice presidency, he mentioned several prospects, concealing their true identities with playful code names: "Celeste," "La Planche," "Madame G." (also "La G."), and "Inamorata." His letters to Theodosia typically mingled serious suggestions to help her improve her mind with lighter musings that gave hints about his private thoughts, and these included bits of gossip as well as his romantic mishaps. Burr remained a keen observer of his social world, and he especially liked to comment on the comings and goings of females in New York, Philadelphia, and elsewhere. After visiting a friend of Theodosia's, for instance, he lamented that the young woman had married a man who was "cold, formal, monotonous, repulsive." The outcome he envisioned for such an ill-conceived marriage—in words a trusted daughter would excuse—was that the pitiable wife should "break her pretty little neck. Yet, on second thought, would it not be better that he break his?" Lighthearted ridicule was a side dish, and sometimes the entrée, in Burr's correspondence with Theodosia.[34]

Burr employed clever allusions when speaking of his courtships: It was his "great love for the finer arts, especially sculpture" that he wanted Theodosia to know about, when he was really telling her about his love of women. In Washington, after failing to meet a woman suited to his taste, he joked: no "busts or statues,"—"is there nothing in that line found in South Carolina?" Rousseau's *Emile* was the immediate source for this particular metaphor, but its original meaning derived from the Greek myth of Pygmalion. Burr reminded Theodosia of the French philosopher's story about the "man who once gave life to marble," and then he provocatively asked: "Why may not this be done again?" For Burr, the *quest* for the perfect companion was apparently as interesting as the *attributes* of the quarry. Over and over again, he wrote about himself as a man who could not do without the delight that the company of accomplished women excited in him.[35]

When not reprimanding Theodosia for her laziness (he called her an "idle slut" for not writing enough), Burr's letters, by and large, took a literary turn. Most of his accounts of flirtations and failed courtships read (quite intentionally) like the fiction of Henry Fielding. Burr titled one of his autobiographical adventures the "story of Reubon and Celeste." "Celeste" was "Inamorata"—that is, they were the same person, the same mysterious woman, available (if perhaps a bit unsettled), and living in Philadelphia. In June 1803, the vice president proposed to her, and she rejected him. But the story is not that simple.[36]

We get a full picture of Burr's literary finesse as he relates the story of Reubon and Celeste. Theirs amounts to a step-by-step record of the eighteenth-century courtship ritual: the friendly visit; dinner with the family; anticipation ("I tremble at the success I desire," he writes); the polite request to "*le père*" for his daughter's hand; the father's assent accompanied by his refusal to "intermeddle"; and then, the "fatal step" of the marriage proposal; rejection, followed by a rapprochement, the clumsy untangling of confused signals; and, at last, the lady's failed attempt to retract her refusal.[37]

Just as in an eighteenth-century comic novel, Burr, as suitor, suffered from a case of mixed signals: he felt he had been turned down, but only after having done his gallant utmost to convince the lady that marriage would place unfair burdens upon her. "Celeste never means to marry," he narrates to Theodosia, assuming both parts in their dialogue. Celeste says: "'firmly resolved.'" Burr replies: "I am very sorry to hear it, madam; had promised myself great happiness; but cannot blame your determination." "No, certainly, sir, you cannot; for I recollect to have heard you express surprise that a woman would marry, &c., and you gave such reasons, and with so much eloquence, as made an indelible impression on my mind." His own words, which had come to her ear, had planted the seed of their breakup.[38]

He had thought the matter was concluded. But a few days after the apparent rejection, a note arrived from Celeste, requesting that he visit her once more. She wished to apologize, she said; her reasons made little sense, though, and Burr found himself in an unusual state—he was speechless. This, in any case, is how he explained it to his daughter:

> *Reubon ought in mercy and in politeness to have taken up the conversation; but he, expecting no such thing, was taken by surprise, and remained dumb, with a kind of half grin. The duette, at this moment, would have made a charming subject for the pencil of Vanderlyn. Celeste was profoundly occupied in tearing up some roses which she held in her hand, and Reubon was*

equally industrious in twirling his hat, and pinching some new corners and angles in the brim.[39]

Burr has painted a delicious scene, perfectly capturing the sexual tension and the polite misunderstanding. It was a romantic comedy of the sort to be taken up, at a later date, by Fred Astaire and Ginger Rogers.

Burr's love life, at least as he described it to Theodosia, was a literary treat, certainly an embellishment, and consistent with his penchant for social satire. Infatuated with his own premeditated self-mockery, he gently chided Theodosia not to "laugh at me so much," and yet that is precisely the effect his comic romantic tales were meant to achieve. His letters to Theodosia reveal the cultural nuances in Burr's romantic pursuits, while he wrapped the women he knew in mystery. After Celeste, he gave his daughter hints of a "serious" courtship with the equally elusive "Madame G." Claiming to have been "coquetted by a wealthy widow," he described "La G." as a mature woman in her forties (his age), whom he admired for her "independence of mind."[40]

Though it is impossible to accurately identify the mysterious women above, there are two others who are clearly flesh and blood—not merely literary fancy. Susan Binney and Madame Leonora Sansay represent Burr's widely divergent relationships with women. Binney seems to have resembled Celeste: she was young (twenty-three in 1801), and well connected (her father was a prominent Boston physician, her brother a successful Philadelphia lawyer). Sansay, whose age cannot be determined, was an exceptional woman. Though American, she spoke French like a native, and she practiced what can only be described as a European style of sexual independence, carrying on affairs during her marriage. Her husband did not approve, but neither did he dissolve the marriage. Sansay seems to have had few inhibitions and, like Burr, she found the time to convert her amorous adventures into pulp fiction.[41]

Burr first mentions Binney in a letter to William Eustis in June 1800, urging his friend to pay his respects to a Miss Binney of Boston "if you have not forsworn all Virtuous women." Despite his daughter's endorsement of the match, the relationship was in shambles by March 1801, when Burr assumed the vice presidency. Burr ended the courtship by telling her the "plain truth and quit honorably."[42]

Only one of his letters to Binney has survived. He wrote her to get her impression of a book he had sent her and a sense of her mind. Though the author had dared to explore one of Burr's favorite subjects—the differences between the sexes—he had failed miserably at convincing him of anything. Instead of bringing clarity, the author was guilty of "jumbling and confounding of sexes," and was "as remote from the truth as the arrogant pretension of male superiority." Burr's final comment to Binney deserves attention: He believed that the task of writing a sober study of the subject was "perhaps reserved for an American pen." Burr may even have imagined himself as that American author—the one person who could write such a radical treatise, to supplement the work of Wollstonecraft.[43]

It is difficult to say precisely when Burr began his relationship with Madame Leonora Sansay, but he met her through his friend William Eustis. He may have known her as early as 1797, well before he met Binney, but it is difficult to know when the affair became serious, although it probably happened before her marriage in 1800. Burr and Madame Sansay remained in contact at least until 1812.

Madame Sansay was married to a French merchant from New York, who was older and a widower. When they married is also a mystery, though Burr dates the union to sometime around 1800—well after he and Eustis had made her acquaintance. Her marriage contract, however, seems not to have had much impact on Madame Sansay's comings and goings: in 1802, as the couple prepared to move to Santa Domingo (now Haiti), she traveled to Washington, meeting with Vice President Burr to request letters of introductions for her trip. Burr asked his uncle Pierpont Edwards to prepare a letter for her, and described her in glowing terms: "you may speak very highly of her talents, her acquirements and her accomplishments—She speaks & writes French & has more sense & information than all the women to be found in St. Dom." Burr's protégé John Vanderlyn completed a portrait of Sansay in 1802. At the same time, Burr and Louis Sansay exchanged letters—the husband expressing a desperate concern as to whether his wife would return to him. He acknowledged outright that he feared his wife was planning to run off with another man, though it seems clear that the suitor was not Burr. Either way, Louis Sansay appealed to Burr to talk to his wife, promising to settle $12,000 on her in case of his death, and this suggests that Burr was acting as the couple's lawyer as well as marriage counselor.[44]

The Sansays reconciled and headed to Haiti. It was here she began to fashion her literary persona, writing highly entertaining letters to the vice president. Along with details of the political upheaval wrought by the Haitian Revolution, she traced the (autobiographical?) romances of a certain "Clara" on the exotic island. Burr's fondness for Leonora Sansay is evident once again in 1804; as he prepared for his duel with Hamilton, he wrote out special instructions to his daughter, establishing that she alone would be able to examine the contents of his correspondence with Madame Sansay. It should be noted, however, that Burr did not consider the Sansay letters to be the most passion-filled among his papers—he kept another bundle, tied with a red string and marked "*Put*," which he wanted immediately burned if he did not survive the duel. He considered his letters to and from Leonora (with the heading "*Clara and mentor*") too embarrassing to be made public at any time, but only because they supplied evidence of his frivolity. As he told Theodosia, "My letters to Clara are in the same bundle. You, and by-and-by Aaron Burr Alston [Theodosia's child], may laugh at *gamp* when you look over this nonsense." Burr's plan was that these letters would someday be read by his grandson, much in the way that the young are still called in to sit through old home movies of their elders in youthful, happier times.[45]

Leonora Sansay was an independent woman. When she returned to America, she settled in Philadelphia, established her own artificial flower shop, and published at least two racy novels. She may have been Burr's on again, off again mistress—it is impossible to do more than speculate. We do know, however, that she openly discussed her sexual liaisons with that liberty provocatively employed by the women of France. Yet she also appears to have been a romantic, putting love ("union of hearts") before the empty gratification of mere physical pleasure. Much like her "mentor" Burr, Sansay imagined that her life was entertaining enough for both a private and public audience. With Leonora, as with Susan Binney, Burr preferred to cast his amours as affairs of the intellect—for him a woman's mind made her more desirable. If Jefferson engaged in a struggle between "Head and Heart" in his famous letter of 1786 to the Anglo-Italian artist Maria Cosway, for Burr there was no need for any such choice—he felt he could have both.[46]

Burr and Eustis shared all kinds of gossip, admired the same women, and yet their most revealing collaboration was one of altruistic action on behalf of a young girl named Susan Lewis. She was the daughter of Maria Reynolds, née Lewis, who had been ruined as a result of her adulterous affair with Alexander Hamilton. In December 1800, Burr implored Eustis to risk his political reputation by finding Susan a home (he would be associating with a family that had been exiled from polite society). "I repeat & do assure you," wrote Burr, "she is to my belief, pure and innocent as an angel." He added, in case Eustis might have questioned Susan's paternity, that she was not his illegitimate offspring: "she has not the most remote affinity to me." Still he was, he said, "under a sacred obligation to protect her."[47]

Burr placed Susan in a boarding school in Boston. His intention was "to give her the kind of education that may enable her to gain a livelihood, if that should depend on her own exertions." But Miss Lewis had other plans. In 1803, she eloped with a young man named Francis Wright, whom Eustis described as a complete cad: "educated to dissipation without acquiring any one decent trait." Three weeks after their elopement, Wright abandoned Susan, and Eustis next discovered her in a house "frequented by young men"—a brothel. Eustis now predicted the worst: "I see nothing to be expected of our unfortunate charge but a gradual declension from reputable life down to what lengths or depths God knows." Although her two protectors refused to abandon her, Susan Lewis seemed destined to repeat her mother's mistakes: eventually married three times and divorced twice, she was ruined by marrying the wrong kinds of men.[48]

Burr's relationships with women were varied and complex. He was not the high-flying libertine that the Hamiltonians claimed him to be: a dangerous man without principles, roaming the streets to fulfill his need for sex, and then abandoning his victims to a life of shame. Burr's way of life can best be described as an American version of the French gallant: through open flirtation, he enjoyed the theatrical aspects of courtship, warded off boredom, and indulged what the French called "small pleasures." Just as his mind was hungry, his sexual appetite partook of a literary passion, if not a pornographic fascination, with sexual conversation; this is evidenced by his secret stash of letters tied up with red string.[49]

Though Burr actively courted a number of women during his widowerhood, he avoided marriage. Whether this was because he never found a woman who could replace Theodosia, or he appreciated his freedom too much to sacrifice any part of it, he seemed content to remain single. That he rejected outright the old canard of the natural superiority of males, however, placed him in a rare class. It is unfortunate that he never wrote the sober treatise on the sexes that he promised. It alone might have placed him in the unique position among the founders of advocating the extension of rights—a modern concept of rights—to women. No other founder even came close to thinking in these terms.

"AN INSINUATING DECEITFULNESS . . . CALCULATED TO FASCINATE YOUTH"

It was not Burr's sexual relationships with young women but his alleged attractiveness to ambitious young men that conditioned the most virulent attacks against him by men within his own party. And it was a British political refugee turned scandalmonger named James Cheetham who, almost single-handedly, orchestrated Burr's fall from political grace. He was a hatter born in Manchester, who quickly learned the contentious "Grub Street" style of satirical and slanderous newspaper writing. Cheetham arrived in New York City in 1798, and within two years, thanks to Burr's assistance, assumed the editorship of the *American Citizen*. It was the only Republican newspaper in the city at the time. But Cheetham left the Burrite fold in 1801, claiming to have become suspicious of Burr's activities.[50]

Matthew Livingston Davis offered a less noble explanation for Cheetham's defection. Davis contended that the editor's talents were up for sale to the highest bidder; in fact, he was more than willing to slander Jefferson, he told Davis, if Burr and his men agreed to pay him the tidy sum of $2,000. Whatever his motives, Cheetham soon became the indispensable tool of DeWitt Clinton, and embarked on a relentless campaign to exile Burr from the Republican Party leadership. Jefferson backed Cheetham: the president was no longer neutral, having chosen sides among the factions vying for power in New York.[51]

In December 1801, Cheetham traveled to Washington City to meet with Madison and Jefferson. He then wrote a letter to the president, detailing all of Burr's supposed intrigues. Burr did try to steal the election, the editor charged, but it was not (as he later contended) through some backroom deal with Federalists during the election tie. He instead claimed that the wily vice president had done his wheeling and dealing long before that:

he had convinced a few electors in New York to drop their votes for Jefferson, giving Burr the edge in the actual presidential election. The source of his story, tellingly, was DeWitt Clinton.[52]

He then went after the Burrites. The editor charged that Marinus Willett had campaigned for Burr (and not Jefferson) in Rhode Island, and that Timothy Greene acted as Burr's "*secret* agency" in South Carolina. John Swartwout, William P. Van Ness, and David Gelston were "entirely devoted to him," and equally intent on bad-mouthing the Jefferson administration. Matthew Livingston Davis was, according to Cheetham, "so perfectly Destitute of an independent mind," and so unmistakably under Burr's command, that he had reviled Jefferson's name all across Manhattan. What, then, was Burr's "little faction" up to? Cheetham concluded that "Burr and his panders" had an "obvious" goal: "It is to bring the present administration into disrepute, and thereby place Mr. Burr in the Presidential Chair."[53]

Cheetham concocted stories. His accusation against the Burrites was really nothing more than a self-portrait. He was servile in his devotion to DeWitt Clinton. He could call Burr an "intriguing and inexplicable man," and in the same breath explain how utterly transparent the vice president was, eager to express "in copious streams to every person who visited him," and to "none . . . more than myself," his dislike of the administration. Lying with apparent ease, Cheetham thus claimed to be Burr's closest confidant. Jefferson could have—and should have—investigated the charges. But he did not. Or perhaps Jefferson did not want to know, because he had made up his mind about Burr already.[54]

Cheetham's campaign did not remain undercover for long. Almost immediately following his trip to Washington, Cheetham wrote the first of many scathing pamphlets against Burr. It centered on a Scotsman, John Wood, formerly a tutor to several prominent families in New York, who had contracted with local printers to write an exposé of the Adams administration. Wood's hastily prepared book was filled with numerous errors and huge portions stolen from other works. And after Burr examined its contents, he discovered that the book contained some dangerous libel. Knowing it hurt rather than helped the Republican cause, Burr decided the book should be suppressed. But the printers had other ideas: they wanted first $1,500, then $2,500 (a not too subtle bribe) to keep the book out of circulation. Wood further contributed to the fiasco by claiming to be Burr's agent.[55]

Cheetham jumped at the opportunity to embarrass Burr. In his May pamphlet, he contended that Burr's motive for suppressing the book was his fear that it might alienate him from his Federalist friends—friends he would need to steal the *next* presidential election from Jefferson. Burr's allies finally decided to put the book on sale in order to show how ridiculous Cheetham's insinuations were, for the book's deficiencies spoke for themselves. But by then, Cheetham was already onto his next attack pamphlet. Now Cheetham was echoing essentially what Hamilton had whispered among his Federalist cronies: that Burr was another "Cataline," whose "malignant, secret, and duplicitous force . . . corrupts whatever it touches." Burr's plot had centered on the election tie. Cheetham likened Burr to Benedict Arnold, the country's most infamous traitor. This Burr had "crouched, and fawned, and surrendered himself" to the Federalists so that he could filch the 1800 election from Jefferson. No longer just a perverted politician, he was a cold-blooded traitor to his party.[56]

Meanwhile, Burr continued to carry on the business of the Senate. In January 1802, Senate Republicans put forward a motion to repeal the Judiciary Act of 1801. This statute infuriated them for good reason: Just before he left office, John Adams had used the act to rush through the appointments of several circuit court justices and to reduce the size of the Supreme Court, making it impossible for Jefferson to put anyone on the high court. Burr kept the repeal motion alive, breaking a tie vote and sending the bill to committee. At the same time, though, he hoped to reduce partisan rancor by giving Federalists an opportunity to review the legislation. He did not dispute the constitutional right of Congress to alter the judiciary system, but he wondered "if it might be constitutionally Moral." Simply put, he saw the dismissal of the twenty-six judges Adams appointed as unfair—a precedent that would condone partisan acts to overturn the judiciary with each new administration. Debate over the repeal did not go on for long. Soon enough, the party in power had the votes they needed, and the repeal passed—despite the lack of unanimity among Republicans, as crystallized in Burr's ambivalence about the repeal.[57]

Though some admired Burr's moderation, the rumors of his waning influence only gained momentum. Federalists gloated over Burr's alienation from the Republican leadership. From both sides now, Burr's every action was under scrutiny. So his appearance on February 22, 1802, at a

Federalist gathering in the national capital to celebrate George Washington's birthday was bound to cause a stir. Invited to give a toast, Burr raised his glass to "The union of all honest men." His toast became the talk of the town. Federalists, revisiting their state of mind during the election tie, once again imagined Burr's words as an offer to "coalesce," as Robert Troup reported. Congressmen John P. Van Ness of New York, Burr's friend and supporter, explained that the entire episode had been blown out of proportion. Burr had actually rejected the Federalists' invitation to dine, dropping by at the conclusion of the meal—by chance, his friend said. Discovering the business at hand, he offered his toast as a courtesy, and then quickly retired.[58]

But Federalists were still looking for signs of Burr's defection. When Hamilton got word of the affair, however, he was furious. And Gouverneur Morris's assessment hardly comforted him: Burr had "little Chance" to be a "Leader of any Party" because, at this point, members of both parties hated him. Even so, Morris had to admit that Burr possessed "considerable Talents for Government."[59]

Burr's consciousness of his waning influence in government was not immediately expressed. He wrote his son-in-law Joseph Alston, in early March, suggesting he was no longer able to predict what direction Congress was moving, even though he was head of the Senate. There was a touch of irony in all that he said: "I dine with the president about once a fortnight, and now and then meet the ministers in the street. They are all very busy: quite men of business. The Senate and the vice president are content with each other, and move on with courtesy." Coolness had settled over Washington, as far as he was concerned. Jefferson was not the same man who, as president-elect in December 1800, told Burr how much he regretted not having him in his cabinet.[60]

Burr's allies were more worried. Congressman Van Ness confided to his brother William in early April that Burr's "influence and weight with the Administration is in my opinion not such as I could wish." Van Ness recognized that DeWitt Clinton, now in the Senate, had the ear of the president. By July, Burr was ready to admit that the situation had deteriorated, noting in a letter to Alston that Clinton was the "instigator" behind Cheetham's publications. Burr warned Pierpont Edwards that his allies were all subject to attack, and it was only a matter of time before Edwards would find himself named as party to "certain imaginary intrigues." Just as predicted, Edwards did not escape Cheetham's wrath. "This knot of knaves cannot long hold together," Burr blasted away to his uncle.[61]

The battle intensified on July 31, 1802, when Burr's loyal friend John Swartwout met DeWitt Clinton on the dueling field in Weehawken, New Jersey, where Burr would eventually face Hamilton. Swartwout accused Clinton of trying to destroy Burr's reputation in order to advance his own political career. In response, Clinton called Swartwout "a liar, a scoundrel, and a villain." Refusing to apologize, Clinton seemed eager to force a confrontation. A date was set, and the two men, along with their seconds, rowed across the Hudson from Manhattan. It was not a pretty affair: A total of five rounds were fired, and Swartwout suffered two leg wounds. Carried to Burr's home, the wounded duelist slowly recovered. But the encounter resolved nothing. Clinton, at one point, offered his hand to Swartwout, but still declared that he would have preferred a chance to shoot at Burr. This affair was not about personal honor; it was a party feud, which Clinton had intentionally provoked. The war of words had now escalated into a confrontation with actual bullets.[62]

After Swartwout's dangerous and unproductive interview with Clinton, the Burrites decided to establish their own newspaper. The *Morning Chronicle* would be edited by Dr. Peter Irving. In August, when the plans for the paper reached Cheetham, he wasted little time in attacking the competition. His chief tactic was to accuse his rival of lacking manliness. He described Irving as a "young man of handsome talents." But of course, Cheetham did not stop there. Dr. Irving, he said, was a sexual pawn of the seductive Burr. "There is a softness," he wrote about the vice president, "an insinuating deceitfulness about him admirably calculated to fascinate youth." By October, Cheetham was directly mocking Irving's paper for its lack of "manliness," comparing it to a "Lady's Weekly Museum." He now called Irving a "beau," who was only capable of sputtering "effeminate attacks"; he went so far as to suggest that Irving might be a woman in disguise, whose whining editorials reminded him of one who suffered from a "female complaint." Making sure everyone understood the insult, in subsequent issues Cheetham would address the physician-editor as "Miss Irving" and "Her Ladyship." It would be his constant refrain over the next two years. Cheetham called the *Morning Chronicle's* output "puerile" and "foolish satire," and Irving's prose mere "tea-party" style, suited to the frivolous tastes of the "dandy."[63]

The intemperate editor was relying on a well-established tradition of political insult. According to eighteenth-century caricature, womanish men were fickle and disloyal, while as men of fashion, dandified politicians could be expected to change party affiliation as easily as they changed their clothes. By comparing the Burrites to beaux, dandies, and foppish boys, he associated them with prodigal dissipation and sexual indulgence—the twin vices of *luxura* and *licentia,* the antithesis of republican virtue.[64]

The theme of sexual inversion, so pronounced in these attacks, conjoined rampant vice and political instability. Add to Cheetham's charge that effeminacy marked the Burrites as amateurs and imposters his dismissal of their youth. They were, in his words, "an impotent faction," nothing more than "angry boys of a juvenile society." One supposedly unsolicited letter to the editor of the *American Citizen* noted the political aberration of the underage Burrites by identifying the letter writer as "old enough to be a Republican, and too old to be a Burrite."[65]

Sexual deviance was the most scurrilous charge in Cheetham's grab-bag of insults. Burr's "precious band," as he called this unnatural faction, was "actuated by personal attachments." They idolized Burr, and were "so extremely close" that they formed an emotionally intimate, sexually uncertain alliance. The homosexual overtones were intentional. Cheetham had conjured the specter of a sodomite plot—a theme popular in the conspiratorial satire of eighteenth-century England—in which Cataline, the notorious Roman traitor and seducer of young men, often figured prominently. Burr's ability to court and corrupt young men endangered the entire party system, polluting the manly bonds that united the Republican Party. The oft-manipulated image of Aaron Burr had reached an unprecedented level of exaggeration.[66]

The men around Burr were an extremely talented group of New Yorkers. Peter Irving had a reputation as a literary scholar, and was active in several social clubs that attracted ambitious young men. He belonged to the "lads of Kilkenny," which assembled at the coffeehouse near the Park Theatre in lower Manhattan. Cheetham claimed that Dr. Irving was but a child, when he was fully thirty years old in 1802, the same age as Cheetham. Cheetham's political hero, DeWitt Clinton, was thirty-three, underscoring the fact that age was not really an issue here. What remains most striking about Burr's core of support is that they were a "band of brothers," in the most literal sense. Peter Irving recruited his younger brother Washington to write for both the *Morning Chronicle* and the *Corrector,* the first significant literary efforts of a man destined to become the most famous American writer of his generation. John Swartwout, age thirty-two, corralled his two younger brothers, Robert and Samuel, into the Burrite fold. Congressman John Van Ness was the same age as John Swartwout; he and his younger brother William were lifelong friends of Burr's. Matthew Livingston Davis as well convinced his brother John to support Burr, and his father-in-law was equally devoted to the cause.[67]

Burr described Dr. Irving as a "decided Republican, but not of the persecuting intolerant sort," whereas Cheetham relied on invective and insinuation. Day by day, the latter's newspaper read like a soap opera, in which the evil Burr was a "proteus," a shape-shifter, using black magic to hide his dishonorable doings of plotting against Jefferson. In the early stages, Burr read the insults but refused to respond. Finally, in September 1802, he followed the advice of New Jersey governor Joseph Bloomfield and drafted a letter (published in various newspapers) calling Cheetham's charges "false and groundless." He stated unequivocally that he had never "advised or countenanced" any opposition to Mr. Jefferson, nor had he "agreed to any terms with the federal party"; and he had never "assented to be held up in opposition to [Jefferson] or attempted to withdraw from him the Vote or support of any Man." Burr said he found it remarkable that "calumny, unsupported by proof or even the authority of Name, could so far receive attention from the public as to require answer or even a denial."[68]

By now, Burr should have known better: slander without proof was pretty much the order of the day. Cheetham claimed he did not even need proof to justify his accusations: "Many, very many, indeed, strongly suspect that [Burr] is guilty of the charge exhibited, but almost all are of the opinion that he has managed the negotiations with so much caution, dexterity, and art, as to defy the production of proof." Rumors alone could convict Burr.[69]

Cheetham claimed that Burr had numerous accomplices in his scheme to steal the presidency: Edward Livingston of New York, James Linn of New Jersey, Abraham Bishop of Connecticut, Pierpont Edwards, Federalist David Ogden—the list went on. During the election tie, Burr and Ogden had traveled on the same stage together, and that was supposed to be evidence enough of a secret deal.[70]

In response, Irving employed a clever defensive tactic. In a hilarious spoof called "The Coach!!!" he wrote:

> *I am astonished the watchful editor has not yet exposed the nefarious intrigues of the Vice President about the* COACH! *The main ground of the matter is this: The Vice President purchased a Coach at second-hand from a federalist. A federalist? A federalist! Oh! Proof incontrovertible! But suppose (for I am not quite certain it is the case) he did not purchase it of a federalist; suppose he obtained it from a* GOOD REPUBLICAN—*still the affair furnishes strong proofs. It shews a manifest desire, by cunning and endeavors, to regain his standing in the opinion of republicans; of which we editors have deprived him. Though he would doubtless prefer purchasing a coach from a federalist, yet he is obliged for the sake of appearances, to give his custom to a republican. Here is proof of his hypocrisy; and surely the man who would dissemble in one instance, would without hesitation, do it in another.[71]*

William P. Van Ness was perhaps the most formidable defender of the vice president. In December 1803, he penned an anonymous pamphlet, signed "Aristides," that took George Clinton to task for being under the influence of his haughty and ambitious nephew. It is probable that Burr had a hand in the pamphlet. It circulated nationally and effectively humiliated DeWitt Clinton, who threatened to sue the printer if he did not reveal the author's name. One thing Van Ness did that was especially pointed was to query why the president had remained silent, refusing to defend his vice president. A few months after "Aristides," Burr took an additional precaution in trying to defend himself: He initiated a libel suit against Cheetham, primarily so as to collect depositions from any and all who could disprove the editor's charges. The move would have made sense had the truth still mattered.[72]

The real power play against Burr occurred in Washington, as DeWitt Clinton maneuvered behind the scenes to remove Burr from the Republican ticket as preparations began for the 1804 presidential election. At first, Clinton imagined that he himself might be selected as Jefferson's running mate in 1804, and that his uncle would retain the governorship of New

York. His principal ally, John Armstrong, put in motion his own secret scheme: George Clinton would run for both the governorship and vice presidency. After winning the second office, Clinton would resign the first, and Robert Livingston could then fill the seat through a backroom deal negotiated in the New York legislature.[73]

Burr had every intention of taking part in the next gubernatorial campaign, and DeWitt Clinton pleaded with Jefferson for a public renunciation of his erstwhile vice president. Jefferson remained detached, denying the younger Clinton immediate gratification. Instead, he deputed Gideon Granger, his postmaster general, to send Clinton a carefully worded letter, assuring him that the president "has requested me to inform you that he never has said he would vote for A.B. [for] vice-prt or Governor. He never has said so." Jefferson wished for the Clintons to keep Burr out of power, but he also wanted to appear above the fray. "I can therefore only brood in silence over my secret wishes," he wrote DeWitt Clinton directly. The president tried to have it both ways: appearing aloof while subtly pulling the strings.[74]

DeWitt Clinton had no need to worry. When the Republican caucus met on February 25, 1804, not a single Republican voted for Burr to return as vice president. Jefferson's silence had sent a strong enough message; southern prejudice against Burr "made the people sufficiently ready to receive impressions to his disadvantage," as one Virginian put it. The caucus went on to nominate the old warhorse Governor George Clinton to replace Burr on the national ticket. And as the *Morning Chronicle* reported, Clinton was the southern candidate, since he received only one vote "north of the Susquehannah." Still, Burr had his supporters, one of whom hailed from— of all places—Virginia. In a private letter, Republican mainstay Littleton Tazewell accused the Republican caucus of being the worst kind of aristocracy. Theirs was, he wrote, "an unauthorized meeting undertaken to decide, that one of the old Servants of the people is no longer worthy of their confidence." They had dismissed Burr, he added, "without specifying any charge against him, or offering any proofs to support it." It may seem odd that anyone from Virginia would defend Burr. But before his untimely death in 1799, Henry Tazewell (Littleton's father) had been quite close to Burr, serving with him in the U.S. Senate. From the younger Tazewell's view, the caucus was guiltier of engaging in intrigue than was the reputedly amoral vice president.[75]

The 1804 governor's election was a nasty and petty campaign. George Clinton refused to run again, and in his place the Clintonians backed Chancellor John Lansing. Other candidates had been considered: New York State Supreme Court Justice Morgan Lewis, and his fellow justice Brockholst Livingston (who had been Burr's friend and political ally until he suddenly abandoned him for the Clintons); Judge John Taylor of Albany; and, of course, DeWitt Clinton, who seemed to imagine that every available office was within his reach. Lansing was the most appealing of these candidates; as a political moderate, he could attract Federalist voters as well as Republicans.[76]

On February 18, two days after Lansing accepted the nomination, Burr's friends gathered at the Tontine Coffee House and announced Burr's plan to run for governor. To the surprise of many, Lansing withdrew that very day, refusing to compete with the vice president. Clinton's men were then forced to scramble to find a replacement. They decided on Morgan Lewis. He had married into the Livingston clan, and was one of the last of the Livingstons to abandon the Federalist Party and join the Clinton faction. In that he was, plainly, a lesser light among the Livingstons, Burr's supporters were optimistic, predicting "certain Success, since the nomination of Lewis."[77]

Burr's enemies were troubled. Hamilton nervously reported that "Burr's prospect has extremely brightened" with Lewis, instead of Lansing, in the race. Hamilton had publicly declared his support for Lansing at a February meeting of Federalists. Speaking to a friendly assemblage, he repeated all the old accusations, and adding one new charge: that Burr's election would encourage New Englanders to endorse the idea of "dismemberment of the Union." Hamilton obliquely alluded to a plot, recently hatched by Federalist congressmen from New England, to secede from the union. Five prominent men backed this plan: Senators Timothy Pickering of Massachusetts, William Plumer of New Hampshire, James Hillhouse and Uriah Tracy of Connecticut, and Representative Roger Griswold of Connecticut. Angered by the extraconstitutional Louisiana Purchase of 1803, and what they saw as the diminishing power of the northern states, they proposed that the New England states ought to attract New York to their idea of a "more perfect union."[78]

This rebel band of Federalists assumed that the exiled vice president would jump at a chance to join them. Several had approached Burr in Washington earlier in the year, and again on April 4, 1804, in New York. But just as before, when Federalists thought that he might become "their" president, Burr refused to give them the answer they were looking for. Granted, as a New Yorker, he shared their concern that the "Northern states must be governed by Virginia or govern Virginia, and that there was no middle course," but he insisted that he "must go on democratically" to obtain a more equitable distribution of regional power within the federal system. For Hamilton, this Federalist overture to Burr was ominous and more extreme than it had been in 1800. Burr was not simply running for governor; he could become the presumptive president of a new, independent country, encompassing all of the land north of the Susquehanna River.[79]

Scandalmongering aside, Burr's gubernatorial campaign was staked on real issues. The Burrites had made a concerted effort to reform the New York City charter, even before Burr announced his run for office. At a Republican meeting in January 1804, they introduced reforms that would democratize city government by reducing property requirements for voters; they wanted the mayor's seat to be an elective office; and they pressed to eliminate the rule that gave greater weight to the votes of the wealthy—a privilege that had kept the city council in the hands of elite Federalists.[80]

Some of these reforms were direct attacks on DeWitt Clinton, who maintained a stranglehold over the city's political machine. But it was not just about Clinton. Burr hoped to revive his role as a democratic reformer, the role he had cultivated during his time in the state assembly, when he sought to place in ordinary voters' hands the power to choose presidential electors. Once again, victory for the lame duck vice president would rest squarely on his ability to win a large majority of New York City's votes.

The situation was delicate for Burr and his supporters. Jefferson had made it clear that he would not interfere in the election, unless one of the candidates blatantly attacked him. While Peter Irving's *Morning Chronicle* did, in fact, point to the Clinton faction's obedience to the ruling Virginians, the Burrite paper avoided any more antagonistic language in alluding to the administration. A number of Burr's supporters expressed their unease. Oliver Phelps, who had been selected as lieutenant governor on Burr's ticket, betrayed his anxiety when he wrote to President Jefferson that "the friends of Mr. Burr" were "much misrepresented." He assured the president that "a great number of influential and active republicans, warm and decided friends to the administration support Col. Burr." Even John Van Ness, who was very close to Burr, voiced frustration, writing his brother William that if Burr "must fall," his friends should not be "dragged along with him." Some of Burr's former allies abandoned him, even his two stepsons: Frederick and John Bartow remained silent during the 1804 election season.[81]

The Burrites repeated the rhetoric of the 1800 campaign, focusing on Burr's superior qualities as a soldier and statesman. He was a man with a "superior soul," far above the "little minded men" who jealously tried to tarnish his reputation with their petty accusations. Irving praised Burr's boldness of character, and his irresistible essence, calling attention to his "open and manly conduct," "his masterly displays of eloquence," and the "commanding dignity of his eye." By celebrating his originality, his unique talents, and the fact that he rose on the basis of merit rather than patronage, Burr's supporters transformed their candidate into a genuine democrat. Morgan Lewis was easy to portray as the "candidate of the associated families" and a man of merely "moderate talents," whose presence on the ticket was explained by his ties to the powerful aristocratic ruling families of New York. Surrounded by the family-based factions of Clintons and Livingstons, Burrites distinguished their candidate as the one "self-made man." His rise was due to his remarkable presence, not a servile, effeminate dependency that came from family or political patronage.[82]

Whereas Burr's defenders portrayed him as a paragon of masculine accomplishment and public virtue, Cheetham's attacks only became more pornographic. He called the Burrites "strolling players," a euphemism for male prostitutes. Burr's home was likened to a bordello, adorned with mirrors on the bedroom walls; there, the *American Citizen* charged, the voyeuristic Burr and his minions indulged in the decadent pleasures of fornication and adultery. If he could be portrayed as heir to Cataline, why not take the next step: and so now, Cheetham called Burr a modern-day Sardanapalus and Heliogabalus, two classical figures with notorious reputations: the first had dressed and behaved as a woman, while the second had a taste for young men with large penises. In one pornographic poem, punning on Burr's name, the versifier made crude allusions to male penetration and sodomy. To make matters worse, the Federalists' 1801 attack handbill (featuring the story of Burr populating the city with prostitutes) was once again circulated—this time by anti-Burr Republicans.[83]

Cheetham could not contain himself. He accused Burr of prostituting himself to a group of black voters by inviting them to his home and supposedly offering them "elegant amusements," that is, exchanging their votes for sexual favors. Amid the sexual tumult, Burr did his best not to care, mustering a droll spirit when he wrote to Theodosia that he planned to send her "some new and amusing libels against the vice president."[84]

But Cheetham's three-year barrage of assaults eventually took its toll. Burr lost the governor's election by 8,700 votes—an embarrassing defeat, because no candidate before him had lost by such a large margin. On May 1, he wrote his daughter, with particular candor, that the "election is lost by a great majority: *tant mieux.*" Burr's reputation (both political and personal) was seriously damaged.

The Federalist editor William Coleman, of the New York *Evening Post,* offered the most balanced explanation for Burr's trouncing. The *American Citizen,* he acknowledged, deserved the credit; the attacks on Burr's "personal character" had been unparalleled, "circulated with an industry and at an expense hitherto unexampled." The Clintons had at the same time succeeded in persuading New York voters that Burr's political career was dead, and that their votes would be thrown away on him. In a way, they were right: Burr would have had little power as governor—his enemies controlled the Council of Appointment and could have overridden any of his patronage decisions. Beyond this, the Federalists, who might have come out in substantial numbers to support Burr against Lewis, in the end did not; and bad weather contributed. As Coleman noted, "Federalists are very much your fair-weather sort of people."[85]

Storm clouds had indeed gathered over his political horizon. It was not that Aaron Burr had done something deceptive or conniving, at this point, to bring on his troubles. His precarious position was the result of several factors that were, essentially, beyond his control. First and foremost, despite what all of our standard history texts assume, there was no national Republican Party in 1800 or 1804; there was a Virginia Republican Party and a New York Republican Party, each of which sought, with jealous determination, to broaden its power. The New Yorkers did not trust the Virginians, and vice versa; their alliance was a tentative one. Burr's success was owing to his role as mediator, uniting the squabbling factions in New York to support the Manhattan Bank, and then again bringing together the Clintons and Livingstons (on his slate of candidates for the assembly) to secure the election of Jefferson. But this role was temporary, and as sectional divisions and factional feuds resurfaced, Burr's unifying role was no longer needed.

Thomas Jefferson was thinking about preparing his most trusted political lieutenant, fellow Virginian and Secretary of State James Madison, to succeed him in the presidency, and for that reason alone he was intent on removing Burr as a contender. In New York, the ambition of DeWitt Clinton knew no bounds, and so he too had to get Burr out of the way. In Clinton's case, the facts speak for themselves: four years later, in 1808, he broke with Jefferson and set up his uncle to run against Madison for the presidency. This maneuver failed. As it turned out, George Clinton, old, incompetent, and no threat to Virginia supremacy, served as a figurehead vice president under Jefferson and then Madison.

Burr had been essential to Jefferson's plans in 1800. His success as a tactician had secured New York and won the election for the Virginian. But when Jefferson handily defeated Rufus King in the 1804 presidential contest, it was clear to all that the Federalists no longer posed a significant electoral challenge to Republican rule. Burr had become expendable. His rival, DeWitt Clinton, lacked the political finesse to unite New York Republicans, let alone build a winning northern coalition. Clinton lacked Burr's qualities—the qualities that the Virginians saw as a hazard, a threat to their sectional dynasty. If the New Yorkers fought among themselves, the Virginians could continue to control the party and the presidency, as they indeed did for the next twenty years. Burr never betrayed his party. In the eyes of his Virginia rivals, who feared his ability to unify northern Republicans, his talents alone betrayed him.

"SYNTAX"

The nastiness of the 1804 governor's race drew Burr and Hamilton into a personal battle. On April 23, Federalist Dr. Charles D. Cooper had published a letter in the Albany newspaper, which included a series of insults that Hamilton had openly declared before a group of prominent men. Why did his insults make it into print? Pure politics. Cooper's letter is best understood as the early republic's version of an attack ad. During the election, Federalists had been divided in their opinions of Burr; those who supported him in the contest with Lewis did everything possible to diminish Hamilton's influence over the voters. For this reason, a rumor began to circulate that Hamilton was indifferent to the outcome of the election. He had supported Lansing, as all knew. When Lansing dropped out and Lewis became a candidate, it was expected that he would not interfere in the race. But Hamilton was not one to beg off. Cooper's letter was published in order to quash the rumor that Hamilton was ambivalent about the election outcome.[86]

Burr did not learn of Dr. Cooper's letter until after the election. On June 18, 1804, he sent Hamilton a brief note. In it, he observed that Cooper had quoted Hamilton as having called Burr a "dangerous man," not to be trusted with "the reins of government." That was not what offended Burr, however. It was another of Cooper's statements: "I could detail to you a still more despicable opinion which General HAMILTON has expressed of Mr. Burr." It was the word "despicable" that drew Burr's attention, a word used at this time to describe socially degraded or "sordid" behavior, which could be considered slander. Cooper's letter provided firsthand testimony that he had heard Hamilton insult Burr's private character. Burr's note to Hamilton began the formal affair of honor that would place the principals paces apart with pistols—the affair that would make Burr, in due course, a notorious figure in American history.[87]

When he sent his aide William P. Van Ness to Hamilton, bearing his note, Burr was not reacting hastily. Rather, as Van Ness explained after the duel, Burr first discussed the Cooper letter with several of his friends, and it was they who advised him to take some action. Burr knew that Hamilton had attacked his private character before; yet he moved slowly while the authenticity of the new reports remained questionable.

With past as prologue, the offended party had certain expectations from his political adversary. Days after the duel, in fact, he explained his mind-set to his loyal Philadelphia friend Charles Biddle: "It is too well known that Genl. H. had long indulged himself in illiberal freedom with my character—He has a peculiar talent of saying things improper and offensive." On two prior occasions, Burr reminded Biddle, out of "delicacy" and a "sincere desire for peace," he had forgiven Hamilton. Why? Because on those occasions Hamilton had understood that he was putting Burr in a position where a challenge was likely to follow, and had seized the opportunity to apologize directly. As Burr put it to Biddle, he had once again expected Hamilton to soften his tone of criticism—to restrain his language—in response to the "generosity of my Conduct." But this time, Burr bemoaned, Hamilton did not meet his expectations: "I have been constantly deceived, and it became impossible that I could consistently with self-respect again forbear."[88]

When Hamilton received Burr's first note, he told Van Ness that the matter required further careful consideration. It took two days for Hamilton to reply, and when he did so, his answer was evasive and disingenuous, and painfully convoluted. He could not "make the avowal or disavowal" that Burr requested, he said, adopting a lawyerly pose by parsing the various meanings of the word "despicable": " 'Tis evident, that the phrase 'still more despicable' admits of infinite shades, from very light to very dark." With amazing hubris, he asked: "How am I to judge of the degree intended? Or how shall I annex any precise idea to language so indefinite?" Instead of addressing the question of honor, Hamilton had decided to argue that the offensive statement was too vague to contain any certain meaning; and thus, he was not bound by the "*inferences*" others might draw from his statements.

Then, Hamilton made a remarkable connection. Cooper's testimonial was part of a larger pattern, and he could not be held accountable for remarks he might or might not have made about a political opponent over "fifteen years of competition." Rather than addressing Burr as an intimate, he was saying, self-protectively, that fifteen years in the national spotlight had opened Hamilton to charges by anyone—any stranger—who might have felt offended by him. The closing line of his response was as provocative as it was brusque: "I trust, on more reflection, you will see the matter in the same light as me. If not, I can only regret the circumstance, and must abide the consequence." It is hard to believe that Hamilton thought he was reducing tensions by composing such a response; in any event, its effect was only to deepen his original insult.[89]

Burr's answer cut through the fog created by Hamilton's indirection. Indeed, his answer provides us with one of the best examples of Burr's incisive intellectualism—his staunchness when it came to dismantling a legal contrivance or exposing an ostentatious political display. He could act, in such instances, with surgical precision. He examined Hamilton's letter carefully, and regretted that he found "nothing of that sincerity and delicacy which you profess to Value." Meeting indirection with direct language, he revealed Hamilton's first mistake, his failure to speak in the tone of a gentleman who championed the code of honor. Hamilton misunderstood honor—honorable men did not hide behind a veil of words, nor pretend that malicious remarks were acceptable to use against a political rival. As Burr neatly stated: "Political opposition can never absolve Gentlemen from the necessity of a rigid adherence to the laws of honor and the rules of decorum." With a bow to republicanism, he added, "I neither claim such a privilege nor indulge it in others." Any true gentleman would have immediately understood the meaning of Cooper's letter and its relationship to Hamilton: "The Common sense of Mankind affixes to the epithet adopted by Dr. Cooper the idea of dishonor; it has been publicly applied to me under the Sanction of your name." Hamilton should have felt an obligation to clear the air, one way or the other, and not to obfuscate. The issue before them had nothing at all to do with "Syntax" or "grammatical accuracy," as Hamilton wished to construe, "but whether you have authorized this application either directly or by uttering expressions or opinions derogatory to my honor." Hamilton could try to dance around what he was responsible for making public, but Burr would not let him off so easily: What mattered was the "effect" of the "calumny," which was both "present and palpable."[90]

On reading Burr's reply, Hamilton fatefully indicated that he had nothing to add or amend to his statement. Van Ness assumed that the next step in the *code duello* was to be taken: Burr would issue his challenge. Nevertheless, as Burr's second, and hoping for an accommodation, Van Ness tried to present Hamilton with a loophole: He asked whether Hamilton could recollect his conversation with Dr. Cooper, thus allowing him to disavow the insults. Many interpreters of the duel have concluded that Hamilton might well have ended the affair here, had he taken Van Ness's advice. But he refused to budge.[91]

Later the same day, however, Hamilton thought about another avenue of approach. He began by asking Nathaniel Pendleton, a friend, to serve as his second. He entrusted Pendleton with a fresh letter for Van Ness, one that

suggested that Hamilton wished to delay, if not avert, the duel both principals had now come to see as probable. So Van Ness put the challenge on hold
and met with Pendleton, who provided a summary of the mysterious conversation that Dr. Cooper had overheard. This was as close as Hamilton was
willing to go in disavowing the insult; he claimed to recall only a conversation that "turned wholly on political topics and did not attribute to Col. Burr,
any instance of dishonorable conduct, nor relate to his private character."[92]

But Hamilton's hopeful comment was then undercut as Van Ness delivered Hamilton's second letter to Burr. There was nothing ameliorating in
it. What Burr saw in it, in fact, was Hamilton's complaining that the demands on him were excessive. Describing Burr's last communication as in
some way "indecorous" (he wrote "rude" in an unsent draft), Hamilton
asked for "greater latitude" in the sort of disavowal he issued. Burr did not
wish to give Hamilton greater latitude; he desired at this point nothing less
than a "general disavowal" of the personal affronts to his character that
Hamilton had habitually leveled against him. Pendleton somehow thought
that Hamilton would oblige Burr. But when Pendleton and Van Ness met
again, the former acknowledged that he was wrong, and that Hamilton
would not issue a general disavowal.[93]

Burr was outraged. As if Hamilton's nitpicking was not bad enough, he
next received a separate paper containing a new explanation from Hamilton
of the conversation Cooper had taken part in. Burr found this revised interpretation of that conversation a "worse libel" than the original Cooper letter,
leaving "injurious impressions" in "full force." As of June 26, further exchanges by letter struck Burr as a pointless exercise. Van Ness told Pendleton
with a sense of finality that only a general disavowal would be accepted.[94]

To this, Hamilton responded angrily, insisting that Burr had made his
initial grievance into something all-encompassing and impossible to reckon
with. He now turned the tables on Burr and accused him of being motivated by a "premeditated hostility." On June 27, the formal challenge was
delivered. Van Ness carried one last clarifying message, in which Burr
stated his position. He said that he had sought to place his grievance in unmistakable but not inflammatory terms, so that Hamilton could find a
means of retracting his "expressions derogatory to [Burr's] honor." But
Hamilton, he explained, had answered not with "magnanimity" but with "a
sort of defiance"; and Burr, as a man of honor, had no choice but to reject

all such evasive posturing. There was nothing left but to deliver to Hamilton "a simple Message." The message—the challenge—was delivered verbally by Burr's second.[95]

What had begun as a formal exchange of letters quickly grew into a jousting match between two unrelenting legal adversaries. It was, in that sense, a battle of "Syntax"—the crossing of verbal lances—and after the first clash neither combatant had fallen from his horse.

Later, it appeared to one interested politician, at least, that Burr had won that first round. After reading the published correspondence, the Virginia Republican John Randolph (who would years later duel Henry Clay) said that he felt the entire affair did Burr "honor," and that Burr could not be "eluded or baffled" by Hamilton's own legal parsing. Hamilton reminded Randolph of a "sinking fox, pressed by a vigorous hound, where no shift is permitted to avail him."[96]

In the process, Hamilton and Burr learned how unalike they really were. Though they both fashioned themselves as "men of honor," they followed different rules. Hamilton figured it was unavoidable that political rivals would come to insult one another; thus, one needed "latitude" in determining whether he had been insulted beyond what was customary in their world. Burr, on the other hand, considered that politics was already such a slippery slope that one had to exercise greater care in what was said about the opposition. Charles Biddle confirmed this: "I never knew Colonel Burr speak ill of any man," he remarked after the duel, "and he had a right to expect a different treatment from what he experienced."[97]

For Burr, honor began with sincerity. For Hamilton, it was protecting one's public reputation—one's public face—at all costs. Sincerity was not nearly as meaningful to Hamilton, who never once in his career appears to have worried that maliciously attacking an enemy might be dishonorable. Over the course of twelve years and probably longer, Hamilton had spoken of Burr in secret, in low and not so low whispers; he displayed little in the way of discretion, whether his target was Jefferson or Adams or Burr or even the loyal Robert Troup. He was accustomed to getting away with his abuse of Burr.

After a certain point in the negotiation, neither man could concede defeat or accept the humiliation of concession. The time for words, for arguments over syntax, was past.

"IF IT SHOULD BE MY LOT TO FALL"

Two weeks would pass before the duelists met at Weehawken on July 11. On the Fourth of July, incredible as it might seem, they socialized together. At a banquet held by the veteran officers of the Society of the Cincinnati, Hamilton stood on a table and sang a rousing military tune. But the gaiety of that evening concealed more serious matters: Death was rare in duels, yet it did happen. Hamilton's eldest son, Philip, had suffered a mortal wound in a duel just three years earlier. So both Hamilton and Burr had to prepare for their interview with that prospect in mind.[98]

If Burr had won the first round, at least rhetorically, Hamilton made a meticulous effort to craft a document for posthumous inspection that would serve to dignify his behavior. To defend himself from the grave, if it came to that, he prepared what is now called his "Apologia," which was later published by Nathaniel Pendleton in the *Evening Post*. Here, Hamilton explained the reasons for his action, but once again avoided yielding to Burr what was demanded: real regret for his behavior. Instead, Hamilton presented an idealized version of himself, while making use of one last opportunity to blacken Burr's name.[99]

Hamilton was a skilled writer. In the "Apologia," he opened with an appeal to men of the cloth, declaring that his "religious and moral principles" made him "strongly opposed to the practice of Duelling." Though in life he had never conducted himself as a religious man, he certainly appreciated the value of establishing his moral purposes here. He referred to his beloved wife and children, and he acknowledged an obligation to his creditors. His following point, however, revealed how contrived and disingenuous the "Apologia" really was. Hamilton wrote: "I am conscious of no *ill-will* to Col. Burr, distinct from political opposition, which, as I trust, has proceeded from pure and upright motives."[100]

Perhaps, if at this moment Hamilton had placed all of his vicious letters about Burr before him, he might have had to alter his plea to posterity. He was weaving a story to explain why the duel had to happen and how he had done everything within his power to avoid it. As Hamilton reconstructed the affair, Burr had made it impossible for him to escape. "There were *intrinsick* difficulties in the thing," he wrote, "and *artificial* embarrassments, from the manner of proceeding on the part of Burr." By "*intrinsick,*" he meant that it was already public knowledge that his "animadversions on the political principles character and view of Col. Burr had been extremely severe." His views were shared by "many others," he insisted, though he was willing to admit that his public statements had spilled over into "unfavorable criticisms on particular instances of the private character of this Gentleman." He made his attacks on Burr's character sound as if they had been incidental and nearly involuntary.[101]

Yet even this defensive pose is a cover story. It was Hamilton who had instigated gossip. It was Hamilton who had invented the decadent Burr. It was Hamilton who had attacked him first (as did his self-protective father-in-law, Philip Schuyler). Hamilton was not, as he pretended, a solitary voice within a large chorus of those denouncing Burr. The truth is that Hamilton began attacking Burr's private character in 1792; and in 1800, he accused Burr of every crime he could bring to mind. Hamilton's charges, all along the way, were outrageous, hypocritical, even hysterical, and not, as he rationalized at the end, occasional political criticisms enunciated with the utmost "sincerity." Though his motives were political, Hamilton's major form of attack was deeply personal, and he showed no constraint in leveling charges against every aspect of Burr's private character. Why did he do it? Because he knew that Burr was an accomplished man of the law and of politics and that the only way he could defeat him was to malign him.[102]

To make himself appear nobler, Hamilton declared in his final public document that he intended to "*reserve* and *throw away*" his first fire (also his second, if Burr was not satisfied after a single shot). Hamilton's avowal has confused many analysts—and is one reason that some have speculated that he had a "death wish." Yet his real purpose was to envelop himself in an aura of moral authority; he believed his righteous bearing would serve to teach Burr a moral lesson: by withholding his fire twice, he would give "a double opportunity to Col. Burr to pause and to reflect." Hamilton knew, too, that he had to justify himself. Why would a man who opposed dueling consent to a challenge? He had to acquiesce, he explained, because it was the only way he could retain the "ability to be in the future [politically] useful." His public reputation mattered more to him than anything else at this affecting moment.[103]

Burr was no less concerned that he should settle his affairs. On the day before the duel, he drafted two letters: one to his daughter, and the second to his son-in-law. He arranged for four executors: John Swartwout and William Van Ness in New York, Theodosia and her husband in South Carolina. Both duelists took stock of their dismal finances. Hamilton was at least $60,000 in debt, which is why he mentioned his creditors as "sufferers" in his "Apologia"; Burr hoped his property would cover his debts, but expected that Alston would assume any that remained outstanding.[104]

Burr, like Hamilton, was thinking of posterity, yet he apparently felt no compelling need to explain his action to the world. He placed his private correspondence in Theodosia's hands, and suggested that her husband might "think it worth while to write a sketch of my life." In material terms, he was only able to leave his friends and family small tokens of affection: a painting of himself for William Eustis; a pair of pistols, some apparel, and his watch to his stepson, Frederick Prevost; and he urged Theodosia to give John Bartow "something—what you please." At this time, Burr still owned slaves: to Peggy Gallatin, he left land worth $250, and implicitly her freedom; he encouraged Theodosia to keep Peter Yates as a valet to her son, since he was "the most intelligent and best-disposed black" he had ever known; and Nancy, "honest, robust, and good-tempered," had to be disposed of as well.

Contemplating the possibility that the letters he was preparing might be his last, Burr felt assured that he could now face death calmly, knowing that his "dearest Theodosia" and his grandson would be cared for. He would live on through his family, he confided to his son-in-law, "if it should be my lot to fall."[105]

"A SORT OF EXILE"

July 11, 1804, broke hot and humid. According to the protocol worked out in advance, Burr was rowed across the Hudson and arrived at the Weehawken dueling ground before Hamilton. He brought with him William P. Van Ness. Hamilton and Nathaniel Pendleton joined them shortly, along with Hamilton's physician, Dr. David Hosack.[106]

The few firsthand reports agree on some of the basic facts. The two men were standing about thirty feet apart, and on Pendleton's command of "*Present!*" they were then both allowed to shoot. Hamilton had provided the

pistols, which were equipped with hair-triggers that made the fire unpredict-
able, and loaded with one-ounce balls that were quite dangerous if they hit
their target. Both seconds later agreed that the duelists fired within seconds
of each other. But they did not agree on one crucial point: who fired first.

Pendleton (influenced by Hamilton's claim that he would withhold his
fire) believed that Burr's shot rang out first, and at that moment Hamilton
fell forward. The ball entered inches above his right hip, passed through
his liver, and lodged in his spine—the sudden shock, according to Pendleton, caused Hamilton to discharge his gun. Van Ness's observations were
more detailed and might be more accurate. He noted that after the first fire,
Burr was jarred, as if he had been struck. His body moved. Then, after
"several seconds" elapsed, Burr fired his pistol, and Hamilton "fell instantly." As Hamilton collapsed, "Burr advanced toward Genl H with a
manner and gesture of regret."[107]

Both Burr and Van Ness felt certain that Hamilton had intentionally
fired his weapon. Before the command to fire was given, he had unambigu-
ously stopped the proceedings so as to test his vision. He leveled his gun
from various positions, judging how the light hit from each. Then, finally,
he put on his spectacles, presumably to improve his aim. It is hard to believe that Hamilton would have indulged in this behavior if, as his earlier
prepared statement avowed, he had no intention of firing his pistol, or he
planned to shoot in the air. If this were the case, why, then, was there any

"Genl. H. . . . . levelled his pistol in different directions to try the light." Excerpt from
Burr's letter to Charles Biddle, July 18, 1804.

need to be concerned about the sunlight? The modern historians who see Burr as the aggressor and Hamilton as a man with scruples ignore this rather telling bit of uncontested information.[108]

Hamilton's wound was fatal, but he did not die until the following day. He was carried back by boat to Manhattan. Burr sent a note to Dr. Hosack, asking about Hamilton's condition, and expressing hope of his recovery. Given large doses of the opiate laudanum to ease his pain, Hamilton spent his last hours trying to convince a local minister to give him communion. He first appealed to Bishop Benjamin Moore of the Episcopal Church, a friend, and then to the Reverend John Mason, of the Presbyterian Church; both men consoled him but refused his request. Moore eventually returned and agreed to administer communion. Why the hesitation? Hamilton had never joined a church, and the ministers were wary of the motivation behind a deathbed confession, especially under the circumstances: dueling was a violation of church doctrine as well as civil law. For the sake of his wife and family, Hamilton wanted to die a "Christian." And so, at two in the afternoon, on July 12, he did. In the weeks that followed, as numerous eulogies were given in his honor, ministers and statesmen alike declared him a religious man.[109]

News of Hamilton's death spread quickly. Burr's enemies mounted a new, even more vicious barrage of attacks. Stories circulated that he had practiced his shot often enough to ensure that his aim would be deadly; he was accused of wearing silk, which was believed to be more resistant to pistol fire—implying, of course, that he was really a coward. One especially ridiculous charge was that he had never even met Hamilton at the dueling site, but had instead, like a criminal, hunted down his prey. Even some Federalists who had previously treated Burr with respect, such as Hamilton's protégé William Coleman, editor of the Evening Post, now classified him as an "assassin." The Burrites were thus no longer a faction but a murder ring; and Burr, their leader, was driven by a narcissistic bloodlust: "Wrapt up in himself—to appease his resentment, and to gratify his ambition," Cheetham wrote in his accustomed style, "he is capable of wading through the blood of his fellow citizens and laughing at the lamentations of widows and orphans."[110]

A grand funeral was organized for July 14, in a manner unseen since the death of Washington four and a half years earlier. A military detail escorted the corpse; melancholy music sounded, as a long train of relatives, friends, and various local officials joined the procession. Atop the coffin lay Hamilton's hat and sword, while his boots and spurs were displayed on his horse; his steed was dressed in mourning regalia as well, and led by two black slaves, who wore white turbans trimmed in black.[111]

A stage was erected in the portico of the Episcopal Church. Hamilton's four sons stood beside Gouverneur Morris, who had been selected to pronounce the funeral oration. When Morris's speech ended, Hamilton's body was carried to the cemetery; there, Bishop Moore performed the last rites, and troops discharged three volleys of gunfire over the grave.[112]

Morris's oration was powerful, yet proved even more successful in print. In his diary, he was surprisingly uninhibited in confiding how difficult it had been for him to draft an appropriate discourse for the occasion. He admired Hamilton, true, but he knew only too well the man's flaws. Should he gloss over Hamilton's illegitimate birth and his martial infidelity? Did it matter that, in Morris's view, Hamilton was "indiscreet, vain and opinionated"? He could not, without real discomfort, reconcile himself to Hamilton's final statement, which did not ring true to him—that the martyr was "in Principle opposed to Duelling, but he has fallen in a Duel." Morris was aware of the growing hostility toward Burr, and having witnessed the French Revolution firsthand, he knew as well the dangers inherent in a mob mentality, and so he was conscious that his words should not excite an "Outrage." How, he wondered, could he do "Justice to the Dead," and at the same time, "not injure the living"?[113]

Burr was shocked by the mounting "persecution." He wrote to Joseph Alston that "thousands of absurd falsehoods are circulated with industry" and the "most illiberal means are practiced to produce excitement"—and, he added, "with effect." To Charles Biddle he sneered that "all our intemperate and unprincipled Jacobins who have been for Years reviling H[amilton] as a disgrace to the Country and a pest to Society" are now "the most Vehement in his praise." Their motive was not to show their "respect to him but, Malice to me." A New York coroner's jury was called not once, but repeatedly, before it was able to obtain an inquest for murder. This was an unprecedented action: first, the duel had taken place in New Jersey, beyond New York's jurisdiction; and besides, no duelist had ever been prosecuted in the past, despite the existing law against dueling. Even Governor

Lewis found the proceedings "disgraceful, illiberal, and ungentlemanly," as John Swartwout informed Burr. Burr was now able to comprehend the fate that awaited him. He admitted to Alston that the duel has "driven me into a sort of exile, and may terminate in an actual and permanent ostracism."[114]

Unsure of what might happen in New York, he decided not to wait for the report of the coroner's jury. On the morning of July 21, he crossed the Hudson, accompanied by his slave Peter Yates and John Swartwout. Swartwout returned to New York and went into hiding, as did William Van Ness. (Matthew Davis and Marinus Willett had been arrested for refusing to give up information about the duel, and Van Ness was subject to a possible indictment as an accessory to Burr's crime.) Burr spent the night at a friend's home in Perth Amboy. The next day he went by carriage to Cranberry, in south-central New Jersey, and from there headed to Philadelphia, where he stayed with Charles Biddle. Efforts to persuade Governor Lewis to extradite Burr from Pennsylvania failed. By the beginning of August, new rumors were surfacing that attempts had already been made to assassinate him. Burr informed Theodosia that these were "mere fables," adding with wonderful sarcasm that those "who wish me dead prefer to keep at a very respectful distance."[115]

Though New York dropped the murder charges, Burr was nevertheless indicted for violating the dueling law. Next, New Jersey called its own grand jury, and indicted him for murder. But dueling was legal in New Jersey! (The court's action is explained by the fact that a party of Federalists was behind the proceedings.) Burr once again exercised his wit, in writing to his daughter that the two states were now battling to determine "which shall have the honour of hanging the vice-president."[116]

The general reaction to the duel was not uniform. In the East, Federalist politicians thought to use Hamilton's stunning death as a means to generate "excitement," or "ferment," as Burr looked on it, and to recover lost ground. William Coleman described Burr not only as a cold and selfish assassin but an "isolated man," devoid of family and national affections. Elevating Hamilton into a martyr and devoted family man, Federalists hoped to regain their claim to moral authority. The Clintons alike were glad to witness Burr's self-destruction as a political force in New York State, especially because there was a cluster of New Yorkers who did not find moral culpability in Burr's actions. In the South and West, Burr would receive widespread credit for having brought down his man in a fair and honorable fight.[117]

His plans were to head south. He had been invited by Pierce Butler to lodge at his plantation on St. Simons, a small island located off the coast of Georgia. Butler was a former Federalist, turned Republican, who recognized the duel as just another affair of honor. For his long trip, Burr was joined by his slave Peter Yates and John Swartwout's younger brother Samuel. The young man was to be his "fellow traveler," as Burr denoted him, over the next two months.[118]

During his southern sojourn, Burr already had in mind to "visit the Floridas for five or six weeks." He sent Theodosia (nowadays with her husband on Alston's rice plantation, The Oaks) detailed letters of his travels, including animated observations about the people he met, descriptions of the geography he traversed, local habits, and other curiosities; he was acting as if he were an anthropologist leisurely studying a strange new land. So she might "better understand" what he wrote to her, he told his daughter to obtain a copy of William Bartram's celebrated *Travels*; the famed eighteenth-century natural historian had journeyed through Florida and Georgia in 1772.[119]

Although Burr was a fugitive, and was occasionally forced to conceal his identity (he told Theodosia to address her letters to "Mr. R. King"), he moved on almost as if nothing had changed. But clearly, a transformation was in progress. Figuring the world of national politics offered no place for Hamilton's killer, he had resolved to channel his energies elsewhere. The Floridas and the Louisiana Territory both captured his attention. As he moved easily through the South, he conjured up an expedition—a new challenge drawing on his military expertise, his mapmaking skill, and an old passion to explore. The ruined vice president would be heard from again.[120]

Aaron Burr in 1802 by John Vanderlyn; General James Wilkinson in 1796 by Charles Willson Peal

Chapter Eight

LITTLE QUID EMPEROR

It is discovered beyond the possibility of doubt, that there has been a dangerous and daring conspiracy afoot . . . carried on by those, and those exclusively, who style themselves "the union of honest men." . . . *Aaron Burr,* the leader of the lawless conspirators, is notoriously known to be the father of the quid faction.

—*Lancaster* [Pa.] *Intelligencer,* Dec. 10, 1806

*O*nce he had killed Hamilton, Burr could do nothing right. At least, that is how the popular imagination today construes the events of 1805–06. Whether he is understood to have planned to enter Mexico with a private army, amid a general U.S. military invasion, or to have "conspired" to detach the restless trans-Allegheny West from the Atlantic-lying Union, his activities after Weehawken have been presented as a psychological mystery the general outlines of which are (or appear) unmistakable. It is only Burr's mind-set—the full nature of his ambition—that has been called into question.

This pivotal episode in the life of the nation has long been presented as a whodunit in which the "who" is known and only the "dunit" or deed, lies in obscurity. To begin with, by labeling Burr's western dealings a "conspiracy," commentators have reached a consensus that there was a single unified project, and that it was headed by one person: Aaron Burr. Modern scholars have done as the journalists of 1805–06 did: they have gathered up scraps of testimony, relied on unsubstantiated rumors, and retold questionable stories, so as to construct a seamless tale. The record must be set straight—not to absolve Burr, but to get at the truth.

What if there was not a carefully laid plot encompassing grandiose and treasonous designs? What if the "Burr Conspiracy" was created by the newspapers, and then inflated by a primary actor in the drama so as to protect himself from possible retribution from Washington? What if the "conspiracy" was created *for* Burr, that is, to fit Burr into? This is not to say that he was an innocent. He was indisputably interested in promoting cross-border filibustering activities to topple Spain's New World governments. But that is not the same as being a traitor.

For those convinced of his treasonous intentions, then and now, this is what he is supposed to have done: With the help of England and Spain, and an army of his own making, he aimed to overthrow the states and territories west of the Alleghenies, and to follow up the domestic victory with a triumphant invasion of Mexico and possibly Spanish Florida. And as if that were not enough, some came to believe that he contemplated marching on Washington to unseat Jefferson.

"ONE OF THE BEST PRESIDING OFFICERS I EVER WITNESSED"

In the winter of 1804–05, before he headed west, Aaron Burr may have been politically wounded but he was still officially vice president. In Washington, he faced his colleagues with the poise he was known for, and on occasion dined peaceably with President Jefferson. With Burr's power in New York much diminished, and the way ahead for the Virginia dynasty of presidents looking clearer, Jefferson was extremely cordial to the man who slew his longtime arch nemesis Hamilton.

The lame duck vice president had returned to Washington to preside over the Senate at impeachment proceedings recently initiated against Supreme Court Justice Samuel Chase, alleged by Jefferson to have made seditious remarks from the bench. Burr's reception at the Capitol was mixed. Federalists close to Hamilton shunned him, of course. But many Republicans welcomed him with open arms. Jefferson invited Burr to several dinner parties, and Madison and Gallatin frequently called at his boardinghouse. Of the Republican leadership, it was Gallatin who spent the most time with Burr, and who clearly continued to treat him as a friend. The treasury secretary was appalled by the duel, not because he considered his friend a murderer but because he knew it spelled "catastrophe" for Burr's career. Gallatin had confided to his wife's brother that he thought Burr blind to the fact that his enemies would use the event to produce "an artificial sensation . . . to deify Hamilton and treat Burr as a murderer." How could someone so smart and capable be at the same time so unsuspecting? Gallatin wondered. How could Burr doubt the resolve of his enemies in plotting his political downfall?[1]

Slander had already made Burr notorious, and so his return to Washington piqued the curiosity of Federalist gadfly William Plumer. The New Englander, who could barely contain his fury over Hamilton's death, watched Burr's every move. He found it remarkable that Republicans of both houses were exceedingly "attentive" to Burr, as Plumer noted in his private journal on November 26. If they had the choice to make over—between George Clinton and Aaron Burr as the number two executive—it would be no contest. Burr would be the man. Or so it seemed to him at that moment. Returning to reality in his journal entry nine days later, the Federalist was convinced that after all that had occurred, Burr would never "rise again." And yet, Plumer concluded, "surely he is a very extraordinary man, & is an exception to all rules."[2]

An exception to all rules. Burr's political enemies routinely drew this kind of portrait of him: he possessed magic; he retained his appeal, even after ruining his career. It was not very different from what Cheetham had written: Burr was a "proteus." Even his supporters could not help but imagine him "incomparable." His audacity amazed.

Jefferson had sparked the Chase impeachment. On May 13, 1803, he wrote to Congressman Joseph H. Nicholson, complaining about the judge's "extraordinary charge" from the bench. In it, Chase had railed against the visionary Jefferson, and the Declaration of Independence, and accused the new administration of provoking lawlessness and civil rebellion. Jefferson had heard about the judge's harangue and had by now developed a strong distaste for Chase; he also was determined to weaken the judiciary, because he considered it a bastion of the Federalist opposition. Why did he complain to Nicholson? The Maryland congressman had already carried out Jefferson's wishes by leading an impeachment of Federalist John Pickering, a federal district judge of New Hampshire, who had been convicted on March 12, 1803, and removed from office.[3]

The Chase trial was a political trial. It was a direct attempt at using impeachment to remove a political enemy. Jefferson said as much to Nicholson, accusing Chase of making a "seditious and official attack on the principles of our Constitution, and on the proceedings of [the] State." Jefferson felt quite comfortable with what he called "selected" prosecutions for sedition. Just a month before his aggressive letter to Nicholson, he wrote to Governor Thomas McKean of Pennsylvania, endorsing the state prosecution of Federalist editor Joseph Dennie. Jefferson did not say that a "general prosecution" was in order, for that "would look like persecution"; but "a selected one" would have a "wholesome effect." Jefferson was repeating the sins of his Federalist foes, who had vindictively exploited the 1798 Sedition Act in order to silence their (Jeffersonian) political opposition.[4]

The Chase case fits a pattern. Republicans were fashioning a doctrine of impeachment that relied on the same English precedent of "bad tendency" that Federalists had used to prosecute Republicans for seditious libel and treason in the 1790s. According to this doctrine, any tendency for political excess could be interpreted as threatening to subvert republican institutions. And, as we shall see, the same impulse was shortly to influence the government's prosecution of Aaron Burr for treason. Jefferson urged on Chase's impeachment, without dirtying his own hands, telling Nicholson that "it is better that I should not interfere." His directive to the Maryland congressman was nevertheless understood. Attacking Jefferson was meant to be viewed as (and prosecuted as) an attack on the republic itself.[5]

Representative John Randolph of Roanoke—not Joseph Nicholson—took the lead in pursuing the impeachment of Justice Chase. In January 1804, he initiated an inquiry into the judge's conduct. The House overwhelmingly voted by 73 to 32 to impeach Chase in early March. And on March 26, one day before Congress went into recess, Randolph skillfully guided the House committee under his direction in presenting several articles of impeachment.[6]

Randolph was not close to his fellow Virginian Thomas Jefferson, but—as he would do many times over during his colorful career—he made the Chase impeachment his own cause. Randolph stood out in the House for a number of reasons: he was known as eccentric and combative, and his sanity was occasionally called into question. In 1804, at thirty-one, he cut an odd figure; standing just over six feet tall, gangly and unwieldy, he had legs that were long and spindly, and his shoulders were abnormally narrow. Randolph was a mesmerizing orator, though his voice was considered "shrill," similar to a woman's. Many commented on his beardless face, one of the several symptoms of a genetic condition known today as Klinefelter's syndrome: Randolph apparently had two X and one Y chromosomes.[7]

The talented, if peculiar, Republican would be taking on Justice Chase, a man with an equally unsettling and imposing demeanor. Chase's white locks ranged down to his shoulders. He was nicknamed "Bacon face" because of a reddish and fleshy visage. He was also compared to the British wit Samuel Johnson, for at sixty-four, he was large, portly, and intimidating. Neither Randolph nor Chase would take kindly to defeat. Both men's antics (and the justice's impressive defense team) promised to make the trial the most spectacular event in Washington that season.[8]

Aaron Burr assumed a critical role in the Chase trial. As presiding officer in the Senate, he was responsible for regulating the proceedings. He alone had to set the tone of the trial. The court first convened on January 2, 1805, and Chase was allowed to respond to the eight articles of impeachment already approved by the House. He was provided with a chair, but William Plumer angrily complained that he should have had a table as well, which Burr refused to provide. Burr had no intention of coddling the judge. He unnerved Chase by interrupting when he saw fit, and Chase was reported later to have been on the verge of tears. Plumer and others may have felt that Burr's behavior amounted to harassment, but his purpose was abundantly clear: he wanted to shame the judge. He had anointed himself a moral enforcer, a part he had once before played so well, when he commanded troops in the Revolutionary War.[9]

Why did Burr do this? Federalists at the time simply thought he was trying to placate Jefferson. But that is not quite correct. A distinct principle directed his behavior: The articles of impeachment brought against Chase had highlighted the justice's greatest flaw—he was a bully. For Burr, this was Chase's real crime. He had made it a habit to hector and badger defense attorneys; he made arbitrary and impulsive rulings; and he took punitive action against grand juries that refused to do his bidding. Over and over, he abused his authority as a judge. In fact, in Article Four of the eight articles, Justice Chase was rebuked for his "repeated and vexatious interruptions" of defense counsel. So Burr had decided—and had every right as president of the Senate—to teach the bully a lesson.[10]

He transformed the Senate chamber into a High Court of Impeachment. After granting the judge a month's delay to prepare his defense, Burr reconvened the court on February 4, and those in attendance were amazed by what they saw. Federalist senator Uriah Tracy claimed that the chamber had been "fitted up in a stile beyond anything which has ever appeared in the Country." The president's raised chair (which Burr occupied) assumed center stage; on the right was a box for the managers (Randolph and his team), and to the left, a similar box for Chase and his defense counsel. Both boxes were covered in green cloth. Benches draped in crimson, placed on each side of the president's chair, were provided for the senators. Additional seats were added to accommodate the hundreds of spectators who came to watch the grand performance. Other boxes were occupied by visiting dignitaries, and a special gallery was built for the "exclusive accommodation of the ladies," as one reporter described it.[11]

The man who shot Alexander Hamilton was in charge of a great national tribunal. This may seem strange to us, but Burr was not relieved of office for having engaged in a duel. During the month-long delay, he had gone to Philadelphia to meet with Governor Bloomfield of New Jersey, conferring on his outstanding indictment for murder in that state. Meanwhile, a group of Republican legislators in Washington signed a petition entreating the governor to intervene on the vice president's behalf. Federalist newspapers, eager to embarrass the administration, savored the irony in observing a man under indictment for murder standing in judgment of a Supreme Court justice.[12]

But Burr refused to be distracted—or deterred. He imposed his will, asking for decorum whenever a disruptive senator strutted about the chamber in the middle of testimony. He even bade one of the defense attorneys to remove his winter coat. And he seemed particularly incensed with those legislators who sat snacking on apples and cake. Outraged, Senator Plumer called the vice president a "pedagogue" for scolding his peers as though they were a pack of unruly schoolboys. "Really, *Master Burr*," Plumer sniped in his journal, "you need a ferule, or birch, to enforce your lectures on polite behavior!"[13]

Plumer was partially right, but he missed the larger point. Burr demanded a high degree of decorum for good reason: etiquette, combined with the presence of ladies in the galleries, would curb partisan excess. He was striving for civility, so that this High Court of Impeachment might achieve something of real value: impartiality. If this was *his* court, Burr wanted reason to rule in it. Given the combustible temperament of his colleagues, he knew that would only happen if he enforced an atmosphere of politeness.

For nearly ten days, Randolph and his team of managers brought forward a long line of witnesses, all of whom recounted episodes of Chase's heavy-handed behavior in his courtroom. Though the defense supplied witnesses as well, Chase himself only made an appearance on the first day. His counsel urged him to sit out the Senate trial, worried that he might let loose with some damaging outburst.[14]

Burr's importance grew as the trial continued. Following the testimony attentively, he asked witnesses to clarify their statements, and made certain the proceedings were not bogged down. If a point of order was raised, he solicited the senators for their opinion, gradually deepening their sense of his impartiality. An observer remarked: "Burr has displayed much ability, and since the first day I have seen nothing of partiality." A Massachusetts Federalist, Samuel Taggart, who was also a clergyman, offered poignant praise: "I could almost forgive Burr for any less crime than the blood of Hamilton for his decision, dignity, firmness and impartiality with which he presides in this tyral [sic]." And then he underscored: "He is undoubtedly one of the best presiding officers I ever witnessed."[15]

Burr watched as the lawyers for Justice Chase unraveled the arguments and exposed the weaknesses inherent in Randolph's case. This was not exceptionally difficult. The managers had proven that Chase was obnoxious, but they had failed to demonstrate that he had committed anything approaching a high crime or misdemeanor.

One of the lawyers to join Chase's team was Charles Lee (no relation to the court-martialed Revolutionary War general of the same name). A Virginian, and one of Burr's Princeton classmates, this Lee had served as attorney general under Washington; later, he would defend Burr at his treason trial. Though not a particularly gifted speaker, Lee nevertheless was convincing in his effort to show how Randolph and the other Republican managers had mangled the law. But it was the Maryland attorney Luther Martin, also a Princeton graduate, a close friend of Chase, and an avowed enemy of Jefferson, who served up the most entertaining forensic performance. In his closing remarks, Martin kept the audience on the edge of their seats for over five hours. He, too, as it happened, would become a major figure on Burr's defense team in the near future.[16]

Former Federalist senator Robert Goodloe Harper also ably defended Chase. Offering a sentimental portrait of the "aged patriot and statesman," Harper succeeded in generating sympathy for the insufferable jurist. At the end of his long closing remarks, Luther Martin set the tone for a valedictory by complimenting the vice president for his "impartiality, politeness and dignity." Randolph, who had been gravely ill during most of the proceedings, closed the prosecution's case with an odd, rambling speech, giving off sparks of brilliance, but not as many as his fits of exasperating digressions.[17]

Burr supervised the vote. Chase was acquitted on all eight articles, surprising even his most ardent defenders. There were twenty-four Republicans and ten Federalists in the Senate, which meant that Chase owed his acquittal to the Republicans who refused to vote along party lines. Six Republicans joined nine Federalists in voting not guilty on all articles. Only one article, the one that specifically addressed Chase's inflammatory charge to the Baltimore jury (which had most infuriated Jefferson), brought Chase close to conviction—4 votes shy of the two-thirds majority that was required. As the voting concluded, Burr calmly announced: "Hence it appears that there is not a constitutional majority of votes finding Samuel Chase, Esquire, guilty, on any one Article." The vice president pronounced the judge's acquittal, and then adjourned the court.[18]

Randolph flew into a rage. He rushed from the Senate chamber to the generally more boisterous House, calling for a constitutional amendment that would allow for the removal of any federal judge by the president on the basis of a simple majority in both houses. His last-ditch effort failed, however, and the quick-tempered Virginia planter would always remember the humiliation he had suffered.

Chase, though acquitted, had been duly chastised. He tempered his courtroom behavior. It would seem that Burr understood the case better than most of his peers. He suspected that Chase would not be impeached if the law was fairly applied. At the same time, he taught the justice a lesson.[19]

"AWAKENED FROM A KIND OF TRANCE"

On March 2, one day after the trial concluded, Burr made his last official appearance as vice president. As president of the Senate, he had one final duty to perform: a farewell speech. All present attested to the sublime power of Burr's address. Many of the men who heard it delivered were moved to tears.[20]

Senator Samuel Mitchill of New York, who was not at all close to Burr, captured these feelings in a letter to his wife written that day:

> When Mr. Burr had concluded he descended from the chair, and in a dignified manner walked to the door, which resounded as he with some force shut it after him. On this the firmness and resolution of many of the Senators gave way, and they burst into tears. There was a solemn and silent weeping for perhaps five minutes.

But the outpouring of emotion did not end there. Mitchill continued:

> For my own part, I never experienced any thing of the kind so affecting as this parting scene. . . . My colleague, General Smith, stout and manly as he is, wept as profusely as I did. He laid his head upon his table and did not recover from his emotion for a quarter of an hour or more. And for myself, though it is more than three hours since Burr went away, I have scarcely recovered my habitual calmness. Several gentlemen came up to me to talk about this extraordinary scene, but I was obliged to turn away and decline all conversation.[21]

Mitchill's rendition of the speech was echoed by others. The Washington Federalist (a paper hardly disposed to treat Burr favorably at this time) gave this laudatory account:

> In this cold relation a distant reader—especially one to whom Col. Burr is not personally known, will be at a loss to discern the cause of those extraor-

dinary emotions which were excited . . . the whole senate was in tears, and so unmanned, that it was half an hour before they could recover themselves.[22]

Two days later, at the President's House, one senator described Burr's speech as "the most extraordinary event" of a lifetime. And another confessed that the performance was strangely spellbinding, causing him to lose all sense of time, so that when Burr finished, the senator felt as if he had "awakened from a kind of trance."[23]

Why was Burr's simple address so moving? His eloquence in the Senate on that day makes sense only if we see in it a clear affirmation of political justice. Burr issued an appeal that echoed the moving prose of William Godwin, one of his favorite writers, husband of the late Mary Wollstonecraft, and author of the acclaimed 1794 novel *Caleb Williams*. His speech was another telling example of how the man Hamilton accused of having no principles was in fact a man deeply imbued with the Enlightenment ideals of truth and justice.[24]

Burr began with a discussion of the rules of the Senate—an appeal to reason—and quickly proceeded to his affecting declaration of sincere respect for the men who sat before him. He apologized if he had ever "wounded the feelings of individual members." He said he felt no anger or resentment, noting only that "on his part he had no injuries to complain of—If any had been done or attempted, he was ignorant of the authors: and if he had ever heard he had forgotten; for he thanked God he had no memory for injuries." At a time when Burr had every reason to feel vindictive, he seized higher ground. He voiced his faith in impartiality, celebrating the Senate as an enlightened forum, a body of equals, where all present could openly discuss their views. This, he explained, was the ideal he had always sought as a public man. He had done his best to behave fairly, "uniform and indiscriminate," and to make sure that in his "official conduct" he had "known no party—no cause—no friend."[25]

The parallel to the final dramatic scene in *Caleb Williams* is quite remarkable. For Godwin, as for Burr, public principle had to trump selfish interest; "sound reasoning and truth . . . must always be victorious over error." The character Caleb is a man caught up in a "nightmare of irrationality," a world riddled with injustice. Made a fugitive, he is relentlessly hunted by his tormentor, the powerfully connected Falkland, who has falsely accused him of a crime and misrepresented his character.[26]

Facing his enemy in the courtroom, Caleb is at peace with himself. He refuses every opportunity to shout down the symbols of power; he foregoes the chance to exact revenge. Like Burr before the Senate, Caleb addresses the magistrate with humility, and overwhelms Falkland with his profound sense of fairness. His only weapon is, in Godwin's words, his "frankness" and the "sovereignty of truth." Falkland's hostility instantly melts away, for as Caleb narrates: "He saw my sincerity; he was penetrated with my grief and compunction. He rose from his seat, supported by the attendants, and—to my infinite astonishment—threw himself into my arms!"[27]

Burr possessed scruples, too. He was a politician, to be sure, but his ability to rise above his resentments moved the Senate in the same way that Falkland had been moved by Caleb Williams. For Burr, there was a vital principle at stake: Only truth and sincerity, he reminded his colleagues, ensured that the Senate would remain a "sanctuary" of liberty, a "citadel" against corruption. He believed the Senate to be the lifeblood of the republic. It rose, he said, above considerations of "merely their personal honor and character." It was the guardian of the "*Law*, of *Liberty* and the Constitution." As he put it, and as it was recorded:

> It is here—it is here—in this exalted refuge—here, if any where will resistance be made to the storms of popular phrenzy and the silent arts of corruption:—and if the Constitution be destined ever to perish by the sacrilegious hands of a Demagogue or the Usurper, which God avert, its expiring agonies will be witnessed on this floor.[28]

After praising the Senate, Burr ended on an emotional note, perhaps melodramatic to our ears, but sounding the language of the literature that prevailed in the first decade of the nineteenth century. He brought up the "afflicting sensations which attended a final separation." He was separating from that august body, and might be heard from no more. For him, at least, a chapter in the history of the republic had come to an end. And so, all he could do was to remind his colleagues of the humanity he believed the collective Senate was capable of exhibiting. Men who believed in the "principles of freedom and social order" were also men of feeling.[29]

At first, Burr's enemies tried to ignore the speech; then they mocked it. William Coleman of New York's Hamiltonian *Evening Post* called reports of the speech a *"hoax."* As more news of the address made its way to New York, James Cheetham's concern grew. Burr's sudden acclaim was inexplicable to him. Given at seemingly his lowest moment, the speech was being called a "sublime" achievement. Disapproval arising from the killing of Hamilton was weakening. Frustrated, Cheetham could only complain that Burr was magically reinventing himself.[30]

Burr's own reaction was subdued. In writing Theodosia, he admitted that he had not prepared an address, but that the ideas he expressed had been on his mind for several days, or at least, that he had "to say something." Though he sent her a copy from the newspapers, he felt that the story had been "awkwardly and pompously told." As he looked out at his colleagues, he explained, his speech had emerged spontaneously: "It was the solemnity, the anxiety, the expectation, and the interest which I saw strongly painted in the countenances of the auditors, that inspired what I said." He had said what he felt—hardly what was expected any more in the rancorous partisan climate of Washington. His candor had unnerved his enemies. Indeed, his candor was what made him unusual.[31]

HAD "TURNED HIMSELF WHOLLY TOWARD MEXICO"

Burr's fascination with the West began long before his duel with Hamilton. He had probably thought about the tremendous possibilities of this territory as early as the 1780s, when he first befriended Augustine Prevost, who had acquired land in Louisiana long before it became part of the United States. In 1803, he had contemplated a trip to New Orleans, discussing the details of it with his boyhood friend Jonathan Dayton, by then a U.S. senator. New Orleans and its environs was alluring to the investor, open to land speculation. Burr saw a chance to recoup his flagging finances.[32]

But now, after leaving office, he had a grander project in mind: In the event of a war with Spain, he would lead a filibuster into Spanish territory. A filibuster was an invasion by a private army without government sanction. There was a loophole for such would-be adventurers: the laws of neutrality, which made filibustering criminal, did not apply during a time of war. He also knew that it was accepted practice for Americans to engage in personal diplomacy, so appeals for foreign assistance were not illegal.[33]

Burr was not alone in viewing filibustering as a necessary means for territorial expansion. Like many American filibusterers before and after him, he used the language of liberty and national pride to justify conquest. In 1775, Richard Montgomery had invaded Canada uninvited, spearheading an offensive inspired by the Revolutionary desire to liberate Canadians from their English colonial oppressors. Other attempts to incite rebellion in Canada were tried by American citizens in 1796 and 1800.[34]

The lure of Spanish lands was just as strong. Long before Burr set his sights on Mexico, the Revolutionary War hero George Rogers Clark united with the French to invade the Spanish-held territory of Louisiana, while Thomas Jefferson, then secretary of state, conveniently looked the other way, unconcerned, he claimed, with "what insurrections should be excited." In 1797, Republican senator William Blount attempted something similar, turning this time to the British as potential allies in ousting the Spanish. And Alexander Hamilton was so enamored with the plan of Francisco de Miranda, who dreamed of liberating South America from Spanish rule, that in 1798, he imagined himself as the conquering hero leading U.S. forces into Mexico.[35]

But for Burr, the above precedents were not enough. His plan required the existence of certain political and military conditions, whereby the United States would be drawn into a war along its southwestern border. He observed such tensions brewing during his vice presidency.

In 1801, Spain had ceded control of the Mississippi and New Orleans to France. Though the strategic port of New Orleans was still administered by the Spanish, Jefferson feared it would momentarily come within Napoleon's grasp. Rumors of massive numbers of French troops arriving in Louisiana heightened his concern. The next year, the Spanish confirmed his fears, refusing to allow Americans to deposit goods at New Orleans. There was no doubt that Jefferson was willing to go to war to secure this crucial commercial hub at the southern end of the Mississippi. The president even dared to make a pact with "harlot England" to force Napoleon out of the American theater.[36]

Warmongering filled the air, in Washington and elsewhere. Even as Jefferson was secretly negotiating an agreement to purchase New Orleans from France, Republicans and Federalists alike clamored for war. In 1803, Senator Samuel Smith of Maryland gave a toast at a dinner held in honor of special envoy James Monroe, who was about to depart for France. In the presence of the French and Spanish foreign ministers, Smith arrogantly lifted his glass with these bold words: "Peace if peace is honorable, war if war is necessary."[37]

In the West, American residents in New Orleans felt the United States should seize the city before French forces arrived. One anxious observer compared the residents of the Crescent City to the Jews awaiting the Messiah. Peter Irving's Burrite newspaper, the *Morning Chronicle,* was one of those encouraging this war frenzy. A writer in its pages argued that the entire militia system should be reorganized, so that the Kentucky militia could take New Orleans and the militias of Georgia and South Carolina could march into Spanish Florida. Burrites justified bold measures with appeals to the "manly feelings of national pride," and America's Revolutionary heritage. Nothing was meant to interfere with America's "national greatness," which meant, of course, the will to expand westward and grow commercially. The Mississippi trade route was key.[38]

As vice president, Burr was keenly aware of the diplomatic shift toward war when he went about collecting information from the U.S. consul in London. He knew exactly how his friends felt. His understanding of the political climate can be gauged from a letter he received from Charles Biddle in 1803. The Philadelphia merchant was primed for war with France and Spain, confidently declaring that "we could do more injury to them than they could do us." Biddle symbolizes how many Americans felt when he compared the simmering conflict to the American Revolution. Back then, his mother had proudly defended her country, he said, in declaring to a British officer that she herself would lead her seven sons into war. Biddle, likewise, pledged his sons, whom "I would much sooner lead to the field than suffer our country to be insulted."[39]

On July 4, 1803, when Jefferson announced that the government had purchased the Louisiana Territory from France for $11.5 million, tensions in the Southwest did not disappear. France may no longer have posed an immediate danger to American interests, but the Spanish continued to be a thorn for security-conscious Americans. Jefferson had originally planned to acquire West Florida (along the Gulf of Mexico) in addition to New Orleans, but this crucial strip of land remained within Spain's colonial domain. There were also significant disputes about the borders. Jefferson tried the same strategy with Spain that had worked with France: military bluster concurrent with negotiation. But there was an important difference. In Jefferson's thinking, as a weak and declining imperial power, Madrid offered little resistance to American expansionism.[40]

The administration assumed that the conquest of Spanish America was inevitable. American expansion was a natural force—private settlement was thought to represent the catalyst by which Madrid would feel obliged to cede its territory. As Madison explained in 1803 to Charles Pinckney, the American minister to Spain, that country could do little to curtail the "growing power of this country, and the direction of it against her possessions within its reach." He added emphatically: "Can she annihilate this power? No. Can she sensibly retard its growth? No." Madison portrayed Spain as a weak woman, with borders so permeable that private American citizens—not the government—would take the lead and lay claim to her possessions. So, what was Burr thinking of doing? Nothing different from what the administration itself was predicting. Jefferson's theory of natural conquest, echoed by Madison and Monroe, opened the door wide for private filibusters. Without calling directly for invasion, Washington was all but giving the green light to private citizens who were contemplating transgressing those borders.[41]

Jefferson's own words reveal how well established this theory was when he wrote to James Bowdoin, his second minister to Spain, in April 1807. In defending his decision to prosecute Burr for treason, the president made a surprising admission: Burr had abandoned the idea of separating the western states, he said, and had "turned himself wholly toward Mexico." This made sense, in his mind. "So popular is an enterprise on that country in this that we had only to lie still, and [Burr] would have had followers enough to have been in the City of Mexico in six weeks." In six weeks? Jefferson was capable of hyperbole. His statement was far from a realistic assessment of Burr's power, for the expeditionary force he had assembled was capable of achieving little, as we shall see; but it is nonetheless significant that Jefferson believed such a conquest possible. It speaks to the fact that people like Burr and Jefferson (and many others) viewed Mexico and Spain's other colonial possessions as vulnerable entities that could be easily toppled by private citizens—it was, to them, a matter of when, not if, it would happen.[42]

A new territorial aggressiveness marked the Jefferson administration's policy. The 1803 Louisiana Purchase had doubled the size of the United States, and Jefferson called this vast expanse his "empire for liberty." For the next three years, war with Spain remained a real possibility; diplomatic relations suffered as each country tried to enforce its contested boundaries. The U.S. and Spanish armies were on the verge of clashing, as both sides engaged in a chess match of provocative moves and countermoves along disputed borders. When Burr looked west in 1804, he considered land investment opportunities, and a filibuster into Mexico, and perhaps Florida, were war with Spain to break out. But to carry off his scheme, he needed allies, the most important of whom were Senator Jonathan Dayton and General James Wilkinson. Both would join him in this daring venture, and it was probably Wilkinson who came up with the idea for a foray into Spanish territory.[43]

Though Burr and Wilkinson probably knew each other from the time of the Revolution, they were not intimates at that early date. With Jefferson's victory in 1801, Wilkinson sought to ingratiate himself with Burr, and for the first time declared himself a Republican. He attended the March inauguration, lobbying for either a War Department post or the governorship of Mississippi Territory. As a man whose entire career involved military commissions and securing patronage, he had served under the first two Federalist presidents, becoming a brigadier general and commander of the U.S. Army by 1796, and was reappointed commanding general in 1800. Two years later, when Congress threatened to take away his military commission, Wilkinson entreated Burr to intervene on his behalf. Burr did another favor for the ambitious general: he helped to place Wilkinson's two sons at Princeton.[44]

Patronage again brought Wilkinson to Burr's door in 1804 when he was angling for the governorship of Louisiana Territory.* He made a surprise visit to New York City in May (two months before the duel), requesting

---

* The Louisiana Purchase was divided in two territories: north of the 33rd parallel was the Louisiana Territory, and south of it the Orleans Territory. Today the 33rd parallel divides the states of Arkansas and Louisiana.

a bed for the night, while inviting the vice president to "see his Maps." Armed with twenty-eight maps, the general was headed for Washington next, where he delivered a lengthy memorial to the president on the current situation in the Louisiana and Orleans territories. The persuasive general succeeded again, becoming governor of the Louisiana territory while retaining his post as army commander. [45]

Patronage and speculation went hand-in-hand in the Louisiana Territory, something that Jefferson was well aware of when he appointed James Wilkinson. Treasury Secretary Albert Gallatin had sized up the new governor of Louisiana, and told the president that he was "extravagant and needy and would not, I think, feel much delicacy in speculating on public money and public lands." Wilkinson was, Gallatin added, not "very scrupulous," but in his lust for land and speculative schemes he was certainly not alone. Wherever a transfer of land had occurred, whether from Indians or by international treaty, speculators descended, beginning with the most politically privileged. [46]

Meanwhile, Burr was making further arrangements in the West. Two of his close relatives (and past financial partners) would find posts in the newly acquired territories: Dr. Joseph Browne, the brother-in-law of Burr's late wife, was named secretary of the Louisiana Territory, and Burr's stepson, John Bartow Prevost, became a superior court judge in New Orleans. Wilkinson and Dayton were bound together by speculative interests, too, because the general's major business partner, Daniel Clark, Jr., U.S. consul in New Orleans from 1801 to 1803, was Dayton's primary contact in the West. [47]

When Burr and Wilkinson met again in Washington, during the winter of 1804–05, they discussed the possibility of a filibuster into Mexico, and there is evidence to suggest that the two were making copies of maps of Florida, Mexico, and the southern frontier. In June, Burr had hoped to meet with Baron Alexander von Humboldt, who was known to have drafted the most complete map of Mexico. He failed to meet the famous German explorer and cartographer, but it is safe to assume that Burr and Wilkinson did their best to get their hands on Humboldt's map. [48]

All the evidence points to the fact that Burr had started thinking about going west well before he lost the governor's race, or faced indictments for murder from his duel with Hamilton. He was not a "desperate man" when he finally reached the Crescent City in 1805. He was in 1805, as he had been in 1803, when he first discussed a trip to New Orleans with Dayton, and as he had always been: a man who undertook action only after deliberate planning. Though his alliance with Wilkinson was essential to his plans, Wilkinson had plans of his own. And those plans, as we shall see, were often at odds with those of the former vice president.[49]

"MEXICO GLITTERS IN OUR EYES"

In 1804, other, even more secret negotiations set the stage for Burr's project. Before he arrived in New York that spring, Wilkinson had become acquainted with two influential Spanish officials: Don Vicente Folch, the governor of West Florida, and Sebastian Calvo de la Puerta y O'Faril, the marqués de Casa Calvo, who remained in New Orleans after 1804, as the Spanish boundary commissioner. These two officials had attended the ceremony that marked the transfer of Louisiana to the United States, and Wilkinson was on hand, too, to watch the American flag replace the French colors over the Place d'Armes.[50]

Wilkinson's intimacy with the Spanish Dons went way back. In 1787, he was put on the Spanish payroll, vowing allegiance to his Catholic Majesty, and acting, for all intents and purposes, as a double agent. He suggested to the Spanish how they might encourage a Kentucky independence movement that would lead to an alliance between Kentucky and Spain. He was also active in constitutional politics in Lexington and Danville, Kentucky, assuming a role in the westerners' bid for statehood, which finally took place in 1792. But the so-called "Spanish Conspiracy" continued to haunt Wilkinson. Rumors about his questionable allegiance followed him through the 1790s, and were part of the War Department's official records; charges would resurface amid the "Burr Conspiracy," and Wilkinson would be investigated by Congress in 1807. He retained his command throughout, and was finally brought forward for court-martial in 1811, when he was completely cleared. As the richest evidence remained buried in Spanish archives, his secret life as a double agent was not discovered until the twentieth century.[51]

In 1804, however, Wilkinson was again looking for money from Spain, asking for $20,000 in back pay for a "pension" he had not received for ten years. In return, he promised Governor Folch of Spanish West Florida valuable information, claiming he could provide "what was concealed in the heart of the President." Wilkinson issued a lengthy memorial, his "Reflections," offering strategic advice to the Spanish on how they could retain their colonial possessions in the face of U.S. belligerence. To keep his identity secret, the document was translated into Spanish, Wilkinson's authorship concealed. In further communications, he was referred to only as "number 13."[52]

Though he received $12,000 for his services in 1804, it is unclear whether the Spanish got their money's worth. This document is more valuable for what it reveals about Wilkinson's self-presentation. Aside from his blustering, Wilkinson adopted a clear strategy in print, namely, to make himself indispensable. The more conflict that arose, the more likely it was that both sides would rely on his advice. In 1804, then, the general supplied information to the Spanish—and to President Jefferson—that served to heighten rather than reduce tensions between the two countries. A boundary dispute loomed, which threatened all-out war. Writing to Jefferson, Wilkinson urged a defense of the U.S. claim to the Rio Grande border separating Louisiana and Mexico, arguing, in other words, that the future Texas was U.S. soil. But writing to Spanish officials, the general described a different scenario. Spain should reclaim control of the west bank of the Mississippi, he suggested, and strengthen its Texas defenses at Nacogdoches and the Sabine River—well north and east of where Jefferson was meant to make a stand. Wilkinson's treachery is instantly recognizable. Two years later, war almost broke out along the Sabine, due to explosive conditions persisting along this border.[53]

Wilkinson also preyed on the worst fears of the Dons. He conjured images of America's overflowing population west of the Alleghenies as a restless force, primed and ready to cross into Spanish territory. If the United States secured its boundary claim along the Rio Grande, all was lost. The flood gates would open to "hardened armies and adventurers, desperadoes who, like the ancient Goths and Vandals," would storm into Mexico. By Goths and Vandals, he meant nothing other than American filibusterers.[54]

Those close to Wilkinson, however, understood his ambition for an Americanized Mexico. Burr and Wilkinson shared a friend in Charles Biddle of Philadelphia: Wilkinson had married Biddle's niece, Ann, back in 1778. Biddle must have known what was on Wilkinson's mind when, in March 1805, he received a letter from the general, predicting that before long he would be, as he put it, "on the high road to Mexico." In his "Reflections,"

Wilkinson himself called Mexico "the most precious jewel of the royal diadem." John Adair, a Kentucky senator, had excitedly informed him not long before his letter to Biddle that "the Kentuckians are full of enterprise" and "greedy after plunder as ever the old Romans were." "Mexico glitters in our Eyes."[55]

Wilkinson was to write a glowing letter of introduction on Burr's behalf to the marqués de Casa Calvo, the same Spanish boundary negotiator who was responsible for paying him handsomely for his "Reflections." It appears that Wilkinson was more than willing to conceal Burr's plans from Spain, at least initially. Wilkinson wanted a filibuster that would succeed, and that would accrue to his benefit and reputation. His backup plan, as it were, was to protect himself in case the filibuster failed. Wilkinson was doing a lot of things at once, all of them designed to secure a prominent (and safe) place for him, regardless who succeeded and who failed.[56]

Under these circumstances, it is less than startling that in the summer of 1804, Burr sent a proposal for cooperation to Anthony Merry, the British minister to the United States. In the form that Merry conveyed Burr's proposal to the foreign secretary in London, the vice president would "lend his assistance to His Majesty's Government in any Manner in which they may think fit to employ him, particularly endeavoring to effect a Separation of the Western Part of the United States from that which lies between the Atlantick and the Mountains, in it's [sic] whole Extent." Beginning with Henry Adams, 125 years ago, many historians have used this communication to damn Burr, without recognizing that it represents only Merry's strategy in attempting to exercise influence on his own government. By no means does it tell the whole story.[57]

We need to start, instead, with the go-between who delivered Burr's message to Merry. Charles Williamson was Scottish-born. He fought on the British side in the Revolution, but became a U.S. citizen and was a member of the New York State Assembly in the 1790s, when he was concurrently the representative of a group of wealthy English investors in the acquisition of over 1 million acres in Ontario and Steuben Counties in the western part of the state. As politically motivated New Yorkers with shared interests in developing unsettled lands, he and Burr had come to know one another fairly well. Both reasonably figured that if British speculators were financing land development in New York (building mills, bridges, and roads, and relying on a sophisticated advertising campaign to attract settlers), then they would likely be interested in assuming a similar role in the new West.[58]

Not surprisingly, Williamson saw Napoleonic ambition as a threat to both British and American interests. In 1803, he approached the British Ministry with his own plan, recommending the creation of a private filibustering force to invade the French West Indies. His force would be made up of Canadian and American recruits, backed by English funds and ships. He viewed South America and Mexico as equally attractive targets. By removing the Spanish from the hemisphere, Williamson believed that the "liberated" countries would quickly become part of an Anglo-American commercial network. Filibustering, thus, was seen as a means for promoting a "free" market, a transatlantic market that served the common interests of England and the United States. And Williamson was not merely a dreamer: he belonged to an influential Scottish family possessing close contacts with members of the British cabinet, one of whom was Henry Dundas, Lord Melville, first lord of the admiralty, who might be called the "patron saint" of filibusterers.[59]

There is one other thing worth knowing about Merry. He and President Jefferson despised one another. In March 1804, well before he knew of Burr's project, Merry had urged his government to follow a course of action that would promote separatist feelings in the American West. Burr must have known this, but was willing to use Merry to further his—and his country's—expansionist ends. As for Merry, when the diplomat reported on Burr's project in 1805, he mentioned his idealistic version of events, highlighting Burr's supposed separatist plan, but he ignored what he thought was unimportant: Burr's plan for ridding Mexico of the Spanish! Meanwhile, it is important to compare Williamson's correspondence with Lord Melville and other British officials: he presented Burr's project strictly as an invasion of Mexico and Florida. Williamson knew what Burr intended, while Merry heard what he wanted to hear.[60]

So, why then would Burr even hint at the idea of separation to Merry, when he had no such intent? Unlike Williamson, who strongly advocated Anglo-American cooperation, Merry loathed the very idea of cooperation with the Jefferson administration, or any kind of joint venture that might accrue to the benefit of the president. He also began the process unsympathetic toward Burr, insofar as he shared many of the biases of the High

Federalists, particularly since the death of Hamilton. He confided in a dispatch to London that the most attractive feature of Burr's plan was that the vice president's "spirit of revenge" might be used against "the present administration."[61]

Charles Williamson sailed to England in the autumn of 1804, where he went about promoting Burr's scheme. Like the indomitable Benjamin Franklin, who spent the better part of two years in the 1770s lobbying the French government to lend material support to the modestly equipped American independence movement, Williamson pleaded with Lord Melville to send Burr money for equipment and military stores, and requested a "small Fleet cruizing in the Gulph of Mexico to keep the Spanish quiet." The Scottish-American lobbyist predicted that if the British government followed his advice and supported Burr, it would soon see "50,000 North Americans, with Col. Burr at their head, far on their March to the City of Mexico."[62]

"TO ORLEANS, AND PERHAPS FURTHER"

In April 1805, Burr finally headed west, traveling overland from Philadelphia to Pittsburgh in the company of his friend Gabriel Shaw, a wealthy New Yorker. Before setting out, he told Theodosia that he contemplated his western tour "with gayety and cheerfulness." This was not to say that his plans were not serious. He explained: "As the objects of this journey, not mere curiosity, or *pour passer le tem[p]s,* may lead me to Orleans, and perhaps further."[63]

In fact, Burr would be gone seven months, covering over 3,000 miles. His itinerary included voyages down the Ohio and Mississippi Rivers, a stop at New Orleans, and a desolate return along the Natchez Trace, which he described as a "vile country," without fresh streams, featuring instead "nasty puddle-water, covered with green scum, and full of amimalculae—bah!" To judge from the pages of Burr's journal to his daughter, the trip made him feel like a dignitary paying a visit to an exotic foreign land. At every stop in Ohio, Kentucky, and Tennessee, he was "received with much hospitality and kindness." And as he descended the Mississippi on an "elegant barge" (supplied by General Wilkinson), he needed no letters of introduction. Just the word of his arrival, and the local elite opened their homes with the "most cordial reception."[64]

Burr was no simple tourist, of course. As an unofficial diplomat, military scout, and land promoter, he went about collecting information,

renewing old contacts and forging new ones, all the while sizing up the political climate. His ultimate plan was to be shaped by what he learned. At
this early stage, he considered several possibilities: Did the West offer speculative ventures for rebuilding his bankrupt finances? Was it possible to
gain the popular support he needed for a filibustering campaign into Mexico? And if the United States did go to war with Spain and he went "further"
than Orleans, as he had hinted to Theodosia, could he rely on Wilkinson
to help him "liberate" Mexico? Overall, could he restore his national political reputation beyond the Alleghenies?

Burr traveled in high style. He arranged for a barge, or in his words "a
floating house, sixty feet by fourteen, containing a dining-room, kitchen
with fireplace, and two bedrooms," to carry him and Shaw down the Ohio.
Along the way, his boat caught up to the barge of Matthew Lyon, the ex-
Vermont congressman. They tied the two barges together and made their
way to Marietta, where Burr visited the famous Indian mounds.[65]

Next he called at the island retreat of Harman and Margaret Blennerhassett, two of the most colorful residents of the Ohio Valley. The couple
had come to America in 1796, fleeing their native Ireland because of the
scandal they had caused: Margaret was both Harman's wife and niece.
Their 179-acre estate lay fourteen miles below Marietta, off the shore of
modern Parkersburg, West Virginia. The Blennerhassett mansion was built
in the grand style of an Irish country home, with serpentine walks and gardens filled with exotic flowers and plants. There the couple devoted their
energies to philosophical pursuits. Harman was an amateur scientist, with
his own laboratory and solar telescope, and his young wife was a product
of Rousseau's *Emile,* raising her children with the same passion for "natural" learning that Burr and his wife had earlier provided for their talented
daughter.[66]

Blennerhassett would eventually become closely involved in Burr's adventure. Burr did not find him the foolish eccentric as others have portrayed
him. The tall, lanky, nearsighted Irishman may have been eccentric in his
tastes and demeanor, but he was also a westerner (by choice, if not by
birth) who would have looked to Mexico as an exciting prospect.[67]

From Blennerhassett Island, Burr made his way to Cincinnati. There he
met with Jonathan Dayton and Senator John Smith of Ohio. They were
backers of the Indiana Canal Company, which planned to construct a canal

to bypass the Falls of the Ohio River, a dangerous series of rapids near Louisville, Kentucky. Burr was one of the directors of the canal company. This speculating venture was little different from the various bridge, road, and land investment schemes he had dabbled in before. His old friend Dayton, a key player, had secured 25,000 acres of land between the Big and Little Miami Rivers. The canal promised to introduce a thriving commercial traffic to the Ohio that would increase the value of this real estate. Wilkinson was involved in this project, too, as was John Brown of Kentucky, who had just retired from the U.S. Senate. The canal venture connected Burr to likeminded men—western power brokers and risk takers, ambitious men interested in commercial growth and expansion. The canal was Burr's first step in starting life over after the vice presidency. Forging a western network, a new base of operations, would enable him to add supporters to his prospective filibuster campaign against Spanish territory.[68]

Burr toured leisurely through Kentucky in May 1805, visiting Eddyville, the home of Matthew Lyon, now a Kentucky congressman. From here, he visited Frankfort, where John Brown entertained him at his home, Liberty Hall. At Lexington, he appears to have crossed paths with John Adair, another U.S. senator who was corralled into Burr's circle. Like Burr and Dayton, Adair had been an officer in the Revolution. In the early 1790s, he served under Wilkinson in a campaign against Indians. He was a readymade filibusterer. It was Adair who had written to Wilkinson, "Mexico glitters in our Eyes."[69]

On May 29, Burr arrived at Nashville, where he was given a hero's welcome. He stayed at the home of Andrew Jackson, whom he had met in the mid- to late 1790s, when the Tennessean served in both houses of Congress. They seemed natural allies. Jackson admired Burr for championing Tennessee statehood during his time in the Senate. Though the roughhewn frontiersman and future president would go on to distinguish himself in the Battle of New Orleans, and then in 1818–19 by invading Spanish territory and forcing the Dons to hand over Florida to the United States, he had yet to accomplish anything militarily in 1805. Still, he held the rank of major general in the state militia, and itched for an opportunity to prove himself. His combativeness was linked to personal feuds, and unspecified threats against Indians yet to be pacified. He was already known for his intense likes and dislikes. At the top of his list of "villains" was General James

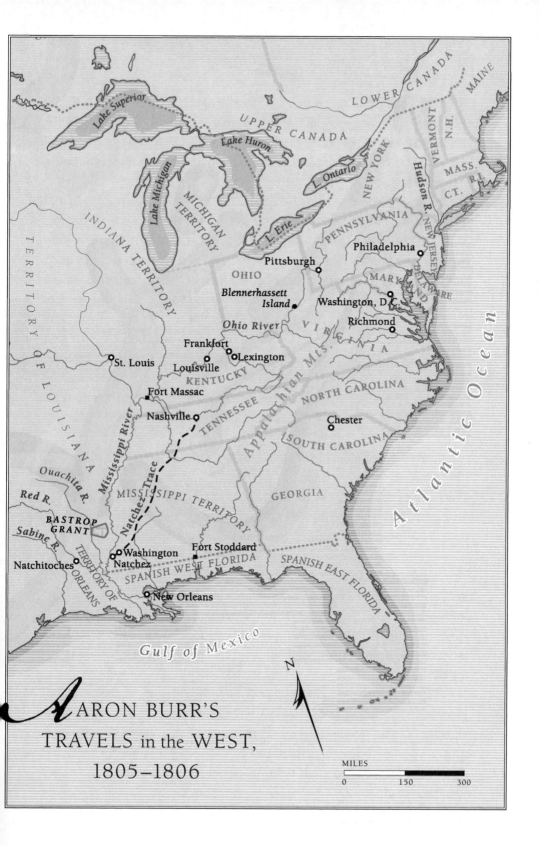

Lake Superior

LOWER CANADA

MAINE

UPPER CANADA

Lake Huron

NEW YORK

VERMONT

N.H.

Lake Michigan

MICHIGAN TERRITORY

L. Ontario

Hudson R.

MASS.

CT. R.I.

INDIANA TERRITORY

L. Erie

PENNSYLVANIA

Philadelphia

NEW JERSEY

Pittsburgh

DELAWARE

TERRITORY OF LOUISIANA

OHIO

MARYLAND

Blennerhassett
Island

Washington, D.C.

Ohio River

VIRGINIA

Richmond

St. Louis

Frankfort

Lexington

Louisville

KENTUCKY

Appalachian Mts.

Fort Massac

Mississippi River

Nashville

TENNESSEE

NORTH CAROLINA

Chester

SOUTH CAROLINA

Ouachita R.

MISSISSIPPI TRACE

Natchez Trace

MISSISSIPPI TERRITORY

GEORGIA

Red R.

BASTROP
GRANT

Sabine R.

TERRITORY OF ORLEANS

Washington

Fort Stoddard

Natchitoches

Natchez

SPANISH WEST FLORIDA

SPANISH EAST FLORIDA

New Orleans

Atlantic Ocean

Gulf of Mexico

N

$\mathcal{A}$ARON BURR'S
TRAVELS in the WEST,
1805–1806

MILES

0   150   300

Wilkinson, who had mistreated a Jackson friend. In 1806, Jackson would shoot and kill a man in a duel; and from that encounter he carried a bullet in his chest for the rest of his life. On some level, he enjoyed violence, and was ready for an adventure that promised him a chance to display courage, defend honor, or just win.[70]

Adding up these western-based allies, Burr was cultivating a formidable following: Smith, Dayton, Adair, Brown, and Jackson were all senators or ex-senators, state leaders, and major speculators; they had military experience and broad connections. Smith and Lyon had contracts to build gunboats for the U.S. Navy. At Jefferson's request, Smith made a special trip to West Florida in 1805, asking residents how they felt about the possibility of becoming part of the United States. Obviously, then, there were no political novices in Burr's widening circle; most were Burr's age, or a bit younger. Collectively, they saw nothing wrong with "revolutionizing Mexico," as they described ridding the West of the "Dons" and making a profit from war. They saw the West as Burr did: the next theater of operations for an expansive young republic, ready to face down any European threat to a destiny they already considered "manifest."[71]

Burr eventually met up with Wilkinson on June 6, at Fort Massac on the Ohio, and the general encouraged Burr to continue on to New Orleans. When he arrived there, he met another old friend, Edward Livingston. Ned Livingston had been the mayor of New York when Burr was vice president; he had defended him against Cheetham's charge that he had tried to steal the election from Jefferson. By 1805, Livingston had remade himself as a distinguished citizen of the new U.S. Territory of Orleans. His importance to Burr had to do with his connection to the Mexican Society of New Orleans. This political club (similar to the democratic societies of the 1790s) advocated the liberation of Spanish-held territory. Burr naturally saw the members of the society as potential boosters and recruits for his filibustering campaign.[72]

"Cheerful, gay, and easy"—that is how Burr described the people of New Orleans. Even the cloistered Ursuline nuns requested an interview with the former vice president, and they entertained him with wit, wine, fruit, and cakes. But this multiethnic city of Creoles, French, Spanish, and Americans was riddled with political factionalism. The Mexican Society was often at the center of controversy. Rumors circulated that the group was planning its own coup of Spanish Florida and Mexico. Many of its members were at odds with the new governor of Orleans Territory, former Tennessee congressman William C. C. Claiborne. Wilkinson despised Claiborne for his relative youth and inexperience and had lobbied against his appointment. In a letter of introduction Wilkinson prepared, which Burr was to present to a Louisiana ally, the general insulted the governor without self-censoring, saying that Burr could be of assistance in relegating that "Idiot black guard . . . to the Devil." Needless to say, Claiborne distrusted Burr for spending too much time with his enemies. Burr also made a misstep during this visit by snubbing the Spanish official the marqués de Casa Calvo. Whether intentionally or not, Burr ruffled the wrong feathers, obliging the Dons to watch him more closely.[73]

He left New Orleans on July 14, traveling through West Florida and along the Natchez Trace. Over the next two months, he retraced his steps, visiting Nashville, Lexington, Frankfort, and Louisville once more. In September, he had one last conference with Wilkinson, in St. Louis. The general dispatched Burr with a glowing letter of introduction to Indiana's territorial governor, William Henry Harrison, pleading with Harrison to arrange Burr's election to Congress. Matthew Lyon had already tried to convince Burr to run for Congress in Tennessee. But neither office seems to have appealed to the reluctant candidate. Burr took an instant liking to Harrison, at any rate, telling Wilkinson that the Virginia-born future president was "fit for other things." He meant, of course, that Harrison was yet another convert to their Mexican venture. By October, Burr was back in Ohio, heading east, and arriving in Washington after one more month on the road. The filibuster idea was still very much alive, as he made his way around the nation's capital in the waning months of 1805.[74]

THE "NEW CATALINA"

It would have been impossible for Burr not to have aroused curiosity and suspicion as he made his way through the West. In early August 1805, the Federalist Philadelphia newspaper *United States Gazette* had published a startling set of queries beginning with "How long will it be before we shall hear of *Col. Burr* being at the head of a *revolution* party on the western waters?" The article insinuated that Burr was already recruiting "adventurous and enterprising *young men* from the Atlantic states" for his project. Why would they join him? One inducement was that Burr's "revolution party" would soon be forming a convention in order to establish a "separate government" among all the "*states* bordering on the Ohio and Mississippi." And that was not all. The writer went on to predict that Burr would seize all the public lands in the West, divide the spoils among the new states, and generously reward his followers with whatever land remained. He would somehow create a prosperous country, and be able to offer tempting land bounties to attract new settlers from the East. Then he would swiftly move southward, liberating Mexico with the help of the British. And he would do it all "in one summer." True, Burr had long been thought capable of extraordinary things; but a scenario this improbable was beyond even Burr's wildest expectations.[75]

In the tantalizing newspaper report, most remarkable is the depiction of Burr's revolution as if it were the launching of a new third political party—a party of the West. He was mobilizing a force of young men and, in this amorphous reconstruction, somehow calling a convention and working within the existing political system; or, at least, willing to do so until his "revolution party" could form a new country.[76]

The writer assumes that Burr could constitute a new version of the old New York Burrites. In the same way that Jefferson would call his electoral defeat of Federalism the "Revolution of 1800," a western party under Burr's direction evoked a whole new political order. Burr's "revolution party" could thus be termed partisan and secessionist at once.

The West was already considered a place ripe for political convulsion, but the *Gazette* article created a different kind of obsession. It did not allude to western separation strictly in terms that easterners were accustomed to reading about—that is, a homegrown rebellion tapping into the "natural" discontent of toughened frontiersmen, living at immense distances from the seats of power, who might respond to Burr's message. Rather, Burr's so-called revolution would come *to* the West from the East, as the result of an influx of ambitious, political informed young men who would carve up the frontier and impose an eastern machine there—Burr's country, with all the built-in instability (moral and managerial) that this implied. The *Gazette* inferred that the former vice president was riding the wave of a radical and dangerous new revolutionary movement. Though exiled from

Jefferson's party, and seemingly ruined in New York, Burr still had a constituency: an Atlantic constituency primed to overrun the frontier.[77]

At the time, Burr claimed that the marqués de Casa Yrujo, the Spanish minister to America, wrote the *Gazette* article. But there is no way to be certain; indeed, it seems far more likely that a knowledgeable American insider was the author. One reason why this makes more sense is that Burr was attacked as a third party leader *before* he went west.[78]

The evidence lies in the meaning of the word "*quid.*" On March 26, 1805, the *Aurora* observed that the vice president was in Philadelphia, where he was "received with more than common cordiality by the *quids.*" The *Quids* (a reference to the Latin *tertium quids,* meaning a "third something") initially described a third party movement in Pennsylvania, within the Republican Party. But the label was to appear over and over again during the next two years, expanding in meaning and accusing Burr of engaging in conspiratorial activities in the West. There were many variations: he was, alternatively, "the father of the quids," the "Little Quid Emperor," "emperor of the Quids," and "Quid emperor." The main organ of Jeffersonian Republicanism in Virginia, the *Richmond Inquirer,* later declared that the only men to be found in Burr's conspiracy were men of a "*third party*" persuasion. To be a third party man was to one of the "*adherents of Burr.*"[79]

The Quid label made sense to impassioned Jeffersonians. Burr had already been smeared as a traitor to his party for supposedly trying to steal the election of 1800 from Jefferson, so it was not much of a leap to imagine him heading a "revolution party" in the West. Moreover, Quids were defectors from both parties, who aimed to create a hybrid party, and this served to reinforce Burr's earlier reputation (invented by his enemies) as a faux Republican. Burr's fateful toast to a "union of honest men," which he gave at the Federalist celebration of George Washington's birthday in 1802, and which was revived by Cheetham to tarnish his name during the 1804 governor's campaign, reappeared in the press to condemn him as a conspirator in 1806.[80]

Here is a plausible scenario: Burr goes west—attracts attention—word gets around—newspapers surmise things—and before anything is really known, his designs are blown out of proportion by self-appointed agents and protectors of the administration. To wit, in an attempt to blame the conspiracy on the opposition party, Republican newspapers remarked on the prominence of Federalists in Burr's camp, such as Jonathan Dayton. This is significant. Despite their hold on the President's House, many Jeffersonian Republicans still imagined themselves in a fight to the finish; if it was not a Federalist plot they feared, it was schism within the party. Burr inspired fears of both at once. What could be worse than a nervy alliance of Federalists and errant Republicans? It was clear that Burr had some big-name Republicans backing him, too: John Smith, Andrew Jackson, and John Brown, to name a few. The Quid theme tapped into existing concerns, equating party dissolution and national disunion.[81]

The "Emperor" label is equally revealing. As early as September 1804, Burr had been mocked in the *American Citizen* when news reached New York of his trip to Pierce Butler's secluded island and Florida. "Does he mean to become *emperor* of the Island of St. Simons?" Cheetham or some other critic asked. The piece went on to suggest that instead of becoming the "Kemper of St. Simon's" (Kemper was an American who had organized a rebellion in Spanish Florida), Burr would set his sights on Louisiana:

> New Orleans and its vicinity seem to be the load-stone to the intriguing, the
> dangerous, the discontented, and worthless of our city. Thither they flock
> like so many Vultures. To raise a rebellion in this quarter against the gov-
> ernment would complete Mr. Burr's Catalinian character.[82]

Calling him "Catalinian" was nothing new, but adding the title of "Emperor" likened him, of course, to Napoleon, the most formidable conqueror of this era. Not long before, Americans had feared that Napoleon's army would take control of New Orleans and the Mississippi—indeed, of the entire West, as then conceived. The title conjured what his enemies felt was Burr's audacity, what Hamilton had called his *"dashing projecting* spirit."

Was he Napoleonic? To his enemies, he was at once aloof and audacious, mysterious and fascinating, a man capable of inspiring inexplicable yet passionate loyalties. Something sexual, something seductive about him attracted vulnerable young men. Similar charges to those raised against Burr in New York by Cheetham, objectifying the Burrites as his soft, womanish, childlike pawns, followed him west. It was typical of the press at this time to recycle old stories and old rumors, if they could be associated with a classical or biblical model of good versus evil. So, with a twist here, a turn there, the exaggerations circulated during the governor's race were converted into a usable model to characterize Burr as a Catalinian conspirator against the American union.

Burr's first trip to New Orleans had caused rumors to swirl, and the gossip did not end when he returned to the east coast in the late fall of 1805. For the next nine months, before returning to the West, Burr spent most of his time traveling between Washington and Philadelphia. After dining with Burr at the executive mansion—on the surface, at least, a completely friendly meeting—Jefferson received two anonymous letters in early December 1805 from an unnamed informant, calling Burr the "new Catalina," who planned to "overthrow the administration." In January 1806, a U.S. district attorney in Kentucky, Joseph Hamilton Daveiss, warned the president about a dangerous conspiracy brewing in the West. Then in February, Daveiss forwarded a more urgent letter, naming Burr as the chief conspirator. Hearing this, Jefferson did nothing. He seemed unconvinced, especially after Daveiss, a Federalist, drew up a list of Burr's accomplices. The list only included prominent Republicans from the western states.[83]

In light of what was to follow—Jefferson's complete acceptance of the notion of a "Burr Conspiracy"—we need to examine this moment carefully. Evidence exists that Burr was interested in working with Jefferson, and in fact that he was thinking of abandoning, or at least delaying, the implementation of his western scheme. Because, at the same time as Daveiss was sounding his alarm to Jefferson, Burr was attempting to get an appointment to the Pennsylvania Supreme Court; and his old allies in New York were trying to resuscitate his political career in that state by muscling in at an opportune moment as the two other Republicans factions—Clintonians and Lewisites—found themselves in a new tug-of-war. At first, Burr's people seized the chance to make an alliance with Governor Morgan Lewis. When that failed, they approached Burr's former (and one might say "natural") antagonist, DeWitt Clinton. This unlikely alliance collapsed almost as quickly as it was formed, but it proved once again that New York electoral politics made strange bedfellows. Finally, amid all the uncertainty, we know that Burr appealed directly to Jefferson for an appointment of some kind (the evidence is in Jefferson's private papers). The president, however, showed no inclination to assist his former vice president.[84]

There are several reasons why Burr might have changed his plans with respect to the West. He learned in Washington that there would be no war with Spain—this was crucial intelligence. Though Jefferson rattled his saber in his annual address to Congress in December, he seemed inclined to avoid military confrontation: secretly, he was pushing a deal to buy the Floridas from the Spanish for $2 million. Burr's hopes for British ships and financing also seemed tenuous. Burr had several meetings with Merry, but the British minister could offer him no assurances that the British cabinet was in any way interested in his project. Nor had Burr heard anything definite from Charles Williamson, his London agent.[85]

Rebuffed, Burr modified his plans, and sometime in the winter of 1805–06, he began to make arrangements to purchase a portion of a large tract of land known as the Bastrop property, which was located near the Ouachita River, in northwestern Louisiana. If an invasion of Mexico was impossible at this moment, he would at least establish a settlement in the region, and bide his time until a filibuster made sense. Burr made a point of writing to Albert Gallatin about his purchase, in effect letting the administration know of his commitment to establishing a presence in the West.[86]

Meanwhile, he attempted (from the East) to foil the Spanish minister to the United States, the marqués de Yrujo, who threatened his still hazy project. Burr sent Jonathan Dayton on a delicate mission to keep Yrujo at arm's length. Dayton pretended to be a double agent, after Wilkinson's example, which makes it quite possible that Wilkinson had suggested the ploy to Burr. Dayton approached the minister with secret information to sell—that Burr intended to lead a western rebellion, and invade the Floridas and Mexico, but had now abandoned that plan. This would not have been news to Yrujo, who had been watching Burr's movements and thought Burr's Mexican plan "ridiculous." But he was not ready for Dayton's further confession when they met a second time. That is when Burr's supposedly two-timing envoy (who now dropped that pose and said Burr had sent him) "divulged" that his employer planned a *coup d'état* against Jefferson, that Burr would infiltrate Washington with his army of adventurers and depose the president, and then seize the public money in the Washington banks; and if he failed to win popular support, he would destroy all the federal ships in the nearby harbor, and flee to New Orleans. There, Burr would declare the independence of Louisiana and the western states from the union.[87]

Why did Dayton offer up such a far-fetched scenario? Because he knew that Yrujo would fall for it. For his "valuable information," Dayton tried to extort $40,000, and in the end netted only $2,500. This was not a ruse to sell false information for personal profit, though some have suspected it was a daring ploy to get the Spanish to unwittingly fund Burr's filibuster. It was nevertheless a calculated effort to knock the Spaniard off balance. It made Yrujo less certain about his original suspicions, and thus more vulnerable to Burr's real agenda: a surprise attack against Mexico, when the time was right.[88]

THE "INQUISITIONS OF EUROPE"

In the spring of 1806, Burr carried on with his plans for a second excursion west. He busied himself recruiting an assortment of new followers, among them New Yorkers, sons of army generals, and foreign adventurers. Dr. Justus Erich Bollmann is an interesting specimen taken from this motley group. A German-born medical doctor, now thirty-seven, he had settled in the United States in 1796, and tried his hand at several business schemes, all of which failed. His romantic, revolutionary tendencies preceded his acquaintance with Burr and his voyage to America: during the French Revolution, he attempted a valiant, if unsuccessful, rescue of the marquis de Lafayette, who was then being held in an Austrian prison. Fluent in English, French, and German, Bollmann was highly educated—just the sort of man we could expect to come to Burr's attention.[89]

Burr left Philadelphia at the beginning of August, proceeding on horseback to Pittsburgh. He sent Bollmann ahead to New Orleans, bearing letters for Edward Livingston and General Wilkinson. Meanwhile, Burr rested at the home of an old acquaintance, Colonel George Morgan. The colonel had been an early speculator in western lands and an avid promoter of western migration. In 1789, the year that the federal Constitution was adopted, he had attempted to found "New Madrid," an American colony sponsored by the Spanish, within Spanish territory. In 1806, Morgan was living at Morganza, his manorial estate south of Pittsburgh. He had two sons: John, thirty-six, was a general in the New Jersey militia; Thomas, twenty-two, was at an age, and of a mind, to find Burr's expeditionary force an attractive prospect.[90]

But Burr misjudged the old colonel. When their dinner conversation turned to the question of the West's future—and the possibility that the eastern states would be unable to stop western secession, if it came to that—Morgan objected to any such suggestion. What happened next is a matter of debate, but Burr said something about the weakness of Jefferson's administration that only made matters worse. Morgan, his sons in tow, expressed irritation, and after his guest had gone dispatched a letter to Jefferson, accusing Burr.[91]

But if the Morgan boys were not attracted to Burr's project, others were. From Pittsburgh, the son of General Presley Neville enlisted, as did the son of Colonel Thomas Butler, a close friend of Andrew Jackson. It was reported later that a "considerable number of single men of conspicuous parentage" had joined Burr from western Pennsylvania.[92]

In New York State, Comfort Tyler served as one of Burr's visible "subalterns." Tyler was one of the earliest settlers in Onondaga County, and a zealous promoter of land development in western New York. In the 1790s, while serving in the state legislature, he had become Burr's political ally. Now, in the summer of 1806, the forty-two-year-old Tyler was calling attention to himself. He suddenly had an "abundance of money," being engaged in some "secret business" for Burr. As he traveled though Pittsburgh and Ohio, he attracted further notice by purchasing provisions and boats, and enlisting "young men of talents & address." Why so much chatter about a wandering New Yorker? Tyler was Burr's Pied Piper, leading a contingent of young men west. He was, in the most literal sense, a Burrite adventurer, a devoted lieutenant in the ex-vice president's expeditionary army.[93]

Burr, after his disappointing encounter with the Morgans, made his way to Blennerhassett Island. Though he stopped here only briefly, the island buzzed with activity. He made contracts with local merchants for supplies, and arranged for the construction of fifteen boats to form a flotilla; the average vessel capable of carrying up to fifty men. In Cincinnati, he met up with Senator John Smith, whose two sons were to join Burr on his expedition. Wasting little time, he went on to see John Brown in Frankfort. By September 24, he was back in Nashville, urging General Jackson to ready the Tennessee militia, and arranging for more boats to be built, and more young men to be recruited. Rachel Jackson's favorite nephew was one of the seventy-five Tennesseans who eagerly signed on to Burr's adventure.[94]

By this time, however, military conditions on the Louisiana-Texas border had changed again. A thousand Spanish troops had crossed the Sabine River at the end of July, and were within ten miles of the U.S. outpost at Natchitoches. This was a taunting gesture, demanding a response. Yet no one acted until General Wilkinson arrived on the scene. Secretary of War Henry Dearborn had ordered Wilkinson, months earlier, to lead reinforcements to New Orleans. But with his typical errant defiance, the general had tarried in St. Louis until August, and did not reach the trouble spot until September 7.[95]

Wilkinson was still pretending to be all things to all people. He dispatched a letter to Dearborn, promising to "drain the cup of conciliation to maintain the peace," adding in the same breath that if "forced to appeal to arms," he would gladly charge ahead, to "soon plant our standards on the left bank of the [Rio] Grand[e] River." But his letters to John Adair and John Smith showed no hesitation whatsoever. He bragged to Adair that at this crucial juncture, there was a fair chance of "subverting the Spanish government in Mexico." And this was only a start, he tempted Smith: for "our conquests" might extend as far west as California.[96]

The new tensions along the border fit into Burr's plans. War fever created exactly the situation he wanted. "All reflecting men consider war with Spain to be inevitable," he wrote Governor William Henry Harrison. He met Theodosia and his son-in-law in Lexington, after the South Carolina couple had enjoyed a pleasant excursion to Blennerhassett Island. Meanwhile, Burr finalized the purchase of the Bastrop property, acquiring 350,000 acres near the Texas border—all prime real estate. There is every indication that Burr planned to settle this tract; he wrote to Benjamin Latrobe, whom he had hoped would design the Indiana canal, asking the architect to join him. Burr took up such subjects as the quality of the soil, his plans for building cabins, but he especially needed Latrobe's engineering skills to construct one road from the Mississippi River to his settlement, and another to the border town of Natchitoches. He offered Latrobe 10,000 acres for his services, insisting that success depended on the architect's sound guidance. "I want your society, I want your advice in the establishments to be made," Burr appealed at the end of October. "In short you have become necessary to my settlement."[97]

Despite his eager efforts, Burr's project began to unravel that autumn.

As his activities gained increasing attention, the cry of conspiracy provided a convenient means of going after Burr's allies. A group suspicious of Blennerhassett organized meetings in nearby Wood County, Virginia (today's West Virginia), accusing the Irish manor lord of mounting an illegal, and possibly treasonous, expedition from his private island. As far away as Michigan Territory, where Burr had never set foot, rumors arose; a newly established bank in Detroit, whose major sponsor was a "perfect quid," was alleged to have been opened solely to channel secret funds to Burr.[98]

Kentucky produced the loudest uproar, primarily because two hack journalists began publishing a scandal sheet—the *Western World*—in the summer of 1806. John Wood, the same writer whose defamatory *History of the Administration of John Adams* had caused Burr so much trouble in New York in 1802, now resided in Frankfort. Along with his fiery coeditor Joseph Monfort Street, Wood used the new paper to fan the flames of an imaginary conspiracy with Burr as ringleader.[99]

Burr's friends and associates came under attacks no less shrill and no less severe. One target was former Kentucky senator John Brown. Dr. Preston Brown, the politician's brother and himself a friend of Burr's, burst into the editor's office, demanding a retraction of the charges. When Street refused, the doctor threatened to "make a *Negro* lash him." This was no isolated incident: Street was known as the "fighting editor" because a good number of his victims presented themselves and demanded satisfaction. John Brown sent Jefferson an impassioned letter, denying the lies printed in the *Western World*.[100]

Despite its lack of credible evidence, and the abusive and sensational style of the *Western World,* the paper became wildly popular, and other newspapers quickly reprinted its stories. One backer of the scandalous paper (at least, it was so conjectured) was U.S. District Attorney for Kentucky Joseph Hamilton Daveiss, who was on a personal crusade to expose what he believed were Burr's conspiratorial activities. After his first warning back in January, Daveiss continued to barrage Jefferson with letters, offering his services to the president. He wrote Secretary of State Madison as well, urging him to pay attention to reports contained in the *Western World.* By early November 1806, he felt confident enough to drag Burr before a Kentucky grand jury.[101]

The rumors were clearly having an effect. A mounting pile of letters sat by President Jefferson, but it was, purportedly, one from his postmaster general, Gideon Granger of Connecticut, which ultimately prompted him to take action. On October 16, 1806, Granger repeated a story told to him by General William Eaton, centering on Burr's grand design of conquering the West and toppling the administration. The general had made a reputation for himself in the Tripolitan Campaign of 1804. He had crossed the Libyan Desert, captured the city of Derna (Darnah), and was on his way to victory at Tripoli, when a peace treaty ended the conflict in North Africa. He had then proceeded to Washington to collect $10,000 he felt the government owed him for his valiant services. In December 1805, he now claimed, Burr had tried to recruit him.[102]

Burr was, of course, preparing for a filibuster, but he was not conspiring to topple the administration. Eaton's word was entirely unreliable. He was given to bouts of drunken excess—one of Burr's biographers has questioned whether he ever met with Burr at all, perhaps having confused a conversation he had with Dayton. Nevertheless, Granger's warning, based on Eaton's account, carried weight. And Granger's motives? He appeared inspired by patriotism, but that is not the whole story; his name had been associated with Burr's conspiracy, thus making his warning to Jefferson more a desperate plea to save his own skin than an accurate assessment of his fear of Burr's intent. And Granger was not alone. In a very short time, John Brown, John Smith, John Adair, and Andrew Jackson would all find themselves scrambling to discredit rumors about their connections to Burr, and to clear their own names.[103]

Jefferson had been slow to react, but now he abruptly called the cabinet together, on October 22, 1806, to discuss Burr. Though he was relying on hearsay, he mentioned that Burr had "opened himself confidentially to some persons," and revealed his "scheme of separating the Western from the Atlantic States, and erecting the former into an independent confederacy." He undercut his supposedly objective assessment by mentioning that Burr had aroused "suspicions, as every motion does of such a Catalinarian [sic] character."[104]

A Catalinian character? Several months earlier, during their last private conference, Jefferson told Burr that he had lost the public's confidence, which was the reason he gave for not appointing his former vice president to a federal office. In response, an incredulous Burr observed "that if we believe a few newspapers, it might be supposed he had lost the public confidence"; but he added, it was "easy to engage newspapers in anything." Jefferson then claimed he did not rely on the newspapers. But clearly he did, for "Cataline" was Cheetham's favorite slur against Burr.[105]

At the October 22 cabinet meeting, the president listed some of the informants who had written to him or to Madison, and referred directly to information they had received through "other channels and the newspapers." With nothing concrete, he persuaded the cabinet that the administration must take drastic action: it must send letters to all the western governors and district attorneys, order them to watch Burr's every move, and "on his committing any overt act unequivocally, to have him arrested and tried for treason, misdemeanor, or whatever other offence the act may amount to." Gunboats would be sent to the fort near New Orleans. And what about Wilkinson? According to Eaton, that devious general was intimately involved as Burr's second-in-command; rumors of his complicity were just as widespread as those against Burr. Jefferson acknowledged that "suspicions of infidelity in Wilkinson" were "very general," and that he had disobeyed Dearborn's orders by failing to head to New Orleans with dispatch.[106]

The cabinet met again on the 24th. Two captains were to be sent with "great discretionary powers" toward arresting Burr. Burr's brother-in-law was to be removed from his post, and John Graham, previously secretary of the Orleans Territory, was to replace Wilkinson as governor of Louisiana. How to deal with Wilkinson was still uncertain.[107]

Jefferson's flurry of activity suddenly came to a halt. On October 25, the cabinet reversed itself. Nothing was to be done, except to send Graham west to spy on Burr, put the governments on guard, and to "arrest him if necessary." This change of plans is inexplicable. The only reason Jefferson gave was that mail had arrived from the West and "not one word is heard from that quarter of any movements of Colonel Burr." That "total silence" somehow "proves he is committing no overt act against the law."[108]

Of course, Jefferson had had no evidence of an "overt act" three days earlier, but it had not stopped him from accusing Burr of treason and a host of other potential crimes. The best explanation for this about-face is that Jefferson's cabinet had persuaded him to slow down. Gallatin was there, and he would not have been eager to jump on the bandwagon and accuse Burr of treason. Jefferson was angry enough to imagine Burr as a "Catalinian character." Maybe it was Eaton's claim that Burr intended to get "rid of the president" that sparked his fury. Still, cooler heads prevailed, and the administration decided to wait until it had real evidence of treason.

Cooler heads did not prevail in Kentucky. District Attorney Daveiss aimed to ruin Burr. On November 5, he presented an affidavit before Judge Henry Innes, charging Burr with having prepared an invasion of Mexico, and demanded that the court issue a warrant for Burr's arrest. He claimed that he had sufficient evidence to prove that Burr intended to separate the western states from the union; even so, there was no law on the books that made such a plot criminal. Daveiss was clearly using the courtroom to shape public opinion. He headed to court, but soon discovered that even in the freewheeling West, innuendo was not enough to sustain a case. It quickly became apparent that he did not have any evidence at all. His legal talents, moreover, were no match for those of Burr and his counsel, Henry Clay.[109]

Clay, twenty-nine, was a rising star in Kentucky. He had just been chosen to succeed John Adair in the U.S. Senate. Burr understood the value of having a respected member of Kentucky's elite at his side. The district attorney was inventing law: he wanted Burr held under bond while he called witnesses and collected evidence. The judge refused this unusual request. Rebuffed, Daveiss returned to normal procedure and requested a grand jury, which the judge granted. Yet Daveiss still brought on no witnesses. Court was dismissed, reconvening on November 12, when, once again, Daveiss came up empty-handed. His so-called key witness was out of town. The jury was dismissed, and Burr went free, for the moment. Two weeks later, the district attorney requested a second grand jury, to convene in early December.[110]

Though Burr had gained the upper hand in the courtroom, the mere act of having charges raised lent legitimacy to the rumors in circulation. He already had received an anxious letter from Senator John Smith, warning him of the "various reports prejudicial to your character." Throughout the month, Burr denied all accusations that he was seeking to dismember the union. After learning that Daveiss had requested a warrant for his arrest, he had written Harman Blennerhassett that the charges were "absurd." He reassured a suspicious Andrew Jackson of his patriotism, and appealed as well to William Henry Harrison and Henry Clay, the latter worrying that his new duties as senator might make it improper for him to further serve as Burr's counsel.[111]

The second hearing began on December 2, when Daveiss charged both John Adair and Burr with planning an invasion of Mexico. The one witness against Adair, whom the district attorney claimed he had interviewed earlier, denied the conversation; he called the statements attributed to him a pack of lies. The case against Adair crumbled, but the prosecutor pressed on. Burr had to answer charges three days later. Having overcome any earlier concerns he might have had, Henry Clay now compared the Federalist-inspired proceedings to the "inquisitions of Europe," and publicly declared that he "did not entertain the slightest idea of his guilt." Burr spoke in his own defense, and dismissed all the stories about him as utterly false.[112]

While Burr sought to rise above the tawdry proceedings, Daveiss increasingly found himself the subject of ridicule. Burr's most vocal critics, the scandalmongers Joseph Street and John Wood, were finally called to testify, and were forced to admit that everything they had printed was rumor and hearsay; they could offer nothing that constituted real evidence. Wood went so far as to say that he had completely changed his mind about Burr; he now believed the ex-vice president had no designs against the union.[113]

As the second hearing concluded, the jury members expressed their disgust with the prosecutor. Not only did they find "no true bill" to indict Burr, they issued a lengthy statement asserting that the district attorney was at best foolhardy and at worst vindictive. They claimed that "there has been no testimony before us which does in the Smallest degree criminate the conduct" of Burr or Adair.[114]

Adding to the circus atmosphere surrounding these proceedings, two balls were held in Frankfort. One was in honor of Burr's vindication; and the other in support of Daveiss's efforts, pompously described in the papers as a ball "in *honor of the* UNION." Joseph Street, still backing the prosecutor, praised the ladies who shunned the ex-vice president. Though the jury had deserted Daveiss, a band of "immovable American ladies" had redeemed him by refusing to dance with the "incomparable Burr."[115]

Dance cards aside, Daveiss's behavior is difficult to explain. He abused the law, declared unsubstantiated rumor to be the equal of concrete evidence, and was intent on using the court system to harass Burr. After his defection from Daveiss, Wood gave the most convincing explanation for the district attorney's behavior: Joseph Hamilton Daveiss held Burr in contempt for killing Hamilton. Though they shared a name, Daveiss and Hamilton were not kinsmen; however, Daveiss was related by marriage to John Marshall, the most influential Federalist in the country since 1800. Revenge may explain why this Federalist district attorney was caught up in his fanatical quest to convict Burr. Partisan politics were deeply personal—and often irrational. As far as Daveiss was concerned, Burr not only had treason in his heart but blood on his hands.[116]

"CRONONHOTON THOLOGOS"

While Burr was battling for his freedom in a Kentucky courthouse, General Wilkinson was staging a farce in New Orleans that would turn the president as well as popular opinion against the former vice president. On November 5, 1806, the same day that Daveiss presented his affidavit for Burr's arrest, the general concluded a truce with Spanish forces on the Sabine River. Now, with no military conflict to exploit, Burr's hopes of an expedition into Mexico ended. War alone had made Burr's plan legitimate in the eyes of the law and in the view of his fellow countrymen.[117]

Wilkinson had been busy preparing for what can only be considered a performance worthy of the calculating Niccolò Machiavelli himself. Wilkinson had a reputation for utilizing his pen along with his sword; a later enemy, Judge James Workman of New Orleans, derisively called him the "CRONONHOTON THOLOGOS OF LETTERS AND WAR." Chrononhotonthologos was a character in a popular 1743 burlesque, whose singular trait was pomposity, whose utterances were bombast. Wherever he was, when Wilkinson delivered his lines, it was invariably an exaggerated drama.[118]

That is not to suggest that Wilkinson was a fool. His peculiar military style borrowed directly from Machiavelli. The American general understood that political success required bold, even theatrical contrivance, and the creation of a viable enemy. Power, to be exercised, required an adversary. As the Spanish vanished from the horizon, in their place Wilkinson declared the presence of an "arch-conspirator": Aaron Burr. To carry out his plans, he manufactured a dire necessity, that is, he created the illusion that Burr posed a discernible threat to New Orleans, and the nation as a whole. By implanting fear, he could demand submission to an unofficial martial law, and in the next few months Wilkinson did everything in his power to subvert the civilian authority in New Orleans.[119]

It is difficult to pinpoint exactly when Wilkinson resolved that he would betray Burr. But on October 22, 1806, he sent off a report and confidential letter to Jefferson that exposed a conspiracy-in-the-making. Though the general claimed that his report came from a "public print," it had actually been forged by Wilkinson himself. The report claimed that as many as 10,000 men had formed a powerful association, and planned to topple New Orleans, invade Mexico, and incite an insurrection capable of sending tremors far enough east to subvert the federal government. Not yet ready to accuse Burr, he claimed that he did not know the identity of the "prime mover."[120]

The general's theatrics did not end there. A month would pass before Jefferson received Wilkinson's first alarm, and the general's emissary was given elaborate instructions on how he should convey it. Only at the moment when he stood before the president was he to dramatically retrieve the communiqué from the "soles of his slipper."[121]

Why did Wilkinson panic? He felt endangered by the mounting rumors that identified him as Burr's principal co-conspirator. And like a true Machiavellian, he found it increasingly difficult to share power with Burr. He would rather act in such a manner as kept him in charge of events as they unfolded; he did not have the patience to wait and see if the former vice president could carry through on his plans. Destroying Burr seemed the only way to divert suspicion from himself and salvage his own tarnished reputation.[122]

He saw the answer to his problem in a document that came into his possession in mid-October 1806. Known as the "cipher letter," this communiqué was hand-delivered to Wilkinson at the Sabine front by a Burr aide, Samuel Swartwout. The younger brother of John Swartwout, Burr's closest New York ally, Sam had been Burr's traveling companion on the trip to South Carolina in 1804. The cipher letter was not written by Burr, but Wilkinson was to claim that it was in order to suit his purposes.[123]

The letter was written in code, the key to which the general alone possessed. It said, in fine, that Burr was en route to New Orleans with a considerable body of men, and that he planned to make use of the British navy in his effort to carry out "our project," by which the letter writer clearly inferred Mexico as the target of an invasion. Wilkinson, however, would twist the facts and claim that Swartwout told him Burr was planning to attack New Orleans itself and "revolutionize" the Louisiana Territory. Wilkinson also doctored the letter, carefully omitting any incriminating references to himself—thus, "our project" became neutral, as "the project."[124]

Believing himself in control and able to utilize the information as he pleased, Wilkinson set his sights on New Orleans. In mid-November, he began to dispatch letters to fellow officers, calling for the city's defenses to be fortified, while urging that all available troops be assembled. He warned his officers not to trust anyone, for he believed secret agents to be roaming the streets. To Governor Claiborne, he warned of a "storm" about to burst in New Orleans, and that he was surrounded by "dangers of which you dream not." In his most bombastic style, he declared that the valiant Wilkinson was on his way to save the city, or perish in its defense.[125]

Wilkinson sent a similar letter to Jefferson, far more theatrical in tone than his October warning to the president. This time he unveiled a "deep, dark and widespread conspiracy," involving virtually everyone imaginable: "young and old, the democrat and the federalist, the native and the foreigner, the patriot of '76 and the exotic of yesterday, the opulent and the needy, the ins and the outs." Demanding martial law, the wily general wanted complete authority over the city of New Orleans, authority that would enable him to arrest Burr's allies, who could dispute his distortion of the facts.[126]

Wilkinson arrived in New Orleans on November 25, and began his brief reign of terror, while Burr, none the wiser, remained enmeshed in legal proceedings in Frankfort, Kentucky. The general gave a rousing speech before the New Orleans Chamber of Commerce in early December, convincing the merchants to impose an embargo, and filling them with fear. Burr's army of 7,000 lawless conspirators were fast approaching, he declared, ready and willing to plunder the city's banks and ransack the city's streets.[127]

While he effectively caused confusion, Wilkinson wasted little time in rounding up a series of suspects. First he ordered the arrest of Swartwout and his traveling companion, Peter V. Ogden. Then he nabbed Erich Bollmann, from whom he had received a duplicate of the cipher letter. After arresting Bollmann, he appeared before the Superior Court, on December 18, to defend his actions. One of Wilkinson's most outspoken critics, the former New York lawyer and politician Edward Livingston, captured the drama of the courtroom scene. Wilkinson arrived in full military attire, his scabbard by his side—"even the spurs were not forgotten." As he stood before the court in full regalia, he threatened to make more arrests, regardless of station or standing, if anyone dared to get in his way. He pointedly accused both Livingston and James Alexander, Bollmann's two lawyers, of being traitors. Shortly after this, the general arrested Alexander, who had been Bollmann's traveling companion. All four men (Swartwout, Ogden, Bollmann, and Alexander) were shipped, under armed guard, to Washington, and charged with misprision of treason (i.e., knowledge of treasonous activities).[128]

Having rounded up most of Burr's associates, the general now aimed to stifle the press and tie the hands of the civil authorities. He arrested Judge James Workman, who had resigned in disgust after Wilkinson repeatedly defied the power of the courts. Judge Workman was targeted because he had urged Governor Claiborne to arrest Wilkinson for his repeated usurpations of the law. The general also placed Ogden's attorney, Lewis Kerr, under arrest, but then released him, because he was close friend of Claiborne's. However, without a second thought, he threw the editor of the local newspaper into prison, preemptively silencing a potentially dangerous critic. And when former Kentucky senator John Adair arrived in town on January 14, 1807, Wilkinson sent two or three companies of soldiers to arrest him at his boardinghouse. As he had done with Bollmann and the others, he quickly dispatched Adair by ship to the east coast. Although the governor had refused to grant Wilkinson the power of martial law, he did nothing to stop the general's high-handed and illegal measures. Thus the inexperienced Claiborne succumbed to Wilkinson's power play and became, in effect, his puppet.[129]

Jefferson finally received the general's first warning about the conspiracy on November 25, more than a month after it was sent. Two days later, the president issued a proclamation, a rather vaguely worded document calling for all "faithful citizens" to desist from participating in an illegal military expedition into Spanish territory. He did not mention the name of Burr. He did not mention Wilkinson.[130]

Wilkinson's second warning (sent in November) made it to Washington on January 1, 1807. Jefferson did not learn about the controversial cipher letter until he received two new letters from the general in mid-January. The president did not take further action until January 22. On that date, at the insistence of Congress, he sent along what information he had, and for the first time he publicly accused Burr of leading an illegal expedition and engineering a conspiracy to separate the western states from the union. While admitting that the information he had was questionable, that it involved a "mixture of rumour, conjectures, and suspicions" making it "difficult to sift out the real facts," Jefferson felt no hesitation in accusing Burr of the most heinous crime imaginable: attempting to destroy his country.[131]

The president also made it clear that Burr's main accuser was trustworthy. In his message to Congress, he praised Wilkinson's display of "the honor of a soldier and the fidelity of the good citizen." This was a crucial turning point. Jefferson knew that the general had not been completely candid with him and had taken gross liberties with the law in New Orleans, but it no longer mattered. He had made a choice. He felt he needed Wilkinson in order to get his hands on Burr. The president had resolved to take the side of "Machiavelli," and whether he admitted it to himself or not, he, not unlike Governor Claiborne, was following the general's lead.[132]

When Wilkinson, on November 12, sent his exaggerated second warning to Jefferson, anticipating Burr's imminent attack on New Orleans, the former vice president was still in Frankfort attending the grand jury hearing. He did not know what forces were already working against him. In Ohio, early in December, Jefferson's federal agent John Graham (who had been sent west to spy on Burr after the October cabinet meetings), now convinced Governor Edward Tiffin to take action against Burr's expedition. So, the Ohio militia seized several of Burr's vessels at Marietta, while in Cincinnati cannons were mounted for the purpose of halting Burr's imaginary army of 20,000, which was rumored to be heading there, along the Ohio River, from Pittsburgh. On the night of December 10, Harman Blennerhassett and Comfort Tyler reacted to warnings from friends and escaped from Blennerhassett Island with four boats; the Wood County militia of western Virginia invaded the island estate the very next day. Havoc ensued as the militia ransacked the property, flagrantly destroying the

Irishman's home, and helping themselves to his wine, acting more like drunken vigilantes than noble patriots called upon to save the nation from a mounting conspiracy.[133]

Burr met up with Tyler and Blennerhassett at the mouth of the Cumberland River near the end of December. At that point, he must have realized that the tide had turned against him. He did not learn of Wilkinson's betrayal until January 10, when he quickly dispatched a letter to Cowles Mead, acting governor of the Mississippi Territory, calling the accusations against him "vile fabrications of a man notoriously the pensioner of a foreign country."[134]

By now, Burr was nearing the old Spanish commercial center of Natchez. Naturally, the news of Wilkinson's duplicity was devastating. His filibuster was a lost cause. More important, he knew that his freedom, if not his safety, was in immediate jeopardy. The general's betrayal, and his subsequent actions in New Orleans, meant that Burr, too, would have to be captured and silenced. Less than two years after presiding over the Senate of the United States, he was now a man on the run. His only chance, as he realized, lay in escaping the general long enough to place himself under the protection of the civilian authorities in Mississippi.

One newspaper claimed that the "little emperor" had been *"outgeneraled"* by Wilkinson, but the truth of the matter is that Wilkinson had outgeneraled both Burr and Jefferson. It was his version of events that now monopolized newsprint, obliging the president to declare to Congress that Burr's guilt was "beyond question." Burr was a fugitive before he had even been indicted for a crime. And so he moved quickly, hoping to evade those who had been deputed by Wilkinson to capture him. A tidy reward was offered. The chase was on.[135]

A romanticized rendition of Burr's capture in 1807

Chapter Nine

WILL O' WISP TREASON

> If I were to name this, I would call it the *Will o' wisp* treason. For though it is said to be here and there and everywhere, *yet it is nowhere.* It only exists in the newspapers and in the mouths of the enemies of the gentleman for whom I appear; who get it put in the newspapers.
>
> —Luther Martin, defense counsel for Aaron Burr, 1807

Betrayed by Wilkinson and pursued by Jefferson, Burr knew he had to quickly seek protection, and his best option was the nearby civil authorities in Mississippi. On January 12, 1807, he opened negotiations with acting Governor Cowles Mead, ensuring he would be tried in the territory—not shipped to New Orleans, which was unofficially under the martial law of the desperate general. A few miles downriver from the settlement of Bayou Pierre, making camp on the Orleans side of the Mississippi, Burr bargained with Mead, while his motley crew waited in wintry weather for four days before agreement was reached. Mead's deputies searched the boats, and instead of finding a cache of weapons found trunks of books. Shaking his head at what he discovered, Mead wrote Secretary of War Dearborn of Burr's anticlimactic surrender: "Thus, sir, this mighty alarm, with all its exaggerations, has eventuated in nine boats, and one hundred men, and the major of these are boys, or young men just from school. . . . I believe that they are the dupes of stratagem, if the asseverations of generals Eaton and Wilkinson, are to be accredited." And that was a big "if," for Mead was convinced that the two generals he named had grossly misrepresented the alarm, if they had not invented it.[1]

A grand jury hearing took place on February 2, in Washington, Mississippi, at the highest court in the territory. Burr's prospects looked promising; the jury issued a presentment two days later and absolved him of all charges. The panel also took the opportunity to disparage Wilkinson, and sharply rebuked local officials for having treated Burr as a prisoner of war.

The jury's action came as no surprise: Burr had been warmly received in Mississippi. Confirming this impression, one of Wilkinson's informants wrote the general that Burr was so popular, acting Governor Mead could barely muster thirty-five men to arrest him, while most of the local militia wished his filibustering "plans might take effect," and if he attacked Baton Rouge, "they would join him."[2]

Though the jury refused to indict him, Burr was not free to go. One of the judges, Thomas Rodney, father of Attorney General Caesar Rodney, insisted that he remain in the vicinity of the court. Rodney's high-handed action put Burr in a dangerous predicament. Wilkinson's henchmen were in the area, ready to nab the so-called "conspirator" and drag him back to New Orleans. Sizing up the situation, Burr determined he had only one choice: to flee. Yet as a lawyer—a very good lawyer—he drafted two letters in defense of his action, which he addressed (while in hiding) to Territorial Governor Robert Williams, who had just resumed his duties. In one letter, he complained of the judge's "vindictive temper and unprincipled conduct" in ordering him not to leave town. And then he protested as "unworthy" the proclamation Williams had issued when Burr refused to show up again in court after having been acquitted. Williams had persisted in calling Burr a fugitive from justice, which he, of course, disputed.[3]

Then Burr vanished. His whereabouts were completely unknown. No one who may have seen him over the next week was willing to expose him. But on February 18, federal land registrar Nicholas Perkins spotted him in the small village of Wakefield, in Alabama Territory, 200 miles from his earlier campsite along the Mississippi, and Burr's fortunes changed dramatically.

It was approximately midnight, and Perkins had been working late at the courthouse, when he heard the sound of horses on the road nearby. He went to the door, as a man on horseback passed at a brisk trot, followed a moment later by another rider who stopped to ask directions to "Major Hinson's." Knowing the difficulty in following this route at night, Perkins warned the man to stay at the tavern. But the rider refused his advice. These were "extraordinary men," Perkins later claimed, riding at such a "late hour in a strange country," and willing to travel on seven or eight miles along bad roads and over dangerous bridges when a comfortable tavern was just around the corner. Their odd behavior made him suspicious. Could they be robbers with a "bad design on Hinson or his property"? he wondered. Then another thought crossed his mind. Might the mysterious rider be Aaron Burr, making his escape through this remote country?[4]

Perkins resolved to follow the men, and he persuaded the local sheriff to accompany him. They discovered the travelers at Hinson's, their horses tied outside the house. The man he had conversed with greeted him again, while the other retreated to the kitchen to warm himself by the fire.[5]

When Perkins finally got a good look at the second guest, he was shocked by his bizarre getup. He wore a slouching white hat with a broad brim, sported a long beard and a checkered handkerchief around his neck, and a great, baggy coat tied with a belt. Hanging from the belt was a tin cup and a butcher's knife. The outfit did not fit the profile of the dapper Burr, known for his stylish dress and genteel manners. But something gave him away: "His eyes," attested Perkins. Burr had glanced at Perkins, then quickly withdrew his gaze; yet the land registrar was convinced he had just identified the stranger. He later testified in court that he had heard "Mr. Burr's eyes mentioned as being remarkably keen, and this glance from him strengthened his suspicions."[6]

Leaving the sheriff behind at Major Hinson's, Perkins rode off to Fort Stoddert, arriving just before sunrise. There, he informed Lieutenant Edmund Gaines of his astonishing discovery, and Gaines agreed to lead a small detail of soldiers back to Hinson's farm. As they approached the house, they came upon Burr, who was accompanied by the sheriff. Gaines asked the unknown rider directly if he was "Colonel Burr," and Burr replied, making no attempt to conceal his identity. After a brief conversation, Gaines arrested him, and they proceeded together to the fort.[7]

Though he had just met Burr hours before, the sheriff was aiding his escape. Major Hinson was harboring a fugitive, as well, yet none of Burr's local supporters was to suffer for their actions. Indeed, for most Alabama settlers the notorious ex-vice president was a hero for his daring filibuster rather than a villain. But to the soldier Gaines, a Virginian, Burr was a wanted man.[8]

Gaines immediately wrote to both Wilkinson and Governor Williams of Mississippi that Burr was in his custody, "in one of our best rooms with a Sentinel at the door." But when a Spanish officer suddenly appeared at the fort, wishing to see Burr, the lieutenant became nervous, worrying that the Spaniard was part of a plot to rescue his prisoner. Burr, however, took his incarceration in stride, requesting nothing more than a few bottles of wine from his Spanish visitor. Gaines then began to make arrangements for Perkins and six other men to escort Burr to the nation's capital. This ad hoc civilian guard pledged its loyalty to the president, and its commitment to Burr's safe conduct. The members of the escort made a practical decision, signing a contract to split the $2,000 reward equally.[9]

Burr began his long trek north and east on March 5. The trip was hazardous and physically demanding for all involved: The party crossed swollen streams and rivers and traversed the rough terrain of the Alabama and Georgia backcountry. Perkins had few concerns until they neared South Carolina, home of the Alstons, who were a powerful clan in the state. If Burr had any hope of escape, it would be here, with the help of his son-in-law.[10]

As the party reached Chester, South Carolina, Burr jumped from his horse. He called out to a group of men, urging them to fetch a local magistrate. He begged them for protection, claiming that he was being held without proper authority. Perkins, a large man, dismounted and forcefully threw Burr back into the saddle. Then the party quickly rode out of town. Understandably less trusting of his famous charge, Perkins hired a gig to convey Burr the rest of the way to Virginia.[11]

On March 25, they arrived in Fredericksburg, at which point Perkins learned that plans had changed. Now Richmond was their destination, and so they backtracked, arriving in the state capital the following day. Gossip about Burr's appearance immediately began to circulate. Virginia congressman John Randolph, who would assume a lead role as foreman of Burr's grand jury, reported that Burr had been spotted en route, still dressed in the odd attire he was captured in, which was described by Randolph as a "shabby suit of homespun, with an old white hat flapped over his face." Jefferson's friends sent the chief executive similar reports, clearly amused by the transformation.[12]

People back east were simply amazed by Burr's capture, finding the story so "strikingly singular," as one newspaper put it, as to surpass "the page of romance." The haughty, elegant Burr, once considered a dandified member of the New York *ton,* was now reduced to an uncouth bumpkin, with "old Virginia leggins" and a tin cup hanging from his belt. In Richmond's Republican newspaper, a debate ensued over his dress; some refused to accept the story that Burr had worn a disguise in order to more easily slip across the border into Spanish Florida. Once again the talk of town, Burr delighted his critics, who could now revel in his humiliation.[13]

"MR. JEFFERSON HAS BEEN TOO HASTY"

The Burr trial featured some of the greatest oratory of the age amid heated exchanges, exhibitions of wit, and incisive demonstrations of legal logic. Though Burr's capture would receive numerous romantic retellings, it was his treason trial that gained the most attention, even acclaim, as one of the great criminal trials in American history. Spectators flocked to Richmond's House of Delegates from places near and distant, jamming the courtroom to witness the prosecution of the former vice president for the high crime of treason. The state summoned over 140 witnesses, though only a few actually took the stand and testified. This was a political prosecution, and so it naturally enflamed public opinion, and consumed more newsprint than any other American court proceeding ever had. Burr's trial was never simply about the law. It was political theater, an elaborate performance designed to mold public opinion as much as to defend public reputations.

On March 30, 1807, at the Eagle Tavern in Richmond, Burr faced his initial examination before Supreme Court Chief Justice John Marshall. But even before the defendant appeared before the judge, political conditions had already determined the direction the proceedings would take. The arguments made in Richmond were, by and large, in response to a series of events that took shape in the months immediately following Jefferson's November 27, 1806, proclamation. During those crucial months from December to March, the furor over Burr's so-called "conspiracy" reached its

height, and a number of related events influenced the prosecution and defense equally.

First, to make its case, the prosecution needed evidence of an "overt
act" of war—necessary to prove treason. The event the prosecution chose
in this effort was the assembly of a small but indeterminate number of men
on Blennerhassett Island, in the days leading up to Harman's escape on December 10. The prosecution wished to give the impression that warlike
conditions existed there.[14]

Accounts in the newspapers, and the message from the governor of
Ohio to the general assembly, underscored the perception that Blennerhassett Island (and the flotilla assembling) was heavily armed. There were
reports of French mercenaries transporting boxes of muskets down the
Ohio River, and of large numbers of men, as many as 20,000, gathering to
feed this astonishing enterprise. The French connection was meant to im-
ply that Burr and his henchmen were consorting with foreigners, who were
not just willing but hell-bent on destroying the union—for the right price.
Blennerhassett, too, was attacked as an Irish royalist, whose loyalty to republican principles was suspect. Rumors circulated that he had authored
several anonymous essays calling for the separation of the western states
from the union.[15]

The obvious (but generally overlooked) question is this: What had
happened in Ohio? A peculiar shift in language was evident in the newspapers and emerged, as well, in the letters of men of local prominence; it was,
as a loyal militia captain wrote to Secretary of War Dearborn, as if Ohio was
making preparations to fight "foreign troops." In the minds of those charged
with Ohio's defense, Burr's expedition had been transformed into a grand
imaginary army, indistinguishable from a foreign enemy. It was the milita-
ristic context—the illusion of a pending war—that made Blennerhassett
Island the centerpiece of the prosecution's case.[16]

On January 18, 1807, one observer captured the tension in Ohio in a
letter he sent to his father, in Virginia: "The minds of the people in general
seem to be very much agitated at the time about a civil war that appears to
be taking place among us." He explained that the president's proclamation
had contributed to this state of affairs, as it was "very copious and unlimited in authorizing and requesting all Governors of states, military officers
down to private citizens to do their best endeavors to bring condign pun-

ishment to all persons contriving or plotting a war against his Catholic Majesty [the king of Spain]." The writer placed Burr at the crux of all these machinations, and wished for the most extreme punishment for the ex-vice president: "I entertain a pleasing hope that I shall soon hear that Mr. Burr is summoned to the bar of Almighty God by the message of a rifle ball through his blood-thirsty heart to give an account of Hamilton's and other innocent blood he is seeking to shed."[17]

These trumped-up threats in Ohio made it possible for those inclined to call Burr a "villain, rascal, thief and highway robber" to see him as a desperate man who could be hunted down and shot like a common criminal. But more important for the coming prosecution, it made Burr the commander of an invading army. His unusual treatment in Mississippi confirmed this view: Burr was not simply arrested there but taken into custody after—the language is important—an "armistice" was reached. Mississippi officials accepted the terms of his surrender as if they had been negotiating with the head of a foreign force.[18]

The flaw in the evidence from Blennerhassett Island, though, was enormous: Burr was not there! At the time the Wood County (Virginia) militia descended on the island, Burr was still in Kentucky, hundreds of miles from the scene of the supposed crime.

If the prosecution scripted its narrative of treason through stories told about Burr's "war" emanating from Blennerhassett Island, the defense followed Burr's lead by drawing on his appearance before the Mississippi grand jury in early February. The dismissal of all charges there (after a rousing defense) resulted because jurors found General Wilkinson's actions in New Orleans to be criminal—not Burr's. In early March, Republican newspapers in the East printed Burr's highly critical letter of Wilkinson, in which he called the general a notorious pensioner of the Spanish—the letter Burr sent to Acting Governor of Mississippi Cowles Mead.[19]

At the same time, other prominent men published their rebukes of the devious general. Edward Livingston exposed Wilkinson's flagrant abuse of the courts and his suspension of habeas corpus in New Orleans, and Ohio senator John Smith printed his denial of ever having heard Burr speak of treason. The most damning attack came from former Kentucky senator John Adair, who called Wilkinson a "petty tyrant" and condemned his abuse of the law as a far more egregious attack on democracy than President Adams's infamous Sedition Acts. As one of the men whom Wilkinson had placed under military arrest and sent east for trial, Adair was a forceful critic; his words carried greater weight after the charges against him were dismissed with the determination that there was no evidence against him. Immediately upon his discharge, Adair demanded that the attorney general conduct a full investigation into his false arrest.[20]

The resentment Adair drummed up found a particularly receptive audience in Washington. The Senate had just passed a bill suspending habeas corpus for a period of three months, only to have its tactic rejected in the House by a vote of 113 to 19. The bill had been conceived in an effort to keep two of Burr's allies—two "conspirators," Samuel Swartwout and Dr. Erich Bollmann—behind bars. Like Adair, they had been sent east by Wilkinson to stand trial, and were being held in a marine barracks, under heavy guard, though no evidence had been presented before a judge.[21]

Their February 1807 hearing was a two-week sideshow, a buildup to Burr's treason trial. Lawyers for the two prisoners requested a writ of habeas corpus and their release from custody, as the two sides debated whether the evidence was adequate to have them held. Chief Justice Marshall presided, laying out his definition of treason. According to the U.S. Constitution, he said, an overt act was required. To hold the men over for trial, it would have to be proven that they had participated in a warlike assembly of men for treasonable purposes. The evidence failed to show this, and so Swartwout and Bollmann were released. But at the same time, Marshall also expanded the meaning of treason, to permit room to consider "constructive treason," as derived from British common law. He said that "all those who perform any part, however minute, or however removed from the scene of action," could be considered traitors. Thus, the chief justice supplied the foundation for both defense and prosecution cases: The state would argue in favor of constructive treason (insofar as Burr was not on Blennerhassett Island), while the defense was left to contend that no evidence existed to suggest that Burr had committed an overt act of treason on Blennerhassett Island or anywhere else.[22]

On February 18, amid the debate over habeas corpus in Congress, Virginian John Randolph took the opportunity to attack Wilkinson. He claimed that the suspension of habeas corpus would have given the general unlimited power—so much power that he could easily have shot Burr or anyone else accused of treason, and been immune from any legal consequences. Randolph's example was not arbitrarily chosen. He probably had heard that Samuel Swartwout was nearly shot by Wilkinson's men when they were bringing him east for trial. "Dead men tell no tales," the colorful congressman warned his colleagues ominously. Because he was rumored to be deeply implicated in Burr's project, Wilkinson had every reason to silence Burr. According to Randolph (who was at that moment the most influential Republican in Congress), he was a renegade general and a potent symbol of military despotism.[23]

This growing sense of public outrage set the stage for Burr's defense. It was obvious that the trial would center on the credibility of two men: Wilkinson and Burr. Wilkinson had made many enemies. And though Jefferson stood by his general, many others saw Wilkinson as a bigger scoundrel and a more serious threat to the republic than the former vice president.

The final factor was the power of the press. The papers circulated unsubstantiated rumors and treated them as facts (indeed, the more outlandish the claim, the more dramatically it was asserted as irrefutable truth), and even the president of the United States was influenced by them. General William Eaton, a star witness for the prosecution, published his account of Burr's plot in a Boston newspaper, and it was widely reprinted across the country. His tale became a kind of talisman for those declaring Burr's guilt. Eaton also assumed a prominent role in the effort to commit Swartwout and Bollman for trial on treason charges. His deposition at their hearing replayed the story he gave to the newspapers, adding detail and spoken under oath. Remarkably, even Burr's much-devoted political lieutenant Matthew Livingston Davis proclaimed in a letter that "if any confidence can be placed in the testimony of Eaton (and I am disposed to believe the greater part of it) Burr had acted in the most weak & childish manner, a great man ever did." Clearly, Burr had ground to make up in winning over the public.[24]

But the newspapers assumed an even more significant role in Jefferson's thinking. He had bought into the Eaton story, as he bought into Wilkinson's strained interpretation of events. Once the president's January 22 message to Congress was published (in which he stated that Burr was guilty "beyond question"), he was entirely committed. His message was accompanied in the papers by a grossly embellished version of the cipher

letter, supposedly drafted by Burr. The same text was printed up as a broadside, entitled "Message of the President of the United States, containing a
Development of the Conspiracy." Jefferson was doing his utmost to shape
public opinion. Lest there be any doubt, his public denunciation seriously
undermined Burr's ability to receive a fair trial. The retired John Adams
observed that there was probably a "lying spirit" at work against Burr, and
that "Mr. Jefferson has been too hasty in his message in which he has denounced him by name and pronounced him guilty." Adams felt the judicial
system should decide Burr's fate, and "if his guilt is as clear as the noonday
sun, the first magistrate ought not to have pronounced it so before a jury
had tried him."[25]

But Jefferson seemed to believe that Burr had been tried in the court of
public opinion, and that it was public opinion, above all, which had crushed
the conspiracy. He wrote to Governor Edwin Tiffin of Ohio on February 2
that "the hand of the people has given the mortal blow to the conspiracy
which, in other countries, would have called for an appeal to armies." A day
later, he reassured Wilkinson that the general's abuses of habeas corpus and
illegal arrests "will be supported by the public opinion."[26]

Jefferson's faith in public opinion only increased as Burr's hearing and
his two trials proceeded. To Virginia congressman William Branch Giles,
the president predicted that the testimony of Eaton and Wilkinson "will
satisfy the world, if not the judges, of Burr's guilt." In more explicit terms,
he told Giles that "letters and facts published in the local newspapers" and
the "universal belief or rumor of his guilt" justified that Burr be committed
for treason; more than that, there was not "a candid man in the United
States" who doubted that Burr had committed an overt act of treason. In
writing to George Hay, who as the U.S. attorney for the Virginia District led
Burr's prosecution, he expressed a similar perspective. When his concern
mounted that Burr might not be convicted, Jefferson urged Hay to present
testimony before the legislature, and "through them the public," as though
the case could be retried before the people. Was this Jefferson blowing off
steam, trying to make a wish come true? Or did he really see the law differently than the other trained attorneys involved in the case? At this point, he
was so certain of Burr's guilt in the court of public opinion that he told Hay:
"before an impartial jury, Burr's conduct would convict himself, were not
one word of testimony to be offered against him."[27]

It seems clear that in the president's construction of democracy, there were times when the rights of the individual were to be subordinated to the will of the majority. Could he possibly mean that public opinion should trump the courts, even when, as in this case, that opinion was mixed with rumor, hearsay, and a "lying spirit," which, as John Adams so trenchantly observed, was part and parcel of democracy? It seems implausible. But that *is* what Jefferson meant: All the evidence contained in his correspondence during these months leads one to conclude that the president wished to submit Burr's fate to the will of the people, whether or not it was just to do so.

Jefferson betrayed his feelings in his last private interview with Burr, in 1806. At that time, he told Burr he had lost the favor of the people, to which Burr responded, discerningly, that this *might* be true only if one relied on the newspapers. But Jefferson *did* rely on the newspapers—that is, on certain Republican papers—when it suited him. (He called the opposition newspapers "polluted vehicles" of information.) In accepting select newspaper stories about Burr, he was unwilling to admit that he might have confused the people's will with his own.[28]

"ABOUNDING IN CRUDITIES AND ABSURDITIES"

On March 30, Burr appeared before Chief Justice John Marshall for an initial examination that would last for three days. Court was held in a private room at the Eagle Tavern. George Hay and Attorney General Caesar Rodney represented the government. Burr, acting as his own counsel, was joined by two prominent Virginia attorneys: Edmund Randolph, who had served as both attorney general and secretary of state under President Washington; and John Wickham, perhaps the most brilliant lawyer of the Richmond bar. Wickham was seven years younger than Burr, born in New York, and this might explain in part how he had found sympathy for his client. Educated in France as well as at the College of William and Mary, he was admired for his polished manners, his wit, and his quickness of legal argument. Wickham presented himself well, as would his client. Two prominent Federalists had loaned Burr $1,000 for new clothes, so that he could be tastefully attired in black silk for the duration of his trials. As Wickham and Burr were the principal architects of Burr's defense, it could not have hurt that the two of them came to court each day in sartorial splendor.[29]

The first day of the examination was brief. Nicholas Perkins gave an account of Burr's capture and his "attempted escape" in South Carolina. District Attorney Hay motioned that Burr be committed on charges of treason and high misdemeanor. Because both sides felt that the public should hear any arguments before the court, Chief Justice Marshall acceded to another motion that court be adjourned and moved from Eagle Tavern to the courthouse for the following day. Burr was released on $5,000 bail, and was free to move around town. When the trial resumed, the courtroom was so packed with curious spectators that Marshall agreed to move the proceedings to the even larger House of Delegates.[30]

Hay opened for the state. He contended that Burr had violated federal law by organizing an expedition against Spain during peacetime; yet that misdemeanor paled in comparison to the charge of treason. The state's entire case rested on three pieces of evidence, the same documents that had been presented in the Swartwout and Bollman hearing: the infamous cipher letter supposedly written by Burr to Wilkinson; an affidavit by Wilkinson; and William Eaton's deposition.[31]

From the beginning, Hay relied on Eaton's narrative of intrigue to convince the court of Burr's guilt. Eaton's account centered on a series of conversations he had had with Burr during the winter of 1805–06, when the two men were living at the same boardinghouse in Washington. During those months, Burr talked about his planned expedition to Mexico. Soon, however, Eaton began to suspect that something more treacherous was being considered, for the colonel's actions seemed, he said, "enveloped in mystery." The general attempted to draw him out—somehow getting Burr to reveal his secret. And what he learned was incredible: Burr had every intention of revolutionizing the western country, separating it from the union, and "establishing a monarchy there, of which he was to be the sovereign, New Orleans to be his capital." The ex-vice president claimed to have inexhaustible resources, willing recruits numbering 10,000 men or more, and assurances that the army would join him. General Wilkinson would be his second-in-command.[32]

But that was not all. Eaton declared that Burr's ambition was not limited to "a deep laid plot of treason in the west." Burr contemplated overthrowing the present government, which he described as weak and impotent. If he could secure an alliance with the naval commanders, "he would turn congress neck and heels out of doors, assassinate the president, seize on the treasury and the navy, and declare himself the protector of an energetic government."[33]

Overwhelmed by this discovery, Eaton decided he could only stop Burr by getting him out of the country. He then approached the president, urging him to give the former vice president some post in London or Cadiz. Reward a traitor? This may seem odd, but Eaton believed that Burr's sense of honor would contain his ambition and ensure his fidelity. Jefferson flatly refused to consider the suggestion, which prompted Eaton to lay open Burr's darker plot to the chief executive. But even this was to no avail: Jefferson felt Burr had little hope of succeeding in the West, because the unwavering loyalty of citizens would foil him. As a final gesture, Eaton let Burr know his true feeling, when he delivered a public toast: "The United States—Palsy to the brain that should plot to dismember, and leprosy to the hand that will not draw to defend our union!" Eaton felt he had behaved honorably, and assumed he would receive the gratitude of his countrymen.[34]

But Wickham observed that Eaton's story sounded "strange." The real question for us, too, is why he would concoct such an outrageous tale. Eaton craved public acclaim and public glory. Senator William Plumer of New Hampshire ranked Eaton, along with Wilkinson, as the vainest two men he had ever met. Even the *American Citizen* (a paper with no interest in protecting Burr) noted Eaton's "weakness and vanity" when it published his questionable revelations about Burr.[35]

Eaton was an army careerist. Thin-skinned and unguarded, he had earlier found himself mired in a court-martial when a fellow officer reported rumors of his misconduct. He left the army at that point, and then used his connections to get an appointment as U.S. consul at Tunis. While there, in 1804, he organized a mongrel filibuster army of Greeks, Italians, and Arabs, which he led 600 miles across the Libyan Desert to capture the city of Derna. Eaton's mission had been to restore the fallen Pasha to his throne, after having been driven into exile by his usurping brother. Upon his return to United States, Eaton met Burr while he was trying to collect money from the government for his military escapades. For his daring, Congress bestowed on him the honorary title of general. The "Hero of Derne" relished the limelight.[36]

Eaton saw himself (much as Wilkinson saw himself) as the savior of the nation. In two letters he wrote to his patron, Senator Stephen Bradley of Vermont, in 1808, discussing whether he should take a commission in the army, Eaton, self-styled dragon slayer, fantasized meeting Burr on the field of glory. If he could not kill Burr in a fair fight, he wanted to earn the public's praise for bringing down the conspiracy. Soon the people would see that he alone had prevented a "civil war," he carped to Bradley. He had stopped Burr's conspiracy from growing into a full-scale revolution.[37]

For men like Eaton, reputation was everything. The larger and more threatening Burr's plot appeared to be, the more important Eaton became. But the honorary general probably suffered from imposter syndrome, never quite certain that his accomplishments would be taken seriously by the nation's most prominent men. His biographer readily admits that Eaton had a way of blurring fact and fantasy. He was restless, ambitious, and before he made it to Richmond in 1807, known for his drunken bouts and large gambling debts. There is little doubt that Burr discussed his expedition with Eaton during the winter of 1805–06, and he most likely tried to recruit him; but that does not alter the evidence pointing to the falsity of Eaton's story. As William Plumer wrote in his journal, it seemed unlikely that Burr, a man known for his discretion would open himself up so foolishly to a man of Eaton's cast.[38]

There is another possibility. Burr might have criticized the president in his conversations with Eaton, or Eaton might have overheard a discussion between Burr and Dayton about the great tale they planned to tell the marqués de Yrujo. Given Eaton's drinking habits, Burr assumed that few people would trust anything the general might say. But it is more likely that Burr said nothing serious to Eaton, and instead Eaton, who heard rumors about Burr, and had listened to Burr disparage Jefferson's administration, created a narrative that placed him at the center of the scenario as Burr's trusted confidant. His vanity and blurred memory best explains the fanciful tale told by the "Hero of Derne."

Hay knew little about the general personally, but he did see that Eaton's story blackened Burr's reputation. In his opening remarks, he took

Eaton's narrative and embellished it. He made Burr's actions sound deeply personal, insisting that Burr's motive was revenge: He hated Jefferson for withdrawing his confidence, and it was this hatred that had inspired him to "establish a monarchy within the territory of the United States." He was cold and ruthless, caring not to temper the "incalculable evils" of his scheme, especially the "bloodshed and desolation which a civil war never fails to produce!" And if that was not enough, Burr had abandoned the "pure and republican principles" he had vowed to defend as "the second officer of the nation." Catalinian conspirator, un-American monarchist, ambitious megalomaniac, bloodthirsty revolutionary, and Judas-like betrayer—this was the government's picture of Aaron Burr. Jefferson's handpicked prosecutor dredged up every horrifying allusion he could imagine—or could borrow from the blotted prose of the papers.[39]

Hay referred to Wilkinson's affidavit of his conversations with Samuel Swartwout, but mainly to confirm what Eaton had said. Then he pointed to the commotions in New Orleans and Ohio as proof of a serious threat, asking: "Was all this occasioned by the approach of one solitary and powerful individual?" Echoing what Jefferson had earlier concluded, Hay contended that "of the treasonable intentions and plans of Mr. Burr therefore there can be no doubt."[40]

When it was his turn, John Wickham quickly exposed the weaknesses in the prosecution's case. He began by asking the most pertinent question: "Is there even one solitary witness who can depose to an overt act of treason?" In the constitutional definition of treason, proof required the testimony of two witnesses to the same overt act. If there was proof of anything, it was that Burr might have been planning an invasion of Spanish lands, which Wickham claimed was not illegal. The country was "in an intermediate state between war and peace," and so a filibuster could easily be seen "as useful" to the United States.[41]

Wickham also wondered aloud why Burr was being tried in Virginia, thereby questioning the prosecution's decision to focus on Blennerhassett Island (which was, technically, within the jurisdiction of Virginia). Where did the prosecution get the idea that an offense had been committed on the island? From the newspapers, of course. Burr's attorney belittled the evidence. Why had no one been brought to testify who witnessed the insurrection? "What kind of invisible army must this have been," Wickham mused playfully, "when in the course of three months not an individual could be found to testify to its existence?"[42]

Eaton was his next target, whom he called a "stranger" to Burr. His retelling of Eaton's story made it appear not only improbable but ridiculous. It "surpasses the bounds of credibility," Wickham declared, that Burr would have made such an outlandish confession as that he planned to establish a monarchy, and separate the western country, let alone "cut the President's throat, & then turn Congress, neck and heels out of doors!" Eaton's behavior defied common sense. He should have viewed Burr as a "madman," but instead he begged the president to place him in a "most responsible and delicate situation," as a foreign ambassador. And what was to be made of Eaton's toast—"Palsy to the brain that should plot to dismember, and leprosy to the hand that will not draw to defend our union!"? Did he expect a public toast to cause Burr to reconsider a dangerous plan? The only conclusion to be drawn, Wickham insisted, was that Eaton "shews an irregular imagination" and a bad memory, his story "strange, passing strange." To rely on such testimony just made the prosecution look as foolish as William Eaton himself.[43]

Edmund Randolph, the elder statesman and Burr's second co-counsel, underscored Wickham's remarks. Prejudices had been propagated "from one end of America to the other," he said, alluding to the role that newspapers played in manufacturing the conspiracy. As to Eaton's statement, it served only a political purpose, inciting fears of "monarchy" among Republicans, especially Virginians. Lest we forget, Burr had been repeatedly caricatured in the newspapers as the "little Emperor"—demonized to conjure the Republicans' worst nightmare.[44]

Next, Burr spoke in his own defense. Turning to the law, he observed that treason "must consist in acts," while the prosecution's warrant relied on mere "conjectures." The commotions that took place in the West could hardly be laid at his feet: "We are told by the President that the people of Ohio were alarmed; and how were they alarmed? He alarmed them. How was he alarmed? By Mr. Wilkinson." The "historical facts" had to speak for themselves. Burr had been "honorably discharged" by three grand juries; and in Mississippi, he pointed out, he was not only acquitted but the clearheaded jury actually "censured the government." And, he added, there was "no alarm in that part of the country."[45]

But his most interesting remarks concerned his promptness to concede to his filibuster plan: even "if it might be said that the designs imputed to me ever did exist," he contended, "it might also be said they were long since abandoned." By the time he descended the river, the equipment he was carrying proved that his object was, by then, "purely peaceable and agricultural." His band of men were on their way to settle the Bastrop property, in Louisiana. He had never considered treason, and repeated what he had said all along: "My designs were honorable and would have been useful to the United States."[46]

With his accustomed directness, Burr addressed Chief Justice Marshall, claiming that the court had three choices: acquittal; commitment for treason; or for misdemeanor. Wasting few words, he said that there was really only one reasonable choice: acquittal. For what the prosecution considered proof was not proof at all, given that the affidavits of Wilkinson and Eaton were "abounding in crudities and absurdities."[47]

The youngest attorney in the courtroom that day wrapped up the prosecution's argument. Caesar Rodney was only thirty-five, and seemed embarrassed by the task before him. He had been a close friend of Burr's, and he admitted as much to the court. But Rodney soldiered on, declaring that a chain of circumstantial evidence proved Burr's guilt, and that the newspapers had firmly implanted in the public mind the certainty of this truth. Yet Rodney was willing to admit that the prosecution probably did not have evidence of an overt act. The only argument he could muster was to compare Burr to Jason, of the Greek legend. In effect, he was leading a band of foolish young men, what he called a "new argonautic expedition," to capture the "golden fleece" in Mexico.[48]

Rodney must have felt some genuine discomfort, for this was the first and only speech he would give at the trial. He left Richmond, and told Jefferson he would have to resign from the case, mentioning family illness as the cause. Rodney's excuse sounds implausible, given that Hay had lost his young wife only a week before the examination. More likely, Burr's former friend simply did not have the stomach for so dubious a prosecution.[49]

All the arguments were made on a single day. Chief Justice Marshall resumed court on April 1, and gave his opinion. He agreed with the prosecution that the evidence provided probable cause that Burr had organized a military expedition against the Spanish territories. Marshall rejected the defense's contention that filibustering was acceptable, refusing to buy into Wickham's argument that the nation was at an "intermediate stage between peace and war."[50]

But treason was a different matter. As it was the "most atrocious crime," and one capable of being manipulated by the "malignant and vindictive passions" common to partisan struggles, Marshall made it clear that, in his judgment, the Constitution offered a precise definition: Treason had to consist in levying war or in giving aid and comfort to the enemy; this high crime required overt acts testified to in open court by two witnesses. For probable cause that Burr had levied war, troops had to have been assembled. Said Marshall, "Treason may be machinated in secret, but it can be perpetuated only in the open day and in the eye of the world."[51]

Marshall chastised the prosecution for failing to collect any witnesses to the crime. If Wilkinson's cipher letter was to be taken seriously, then the prosecution ought to have produced evidence that a grand army assembled in or around the month of July, when Burr was alleged to have written the letter in question. The letter could be read as proof of a treasonable design, but that design had to have "ripened into the crime itself by actually levying war." In the law, intentions did not equate to actions. So, if Swartwout's declaration (in Wilkinson's affidavit) was true, and Burr was scouring the country from New York to the western states, raising an army of 7,000, then, Marshall inquired, "What could veil his troops from human sight?" Following Wickham's logic, Marshall agreed that "an invisible army is not an instrument of war." More than five weeks had passed since his ruling in the Bollman-Swartwout case, in which he had made the same argument. If treason existed, he asked provocatively, "Why is it not proven?"[52]

The chief justice's decision was damning for the prosecution. He not only rejected the evidence as probable cause of treason but implied that if Burr had really organized an insurrection, there should be ample testimony to that fact. He directly, pointedly, questioned whether this invisible rebellion had ever occurred. In effect, he was calling Wilkinson's bluff. Where was the grand army descending the Mississippi that threatened New Orleans? It had never materialized. And if it had, why was the government unable to find single witness to its existence?[53]

Thus, Marshall concluded that Burr could not be committed for treason, though he could be held for carrying out a military expedition. Finally,

Marshall gave the prosecution some ground to recoup their losses: If the prosecution collected the right kind of evidence, it could seek an indictment against Burr for treason. With that understanding, Burr was released on bail of $10,000, and his next appearance before the court was set for May 22.[54]

"THE ACQUITTAL OF COLONEL BURR WILL BE A SATIRE ON THE GOVERNMENT"

Jefferson fumed when he learned of Chief Justice Marshall's ruling. He was convinced that the Federalists and a "little band of Quids" were orchestrating their own conspiracy. His enemies were banding against him, using the judiciary and attacking Wilkinson for his abuses of civil liberties, in order to save Burr's neck. In two letters written in April, one to James Bowdoin, minister to Spain, and another to the Republican stalwart William B. Giles, Jefferson repeated his six-year-old complaint that Federalists on the High Court were a corrupting influence in government.[55]

Jefferson thought he saw a pattern. The administration had recently lost another high-profile filibustering trial, the July 1806 case of Samuel G. Ogden and William S. Smith, and this colored his view of the Burr proceedings. Ogden and Smith (the latter being John Adams's son-in-law) were associates of the Venezuelan adventurer Francisco de Miranda, who outfitted a filibuster with the help of American recruits and dollars. Ogden and Smith were tried in federal court in New York and acquitted of the charge of equipping Miranda's expeditionary force. The jury felt that the two men had done nothing illegal. Miranda was a charismatic figure, who had won the admiration of Washington, Adams, and Hamilton—another reason for the Virginian to distrust him. But Miranda was never an associate of Burr's; in fact, the two men distrusted each other. As Jefferson reviewed the case, he came to believe that Federalists had shielded Ogden and Smith from conviction and now, with more legal chicanery, the Federalist chief justice was thwarting Burr's prosecution. In April, his suspicions were confirmed when he discovered that Marshall had attended a lavish dinner at John Wickham's, and Burr was one of the guests.[56]

Jefferson had long distrusted Marshall, a fellow Virginian. The two men had a common heritage as members of the Randolph dynasty—one of the first families in the Commonwealth of Virginia. They carried themselves with the casual air and dress that was the fashion of the Virginia gentry. But that was where the similarity ended. They were fierce partisan opponents, and intensely disliked one another. Marshall was younger—in fact, the same age as Burr. He was jovial and outgoing, whereas Jefferson was reticent and retiring. The chief justice had just published the fifth and final volume of his biography of George Washington, which celebrated Federalism while disparaging Jefferson and the Republican Party. Both Marshall and Jefferson saw the other as a spoiler, capable of subverting the foundational principles of republican governance.[57]

As the presiding judge at Burr's hearing, Marshall did not have to do much to get under Jefferson's skin. As for Jefferson, Marshall's refusal to commit the former vice president for treason was pure effrontery. The wily jurist had dared to shield a traitor—using his bag of legal tricks, as Jefferson put it, "to throw dust in the eyes of his audience." Marshall had ridiculed the prosecution for failing to prove an overt act, which Jefferson felt Burr's conduct had decidedly shown.[58]

Jefferson believed that the chief justice had overstepped himself, and he predicted a public backlash. He thought the legislature would be stirred into action, and would pass an amendment to weaken the Supreme Court, effectively stripping the justices of their lifetime appointments—or at least, making it easier to remove them. Jefferson fantasized that if Marshall persisted in blocking Burr's conviction, "the day is never far distant," as he wrote to Giles, "when the people will remove him." Through obstructionist actions, Marshall would inadvertently bring down the Supreme Court. Jefferson's undisguised animosity was directed at two targets: the "crooked gun" Aaron Burr and the legal con artist John Marshall.[59]

Jefferson may have lost his objectivity with regard to Burr's case, but he certainly had not lost his desire to win. In the weeks leading to the grand jury's May 22 meeting, he redoubled his energies. The federal government sent out agents to find witnesses, collect depositions, and round up anyone who might be able to testify against Burr, whether or not that person was a credible witness. The administration spent nearly $100,000 in the attempt to convict Burr, a sizable sum for a president who had long opposed a strong central government Jefferson relied on executive privilege when he sent Hay a batch of blank pardons, and urged the prosecutor to give complete immunity to any of Burr's so-called "accomplices" who could be persuaded to testify against him.[60]

Burr saw the forces arrayed against him. He wrote to his daughter in mid-May that "the most indefatigable industry is used by the agents of the government, and they have money at command without stint." He assured Theodosia, "if I were possessed of the same means, I could not only foil the prosecutors, but render them ridiculous and infamous." In this game of cat and mouse, Burr understood that public opinion was the state's most valuable weapon, writing in the same letter: "The democratic papers teem with abuse against me and my counsel, and even against the chief justice." He refused to shield his daughter from the truth, telling her bluntly that the odds were against him: "Nothing is left undone or unsaid, which can prejudice the public mind, and produce a conviction without evidence." He thought the chances were good that he would be convicted on the basis of prejudice—on the basis of lies that Jefferson had convinced himself he believed.[61]

When the grand jury convened on May 22, Burr had added two new lawyers to his team: Benjamin Botts, a member of the Virginia bar; and John Baker, who said little but was well versed in local politics and had the ability to size up potential jurymen. They would be joined later by another Virginian, Charles Lee, who had been attorney general under Washington after Edmund Randolph. Finally, Burr took on Luther Martin of Maryland, without a doubt the most interesting member of his defense team. Know as "Old Brandy Bottle" for his alcoholic excesses, Martin was a strange mixture of crudeness and cunning. His manners were brusque, which may be why Jefferson derisively called him a "federal bull-dog"; or maybe it was because he was a lawyer who could sink his teeth into his prey and never let go. He outmaneuvered his opponents by having the last word, and that last word was often biting and sarcastic. Martin was man of great passion and boundless energy; his love of drink, rather than slowing him down, seemed to fuel his always entertaining performances in the courtroom.[62]

The prosecution had also changed its lineup. Hay was now joined by Alexander McRae, lieutenant governor of Virginia, described as dour and abrasive, but whose loyalty to Jefferson was unwavering. In contrast to the workmanlike Hay or the stern McRae, William Wirt, the third man at the prosecution table, was a scrappy young attorney who came to Jefferson's attention after marrying the daughter of one of his neighbors. At thirty-four, Wirt was over six feet tall and considered handsome. The famous portrait artist, Saint-Mémin, who was present in Richmond during the trial, captured Wirt as almost a Byronesque figure, with a massive head of curly locks and Roman features. Wirt had literary pretensions besides. His *Letters of the British Spy* (1803) told the story of a fictitious Englishman who was in Virginia seeking to understand the character of the people. In this often-re-printed work, Wirt showed his passion for the study of eloquence, especially courtroom eloquence; he admired most the "resistless enthusiasm of unaffected passion, which takes the heart by storm." He understood courtroom oratory as a self-conscious strategy designed to stir up sensations. He also recognized that trials were a form of medieval combat, opponents crossing verbal lances, or engaging in what he called "forensic digladiation" to prove their manly prowess. The theatrical styles of Luther Martin and William Wirt mattered, because this was a case in which winning over the public was just as important as persuading the judge.[63]

Burr wasted little time unsettling the prosecution. He began by protesting jury selection, his suspicions aroused when he learned that his good friend John Taylor of Caroline had been dropped from the jury pool. Next he insisted on the right to challenge jurors, and to eliminate any who showed extreme bias against him. Two jurors at the top of his list were William B. Giles, who had spearheaded the effort in the Senate to suspend habeas corpus, and Wilson Cary Nicholas, whom Burr blasted in a letter to Theodosia as "my vindictive and avowed personal enemy—the most so that could be found in this state." Nicholas, along with DeWitt Clinton, had led the charge to exile Burr from the Republican leadership. So Giles and Nicholas agreed to step down, while grumbling about their own mistreatment.[64]

Still, the jury panel was stacked against him, composed of twenty Jeffersonians and four Federalists. Sixteen of these were chosen to serve on the grand jury. His few challenges were symbolic at best.[65]

As in the Chase trial, Burr had every intention of transforming the courtroom into his classroom. But in this instance, he wished to teach a lesson on political persecution, and to demonstrate that justice only existed when the lone individual could successfully confront the tyrannical hand of state power. He had already revealed his approach in a letter to Theodosia, asking her to compose an essay containing all the episodes in ancient history when "a man of virtue and independence, and supposed to possess great talents," had become "the object of vindictive and unrelenting persecution." And after the grand jury had been selected, when the prosecuting attorney Hay insisted that Burr should be kept on the "same footing with every other man charged with a crime," Burr responded indignantly: "Would to God I did stand on the same ground with every other man." Though Marshall tried to temper the outburst, Burr had already succeeded in making his point.[66]

Over the next couple of days, the prosecution went on the offensive. Hay made a motion to commit Burr for treason, and the defense cried foul. Wickham was so furious that he threw Wilkinson's affidavit on the table, muttering that it was a pack of lies. The prosecution's key witness, the boisterous general, was still missing, and yet Hay was still dredging up the old charge of treason based on nothing but what Wickham called "floating rumours." And what did he mean? There was talk around Richmond that Burr would panic and flee the scene when Wilkinson, the so-called "savior of the nation," was about to make his grand entrance. By committing Burr for treason, Hay figured he could prevent Burr's flight while portraying him as a coward, afraid of his chief accuser.[67]

No one, in fact, knew where Wilkinson was. Hay made excuses for him, reminding people of the general's age and unwieldy size. Burr's attorney, Edmund Randolph, could not let the comment pass without his own retort: even "the gigantic 'bulk' of the general himself" was a poor excuse for his tardiness. And so, meanwhile, the defense also took aim at the Jefferson administration, criticizing the president for labeling Burr a guilty man in his message to Congress, thus contributing to the defendant's mistreatment.[68]

The prosecution flew into a rage. This was not a contest between Burr and Jefferson, William Wirt countered. Impatient with defense claims of persecution, he spoke in a sarcastic tone: "Oh no, sir, colonel Burr indeed has been oppressed, has been persecuted"—so why don't we just extend him every privilege and trust that he will not escape? Had the defense forgotten that its client had been a fugitive? Precautions were necessary: "This would really be carrying politeness beyond its ordinary pitch."[69]

Burr was not deterred. He launched into a speech justifying his criticism of the president. "Surely it is an established principle, sir," he said, "that no government is so high as to be beyond the reach of criticism." In an attempt to destroy a man, vigilance was necessary. Burr went on to cite violations of the law, reminding the court that his "friends had been every where seized by the military authority; a practice truly consonant with European despotisms." Burr's allies in New Orleans had been dragged before tribunals, and forced to give testimony; Burr's own papers and property had been unlawfully seized, and his letters stolen from the post office. Speaking in the third person, Burr went on: An "order had been issued to kill him, as he was descending the Mississippi." All the while the government looked the other way. And now Burr remarked, with undisguised irony, "nothing seemed too extravagant to be forgiven by the amiable morality of this government." The sacred right of habeas corpus had been threatened, and this not only affected him but "concerned the whole nation."[70]

The state case was flawed, Burr further contended, because it rested on a perverted definition of war. The defendant, as his own counsel, spoke directly. The trial transcript explains:

> Our president, said Mr. Burr, is a lawyer, and great one too. He certainly ought to know what it is, that constitutes a war. Six months ago, he proclaimed that there was a civil war. And yet, for six months they have been hunting for it, and still cannot find one spot where it existed. There was, to be sure, a most terrible war in the newspapers; but no where else. . . . At length, however, the Spaniards invaded our territory, and yet, there was no war. But, sir, if there was a war, certainly no man can pretend to say, that the government is able to find it out.[71]

Jefferson had concealed the war with Spain, which Burr claimed was a *real* war. And in its place, the government had manipulated the truth once again and manufactured an invisible civil war.

The battle over Burr's commitment for treason took an entire week. On May 28, the prosecution dropped the motion for commitment, and Burr agreed to pay additional bail. "Still waiting for Wilkinson," Burr wrote to Theodosia a week later, "and no certain accounts of his approach." John Randolph, the eccentric who had been selected as foreman of the grand jury, complained that it had nothing to do. Court was adjourned until

June 9, giving both sides an opportunity to stir up even more rancorous debate.[72]

On that date, Burr made a proposal that caught the prosecution completely off guard. He felt it was necessary to his defense to have as evidence General Wilkinson's October 21 letter to Jefferson, and Jefferson's reply. So he requested both, as well as copies of orders issued by the army and navy that pertained to his case. He was especially interested in an order issued by the secretary of the navy instructing a lieutenant to "destroy his person and property." This letter had already been published in the newspapers. If this order had in fact been issued, Burr felt it would justify his flight from Mississippi. Secretary of Navy Robert Smith had refused to forward the relevant papers up to now; so Burr was compelled to take further action. He asked the court to issue a subpoena *duces tecum* (to the president). This meant that Jefferson had to deliver the papers, and if necessary, deliver them in person. But as Burr made clear, he only wanted the papers, and had no intention of forcing Jefferson (or any cabinet member) to appear in court.[73]

Hay was baffled. At first, he said that he would supply the papers, though he felt the subpoena was uncalled for. Then he became annoyed, and decided to dispute Burr's right to pursue this course of action. The following day, Luther Martin stepped in and gave one of his grand orations. "This is a peculiar case," he intoned. President Jefferson had imperiously prejudged Aaron Burr, when he declared that there was "no doubt" as to his guilt. By taking this aggressive action, the president had placed himself in the middle of the case; he had bullied Burr with his accusations, usurping the power of the court system to decide his fate. "He had assumed to himself the knowledge of a Supreme Being himself," Martin pointed the finger, "and pretended to search the heart of my highly respected friend."[74]

Martin's client, his highly respected friend Burr, made no remark as his lawyer stepped up his impassioned appeal. Had Jefferson callously used the cry of treason to enhance his political reputation? He had called Burr a traitor "in the face of the country"; and the nation had "rewarded" the president for doing so. This was indecent, said Martin. It was evidence of Jefferson's arrogance, and perhaps a crime as well. The president had "let slip the dogs of war, the hell-hounds of persecution, to hunt down my friend."[75]

Wirt was livid, or certainly that is what his words at this moment suggest. Wilkinson's letter had no bearing on Burr's case, he insisted. And whatever "bloody orders" might have been issued, "Burr had placed himself in a state of war with his country." In that case, it would have been a "great and glorious virtue" to kill the traitor. If Burr's attorneys were to claim that the government had behaved dishonorably, then, Wirt scoffed, "let them clear the skirts of their client." "Let them prove his innocence," he dared, momentarily forgetting that basic tenet of the law: innocent until proven guilty. Proof of Burr's innocence would be "the most eloquent invective which they can pronounce against the prosecution."[76]

Wirt's outburst showed how effectively Luther Martin had baited the prosecution. Wirt had confirmed rather than disproved the defense's contention that the government had a vendetta against Burr. Foolishly, he had raised the outlandish argument that the militia had a right to kill Burr simply on the presumption of his guilt. Just as Jefferson had done, Wirt, a future U.S. attorney general, had twisted the rule of law in contending that Burr's guilt was so irrefutable that bringing him to trial was superfluous.

Wickham could hardly believe what he had heard Wirt say. Did he really mean that "the *acquittal of Colonel Burr will be a satire on the government*"? It was a sad day when the president's handpicked prosecutor confessed "that the character of the government depended on Burr's guilt." To Wickham, Burr could be acquitted without the federal government collapsing, morally or otherwise.[77]

So the defense had decided on a strategy: Martin would go for the jugular, and Wickham take the higher ground. At this point, Wirt found himself backed into a corner. He must have recognized that his arguments had played into the defense's hands. In this round of forensic digladiation, when Hay and McRae were not in the least agile, Wirt, the government's best and brightest, could not keep pace.

Wickham made it clear that Wilkinson's letter was crucial. "He is the pivot on which this prosecution turns," he keenly observed. The prosecution had no case without the general, and so the defense had every reason and every right to challenge his credibility—to prove the "falsehood of his testimony." Given his tyrannical conduct in New Orleans, the general was not, Wickham remarked slyly, "so immaculate as the government."[78]

Next, Edmund Randolph took a series of swipes at Wilkinson, whom he described as a desperate man, willing to distort the truth in a frantic attempt to salvage his own reputation. By having Wilkinson's original letter physically in court, Randolph said he would be able to show the general as he really was, and make certain that he would no longer be "worshipped as the political Messiah of America." As for Jefferson, his principal crime lay in shielding such a character.[79]

Finally, Burr entered the fray. He claimed that he had little interest in defaming the government. He denied that he had encouraged his attorneys to do so, either. At this point Martin chimed in, saying that Burr had encouraged restraint, and that any severe comments were his alone. Burr explained that he was requesting General Wilkinson's letter because he was looking for "facts," and that the letter would show no evidence of treason. He clarified, too, that Jefferson's proclamation, based as it was on Wilkinson's October 21 letter, made no mention of treason. The only issue at hand at that time was whether an attack on Spanish territories had been intended. Had there been any suggestion in the president's mind that Burr was part of a treason plot, Jefferson certainly would have said so. And so, Burr concluded, the facts disproved the prosecution's logic.[80]

On June 13, after hearing from both sides, Marshall ruled that Burr had the right to request a subpoena *duces tecum*. The court then issued Burr's subpoena to Jefferson. The president complied, up to a point; he gave Hay permission to hand over Wilkinson's letter and any other documents pertaining to Burr's case, though he reserved the right to withhold any information considered confidential. At the same time, he shifted his anger toward Luther Martin. He thought he could badger Martin into revealing what he knew about Burr's conspiratorial activities, by supplying a communication he had received from a Martin acquaintance in Maryland, which attested to Martin having expressed his support for Burr's plan to sever the West from the union. Thus the president thought he might be able "to commit Luther Martin," along with Burr. He could silence Martin, if not convict him of misprision of treason (knowledge of treasonous activities). This was Jefferson at his most obsessed, believing that anyone who could effectively defend Burr—he was now calling Martin "this unprincipled and imprudent federal bull-dog"—had to be no less than Burr's accomplice. To Jefferson, apparently, the reason that Martin sounded so persuasive was that he knew what Burr was up to all along.[81]

"MAMMOTH OF INIQUITY"

On the same day that Chief Justice Marshall delivered his opinion on Burr's subpoena, several witnesses were sworn, including the flamboyant General Eaton. Burr later wrote Theodosia that when the general came out of the jury room, he was in "such a rage and agitation that he shed tears, and complained bitterly that he had been questioned as if he were a villain." Burr drolly added to his report, "How else could he had been questioned with any propriety?"[82]

But the swearing-in process was delayed when the prosecution's surprise witness, Dr. Erich Bollmann, arrived in court. The German-born Bollmann had been one of two messengers who carried the cipher letter (supposedly written by Burr) to Wilkinson, and had been arrested and sent to trial along with Samuel Swartwout. Some months before the trial, he had approached Jefferson for a private interview, wherein he hoped to convince the president that the newspaper charges had been grossly exaggerated. Burr's only plan, he told Jefferson, was an expedition against Spanish possessions. Jefferson persuaded Bollmann to put his statements into writing, which he did. Later, Bollmann publicly regretted having gone to Jefferson; he explained, in the newspapers, that English was not his native language, and some of his statements might be misleading. He was dismayed that Jefferson had used his statements against Burr after having given his "word of honor" to keep the matter private. Finally, Jefferson directed George Hay to give Bollmann full immunity in return for agreeing to testify against Burr.[83]

Prior to Bollmann's appearance in court on June 13, Hay offered him the presidential pardon. He said nothing. Hay tried once more, dramatically, before the packed courtroom, to dangle, as Burr put it, "a pardon under the great seal and with the sign manual [hand signature] of *Thomas Jefferson*." At this moment, Luther Martin interjected: "It had always been Doctor Bollmann's intention to refuse this pardon," though he had not done so until now because "he wished to have this opportunity of publicly rejecting it." Hay asked again, and again, but his witness consistently refused to change his mind.[84]

Martin contended that a pardon was an admission of guilt, and that was why Bollmann refused it. Here was a man with a heroic reputation, having done "so much to rescue the marquis la Fayette from imprisonment," and who "bears too great a regard for his reputation" to "abandon his honour through a fear of unjust persecution." Martin had turned the courtroom into a morality play, and Bollmann, who had gone to prison after his attempted rescue of Lafayette failed, was exhibiting the same kind of courage in his commitment to Burr. This, according to Martin, was the definition of "manly loyalty."[85]

The battle over dueling reputations reached its crescendo the following Monday. On the fateful day of June 16, the proud General James Wilkinson marched into court. He had arrived in Richmond prior to the weekend, with an entourage consisting of several young officers and ten or so witnesses in tow whom he had rounded up to testify before the grand jury. Wilkinson was known for pomp and circumstance. We can take an educated guess as to his appearance on the basis of an 1804 description, when the portly general was seen riding through Washington in an ornate uniform of his own design. His saddlecloth was of leopard skin, and his stirrups were made of gold. Gold braids, shiny buttons, the insignia of military office, and a large sword swinging from his side topped off his regalia. That was how he strode into the courtroom: in high style and clad in his military finest.[86]

It was the moment the spectators had been waiting for. Wilkinson and Burr had not crossed paths since the former had accused the latter of treason. In the florid prose that befit the pomp of Wilkinson, he described their courtroom dance to Jefferson. "I saluted the Bench & in spite of myself my Eyes darted a flash of indignation at the little Traitor," he gallantly recounted, assuring the president that "this Lyon hearted Eagle Eyed Hero, sinking under the weight of conscious guilt," was no match for him. "With haggard Eye," he noted of Burr, "he made an Effort to meet the indignant salutation of outraged Honor, but it was in vain." Wilkinson believed that Burr's "audacity" had failed him, so that the defendant "averted his face, grew pale & affected passion to conceal his perturbation."[87]

Wilkinson was living in his own world if we can go by the less self-interested (though still subjective) account of Washington Irving, who was close by. Still a relative unknown, the future author of such great American short stories as "Rip Van Winkle" had been sent to Richmond to cover the trial. His report brilliantly captured those qualities that made his fellow New Yorker's reputation as the "incomparable Burr." Irving described how

Wilkinson strutted into court, and halted when he stood parallel to Burr, who just then was seated and conversing with one of his counsel. "Here he stood for a moment swelling like a turkey cock, and bracing himself up for the encounter of Burr's eye," Irving observed. Burr took no notice of him until the judge instructed the clerk to swear in General Wilkinson. Irving gave a detailed account of what happened next:

> *At the mention of the name Burr turned his head, looked him full in the face with one of his piercing regards, swept his eye over his whole person from head to foot, as if to scan its dimensions, and then coolly resumed his former position, and went on conversing with his counsel as tranquilly as ever. The whole look was over in an instant; but it was an admirable one. There was no appearance of study or constraint in it; no affectation of disdain or defiance; a slight expression of contempt played over his countenance, such as you would show on regarding any person to whom you were indifferent, but whom you considered mean and contemptible.*[88]

Burr was second to none in dismissing an adversary with a well-timed glance.

Burr's disciplined audacity was a rare and valuable quality for a political actor. He exhibited that subtle elegance, typified by Beau Brummell, which defined masculine sociability in a modernizing age. Brummell was the most distinctive trendsetter in England, a cultural celebrity, who had come to be part of the inner circle of the Prince of Wales. He was known for his meticulous control of every gesture, and especially for his dismissive gaze—the mark of masculine prowess. Brummell was a younger man, but like Burr he was small and slender. To Irving, a theatergoing aesthete who had traveled to England and the Continent, Burr possessed this distinctly modern style of self-presentation. He was, in that sense, the American version of Beau Brummell. Both men mastered the "effortless effort," a trait that is more readily associated in modern times with such Hollywood legends as Humphrey Bogart and Clint Eastwood. This is a significant statement, because it is the only way we can truly comprehend the intangible in Burr's personality that his admirers found so irresistible and his enemies saw as dangerously seductive.[89]

Wilkinson, of course, represented the opposite personality type: Old

World values of the eighteenth century, which measured worth according to rank, pomp, uniforms, and other surface indices. Burr had a distinct advantage over Wilkinson in the courtroom. He was not just a lawyer—he was in his element. Wilkinson was in a place where he could no longer throw his weight around and behave as a petty tyrant, as he had done in New Orleans. And his protector, Jefferson, was far away. Burr might have been on trial, but Wilkinson was certainly in the spotlight.

Wilkinson was interrogated by the grand jury for four long days. Eventually he was forced to admit that he had altered his copy of the cipher letter. The opening sentence was missing, the gist of which implicated the general as Burr's confidant; Wilkinson had erased several other words and replaced them with innocent-sounding language. Congressman John Randolph, the jury foreman, was predisposed to distrust the general, and sternly insisted that Wilkinson remove his sword upon entering the jury room—a move that symbolically unmanned the proud soldier. Randolph had listened skeptically to Wilkinson's self-aggrandizing account of his actions in New Orleans, so that now, upon learning that Wilkinson had tampered with the evidence, he resolved that this "mammoth of iniquity," as he called him, should be indicted for misprision of treason. A vote was taken on the matter, and of the sixteen jurors, seven pushed for indictment. Thus Wilkinson escaped a share in Burr's fate by 2 votes.[90]

No member of the distinguished jury thought that Wilkinson was innocent. Randolph gave his undisguised opinion: "Wilkinson is the only man I ever saw who was from the bark to the very core a villain." The congressman was certain that Wilkinson was only saved because of his close connection to President Jefferson. And though they were both Virginia Republicans, there was no love lost between Jefferson and Randolph. He had supported the president during the election of 1800, but was now a defiant critic. In addition to wishing for Wilkinson's indictment, he felt as strongly that Jefferson should be rebuked for sheltering this "mammoth of iniquity."[91]

Nearly fifty men were paraded before the grand jury. In addition to Generals Wilkinson and Eaton, the witness list included navy commodores, low-ranking soldiers, such trusted associates of Burr's as Andrew Jackson, Erich Bollman, and Samuel Swartwout, plus several of Harman Blennerhassett's servants. Among these, Swartwout proved to be a particularly compelling witness; several jurors later attested to his candor and innocence, which only added to their distrust of General Wilkinson.[92]

In spite of such performances as Swartwout's, the grand jury did what was expected. On June 24, it issued bills of indictment for treason and misdemeanor against Burr and Harman Blennerhassett. Additional indictments were issued one day later for Jonathan Dayton, Senator John Smith of Ohio, Comfort Tyler (who had been so prominent in recruiting for Burr's enterprise), and two minor members of Burr's expeditionary army. Nevertheless, the grand jury had no intention of endorsing Wilkinson's reign of terror in New Orleans insofar as Bollman, Swartwout, John Adair, Peter Ogden, and James Alexander (all sent east by the general) escaped indictment.[93]

The indictments revealed the prosecution's strategy. So as to convince the jury that any assembly of men was proof of treason, Burr's two alleged crimes were merged. The indictments were founded on the allegation that on December 10, twenty or thirty men stopped at Blennerhassett Island on their way down the Ohio; it was their intent to take temporary possession of New Orleans on their way to Mexico. Never mind that this group was unarmed and neither used nor threatened force. A war of some kind was underway—*by construction of law*—and centered on Blennerhassett Island. Though Burr was not on the island, the indictment claimed that he was. As to this particular, Burr wrote his daughter that "not a man on the jury supposed this to be true." It was a faulty indictment.[94]

Since there was no bail allowed for one accused of treason, Burr spent two nights in the city jail. His attorneys complained to Chief Justice Marshall that the miserable conditions in the jail were endangering his health, and making it difficult for them to consult with their client. By order of the court, Burr was then moved to Luther Martin's residence, where he was confined to the front room. The windows were barred, the door padlocked; seven men guarded the house to prevent him from escaping.[95]

On the last day of June, Burr was moved to the state penitentiary, located on the outskirts of Richmond. He would be joined there by Harman Blennerhassett after the latter was transported from the West and brought to Richmond to stand trial. Meanwhile, Burr had the top floor to himself, and guests of both sexes flocked to see him. Local women showered him with gifts of oranges, lemons, apricots, cream, and butter. No less than

William Wirt's mother-in-law supplied the prisoner with homemade treats. According to Washington Irving, the fair sex was hoping for his acquittal. Republican newspaper editor William Duane of the Philadelphia *Aurora* mockingly referred to the "emperor of the penitentiary." There was some truth in this description. Blennerhassett would write with amazement, "Burr lives in great style, and sees much company in his gratings, where it is as difficult to get an audience as if he really were an Emperor."[96]

As the men and women of Richmond rallied to Burr's cause, Wilkinson accordingly became the laughingstock of the town. Another man who was never known to be shy about expressing his resentments was Andrew Jackson, who proclaimed to any who would listen that James Wilkinson was a scoundrel. The Tennessean was convinced that the trial was nothing but an example of political persecution. The great democrat Jefferson, whom he had previously esteemed, he now considered a dupe, if not corrupted as a result of his alliance with Wilkinson.[97]

Samuel Swartwout echoed Jackson's ridicule of Wilkinson. He insisted that the unprincipled general had stooped so low as to steal his gold watch in New Orleans, when he placed him under arrest. Here in Richmond, Swartwout confronted his erstwhile captor, literally pushing him into the street and challenging him to a duel. Wilkinson refused to settle the dispute through an affair of honor or any other way; in the vocabulary of the duelist, Swartwout branded him a "coward" and "poltroon" in a statement printed in the *Virginia Gazette* and picked up by other newspapers. A caricature of Wilkinson made the rounds in Richmond that summer: he was Falstaff, the bumbling, rotund, and foolish sidekick of King Jefferson.[98]

"WHO IS BLENNERHASSETT?"

On August 3, 1807, before a large crowd that filled the House of Delegates, Aaron Burr's treason trial began. The unbearable summer heat could not keep the curious away from what was becoming the greatest spectacle in the short history of the republic. As he strode into court, Burr was accompanied by his son-in-law, Joseph Alston. This show of family loyalty was important. Alston had embarrassed both Burr and himself when a letter he wrote to the governor of South Carolina, disavowing any knowledge of Burr's treasonous intentions, appeared in the newspapers. Alston had seemed more anxious to save himself than to repudiate Burr's accusers, but he made up for his lapse of judgment by publishing a condemnation of Burr's mistreatment. If there had been any tension between Burr and Alston, it did not last. On Burr's request, Theodosia and her husband hastened to Richmond to lend their support, and they would remain by his side until the end of the trial.[99]

Jury selection did not get underway until the second week. Once again, it was next to impossible to find an impartial juror, let alone twelve. During the first two days, forty-eight men were examined and only four accepted. Hay concluded that only a "solitary hermit" could have not formed an opinion about Burr's guilt or innocence. Burr decided to speed things along by agreeing to take eight men from the second panel of forty-eight, though he recognized the bias among some of them.[100]

This was a risky proposition, of course. Yet Burr had already calculated that his fate really would be in Justice Marshall's hands. The chief justice had the sole authority to determine what evidence was admissible, and to prescribe the standard of proof needed to satisfy the court's definition of treason. The entire trial centered on whether Marshall would endorse—or reject—the idea of "constructive treason."

As the indictment made clear, the prosecution's entire case rested on proving that something akin to war—by *construction of law*—had occurred on Blennerhassett Island on December 10, 1806. From the state's perspective, it did not matter whether Burr was on the island at that time or not. In constructive treason, at least in theory, all are principals, and there are no accessories; that is, guilt is supposedly equally distributed among the participants. Of course, the prosecution only used this legal fiction to get around the fact of Burr's absence from the island on the night in question. According to the state's scenario, Burr was the mastermind, and as such, his intentions could be manifest in the actions of his agents. It was the prosecution's strategy to argue that Burr was the principal *in absentia,* the puppet master pulling the strings of Harman Blennerhassett. Consequently, the eccentric Irishman, who was indisputably present on the island, was now no less important than Burr to the state's case.

The jury having been seated, Hay delivered his opening remarks, summarizing the strategy of the prosecution. In laying the foundation for constructive treason, Hay quoted Marshall's opinion in the Bollmann-

Swartwout case, reminding the chief justice of his own language. Marshall had ruled that "all those who perform any part, however minute, or however removed from the scene of the action" are "to be considered traitors." In other words, all were principals. Burr could be hundreds of miles away, and still be guilty. Then Hay argued that an overt act of treason need not necessarily look like war. *It did not require the use of force, armed men, or any evidence that military hostilities had occurred.* All that mattered was that an assembly of men with a "treasonable design" had gathered on Blennerhassett Island.[101]

What Hay meant to prove was that a "treasonable design" had originated with Burr. For two years, Burr had traveled the country, criticizing the government and stimulating discontent, as he pushed forward his grand scheme, in Hay's words, "of establishing an empire in the west." As the plot thickened and the conspiracy took shape, it was Blennerhassett who became the linchpin of Burr's grand design. Hay next reminded the jury that Blennerhassett was the author of several articles that called for separation of the West from the union. More important, on that December night, the Irishman had led an assembly of men from his island to a rendezvous with Burr at the mouth of the Cumberland River, and together they headed to New Orleans. At this crucial juncture, Hay contended, the treasonous assembly was "under the command of Burr *and* Blennerhassett" (italics added). As his proxy on the island, and as his co-commander along the Ohio and Mississippi Rivers, Blennerhassett was Burr's right-hand man—and a vehicle for Burr's treasonous intentions and designs.[102]

Hay also used this opportunity to portray Burr as a man without a country. He lacked a sense of patriotism, and represented no constituency; he had no loyalty to anyone but himself. In the East, before his second trip to the West, Burr was alleged to have told potential recruits that westerners would "meanly and tamely acquiesce" to a new government. Perhaps even a monarchy. West of the Alleghenies, Burr told a different story, urging his hearers to free themselves from the oppressive easterners. He was suggesting that the Atlantic states merely thought of the West as a source of tax dollars, which amounted to little more than "a state of colonial dependence."[103]

Here Hay revived Cheetham's imagery, in effect labeling Burr a "proteus," as Cheetham had, that is, a man who shaped his conversation as a tool of seduction. In the initial examination, he had already described Burr as a man who turned to conspiracy in retaliation for Jefferson having withdrawn his confidence in his vice president. He was, in this way, like a spurned lover, a vindictive woman. Republican theory from the time of Niccolò Machiavelli had conceived of reckless ambition as the goddess Fortuna, a feminine power that was subversive, mysterious, capricious, and devoid of conscience. Burr, so his enemies claimed, possessed all of these traits in abundance, which the prosecution never grew tired of repeating.[104]

After his opening remarks, Hay called his first witness, General William Eaton. Immediately, Burr rose and objected, claiming the prosecution had first to prove an overt act of treason, and Burr figured that Eaton knew nothing about the events on Blennerhassett Island. The challenge sparked debate that continued until the end of the day. Wirt said that the prosecution had every right to present its evidence in a chronological fashion, developing the conspiracy "from its birth to its consummation." Luther Martin dismissed Wirt's logic by arguing that it made no more sense than proving a motive for murder before a corpse had been found.[105]

Marshall gave his opinion the following morning, ruling that he would only exclude evidence that "does not appear relevant." He permitted the prosecution to carry on, but made it clear that Eaton's testimony, or that of any other witness, must relate to the overt act of treason. He was giving the prosecution a warning: proving intention alone was insufficient. The testimony must have some connection to the crime charged, as stated in the indictment.[106]

Eaton returned to the stand. He retold his story one more time. Owing to Marshall's ruling, his inflammatory account of Burr's threat to assassinate Jefferson was dropped. On cross-examination, Burr forced him to admit that the government had finally paid him the $10,000 claim he had demanded for his North African filibuster. A payoff? Maybe. This was, in any case, the impression the defense wished to leave in the minds of the jurors.[107]

The flamboyant general had become even more of an outcast than Wilkinson. Blennerhassett recorded in his journal: "the once redoubted Eaton had dwindled down in the eyes of this sarcastic town, into a ridiculous mountebank." Eaton was regularly seen "strutting about the streets, under a tremendous hat, with a Turkish sash over colored clothes," and his drinking bouts were by now legendary. Amazingly, he openly copulated with a prostitute at a local tavern before leaving town. He was dressed as a Turkish prince and she had donned a harem costume. The "Hero of Derne" had become a lewd and pathetic wretch in Richmond.[108]

The next prosecution witness was retired Commodore Thomas Truxton, who had long been a close friend of both Burr and Wilkinson. He earned national fame during the Quasi-War (1798–99), defeating two heavily armed French warships. The commodore was not a man to be trifled with. He was shocked by the news that he had been implicated in Burr's conspiracy, and that his name had been mentioned in the infamous cipher letter. Anxious to reclaim his honor, he dispatched a letter to Jefferson, followed by an unsolicited note to Burr's grand jury, denying any role in the affair. He begged Burr to clear his name. Eventually, after Burr convinced him that he was not the author of the cipher letter, Truxton turned his wrath on Wilkinson, who he believed had framed Burr. He blasted the general as a "base hypocrite," accusing him of double-dealing and of dragging his name through the mud. In Richmond, before a large crowd, the commodore came upon General Wilkinson and turned from him in disgust. He may not have pushed him, as Swartwout had done, but his snub was just as damning.[109]

Truxton did little to help the prosecution. In fact, his testimony actually benefited the defendant. As he recounted his conversations with Burr, he asserted that he had never heard him say anything remotely treasonous. To the contrary, his discussions confirmed Burr's account: in the event of a war with Spain, he intended to lead a filibuster into Mexico. Truxton was equally knowledgeable about Burr's contingency plan, which Hay had dismissed as a mere cover story: if war did not materialize, then Burr had every intention of settling on the Bastrop property. Truxton again confirmed Burr's version.[110]

This seasoned naval commander was unflappable on the stand. Pressed by the prosecution concerning Burr's "promise" to make him an admiral, he stated several times that he could not remember whether Burr "wished to see or make me an admiral." On cross-examination, when Burr asked if they had been intimate, and whether he had ever heard him utter a disunionist sentiment, Truxton replied: "There seemed no reserve on your part. I never heard you speak of a division of the union." Truxton also apprised the court that Burr had told him that the president was not privy to his plans. Thus, Burr came off as a candid man who was neither mysterious nor capricious, and this undermined the prosecution's portrayal of the defendant as a deceptive schemer.[111]

Peter Taylor was the next prosecution witness to take the stand. He was a poorly educated Englishman, who had been hired as the Blennerhassetts' gardener. His testimony was intended to demonstrate the conspiratorial connection between Burr and Blennerhassett. On the stand, he asserted that Mrs. Margaret Blennerhassett had sent him down the Ohio River to warn her husband that the Wood County (Virginia) militia was threatening to raid their island, and that he might be in danger if he tried to return home. Taylor searched for his employer in Chillicothe and Cincinnati, before meeting up with Blennerhassett and Burr in Lexington, Kentucky. It was the one and only time that Taylor encountered Burr in person. Sometime later, Blennerhassett convinced his gardener to join in the expedition to settle the Bastrop property, in Louisiana. According to Taylor, when he asked Blennerhassett what seeds to bring along, the reply was "None." When pressed, his master confessed that their real project was to take Mexico and to establish a new empire. Taylor recreated Blennerhassett's remarks for the court: "Peter," the Irishman was meant to have said, "Colonel Burr would be the king of Mexico, and Mrs. Alston, daughter of Colonel Burr, was to be the queen, whenever Colonel Burr died."[112]

Taylor further claimed that Burr's young recruits had been lured into the expedition with false promises of settling the Bastrop property. Whether they wanted to or not, they were all expected to participate in the Mexican invasion. If someone refused, Blennerhassett would "stab" any man who defied orders. As unlikely as this scenario sounds, Blennerhassett was meant to have revealed to Taylor that the conspirators' ultimate design was to provoke the western states to leave the union. Finally, Taylor testified that Blennerhassett had sent him to buy guns, ordering him to burn the letter he carried on this errand, because he recognized that it contained "high treason."[113]

Obviously, Taylor's testimony was brimming with accusations of treason, though most of these were directed against Blennerhassett. He was portrayed as Burr's co-conspirator and a ruthless commander. It was Taylor's testimony that had led to his employer's indictment, for the gardener had already told the same inflammatory story to the grand jury. Margaret Blennerhassett, when she learned of Taylor's betrayal, wrote to her husband in disgust that he was "confined in a prison in the dogdays, and by the perjury of a wretch not many degrees from a brute!" Theodosia later joked about Taylor's absurd testimony by referring to the Mexican people as her "subjects."[114]

The prosecution seemed perfectly comfortable putting the entire Blennerhassett household on trial. Taylor was just the first of three hired servants put on the stand, and a subpoena was even issued for Margaret to appear as a witness for the prosecution. To the prosecution, the Blennerhassetts were the perfect marks in the conspiracy Burr had hatched. One potential juror from Wood County, Thomas Creel, claimed that "Burr had seduced Blennerhassett" and had used "the medium" of his wife to do so. Creel's comment extended the public's fascination with this family, which grew into a full-blown fabricated romance. As one version of the story was told, Burr was bedding Margaret while her unsuspecting, nearsighted husband played his flute in the study.[115]

The Blennerhassetts were perfect targets for another reason: class anger. On their grand estate on the Ohio River, they lived like British royalty. Harman was known as snobbish, and his wife attracted considerable attention for her horseback riding—another sign of aristocratic breeding. She rode a white horse, dressed in a bright scarlet habit adorned with gold buttons, and topped off by a white beaver hat with ostrich feathers. The couple owned at least a dozen slaves, in addition to hiring a sizable number of white servants. It is not surprising that their more humble frontier neighbors would resent them. When the Wood County militia ransacked the Blennerhassett estate, these were drunken soldiers toppling a symbol of class privilege. And thus, the civil war that the prosecution claimed was brewing on Blennerhassett Island was in fact something other: a minor skirmish in a simmering class war on the early American frontier.[116]

Colonel George Morgan and his two sons, militia general John Morgan and the younger brother Thomas, were the next prosecution witnesses. According to the Morgans, Burr had said many things that sounded treasonous when he visited the colonel's estate, Morganza, outside Pittsburgh, in the summer of 1806. At dinner, Burr predicted that the western states would soon leave the union, and he disparaged the "weakness and imbecility of the federal government." In fact, Burr had gone so far as to claim that the administration was so weak that with two hundred men, "he could drive the president and congress into the Potowmac." The Morgans were called to testify for one reason: their story confirmed Eaton's. Burr appeared to be plotting disunion, boasting that he could overthrow the government—just as Eaton had claimed—by turning "Congress neck and heels out of doors."[117]

As in the case of Eaton, this was not the first time Colonel Morgan presented himself as one who had saved his country from a conspiracy. In 1788, he had warned of a plot by the lieutenant governor of Canada to engineer a rebellion in the western states. That was then. Now in his mid-sixties, Morgan had less credibility. In the fall of 1806, when Pennsylvania chief justice William Tilgham, General Presley Neville, and Judge Samuel Roberts visited him and listened to his account of his meeting with Burr, it was obvious to the visitors that Colonel Morgan's mind exhibited signs of "delirium." Tilgham apprised Governor McKean of Pennsylvania of his interview with Morgan. The governor did not take Morgan's statements seriously, and therefore felt no need to warn President Jefferson that Burr might be up to something.[118]

It was just as clear that the Morgans had been coached, or had otherwise reshaped their testimony to accord with Eaton's well-publicized deposition. For example, when Justice Tilgham interviewed Morgan, there was no mention of Burr's having uttered the offensive remark (which sounded most like Eaton) that with two hundred men, he could drive the president and Congress into the Potomac. It also seems likely that the two sons were protecting their father by echoing his testimony. During cross-examination, Burr brought up Colonel Morgan's state of mind and forced one of his sons to admit that the colonel was "old and infirm," though he would not acknowledge "delirium." Burr insisted (in a private letter) that the Morgans were lying and the conversations had never taken place, but he refrained from accusing the Morgans of lying in the courtroom. It was enough to cast doubt.[119]

Six additional witnesses followed. They included servants, the Blennerhassetts' neighbors, and others who were on or near the island on December 10. It was another of the Blennerhassetts' unfaithful servants, Jacob Allbright, who proved most valuable to the prosecution. He claimed to have actually observed something that resembled the use of force on the island. On the night in question, he said, General Tupper of the Ohio militia arrived on the island and tried to arrest Blennerhassett. When he put his hand on the Irishman, seven or eight of the men raised their muskets to stop him. Tupper was then forced to leave at gunpoint.[120]

Burr and his defense team aggressively challenged Allbright's testimony, asking the witness to identify Tupper in the courtroom. Tupper's deposition had directly refuted everything Allbright had said, and the prosecution, of course, did not call Tupper to the stand for this reason. Blennerhassett's groom, William Love, disputed Allbright's testimony, swearing that Tupper's visit was perfectly friendly and without incident. Altogether, this round of testimony proved contradictory and confusing: some witnesses reported seeing rifles, the making of bullets, sentinels posted, and a military watchword in use, while others saw no signs of military array or activity whatsoever. And as the defense reminded the jury, not a single witness saw Burr on the island.[121]

One Dudley Woodbridge, a prosecution witness, inadvertently provided comic relief. He was Blennerhassett's business partner, whom Burr had hired to requisition provisions and boats. Cross-examining Woodbridge, Burr asked whether it was not "ridiculous" for Harman to be engaged in a military enterprise, when the nearsighted man could not distinguish a human from a horse at ten paces. And when Wirt had his turn, and asked Woodbridge whether Blennerhassett was a man of "vigorous talents," the witness could not help but say that "he had every sense but common sense." This was not the ideal candidate to share command of an incipient revolution.[122]

Burr had had enough, and he rose to object to any further "collateral" testimony. The defense then moved to halt testimony. Wickham addressed the court, offering what many observers at the time considered to be "the greatest forensic effort of the American bar." Over the course of this day and the next, he dissected the flawed logic of the prosecution. Its first mistake was trying to convict Burr of treason when he was not present on Blennerhassett Island. Hay and his team were attempting to prove that Burr was a "traitor by relation," his guilt derived from the acts of Blennerhassett and others. Trying to convict Burr by such "artificial rules of construction" was, for Wickham, a misrepresentation of the laws concerning treason.[123]

Wickham's major thrust was to disprove the premise that all were principals in treason. He meticulously reviewed pertinent British cases, pointing out that the few precedents that existed were pre-Enlightenment episodes. Jefferson's prosecution team was inadvertently replicating a few infamous cases of despotism under a monarchy. For instance, as David Hume recorded in his *History of England,* Lady Lisle had been convicted of treason (as an accessory) for having harbored a man who was subsequently charged with treason. As she was the widow of another traitor, the judge identified her as a "traitor by relation." This was a case of judicial retribution and nothing more. In Burr's trial, a similar mismanagement was underway. The precedent that the state was endorsing was in fact a notorious example of political persecution.[124]

Here Wickham upped the ante. He raised a series of old English laws that equated treason with seduction. It was traditionally understood that sleeping with a female relative of the king constituted treason. Suppose, Wickham said, a female had acted as accomplice to a male traitor by participating in the treasonous act of defiling a royal personage. Not only was the female accomplice not present, but she also lacked the physical attributes to engage in the commission of the crime. To assume that all are equal participants in the crime was thus an outrageous proposition, and so "constructive treason" in effect approved what was illogical and unimaginable: a woman copulating with another woman. Wickham compared the "physical impossibility" of a woman becoming a man to the prosecution's contention that Burr was in two places at once. He was either on the island, or not—and everyone knew he was not there. To be absent from the island was to be innocent of the charge in the indictment.[125]

Furthermore, Burr could not be convicted as an accessory until Blennerhassett—the principal—was first convicted. The prosecution would have to prove an overt act of treason by Harman Blennerhassett. As Wickham made clear, insofar as twelve witnesses had failed to put Burr on the island, or to prove his participation in an overt act of war, then Justice Marshall was under an obligation to step in, clarify the constitutional definition of treason, and preserve the integrity of the court by instructing the jury that the indictment against Burr was fatally flawed.[126]

The prosecution now had only one recourse left. It had to diminish the importance of Blennerhassett Island as a staging area for war, while retaining it as the site of Burr's seduction of the island's owner. Though both McRae and Hay tried to answer Wickham, only Wirt was able to steal the stage. A portion of his speech, in fact, was remembered long after the trial as "Who is Blennerhassett?" It was reprinted in newspapers in 1807, and recited by schoolchildren into the twentieth century. The speech was remembered less for Wirt's legal erudition than for his literary eloquence. He began by arguing that Blennerhassett Island was a mere "atom" in the sprawling conspiratorial scheme led by Burr, which extended from New York to New Orleans. It was ridiculous, he said, to think that Blennerhassett was the principal, and Burr merely an accessory. Burr was demonstrably behind the plot, "a soldier bold, ardent, restless and aspiring, the great actor whose brain conceived and whose hand brought the plan into operation." It was inconceivable that Burr would consent to being the "cat's paw" of any man, let alone Blennerhassett.[127]

"Who is Blennerhassett?" Wirt asked. He was a man of letters, seeking solitude on his beautiful island, which he had transformed into a romantic oasis. He lived surrounded by books, music, and a lovely wife "to crown the enchantment of the scene." Into this place the "destroyer" comes, changing "paradise into hell." Burr had invaded. Burr had transgressed. Burr was the principal, the stranger who found a way into the Irish dilettante's heart, "by the dignity and elegance of his demeanor, the light and beauty of his conversation, and the seductive and fascinating power of his address." The island was Eden, the symbol of Adamic and masculine innocence, and Burr, of course, was the seducer, the serpent.[128]

Wirt had brought together all the old images of Burr. Here was Cataline, luring young and potent men, and causing them to love the person of Aaron Burr. Wirt calls them men of "youthful ardor." The New York Burrites had been "young boys," and those young men who were drawn into Burr's western conspiracy were again being painted as sexual pawns. Since the Hamilton duel, Burr had been repeatedly accused of tearing apart the family hearth. All Wirt was doing different was constructing Burr as a dandified Satan. He had bewitched the Irishman. And thus, his crime was not so much an act of war as an act of seduction. His revolution was as erotically charged as it was corrupt.[129]

Benjamin Botts, the youngest member of the defense team, spoke next. Instead of relying on "sleeping Venus" and "voluptuous nakedness," as he sarcastically described Wirt's alluring prose, he had at his disposal only the dry doctrines of the law. The courtroom burst into laughter. Hay tried to offer rebuttal, but at this point the trial was all but over.[130]

Luther Martin spoke for over fourteen hours to close for the defense. He directed his attack against the prosecution's weak attempt to divert attention from the constitutional definition of treason. He would not permit Hay and his colleagues to pretend that the error in the indictment was not a glaring one. Martin deftly referred to the prosecution's strategy as the "*Will o' wisp* treason." And he added, "though it is said to be here and there and everywhere, *yet it is nowhere.*" The term "will-o'-the-wisp" derived from European folklore; also called "fool's fire," it referred to ghostly lights that hovered over bogs, only to disappear when approached, and was used metaphorically to convey a thing that was confounding or even maliciously invented. Martin accused the prosecution of chasing an illusion, imagining a sinister plot that never existed.[131]

On August 31, after eight days of argument, the chief justice rendered his decision. He dismissed the indictment as flawed, asserting that the prosecution had failed to prove an overt act of war. There would be no more witnesses, only the jury's verdict, declared the next day. "We of the jury say that Aaron Burr is not proved to be guilty under the indictment by any evidence submitted to us. We, therefore, find him not guilty." Burr wanted an unambiguous statement, and objected to the unusual language. There remained one obstinate juror who refused to accommodate him. Marshall indicated that the verdict would be reported as "not guilty."[132]

Wirt blamed the chief justice for the outcome of the trial, writing to his friend, Jefferson's nephew Dabney Carr: "Marshall has stepped between Burr and death." But even a strident Jeffersonian like Thomas Ritchie, editor of the *Richmond Enquirer,* admitted that Burr was "virtually acquitted on the indictment." Eight days after having been found not guilty, Burr faced a new trial. This time, however, he was being charged with a misdemeanor for having attempted a filibuster. Fifty witnesses were examined, and less than a week later, the jury delivered a verdict of not guilty. At this point, the same prosecution team that had managed the Richmond trial now sought to commit Burr on charges of treason and misdemeanor in Ohio or Kentucky. In the course of a new round of testimony, Wilkinson was recalled, and under cross-examination—and let us use Burr's own words here—"acknowledged, very modestly, that he made certain alterations" in the cipher letter.[133]

During this period, Burr remained out on bail in Richmond. On October 20, Marshall ruled there was not enough evidence to try Burr for treason again, but that Burr and Blennerhassett could be committed for trial in Ohio on the misdemeanor charge. But by this time, even George Hay was tired of the proceedings and admitted that he was fed up with Wilkinson. He wrote to Jefferson that his confidence in the general was "shaken, if not destroyed." He expressed regret that the administration had put so much faith in a faithless man. "I am sorry," Hay told the president, "because you have expressed opinions in his favor; but you did not know then what you soon will know." Jefferson would be obliged, on some level, to accept his error of judgment. At last, after almost seven months of heated deliberation and courtroom drama, the trials of Aaron Burr ended.[134]

"I NEVER BELIEVED HIM TO BE A FOOL"

In the end, the entire rationale for charging Burr with treason in the so-called "Burr Conspiracy" rested on Wilkinson's word and the infamous cipher letter. Yet this crucial piece of evidence was altered. Burr insisted he never wrote the letter. And he didn't, in fact. Jonathan Dayton did. Recall that the cipher letter implicated Burr in a conspiracy that Wilkinson said involved an attack on New Orleans. The closest Wilkinson ever came to admitting that Burr did not write the cipher letter was in a letter to Charles Biddle, which he sent during the grand jury proceedings. In Biddle's words, the general confided in him that "the letter from Dayton was more explicit, more corruptious & treasonable than Burr's." (Dayton had written a cover letter to accompany the cipher letter, both of which were delivered at the same time to Wilkinson by courier Samuel Swartwout.) Wilkinson was accusing Dayton of putting treasonous ideas on paper, and Wilkinson could not have mistaken Dayton's handwriting or writing style for that of Burr. But it was not in the general's interest to point the finger at Dayton. He needed evidence against Burr, so he purposely manufactured it.[135]

Throughout the trial and in its aftermath, Jefferson stood by Wilkinson. It is, perhaps, more accurate to say that Jefferson stood by his decision to prosecute Burr, and to do so meant that he had to defend the general. In

1812, as a private citizen, he wrote a revealing letter to James Monroe, in which he rationalized that he had never really trusted Wilkinson except in this one instance, when Wilkinson accused Burr of treason![136]

Jefferson's real feelings about Burr are hard to pin down. In 1807, he called him many things. He compared him to Don Quixote, a wild-eyed dreamer; elsewhere, he dismissed him as a "crooked gun." To Colonel George Morgan, he projected that if Burr's treason trial went as he thought it would, "there can be no doubt where his history will end." There is only one way to read this statement: Burr would soon be hanging from the gallows. To another correspondent, he portrayed Burr's life as a morality tale that fixed the "value of honesty"; here he wrote melodramatically: "With that, what might he not have been!" To New Yorker Robert Livingston, he had no more to say about his former vice president than this petty aside: "Burr has indeed made a most inglorious exhibition of his much over-rated talents."[137]

A crucial question remains. Why did Jefferson never confront Burr in person? During the winter of 1805–06, Jefferson received warnings from Kentucky district attorney Joseph Hamilton Daviess, caught wind of other anonymous accusations, and is supposed to have had a private conference with General William Eaton, in which the "Hero of Derne" exposed Burr's treachery. Yet during this same period, Jefferson dined with Burr at the President's House on at least two occasions. They met for a private conference in March 1806. Why did Jefferson not intimate to Burr that some were accusing him of treason? Why did he not offer Burr an opportunity to explain himself and elaborate on his future plans? Of course, we must also ask: Why did Burr not let Jefferson know that he was considering a filibuster? The point is, a few frank words over a glass of wine might well have changed the course of history, and averted the outstanding farce that was Burr's treason trial.[138]

Burr's fatal flaw was twofold. He trusted Wilkinson, and did not adequately understand Jefferson. Knowing that rumors tended to circulate, he should have figured that the president would eventually form suspicions concerning his activities in the West. What made him think that an unauthorized filibuster would be welcomed by the administration? At the very least, his boldness was a usurpation of Jefferson's executive authority in the conduct of state diplomacy. No matter what their intimate dinners consisted of, Jefferson had unmistakably shown that he wanted to neutralize Burr's power within the Republican Party, if not exile him from it. How could Burr so thoroughly misinterpret Jefferson's thin-skinned political character, in ignoring the fact that the president could not tolerate Burr's transformation into a national hero—which is what would have occurred if he had successfully led a filibuster into Mexico.

We can glean from the always quotable ex-President John Adams how Burr's activities, as reported in the newspapers, were received by much of the general public. Adams observed that Burr had to be "an idiot or a lunatic." He knew something more of Burr than the average American, to be sure, and in writing to a fellow signer of the Declaration of Independence, Benjamin Rush, he unflinchingly stated: "I never believed him to be a fool." In this, Adams was only partially right. Burr never planned the grand conspiracy that attached to him, and neither did he seriously contemplate the assassination of the president or his own installation as emperor of Mexico. But it seems undeniable that he was foolish in his dealings with Jefferson. He stubbornly refused to see that his filibuster could not succeed without Jefferson's acquiescence. And Jefferson never gave him anything close to a nod signifying his support.[139]

A whimsical-looking Aaron Burr in 1826 by Henry Inman

Chapter Ten

THAT STRANGER WAS AARON BURR

It happened that some gentlemen who belonged to the bar, had commenced a controversy on some point in law, very near an old gentleman. He occasionally regarded them with a look, as if to penetrate the recesses of their soul; and then resumed his posture. At length, a young smart, with a significant glance accosted him: "Old gentleman, what is your opinion?" The man of silence and mystery spoke—and lo! What was our astonishment! His countenance . . . brightened with intelligence; the loftiest eloquence flowed from his tongue . . . the halo of genius shone around him. . . . All eyes were fixed on the extraordinary stranger—all desire to know his name. Inquiry was made—reader! That stranger was *Aaron Burr.*

   —*New-York Mirror,* and *Ladies' Literary Gazette,* 1825

While Burr was technically free after his trials in Richmond ended, he was soon hounded by his numerous creditors. Former friends and supporters pressed for repayment of loans, or bills they had honored, wasting little time in bringing $36,000 in civil suits against him. But Burr seemed undeterred, determined as ever to reinstate his plans for a filibuster; he made arrangements to travel to England for just this purpose.

This may seem strange given all he had been through, but Burr must have felt that he could justify himself if he could still succeed with his scheme.[1]

After Justice Marshall's final ruling on October 20, Burr left Richmond for good and headed to Philadelphia. He stopped in Baltimore along the way, only to find that news of his presence had sparked the fury of local Republicans. A handbill, filled with incendiary satire, announced that four "choice spirits" would be given a mock execution on November 3. First on the list was Chief Justice Marshall for his "capers in open court," followed by Aaron Burr, "His Quid Majesty, charged with the trifling fault of wishing to divide the union." Harman Blennerhassett, who was also in Baltimore at the time, was targeted for "conspiring to destroy the tone of the public fiddle." And finally, "*Lawyer* Brandy-Bottle," Luther Martin, for his scandalous prediction that Burr would divide the union in less than six months.[2]

There was genuine danger. Baltimore's mayor provided Burr and his traveling companion Samuel Swartwout with an armed escort to the public stagecoach. The two men were hurried out of town. Two troops of horse and police assembled to make sure the mob did not get out of hand. Blennerhassett, curious to see what would happen, stayed behind to watch the commotion from a window in Luther Martin's home. Around 1,500 people gathered outside, shouting and cheering, as effigies of Marshall, Burr, Blennerhassett, and Martin were hung (and later burnt) to the delight of the crowd. Before Martin went up in flames, one of the bystanders suggested one last draught of brandy for the condemned man, to ease his fear of death. It was done, as the crowd cheered.[3]

In Philadelphia, Burr may have gone into hiding, mainly from his creditors. His caution was prudent; his movements were watched closely. Certain newspapers published rumors that he had already initiated a "renovated enterprise under the auspices of a foreign government." Meanwhile, his relationship with Blennerhassett soured. By the end of November, Blennerhassett informed his wife, "I have broken with Aaron Burr on a writ," joining the long list of creditors suing the former vice president.[4]

Blennerhassett's anger did not let up. Four years later, he tried to blackmail Joseph Alston, threatening to write a tell-all book if the South Carolinian refused to cover Burr's obligations. Taking his family to Mississippi Territory, he faced more financial mishaps when his new cotton plantation failed in 1814. He moved to Canada, then to England, only to die in obscurity in 1831. But the Irishman was not the tragic pawn, as Wirt had portrayed him in the Richmond courtroom. Like many others of his generation who had acquired and lost fortunes, he was a romantic, a dreamer, and a frontier entrepreneur. These were the traits that had drawn him to Burr's expedition in the first place. Yet the two adventurers never saw each other again once they parted ways in 1807.[5]

To handle his civil suits, Burr retained the young lawyer Nicholas Biddle. He was the son of his old friend Charles Biddle, and a graduate of Princeton, who had just returned from France, where he was serving as the private secretary to John Armstrong, the U.S. minister. At twenty-one, Biddle was just beginning his distinguished career as a man of letters (he would shortly begin editing the Lewis and Clark journals) and would go on to establish himself as leader of the financial community. In fact, as president of the Bank of United States from 1823 to 1836, Nicholas Biddle would be the second most powerful man in the country after the president. Despite the scandalous repercussions of the conspiracy and treason trial, Charles Biddle and his family had never distanced themselves from Burr. Burr was considered part of their family, having done everything in his power (when he had power) to promote the careers of Biddle's sons. It was Biddle's enduring network of personal friendships that now kept Burr out of debtor's prison.[6]

Burr continued to plan his trip to England. His first order of business was to reestablish contact with Charles Williamson, his Scottish agent. In November, he supplied David Meade Randolph, a Federalist he had befriended in Richmond, with a letter of introduction to Williamson. At the same time, he made arrangements for Samuel Swartwout to head to Great Britain before him, and act as his confidential agent. (Though there is no evidence that Williamson and Burr corresponded during Burr's second trip out west, it seems apparent that Williamson kept abreast of Burr's activities.) In April 1807, when Williamson learned of Burr's arrest and trial, he concluded that the filibuster failed because Burr had abandoned his original plans to satisfy an Anglo-American effort to open up Mexico to commerce they could jointly control. Williamson must have believed that Burr had opted instead to work counter to London's interests.[7]

But before long, he learned that Wilkinson had deceived Burr and that Wilkinson had been bribed by the Spanish. Thus Burr did not have to be perceived as an enemy of Great Britain. Actually, Williamson did not know where Burr stood, but in writing to the Lord Justice Clerk, another enthusiastic supporter of filibusters, he assured that Burr would "extricate himself from the present embarrassment." Given Burr's "pride and ambition," he felt certain that the former vice president would rise above his difficulties.[8]

So, in spite of the unfavorable reports he had heard, Williamson remained eager to assist Burr in reviving his filibuster. Williamson was there to greet Swartwout when the young associate appeared on his London doorstep in February 1808. Swartwout convinced him that Burr still commanded a following back in America, and that conditions were ripe for action. Both Swartwout and David Randolph told Williamson that many Americans feared a French invasion of Florida and New Orleans. Williamson used this intelligence to press his own plans for an Anglo-American expedition into the Spanish colonies, insisting that England must strike first, before the French swallowed up New Spain. This is how Williamson smoothed the way for Burr's approach to the British Ministry, well before his friend set foot in England.[9]

In January 1808, Burr faced his last legal entanglement arising from his western expedition when he and Blennerhassett were indicted in the United States District Court at Chillicothe, Ohio. Marshall had left open the possibility that the two men could be tried again in Ohio for the misdemeanor crime of planning an invasion of the Spanish colonies. Though the indictment did not hold up, and charges were never pressed, President Jefferson still held out hope. Writing to Senator Edward Tiffin of Ohio, he imagined Burr bent on revenge, selling his talents to any country at war with the United States. The president predicted: "If we have war with Spain, he will become a Spanish General. If with England, he will go to Canada and be employed there. Internal convulsion may be attempted if no game more hopeful offers." Amid mounting criticism of General Wilkinson—a court-martial was now underway—the president felt more than ever compelled to justify his pursuit of Burr.[10]

In April, Burr traveled to New York City. He took the precaution of using an assumed name, a practice he would continue even after his arrival in England. Theodosia came to New York to see her father once more before his voyage. He requested that she assist him with a ruse meant to misdirect any who might be watching him. Her job was to place a notice in the papers that her father had been spotted on his way overland to Canada. Then, on June 9, using the name "H. G. Edwards," Burr boarded the *Clarissa Ann,* a packet headed to Nova Scotia, and thence to England. At least one of the thirty-six passengers knew him: Alexander Charles Williamson, the son of his Scottish agent. Their voyage together could hardly have been a coincidence.[11]

The ship made a brief stop in Halifax, where Burr collected letters of introduction from Sir George Prevost. Sir George was the youngest son of General Augustine Prevost, with whom Burr had developed a close relationship in the 1780s. As a relative of his late wife, Prevost was more than willing to open doors for Burr in England. He gave Burr a letter to be presented to local British officials, to permit "H. G. Edwards" to proceed without delay to London.[12]

The *Clarissa Ann* docked at Falmouth on July 13, and three days later Burr was in London. Secretary of State Madison was soon apprised of his arrival, when the American minister informed him that the object of Burr's visit (as far as he had heard) was to gain British support for a renewed assault on Spanish America. Madison may not have even have told President Jefferson of this report, knowing of the president's exaggerated concern that Burr might lead a foreign army into a war with the United States.[13]

"WE WILL REFORM"

Burr desperately needed as many influential friends as he could win over, who could pull strings to protect him, and help him get around the restrictions he faced as an alien. Charles Williamson, his chief advocate, was not in England at this time. He had been sent to Jamaica on a diplomatic mission. "Your absence is extremely distressing and embarrassing," Burr wrote to his friend in July, admitting that "it is a contingency against which I had made no provision." He befriended John Reeves of the British Alien Office, the department concerned with supervising foreign residents. When Burr made his formal declaration to Reeves, as all aliens were required to do, he made the point of dropping the names of some powerful men. "I am known personally to Lord Mulgrave and Mr. Canning, to whom the motives of my visit have been declared. Those reasons have long been known to Lord

Melville." Mulgrave was the first lord of the admiralty, Canning the foreign secretary; Burr had met both men during his first week in London.[14]

The political landscape had dramatically changed in England over the past few months. In March, Napoleon had invaded Spain, forcing Charles IV of Spain and his son to abdicate. By June, the French emperor had extended his nation's hold over Spain as his brother, Joseph Bonaparte, assumed the throne. Burr admitted to Williamson that the "new state of things defeats, for the present, the speculations we had proposed, yet it opens new views." By this he probably meant that the British saw Spain as a French puppet, and so London might support independence movements in Spain's American colonies. Indeed, Williamson was in Jamaica in order to encourage the British governor that he should open channels of communication with the Cuban government, convincing it to resist Napoleon at all costs. And Williamson imagined that Burr would have a role to play in unfolding events. He suggested that the New Yorker might advise the British cabinet of "what means would most certainly prevent the French in the present crisis from having command of the Floridas and Mexico." Flattering his friend, Williamson told Burr, "No man can give so valuable information as yourself."[15]

But the moment soon passed. In July, the British government issued a proclamation of peace with the Spanish insurgency because it saw the emergence of Spanish Juntas organizing against Napoleonic rule. As the chief ally of the Spanish Juntas, London was obliged to reverse its course, and resisted the temptation to back any existing scheme to liberate Latin America.[16]

If Burr had little success impressing British officials, he did not give up hope. He collected his maps, continued to make his social rounds, and eventually nestled under the wing of his most important new friend, Jeremy Bentham. By August, he was lodging at Bentham's London residence, known as "the Bird Cage," and making regular trips to his country estate. Bentham was one of the most innovative English philosophers of his day, and a political radical. Rather than practice law, he became its foremost critic, rejecting abstract understandings in favor of tested principles. He was, like Burr, a rationalist.[17]

Burr was already well versed in Bentham's writings when, in 1803, he read Pierre-Etienne-Louis Dumont's French translation, *Traités de législa-*

tion civilé et pénale. Dumont was Swiss and a friend of Albert Gallatin's, which may explain how Burr learned of Bentham in the first place. And Bentham, in fact, knew of Burr's interest in his work long before they met. An English bookseller had informed him. Burr was Bentham's first American champion. The English philosopher returned the compliment, adjudging that Burr was "better qualified to pursue my ideas, as well as better disposed for it than any man I have yet met with, or ever expect to meet with."[18]

To say that Burr was enthralled with Bentham is not an exaggeration. He sent Theodosia a bust of the reformer, and convinced her to make a project of translating into French some of his unpublished work. Once, when Bentham left Burr alone in the Bird Cage for a period of weeks, Burr went so far as to climb into his host's dingy attic and retrieve a number of manuscripts. Writing to Bentham, he described himself as a "coalheaver," returning downstairs from the chaotic mass of cobwebs and dirt with his precious find. The two men routinely discussed a wide range of social issues, from prison reform and poor relief to international law and democracy. Bentham was a feminist, as Burr was. He defended women's right to suffrage and divorce, recognizing that women as well as men had an equal claim to happiness. Infanticide and homosexuality were also topics of conversation. When the translator Dumont finally met Burr, he remarked that he was just like Bentham, "always in such a hurry!"[19]

No two men could have been better intellectually suited for one another. Bentham was the principal architect of Utilitarianism, which advanced the doctrine that government should serve the "greatest happiness of the greatest number." As an uncompromising rationalist, he firmly believed that all institutions, laws, or policies had to be based on objective standards. Government legislation and moral principles should be defined scientifically, empirically, rather than by such vague concepts as "natural rights." Bentham unsparingly attacked Jefferson's Declaration of Independence as a hodgepodge of "rhetorical nonsense—nonsense upon stilts." He believed that human behavior, like the laws of physics, could best be explained by two universal conditions: the forces of pleasure and pain. Calculating human needs, then, was the key to measuring genuine political interests.[20]

These ideas appealed to Burr because they substantiated his own intellectual odyssey. As a boy at Princeton, he had become a convert to the

Scottish Utilitarian thought of John Witherspoon, absorbing, too, the legal reform ideals of Cesare Beccaria, who loomed large in Bentham's pantheon. In 1791, as attorney general of New York, Burr had proposed his own Utilitarian reform of criminal law. His attraction to the educational psychology of Jean-Jacques Rousseau and Mary Wollstonecraft also made him susceptible to Bentham.[21]

At their core, Enlightenment *philosophes* like Rousseau and Wollstonecraft were behaviorists, believing that social conditions shaped human behavior. For Bentham, as for Burr, government should be organized around the usefulness of its policies, and legislators should strive to act as scientists, discussing laws dispassionately and rising above partisan rancor. So, in many ways, Burr had already practiced Bentham's ideas. His management of the election of 1800 is a perfect example; at a crucial moment, he orchestrated political victory—not by abusing his opponents or manipulating human passions but by focusing on election strategy as problem solving. Bentham's philosophy made perfect sense to Burr.

But Burr also appears to have influenced Bentham. In 1809, when his friendship with Burr had just blossomed, the English philosopher wrote his "Plan for Parliamentary Reform," calling for universal suffrage, secret ballots, and equal electoral districts. He also made a convincing case for the irrationality of denying women the right to vote. It cannot be absolutely said that Burr alone had convinced him, but it is certainly significant that Bentham's rallying cry took shape at this time: that English reformers should "look to America" in building their own democracy.[22]

Burr was also drawn to Bentham's radical plan of penitentiary reform, called "the Panopticon." It was a new style of prison that kept all the inmates under constant surveillance; a central observation tower was placed in the middle of a circular-shaped institution, in which guards watched the prisoners in their cells through transparent walls. The Panopticon grew out of the Enlightenment fantasy that human beings could be remade, and the prison rebuilt as a social laboratory. Bentham saw it as a more humane solution than the current British practice of sending criminals to a penal colony in Australia.[23]

Burr wrote to Theodosia that he was "charmed" with the Panopticon, and urged her to press her husband to present the design to the South Carolina legislature, knowing that the state was planning to build a penitentiary.

He confidently assured Bentham that "the Panopticon shall be known in America." Burr's curiosity about the Panopticon was sparked by the same impulse that had earlier drawn him to the Cayuga Bridge project. Recall that he had overseen the building of military fortifications for New York Harbor. That South Carolina would take this bold step was wishful think-ing. His daughter understood southerners much better than her father. "I have not the least expectation that the plan will be adopted," she wrote to him. "In South Carolina there is less enterprise, less public spirit, than in any other state; and that, Heaven knows, reduces it low enough." South Carolina was not New York.[24]

Burr was also animated by a project that combined Bentham's reform ideas with his own plans for Latin American liberation. He saw an oppor-tunity to introduce democratic forms of government in Spain because the Juntas had rejected monarchy and Bonapartism. Burr wanted to get Ben-tham's writings into the hands of the marqués de Yrujo, who was now in London and a supporter of the Juntas. He hoped that Yrujo would be willing to distribute Bentham's writings on legislative reform. In a memorandum Burr prepared, he offered an overview of ancient and modern assemblies, highlighting Bentham's legislative reforms. He insisted that Spain should look to America, not Europe, for its best democratic model. But this utopian reform plan failed, too. Yrujo was no liberal or revolutionary. Burr wrote to Bentham that the "horrors of innovation" scared the Spaniard, and anything "tainted with democratic infection" was "odious and alarming" to him.[25]

In September, Burr enthusiastically declared to Bentham, "by the help of God, and of you, we will reform," but by October his optimism was wan-ing. He learned that Charles Williamson had died of yellow fever as his ship sailed from Cuba to England. And though he had rekindled an acquaintance with Anthony Merry, Merry could do little for him now. Burr's disappoint-ments mounted when he learned that his daughter was gravely ill.[26]

Theodosia had suffered a growing list of medical ailments since the birth of her son in 1802. In a letter to Dr. William Eustis, she summarized her condition: a partially prolapsed uterus and irregular menstrual periods, accompanied by "offensive" discharges and painful cramps. She had devel-oped rheumatism, and believed that her womb was "obstructed." But what troubled her most were the mental afflictions. Night and day, she suffered "hysteric fits," saw flashing lights, heard strange noises, all of which made it impossible for her to think, let alone read a book or carry on an intelligent conversation. There seems little doubt that she was suffering from a severe uterine infection and the same physical ailments that had plagued her mother.[27]

Burr was convinced that she must come to England. He had consulted with an English expert on "female complaints," who offered a cure. But Theodosia was not well enough to make a winter voyage, and refused to travel. She attempted to reassure her father that she was able to tough it out. But Burr was not fooled.[28]

At this moment, he began to consider returning to the United States. He was already anticipating March 1809, when Jefferson retired and "the persecutions will be less vindictive," as he wrote to his friend Timothy Green. He saw little hope for "X," the secret name he gave to his filibuster. Burr was confident that he had a way to negotiate with his remaining creditors, and thus there was nothing to keep him from sailing home.[29]

"FOLLIES"

But he did not sail. Instead, he made plans to visit Scotland, hoping to renew acquaintance with friends and relatives of the late Charles Williamson. There would be nothing routine about this trip, however, because London had grown suspicious of Burr's comings and goings; only Britons could travel freely. Following the advice of John Reeves of the British Alien Office, he submitted a claim of British nationality: having been born in colonial America! Burr's unusual ploy became the talk of London. (As word reached the United States, Burr's already tarnished name suffered added abuse; even his daughter found the news of his alleged transfer of national allegiance incredible.) But it was just a ploy.[30]

While the top law officials of the land considered how to handle the matter, the petitioner headed north to Edinburgh, where he remained for some weeks, meeting and greeting, and leading what he himself admitted to Bentham was "a life of the utmost dissipation." The Lord Mayor gave him a public welcome, and he hobnobbed with such literary giants as Walter Scott (at this point a celebrated poet but not yet a novelist) and Henry Mackenzie, author of the sentimental classic *The Man of Feeling*. In an invaluable journal that he kept at this time, Burr also preserved a record of his sex life.[31]

Burr's journal recorded his every move and described everyone he met, indulging the same literary impulse that he had shown earlier, when, for his daughter's reading pleasure, he humorously portrayed his failed courtships. In a sparse but lively style, he transformed the people he met into literary characters: the women are funny, flirtatious, alternately sad and coy, and he is impressed by their tasteful attire and smart conversation. Numerous "follies," sexual or otherwise, are sprinkled through his voluminous European journal, which filled nearly 1,000 pages when it was published after his death.[32]

To convey the flavor of Burr's gossipy journal, take as an example his dealings with an Italian sculptor in London. The artist made a bust of Bentham, and a face mask of Burr to boot. When the mask was removed, Burr discovered, to his chagrin, a purple mark on his nose. He tried many remedies, but nothing removed the stain. He then cursed the Italian for the "nose disaster," self-conscious about being seen in public and hoping to "sleep off his nasology." He wrote that he would "see no signora till the proboscis be in order."[33]

There is something modern about the inner dialogue in Burr's journal. Perhaps this is why later readers have had had such a difficult time with this document. It is written as a conversation with his daughter, something for her entertainment. But what makes it different from his earlier letters is his openness with regard to his sex life. He is too casual, too matter-of-fact, for a Victorian or post-Victorian audience. To later generations, he appears indiscreet, if not immoral. We must understand that sexuality was neither sinful nor savage for men of the Enlightenment; instead, sexual enjoyment was acceptable and refined, a "rational" pleasure. Even women supposedly benefited from sexual openness. That is what Mary Wollstonecraft believed, when she stated that "false delicacy" kept women hopelessly ignorant about their bodies. It is not at all surprising that Burr should have felt perfectly at ease in writing to his daughter about sex.

He is intentionally playful in the pages of this journal. He crafts a sexual cipher for himself, inventing code words to describe the different types of women he encountered, classifying them according to age, marital status, sexual experience, and occasionally nationality. One favorite term for illicit sex was "muse." This was possibly a double entendre for "amusement"; *muse* was the French word for animals in heat, or the rutting season. He also denoted sex as "follies" and "accidents," and often recorded his encounters in shorthand. Here is a typical entry: "Vis. inv. pr. U. pa. bi. jo. ma. bi. fa," which stood for "visitai invite plusieurs fois une jungfru pas bien jolie mais bien faite" (after repeated invitations, I had sex with a Swedish maid who was not very handsome, but well built). He tended to mention the circumstance leading to the amorous adventure (in other cases, his resolve not to take advantage of the opportunity); the amount of money paid; and sometimes how long the event lasted.[34]

Nothing was off limits. His journal vividly captured the multifarious sexual landscape of Europe, including prostitutes, chambermaids, "sirens," and manipulative French women who love only "in the head" but give no more of themselves. On December 21, 1808, the same day he boarded the stage in London for his trip to Scotland, he joked that he had been "amused for an hour with a very handsome young Dane." Then he added to his fictive reader Theodosia, "Don't smile. It is a male." On the same day that he returned from Scotland, he noted that two young men had approached him, but that he kept his distance—the insinuation being that they had propositioned him. There is little shame in his journal. The only time he begged for "penitence and contrition," promising never again to frequent prostitutes, was when he feared that he had exposed himself to venereal disease. It was not long before he broke this promise to himself.[35]

Burr's sexual diary was not unique. As a bachelor in Virginia, in 1770, Thomas Jefferson used Shelton's tachygraphical alphabet to record in code what appear to be sexual liaisons. James Wilson, a renowned jurist and a signer of the Declaration of Independence, was reputed, however falsely, to have kept a sexual diary. And Samuel Boswell, one of the most famous journalists of the time, recorded in excruciating detail his numerous sexual escapades. Burr's curt descriptions were neither pornographic nor salacious; their brevity made them almost sociological. More to the point, he wrote so as to monitor himself, putting pen to paper to curb his excesses. The literary invention of his daughter represented his conscience. She never saw the journal. His method was not so different from that of Benjamin Franklin, who kept a moral accounting system of his virtues and vices (chastity made his list), and who made sure he struck a balance at the end of the month. As a true Benthamite, Burr treated sex as natural and pleasurable; and he was empirically bent on maintaining a personal sexual timetable. After ten days, he noted at one point, he was "scarcely fit for society" and began to treat people brusquely. And what had caused this "irritability"? "The want of muse," of course.[36]

Burr's journal is remarkable for its openness. Its pages contain moments of unmitigated vanity. His humor is infectious, too, and he shares even his most outrageous dreams. Awakening one morning, he scratched out: "Dreamed engaged to marry a huge ugly beast." The longtime widower's independence was so threatened that his subconscious mind "deliberated whether to blow out brains or perform engagement."[37]

Burr enjoyed Scotland, and not only because of "dissipation." He admired the fact that the women engaged in public gatherings as equals, holding their own in political debates or intellectual discussions. The reformer from America regaled his Scottish acquaintances with ideas about Benthamite legal reform. For his efforts, Bentham nicknamed him "Hercules Burr."[38]

During the first week of February 1809, he rushed back to London in order to sit down with Lord Melville, the patron saint of filibusterers. He appreciated Melville's frank and "free conversation," boldness, and "manly" character. Melville was no longer the powerful statesman he once was, and Burr knew that he was chasing false hopes. He satirized his journey to Scotland as the "Adventures of Gil Blas Monheagungk De Manhattan," borrowing from a famous eighteenth-century picaresque novel. Here a man from the lower classes used his wits to rise to social prominence. Burr was beginning to present himself as an American savage, out of place among the political elite, and unable to exercise much control over his life. Whether he admitted to himself or not, sex was one of few things he could control.[39]

His vulnerability became painfully clear on April 4, when he was arrested. His belongings and papers were confiscated. "They have everything," he recorded. "No plots, or treasons, to be sure, but what is worse, all my ridiculous journal." No charges were filed; Burr was simply being harassed. For members of the British Ministry, he had become a dangerous alien, whose activities appeared suspicious. Two days later, his possessions were returned. He was released, but at the same time ordered to leave the country.[40]

Furious, Burr blamed Lord Liverpool most of all for having orchestrated his arrest. He tried to petition for a reconsideration of the departure order but found himself unable to address "my lord." This is what he meant when he said he felt alienated, because the words "my lord" stuck in his "savage throat." In the end, he was able to take out a passport in his own name and travel at the government's expense, selecting Sweden as his destination. We cannot determine precisely why Burr was expelled from Great Britain, though he blamed "Jefferson, or the Spanish Juntas, or probably both." By now he had given up on the idea of aligning with the Spanish Juntas, figuring them as terminally undemocratic.[41]

So he said his good-byes. In addition to Bentham, he paid a visit to William Godwin, from whom he requested the name of the painter who did a likeness of his dead wife, Mary Wollstonecraft: "I wish to have my daughter's copied in the same style." Despite all his tribulations, he carried on as a tourist, collecting souvenirs for Theodosia and her son. As he made final preparations, he dubbed himself a "pilgrim." On April 25, he set sail. He entered the Swedish capital not as an American exile or *prisonier d'état* but as a visiting dignitary.[42]

"PASSING TO ANOTHER PLANET"

Burr was fascinated with Sweden. He visited museums and art galleries, studied the language, and closely examined the laws. He had befriended Henry Gahn, the Swedish consul in New York City, and now sought out members of Gahn's family who were leading figures in the scientific and medical community. His social calendar included historians, geographers, jurists, and prominent politicians. Burr gained access to the Society of Nobles, an exclusive club which housed an extensive library. Welcomed by the Swedish regent, he felt honored and foolish at the same time. "You would have laughed," he jotted down in the journal intended for Theodosia, thinking his appearance silly, "with a sword and immense three-cornered hat."[43]

He praised the openness of Swedish society, writing his daughter:

"Honesty is not a virtue here; it is a mere habit." Unlike England, where nothing seemed to protect a person against fraud and theft, Burr described Sweden feeling as if he was "passing to another planet." Doors were left unlatched. Young girls, with no fear for their safety, were sent on errands "at all hours of the night." He was impressed by the liberality that prevailed: "There is no country with whose jurisprudence I am acquainted in which personal liberty is *so well secured*," he wrote to Henry Gahn. "Civil justice is administered with so much dispatch and so little expense." Burr momentarily considered writing a book on the Swedish success story, as few outside Sweden knew anything about its remarkable legal tradition.[44]

He spent five delightful months in Sweden, hoping to make Russia his next destination. But this time it was John Quincy Adams, the American minister in St. Petersburg, who stood in his way, refusing to approve his passport. Unlike most Federalists, Adams had opposed Burr during the treason trial. In 1808, as a member of the Senate, he led a vindictive campaign against Burr's ally John Smith, who stood trial for impeachment. (Smith had earlier been indicted as Burr's co-conspirator in Richmond, but the charges were dismissed.) Adams's tacit reward for supporting Jefferson's administration was his appointment by incoming President James Madison to the diplomatic post.[45]

Rebuffed but hardly deterred, Burr set his sights on Denmark, hoping to make his way to Germany, and possibly France. He reached Copenhagen on October 23. There, he met more European intellectuals, most notably the German literary critic Friedrich von Schlegel, who had published a major treatise on political neutrality which Burr had read and respected. He was nearly broke in Denmark when, to his surprise, a Swedish acquaintance forwarded a gift of 1,000 marks. Along with the needed funds, the Swede sent a note expressing thanks to "Providence" for having enabled him to enjoy the company of a man he had long esteemed, and "now loved." Burr recorded in his journal: "Did you ever hear of any thing equal to this, except in novels?" He had acquired a long list of admirers, making his stay among the "kind and amiable Swedes" the high point of his European tour. But Burr had still not given up on "X" (his filibuster idea), and so he now turned his attention to Germany as the most likely point of access to France, where he thought his plan could be pressed forward.[46]

"AN AMERICAN NAPOLEON"

By the middle of November, Burr was in the vicinity of Hamburg, where he sensed hostility from the community of Americans living there. He was in need of financial support again, and clearly felt that the comforts of Sweden were not to be replicated. Just as he had used his connection to the Swedish consul in New York to cement his welcome in Stockholm, he now sat waiting for a response from the comte d'Hauterive, former French consul in New York, on whom he was relying to secure permission to enter France. At this time, a foreigner could not simply travel across France on the basis of a single passport, but was obliged to petition to travel from one place to another within the country. Only the minister of police could grant him entry into Paris.[47]

So Burr spent Christmas 1809 in Göttingen, where he learned of a development: the emperor Napoleon had thrown his support over to the independence movement in Mexico and other Spanish colonies. On hearing the news, Burr added a sarcastic phrase to his private journal: "Now, why the devil didn't he tell me of this two years ago?" After the first of the year, the wanderer made his way into Weimar, where the aristocracy gave him a warm welcome based on recommendations from respectable Swedes. He was made aware that his past was known in every detail—the duel, his "treasons," and his "gallantries"; but this did not seem to bother most. He met the brother of Alexander von Humboldt, whose map of Latin America had figured in the so-called "conspiracy"; and he experienced a certain coolness from the illustrious Johann Wolfgang von Goethe. One of the ladies at the Weimar court was Henriette von Knebel, who described the "short and lean" visitor, now fifty-three, as a great curiosity. He "likes to talk in his anglicized French," she told her brother, "and his eyes are sparkling." Burr must have put forward some of his opinions on the abilities of the female sex, insofar as she wrote in response to their conversation: "I should not want to place my fate in his keeping, although he has a great respect for our sex." As interestingly, she drew a comparison that others might have thought of in political terms, but she clearly considered merely physical. He resembles, she said, "an American Napoleon."[48]

Rather than wait, Burr inched closer to the French border. At the beginning of February 1810, he was granted a passport to go to Paris, arriving there on the 16th. "My head being so full of X matters," he confided to his journal en route, he immediately made contact with high-level officials: the comte de Volney was an old friend, formerly posted to the United States. He glided from one introduction to the next.[49]

He had several conversations with one well-connected official who had ties to the foreign secretary, and the latter then submitted a summary of these meetings to Napoleon. In short, Burr's goal, expressly stated, was to take Florida and use it as a base of operations to attack Mexico, and possibly the Bahamas, Cuba, and Jamaica. He allowed that the plan would succeed if the United States were at war with Great Britain—something that loomed on the near horizon in 1810—and there was, he felt, a good chance that Canada could be persuaded to seek independence at the same time. All he wanted from Napoleon, in order to effect this plan, was two or three frigates. He was clear in stating that he did not intend to conquer the Spanish colonies, nor divide the United States, but only to spur independence movements in the former. He also expected France to approve the outcome in Florida—that it would become a part of the United States.[50]

But by the end of March, Burr felt he was getting nowhere with his proposals, and arranged to meet with the brother of the emperor, Jérôme Bonaparte. At their April 4 interview, Burr spoke in earnest; but this meeting, too, appeared to him a dead end. He remained in Paris three more unproductive months, and finally decided to apply for a passport to return to the United States. His request was denied, and he now termed himself: "Me voilà prisonier d'état et presque sans sous!" (Here am I a prisoner of the state and nearly penniless).[51]

Trapped in Paris, Burr found ways to pass the time. He was reunited with the talented John Vanderlyn, the American artist who had been his protégé back in New York. They dined together, toured the gardens of Versailles, attended the opera—and even pursued "muse" as a pair. As a regular guest at Vanderlyn's studio, Burr the connoisseur eyed the models and judged his friend's latest projects. He also dabbled in a few highbrow liaisons. A Madame Z entered his life, and prompted some intellectual foreplay at the very least; they indulged in sexual banter about a "'traveller's pen,' said to be *without end.*" He politely demurred when another woman offered to make him a kept man, holding out the promise of a "little room looking into the garden." His dwindling resources obliged him to take on tasks he would not have deigned to perform before. At a low point, he agreed to translate a book (unnamed) into French for 100 *louis*. The "curious part of the story" involved Burr himself, as he noted in his journal; though it was a work containing "abuse and libels," he did not contest it. He simply translated what he saw. Perhaps his body was not for sale, but in at least this one instance, his reputation was.[52]

His long delay in Paris is traceable to his growing list of American enemies. John Armstrong, the current minister to France, was, as Burr described him to a French friend, "for many years . . . my personal and political enemy." As an ally of DeWitt Clinton, he had worked behind the scenes to ruin Burr's standing among New York Republicans. As if Armstrong's power was not enough, the American consul in charge of passports was Alexander McRae, the Virginia lawyer and loyal Jeffersonian who had served as one of the prosecutors during Burr's treason trial. By October 1810, Burr judged that most Americans in Paris had "entered a combination" against him. Anyone who talked to him was "shunned," and even ships' captains refused to deliver his letters. Vanderlyn alone stood by him, expressing nothing but "pity and contempt" for those Americans who sheepishly followed the herd.[53]

Burr pressed on. With Vanderlyn's assistance, and a few new powerfully placed French acquaintances capable of pulling the necessary strings, he was able to get a passport to Amsterdam in the spring of 1811. His trip there was spurred by an opportunity to speculate in Holland Land Company shares—the same group he had invested in back in New York in the 1790s. In Amsterdam, he found a ship's captain willing to bring him back to America; so he rushed back to Paris for a new passport, only to face more red tape. It was not until September 28 that Burr finally set sail on the *Vigilant*.[54]

He was deeply apprehensive about returning home. Waiting in Holland, he feared that the "country which I am so anxious to re-visit will perhaps reject me with horror." He had counseled his daughter on how she might smooth the way for his homecoming. Theodosia had already appealed to Dolley Madison, reminding the first lady that her father was "once your friend," and the "President only can restore him to me and to his country." Though Dolley sent a warm reply, she explained that she could do nothing.[55]

Theodosia also appealed to Madison's secretary of war, William Eustis. He had been Theodosia's doctor and Burr's longtime friend, and had just married Caroline Langdon, a close friend of Dolley Madison's. Yet the "corn curer," as Theodosia had derisively called him in a letter to her father, proved a "fair-weather friend . . . afraid of everything; of nothing."[56] Next, she issued an impassioned plea to Treasury Secretary Albert Gallatin, one of her father's oldest political allies:

> Recollect that I have seen my father dashed from the high rank he held in the minds of his countrymen, imprisoned, and forced into exile. Must he ever remain thus excommunicated from the participation of domestic enjoyments and the privileges of a citizen; aloof from his accustomed sphere, and singled out as a mark for the shafts of calumny? What benefit to the country can possibly accrue from the continuation of this system? Surely it must be evident to the worst enemies of my father, that no man, situated as he will be, could obtain any undue influence, even supposing him desirous of it.[57]

Here we see Theodosia at her most impressive, and most strategic, arguing with the same intellectual force that any male politician might bring to bear in a like situation. She made Burr's case as well as it could be made, citing the cruel and perverse, if not irrelevant, "system" of political abuse that wrongly equated his fall from power with the loss of his rights as a citizen. But her arguments fell on deaf ears. Gallatin would do nothing, and did not even deign to answer her letter.

To make matters worse, though Burr and his daughter were far from the nation's capital (she moved between New York and South Carolina), nothing could curtail the wild rumors that circulated. Some in Washington were gossiping that Theodosia had been abandoned by her husband, and that the two were separated. Later, even nastier rumors would suggest that Alston had been abusing his wife. Others in government circles whispered that Burr was now "deranged," wandering through Europe like a madman.[58]

Although Theodosia encouraged her father to return home and take his stand "in the midst of the tenth legion" (by which she meant the old Burrites), she must have been aware, as he was, that there would be no political future for him. Many of his friends had already deserted him; Robert Swartwout was one of the few who continued to defend him. Aaron Burr was not a man who succumbed to defeat easily, but neither did he try to deny the facts. As his daughter had admitted to Gallatin, he would never again have any "influence" in America.[59]

Burr had sailed from the northern coast of Holland aboard the *Vigilant,* but he did not arrive in America when that ship did. A British vessel ordered the *Vigilant* to dock at Yarmouth on October 9, and Burr, preferring not to remain on a crowded ship filled to the gills with sailors, pigs ("one hundred other quadrupeds and bipeds"), and luggage, requested permission to go into London. When in January 1812, the ship was finally approved to sail, its destination had been changed to New Orleans, which was out of his way; but he was desperate to sail, having paid his fare in advance. Then the captain was soon forced, by what Burr described as the "malice of agents," to drop him from the passenger list. He tried other American vessels, only to find that they, too, would not take him, fearing some form of retaliation from the U.S. government.[60]

He finally scraped together all the money he could, borrowing from friends and even enemies, and bought passage on the *Aurora,* using the alias "Adolphus Arnot." This British packet was headed for Boston, taking to the sea on March 28, 1812. Two days before departure, aware of increasing tensions between the United States and Great Britain, Burr wrote brusquely in his journal: "I hope never to visit the country again, unless at the head of fifty thousand men. I shake the dust off my feet, adieu, John Bull!" The ill-treated adventurer was feeling decidedly American as he headed home.[61]

"TO FILL HIS LORDSHIP'S TANKARD"

Five weeks later, Aaron Burr came ashore in Boston. There he tarried for several weeks, uncertain whether he could return to New York unmolested by his creditors. On May 30, he sailed for Manhattan, taking the necessary precautions to conceal his identity, and slipped into the city seven days later. He sought out Samuel Swartwout, who arranged for Burr to stay with his brother Robert until he could get himself more permanently settled. From John Wickham, Burr learned that no action had been taken against him in the misdemeanor indictment in Ohio, and so he had nothing to fear from that quarter. In July, he discreetly announced in the newspapers the opening of his law office at 9 Nassau Street. With the help of his longtime business associate Timothy Green, Burr was able to put together a law library and open his doors for business.[62]

But that same month he received catastrophic news. His only grandson and namesake, Aaron Burr Alston, had died. He was only eleven years old. A devastated Theodosia wrote to her father: "There is no more joy for me, the world is blank, I have lost my boy, my child is gone forever." She was overcome with grief, and Alston worried about her health. "My present wish," he begged of Burr, "is that Theodosia should join you . . . as soon as possible." Alston knew his wife well enough that he could imagine how a change of scene and her father's company would aid in her recovery. Burr agreed, fearing for his daughter's fragile constitution. He wrote ominously to Bentham at this time: "I have reason to apprehend that she will not long survive."[63]

Plans were made for Theodosia to come north alone. Alston was unable to accompany his wife. The United States had declared war against Great Britain in June, and he was in command of the South Carolina militia. He would shortly stand for election, and win the governorship in December 1812. So, at Burr's request, Timothy Green agreed to act as Theodosia's escort. Green arrived in Charleston in late November, only to discover that his traveling companion was "very low, feeble, and emaciated," and, as he prepared her father, suffering from an "incessant nervous fever." A long coach ride was out of the question, so they purchased passage on the *Patriot,* a swift schooner that was equipped to reach New York in less than a week. The ship set sail on December 31.[64]

Theodosia Alston never reached New York. The *Patriot* was lost at sea somewhere off the coast of the Carolinas. But Burr did not know until sometime later that there had been a violent storm, and he convinced himself, meanwhile, that because his daughter, her maid, and her escort were probably the only passengers on the chartered privateer (loaded with a shipment of Alston's rice crop), the boat may have been pressed into service in the West Indies, searching for British prey. This was, after all, a common resort in warfare at the time. But by February 1813, Alston cried out in a letter to Burr: "My boy—my wife—gone, both!" Both men had to come to terms with the tragedy.[65]

With his daughter and grandson gone, Burr tried to build a new life in

New York. Since his return, he had been devoting himself "exclusively to the business of my profession," as he wrote to a fellow New Yorker. He was spending a great deal of his time in the state capital of Albany. There he re-established himself before the New York Supreme Court, and breathed easy upon being given what he felt was a "courteous and flattering" recep-tion, after his long hiatus.[66]

In Albany, where he had often worked as a lawyer in the prime of his career in the 1790s, he now reconnected with the Yates family. Robert Yates had run for governor unsuccessfully, and sat on the state supreme court. In befriending his son, John Van Ness Yates, a fellow attorney and the recorder for the city of Albany, Burr took both John and his young wife Eliza under his wing. Eliza was acting as her husband's secretary, sending Burr drafts of the revised laws of New York. Her husband had been ap-pointed to the legislature to add notes to the laws, and he was relying on Burr to review his work. Burr also took a greater interest in Theodosia's cousins, Phoebe and Kate Bartow, to whom he also sent books, and to whom he wrote sweetly taunting letters. He told Kate: "If you dare grow ugly, Lord, how I will hate you." His tone resembled the playful banter he had used with Theodosia, whom he had jokingly called a "hussy."[67]

And he became the mentor of Catherine B. Thompson, another woman who filled the void left by the death of his daughter. It is unclear how they met. Her father Alexander Thompson died in 1813, and Burr may have played some part in settling his estate. Their relationship was largely intel-lectual; he urged her to read Bentham's writings, which she did, and he shared with her his interest in the work of Mary Wollstonecraft. Elizabeth wrote to Burr that she considered Wollstonecraft "more excellent in her er-rors than others are in their perfection." She called her new, older friend the "great mogul," in consideration of his wide-ranging intellectual inter-ests. Catherine Thompson was unmarried, with a large family; she was a few years older than Theodosia, and later became a schoolteacher. She had a niece who adored Burr. There is something else that ought to be said: Burr needed the company of women, and he adored children, looking for ways to recreate, however imperfectly, a sense of family, and intimacy, that had been lost to him.[68]

His concern for women was manifest in his law practice. Widows and desperate housewives alike appealed to him for redress. He may have been, in fact, the very first American lawyer to specialize in family law. His duties included more than pleading a case; he counseled the women who came to him, and gave charity to them. Indeed, it was not unusual for his female clients to ask for money. It is more than a coincidence that all of Burr's divorce clients were women. It is equally apparent that they selected him because of his reputation as a man who identified easily with women's issues.[69]

Burr's most interesting case involved Rebecca Blodget, the widow of Samuel Blodget. Her husband had been one of the greatest "high-flying" speculators of the 1790s. He made a fortune in marine insurance, founded several banks, and was a key player in the commercial development of the District of Columbia, when it was not yet the nation's capital. He was a Renaissance man, a "projecting Genius," in the words of George Washington, who, as an architect, designed the Bank of the United States in Philadelphia in 1795, and published the first major treatise on American economics. But his glory days did not last. In 1802, Blodget's business partners sued him, a considerable amount of his property was sold, and he ended up in debtor's prison. In 1813, one year before his death, more of his property was sold to cover his enormous debts.[70]

As her husband's property went up for sale, Rebecca Blodget tried to salvage what she could. In 1814, the year she first contacted Burr, she was forty-two and had four children to provide for, ranging in age from twenty-one to fifteen. She was a proud woman, as she described herself, and had once been a leading light of Philadelphia society. Her father, the Reverend William Smith, had been provost of the University of Pennsylvania and in 1790 delivered the official eulogy upon Benjamin Franklin; her mother, Rebecca Moore Smith, was part of the female literati. When the younger Rebecca married Blodget in 1792, she was known for her wit and beauty. It is clear that she knew Burr from his time in the Senate, and Burr was, of course, acquainted with her husband's record of accomplishment.[71]

Her reason for contacting Burr was simple: She needed help to regain control of a piece a property in New York. This land had been given to her by her father. It was her "unfeeling brothers," as she put it in a letter to Burr, whose "souls are not larger than peas," who retained control of her land, because it was attached to a larger holding in their possession. Burr devised a solution: She would sell her 1,000 acres of this land to his law partner, forcing her brothers to partition the larger holding, so she could then recover her property. In this he succeeded through clever maneuvering.[72]

But her problems did not end there. Her husband had left her with nothing. She was virtually squatting in a barn near Lancaster that she had once owned—a piece of property, she claimed, that she had been "cheated out of" by her husband. She was constantly hounded and abused by her husband's creditors. She called one a "lazy brute," who refused to see her when she called at his home, telling his servant to say that he was asleep. With incredulity in her tone, she asked Burr: "Do you ever sleep in the day?" She admitted to feeling resentment about her less than ideal marriage: "Mr. B. died as he lived," she wrote to Burr, "you know how he lived & I will spare myself the pain of saying how he died."[73]

The principal difference between Burr and Blodget was that the former had found a way to stay out of debtor's prison. How he did so is a further testament to his talent as a lawyer and negotiator: Burr was able to keep one step ahead of his creditors, and to appease them well enough that they never pressed for prison time. He waged such a battle in 1814, telling his son-in-law at that time: "my old creditors (principally the holder of the Mexican debts) came upon me last winter with vindictive fury." He was held for bail "in large sums," and figured he would be going to prison. But somehow he avoided it. For the rest of his life, Burr was never free from creditors. He was sued many times, by former friends like David Gelston and old clients like Louis Le Guen.[74]

Burr looked to the state legislature to ease his financial burdens. In February 1814, he began to lobby—in his words, make "out-door preparations"—for a bill to grant him compensation, in the form of a land grant, for his military service during the Revolution. His rationale, as he explained it to a lawyer who he hoped would promote his cause, was that he had served four years in the army without any subsequent compensation, and that his services "were principally in this state." Burr's request was patterned on veteran appeals that state legislatures and Congress itself were hearing: his health had suffered from the exigencies of war, and he was suffering financially, at a time in life when it was difficult if not impossible "to commence a new career." His was not exactly a new career, but to stay solvent he would have to practice law until he was eighty years old.[75]

Burr's bill was defeated in April. He blamed its failure on the Federalist

"Junto" in the Senate, and he was partially right: James Cochran, the first cousin of Alexander Hamilton's widow, had led the opposition. Burr did have more than a few genuine supporters: ten Republicans backed the bill, including his old rival Morgan Lewis and a new ally, Martin Van Buren. Burr made a special appeal to Van Buren, claiming that a land grant from the state was the "only hope which I have of being able to keep out of prison." And it is clear that Van Buren was responsive, meeting with Burr and warmly acknowledging his "particular politeness & friendly solicitude." Burr, too, proved himself willing to employ his skills on behalf of his new benefactor. In the summer of 1814, he helped Van Buren draft the "Classification Bill," meant to establish a state militia draft. Though the bill was never implemented because the War of 1812 was ending, it was still a landmark piece of legislation, a "most energetic war measure" in what had become an unprofitable war for the United States.[76]

A second attempt to get a bill passed failed, too. The committee praised Burr as an "active, zealous and intelligent officer," but correctly concluded that his petition ought to receive attention from the national legislature, as he had not served in the lines of the state militia. This was only the beginning of his fight to secure compensation for his military services. He would turn to the federal government next, but only after new legislation was passed in the 1820s, extending pension benefits.[77]

His friendship with Van Buren proved to be a lasting one. Though they had known one another since 1803, when Van Buren was a protégé of the Van Ness family of Kinderhook, the younger man broke with the Van Nesses at the time of the governor's race in 1804, supporting Morgan Lewis over Burr, a decision that earned him William Van Ness's personal enmity. Yet this early betrayal mattered little ten years later. The two men had much in common. Van Buren came to promote commercial republicanism, and adopted a political style that openly embraced the machinery of parties. They worked together on several high-profile law cases, and Van Buren was a firm believer in legal positivism (a Utilitarian approach to law and legislation), so one can only wonder if Burr encouraged him to read Jeremy Bentham. The resemblance between the two men extended to their personal appearance: each was of small build, dressed meticulously, and was called a "dandy." Rumors later circulated that Van Buren was Burr's bastard child. He was not.[78]

The similarity between the two men had to do with politics, not genes. Both men rose in the Republican Party as outsiders, that is, without a powerful family faction to press their careers. They found the art of negotiation and compromise sensible. Van Buren's support of commercial republicanism was in fact the mantra of the Burrites. That Van Buren was called "the Little Magician" reflected the same unease that Burr's enemies voiced when they called him a "proteus." The reason Van Buren succeeded where Burr failed is that by the 1810s there were more men like him—like them—men who appealed to those outside the elite families who so long dominated state politics. This makes the short-lived Burrites a phenomenon destined to thrive in politics: not a disruptive third wheel, as their enemies charged, but the first truly democratic political organization in New York, offering a sensible alternative to the ruling family factions.

Burr left hints about what he thought of the Madison administration. While he was in Europe, Theodosia had sent reports about the worsening economy, and the turnover in his cabinet. Erich Bollmann had let him know that Madison was endorsing a filibuster takeover of West Florida. Days before he sailed home from England, Burr became aware that war fever had stuck in the United States; but he assessed little would come of it. Belittling the new generation in Congress, he added: "I treat their war-prattle as I should a bevy of boarding-house misses who should talk of making war." Not only did he scoff at the so-called "War Hawks," he also felt confident that Madison could never be an effective commander in chief. It is reasonable to conclude that after the war got underway, Burr was not impressed by the administration's handling of it.[79]

As Burr sat out the war, Secretary of War James Monroe envisioned the U.S. forces occupying both East Florida and the full extent of British North America. There was a familiar ring to this expansionist strategy: It was identical to Burr's proposal to Napoleon for ridding North America of the British. But Madison's three secretaries of war—William Eustis, James Monroe, and John Armstrong—all failed to create an efficient military bureaucracy. Given his own military experience and organizational skills, it is a safe guess that Burr was thinking that he would have been a better war president than the unmartial Madison.[80]

If Burr wrote little about Madison that survives, he certainly did not remain silent after he learned that Monroe was next in line for the presidency.

In a November 1815 letter to his son-in-law, Burr launched into a harangue against Monroe, calling the man and his nomination "equally exceptional & odious." He regarded congressional caucus nominations as "hostile to all freedom & independence of suffrage." He remembered all too well that in 1804, the Republican caucus had acted as a corrupt clique, an unjust aristocracy, when it stripped him of the vice presidency.[81]

Perhaps the best explanation for Burr's annoyance and impatience was his residual disappointment in the Virginians who, standing with Jefferson, had caused his descent from power within the Republican Party. The Virginians had mastered what he called "one of the principal Arts . . . which has been systematically taught by Jefferson," the promotion of "state dissensions—not between repub[lican] & federal—that would do them no good, but Sc[h]isms in the repub[lican] party." In this, Burr was basically correct. Jefferson had employed his "southern" strategy against Burr, just as Madison undermined DeWitt Clinton, his opponent in the 1812 election, by using patronage to strengthen his rivals in New York.[82]

But Burr's real venom was directed at James Monroe. He called the last president in the Virginia Dynasty "naturally dull & stupid—extremely illiterate," "indecisive . . . pusillanimous & of course hypocritical." He was unsparing in his criticism of Monroe's military career, observing that he never "commanded a platoon nor was ever fit to command one." He pointed out that during the Revolution, Monroe was a sycophant. As the aide-de-camp to Lord Stirling, who was "regularly drunk from Morning to Morning, Monroe's whole duty was to fill his Lordship's Tankard and hear with indications of admiration his Lordship's stories about himself." This was damning stuff—and Burr was not finished. As a lawyer, Monroe was "far below Mediocrity," never rising to the "Honor of trying a Cause of the Value of an hundred pounds." But Monroe's elevation, despite his lack of ability, was not anomalous, according to Burr. Rather, his was "a character exactly suited to the View of the Virginia Junto," which maintained itself on sycophancy, instead of recruiting men of "Talent and Independence."[83]

Burr wanted ex-Governor Alston to lead other southern politicians in a surprise attack to outflank the Virginians. Republicans, he insisted, must choose a man of "firmness and decision," and, he said notably, "That man is Andrew Jackson." He felt that the hero of the Battle of New Orleans was the best candidate to defeat Monroe and break the stranglehold that the

Virginians had on the party. It could succeed, Burr advised Alston, if Jackson's nomination was kept secret, and only announced at the last moment before the caucus met. Confident that his plan would work, Burr commanded Alston to "emerge from this state of Nullity" and prepare for battle. "You owe it to yourself—you owe it to me—you owe it to your country— you owe it to the Memory of the dead." These were fighting words.[84]

At this moment, Burr was a better prognosticator than even Martin Van Buren, Jackson's future secretary of state and vice president, who would not support the Tennessean for another decade. In 1815, New Yorkers were divided between two possible challengers to Monroe: their governor, Daniel Tompkins, or Secretary of War William Crawford of Georgia. Jackson ended rumors of his run for the top office only days before Burr penned his letter to Alston. Jackson had just visited ex-President Jefferson, and some have speculated that it was Jefferson who persuaded him to withdraw.[85]

Burr did not hear back from Alston until February 1816. Apologizing for his tardy response, the younger man acknowledged that he sympathized with Burr's position, but lacked the "spirit, the energy, the health" to engage in so desperate a political battle. He had been unable to attend the fall session of the South Carolina legislature, due to sickness and depression. Politics had little interest for him anymore: "I feel too much alone, too entirely unconnected to the world, to take much interest in anything." As a "miserable remnant" of his former self, Alston was unknowingly bidding farewell to his father-in-law. His condition worsened, and he died in September, surviving his wife by only three years.[86]

As for Burr, when he wrote to Alston disparaging Monroe, he had just turned sixty—he was two years older than Monroe. Unwilling to keep his opinions to himself, he had hoped for a political surrogate in Alston of South Carolina. But Alston was dead at thirty-seven, allowing the Virginia "mediocrity" to enter office.

"A HALO OF GENIUS SHONE AROUND HIM"

Burr did not lose his interest in Latin America. He joined a circle of South American revolutionary exiles in New York and Philadelphia. José Alvárez de Toledo, a leader of Mexican insurgents living in New York, wrote to Burr in September 1816, asking him to "assume the management of our political and military affairs." Though this offer might sound as though Burr was being handed the presidency of Mexico (should the revolution succeed), Toledo had no power at this time to make any such offer. He was simply one of many revolutionaries and fellow travelers who were promoting independence for Latin America and looking to the United States for support. And he knew enough of Burr that he would be receptive to his plea.[87]

After returning to the United States, Burr's strongest ties to the Latin American insurgency came by way of two Englishmen: John Alderson and Robert Cartmel. Alderson had established a commercial operation in Venezuela, maintaining close ties to Simón Bolívar, the famed "Liberator" of South America. In 1817, while living in Philadelphia, Alderson established himself as part of a network of Latin American revolutionary refugees, and he brought Burr into the fold. He even supplied Burr with a Spanish tutor.[88]

Cartmel was another English merchant who had set up businesses in Colombia and New York. He became acquainted with Burr in 1817. Two years later, when Cartmel found himself in New York debtor's prison, Burr acted as his attorney. The two became intimates, not just business partners, exchanging warm letters over a decade.[89]

After leaving New York, Cartmel headed for Cuba. But around 1823, he returned to the northern Colombian port of Carthagena. One venture that succeeded in enticing Burr was a steamboat company. With another New Yorker, Samuel Chester Reid, a naval hero of the War of 1812, Burr backed a scheme to sell steamboats to a contractor with exclusive navigational rights along Colombia's Magdalena River. Burr sent Reid designs of passenger vessels, based on the boats that were being used on the Erie Canal. Clearly, Burr had not yet given up on speculative opportunities, just as he enjoyed the risk—the thrill—of backing revolutionaries whose goals harmonized with his own.[90]

He may still have been dreaming about Latin America, but he devoted most of his energy to the practice of law. Here he liked to try new tactics, which, as he told his junior associate Gurdon W. Lathrop, had always brought him "great honor as an attorney," as well as, he admitted, "much criticism" and "much mirth." He was drawn into an old battle involving the heirs of George Croghan. Back in the 1780s, he had crossed swords with Alexander Hamilton in protecting the interests of Augustine Prevost—

Croghan's son-in-law and heir—over William Cooper's claim to the Otsego tract. But now, three decades later, Burr sought a new way to challenge the status of land titles. In what he described as an "extraordinary suit," he drew up a list of 500 names of actual occupants of the land, preparing a case with "500 defendants." This tactic anticipated what lawyers later would use in class action suits: the threat of a large numbers of litigants to force some kind of settlement.[91]

His most elaborate litigation involved the heirs of Medcef Eden, Jr. Eden was the son of a wealthy brewer in New York City who had owned a large amount of Manhattan real estate. Medcef and his brother Joseph had squandered their father's fortune after his death in 1798, and according to Burr, had been tricked out of their inheritance. In 1815, Burr tracked down the impoverished Medcef Eden in Westchester County; his brother had died two years earlier. The surviving brother had recently married Rachel Maltbie, a widow with three daughters—Sally Ann, Elizabeth, and Rebecca. So, for the next decade, Burr devoted himself to recovering the lost legacies of this family. He moved the Edens into his home, and when Medcef Eden died in 1819, Burr became the executor of his will and the guardian of his three stepdaughters—now Medcef's heirs.[92]

Initially, Burr took on this case because it offered an impossible challenge. He needed to find a way to weaken the land titles, and began with a small farm owned by one John Anderson, recovering it for the Eden estate. The case created a precedent, in establishing that the Eden brothers had been fraudulently deprived of their land by so-called usurers and money brokers. Burr then issued a series of writs of ejectment against the holders of city lots, reclaiming titles to the Eden estate piece by piece.[93]

Burr also mobilized an effective legal team, relying on the same skills that had made him a successful political organizer. He drew in Martin Van Buren and another prominent New York attorney to help transfer the property to Eden's widow. Burr even recruited one of the great orators of the time, Daniel Webster, to join this fight. In the end, he won several key judgments in this prolonged legal contest. But it was not until 1828 that was he finally able to secure some profits from the estate for Eden's heirs.[94]

His handling of the Eden case confirmed Burr's reputation as a leader of the bar. He acquired an almost legendary status, as an "old gentleman" capable of astonishing much younger attorneys with his "loftiest eloquence" on points of law. In the *New-York Mirror,* and *Ladies' Literary Gazette,* Burr was still a mysterious "stranger" but he was not a villain—he was instead the incomparable Burr once again, and a "halo of genius shone around him" when untangling some impossible legal problem.

The Eden matter, however, assumed personal meaning for him, because Eden's widow and his two younger daughters became part of Burr's surrogate family. In 1823, Burr wrote affectionately of his growing brood to a friend, describing himself as a "housekeeper with all my Children about me." As one might expect, he ensured that the two girls received a rigorous education, and that they married well. Rebecca married John Lynde Wilson, a longtime political associate of Burr and a former governor of South Carolina—shades of Theodosia. And when Elizabeth left the roost in 1828, she married Isadore Guillet, a man of taste and breeding, who had once served as *Secretaire-Interprete* in the French Ministry of Foreign Affairs.[95]

Burr also adopted two sons, both reputed to have been his biological children. Aaron Burr Columbe (who later changed his name to Aaron Columbus Burr) was the son of a Frenchwoman who arrived in the United States around 1815. Though a less impressive student than Burr would have liked, he responded to Burr's dream of Latin American adventure. In the decade before the Civil War, with the help of none other than Abraham Lincoln, he promoted a plan to colonize freed slaves on a tract of land in Honduras.[96]

Burr's second adopted son, Charles Burdett, born in 1814, benefited from the best educational opportunities. Following in Burr's footsteps, he joined the senior class at Princeton, and graduated in 1829. Burr relied on old contacts (Captain James Biddle, son of Charles Biddle) to secure Burdett a commission in the U.S. Navy. Burr was hoping he might join the crew of a "polar Expedition." But his adopted son had little interest in either maritime exploits or the law. He ended up pursuing a literary career, first as a newspaper reporter, and then as a writer of popular fiction. In 1860, he published a quasi-biographical account of Burr's life, *Margaret Moncrieffe: The First Love of Aaron Burr,* thus contributing to the romantic mythology that surrounded his stepfather's private conduct.[97]

In his later years, Burr showed that he had not given up his literary aspirations, either. He talked about writing a revisionist history of the American Revolution—a tantalizing notion, a worthy project. He claimed to have lost his notes when Theodosia disappeared at sea, and came to feel that his history would simply be too shocking, and so unlike the "received history" authored by his former colleagues in government, that no one would believe it.[98]

He did, however, revive a dramatic piece of his past in 1830, when he lent his assistance to Richard H. Bayard, the son of James A. Bayard. Young Bayard was attempting to clear his father's name—the elder Bayard having always been associated with the backroom bargaining that secured Jefferson the presidency in 1801. Thomas Jefferson Randolph had published his grandfather's papers in several volumes during the previous year, and had struck a nerve. In the collected notes called the *Anas*, Jefferson had flatly denied having made any deal with Bayard to settle the election tie of 1800–01. Richard Bayard found a political ally to defend his father on the Senate floor, and now he wanted conclusive proof. So he sought Burr's help, asking for a copy of a deposition made by his father, in which the election crisis was detailed. Burr tracked down the deposition, and discussed the matter with his former political lieutenant, Matthew Livingston Davis. Armed with these depositions, Bayard refuted Jefferson's words in print. Bayard's defense may be the first documented argument in a scholarly debate, which persists to this day, as to whether Jefferson negotiated with Federalists to end the tie.[99]

Jefferson's papers not only annoyed the younger Bayard but the politically ambitious Davis, too. Davis considered writing his own account of the election of 1800. His notes, which survive, offer a running commentary on his reading of Jefferson. To Davis, Jefferson claimed to disdain parties, yet he diligently enforced party lines; he declared that he never wrote for the newspapers, and then used Madison to do his dirty work. No doubt Davis's emotionalism served as the catalyst for his eventual decision to edit Burr's papers. He wanted to vindicate Burr, and to salvage the reputations of men like himself who had rallied to Burr's cause.[100]

If Burr had lost his taste for historical revisionism, he still cared about his military legacy, and he still sought to secure his pension. He relied on old friends such as Aaron Ogden and younger allies such as Van Buren to come to his aid. In 1828, at the age of seventy-two, he prepared several declarations of military service, and repeated the procedure after one was lost in a fire in the Treasury Department; he collected testimony from surviving soldiers, and even hunted down General Washington's letters from the first president's biographer, Jared Sparks. Still unpaid, but retaining his sense of humor, Burr wrote to Van Buren in 1834: "I have no prospects of growing richer or younger." Van Buren took action on his behalf, and Ogden played a crucial role in working Burr's claim through the system. Finally, two years before his death, Burr received his pension from the government. It amounted to $3,300. The money was probably less important to him than the principle of defending his military reputation.[101]

Burr's relationship with Ogden was a telling reminder of his unwavering loyalty to old friends. Even in 1828, when Burr enlisted him to help secure his military pension, Ogden's finances were in worse shape than Burr's. His mansion in Elizabethtown, New Jersey, had been repossessed, and his vast wealth had vanished. Burr came to his rescue after Ogden was imprisioned for debt, convincing the New York legislature to pass a law forbidding jail time for verterans of the Revolution.[102]

Ogden and Dayton—and Burr—had all been friends since childhood. It had come to this: Though Ogden was a Federalist most of his life (serving under Alexander Hamilton as deputy quartermaster general during the Quasi-War of 1798–99), he switched parties in 1828, voting for Andrew Jackson. It may have been Burr who persuaded him. While Burr never asked for or received any patronage from Old Hickory, the new president made Ogden the revenue collector for Jersey City.[103]

Burr tried to make amends with certain other people from his past. After Luther Martin suffered from a paralytic stroke in 1819, losing his intellectual rigor and his mental focus, Burr took him in and cared for him during the last three years of his life. He also provided a piece of property to the son of Benjamin Botts, another of Burr's earlier counselors, who had perished in a fire in a Richmond theater in 1811. And in 1834, Burr was still helping Rebecca Blodget by giving her advice on how she might collect information on his husband's military career so that she could secure her widow's pension.[104]

"MADAME OF THE HEIGHTS"

Burr's generosity is demonstrable, but so is his poor judgment. He was seventy-seven when he made a decision he would soon regret. On July 1, 1833, he married Eliza Jumel, a wealthy widow, in New York. Theirs was a match that contained all the ingredients of a scandal; there probably were not two people in New York whose lives (independently of one another) provoked a comparable amount of gossip, and whose legacies would be so tarnished by half-truths.

"Madame Jumel," as she was known, was fifty-eight at the time of her marriage to Burr. One archivist summed up her life this way: "born a bastard, in youth a prostitute, in middle age a social climber, died an eccentric." It is difficult to get a clear picture of who she really was because most of the information about her early life comes from a legal battle over her estate that took place in 1865, in which interested parties did everything possible to paint her in an unflattering light. Yet it must also be said that Jumel contributed to the problem, unsubtly manipulating the truth in an effort to improve her image.[105]

To rise in society, this ambitious woman had to rewrite her past. Born Betsey Bowen in Providence, Rhode Island, she was in fact not illegitimate, though her father's death when she was eleven plunged the family into poverty. There is credible evidence, however, that Betsey worked as a prostitute, giving birth to a child out of wedlock in 1794. (She later tried to conceal this by claiming to have married a French sea captain.) At some point, she made her way to New York, pursuing a career as a "supernumerary," or extra, on the stage. Described as a blond beauty, she became the mistress of the prosperous wine merchant Stephen Jumel, and lived with him for several years before they married in 1804.[106]

This marriage was at no point a conventional one. Beginning in 1815, the couple took an extended tour of France, where Madame Jumel gained notoriety as an art collector as she hobnobbed in royal circles. The marriage grew into a business partnership; the couple spent many years apart, and after Eliza secured her husband's power of attorney, she took an active role overseeing his business interests in the United States. She was unmistakably ambitious, and displayed business savvy. But she was also capable of malice, and was known for telling insulting stories about her husband.

In sum, she was neither a mere gold digger nor a loving wife. By the time Burr met the widow Jumel, she had successfully transformed herself into a *grande dame* of the Old World, riding through Manhattan in an elegant carriage, decorating her home with the finest in European furnishings, and establishing herself as a connoisseur and patron of the arts.[107]

Eliza and Burr met when she was settling her estate, after her husband died, in 1832. They had another connection, too, because Nelson Chase, the husband of her adopted niece, worked in Burr's law office. Their marriage began pleasantly enough. Burr received letters of congratulations, and to one of these he replied that he considered the well-wisher's amusing letter a "sort of Epithalamium," or love poem. But given the couple's advanced years, he lightly added that no one was summoning the "loves or graces" to their marriage feast. They went on a honeymoon to New England, visiting Burr's Connecticut relatives, also attending to business while in the neighborhood—Jumel owned stock in a toll bridge company in Hartford. What happened next is a matter of dispute. Six months after they wed, the Burrs separated, and a year after that, Jumel sued for divorce.[108]

The divorce action was nothing short of a circus, the classic "He said, she said" affair. Jumel charged her new husband with adultery (with various females, she alleged, but with one woman in particular, Jane McManus). Burr countered, accusing Jumel of carousing with several different men, including a coachman. Both parties rounded up witnesses of questionable character to testify, and charges of perjury were made.[109]

The adultery complaint was both necessary and ludicrous. It was virtually impossible to get a divorce in New York without proof of adultery. And it is clear, in this instance, that Jumel was able to bribe a former servant of Burr to testify against him. Mariah Johnson claimed to have witnessed at least two specific encounters between her employer and McManus. The first time, she said, she accidentally walked in on the pair, and caught Burr with his hand under her clothes, his trousers down—and saw McManus's "nakedness." The second time, Johnson had to climb onto the roof of a shed in order to peer through a window as the two engaged in "their mean act." If the story of her spying was not comical enough, Johnson also testified that McManus had screamed, "Oh la! Mary saw us."[110]

Johnson's testimony was neither objective nor ultimately persuasive.

She admitted to calling McManus a whore, and she acknowledged that Madame Jumel and her niece had consulted with her about the divorce action. This is not to say that, at seventy-seven, Aaron Burr could not have been a sexually active man; but the idea that he was bedding a twenty-six-year-old woman seems far-fetched—except for a man with Burr's reputation.[111]

And who was the other woman? She was a bookkeeper with a passion for filibustering that matched Burr's. Her father was a land agent for Samuel Swartwout, Burr's adventure-bound friend from his days as a candidate for governor, who carried messages for Burr the filibusterer. The McManus clan had devised a scheme to settle German immigrants in Texas, a plan not unlike what Burr had tried with the German Company in Canada in the 1790s. Burr was impressed with Jane McManus's courage and daring; he wrote to her in 1832 that her "enterprise has something of the air of Romance and Quixotteism." These words were not meant to deter her, however. He told her to keep a journal of everything that happened, and he gave her a bit of history besides. There had been another young woman who, in 1785, established a colony on Seneca Lake, 100 miles from the nearest white settlement. The colony flourished, she became wealthy, and, as Burr explained, it had since become "a monument of her intelligence her courage and her discretion." But at the same time, he told McManus to be careful, for the woman in question had become mildly despotic (his words) in directing an enterprise of this kind. He hoped that McManus would "do better!"[112]

Jane McManus was no fool, nor was she a prostitute. She had valid reasons for visiting Burr: she needed a letter of introduction, which he provided. He wrote to Judge Workman, a supporter of Mexican liberation whom Burr knew from his time in New Orleans—a letter that reveals the real nature of his relationship with the young female adventurer. Burr told Workman that he had been friendly with McManus's father, giving him advice on where to buy land in Texas. McManus was not a woman interested in "gallantry," he explained. "She is a woman of business." He praised her for her judgment and discernment, "a talent peculiar to her sex," and claimed that she possessed something "more rare" among women: "courage, stability and perseverance." For such a woman to be throwing herself at an old man—and others signed affidavits during the divorce proceedings attesting to the fact that she was at Burr's home all hours of the night—was to risk a reputation that she cared about deeply. It seems unlikely that she would trade sexual favors for a pair of shoes, or a side-saddle, as Mariah Johnson testified. McManus was named by Jumel as a correspondent because as the divorce proceedings began, she was in New Orleans and unavailable to defend herself.[113]

Burr finally relented, agreeing not to contest the divorce. But he did not admit to the charges. He also refused to pay any alimony. Therefore, this divorce could hardly have been about anything other than money and power; sex was immaterial. Jumel had charged in the bill that Burr was attempting to defraud her of property, rents, and profits, and pay off his debts, "without her consent." Burr countered that he did nothing without her approval, and that he had left her home simply to escape her "violent and ferocious temper" and her "abusive and insulting conduct" toward him, which she persisted in even when he was in "low health." To suggest that Burr was stripping her of her fortune, or foolishly wasting her money by making bad deals, was merely the gossip that Jumel spread about him. It is more likely that "Madame of the Heights," as Burr called her, was unwilling to surrender any piece of her authority as a woman of business. She expected him to play the consort, and when he challenged an opinion, she became abusive and ill-tempered.[114]

When the Chancery Court finally ruled on the case, it approved of the divorce. Burr was not at all pleased and made one last attempt to refute the ruling. He noted that the evidence presented (i.e., the sexually related charge) was "inconsistent" and full of contradictions, and that because of his "great age . . . being nearly of the age of about 80 years," what she accused him of was "according to the law of nature impossible." He was no prude, of course; he had been open about his sex life with his daughter. He had adopted several children, among whom may have been his biological children, or they could have just as easily been orphans he took in. In preparing his will in 1835 (amid the divorce proceedings), he recognized as heirs two daughters, Frances Ann, age six, and Elizabeth, age two. If he had been adulterous, he surely would have acknowledged the facts. In this case, though, he simply refused to be bullied. Jane McManus felt the same way and saw to it that the state of New York indicted Mariah Johnson for perjury.[115]

He died, as it happened, on the day of the final divorce decree, September 14, 1836. Months earlier, he had suffered a major stroke, which paralyzed his legs. Indeed, during those last two years, under the cloud of Madame Jumel's divorce action, he showed signs of decline. He lived for a time in a Manhattan boardinghouse, and in 1836 was moved to another, on Staten Island, so that he could be close to his Edwards cousins. As a divorced man, Aaron Burr was not to receive justice. He did not live to see his name cleared.[116]

Burr got justice in one sense. He outlived all of those who attacked and defeated his political chances—Hamilton, Jefferson, DeWitt Clinton, William Wirt, even James Cheetham. Returning to New York, where his career began, he lived out his life as a successful attorney. He was not alone in his last years, or even in his last days; but in the larger sense this astute political thinker and strategist had long since disappeared from the political scene, if not the social register as well. He remained, perhaps, a curiosity, but he never again influenced national affairs. His time was a hallowed time in the minds of those who led the government of the United States in the mid-1830s, for they looked back on the old revolutionaries, sentimentally, as a superior breed. Yet Aaron Burr would only live on through his contested legacy, over which he exercised no control.

Epilogue:
HE USED NO UNNECESSARY WORDS

*A*aron Burr, Jr., was buried where his signs of promise were first displayed, at Princeton, beside his greatly respected father, Aaron Burr, Sr., a former president of that university. As a youth at Princeton, Burr had exhibited many of the characteristics that would attach to him in later years: he was cool, adroit, and confident. Certainly there was nothing in his background to suggest that he would be vilified in history as a plotter and a murderer.

In these pages, no attempt has been made to excuse anything that Burr did, but rather to clarify the conduct of politics in the early republic. In that sense, he was no better, no worse, than those with whom his name is most commonly linked, Alexander Hamilton and Thomas Jefferson. In moral terms, it is arguable that he behaved with greater honesty and directness than they did—something that is often overlooked in such comparisons. Hamilton and Jefferson were notable as statesmen, but their treatment of Burr as a rival shows unmistakably that they felt threatened by him; not by any discernible immorality, as they pretended, but by his potential popularity, detrimental to their ambition. Politics, then as now, causes "great" men to speak irrationally and act deviously.

Hamilton and Jefferson have always had their defenders. Burr did not have a protective posterity to project his "greatness" through the ages. Many of his personal records went down with the *Patriot* when Theodosia drowned. So the historical record is incomplete. Jefferson's writings presently occupy thirty-three modern volumes (in a project that commenced in 1950), and are still being compiled and edited, down to the last detail. Hamilton's writings are contained in twenty-seven published volumes. Burr's in two. Historians, as a result, have found Burr to be a man of mystery, and many (nearly all) have insisted that he had no political philosophy to compare with, or rank alongside, Jefferson, Hamilton, and the other traditional "founding fathers."[1]

The record clearly shows that this assumption is ridiculous. Minimizing Burr's achievements, or the quality of his mind, merely reminds us how imperfect historical memory is. Burr not only possessed political genius, he was a popular organizer and active thinker, a busy legislator, and a man of progressive ideas. But he was also a man of his time, which meant that his financial speculation was what we would call unsound. Both Hamilton and Jefferson, with all their advantages, died in debt, leaving their families to fend for themselves. This is the light in which we must view Burr's filibustering activity as well. Filibustering does not comport with modern mythology about the founders, and so his efforts are too easily dismissed as signs of unpredictable behavior. Too little attention is paid to the passion for territorial expansion. From the time of the American Revolution, political leaders embraced conquest, generally under the guise of liberating the colonial possessions of Canada, Louisiana, and Mexico. Burr's thinking on the West was little different from Hamilton's, Jefferson's, or Madison's. To ignore the western ambitions of the founders is an ahistorical reading of Burr's world, where efforts to expand the size of the nation were widely endorsed by many Americans.

One who knew him after his star had faded, after he had returned to the practice of law in New York, spoke of Burr with authority. He was John Greenwood, Burr's law clerk from 1814 to 1820, speaking as a judge in 1863. He knew Aaron Burr as a man who could never be idle, a man who rose early and worked conscientiously through the day and often into the evening; a man of "courtly" manners, but equally adept as a storyteller, with few unpleasant memories (or so it appeared); a man who possessed an infectious laugh and who would "go any length to serve a friend." He knew Burr, too, for his personal habits: as a constant cigar smoker, for instance— he had extra long cigars made especially for him. He credited Burr for his "quick, penetrating, and discerning" mind, which the smoke that swirled about him did not cloud.

Burr, he said, did not speak of Hamilton. He did not try to justify himself in this or any other matter deriving from his years in the political limelight. He was frequently noticed, and sometimes accosted, and though he knew he was spoken ill of, he withstood it all without ever flinching. Similarly, as a courtroom performer, Aaron Burr was not loud or demonstrative, but thorough and effective. He could not be cowed by another attorney; he was "never submissive, and he used no unnecessary words." Greenwood was impressed by this—by Burr's extraordinary self-possession—in that "under the most trying circumstances . . . he probably never knew what it was to fear a human being."[2]

It is hard to match this characterization. When we speak of Thomas Jefferson, we automatically recur to such texts as the Declaration of Independence. For Jefferson's fame resides in his ability to persuade, or inspire, with his pen. But Jefferson, though he had a rich legal mind, was not a noteworthy courtroom attorney; there he found no inspirational message. In most of his letters and all of his public texts, he made multiple drafts before thoughtfully releasing them to public scrutiny. Alexander Hamilton, whose passions and intelligence were equally in evidence, lost control of words all too often—even his staunch defenders have acknowledged this as a decided weakness.

In the case of Aaron Burr, however, Greenwood captures a critical facet of the politician as well as the attorney, when he states that "he used no unnecessary words." He did not go public, as Hamilton did, attempting to defend himself from attack by spilling words in the newspapers or in self-serving pamphlets. He did not write a partisan history, as Jefferson attempted, though unsuccessfully, by repeatedly soliciting sympathetic political writers during and after his presidency. Burr's chief talent—indeed, one reason why he might have made a highly effective, distinctly moderate national executive in a time of political passions—was his clarity of purpose, as expressed in rational, dispassionate words. Though for 200 years he has been accused of fomenting disorder, his actual restraint with language is the Burr missing from modern historical narratives.

"THE ODD MAN OUT"

Incredibly, much of the image of Burr that we know today is taken from rhetorical attacks of enemies and fiction. For those who hated him, Burr was a satanic figure, the fallen angel, narcissistically driven by ambition, inherently evil and congenitally cursed. The Federalists were the first to compare Burr to Satan, but it was William Wirt who gave literary force to this notion in his famous oration during the 1807 treason trial, painting Burr as the foul fiend who despoiled Blennerhassett's Eden. A devilish Burr reappeared in the first drama about his treasonous plot, *The Conspiracy; or the Western Island* (1838), and it made numerous curtain calls, the most famous being the 1931 Broadway rendition of Booth Tarkington's *Colonel Satan, or a Night in the Life of Aaron Burr.* A twist on the same concept came in Gertrude Atherton's novel *The Conqueror* (1902), a fictional biography of Hamilton which supplies the damning indictment of Burr. As a kind of Dorian Gray, Burr was corrupted by what Atherton called "congenital selfishness," and his evil so chillingly cold and glacial in scale that he could be seen as the visible part of a "dazzling and symmetrical" iceberg, "its deadly bulk skulking below the surface." Acknowledging Burr's allure among susceptible women, Atherton noted that he was "handsome, magnetic, well-bred, and polished." But like Lucifer or the "Great Imposter" (and as a possible precursor to the infamous Jack the Ripper), Burr knew how to adopt a gentlemanly pose that concealed a monster's desire. Again in Atherton's words, he "studied women with the precision of a vivisectionist." As late as 1955, in *Aaron Burr's Dream for the Southwest,* playwright Thomas Sweeney could still imagine Burr as a hypersexualized and insane genius (with twenty or more bastard children), a weird blend of Dr. Frankenstein and Hugh Hefner.[3]

In the hundreds of stories told about Burr after his death, writers vary as to whether they admire or despise him, but there is one point they generally agree on: He was a man capable of conquering and ravishing men as well as women. Lest the inference be misconstrued, to be ravished is to be enchanted—hypnotically entranced and brought into a state of submission before the object of affection. Virtually every account of Burr's life describes a man of unquenchable desires: for power over men, and for the hearts of women.

Ron Chernow's *Alexander Hamilton* (2004) continues in this tradition, calling Burr an assassin ("He shot to kill"), despite an abundance of contrary historical evidence. Chernow invents a remorseless Burr, casually bedding his mistress nine days after Hamilton's demise. He claims that

Burr was "such a dissipated, libidinous character" that whatever Hamilton might have said to provoke the duel was justifiable. Of course, it should now be clear that Hamilton was not one degree less libidinous than Burr, should such things matter to history.[4]

Even for those novelists who did not conceive of Burr as demonic, many still imagined him as a man of unhealthy drives, of relentless ambition, a man who was ruled by his body instead of his mind. In his two-volume novel based on Burr, *Burton: or, The Sieges* (1838), the Reverend Joseph Holt Ingraham explained the origin of his subject's conspiracy-driven downfall. As the rake turned traitor, Burr's early debaucheries prefigured his later grand scheme; his conquests on the "sofa" were merely a rehearsal for his imperial ambitions against a supine West. Such early accounts are not surprising, for at the time of his death, Burr was known as the nation's most successful "ladies' man"; the publication (also in 1838) of his private journal provided information about his sexual life that his well-protected peers did not have to submit to posthumously.[5]

The theme of enchantment and seduction was also applied to Burr's relationship with his daughter, which for many fictional writers amounted to his greatest obsession. Some writers actually blamed Theodosia for his fall from grace. In *Famous Belles of the Nineteenth Century* (1901), Virginia Peacock claimed that the moment Theodosia was married to Joseph Alston— and thus no longer the sole admirer of Burr—"the retrogressive period of Burr's life began." In *The Magnificent Adventure* (1916), Emerson Hough fashioned Burr into a pimp by persuading his daughter to seduce Meriwether Lewis and foil the Lewis and Clark expedition. Others claimed that a "consuming love" for his daughter lured Burr into that "wild and dazzling dream of a Mexican empire." In *My Theodosia* (1941), Anya Seton hinted at incest, but stopped short of making the claim outright. Gore Vidal's best-selling *Burr* (1973) implied that incest was the motive for the famous duel with Hamilton. Burr issued his challenge because Hamilton had spread malicious lies about the father and daughter's unnatural love.[6]

Sexual rivalry, born of jealousy, is another stock theme in the posthumous career of Aaron Burr. It forms the basis of Jerome Dowd's 1884 play, *Burr and Hamilton: A New York Tragedy*. Yet the most humorous portrayal of rivalry and jealousy among the founders has to be Charles Nirdlinger's play *The First Lady of the Land* (1914). In a story ostensibly about Dolley

Payne Todd prior to her marriage to James Madison, Nirdlinger gives Burr top billing among her suitors, and highlights his wit and debonair style. Here the reticent Madison fears losing his future wife to the irresistible Burr. Jefferson, whose character never appears on stage, is constantly running to play his fiddle in order to hide his fear of Burr and women.[7]

Modern popularizers have responded to this old theme of sexual competition, adding a heavy dose of psychological jargon. In his *Burr, Hamilton, and Jefferson: A Study in Character* (1999), former Nixon appointee to the National Parks Service Roger Kennedy contends that Hamilton was Burr's "fatal twin," a variation on the Cain and Abel parable, or Romulus and Remus, who were actual twins. Consumed with envy, his Hamilton is a suicidal masochist: "He arranged to have Burr kill him," writes Kennedy. Similarly, Arnold Rogow's *A Fatal Friendship: Alexander Hamilton and Aaron Burr* (1998) reduces the duel to Hamilton's maladjusted personality and flawed "character structure." As in Kennedy's vision, the duelists are mirror images of each other. But for Rogow, Hamilton's death wish is rooted in his denial of an "underlying homoerotic" attraction to Burr. Hamilton's inner demons (in this case, his gay identity) consume him.[8]

All of these themes can be traced back to the 1790s and 1800s. As early as 1795, Federalists attacked Burr as a man overwrought with jealousy over Hamilton's fame and success. The sexually specific identification of Burr with the Roman pervert Cataline was first used by Hamilton, then by the editor James Cheetham, and eventually by Jefferson; this seemed to be a convenient means of portraying Burr as a man driven by passions—ruled by his body. Recall that the Roman general had a reputation that included slaughtering his son, wife, and brother, and sleeping with young men, his sister, and daughter. This is also why Gore Vidal's hunch that incest led to the Burr-Hamilton duel was not pure invention. It was already a part of the gossip Hamilton had circulated against Burr.

But even the aggressively masculine image of Burr—whether as a satanic or a libertine predator—does not encompass the range of his sexualization. Fiction writers have as easily gravitated to the inverse image of the dandy/dilettante. In 1901, in *A Dream of Empire of the House of Blennerhassett,* William Henry Venable had Burr playing the fop. As a "Brummel[l] of exterior properties," he was satirized for his meticulous attention to dress, his polished boots, and his (implicitly feminized) clean-shaven face. By this time, Brummell, too, had become a caricature, no longer invoking the masculine ideals of restraint and audacity so admired in the early nineteenth century. This dandified Burr exudes sexuality from every pore. He is not simply a ladies' man but a sexual hybrid, especially alluring to young boys. The celebrated southern writer Eudora Welty captured this theme in her story "First Love" (1943). It is told from the perspective of a young deaf boy who, upon seeing Burr for the first time, cannot but react in sexual terms— he says he feels ravished. As the boy watches the crowd at Burr's trial in Mississippi, the courtroom becomes a stage: Burr is a dazzling orator, a man of gestures, the embodiment of sexual energy.[9]

Of course, when Federalists attacked Burr as a man of surfaces, they intended only a slur against the Burrite party by uncovering his allure among young men. When Burr ran for governor in 1804, these Burrite "boys," dandies and "strolling players," were likened to male prostitutes. This is not to say that Burr was not fascinating; he was. But he was also frank and reasonable. The objectification of Aaron Burr instructs us that politics in the early republic was a highly personalized competition. Performances mattered. The classic showdown between Burr and Wilkinson during the treason trial was infused with competing ideals of masculine behavior.

In that year of 1807, an anonymous Federalist writer captured this problem perfectly. In his "Portrait of Burr," he claimed that there was "no human creature more reserved, mysterious, and inscrutable"—echoing what Cheetham had written. Recall again that the unprincipled editor had contended that no proof was necessary to show that Burr had tried to steal the 1800 election from Jefferson because, as a rule, Burr wrapped his every action in mystery. Many historians have followed this rule of thumb, arguing that circumstantial evidence is proof enough to assert Burr's backroom dealing over the winter months of 1800–01. In the 1807 "Portrait," the Federalist writer also described Burr as the "epitome" of "Chesterfield and the graces." To the ladies, he is "all attention . . . he gazes on them with complacency and rapture"; he displays "those captivating gestures . . . those dissolving looks, that soft, sweet, and insinuating eloquence, which takes the soul captive before it can prepare for defence." Burr was "exemplary, an illustrious instance of the capriciousness of popular admiration." He was all show and no substance. He had a feminine allure, soft and sweet—a "proteus" indeed, who could sexually transform himself while in the company of his male and female admirers.[10]

We may not understand this language as particularly insulting, or possessing the power to intimidate, dismiss, or castigate as much as the overt sexual slurs related above. But, in fact, Burr's contemporaries read the Chesterfieldian caricature as the deepest cut in a man's reputation, and fatal to his public career. It convicted Burr of emptiness, of being all smoke and mirrors. This is another critical caricature that still finds its way into modern historical prose, justifying the position that Burr was a man without ideas—a faux founder at best. Calling him an "enigma" is another way to reduce him to a trivial mystery or a pale riddle. His insignificance is a given. He may be used to add color to the founders' story; he may be introduced as a diversion within the larger story. That is precisely what has happened.

The consensus among historians seems to be that Burr was never at the center of any "real" political activity except as an operative, a man who was skilled in a certain kind of strategy but who was otherwise devoid of ideas or beliefs. Hamilton's self-serving charge that Burr lacked principle, combined with the political satire and lurid fiction that painted him and his supporters as dandified politicians, has actually taken the place of real historical scholarship. Joseph Ellis sums up the consensus view in his *Founding Brothers* (2000): "And Burr, if I have him right, is the odd man out with the elite of the early republic, a colorful and intriguing character to be sure, but a man whose definition of character does not measure up to the standard."[11]

But we now know that Burr was more than a colorful character. And he was at least equal to the "standard" among the founding elite. His distorted life story shows, too, that sexuality was part of the political vocabulary of the founders. Historians have long since fallen prey to the trap of conflating Burr's real sexual behavior with the political attacks of his enemies. They have allowed a two-dimensional portrait of Burr to serve as a foil, and have used him merely to lift up the character of other founders.

The facts are indisputable: Aaron Burr was at the center of nation building and was a capable leader in New York political circles at a crucial period. Burr's life was not only about sex; and yet sexuality was the stuff of politics. One need only read Hamilton's constitutional theory in *Federalist No. 6* to discover how readily sexual corruption (i.e., seductive women) could be equated with disunion. And Hamilton wrote these words long before he saw Burr as a threat to his political party or his personal ambitions. If one reads the newspapers, rather than simply relying on the published papers of prominent founders (Hamilton, Jefferson, and Adams), it soon becomes clear that sexual satire pervaded politics. The sexualization of Aaron Burr was a means for his opponents to increase their political capital, because the vocabulary to do so was already a part of the political scene—not because of Burr's particular shortcomings.[12]

Burr was, in fact, the "odd man out," but not because he lacked character. He was odd because he was the only founder to embrace feminism. He was one who truly believed and adhered to the ideal that reason should transcend party differences. He was unique in that he refused to slander his political enemies behind their backs. He displayed an insatiable intellectual curiosity and read widely; his faith in Utilitarianism made him remarkably modern in imagining daring possibilities for social and political change. He consistently embraced an inclusive definition of democracy, defending freedom of speech, promoting the expansion of suffrage and economic rights to the middling classes, and battling prejudice against aliens, free blacks, petty criminals, and women. His moving words (in opposition to a law to disenfranchise aliens) before the New York Assembly in 1799 are worth repeating, for they remind us of his idealism:

> *America stood with open arms and presented an assylum to the oppressed of every nation; we invited them with the promise of enjoying equal rights with ourselves, and presented them with the flattering prospect of presiding in our councils and arriving at honour and trust; shall we deprive these persons of an important right derived from so sacred a source as our constitution[?][13]*

The evidence shows that as a proponent of equal rights, there was no one among the founders any more enthusiastic—any more genuine—than Burr.

Aaron Burr's life represents the antidote to lazy history. His experiences, his mistakes, and his radical insights combine to give us a better picture of the political culture that defined his generation. To conceive of

Washington, Adams, Jefferson, and their ilk as they were on their best day is to compress the life of any modern president into the most memorable line in an inaugural address that someone else wrote for him. The founders were far more numerous than popular history suggests, and far less righteous and dignified. The historic memory does not hold much history. That is why Burr, the fallen founder, is more representative than one might otherwise imagine.

The founders contributed wisdom and often exhibited courage. But to remove them from political time as if they were ever, on a single day, holy men or paragons of virtue misses their true vocation and their true motivation. They did not live inside an impossibly romantic political forum where great minds communed on a regular basis to remind each other of their noblest ideals. They did not spend the bulk of their time sitting at their desks writing treatises, or standing before their congressional peers making sublime speeches. The lawyers among them were more typically engrossed in the ugly details of a property case, or in a dogged debate inside a courtroom; the many speculators among them mulled over the looming threat of debtor's prison. They spent their time engaged in the polite banter of the tea parlor, and indulged in secret sexual trysts with prostitutes, mistresses, and, in the South, slaves.

These were our founders: imperfect men in a less than perfect nation, grasping at opportunities. That they did good for their country is understood, and worth our celebration; that they were also jealous, resentful, self-protective, and covetous politicians should be no less a part of their collective biography. What separates history from myth is that history takes in the whole picture, whereas myth averts our eyes from the truth when it turns men into heroes and gods.

NOTES

PREFACE

1. Two books demonstrate Burr's unparalleled role in popular literature. Samuel H. Wandell, *Aaron Burr in Literature* (London, 1936); and Charles J. Nolan, Jr., *Aaron Burr and the American Literary Imagination* (Westport, Conn., 1980); and for pornography featuring Burr, see *The Amorous Intrigues and Adventures of Aaron Burr* (New York, 1861). Some extremely talented writers (Harriet Beecher Stowe, Eudora Welty, and Gore Vidal) have made Burr into a fictional subject, in part because of Burr's controversial legacy.

2. To be clear, Mary-Jo Kline as editor of *Political Correspondence and Public Papers of Aaron Burr,* 2 vols. (Princeton, N.J., 1983) (cited hereafter as *Burr Papers*), has performed a tremendous service for scholars in compiling and annotating Burr's key political texts. But Kline's edited volumes did not address his personal life or try to offer a complete picture of Burr as a historical figure. Refusing to do the research, modern historians have routinely failed to examine Burr's papers on microfilm (27 reels), and many have ignored, or paid scant attention to, Kline's edited volumes.

3. Treatments of Burr tend to see him as either a tragic figure or evil incarnate. Most biographers, even those sympathetic to their subject, portray him as a man without a political philosophy. Burr has been cast as an opportunist, or as a man who was somewhat mentally unstable. His political mistakes have been explained as a result of his almost childlike naïveté about political enemies. And his most recent biographer, Milton Lomask, has repeated the common portrait of him as Chesterfieldian gentleman, with a need to be constantly entertained. Others see him as harmless but insubstantial. Many later studies rely on James Parton, whose 1857 biography (and later editions) are filled with inaccuracies and unsubstantiated half-truths. See Parton, *The Life and Times of*

Aaron Burr, 2 vols. (Boston and New York, 1892); Samuel Wandell and Meade Minnigerode, *Aaron Burr: A Biography compiled from rare, and in many cases unpublished, sources,* 2 vols. (New York, 1925); Nathan Schachner, *Aaron Burr: A Biography* (New York, 1937); Herbert S. Parmet and Marie B. Hecht, *Aaron Burr: Portrait of an Ambitious Man* (New York, 1967); and Milton Lomask, *Aaron Burr: The Years from Princeton to Vice President, 1756–1805* (New York, 1979) and *Aaron Burr: The Conspiracy and Years of Exile, 1805–1836* (New York, 1982).

CHAPTER ONE

1. Philip Schuyler to Alexander Hamilton, Jan. 29, 1792, in Harold Syrett, ed., *The Papers of Alexander Hamilton,* 27 vols. (New York, 1961–87), X: 579–81.
2. See Eleanor Pearson DeLorme, "Gilbert Stuart: Portrait of an Artist," *Winterthur Portfolio* 14 (1979): 339–60; and Richard McLanathan, *Gilbert Stuart: The Father of American Portraiture* (New York, 1986), 49, 63, 78–79.
3. Jay Fliegelman, *Prodigals and Pilgrims: The American Revolution Against Patriarchal Authority, 1750–1800* (New York, 1982), 208.
4. Matthew L. Davis, ed., *Memoirs of Aaron Burr,* 2 vols. (New York, 1836), I: 25–26.
5. See "To all Independent Electors," *The Corrector,* April 26, 1804.
6. Carol F. Karlsen and Laurie Crumpacker, eds., *The Journal of Esther Edwards Burr, 1754–1757* (New Haven, 1784), 188.
7. Suzanne Geissler, *Jonathan Edwards to Aaron Burr, Jr: From the Great Awakening to Democratic Politics* (New York, 1981), 20, 28, 37, 58–60.
8. *Ibid.,* 85–86.
9. *Ibid.,* 87–89, 90; Karlsen and Crumpacker, eds., *The Journal of Esther Edwards Burr,* 257.
10. Burr's sister was named after Esther's mother, Sarah, but was called Sally. In another entry, she described "Little Aaron" as a "fine quiet child." See *ibid.,* 198, 247.
11. *Ibid.,* 228–29.
12. Geissler, *Jonathan Edwards to Aaron Burr,* 95–97, 101; Karlsen and Crumpacker, eds., *The Journal of Esther Edwards,* 295.
13. Aaron Burr (hereafter AB) to Theodosia Burr, January 4, 1799, in Mark Van Doren, ed., *Correspondence of Aaron Burr and his Daughter Theodosia* (New York, 1929), 46–47.
14. Geissler, *Jonathan Edwards to Aaron Burr,* 97, 101–02; and William H. Edwards, *Timothy and Rhoda Ogden Edwards of Stockbridge, Mass., and Their Descendants: A Genealogy* (Cincinnati, 1903), 20.
15. Davis, ed., *Memoirs of Aaron Burr,* I: 26; Schachner, *Aaron Burr,* 20; Parton, *Life and Times of Aaron Burr,* I: 53.
16. Geissler, *Jonathan Edwards to Aaron Burr,* 54, 59, 86, 94.

17. *Ibid.*, 99, 102, 104.

18. Gordon Wood, *The Radicalism of the American Revolution* (New York, 1992), 17, 22.

19. Geissler, *Jonathan Edwards to Aaron Burr,* 15–16, 98–99.

20. *Ibid.*, 101, 103; Edwards, *Timothy and Rhoda Ogden Edwards,* 20.

21. Carl E. Prince, Mary Lou Lustig, and David William Voorhees, eds., *The Papers of William Livingston, Vol. 5: April 1783–August 1790* (New Brunswick, N.J., 1988), V: 562, 589; Maxine N. Lurie, "New Jersey Intellectuals and the United States Constitution," *Journal of Rutgers University Library* 49 (1987): 66–67; Geissler, *Jonathan Edwards to Aaron Burr,* 54–57.

22. Edwards, *Timothy and Rhoda Ogden Edwards,* 18; Prince et al., eds., *The Papers of William Livingston,* V: 570, 572–73; see also Princeton Undergraduate Alumni Index, 1773.

23. Walter R. Fee, *The Transition from Aristocracy to Democracy in New Jersey, 1789–1829* (Somerville, N.J., 1933), 9; Prince et al., eds., *The Papers of William Livingston,* V: 510–11, 537; Kline, ed., *Burr Papers,* I: 487–88, 490.

24. Nathan Schachner, *Alexander Hamilton* (New York, 1946), 28–30.

25. Davis, ed., *Memoirs of Aaron Burr,* I: 26–27; and Sheldon S. Cohen and Larry R. Gerlach, "Princeton in the Coming of the American Revolution," *New Jersey History* 92 (1974): 71.

26. Thomas Jefferson Wertenbaker, *Princeton, 1746–1896* (Princeton, N.J., 1946), 106–07; Paul Wallace, *Princeton Sketches, the Story of Nassau Hall* (New York, 1893), 5–8; Frances L. Broderick, "Pulpit, Physics, and Politics: The Curriculum of the College of New Jersey, 1746–1794," *William and Mary Quarterly* 6 (January 1949): 43, 62.

27. Mark A. Noll, *Princeton and the Republic, 1768–1822: The Search for a Christian Enlightenment in the Era of Samuel Stanhope Smith* (Princeton, N.J., 1989), 28; Ashbel Green, *The Life of the Revd John Witherspoon, D.D., LL.D. with a brief review of his writings; and a summary estimate of his character and talents,* ed. Henry Littleton Savage (Princeton, N.J., 1973), 146–47, 258.

28. See L. Gordon Tait, "John Witherspoon as Sage: 'The Druid Essays of 1776,'" *New Jersey History* 100 (1982): 35; Edward S. Fody, "John Witherspoon: Advisor to the Lovelorn," *Proceedings of the New Jersey Historical Society* 84 (1966): 239–49; Noll, *Princeton and the Republic,* 52; Green, *The Life of Revd John Witherspoon,* 266. Witherspoon rejected the argument that piety and politeness were opposed; see Christopher Castiglia, "Pedagogical Discipline and the Creation of White Citizenship: John Witherspoon, Robert Finley, and the Colonization Society," *Early American Literature* 33 (1998): 199.

29. Broderick, "Pulpit, Physics, and Politics," 61.

30. *Ibid.*, 61–62. The policy of opening the stacks to all students except freshmen preceded Witherspoon. John Davies (president of the college from 1759 to 1761) made the case that "if they have books always in hand to consult upon

every subject," both students and faculty would engage in "a more thoro' discussion, in their public Disputes, in the Course of their Private Studies, in Conversation," and this "will enable them to investigate TRUTH thro' her intricate Recesses" and to "guard against the Strategems and Assaults of Error." See David W. Robson, *Educating Republicans: The College in the Era of the American Revolution, 1750–1800* (Westport, Conn., 1985), 66–67.

31. *Philip Vickers Fithian: Journal and Letters, 1767–1774,* ed. John Rogers Williams (Princeton, N.J., 1900), 256–57.

32. See James McLachlan, "The *Choice of Hercules*: American Student Societies in the Early 19th Century," in Lawrence Stone, ed., *The University in Society* (Princeton, N.J., 1974), II: 472; Leon Jackson, "The Rights of Man and the Rites of Youth: Fraternity and Riot at Eighteenth-Century Harvard," *History Higher Education Annual* (1995): 30, 32; Wallace J. Williamson III, *The Halls: A Brief History of the American Whig-Cliosophic Society of Princeton University* (Princeton, N.J., 1947), 6–8.

33. Burr's classmates included many destined for prominent political careers: James Madison was elected fourth president of the United States; Paterson and Oliver Ellsworth were both appointed to the U.S. Supreme Court; Reeve was elevated to chief justice of the Connecticut Supreme Court; nine graduates attended the Constitutional Convention; Hugh Henry Brackenridge and Philip Freneau became newspaper editors and nationally renowned poets; William Bradford was U.S. attorney general under Washington; and Brackenridge was elected to the Pennsylvania state legislature and appointed to a judgeship in the Pennsylvania Supreme Court. For the importance of secret confidences, see Jackson, "The Rights of Man and the Rites of Youth," 35; also see *Philip Vickers Fithian,* 257.

34. Davis, ed., *Memoirs of Aaron Burr,* I: 41.

35. Williamson, *The Halls,* 10.

36. Moses Allen to AB, Jan. 23, 1772, Burr Papers, microfilm, reel 1.

37. Jackson, "The Rights of Man and the Rites of Youth," 32; Paul Clarkson and R. Samuel Jett, *Luther Martin of Maryland* (Baltimore, 1970), 16; John E. O'Connor, *William Paterson: Lawyer and Statesman, 1745–1806* (New Brunswick, N.J., 1979), 23.

38. Paterson wrote with a touch of irony to Burr: "forbear with me whilst I say, *that you cannot speak too slow*"—William Paterson to AB, Jan. 17, 1772; for his handwriting, see William Paterson to AB, Oct. 26, 1772, Burr Papers, microfilm, reel 1.

39. William Paterson to AB, Oct. 26, 1772; see also Andrew Burstein, *The Inner Jefferson: Portrait of a Grieving Optimist* (Charlottesville, Va., 1995), 46; and Frank Brady, "Tristram Shandy: Sexuality, Morality, and Sensibility," *Eighteenth-Century Studies* 4 (Autumn 1970): 44.

40. Burr, "On Honor" [ca. 1772], Burr Papers, microfilm, reel 1; the original of this essay is available in Special Collections and Rare Books, Princeton Library,

Princeton, N.J. (quotes are from the original). Paterson routinely lent his compositions to other students. This practice was not seen as unethical: the goal of education was to acquire a mastery of the material and gain a command of the language, not to display originality—which was a nineteenth-century romantic ideal. John O'Connor argues that Paterson lent his compositions to curry favor with men from important families. See W. Jay Mills, ed., *Glimpses of Colonial Society and the Life at Princeton College, 1766–1773* (Philadelphia, 1903), 18, 139; and O'Connor, *William Paterson*, 15, 22.

41. "On Honor."
42. Princeton was "the premier Patriot college." From Witherspoon's classes, half of the students fought in the war, and a small number (two of 178) identified themselves as Loyalists; forty-one of this distinguished group went on to hold prominent political posts in state and national governments. See Robson, *Educating Republicans*, 69–70.
43. Davis, ed., *Memoirs of Aaron Burr*, I: 40.
44. Rush paraphrases one of the maxims of the seventeenth-century French statesman Cardinal Richelieu: "That an unfortunate and an imprudent person were synonymous terms." See Benjamin Rush to John Adams, Apr. 3, 1807, in John A. Schutz and Douglass Adair, eds., *The Spur of Fame: Dialogues of John Adams and Benjamin Rush, 1805–1813* (San Marino, Calif., 1980), 77.

CHAPTER TWO

1. For the identification of Matthias Ogden, see the *Key* that was sold with the engraving, published in 1798, in John Hill Morgan, ed., *Paintings by John Trumbull at Yale University of Historic Scenes and Personages Prominent in the American Revolution* (New Haven, Conn., 1926), 32–33. Ogden was wounded at the time Montgomery led the surprise attack on Quebec. See "Journal of Isaac Senter," in Kenneth Roberts, ed., *March to Quebec* (New York, 1938), 233–34.
2. Hugh Henry Brackenridge, "The Death of General Montgomery, in Storming the City of Quebec. A Tragedy" (Norwich, Conn., 1777), 15, 38; see also Ginger Strand, "The Many Deaths of Montgomery: Audience and Pamphlet Plays of the Revolution," *American Literary History* 9 (1997): 14–15.
3. Brackenridge, "The Death of General Montgomery," 16, 34–36.
4. For a description of Congress's Report on the Memorial for General Montgomery, issued on Jan. 25, 1776, and the earlier discussion on Jan. 18 in which Burr was favorably singled out, see Edmund C. Burnett, ed., *Letters of Members of the Continental Congress* (Washington, D.C., 1921), I: 318, 328; Benedict Arnold to General Wooster, Dec. 31, 1775, in Roberts, ed., *March to Quebec*, 103; and William Bradford, Jr., to AB, Jan. 24, 1776, in Davis, ed., *Memoirs of Aaron Burr*, I: 75.

5. Charles Royster, *A Revolutionary People at War: The Continental Army and American Character, 1775–1783* (Chapel Hill, N.C., 1979), 25, 188; John F. Ferling, *The First of Men: A Life of George Washington* (Knoxville, Tenn., 1988), 177–78, 200, 225–37, 250–52.

6. Samuel Spring to AB, May 15, 1772, in Burr Papers, microfilm, reel 1; Geissler, *Jonathan Edwards to Aaron Burr,* 111–13; Timothy Edwards to AB, Feb. 11, 1774, in Davis, ed., *Memoirs of Aaron Burr,* I: 46.

7. Davis, ed., *Memoirs of Aaron Burr,* I: 58; Geissler, *Jonathan Edwards to Aaron Burr,* 134–36; Lomask, *Aaron Burr: The Years from Princeton to Vice President,* 37.

8. See John Hancock to Richard Montgomery, Nov. 30, 1775, in Paul H. Smith, *Letters of Delegates to Congress, 1774–1789* (Washington, D.C., 1976–88), 2: 414–15; and Michael P. Gabriel, *Major Richard Montgomery: The Making of an American Hero* (Madison, N.J., 2002), 12, 72, 85–86, 143, 150, 173–200.

9. See "On Music" [ca. 1772], in Burr Papers, microfilm, reel 1. For an account of the sermon, see Joel T. Headley, *The Chaplains and Clergy of the Revolution* (Springfield, Mass., 1861), 91–92.

10. Though Burr is not mentioned by name as visiting the tomb, he was probably there. Samuel Spring and Burr were close friends from college. His name was probably omitted because Spring and Burr later had a falling out over religious differences. For an account of the visit to Whitefield's tomb and the bad blood between the two men, see Headley, *The Chaplains and Clergy of the Revolution,* 93, 106.

11. Royster, *A Revolutionary People at War,* 24.

12. Peter Colt to AB, Sept. 11, 1775, in Davis, ed., *Memoirs of Aaron Burr,* I: 64; see also the letter from Dr. James Cogswell to AB, Sept. 9, 1775, ibid., 63–64; and from his brother-in-law, Tapping Reeve to AB, Sept. 9, 1775, and AB to Sally Burr Reeve, Sept. 18, 1775, in Burr Papers, microfilm, reel 1.

13. *Journal of Matthias Ogden in Arnold's Campaign Against Quebec* (Morristown, N.J., 1928), 5, 6–7. Ogden's spelling and punctuation have been corrected in this printed version. The original is in possession of the Washington Association of New Jersey. Large portions of the journal are reprinted in Wandell and Minnigerode, *Aaron Burr,* I: 46–50, esp. 48–49.

14. For his reference to Ogden, see Benedict Arnold to Mr. Jos. Terry, Nov. 20, 1775; it is also obvious that Arnold used Ogden as a messenger before Burr— see Benedict Arnold to Messrs. Prince & Haywood, Nov. 20, 1775; and for for his letter of introduction for Burr, see Benedict Arnold to General Montgomery, Nov. 30, 1775, all in Roberts, ed., *March to Quebec,* 94, 101; see also Davis, ed., *Memoirs of Aaron Burr,* I: 66, 69, and Wandell and Meade Minnigerode, *Aaron Burr,* I: 52–53.

15. Gabriel, *Major Richard Montgomery,* 50–54, 56–59, 77.

16. Washington Irving, *The Life of George Washington,* Part I (1855–59), in *The Works of Washington Irving* (New York, 1897), 12: 508; and John Joseph Henry,

An Accurate and Interesting Account of the Hardships and Sufferings of that Band of Heroes, who traversed the Wilderness in the Campaign against Quebec in 1775 (Lancaster, Pa., 1812), 98, 134; for a similar description of Montgomery, see "George Morison's Journal," in Roberts, ed., *March to Quebec,* 534.

17. Gabriel, *Major Richard Montgomery,* 108, 125, 148–49.

18. In a previous letter from Janet Montgomery, she wrote: "Besides, having this opportunity, I would wish to assure Colonel Burr of the very respect I have for those gentlemen whom General Montgomery professed to esteem; among which, sir, I am told you was not the least. To be by him distinguished argues superior merit." See Janet Montgomery to AB, Dec. 25, 1778, and Mar. 7, 1779, in Davis, ed., *Memoirs of Aaron Burr,* I: 139, 169.

19. Gabriel, *Major Richard Montgomery,* 115–16, 140.

20. *Ibid.,* 143.

21. Henry, *Band of Heroes,* 72–73.

22. Mills, ed., *Glimpses of Colonial Society and Life at Princeton,* 22; O'Connor, *William Paterson,* 23, 26; "John MacPherson," in James McLachlan, ed., *Princetonians, 1748–1768* (Princeton, N.J., 1976), I: 574–78. Montgomery's trust in MacPherson is indicated by his decision to have him and Arnold, under a flag of truce, deliver the terms of surrender to the governor of Quebec on Dec. 15. See Gabriel, *Major Richard Montgomery,* 149.

23. Gabriel, *Major Richard Montgomery,* 154, 156–58, 161–63; Davis, ed., *Memoirs of Aaron Burr,* I: 71.

24. According to British sources, thirteen bodies were recovered from that spot. See Gabriel, *Major Richard Montgomery,* 162, 166, 171; and Craig L. Symonds, *A Battlefield Atlas of the American Revolution* (Baltimore, Md., 1986), 23.

25. Donald Campbell to Robert R. Livingston, Mar. 28, 1776, printed transcript, Robert R. Livingston Papers (MG 23 B40), National Archives of Canada. I would like to thank the archivist Sandy Ramos for sending me this document.

26. Everett Somerville Brown, ed., *William Plumer's Memorandum of Proceedings in the United States Senate, 1803–1807* (London, 1923), 612; see also James Thompson's Report, Aug. 16, 1828, in *New Dominion Monthly* 17 (1875): 403; and Gabriel, *Major Richard Montgomery,* 171.

27. Henry places Spring in the hospital—*Band of Heroes,* 116. All biographical studies of Burr have treated Spring's account as factually accurate, without considering the conflicting accounts of the assault. See Wandell and Minnigerode, *Aaron Burr,* I: 55; Schachner, *Aaron Burr,* 42; Lomask, *Aaron Burr: The Years from Princeton to Vice President,* 41; and Geissler, *Jonathan Edwards to Aaron Burr,* 144.

28. See Davis on Trumbull's painting and Colonel Richard Platt to Commodore Valentine Morris, Jan. 27, 1814, in Davis, ed., *Memoirs of Aaron Burr,* I: 71, 177. Platt's 1814 letter was part of the certification supporting Burr's claims for

compensation from New York—see Kline, ed., *Burr Papers,* I: 31, 189, 283–85; II: 194, 1206, 1212–13; see also Henry, *Band of Heroes,* 181. Campbell wrote in his letter: "I could wish not to open the Wounds afresh by entering on the subject, But from the neglect or Design of the Messenger (& others) who was by me Dispatched to Montreal & Congress, in permi[t]ing a false & base insinuation to Appear against me . . . makes it necessary for the Satisfaction of Friends of the Deceased & the Living, to have the Truth & [a] fair State [ment] of that day known." Campbell was clearly interested in telling his version of the story to defend his honor. See Campbell to Livingston, Mar. 28, 1776; and Gabriel, *Major Richard Montgomery,* 241, note 39.

29. Montgomery used the Latin phrase in his letter *Adaces Fortuna jubat.* Gabriel translates this phrase as "fortune favors the courageous," but "audacious" is closer to the original Latin meaning—see Gabriel, *Major Richard Montgomery,* 155, 170. For casualty list, see Roberts, ed., *March to Quebec,* 27–40.

30. Reeve had not initially supported Burr's decision to join the army. See Tapping Reeve to AB, Sept. 9, 1775, in Burr Papers, microfilm, reel 1; and Tapping Reeve to AB, Jan. 27, 1776, in Davis, ed., *Memoirs of Aaron Burr,* I: 75–76. For "Timothy Edwards . . . design of entering the service," see John Pierce to AB, Feb. 11, 1776, and Joseph Bellamy to AB, Aug. 17, 1775, and Mar. 3, 1776, in Burr Papers, microfilm, reel 1.

31. William Bradford to AB, July 30, 1776, and Theodore Sedgwick to AB, Aug. 7, 1776, Burr Papers, microfilm, reel 1. Bellamy expressed a similar desire to join the army in another letter, claiming that along with his other friend, Jimmy Cogswell, "we should form a happy triumvirate"—see Joseph Bellamy to Burr, Aug. 18, 1775, Burr Papers, reel 1. William Bradford (1755–95) was a member of the prominent family of colonial and Revolutionary printers in Philadelphia; he served as attorney general of Pennsylvania, and in 1794, as U.S. attorney general under President Washington. Theodore Sedgwick (1746–1813) attended Yale College, and was admitted to the bar in 1766. He was elected to the Massachusetts State House of Representatives and state senate, served as a member of the Continental Congress, was sent as a delegate to the state convention that adopted the federal Constitution in 1788, and later was elected to Congress, served in the Senate, and was a judge of the Supreme Court of Massachusetts from 1782 to 1813. Sedgwick, like Bradford, was inspired by Burr's bravery; he joined the second expedition against Canada in 1776.

32. See Emmanuel Kant, *Critique of Judgment* (1781; Oxford, 1952), 112–13. Hugh Blair's *Lectures on Rhetoric and Belle Lettres* was originally published in 1783; for quotations, see Hugh Blair, *Lectures on Rhetoric and Belles Lettres* (Philadelphia, 1852), 263–64.

33. General Orders, George Washington, July 2, 1776, in John C. Fitzpatrick, ed., *The Writings of Washington,* 29 vols. (Washington, D.C., 1931–44), 5: 211; Royster, *A Revolutionary People at War,* 11, 25–26, 216, 219, 228; Holly A.

Mayer, *Belonging to the Army: Camp Followers and Community During the American Revolution* (Columbia, S.C., 1996), 3; Lawrence Delbert Cress, "An Armed Community: The Origins and Meaning of the Right to Bear Arms," *Journal of American History* 71 (June 1984): 22–42.

34. Charles Robert Kemble, *The Image of the Officer in America* (Westport, Conn., 1973), 20; George D. Massey, *John Laurens and the American Revolution* (Columbia, S.C., 2000), 82; and Royster, *A Revolutionary People at War,* 91, 289, 123–25. Officers attacked their rivals with class and sexual slurs, as Henry Beekman Livingston did when he published a nasty handbill mocking General Alexander McDougall. See Roger J. Champagne, *Alexander McDougall and the American Revolution in New York* (Schenectady, N.Y., 1975), 124–25.

35. For an account of his daring navigation of the Kennebec River and Dead River, see AB to Timothy Edwards, Nov. 22, 1775; and for his stay at Fort Weston, see AB to Sally Burr Reeve, Sept. 24, 1775, Burr Papers, microfilm, reel 1.

36. AB to Sally Burr Reeve, Sept. 24, 1775, and AB to Sally and Tapping Reeve, Feb. 1776, in Burr Papers, microfilm, reel 1.

37. AB to Sally Burr Reeve, Feb. 1776, in Burr Papers, microfilm, reel 1.

38. Matthias Ogden to AB, Mar. 20, June 5, 1776, and AB to Matthias Ogden, June 18, 1776, in Davis, ed., *Memoirs of Aaron Burr,* I: 77–78, 81–82; and Benedict Arnold to the Honorable Continental Congress, Jan. 24, 1776, in Roberts, ed., *March to Quebec,* 118.

39. AB to Matthias Ogden, Mar. 7, 1777, in Davis, ed., *Memoirs of Aaron Burr,* I: 109.

40. *Ibid.*

41. Judith L.Van Buskirk, *Generous Enemies: Patriots and Loyalists in Revolutionary New York* (Philadelphia, 2002), 15–16; Champagne, *Alexander McDougall,* 109, 114; Ferling, *First of Men,* 150, 152; Lomask, *Aaron Burr: The Years from Princeton to Vice President,* 43.

42. Ferling, *First of Men,* 153, 160; Van Buskirk, *Generous Enemies,* 18.

43. Ferling, *First of Men,* 165, 167; John Niven, *Connecticut Hero: Israel Putnam* (Hartford, Conn., 1977), 72.

44. Matthias Ogden to AB, June 5, 1776, in Davis, ed., *Memoirs of Aaron Burr,* I: 80–81.

45. Burr's nineteenth-century biographer James Parton depicted their meeting as a clash of irreconcilable personalities, but there is no evidence to substantiate this view—see Parton, *Life and Times of Aaron Burr,* I: 84–84.

46. Niven, *Connecticut Hero,* 7–8.

47. Ferling, *First of Men,* 168–69.

48. *Ibid.,* 169–71; Niven, *Connecticut Hero,* 73–74.

49. Niven, *Connecticut Hero,* 73–74; Ferling, *First of Men,* 171; and for the location of the redoubt, see Henry P. Johnson, *The Campaign of 1776 around New York and Brooklyn* (Brooklyn, N.Y., 1878), 88.

50. See letter from Benjamin D. Silliman to Edward F. De Lancy, Jan. 22, 1876, in Thomas Jones, *History of New York during the Revolutionary War, and of the Leading Events in the Other Colonies at that Period* (New York, 1879), I: 608–09; and Katharine Hewitt Cummin, *Connecticut Militia General: Gold Selleck Silliman* (Hartford, Conn., 1979), 44. For the qualities expected of officers, see one of the most popular military guides published during the American Revolution, Thomas Simes, *The Military Guide for Young Officers* (Philadelphia, 1776), 6–7, 175, 192. However, there was another account, in which Burr was portrayed as far more aggressive and arrogant who won over the troops with his forceful resolve. This report was given by two former soldiers in 1814 who admired Burr's brashness in outmaneuvering a superior officer. See "Certificate from Isaac Jennings and Andrew Wakeman," in Davis, ed., *Memoirs of Aaron Burr,* I: 103–04.

51. Ferling, *First of Men,* 172–73, 175; Niven, *Connecticut Hero,* 75; and Adrian C. Leiby, *The Revolutionary War in the Hackensack Valley: The Jersey Dutch and the Neutral Ground, 1775–1783* (New Brunswick, N.J., 1962), 59–60.

52. Ferling, *First of Men,* 175–77; Niven, *Connecticut Hero,* 75.

53. AB to Mrs. Edwards, Sept. 26, 1776, and AB to Timothy Edwards, Aug. 10, 1776, in Davis, ed., *Memoirs of Aaron Burr,* I: 97, 106–08.

54. Niven, *Connecticut Hero,* 7, 69, 76–77. For Burr's military duties under Putnam, and his intelligence work (drafting a detailed report of the Battle of New Brunswick), see Israel Putnam to John Neilson (all in Burr's handwriting), Jan. 26, Feb. 13, Mar. 15, Mar. 30, 1777; AB to Colonel Samuel Forman, Apr. 1, 1777; and "Report: Enemy at Brunswick—signed by A. Burr," in Burr Papers, microfilm, reel 1.

55. AB to William Paterson, July 26, 1776, in Davis, ed., *Memoirs of Aaron Burr,* I: 85.

56. AB to Mrs. Edwards, in *ibid.,* I: 107.

57. General Washington to AB, June 27, 1777, Burr Papers, microfilm, reel 1.

58. Royster, *A Revolutionary People at War,* 200; Prince et al., eds., *The Papers of William Livingston,* V: 570–71.

59. AB to General Washington, July 20, 1777, in Burr Papers, microfilm, reel 1.

60. Royster, *A Revolutionary People at War,* 199–200.

61. Previous biographers have exaggerated the "imperious" and "icy" tone of this letter because they have failed to compare it to other complaints that Washington received from officers. See Schachner, *Aaron Burr,* 54; Lomask, *Aaron Burr: The Years from Princeton to the Vice President,* 52; and for a more balanced view, see Kline, ed., *Burr Papers,* I: lxii–lxiii.

62. Champagne, *Alexander McDougall,* 120.

63. Ferling, *First of Men,* 204–05, 207–08, 210–12; Symonds, *A Battlefield Atlas,* 53.

64. It is clear that the story of his successful sortie was making the rounds among officers. Another officer wrote to Burr, congratulating him on his "good for-

tune," and commenting that he had heard "various accounts about the manner in which you executed the plan." See T. Yates to AB, Sept. 20, 1777, and two later accounts, "Statement of George Gardner" (1813) and "Lieutenant Robert Hunter to Gabriel Furman, Esq., Member of Assembly," (1814), all in Davis, ed., *Memoirs of Aaron Burr*, I: 113–16, 117–18. See also "Eyewitness to Battle: Alexander Dow's Account of a 1777 Skirmish and the 1778 Battle of Monmouth," *Brigade Dispatch* 29 (Spring 1999): 15; Leiby, *The Revolutionary War in Hackensack Valley*, 137–38; and Jared Lobdell, "Paramus in the War of the Revolution," *Proceedings of the New Jersey Historical Society* 78 (July 1960): 166.

65. Champagne, *Alexander McDougall*, 120–21; Niven, *Connecticut Hero*, 77. For Malcolm's reference to "militia intractables," see William Malcolm to AB, Feb. 26, 1778, and AB to William Malcolm, Sept. 14, 1777, Burr Papers, microfilm, reel 1.

66. Niven, *Connecticut Hero*, 78, 81–83; see also William Malcolm to AB, Feb. 26, 1778, in Burr Papers, microfilm, reel 1.

67. James Mitchell Varnum to AB, Oct. 1, 1777, Burr Papers, microfilm, reel 1; Symonds, *A Battlefield Atlas*, 59; Ferling, *First of Men*, 213, 217–20.

68. For the reference to the "rascally inhabitants" and "villains who carry provisions to the enemy," see Alexander Scammell to AB, Feb. 3, 1778, Burr Papers, microfilm, reel 1.

69. Royster, *A Revolutionary People at War*, 75, 77, 80; Simes, *The Military Guide for Young Officers*, 2.

70. See letter "From Robert Hunter to Gabriel Furman, Esq., Member of the Assembly" (1814), in Davis, ed., *Memoirs of Aaron Burr*, I: 116, 120. The Gulph or Gulph Mills was 5.25 miles ESE of Valley Forge.

71. Davis claims that Burr "nearly severed it from his body," and the "arm of the mutineer was next day amputated"—*Memoirs of Aaron Burr*, I: 120–21. For officers hitting soldiers and soldiers' undermining their authority, see Royster, *A Revolutionary People at War*, 79. A friend of Burr's faced a similar situation. In 1776, Captain Joseph Bloomfield, a company commander in the Third New Jersey, when trying to apprehend a drunken soldier, severely beat the man with the flat of his sword. The very next day both men were subject to a court-martial. See Mark E. Lender and James Kirby Martin, eds., *Citizen Soldier: The Revolutionary War Journal of Joseph Bloomfield* (Newark, N.J., 1982), 13, 103.

72. Wandell and Minnigerode, *Aaron Burr*, 69–70; Schachner, *Aaron Burr*, 57–58; Lomask, *Aaron Burr: The Years from Princeton to Vice President*, 56. The story from Davis is also repeated in William S. Baker, "The Camp by the Old Gulph Mill," *Pennsylvania Magazine of History and Biography* XVII (1893): 426–27. For Corporal Haddock's court-martial, see Feb. 29, 1778, Burr Orderly Book, Mar. 1778 (this book includes entries for February); for the two cases involving a soldier pointing a loaded musket at an officer and an officer abusing a captain

while suppressing a riot, see General Court Martial, May 19, 1778, Burr Orderly Book, Apr. 20 to May 22, 1778; and for the men charged with "riotous
and mutinous manner" for entering Colonel Craig's house "with drawn swords,"
see General Court Martial, June 18, 1778, Burr Orderly Book, June 17 to July
28, 1778. All in Burr Papers, microfilm, reel 12.

73. Previous biographers have either ignored or failed to analyze in a systematic fashion Burr's orderly books. The orderly book was the most basic document of the
Continental Army, providing detailed accounts of court-martial cases. Better than
any other source, his orderly books accurately record Burr's approach to military
discipline. For Malcolm's absence from the regiment, see "From Lieutenant Robert Hunter to Gabriel Furman" (January 1814), in Davis, ed., *Memoirs of Aaron
Burr,* I: 112, 116; see also William Malcolm to AB, Oct. 17, 1777, Feb. 26, 1778,
and a letter [dated 1778–79], all in Burr Papers, microfilm, reel 1. For the Michael
Brannon court-martial on May 22, 1778, see Orderly Book, Apr.–May 1778. In
the case of Corporal Robert Haddock, he was sentenced to 40 lashes for "m[alo]lent
and threatening behavior to Lt. Col. Burr," but given 100 lashes for neglect of
duty. Burr approved the sentence—see Court Martial, Feb. 29, 1778, Burr Orderly Book, Mar. 1778 (also includes entries for February), Burr Papers, microfilm,
reel 12.

74. Brigade Court Martial, Mar. 2, Burr Orderly Book, Mar. 1778, Burr Papers,
microfilm, reel 12.

75. Feb. 16, 1779, Burr Orderly Book, Jan. 15 to Feb. 28, 1779, Burr Papers, microfilm, reel 12.

76. See Burr's orders for Feb. 11, 1779, in Orderly Book, Jan. 15–Feb. 28, 1779,
Burr Papers, microfilm, reel 12; and Samuel Young, "Aaron Burr as a Soldier.
A Letter from Judge Young of Westchester County, New York," *Historical Mag-
azine* 9, 2nd ser. (June 1871): 887. For another example of Burr's moralistic
reasoning, see the court-martial sentences of David Burns and Henry Holmes.
Both men were charged with desertion and enlisting in another regiment; but
Burr, president of the proceeding, gave a harsher penalty of 100 lashes to
Burns. The commander of the brigade fully approved of this sentence because
"it appears the latter [Holmes] was made drunk and inticed away by a villain."
See Brigade Court Martial, June 15, 1778, Burr Orderly Book, May 23–June
16, 1778, Burr Papers, microfilm, reel 12.

77. Ferling, *First of Men,* 241–42, 244.

78. *Ibid.,* 244–45; Mark Edward Lender, "The Battle of Monmouth in the Military
Context of the American Revolution," in Mary R. Murrin and Richard Wal-
dron, eds., *Conflict at Monmouth Court House* (Trenton, N.J., 1983), 14–15.

79. Burr explained his physical problems in his letter to Washington requesting a
furlough. In his letter of resignation, he again referred to his health as the reason for his decision to leave the army—see Davis, ed., *Memoirs of Aaron Burr,*
I: 128, 136, 168. Lee's first letter was incorrectly dated July 1, though in the

published Lee Papers it is dated June 30—see Major General Charles Lee to General Washington, June 28, 1778, George Washington Papers, Library of Congress; see also *The Lee Papers* (4 vols.) in *The Collections of the New-York Historical Society* (New York, 1872–75), II: 435–36.

80. General Lee to AB, Oct. 1778, in Davis, ed., *Memoirs of Aaron Burr,* I: 135; also in *Lee Papers,* III: 238–39; and see Orderly Book, Mar. 1778, Burr Papers, microfilm, reel 12.

81. Davis, ed., *Memoirs of Aaron Burr,* I: 135. Lee was less coy in his letter to political ally Benjamin Rush. He brusquely dismissed Washington's account of the Battle of Monmouth Court House as "a most abominable damn'd lie," and claimed his "Court Martial was a Court of inquisition"—see Lee to Benjamin Rush, Sept. 29, 1778, in *The Lee Papers,* III: 236–37.

82. Ferling, *First of Men,* 228–30.

83. Lee to General Washington, June 28, 1778, and Lender, "The Battle of Monmouth," 19.

84. AB to Tapping and Sally Burr Reeve, Mar. 1, 1779, Burr Papers, microfilm, reel 1; Massey, *John Laurens,* 124–26.

85. Uday Hay to AB, Feb. 13, 1779, in Burr Papers, microfilm, reel 1; and see Charles Lee to Miss Rebecca Franks, Dec. 20, 1778, in *The Lee Papers,* II: 287–81.

86. See "To the Printer of the Virginia Gazette," [1775], which was reprinted in the *New Jersey Gazette* on Dec. 31, 1778, as an attack on Lee, and Robert Troup to Chief Justice Jay, June 29, 1778, in *The Lee Papers,* II: 297–300, 429. Also see General Court Martial (held June 2, 1778) recorded for June 6, 1778, in Orderly Book, May 23–June 16, 1778, Burr Papers, microfilm, reel 12.

87. See AB to General Washington, Oct. 24, 1778, and Washington to AB, Oct. 26, 1778, in Davis, ed., *Memoirs of Aaron Burr,* I: 136–37; Colonel Robert Troup to Major General Gates, Jan. 3, 1779, in *The Lee Papers,* III: 290; and Champagne, *Alexander McDougall,* 124–25, 175–79. And for courts-martial, see Orderly Book, June 17–July 28, 1778. For "spirit of discord," see Sept. 25, 1778, in Orderly Book, Aug. 2–Oct. 10, 1778, Burr Papers, microfilm, reel 12.

88. Davis, ed., *Memoirs of Aaron Burr,* I: 112, 115, 138.

89. Sun Bok Kim, "The Limits of Politicization in the American Revolution: The Experience of Westchester County, New York," *Journal of American History,* vol. 80, no. 3 (Dec. 1993): 877–87, 880; and "Petition of Inhabitants of Westchester County," Dec. 23, 1776, in *Calendar of Historical Manuscripts Relating to the War of the Revolution, in the Office of the Secretary of State,* 2 vols. (Albany, 1868), I: 563.

90. Kim, "The Limits of Politicization in the American Revolution," 885; and see Feb. 16 or 17, 1779, in Orderly Book, Jan. 15–Feb. 28, 1779, Burr Papers, microfilm, reel 12.

91. AB to General McDougall, Jan. 13, 1779, in Davis, ed., *Memoirs of Aaron Burr,* I: 142–43.

92. *Ibid.,* 143.

93. AB to General McDougall, Jan. 12, 13, 1779, in *ibid.,* I: 141–43.

94. See AB to General McDougall, Jan. 12, 1799, and AB to Lord Stirling [William Alexander], July 4, 1778, in *ibid.,* I: 129, 142; and Lord Stirling to AB, June 3, 1778, and July 6, 1778, AB to John Leake, Jan. 17, 1779, AB to General McDougall, Jan. 22, 1779, in Burr Papers, microfilm, reel 1. For the spy network, see Champagne, *Alexander McDougall,* 156.

95. Samuel Young, "Aaron Burr as a Soldier," 885; and AB to General Malcolm, Jan. 21, 1779, and General McDougall to AB, Feb. 6, 1779, in Davis, ed., *Memoirs of Aaron Burr,* I: 148, 151.

96. Samuel Young, "Aaron Burr as a Soldier," 885, 886.

97. Richard Platt to AB, Jan. 20, 1779, in Burr Papers, microfilm, reel 1.

98. AB to Peter Colt, Jan. 21, 1779, and AB to Major John Bigelow, Jan. 21, 1779, in Burr Papers, microfilm, reel 1.

99. AB to General McDougall, Feb. 18, 1779, Burr Papers, microfilm, reel 1.

100. AB to General Washington, Mar. 10, 1779, Burr Papers, microfilm, reel 1.

101. AB to General McDougall, Feb. 18, 1779, Burr Papers, microfilm, reel 1.

102. AB to Rufus Putnam, Feb. 17, 1779, Burr Papers, microfilm, reel 1.

103. *Ibid.*

104. AB to Sally Burr Reeve, Apr. 25, 1779, Burr Papers, microfilm, reel 1.

CHAPTER THREE

1. William Paterson to AB, Oct. 26, 1772, Burr Papers, microfilm, reel 1. Thaddeus Dod was not the only Princeton student forced to marry a woman because she was pregnant. Madison and Bradford also discussed Andrew Bryan, who found himself in a similar situation. See William Bradford to James Madison, Mar. 4, 1774, and James Madison to William Bradford, Apr. 1, 1774, in Thomas A. Manson and Robert Rutland, eds., *The Papers of James Madison,* 17 vols. (Chicago and Charlottesville, Va., 1962–1991), I: 109, 111–12; and Robert Stewart to Aaron Burr, Feb. 7, 1774, Burr Papers, microfilm, reel 1. See also "Thaddeus Dodd" and "Andrew Bryan," in Richard A. Harrison, ed., *Princetonians: A Biographical Dictionary, 1769–1775* (Princeton, N.J., 1980), II: 191, 283–85. For anti-matrimonial satire about mismatched couples (the old marrying the young), see Cornelia Dayton, "Satire and Sensationalism: The Emergence of Misogyny in Mid-Eighteenth-Century New England Papers and Almanacs," Paper presented to the New England Seminar at the American Antiquarian Society, Worcester, Mass., Nov. 15, 1991, 16. And for anti-matrimonial and anti-clerical erotica, see Peter Wagner, *Eros Revived: The Erotica of the Enlightenment in England and America* (London, 1988), 144–46, 72–86. The novels of Laurence Sterne and Tobias Smollett also show the influence of anti-Catholic erotica, which might have shaped the Princeton students' bawdy humor about the monk.

2. Geissler, *Jonathan Edwards to Aaron Burr, Jr.,* 111–13.

3. AB to Sally Burr Reeve, Jan. 17, 1774, Burr Papers, microfilm, reel 1.

4. AB to Sally Burr Reeve, Jan. 20, 1774, Burr Papers, microfilm, reel 1.

5. Geissler, *Jonathan Edwards to Aaron Burr,* 111–12. See Roy Porter, "Mixed Feelings: The Enlightenment and Sexuality in Eighteenth-Century Britain," in Paul-Gabriel Boucé, ed., *Sexuality in Eighteenth-Century Britain* (Manchester, 1982), 5, 12, 14 (note 14); and Miriam Williford, "Bentham on the Rights of Women," *Journal of the History of Ideas* 36 (Jan.–Mar. 1975): 172.

6. AB to Sally Burr Reeve, Jan. 17, 18, 1774, and Joseph Bellamy, Jr. to AB, Aug. 17, 1775, in Burr Papers, microfilm, reel 1; Geissler, *Jonathan Edwards to Aaron Burr,* 111–13.

7. AB to Sally Burr Reeve, Jan. 17, 1774, Burr Papers, microfilm, reel 1.

8. Wandell and Minnigerode, *Aaron Burr,* I: 126. For the stylistic features that Burr imitated in his writing, see Ian Watt, "From the Rise of the Novel: Studies in Defoe, Richardson, and Fielding," in Michael McKeon, ed., *Theory of the Novel: A Historical Approach* (Baltimore and London, 2000), 455–56, and Joanne Cutting-Gray, *Woman as "Nobody" and the Novels of Fanny Burney* (Gainesville, Fla., 1992), 21–23.

9. Adam Sisman, *Boswell's Presumptuous Task: The Making of the Life of Dr. Johnson* (New York, 2000), 29; and see *A New Fortune-Book, Being a New Art of Courtship, open'd for Young Men and Maids, Widows, Widowers, and Batchelors* (Cirencester, U.K., 1770).

10. For colonial American attitudes, see Howard P. Chudacoff, *The Age of the Bachelor: Creating of an American Subculture* (Princeton, N.J., 1999), 21; and "Scipio," [1784], in Prince et al., eds., *The Papers of William Livingston,* V: 98–100.

11. Joseph Bellamy, Jr., to AB, Feb. 8, 1775, Burr Papers, microfilm, reel 1.

12. AB to Sally Burr Reeve, July 1775, in Burr Papers, microfilm, reel 1.

13. AB to Matthias Ogden, Feb. 2, 1775, in Davis, ed., *Memoir of Aaron Burr,* I: 50–51.

14. AB to Matthias Ogden, Mar. 12, 1775, in *ibid.,* I: 53.

15. *Ibid.,* I: 52; on the importance of women as arbiters of young men's reputation, see Donna DeFabio Curtin, "The *gentlest,* most *polished,* most *beautiful* part of the creation: Men, Women, and Genteel Culture in the Early American Northeast, 1720–1800," Ph.D. Dissertation, Brown University, 1999.

16. AB to Matthias Ogden, Mar. 12, 1775, in Davis, ed., *Memoirs of Aaron Burr,* I: 52–53.

17. AB to Matthias Ogden, Feb. 2, 1775, in *ibid.,* I: 51–52.

18. Greissler, *Jonathan Edwards to Aaron Burr,* 134–35.

19. Chesterfield did not endorse whoremongering. He also did not believe in showing outright meanness toward women, but he felt little respect for them; women, he believed, had to be indulged. They should never be insulted as a

group, but they were mainly social pawns that men had to learn how to manipulate in order to avoid their wrath or secure their sexual favors. See *Letters Written by the Late Right Honourable Philip Dormer Stanhope, Earl of Chesterfield, to his Son* (London, 1806), I: 218, 287, 294–95, 316–17, 371–73.

20. AB to Sally Burr Reeve, July 1775, Burr Papers, microfilm, reel 1.

21. Edward G. Williams, "The Prevosts of the Royal Americans," *Western Pennsylvania Historical Magazine,* vol. 56, no. 1 (Jan. 1973): 16.

22. AB to Sally Burr Reeve, Sept. 24, 1775, and AB to Sally and Tapping Reeve, Feb. 1776, Burr Papers, microfilm, reel 1; and for camp life, see Mayer, *Belonging to the Army,* 59.

23. Mayer, *Belonging to the Army,* 59–61, 63–64, 66; Royster, *A Revolutionary People at War,* 59–61; General Court Martial, June 2, 1778, Orderly Book, May 23–June 16, 1778, Burr Papers, microfilm, reel 12.

24. Mayer, *Belonging to the Army,* 54–56, 147–49, and Davis, ed., *Memoirs of Aaron Burr,* II: 434; Paul David Nelson, *William Alexander, Lord Stirling* (Tuscaloosa, Ala., 1987), 123; Pierre Etienne DuPonceau, "Autobiography," *Pennsylvania Magazine of History and Biography* 63 (1939): 209, 213.

25. Ferling, *First of Men,* 240–41; on the Mischianza, see Jones, *History of New York During the Revolutionary War,* I: 241–52.

26. For a discussion of the Galloway incident, see Judith Van Buskirk, "They Didn't Join the Band: Disaffected Women in Revolutionary Philadelphia," *Pennsylvania History* 62 (1995): 520.

27. In a letter to his sister and Tapping Reeve, Burr wrote: "I am in raptures with your confiscating law"—see AB to Sally and Tapping Reeve, Feb. 1776, Burr Papers, microfilm, reel 1.

28. "The Prevosts: Late Colonial and Revolutionary War," The Hermitage, Ho-Ho-Kus, N.J.

29. On the property one home was called "The Hermitage," the second one "Little Hermitage." Theodosia's widowed mother, Ann de Visme, purchased the Hermitage, while Theodosia and her husband owned the Little Hermitage. "The Prevosts: Late Colonial and Revolutionary War"; and Bernard C. Steiner, ed., *The Life and Correspondence of James McHenry* (Cleveland, 1907), 22–23; and Dorothy Valentine Smith, "'Mrs. Prevost Requests the Honor of His Company,'" *Manuscripts* XI (Fall 1959): 27, 30.

30. Van Buskirk, *Generous Enemies,* 73–74.

31. "The Prevosts: Late Colonial and Revolutionary War"; see also Ray Swick, *An Island Called Eden: The Story of Harman and Margaret Blennerhassett* (Parkersburg, W.Va., 2002), 35; for one extant letter in French, see Theodosia Prevost to AB, Dec. 24, 1781, in Burr Papers, microfilm, reel 1; for his suggestion that she read abbé Mably's book on the U.S. Constitution in French, then he will not have to read it, see AB to Theodosia, May 22, 1785, in Davis, ed., *Memoirs of Aaron Burr,* I: 266.

32. The story was printed in *The Corrector* on April 18, 1804. Theodosia's talents were rare indeed. One historian claims that scant evidence exists for American women playing crambo. See David S. Shields, *Civil Tongues and Polite Letters in British America* (Charlottesville, Va., 1997), 165, 168–69.
33. "The Prevosts: Late Colonial and Revolutionary War Era."
34. James Monroe to Theodosia Prevost, Nov. 8, 1778, in Davis, ed., *Memoirs of Aaron Burr,* I: 184–85.
35. Samuel Bradhurst III was Theodosia's relative. Dr. Bradhurst was an officer in the New Jersey militia, captured in mid-1777; see "The Prevosts: Late Colonial and Revolutionary War Era." For the practice of giving officers paroles, see Van Buskirk, *Generous Enemies,* 74, and Nelson, *William Alexander, Lord Stirling,* 134.
36. Wandell and Minnigrode, *Aaron Burr,* I: 88.
37. See Robert H. Harrison to AB, Aug. 1, 1778; Robert Benson to AB, Aug. 2, 1778; and pass issued by Governor George Clinton for Burr to escort the three men behind enemy lines, with a note by Burr adding the names of Theodosia and Catherine De Visme, Burr Papers, microfilm, reel 1.
38. On the gift from the queen of France, see George Washington to the marquis de Lafayette, Aug. 10, 1778, in Louis Gottschalk and Shirley A. Bill, eds., *The Letters of Lafayette to Washington, 1777–1791* (Philadelphia, 1976), 136–67, and "The Prevosts: Late Colonial and Revolutionary War Era"; on Burr's account of his escort of the Tories, see AB to George Clinton, Aug. 19, 1778, in Burr Papers, microfilm, reel 1.
39. William Paterson to AB, Aug. 31, 1780; and for letters from Paterson about Theodosia, see Paterson to AB, Jan. 29, 1779, and Paterson to AB, Sept. 29, 1779, in Davis, ed., *Memoirs of Aaron Burr,* I: 148–49, 188, 211–13; see also "The Prevosts: Late Colonial and Revolutionary War Era," and O'Connor, *William Paterson,* 107.
40. "The Prevosts: Late Colonial and Revolutionary War"; and O'Connor, *William Paterson,* 106–07.
41. AB to Sally Burr Reeve, Apr. 25, 1779, in Burr Papers, microfilm, reel 1.
42. See Harry Ammon, *James Monroe: The Quest for National Identity* (Charlottesville, Va., 1990), 13–14; Davis, ed., *Memoirs of Aaron Burr,* I: 128; and Wendell Edward Tripp, Jr., *Robert Troup: A Quest for Security in the Turbulent New Nation, 1775–1832* (New York, 1982), 27–30.
43. AB to Sally Burr Reeve, Nov. 5, 1778, and AB to Sally Burr Reeve, Apr. 25, 1779, Burr Papers, microfilm, reel 1. In extremely romanticized terms, the depth of Burr's affections for his sister are evidenced by another letter in which he wrote of the death of his friend Joseph Bellamy: "My faithful Correspondent my best, my, (almost) only Friend, is, alas, no more—J. Bellamy's death gave me Feelings, which few Deaths can ever renew; But why this to a Sister who feels more for a Brother than herself—my Pen and Heart you know were ever

nearly allied." AB to Sally Burr Reeve, June 8, 1777, Burr Papers, microfilm, reel 1.

44. For Troup's description of his conversation with the Livingston sisters, see Robert Troup to AB, May 23, 1780, in Davis, ed., *Memoirs of Aaron Burr,* I: 205; Thaddeus Burr to AB, Aug. 12, 1780, and William Paterson to AB, Mar. 18, 1779, in the Burr Papers, microfilm, reel 1; and O'Connor, *William Paterson,* 89.

45. "The Prevosts: Late Colonial and Revolutionary Era"; and Elizabeth Duval to Theodosia Prevost, Nov. 3, 1779, in Burr Papers, microfilm, reel 1. Burr sent a series of letters about his health from the Hermitage between October and December, indicating he was spending a great deal of time there—see AB to Jeremiah Wadsworth, Oct. 22, Oct. 27, and Dec. 1779, in Burr Papers, microfilm, reel 1.

46. Catherine De Visme to AB, Dec. 30, 1781, in Burr Papers, microfilm, reel 1; New York *Royal Gazette,* Dec. 19, 1781; and "The Prevosts: Late Colonial and Revolutionary Era."

47. AB to Tapping and Sally Burr Reeve, July 24, 1780, in Burr Papers, microfilm, reel 1; "The Prevosts: Late Colonial and Revolutionary Era." Dorothy Valentine Smith was one of the first researchers to carefully review the documents relating to Burr's early relationship with Theodosia. However, writing in the 1950s, she could not accept the idea that Theodosia would have engaged in a sexual affair with Burr. Lomask repeats Dorothy Smith's conclusion in his 1979 biography, writing that Theodosia kept their "increasingly warm relationship on an intellectual plane." For some reason, Lomask ignores Paterson's letter. He claims that Burr knew of Prevost's poor health a year or more before the announcement of his death. But that does not explain why Paterson talked of marriage long before Prevost contracted yellow fever in Jamaica. See Smith, "Mrs. Prevost Requests," 30; Lomask, *Aaron Burr: The Years from Princeton to the Vice President,* 67, 79–80.

48. AB to Theodosia Prevost, Dec. 3, 5, 1781, in Davis, ed., *Memoirs of Aaron Burr,* I: 232–33.

49. Theodosia Prevost Burr to AB, May 22, 1785, in *ibid.,* I: 267–67.

50. Witherspoon wrote a series of letters on marriage published in the *Pennsylvania Magazine* in 1775–76; see Fody, "John Witherspoon: Advisor to the Lovelorn," 239–49; see also Katherine Sobba Green, *The Courtship Novel 1740–1820: A Feminized Genre* (Lexington, Ky., 1991), 63–66; and Mary Wollstonecraft, *A Vindication of the Rights of Woman* (1792), ed. and intro. Miriam Brody (New York, 1992), 51–52, 112–13.

51. For the invalid reference, see AB to Jeremiah Wadsworth, Oct. 22, 1779, and for "eye trouble," see AB to John McKesson, July 31, 1790, in Burr Papers, microfilm, reel 1; see also Robert Troup to AB, Feb. 19, 1780, in Davis, ed., *Memoirs of Aaron Burr,* I: 196; Lomask, *Aaron Burr: The Years from Princeton to the Vice President,* 103.

52. See AB to Paterson, Feb. 16, 1780, Robert Troup to AB, Oct. 23, 1780, and Feb. 19, 1780, and AB to Theodosia Prevost, Dec. 3, Dec. 6, 1781, in Davis, ed., *Memoirs of Aaron Burr,* I: 193–94, 214, 232–33.

53. For a reference to Theodosia's "incurable disorder of the uterus," see Joseph Browne to AB, Jan. 13, 1783, Burr Papers, microfilm, reel 1; and for references to her illness and melancholy, see AB to Theodosia Prevost, Dec. 23, 1781, AB to Theodosia Prevost Burr, Apr. 1785, and May 1785, and Theodosia Prevost Burr to AB, May 1785, in Davis, ed., *Memoirs of Aaron Burr,* I: 242, 255, 258; Lomask, *Aaron Burr: The Years from Princeton to the Vice President,* 103; Schachner, *Aaron Burr,* 82, 130.

54. Thomas Smith to AB, March 1, 1781, in Davis, ed., *Memoirs of Aaron Burr,* I: 223; Lomask, *Aaron Burr: The Years from Princeton to Vice President,* 32–33, 73–75.

55. AB to Paterson, Feb. 16, 1780, in Davis, ed., *Memoirs of Aaron Burr,* I: 193–94.

56. AB to Peter Colt, July 17, 1782, in Burr Papers, microfilm, reel 1.

57. Theodosia Prevost to AB, May 1781, in Davis, ed., *Memoirs of Aaron Burr,* I: 226–27.

58. AB to Theodosia Prevost, Dec. 6, 1781, in *ibid.,* I: 234.

59. Theodosia Prevost to AB, Feb. 12, 1781, in *ibid.,* I: 224–25.

60. Wollstonecraft, *Vindication of the Rights of Woman,* 48, 103, 122. After reading this work, which he called a "book of genius," Burr told Theodosia that the author had "successfully adopted the style of Rousseau's Emilius"—AB to Theodosia Prevost Burr, Feb. 16, 1793, in Davis, ed., *Memoirs of Aaron Burr,* I: 363.

61. *Ibid.,* I: 99, 123, 148.

62. For the eighteenth-century ideal of friendship, popularized by Joseph Addison in *The Spectator,* see Michael G. Ketcham, *Transparent Designs: Reading, Performance, and Form in the "Spectator" Papers* (Athens, Ga., 1985), 123; see also AB to Theodosia Prevost Burr, May 19, 1785, Theodosia Prevost Burr to AB, May 22, 1785, and June 30, 1791, in Davis, ed., *Memoirs of Aaron Burr,* I: 264, 267–68, 294.

63. Marriage certificate of Burr and Theodosia, Burr Papers, microfilm, reel 1; Lomask, *Aaron Burr: The Years from Princeton to the Vice President,* 78–79.

64. "The Prevosts: Late Colonial and Revolutionary War"; Theodosia Prevost Burr to Sally Burr Reeve [July 1782], and William S. Livingston to AB, July 10, 1782, in Burr Papers, microfilm, reel 1.

65. Burr first arranged for a tutor before their marriage—see AB to Major R. Alden, Feb. 15, 1781, in Davis, ed., *Memoirs of Aaron Burr,* 222; and Theodosia Prevost Burr to Tapping Reeve, Aug. 3, 1788, Burr Papers, microfilm, reel 2; Lomask, *Aaron Burr: The Year from Princeton to the Vice President,* 98–100.

66. Timothy Edwards to AB, Apr. 28, 1783, Burr Papers, microfilm, reel 1; Lomask, *Aaron Burr: The Years from Princeton to Vice President,* 107–08.

67. AB to Theodosia Prevost Burr, Apr. 1785, and Theodosia Prevost Burr to AB, Sept. 27, 1785, in Davis, ed., *Memoirs of Aaron Burr,* I: 252, 271.

68. AB to Theodosia Prevost, Dec. 7, 1781, Oct. 29, 1784, and Dec. 15, 1791, in *ibid.,* I: 235, 248, 311.

69. AB and Theodosia Prevost Burr to Tapping Reeve, Aug. 3, 1783, in Burr Papers, microfilm, reel 1; Theodosia Prevost Burr to AB, June 30 and July 23, 1791, in Davis, ed., *Memoirs of Aaron Burr,* I:294, 300.

70. AB to Theodosia Prevost Burr, Nov. 14, 1791, Dec. 13, 1791, Feb. 19, 1792, in Davis, ed., *Memoirs of Aaron Burr,* I: 306, 310, 315–16.

71. On patronage, see AB to Theodosia Prevost Burr, Nov. 14, 1791, and Theodosia Prevost Burr to AB, July 27, 1791, in Davis, ed., *Memoirs of Aaron Burr,* I: 301, 307. For women's role in political patronage in general, see Catherine Allgor, *Parlor Politics: In Which the Ladies of Washington Help Build a City and a Government* (Charlottesville, Va., 2000), 128–46; and for an example of a representative's wife who was politicking at home while her husband sat in Congress, see William C. diGiacomantonio, "A Congressional Wife at Home: The Case of Sarah Thatcher, 1787–1792," in Kenneth R. Bowling and Donald R. Kennon, eds., *Neither Separate Nor Equal: Congress in the 1790s* (Athens, Ohio, 2000), 174–76.

72. AB to Theodosia Burr, July 27, 1791, in Davis, *Memoirs of Aaron Burr*, I: 301.

73. AB to Theodosia Prevost Burr, Dec. 23, 1781, Theodosia Prevost Burr to AB, Mar. 25, 1783, Mar. 22, 1784, Sept. 25, 1785, in Davis, ed., *Memoirs of Aaron Burr,* I: 242, 245, 248, 271. For the connection between opium and romantic allusions, see Alethea Hayter, *Opium and the Romantic Imagination* (London, 1968), 24, 42, 48.

74. For Theodosia's knowledge of Latin, see AB to Theodosia Prevost, June 15, 1781; also AB to Theodosia Prevost Burr, Dec. 4, 1791, in Davis, ed., *Memoirs of Aaron Burr,* I: 230, 308–10.

75. Jean-Jacques Rousseau, *Emile, or On Education* (1762), trans. Barbara Foley (New York, 1911) and updated by Grace Roosevelt (New York, 2002), 1–2.

76. Theodosia Burr to AB, Aug. 28, 1785, in Davis, ed., *Memoirs of Aaron Burr,* I: 268–69.

77. G. J. Barker-Benfield, *The Culture of Sensibility: Sex and Society in Eighteenth-Century Britain* (Chicago, 1992), 276–79.

78. AB to Theodosia Burr, Feb. 8, 1793, in Davis, ed., *Memoirs of Aaron Burr,* I: 361–62.

79. AB to Theodosia Burr, May 19, 1785, July 17, 1791, Oct. 30, 1791, and Theodosia Prevost Burr to AB, July 23, 1791, in Davis, ed., *Memoirs of Aaron Burr,* I: 264, 296–97, 298–99, 304–05; and AB to Theodosia Burr, Dec. 1, 1791, "AB to Theodosia, Plan for Journal," Dec. 16, 1793, AB to Theodosia Burr, Jan. 16, 1794, Jan. 23, 1794, and June 7, 1794, in Van Doren, ed., *Correspondence*

of Aaron Burr and his Daughter Theodosia, 3, 8, 12–13, 18–19; Geissler, *Jonathan Adams to Aaron Burr,* 155–56.

80. AB to Theodosia Burr, Dec. 16, 1793, Jan. 7, 8, 14, 23, 1794, Sept. 28, 1795, in Van Doren, ed., *Correspondence of Aaron Burr and his Daughter Theodosia,* 7, 12–14, 16–19, 41–42.

81. AB to Theodosia Prevost Burr, Feb. 8, 15, 16, 1793, in Davis, ed., *Memoirs of Aaron Burr,* I: 362–63.

82. AB to Theodosia Burr, Sept. 17, 1795, Jan. 4, 1799, Jan. 30, 1800, in Van Doren, ed., *Correspondence of Aaron Burr and his Daughter Theodosia,* 36, 48, 54.

83. AB to Theodosia Burr, Jan. 4, 1799, in *ibid.;* Lawrence E. Klein, *Shaftsbury and the Culture of Politeness: Moral Discourse and Culture Politics in Early Eighteenth-Century England* (Cambridge, UK, 1994), 6, 98, 146, 211; C. Dallett Hemphill, *Bowing to Necessities: A History of Manners in America, 1620–1860* (New York, 1999), 117.

84. Wollstonecraft, *Vindication of the Rights of Woman,* 202; Klein, *Shaftsebury and the Culture of Politeness,* 6, 45, 83.

85. John Doris to [?], 1798, "Burr's Brief," New York Public Library, cited in Geissler, *Jonathan Edwards to Aaron Burr,* 158–59.

86. AB to Theodosia Burr, Sept. 17, 1795, in Van Doren, ed., *Correspondence of Aaron Burr and his Daughter,* 36.

87. AB to Theodosia Burr, Jan. 4, 1799, in *ibid.,* 46–47.

88. It is important to remember that single, propertied women were allowed to vote in New Jersey from 1776 to 1807. AB to Theodosia Prevost Burr, Jan. 23, 1797, in *ibid.,* 44.

89. AB to Theodosia Burr, Feb. 16, 1793, in Davis, ed., *Memoirs of Aaron Burr,* I: 363.

CHAPTER FOUR

1. Theodosia Prevost Burr to AB, July 23, 1791, in Davis, ed., *Memoirs of Aaron Burr,* I: 298. For the three factions, see Jabez D. Hammond, *The History of Political Parties in the State of New York,* 2 vols. (Albany, N.Y., 1842), I, 48, and Alfred Young, *The Democratic Republicans in New York* (Chapel Hill, N.C., 1967), 34, 36.

2. George Dangerfield, *Chancellor Robert R. Livingston of New York, 1746–1813* (New York, 1960), 185–86, 277–78.

3. Parton, *Life and Times of Aaron Burr,* I: 169.

4. Young, *The Democratic Republicans,* 42, 46–49, 163, 278, 431.

5. Sidney I. Pomerantz, *New York An American City, 1783–1803* (New York, 1938), 397; Paul M. Hamlin, *Legal Education in Colonial New York* (New York, 1939), 90.

6. Edwin G. Burrows and Mike Wallace, *Gotham: A History of New York City to the 1890s* (New York, 1999), 265, 270.

7. Julius Goebel, Jr., ed., *The Law Practice of Alexander Hamilton,* 5 vols. (New York, 1964–81), I: 197–202; Burrows and Wallace, *Gotham,* 267.

8. On Duane, see Leo Hershkowitz, "Federal New York: Mayor's of the Nation's First Capital," in Stephen L. Schechter and Wendell Tripp, eds., *World of the Founders: New York Communities in the Federal Period* (Albany, N.Y., 1990), 30–32; Edward P. Alexander, *A Revolutionary Conservative: James Duane of New York* (New York, 1938), 158. For the "harvest" for lawyers, see Alexander Hamilton (hereafter AH) to Gouverneur Morris, Feb. 21, 1784, in Syrett, ed., *The Papers of Alexander Hamilton,* III: 512.

9. Goebel, ed., *The Law Practice of Alexander Hamilton,* I: 215–16, 220; AH to James Duane, Aug. 5, 1783, AH to Robert Livingston, Aug. 13, 1783, and AH to Gouverneur Morris, Feb. 21, 1784, in Syrett, ed., *The Papers of Alexander Hamilton,* III: 430–31, 512; E. Wilder Spaulding, *New York During the Critical Period* (1932), 123.

10. Burr handled sixty-three cases before the Mayor's Court in 1784. Until 1791, when he represented his last case before that court (until resuming practice in 1813), most of his cases involved defending debtors or collecting debts. For specific cases, see *Mary Clarke v. Somandyke,* Dec. 9, 1786, *John Jay v. William Ivers,* July 12, 1788. Burr also handled five cases for William Malcolm between 1784 and 1790; see New York City Mayor's Court (hereafter NYCMC), Burr Papers, microfilm, reel 13. For a letter from a debtor, see Grant Cottle to AB, Oct. 6, 1787, Burr Papers, microfilm, reel 1; see also Bruce Mann, *Republic of Debtors: Bankruptcy in the Age of American Independence* (Cambridge, Mass., 2002), 99.

11. Burr handled a total of eighteen cases under the Trespass Act. Clients did not always get the sum they sued for. Though Burr's client Obadiah Wells sued for £500, the jury only awarded him £40. See Minutes, NYCMC, Mar. 1, 1786, and *Obadiah Wells v. John Folk,* Feb. 10, 1784, NYCMC, Feb. 10, 1784. Burr handled two Trespass Act suits for John Jay's family before the New York Supreme Court. See NYCMC and New York Supreme Court (NYSC), Burr Papers, microfilm, reels 13 and 15; and Goebel, ed., *The Law Practice of Alexander Hamilton,* I: 266.

12. William Malcolm to AB, July 15, 1783, Burr Papers, microfilm, reel 1. Burr handled a case for Marinus Willett; see *Marinus Willett v. George and Susannah Turnbull,* Nov. 5, 1789, in NYCMC, Burr Papers, microfilm, reel 13. For the friendship and "violent Whig" credentials of Willett, Lamb, and Malcolm, see Isaac Q. Leake, *Memoir of the Life and Times of General John Lamb* (Albany, N.Y., 1850), 205–06, and Young, *The Democratic Republicans,* 67.

13. Burr handled thirteen cases of assault and battery (assault and trespass) in the Mayor's Court between 1784 and 1788. For the case of assault and imprisonment, see *George Higday v. Martin Macaboy,* Dec. 27, 1784, NYCMC, Burr

Papers, microfilm, reel 13. This case was identical to that of *Joshua Hartt v. Townshend Wickes,* NYSC, 1787, in which Hamilton represented the Loyalist defendant—see Goebel, ed., *The Law Practice of Alexander Hamilton,* I: 517.

14. Burr handled three slave cases—all in 1784. The case involving the female slave was *Thomas Stevenson v. John Lake,* May 11, 1784, NYCMC, Burr Papers, microfilm, reel 13; see also Shane White, *Somewhat More Independent: The End of Slavery in New York City, 1770–1810* (Athens, Ohio, 1991), 1, 4; and William Strickland, *Journal of a Tour in the United States of America, 1794–95* (New York, 1971), 228–30.

15. See *Lazarus and Amos Hadden v. Bartholomew Griffin and John Barker,* May 21, 1796, New York Chancery Court (hereafter NYCC), Burr Papers, microfilm, reel 20. Burr proposed the following revised wording for the bill: "That from and after the passing of this act, all Negro, Mulatto, Indian, Mustee, or other person of whatsoever description, age, or colour, now holden, or claimed as slave or slaves, by any citizen or inhabitant of this State, shall be, and hereby declared absolute free." See *Journal of the Assembly of the State of New York,* 8th sess. (1785), 53–54, 76–77.

16. See AB to Theodosia Prevost Burr, Dec. 14, 1781, and AB to his daughter Theodosia Burr, Mar. 7, 1794, in Davis, ed., *Memoirs of Aaron Burr,* I: 237, 377.

17. In 1790, 27 of 120 members of the New York Manumission Society were listed in the census as owning slaves. The best known slaveholder was John Jay, who served as president of the organization for many years. Burr was not listed as a member of the society. See White, *Somewhat More Independent,* 81–82; also Robin Brooks, "Melancton Smith: New York Anti-Federalist, 1744–1798," Ph. D. Dissertation, University of Rochester, 1964, 282.

18. This observation was not made in a letter to Burr, but in a letter from Macomb to another of Burr's clients, William Constable. See Alexander Macomb to William Constable, Jan. 11, 1792, Constable Papers, Vol. 3, New York Public Library; and Davis, ed., *Memoirs of Aaron Burr,* II: 14, 18–19. For Burr's insistence on collecting all the necessary papers, see AB to Tapping Reeve, Dec. 10, 1785, *John Kelly v. AB and Anne De Visme,* Sept. 21, 1785, NYCC, and Burr's case notes, NYSC, in Burr Papers, microfilm, reel 1, 16, 18.

19. AB to Theodosia Prevost Burr, July 17, 1791, in Davis, ed., *Memoirs of Aaron Burr,* I: 297.

20. Parton, *Life and Times of Aaron Burr,* I: 151–52; see also Davis, ed., *Memoirs of Aaron Burr,* II: 21.

21. AB to Jeremiah Wadsworth, Sept. 14, 1785, in Kline, ed., *Burr Papers,* I: 17; Francis A. de La Rochefoucault-Liancourt, *Travels through the United States of North America, the Country of the Iroquois, and Upper Canada, in the Years 1795, 1796, and 1797. . . .,* 2nd ed. (London, 1800), 1: 261; William Priest, *Travels in the United States of America* (London, 1802), 132; and Shaw Livermore, *Early American Land Companies* (New York, 1939).

22. Washington had pursued various land speculations before the Revolution, but he did not collect on his investment until after the war. He was the surveyor on bounty lands, and kept the best lands for himself, also persuading veterans to sell their shares to him. In the end, he acquired 20,147 acres. After the war, he invested in New York lands, revived his Ohio Company, and invested heavily in lands near Mount Vernon. His frontier lands totaled 60,000 acres in the West. He had landholdings in West Virginia, Pennsylvania, Ohio, and Kentucky, and realized $50,000 in profits from selling tracts of the frontier lands between 1795 and 1799. He also invested in several canal schemes and government securities. See Ferling, *First of Men,* 69–73, 331–35, 489–90, and Dangerfield, *Chancellor Robert R. Livingston,* 253; Robert Frances Jones, "The Public Career of William Duer: Rebel, Federalist Politician, Entrepreneur, and Speculator, 1775–1792," Ph.D. Dissertation, University of Notre Dame, 1966, 193–99, 204, 208; for satire of Hamilton as "Magnus Apollo," see *New-York Journal,* June 11, 1790.

23. For James Monroe, see Robert D. Arbuckle, *Pennsylvania Speculator and Patriot: The Entrepreneurial John Nicholson, 1757–1800* (University Park, Pa., 1975), 85; for the term "plunged head and ears," see Melancton Smith to Andrew Craigie, Oct. 1787, quoted in Brooks, "Melancton Smith," 142; and for Troup and Livingston's involvement in the Million Dollar Bank and Troup's numerous land ventures, see Tripp, Jr., *Robert Troup,* 138–41, 148–79.

24. See Peter Colt to AB, Sept. 17, 1787, in Kline, ed., *Burr Papers,* I: 30–31; Geissler, *Jonathan Edwards to Aaron Burr,* 15; Davis, ed., *Memoirs of Aaron Burr,* I: 205–07; and "Deed to William Malcolm and AB for Manhattan Property," Dec. 13, 1785, Burr Papers, microfilm, reel 1.

25. Brant's second wife was another daughter of George Croghan—see Kline, ed., *Burr Papers,* I: 3–4, 83; Williams, "The Prevosts of the Royal Americans," 20–25.

26. Burr pledged his assistance to Prevost in 1784—see AB to Augustine Prevost, Jan. 6, 1784, Burr Papers, microfilm, reel 1. Burr moved for an attachment against the sheriff for contempt in violating the injunction. Goebel offers a weak defense of Hamilton in this affair: "In the absence of documentation it cannot be assumed that Hamilton in any way perpetrated a fraud upon the court. As to the controversial sheriff's sale of Croghan's remaining Otsego lands in 1786, no attempt was ever made to set it aside, to the best of our knowledge, and the contempt proceeding was never pressed. We suspect that it was the Cooper and Craig, a 'hardnosed' pair, who pressured Sheriff Clyde to proceed with the sale in violation of the injunction issued out by the Chancery, and not Hamilton. If Hamilton did counsel his clients and the sheriff to disregard the Chancellor's order, he violated the terms of the injunction and acted in an unethical manner." See Goebel, ed., *The Law Practice of Alexander Hamilton,* IV: 78–89, 91–104, 113; Williams, "The Prevosts of the Royal Amer-

icans," 25–26; and Alan Taylor, *William Cooper's Town: Power and Persuasion on the Frontier of the Early American Republic* (New York, 1995), 66–70.

27. See William Cooper to AB, Nov. 19, 1787, in Kline, ed., *Burr Papers,* I:32; Goebel, ed., *The Law Practice of Alexander Hamilton,* IV: 105. For the mutual affection between Burr and Prevost, see AB to Augustine Prevost, Jan. 9, 1784, and Aug. 1785, and for Burr's letters offering advice, AB to Augustine Prevost, Mar. 26, 1789, and Apr. 5, 1789. Prevost even purchased gifts for the Burr family; see "Augustine Prevost: memorandum of Sundry articles . . . sent to Col. Burr's Family," [1783–91?]; and for Burr's desire to live in the country, see AB to Augustine Prevost, Mar. 26, 1789, Burr Papers, microfilm, reel 1; see also Williams, "The Prevosts of the Royal Americans," 28–29.

28. See Burr's letters to William Cockburn, the surveyor, May 24, 1784, and Burr's interest in the "Georgia or Misicipi Lands," AB to Augustine Prevost, Mar. 12, 1787, in Kline, ed., *Burr Papers,* I: 9–11. See also AB to William Cockburn, Oct. 24, and Aug. 23, 1784. And for a letter about selling his Katskill lands, or getting compensation for his western lands, see AB to Augustine Prevost, June 7, 1790, in Burr Papers, microfilm, reel 1; and Williams, "The Prevosts of the Royal Americans," 33–34.

29. Kline, ed., *Burr Papers,* I: 38–39; Dixon Ryan Fox, *Yankees versus Yorkers* (New York, 1940), 185.

30. Kline, ed., *Burr Papers,* I: 39–42, 36.

31. *Ibid.,* I: 45. See Parton, *Life and Times of Aaron Burr,* I: 51–52; Wandell and Minnigerode, *Aaron Burr,* I: 22; Schachner, *Aaron Burr,* 19. Lomask also rejects this view of Uncle Timothy as stern Calvinist, but does not address his career as a speculator; see Lomask, *Aaron Burr: The Years from Princeton to the Vice President,* 22–23.

32. Pierpont Edwards to AB, July 31, Aug. 8, 1785, Burr Papers, microfilm, reel 1.

33. See AB to Pierpont Edwards, Aug. 13, 1785, Burr Papers, microfilm, reel 1. Some historians have dismissed the story of Pierpont's infidelities, but this letter speaks for itself. For a defense of Edwards, see "Pierpont Edwards," in James McLachlan, ed., *The Princetonians, 1748–1768,* I: 641–42; and for a study which acknowledges his sexual affairs, see Charles A. Heckman, "A Jeffersonian Lawyer and Judge in Federalist Connecticut: The Career of Pierpont Edwards," *Connecticut Law Review* 28 (Spring 1996): 4–5.

34. John Adams to Benjamin Rush, Jan. 25, 1806, in Schutz and Adair, eds., *The Spur of Fame,* 48; "Pierpont Edwards," in McLaughlin, ed., *The Princetonians 1748-1768,* I: 641–42; Heckman, "A Jeffersonian Lawyer," 45.

35. Heckman, "A Jeffersonian Lawyer," 2, 9.

36. Burr did not take his seat in the assembly until Nov. 5, 1784—see *Journal of the Assembly of the State of New York,* 8th sess. (1784), 37.

37. See Champagne, *Alexander McDougall,* 185–99, 209–11; see also Kline, ed., *Burr Papers,* I: 4.

38. Champagne, *Alexander McDougall,* 201.

39. Davis, ed., *Memoirs of Aaron Burr,* I: 249–51; see also *Journal of the Assembly of the State of New York,* 8th sess. (1785), 39, 78–79.

40. See Saul Cornell, *The Other Founders: Anti-Federalists and the Dissenting Tradition in America, 1788–1828* (Chapel Hill, N.C., 1999), 83, 85, 98; Brooks, "Melancton Smith," 176–80.

41. Burrows and Wallace, *Gotham,* 292, 295.

42. Oliver was a merchant from Ulster County, who served with Burr in Malcolm's regiment in 1777–79—see AB to Richard Oliver, July 29, 1788, in Kline, ed., *Burr Papers,* I: 33–34.

43. See *New-York Journal,* Apr. 30, 1788.

44. Davis refers to a 1788 handbill with Burr as a candidate for the assembly, including "William Denning, Melancton Smith, Marinus Willett, and Aaron Burr"—Davis, *Memoirs of Aaron Burr,* I: 286. For the same handbill and notices in the newspapers, see *New-York Journal,* May 1, 1788; and for the poor showing of Anti-Federalist candidates in New York City as compared to Federalists, see *New-York Journal,* June 7, 1788; and Brooks, "Melancton Smith," 167, 169.

45. AB to Theodore Sedgwick, Oct. 30, 1788, in Kline, ed., *Burr Papers,* I: 36–37; Young, *The Democratic Republicans,* 119.

46. See *Thomas Greenleaf v. William S. Livingston,* Oct. 1788, NYSC Cases, Burr Papers, microfilm, reel 15; Leake, *Memoir of the Life and Times of General John Lamb,* 332–36; and Young, *The Democratic Republicans,* 120–21.

47. Young, *The Democratic Republicans,* 120. For Lawrence as swing vote along with Smith, see Brooks, "Melancton Smith," 239. For Lawrence's veneration of Burr, see Nathaniel Hazard to Alexander Hamilton, Sept. 30, 1791, in Syrett, ed., *Hamilton Papers,* IX: 246–47. Lawrence and William Smith Livingston were Princeton graduates. Livingston was one year older than Burr, and they both graduated in 1772—so they obviously knew each other. Lawrence was younger (born in 1761); he was a member of the class of 1783, accepted to the New York bar on Aug. 1, 1786—four years after Burr. Livingston was admitted to the New Jersey bar in 1780, and needed Burr's help to get an injunction lifted so he could practice in New York. He had an office on Wall Street by 1786. Given Burr's previous friendship with Livingston, he could have represented him—but he did not. See "William Smith Livingston," in Harrison, ed., *Princetonians, 1769–1775,* III: 236–40; "Nathaniel Lawrence," in Richard A. Harrison, ed., *Princetonians, 1776–1783,* III: 425–29.

48. Thomas E.V. Smith, *The City of New York in the Year of Washington's Inauguration, 1789* (New York, 1889), 220–22; Young, *The Democratic Republicans,* 149.

49. AB to Augustine James Frederick Prevost, Apr. 22, 1789, in Burr Papers, microfilm, reel 2; Edgar Mayhew Bacon, "Washington's Inauguration in the First Federal Capital," in *History of the State of New York.* Vol. 5: *Conquering the Wil-*

derness (New York, 1934), 86; Smith, *The City of New York,* 229; and Young, *The Democratic Republicans,* 150.

50. See "To the Supervisors of the City of Albany, in the County of Albany" [signed by Alexander Hamilton, Chairman], *Daily Advertiser,* Feb. 20, 1789; and "To the Freeholders of the State of New York," *New-York Journal,* Mar. 26, 1789. For the nominating committee, see *Daily Advertiser,* Feb. 21, 1789; for rumors of Burr's possible candidacy for Congress, see *Daily Advertiser,* Feb. 20, 1789. This rumor appeared a day before his name was listed on the nominating committee for Yates.

51. Hamilton signed his letters "H.G." See "Letter I," "Letter II," "Letter III," *Daily Advertiser,* Mar. 10, 11, 12 1789. In "Letter III," he even accuses Clinton of stealing the election from Schuyler in 1777: "So far is the first report from being true, that it is a fact notorious to those who were acquainted with the transactions of the period, that in the very first election for Governor in this state, General Schuyler was a competitor with Mr. Clinton for the office, and it is alleged would have been likely to prevail, had not the votes of a considerable body of militia, then under the immediate command and influence of the latter, turned the scale in his favour."

52. The "sphere" argument was popular during the ratification debate. See a letter signed "Honestus," *New-York Journal,* Apr. 28, 1788; for attacks on Clinton's decorum, see "To the Supervisors of the City of Albany, in the County of Albany," *Daily Advertiser,* Feb. 20, 1789; and for the ensuing debates on Clinton's "hospitality," see "To the Freeholders of the Southern District," *Daily Advertiser,* Mar. 21, 1789; "To the Electors of the County of Ulster," *New-York Journal,* Apr. 2, 1789; and *New-York Journal,* Apr. 23, 1789; also Young, *The Democratic Republicans,* 139. See also Kenneth R. Bowling, "New York City, Capital of the United States, 1785–1790," in Schechter and Tripp, eds., *World of the Founders,* 13–17; Allgor, *Parlor Politics:* 18–20; and Rufus Griswold, *The Republican Court, or American Society in the Days of Washington* (New York, 1855), 215.

53. Young, *The Democratic Republicans,* 131, 145.

54. For Burr's cases as attorney general, see NYSC Cases, Burr Papers, microfilm, reels 15 and 16; for his reference to rape, see AB to ?, May 12, 1791, Burr Papers, microfilm, reel 2; and Kline, ed., *Burr Papers,* I: 47–48.

55. Burr's reform ideas were similar to those of his Princeton classmate, William Bradford, Jr., who was appointed to the Pennsylvania Supreme Court in 1791, and published a pamphlet on felony law reform in 1793. See "William Bradford, Jr.," in Harrison, ed., *Princetonians: 1769–1775,* II: 185–91; and Bradley Chapin, "Felony Law Reform in the Early Republic," *Pennsylvania Magazine of History and Biography* 113 (1989): 164–65, 172.

56. See "Observations of the Attorney General," Mar. 2, 1791, in Kline, ed., *Burr Papers,* I: 72–76.

57. Twelve of the fourteen state senators had been Anti-Federalists; David Gelston put forward the nomination, while Dr. Thomas Tillotson, Chancellor Livingston's brother-in-law, sealed the deal. See *New-York Journal,* Jan. 20, 24, 1791; Young, *The Democratic Republicans,* 189–91.

58. Hamilton admitted to Livingston's brother-in-law, Morgan Lewis, that he had blocked Livingston's appointment to Washington's cabinet or another high office—see Young, *The Democratic Republicans,* 159–61, 189–90.

59. Joanne B. Freeman, "The Art and Address of Ministerial Management: Secretary of the Treasury Alexander Hamilton," in Bowling and Kennon, eds., *Neither Separate Nor Equal: Congress in the 1790s,* 273, 276–78.

60. Robert Troup to AH, June 15, 1791, and Nathanial Hazard to AH, Nov. 25, 1791, in Syrett, ed., *Hamilton Papers,* VIII: 478–79, IX: 529–31.

61. Schuyler was livid over his defeat, taking his slight no better than Livingston had when President Washington spurned him. He became even more committed to defeating Clinton, and deeply resented Burr. Hamilton had been outmaneuvered—and he certainly did not take kindly to defectors. William Smith Livingston (the ax-wielding parade marshal who had attacked Greenleaf's shop) left the Federalist band, and Hamilton called him "that Whore in politics." Jefferson later lured Pennsylvanian Tench Coxe, the assistant secretary of the treasury, Hamilton's chief aide, into the Republican camp. After this, Hamilton did everything within his power to destroy Coxe. See Young, *The Democratic Republicans,* 161, 192; Don R. Gerlach, *Philip Schulyer and the Growth of New York, 1733–1804* (Albany, N.Y., 1968), 36; Syrett, ed., *Hamilton Papers,* XIII: 480–81; and Jacob E. Cooke, *Tench Coxe and the Early Republic* (Chapel Hill, N.C., 1978), 156, 330.

62. AB to Theodore Sedgwick, Jan. 20, Feb. 3, 1791, in Burr Papers, microfilm, reel 2.

63. See *Albany Register,* Feb. 13, 1792; and Kline, ed., *Burr Papers,* I: 93–97.

64. AB to Theodosia Prevost Burr, Feb. 19, 1792, in Davis, ed., *Memoirs of Aaron Burr,* I: 315; Kline, ed., *Burr Papers,* I: 101–03. On St. Clair, see Ferling, *First of Men,* 406–07.

65. See "Governor's Election," *Albany Register,* Feb. 13, 1792; for the three-man race, see *New-York Journal,* Feb. 15, 1792, and Young, *The Democratic Republicans,* 280.

66. A letter signed "A Plain Farmer," *Daily Advertiser,* Feb. 16, 1792.

67. See James Fairlie to Robert Yates, Feb. 8, 1792, Misc. Mss., Fairlie Papers, New-York Historical Society; and Robert Ernst, *Rufus King: American Federalist* (Chapel Hill, N.C., 1968), 67–69; Schachner, *Alexander Hamilton,* 8, 102–05.

68. Peter Van Gaasbeek to AB, March 28, 1792, in Kline, ed., *Burr Papers,* I: 103.

69. Young, *The Democratic Republicans,* 234, 237, 239; Kline, ed., *Burr Papers,* I: 77–86; Davis, ed., *Memoirs of Aaron Burr,* I: 329–30.

70. Jones, "The Public Career of William Duer," 261–63, 282, 287.

71. Young, *The Democratic Republicans*, 305–06.

72. See AB to Tench Coxe, June 12, 1792, and AB to Jacob Delamater, June 15, 1792, in Kline, ed., *Burr Papers*, 124–26; Young, *The Democratic Republicans*, 309.

73. Robert Troup to John Jay, June 10, 1792, cited in Tripp, *Robert Troup*, 105; see also letter of William Willcocks, *Daily Advertiser*, June 14, 1792; *New-York Journal*, June 30, 1792; Young, *The Democratic Republicans*, 304, 310–11; and Kline, ed., *Burr Papers*, I: 111–12.

74. See AB to Jacob Delamater, June 15, 1792, in Kline, ed., *Burr Papers*, I: 109, 126; Burr was defended (probably by a friend) in the newspapers on similar grounds, claiming that "In this business Col. Burr stands clear of the charge of party; he had been opposed to Governor Clinton, and of course did not favor his interest." See "To the People of the State of New York," signed "Columbianus," in *New-York Journal*, Aug. 11, 1792; also Young, *The Democratic Republicans*, 309.

75. Young, *The Democratic Republicans*, 85–86, 305; Brooks, "Melancton Smith," 211.

76. As I noted before, Burr had faced Cooper's unscrupulous dealings in the legal battle over the Otsego Patent in 1785. Richard Smith was one in a long line of corrupt sheriffs under Cooper's thumb. For the accusations of fraud and corruption by the canvassers, see "The Reasons Assigned by the Majority of the Canvassers, in Vindication of their Conduct," first published June 15, 1792, reprinted in *An Impartial Statement of the Controversy, Respecting the Decision of the Late Committee of Canvassers* (New York, 1792), 19, in Burr Papers, microfilm, reel 3. Though the "Reasons" was published after Burr drafted his opinion, it is evident that Burr was well aware of the charges of corruption. In his opinion, he wrote that based on the affidavits, Richard Smith "knew of the appointment of Mr. Gilbert." He suggests here that Smith blatantly held onto the position. Thomas Greenleaf had filled his paper, the *New-York Journal*, with affidavits attesting to intimation by Cooper before the canvassers made their decision—see letter signed "A.B.," *New-York Journal*, June 2, 1792. Melancton Smith wrote a letter to the papers about the "fraud and corruption" in Otsego—see letter signed "Lucuis" in *New-York Journal*, June 30, 1792. David Gelston led the investigation of Judge Cooper in the state assembly—see Young, *The Democratic Republicans*, 296, 300–01, 321–22; Brooks, "Melancton Smith," 211; Taylor, *William Cooper's Town*, 175–80.

77. Kline, ed., *Burr Papers*, I: 112–13, 126–29, 132–33.

78. AB to James Monroe, Sept. 10, 1792, in Kline, ed., *Burr Papers*, I: 135–37.

79. AH to unknown, Sept. 26, 1792, in Syrett, ed., *Hamilton Papers*, XII: 480.

80. AB to Jacob Delamater, June 15, 1792, in Kline, ed., *Burr Papers*, I: 125.

81. See AB to John Trumbull, Aug. 20, 1972, Peter Colt to AB, Sept. 5, 1972, and AB to Theodore Sedgwick, Oct. 14, 1972, in Kline, ed., *Burr Papers*, I: 131–35, 140–42.

82. AB to Theodore Sedgwick, Oct. 14, 1792, in Kline, ed., *Burr Papers,* I: 140–41.

83. The rebuttal to Burr's pamphlet was entitled *An Appendix to the Impartial Statement of the Controversy Respecting the Decision of the Late Committee of Canvassers* (New York, 1792); not only did this include Trumbull's opinion, but even his boyhood friend, Aaron Ogden, signed on to an opinion criticizing Burr. See Kline, ed., *Burr Papers,* I: 114.

84. Benjamin Rush to AB, Sept. 24, 1792, in Kline, ed., *Burr Papers,* I: 137–38; and Noble E. Cunningham, "John Beckley: An Early American Party Manager," *William and Mary Quarterly,* 3rd ser., 13 (Jan. 1956): 40–52, esp. 41. See also Jeffrey L. Pasley, "'A Journeyman, Either in Law or Politics': John Beckley and the Social Origins of Political Campaigning," *Journal of the Early Republic* 16 (Winter 1996): 531–69.

85. Benjamin Rush to AB, Sept. 24, 1792.

86. John Nicholson to James Madison, Oct. 3, 1792, The James Madison Papers, Library of Congress. See also Noble Cunningham, *The Jeffersonian Republicans: The Formation of Party Organization, 1789–1801* (Chapel Hill, N.C., 1957), 46.

87. Melancton Smith and Marius Willett to James Monroe and James Madison, Sept. 30, 1792, The James Monroe Papers, Library of Congress; and AB to John Nicholson, Oct. 7, 1792, in Kline, ed., *Burr Papers,* I: 139. Clinton broke the tie on the Council of Appointment in favor of appointing Burr an associate justice to the state supreme court on Oct. 2. Burr's letter of introduction for Smith was dated Oct. 7. See Young, *The Democratic Republicans,* 328; also Schachner, *Alexander Hamilton,* 308.

88. Arbuckle, *Pennsylvania Speculator and Patriot,* 78–79, 85; Cunningham, *The Jeffersonian Republicans,* 49. Monroe purchased 100,000 acres of land in the Kentucky Territory, and planned a venture with Madison for land in Genesee Valley, New York. See Ammon, *James Monroe,* 38–39, 78.

89. Monroe and Madison to Smith and Willett, Oct. 19, 1792, James Monroe Papers; see also James Monroe to James Madison, Oct. 9, 1792, in Stanislaus Hamilton, ed., *The Writings of James Monroe,* 7 vols. (1889–1903; AMS, 1969), I: 242.

90. Monroe voiced his concerns by suggesting that the New Yorkers were placing their state and regional interests above "union," though he noted that they had made no effort to garner northern support for Burr. James Monroe to Thomas Jefferson, June 14, 1792, and James Monroe to James Madison, Oct. 9, 1792, in Hamilton, ed., *Writings of James Monroe,* I: 237–38, 242.

91. Young, *The Democratic Republicans,* 332.

92. AH to Gouverneur Morris, Dec. 24, 26, 27, 1800, and Jan. 16, 1801; AH to Oliver Wolcott, Dec. 16, 1800; and AH to Theodore Sedgwick, Dec. 22, 1800; for the earlier letters, see AH to unknown, Sept. 21, 1792, and AH to unknown, Sept. 26, 1792, in Syrett, ed., *Hamilton Papers,* XII: 408, 480.

93. AH to unknown, Sept. 21, 1792.

94. *Ibid.* Duer owed between $1,583,000 (estimated by the Federalist paper, *The Gazette of the United States*) and $3 million. There is no evidence that Hamilton asked Duer to resign; he left because he felt he could promote his schemes better outside of the government. In 1792, he begged Hamilton for help after the U.S. district attorney brought suit against him for the settlement of his accounts, which had been left unpaid largely due to Hamilton. After Duer entered prison, Hamilton never visited him, and only communicated by mail; he made several small loans, but had abandoned his friend by May. Hamilton's other close friend, Robert Troup, resembled Duer, investing in schemes like the Million Dollar Bank in 1791. Troup's finances were precarious through the 1790s, and he was on the brink of ruin in 1798. At the time of his death, Hamilton's friends organized a subscription of $100,000 to pay for his debts and provide for his family. See Jones, "The Public Career of William Duer," 269, 277–78, 289; Tripp, *Robert Troup,* 140–41, 178; and for Hamilton's debts, see Mitchell, *Alexander Hamilton,* 547–53.

95. Hamilton was receiving reports on Burr's activities. As early as 1791, Nathaniel Hazard claimed that Smith, Nathaniel Lawrence, and Miles Hughes all "dislike Clinton," and that Lawrence was a great admirer of Burr. After the election controversy, Troup reported to John Jay that the New York Federalists were "determined to rip him [Burr] up." See Nathaniel Hazard to Alexander Hamilton, Sept. 30, 1791, in Syrett, ed., *Hamilton Papers,* IX: 246–47; and Young, *The Democratic Republicans,* 328.

96. The first two letters were written on Sept. 21 and 26, and his letter to John Steele on Oct. 15, 1792; see Syrett, *Hamilton Papers,* XII: 568–69. John Steele of North Carolina was a moderate Federalist; he served two terms in the U.S. Congress and was appointed comptroller of the treasury in 1796 (Kline, ed., *Burr Papers,* II: 671). Burr may have been friendly with Steele, as suggested in a letter to Benjamin Rush in which he says, "your cheerful friend Mr. Steele was about ten days in town." See AB to Benjamin Rush, Aug. 20, 1793, Burr Papers, microfilm, reel 3.

97. Schachner, *Alexander Hamilton,* 364–65.

98. *Ibid.,* 366–69.

99. See AB to Theodosia Prevost Burr, Oct. 30, 1791, in Davis, ed., *Memoirs of Aaron Burr,* I: 304. Jacob Katz Cogan identified the relationship between Burr and Maria Reynolds's daughter in "The Reynolds Affair and the Politics of Character," *Journal of the Early Republic* 16 (Fall 1996): 416. Burr handled two divorce cases in 1790, one involving prominent members of the Livingston clan. In each case, Burr represented the wife. In the Livingston case, the wife charged her husband with committing adultery with the same woman for three years. See *John Strang v. Anne Lousberry Strang* [Apr. 20, 1790] and *Anne Horne Livingston v. Henry Beekman Livingston,* Dec. 7, 1790, NYCC cases, Burr Papers, microfilm, reel 19.

100. For the list of congressmen and the residences, see Dorcus K. Helms, "An Uneasy Alliance: The Relationhip between Jefferson and Burr: 1791–1807," M.A. Thesis, North Texas State University, 1979, 5; also Kenneth R. Bowling, "The Federal Government and the Republican Court Move to Philadelphia, November 1791–March 1791," and Anna Coxe Toogood, "Philadelphia as the National Capital, 1790–1800," both in Bowling and Kennon, eds., *Neither Separate nor Equal: Congress in the 1790s,* 5, 8, 38–39.

101. Bowling, "The Federal Government and the Republican Court," in Bowling and Kennon, eds., *Neither Separate Nor Equal: Congress in the 1790s,* 5, 9, 17–21.

102. Abigail Adams to Abigail Smith, Nov. 21–28, Dec. 26, 1790, in Charles F. Adams, ed., *Letters of Mrs. Adams, the Wife of John Adams* (Boston, 1840), 209–11; Wendy A. Nicholson, "Making the Private Public: Anne Willing Bingham's Role as Leader of Philadelphia's Social Elite in the late Eighteenth Century," M.A. Thesis, University of Delaware, 1988, 2, 4–6, 22–25; and Elizabeth M. Nuxoll, "The Financier as Senator, Robert Morris of Pennsylvania, 1789–1795," in Bowling and Kennon, eds., *Neither Separate Nor Equal: Congress in the 1790s,* 116–19, 122.

103. Nicholson, "Making the Private Public," 47–49, 52–54; Bowling, "The Federal Government and the Republican Court," in Bowling and Kennon, eds., *Neither Separate Nor Equal: Congress in the 1790s,* 22–23.

104. AB to Theodosia Prevost Burr, Oct. 27, 1791, and Dec. 27, 1791, in Davis, ed., *Memoirs of Aaron Burr,* I: 303, 313.

105. Theodosia Prevost Burr to John Bartow Prevost, Mar. 23, 1792, in Burr Papers, microfilm, reel 3.

106. AB to Theodosia Prevost Burr, Feb. 8, 1793, in Davis, ed., *Memoirs of Aaron Burr,* I: 362.

107. AB to Theodosia Prevost Burr, Dec. 27, 1791, in *ibid.,* I: 313; and AB to Pierpont Edwards, [Oct.–Nov. 1791]; and *James and Elizabeth Monroe, Nicholas and Hester Gouverneur, and Thomas and Mary Knox v. John Kortright,* Nov. 15, 1794, NYCC Cases, Burr Papers, microfilm, reels 2 and 20.

108. For a copy of Dolley Payne Todd's will in Burr's handwriting (dated May 13, 1794), see Burr Papers, microfilm, reel 3; see also David B. Mattern and Holly C. Shulman, eds., *The Selected Letters of Dolley Payne Madison* (Charlottesville, Va., 2003), 15–16.

109. See "A Fair Correspondent," *Albany Register,* Mar. 17, 1794, cited in Young, *The Democratic Republicans,* 350, 362. For the political role of fashion in Revolutionary France and the United States in the early republic, see Susan Branson, *These Fiery Frenchified Dames: Women and Political Culture in Early National Pennsylvania* (Philadelphia, 2001), 69–72.

110. James Roger Sharp, *American Politics in the Early Republic: The New Nation in Crisis* (New Haven, Conn., 1993), 79, 82–83; Young, *The Democratic Republicans,* 353, 357.

111. AB to John Nicholson, July 16, 1793, in Kline, ed., *Burr Papers,* I: 156–57; and John Steele to Alexander Hamilton, Apr. 30, 1793, in Syrett, ed., *Hamilton Papers,* XIV: 358–59.

112. For his praise of the new French Constitution, see AB to Theodosia Prevost Burr, Dec. 15, 1791, in Davis, ed., *Memoirs of Aaron Burr,* I: 312. Burr sent his friend Jacob Delamater the fifth volume of Rousseau's *Confessions;* see AB to Jacob Delamater, Nov. 20, 1793, in Burr Papers, microfilm, reel 3; and Richard N. Côte, *Theodosia Burr Alston: Portrait of a Prodigy* (Mount Pleasant, S.C., 2003), 91–93.

113. Young, *The Democratic Republicans,* 354, 393–94; and Albrecht Koschnik, "The Democratic Societies of Philadelphia and the Limits of the American Public Sphere, circa 1793–1795," *William and Mary Quarterly* 58, ser. 3 (2001): 615–36.

114. See Thomas Jefferson to AB, Jan. 20, 1793, and "Motion on the Letter to the French Republic" [Apr. 24, 1794], and AB to James Monroe, May 30, 1794, in Kline, ed., *Burr Papers,* I: 145–46, 178–79, 180–81; and William Howard Adams, *Gouverneur Morris: An Independent Life* (New Haven, Conn., 2003), 231, 234.

115. Monroe confided to Jefferson that Washington opposed Burr for reasons of a "personal nature," but he does not explain what those reasons might have been. See James Monroe to Thomas Jefferson, May 26, 1794, The Thomas Jefferson Papers, Library of Congress; Adams, *Gouverneur Morris,* 249; and Theodore Sedgwick to Jonathan Dayton, Nov. 19, 1796, in Syrett, ed., *Hamilton Papers,* XX: 407.

116. AB to Pierpont Edwards, May 24, 1794, Burr Papers, microfilm, reel 3; Kline, ed., *Burr Papers,* I: 181–82; Lomask, *Aaron Burr: The Years from Princeton to Vice President,* 197. Burr wrote a similar letter to Timothy Edwards, that "my once amiable and accomplished wife had died." See AB to Timothy Edwards, May 24, 1794, personal collection of Brian D. Hardison, who generously sent me this letter.

117. Theodosia Burr to John Bartow Prevost, Mar. 23, 1792, Burr Papers, microfilm, reel 3; and for the phrase "Poor Coln Bur has Lost his Wife," see Catherine Coles to Dolley Payne Todd [Madison], June 1, 1794, Letters of Dolley Madison, 1794–1837, Special Collections, University of Virginia, Charlottesville, Va.; also cited in Mattern and Shulman, eds., *Selected Letters of Dolley Payne Madison,* 28.

CHAPTER FIVE

1. Though the figure was first identified as Jefferson, Noble Cunningham, one of the foremost historians on the rise of the Republican Party, claims it could just as easily be Burr—see Noble E. Cunningham, *The Image of Thomas Jefferson in*

the *Public Eye: Portraits for the People* (Charlottesville, Va., 1981), 113. Another scholar has argued that the figure is Israel Israel, a wealthy stable owner and tavern keeper, and prominent member of the Democratic Society of Philadelphia. The attacks against him as a greedy broker are anti-Semitic slurs. Still, Swanwick is a better candidate for the figure. Israel was six feet tall (like Jefferson, who was six feet two and a half) and the character is not: he is standing on an elevated podium. Swanwick was known as an orator; Israel was not. The Shakespearean reference points to Swanwick rather than Israel. And Swanwick was a wealthy import-export merchant actively involved in the dry goods trade, which is referred to in the speech given by the figure. On Swanwick (1759–98) and his identification in the cartoon, see Ronald Baumann, "John Swanwick: Spokesman for Merchant-Republicanism in Philadelphia," *Pennsylvania Magazine of History and Biography* 97 (Apr. 1973): 164; and Baumann, "The Democratic-Republicans of Philadelphia: The Origins, 1776–1797," Ph.D. Dissertation, Pennsylvania State University, 1970, 503. See also William Pencak, "Jews and Anti-Semitism in Early Pennsylvania," *Pennsylvania Magazine of History and Biography* 124 (July 2002): 398–400.

2. See Baumann, "John Swanwick," 139–42, 148–50; Henry Adams, *Life of Albert Gallatin* (1879; New York, 1943), 188.

3. Baumann notes that Swanwick had acquired tremendous wealth: he owned thirteen ships, many shares of bank stock, urban real estate, and a 200-acre estate. In the cartoon, he is mentioned as crushing other merchants in the dry goods trade. This is a reference to Swanwick's ability to establish new overseas markets in China, India, Germany, and France, while his competitors, by staying within the British trade network, languished in the 1780s. See Baumann, "John Swanwick," 133, 142–43; and Baumann, "The Democratic-Republicans," 502–04.

4. For Burr's membership in the New York Democratic Society, see Philip S. Foner, ed., *The Democratic-Republican Societies, 1790–1800* (Westport, Conn., 1976), 200. Like Burr and his supporters, Swanwick shared the same belief in commercial Republicanism; see Baumann, "John Swanwick," 139–53.

5. Genet is the doll-like figure, dropping coins into the hand of the man seated on the floor—see Pencak, "Jews and Anti-Semitism," 400.

6. Richard Welch, *Theodore Sedgwick, Federalist: A Political Portrait* (Middleton, Conn., 1965), 130–31; Cunningham, *The Jeffersonian Republicans,* 63, 66; and Ferling, *First of Men,* 449–53.

7. Kline, ed., *Burr Papers,* I: 160; see also "Petition against the election of Albert Gallatin," Dec. 2, 1793, National Archives and Records of Administration, Records of the U.S. Senate, Washington, D.C.

8. Adams, *Life of Albert Gallatin,* 83, 87–88, 91–93, 95–96; see also Ernest, *Rufus King,* 195.

9. For Taylor's note, see Burr Papers, microfilm, reel 1; Kline, ed, *Burr Papers*, I: 170. Coverage of the Senate hearings appeared in the *American Minerva,* the *Gazette of the United States,* the *Philadelphia Gazette,* and the New York *Daily Advertiser,* to name just a few. For a report that the public Senate hearings attracted a "crowded audience the whole time," see *Pittsburgh Gazette,* Mar. 8, 1794.

10. See coverage of the Senate hearings in the *American Minerva,* Feb. 28, 1794.

11. Gallatin also spoke in his own defense; yet his argument was very different from Burr's definition of citizenship—Albert Gallatin to AB [before Feb. 27, 1794], in Kline, ed., *Burr Papers,* I: 165. For a discussion of Gallatin's arguments, see James H. Kettner, *The Development of American Citizenship, 1608–1870* (Chapel Hill, N.C., 1978), 233–34.

12. See the notes taken by Gallatin and King on Burr's remarks in Kline, ed., *Burr Papers,* I: 168–69, 173–74.

13. Burr's arguments in part reflected the constitutional idea of "volitional allegiance," popular during the Revolution. But that model was never applied to foreign-born residents. Congressman Theodore Sedgwick best expressed the Federalist stand on citizenship in December 1794, when the House debated revising the Naturalization Law. Sedgwick argued that native-born Americans had years of training, in schools and community life, that prepared them for the duties of citizenship. Anglo-American culture had to be learned through years of experience. See Kettner, *The Development of American Citizenship,* 194, 232–35; Welch, *Theodore Sedgwick,* 133–34.

14. See AB to Samuel Smith, Dec. 17, 1800, in Kline, ed., *Burr Papers,* I: 472.

15. For vote, see *American Minerva,* Mar. 13, 1794; see also John Adams to Abigail Adams, Mar. 2, 1794, in Adams, ed., *Letters of John Adams, Addressed to his Wife,* II: 145. A later account praised Burr for a "discourse of considerable ingenuity"; see [Joseph] *Delaphlaine's Repository . . . ,* 2 vols. (Philadelphia, 1815–18), I: 183, quoted in Kline, ed., *Burr Papers,* I: 170; and Ammon, *James Monroe,* 110.

16. See Adams, *Life of Gallatin,* 100–01, 109.

17. AB was ordering and recommending Bentham's writings as early as 1803, long before he met him in 1808—see Kline, ed., *Burr Papers,* II: 767–68, 1057; Adams, *Life of Gallatin,* 289; Raymond D. Walters, Jr., *Albert Gallatin: Jeffersonian Financier and Diplomat* (New York, 1957); also AB to Theodosia Burr Alston, Sept. 9, 1808, in Van Doren, ed., *Correspondence of Aaron Burr and his Daughter Theodosia,* 242.

18. As Gallatin wrote: "My advantages consisted in laborious investigation, habits of analysis, thorough knowledge of the subjects under discussion, and more extensive general information"—Adams, *Life of Gallatin,* 154, 156.

19. William B. Hatcher, *Edward Livingston: Jeffersonian Republican and Jacksonian*

Democrat (University, La., 1940), 25, 28–32, 36; see also "Edward Livingston," in Harrison, ed., *Princetonians, 1776–1783,* II: 333–35.

20. Joseph Charles, "The Jay Treaty: The Origins of the American Party System," *William and Mary Quarterly,* 3rd ser., 12 (Oct. 1955): 589–90, 92–93; Young, *The Democratic Republicans,* 366–67; Ferling, *First of Men,* 437–38.

21. For Burr's leadership in the opposition against Jay's appointment, see John Jay to Sarah Livingston Jay, Apr. 20, 1794, in John Jay Papers, Columbia University, New York; see also Kline, ed., *Burr Papers,* I: 177–78.

22. For Burr's recommendation of his stepson, see AB to James Monroe, May 30, 1794. Burr continued to write to Monroe, and send him the latest news; see AB to Monroe, July 5, Aug. 2, Sept. 11, Dec. 24, 1795; and for Tazewell and Mason's relationship to Burr, AB to Henry Tazewell, Sept. 3, Oct. 11, 1795, in Kline, ed., *Burr Papers,* I: 180, 212, 223–30; see also Ammon, *James Monroe,* 92.

23. Charles, "The Jay Treaty," 592; Ferling, *First of Men,* 456; Mitchell, *Alexander Hamilton,* 333; Kline, ed., *Burr Papers,* I: 212.

24. Charles, "The Jay Treaty," 594; Ernest, *Rufus King,* 206; Kline, ed., *Burr Papers,* I: 219–20. For a somewhat less critical view of the Jay Treaty, see Sharp, *American Politics in the Early Republic,* 117.

25. See Albert Gallatin to Hannah Gallatin, June 29, 1795, in Adams, *Life of Albert Gallatin,* 151; AB to George Washington, June 16, 1795, in Kline, ed., *Burr Papers,* I: 212–15, 218–19.

26. See "Franklin—No. XI," *Argus,* May 26, 1795; "From a Correspondent," [reprinted from the *Aurora*], *Argus,* June 20, 1795; "From a Correspondent," [reprinted from the *Aurora*], *New-York Journal and Patriotic Register,* June 20, 1795.

27. Charles, "The Jay Treaty," 595. Greenleaf did publish the copy from the *Aurora,* but he published it at the same time he published the motions by Burr and Tazewell. Rufus King claimed that Burr been circulating his copy among his constituents—see *Argus,* July 3, 1795. For Burr's motions, see *Argus,* July 4, 1795, and *New-York Journal and Patriotic Register,* July 4, 1795. For a report on King's claims of Burr circulating his copy of the treaty, see *New-York Journal,* Dec. 19, 1795.

28. See *Argus,* July 6, 1795; *New-York Journal and Patriotic Register,* July 8, 1795.

29. *The Democratiad* (Philadelphia, 1795), 10–11.

30. *Aristocracy* (Philadelphia, 1795). Charles E. Modlin was the first to identify this poem as an attack on Burr—see Modlin, "Aristocracy in the Early Republic," *Early American Literature* 6 (1972): 252–57.

31. *Aristocracy,* 15.

32. Oliver Wolcott, Sr., to Oliver Wolcott, Jr., Mar. 25, 1795, in George Gibbs, ed., *Memoirs of the Administrations of Washington and John Adams Edited from the Papers of Oliver Wolcott* (reprint New York, 1971), I: 179; see also *Aristocracy,* 9.

33. For the burning of Jay's portrait, see *New York Journal*, July 22, 1795; also Fisher Ames to Oliver Wolcott, Jr., Sept. 2, 1795, in Gibbs, ed., *Memoirs of the Administrations*, 1: 229; Young, *The Democratic Republicans*, 449, 450–53.

34. Young, *The Democratic Republicans*, 394, 418; Ernst, *Rufus King*, 203; Foner, ed., *The Democratic-Republican Societies*, 200.

35. AB to Henry Tazewell, Sept. 3, 1795, in Kline, ed., *Burr Papers*, I: 226. The New York Democratic Society published a defense of their organization in the *New-York Journal* on May 28, 1795. In its defense, the society employed the same terms that Burr had used to justify his actions during the 1792 election controversy: that is, every citizen has the right to express his opinions, and "to hear and impartially weight the arguments on both sides of the question." See Young, *The Democratic Republicans*, 415–16.

36. *Democratiad*, 10; *Aristocracy*, 14.

37. See Philip Schuyler to Rufus King, Dec. 16, 1794, box 5, folder 7, King Papers, New-York Historical Society, New York, N.Y.; Young, *The Democratic Republicans*, 430; Kline, ed., *Burr Papers*, I: 202.

38. Young, *The Democratic Republicans*, 430, 441.

39. James Madison to James Monroe, Dec. 4, 1794, in Mason and Rutland, eds., *The Papers of James Madison*, XV:408.

40. Young, *The Democratic Republicans*, 436, 136; see chapter four: "An Unprejudiced Mind."

41. Young, *The Democratic Republicans*, 431.

42. See Peter Van Gaasbeek to Stephen Van Rensselaer, Dec. 30, 1794, in Kline, ed., *Burr Papers*, I: 185–87, 202–05.

43. See Philip Schuyler to Rufus King, Dec. 16, 1794, in King Papers, box 5, folder 7, New-York Historical Society; and Young, *The Democratic Republicans*, 431–34.

44. Young, *The Democratic Republicans*, 430.

45. Federalist Daniel Hale wrote Rufus King that "Burr's creatures are indefatigable thro the whole state." Burr relied on friends, but not that alone. In the *Albany Gazette*, one of his critics claimed Burr made "*unusual* friendly visits in the Middle, Eastern and Western districts of this state," supposedly riding circuit in the four counties, acting as "*deputy prosecutor* for the people." See Daniel Hale to Rufus King, Dec. 23, 1794, in King Papers, box 5, folder 7, New-York Historical Society; and *Albany Gazette*, Dec. 8, 1794; see also Kline, ed., *Burr Papers*, I: 187.

46. See *American Minerva*, Nov. 13, 1794, and *Albany Gazette*, Dec. 8, 1794.

47. *American Minerva*, Apr. 16, 1794.

48. AB to Henry Tazewell, Sept. 3, Oct. 11, 1795, in Kline, ed., *Burr Paper*, I: 226–27, 229.

49. Dumas Malone, *Jefferson and the Ordeal of Liberty* (Boston, 1962), 276–77; Cunningham, *The Jeffersonian Republicans*, 86–87. The rumors about the meet-

ing hit the newspapers in October 1796, but Federalists were already blaming Jefferson and Burr for orchestrating the opposition against the Jay Treaty in order to subvert the Federalists and win the next presidential election. See Chauncey Goodrich to Oliver Wolcott, Sr., Apr. 12, 1796, in Gibbs, ed., *Memoirs of the Administrations of Washington and Adams*, I: 326. This claim by Goodrich was made several months before Republicans had officially decided on Burr as Jefferson's running mate, which was determined in July 1796.

50. For the absence of party machinery, except in Pennsylvania, see Cunningham, *The Jeffersonian Republicans*, 112, 114.

51. Adams assumed he would be the "heir apparent" as early as January 1796, but Federalist Party leaders reached this decision by spring. Madison admitted to Monroe that Jefferson had to be prodded to run, but his candidacy was confirmed by May. See Sharp, *American Politics in the Early Republic*, 142; also James Madison to James Monroe, Feb. 26, 1796, and May 14, 1796, in J. C. A. Stagg, ed., *The Papers of James Madison* (Charlottesville, Va., 1989), XVI: 232–33, 358.

52. Richard McCormick observed that the Republicans were "indifferent on the matter of the vice-presidential candidate." Federalists also saw the contest as a battle over the presidency alone. Hamilton's plan to place Pinckney over Adams reflects his indifference to the vice presidency; he was not selecting a running mate for Adams, but another presidential candidate. One Federalist, Oliver Wolcott, believed that Jefferson would be more dangerous as vice president than as president, because he would serve as "the rallying point of faction and French influence." See Richard McCormick, *The Presidential Game: The Origins of American Presidential Politics* (New York, 1982), 52–57; and Oliver Wolcott to Oliver Wolcott, Sr., Nov. 27, 1796, in Gibbs, ed., *Memoirs of the Administrations*, I: 400.

53. Stephen G. Kurtz, *The Presidency of John Adams: The Collapse of Federalism, 1795–1800* (New York, 1957), 92, 94–95, 186, 203.

54. *Ibid.*, 93; see also L. H. Butterfield, ed., *Diary and Autobiography of John Adams*, 4 vols. (Cambridge, 1961), 3: 229. Ulrich Phillips reinforces this view, describing Butler as the "personification of sectionalism"—see Phillips, "The South Carolina Federalists, II," *American Historical Review*, 14 (July 1909): 731. Though Butler was five years older than Burr, he carried certain liabilities: he had been born in Ireland, and had been a major in the British army until 1773. He did not, however, play an active military role in the Revolution. On the other hand, he was prominent planter and had extensive service in state government and the Continental Congress before his election to the Senate—see Billy Bob Lightfoot, "The State Delegations in the Congress of the United States, 1789–1800," Ph.D. Dissertation, University of Texas, 1958, 1021, 1023–24.

55. Federalist William Loughton Smith, who reported on the meeting, claimed that Senate Republicans felt that Langdon had "no influence." Livingston was supposedly put forward because the Virginians liked his *Cato* letters against the Jay Treaty. But Livingston had not held elected office in the 1790s; he was not known as a Republican leader. Livingston was an unlikely candidate because, as his biographer notes, his personal style had a way of "arousing the keenest hostility." See William Loughton Smith to Ralph Izard, May 18, 1796, in "South Carolina Federalist Correspondence," *American Historical Review* 14 (July 1909): 780; see also Dangerfield, *Chancellor Robert R. Livingston,* 209, 228, 245–46. For Clinton as a "safe" candidate, see chapter four: "An Unprejudiced Mind"; and for Burr's voting record, see Mary P. Ryan, "Party Formation in the United States Congress, 1789 to 1796," *William and Mary Quarterly,* 3rd ser., 28 (Oct. 1971): 532.

56. See excerpt in Wolcott's papers, in Gibbs, ed., *Memoirs of the Administration,* I: 379–80; and Jefferson to Madison, Apr. 27, 1795, in Stagg, ed., *Papers of James Madison,* 16: 1–2. James Roger Sharp notes how the word "southern" was later changed to "republican." Either Jefferson changed it when preparing his papers for the historical record because the word was embarrassing, or it was altered after his death. See Sharp's "Unraveling the Mystery of Jefferson's Letter of April 27, 1795," *Journal of the Early Republic* 6 (1986): 411–18; also Sharp, *American Politics in the Early Republic,* 144.

57. See John Beckley to James Madison, June 20, 1796, in Stagg, ed., *Papers of James Madison,* 16: 371.

58. *Ibid.* Tennessee and Kentucky stood by Burr: both states gave Jefferson and Burr an equal number of votes: 4 each from Kentucky and 3 each from Tennessee—"John Brown," in Harrison, ed., *Princetonians, 1776–1783,* III: 217–22; and Kline, ed., *Burr Papers,* I: 257–63.

59. Chauncey Goodrich to Oliver Wolcott, Sr., May 13, 1796, in Gibbs, ed., *Memoirs of the Administrations,* I: 338–39; Frank Monaghan, *John Jay* (New York, 1935), 255–61; and "John Brown," in Harrison, ed., *Princetonians, 1776–1983,* III: 220.

60. William H. Masterson, *William Blount* (Baton Rouge, La., 1954), 307, 316–23; "John Brown," *Princetonians,* 220–21.

61. Rufus King to AH, May 2, 1796, in Charles R. King, ed., *The Life and Correspondence of Rufus King,* 6 vols. (1895), II: 46.

62. John Beckley to James Madison, June 20, 1796, in Stagg, ed., *Papers of James Madison,* XVI: 371–72; for information on James Swan, see also AB to James Monroe, July 5, 1795, in Kline, ed., *Burr Papers,* I: 223–25.

63. See John Beckley to James Madison, Oct. 15, 1796, in Stagg, ed., *Papers of James Madison,* XVI: 409. For Federalist worries in Connecticut, see Chauncey Goodrich to Oliver Wolcott, Sr., May 6, 1796, in Gibbs, ed., *Memoirs of the*

Administrations, I: 337. See also AB to Pierpont Edwards, Nov. 22, 1796, in Kline, ed., *Burr Papers,* I: 273.

64. Thomas Jefferson to James Monroe, July 10, 1796, The Thomas Jefferson Papers, microfilm, Library of Congress; see also Kurtz, *The Presidency of John Adams,* 103–04; John Beckley to James Madison, June 20, 1796.

65. See Theodore Sedgwick to AH, Nov. 19, 1796, with enclosures (Dayton to Sedgwick, Nov. 12 and 13, 1796), in Syrett, ed., *Hamilton Papers,* XX: 403–04; and William Blount to John Sevier, Sept. 26, 1796, in Kline, ed., *Burr Papers,* I: 268.

66. John Adams to Abigail Adams, Dec. 12, 1796, Adams Family Papers, Massachusetts Historical Society, Boston.

67. John Beckley to James Madison, Oct. 15, 1796, in Stagg, ed., *Papers of James Madison,* XVI: 409; and Stephen Higginson to AH, Dec. 9, 1796, in Syrett, ed., *Hamilton Papers,* XX: 438.

68. [Richmond] *Virginia Argus,* printed in [Richmond] *Virginia Gazette and General Advertiser,* Oct. 12, 1796, quoted in Arthur Scherr, "The 'Republican Experiment' and the Election of 1796 in Virginia," *West Virginia History* 37 (1976): 89.

69. Virginian Joseph Jones informed his nephew James Madison after the election that Republican electors (all but one) were warned of the "hazard of voting for P[inckney]" and directed to use their second vote on "some other person." By then, Burr was completely out of the picture—see Joseph Jones to James Madison, Dec. 9, 1796, in Stagg, ed., *Papers of James Madison,* XVI: 423–24. John Adams received similar reports, writing that the "Southern Gentlemen with whom I have conversed, expressed more Affection for me than they had ever did since 1774. They certainly wish Adams elected rather than Pinckney. Perhaps because Hamilton and Jay are said to be for Pinckney." See John Adams to Abigail Adams, Dec. 12, 1796, Adams Family Papers.

70. For Burr's warning to Massachusetts elector Elbridge Gerry, see AB to Elbridge Gerry, Nov. 30, 1976, in Kline, ed., *Burr Papers,* I: 278; and for his later complaint against the Virginians, see Hannah Gallatin to Albert Gallatin, May 12, 1800, in Adams, *Life of Albert Gallatin,* 243; Kurtz, *The Presidency of John Adams,* 202.

71. AH to Rufus King, Dec. 16, 1796, in King, ed., *The Life and Correspondence of Rufus King,* II: 126; Chauncey Goodrich to Oliver Wolcott, Sr., Dec. 17, 1796, in Gibbs, ed., *Memoirs of the Administrations,* I: 413; Kurtz, *The Presidency of John Adams,* 204; and Abigail Adams to John Adams, Dec. 25, 1796, Adams Family Papers. North Carolina was not as bad as Virginia; there Jefferson received 11 to Burr's 6 electoral votes. The rest went to Federalists: Iredell (3), John Adams (1), C. Pinckney (1), T. Pinckney (1), and Washington (1).

72. H. H. Simms, *Life of John Taylor* (Richmond, Va., 1932), 64; and Kurtz, *The Presidency of John Adams,* 198.

73. Robert Troup to Rufus King, Jan. 28, 1797, in King, ed., *Life and Correspondence of Rufus King,* II: 135–36.

74. Theodore Sedgwick to Rufus King, Apr. 9, 1798, in *ibid.,* II: 311, 313; see also Mann, *Republic of Debtors,* 191.

75. AB to Theodore Sedgwick, Jan. 2, 1797, Burr Papers, microfilm, reel 3.

76. For Greenleaf's betrayal of Morris and Nicholson, see Arbuckle, *Pennsylvania Speculator and Patriot,* 118–19, 137; for Greenleaf's underhanded dealing with Burr, see Kline, ed., *Burr Papers,* I: 290–91; on the legal proceedings involved in the Angerstein tract, see Goebel, ed., *The Law Practice of Alexander Hamilton* IV: 172–74; and *AB v. Angerstein,* May 3, 1799, in Burr Papers, microfilm, reel 20. There is some dispute over the value of £24,000 sterling; Goebel set the penalty at $106,000, while Mary-Jo Kline claims it was $90,000; in a private letter from Hamilton, he makes it $80,000—see Goebel, ed., *op. cit.,* 174, 176, note 37; Kline, ed., *Burr Papers,* II: 740, note 1; AH to John Rutledge, Jr., Jan. 4, 1801, in Syrett, ed., *Hamilton Papers,* XXV: 292–98.

77. Burr had borrowed money from Marinus Willett, and in 1798, he wrote a revealing letter about the state of his finances: "For the present, you know how little in my power—The enclosed in the very last dollar I have—." See AB to Marinus Willett, Mar. 26, 1798, his various promissory notes to Willett, and Burr's "Account with John Lamb, 1795–97," in Burr Papers, microfilm, reels 3 and 4; see also Kline, ed., *Burr Papers,* I: 291, 296; and Leake, *Memoir of the Life and Times of General John Lamb,* 124–26, 131.

78. Arbuckle, *Pennsylvania Speculator and Patriot,* 58–60, 187–89, 193–94, 199.

79. AB to James Greenleaf, Jan. 17, 1796, and AB to John Nicholson, Mar. 18, 1798, Burr Papers, microfilm, reels 3 and 4. Burr repaid part of his notes that Nicholson had endorsed, but he probably still owed him money, even after Nicholson's death in 1800. After the impeachment trial, Nicholson was sued by the state of Pennsylvania for monies unaccounted for during his tenure as comptroller-general. He also had to deal with the U.S. government in the suit over the protested note (involved the U.S. Bank) that Burr had signed to Nicholson. In trying to arrange some kind of payment agreement, he allowed the U.S. government to retain $5,000 of Burr's notes—see John Nicholson to AB, Mar. 14, 1797, Burr Papers, microfilm, reel 4. Nicholson asked Burr to serve as his defense lawyer during his impeachment trial. Burr declined, but did act as his consultant—see Arbuckle, *Pennsylvania Speculator and Patriot,* 57.

80. See AB to John Lamb, Jan. 12, 1798; see also Deed to Sir John Temple, June 17, 1797 (inventory of his household furnishings), and Lease to William Martine, June 30, 1797. Lamb preferred that Burr find another way to repay his debts, and sent a letter releasing him from the obligation to settle his debts with the proceeds of his house. But Burr seemed intent on scraping together whatever funds he could to rescue his friend. See John Lamb to AB, Mar. 29, 1797, and the constant exchange of letters between Burr and Lamb about his

finances, and Burr's "Account with John Lamb, 1795–97," in Burr Papers, microfilm, reels 3 and 4; also Kline, ed., *Burr Papers,* I: 296–97.

81. See AB to John Lamb, Jan. 12, 1798. Burr and his friends expressed similar emotions. In one letter, Van Gaasbeek wrote, "I would sooner sacrifice every farthing than to wound the reputation of one so deserving a Friend." Burr's philosophy for dealing with debts was best expressed in a letter to Oliver Phelps who was trying to collect money from Thomas Morris. Burr wrote: "You are acquainted with his distress and I presume are not disposed to add to them from mere revenge—indeed I know you to be incapable of acting from such motives on any occasion—Your object is doubtless to secure your debt and you are perfectly justified in taking every legal measure to attain this end—At the same time, if you can get better and sooner paid by concord than hostility, I am sure you would prefer it. It is my opinion that you can—If Mr. Morris be driven to the last extremity, you may probably lose your debt—He has friends who are willing, at present, to aid him to a certain extent." Burr's point was that negotiation, and some concession on the part of the lender, was far better than extreme measures to destroy the debtor. See Peter Van Gaasbeek to AB, Feb. 1, 1797, and AB to Oliver Phelps, Dec. 15, 1799, in Burr Papers, microfilm, reel 4; and on sureties, see Mann, *Republic of Debtors,* 16.

82. For a description of the estate, see Isaac Newton Phelps Stokes, *Iconography of Manhattan Island,* 6 vols. (New York, 1926), V: 1340; see also Allgor, *Parlor Politics,* 60; and for furnishings, Deed to Sir John Temple, June 17, 1797, Burr Papers, microfilm, reel 4.

83. Burr is listed as a resident in Richmond Hill in the 1793 and 1774 in the *New York City Directory and Register* (1793, 1794), 22, 27; see also Schachner, *Aaron Burr,* 122, and for mention of the gallery, the Deed to Sir John Temple, June 17, 1797.

84. For Davis, see Schachner, *Aaron Burr,* 121; Lomask, *Aaron Burr: The Years from Princeton to the Vice President,* 110; and John Davis, *Travels in Four and a Half Years in the United States of America* (reprint 1909), 26; for Brant, see AB to John Vanderlyn, Feb. 28, 1797, in Burr Papers, microfilm, reel 4; for the comte de Volney, see Parton, *Life and Times of Aaron Burr,* I: 154, and Kline, ed., *Burr Papers,* II: 1097; and for Nathalie-Marie-Louise-Stephanie-Beatrice de Lage de Volunde (1782–1841), see Côté, *Theodosia Burr,* 93, and Kline, ed., *Burr Papers,* I: 280.

85. Burr acquired Richmond Hill by signing a sixty-nine-year lease from the Episcopal Trinity Church on May 1, 1797. Though he had occupied the estate for several years, the lease was not signed until a month and a half before he sold his furnishings. Burr assigned the lease to John Jacob Astor of Richmond Hill in 1803, along with the deed to several lots. See Deed to Sir John Temple, June 17, 1797, and Lease to William Martine, June 30, 1797, "Assignment of lease to John Jacob Astor of Richmond Hill property," Oct. 22, 1803," and "Deeds

of Lots on Bedford & Downing Streets to John Jacob Astor," Nov. 18, 1803, Burr Papers, microfilm, reels 4, 5. See also Schachner, *Aaron Burr,* 125.

86. Theodosia Burr to John Bartow Prevost, Aug. 30, 1799, Burr Papers, microfilm, reel 4.
87. Theodosia Burr to John Bartow Prevost, June 17, 1799, in Burr Papers, microfilm, reel 4; Maria Nicholson to Hannah Gallatin, Feb. 5, 1801, in Adams, *Life of Gallatin,* 245; and Côté, *Theodosia Burr,* 112.
88. AB to John Lamb, Mar. 31, 1797, and AB to Pierpont Edwards, Oct. 30, 1797, in Burr Papers, microfilm, reel 4.
89. William Loughton Smith to Ralph Izard, Nov. 8, 1796, in "South Carolina Federalist Correspondence, 1789–1797," 785; AH to John Rutledge, Jan. 4, 1801, and AH to James McHenry, Jan. 4, 1801 (same enclosure on AB to both men), in Syrett, ed., *Hamilton Papers,* XXV: 292–98. Hamilton owed at least $60,000 according to Gouverner Morris at the time of his death, and his assets, at best, were estimated at $40,000. Yet Morris and Hamilton's other friends felt that $100,000 should be raised by subscription to cover Hamilton's debts and support his family—so his debts might have been more or his assets much less. See Mitchell, *Alexander Hamilton,* 547–53; and Ron Chernow, *Alexander Hamilton* (New York, 2004), 724.
90. Burr became involved in the German Company in 1794. See Kline, ed., *Burr Papers,* I: 221–22; and Robert Liston and John Graves Simcoe quoted in Alan Taylor, "A Northern Revolution in 1800? Upper Canada and Thomas Jefferson," in James Horn, Jan Ellen Lewis, and Peter S. Onuf, eds., *The Revolution of 1800: Democracy, Race, and the New Republic* (Charlottesville, Va., 2002), 386–87.
91. Taylor, "A Northern Revolution," 390, 396, 399.
92. See Kline, ed., *Burr Papers,* I: 316–17.
93. See Adams, *Life of Gallatin,* 186; Ammon, *James Monroe,*157; Thomas Jefferson to AB, June 17, 1797, and his reply, AB to Thomas Jefferson, June 21, 1797, in Kline, ed., *Burr Papers,* I: 298–301. For Jefferson's earlier letter to Burr concerning his friend, Dr. Currie, see Thomas Jefferson to AB, Jan. 7, 1797, and other letters from Jefferson in 1798 and 1800 on Currie's case in Burr Papers, microfilm, reel 4.
94. AB to William Eustis, June 12, 1797, in Kline, ed., *Burr Papers,* I: 297.
95. See AB to James Monroe, Aug. 9, 1797, in *ibid.,* I: 311; Ammon, *James Monroe,* 160–61, 168–69. For the dinner and toasts, see New York *Daily Advertiser,* July 15, 1797.
96. David Gelston's Account of an Interview between Alexander Hamilton and James Monroe, July 11, 1797, in Syrett, ed., *Hamilton Papers,* XXI: 159–62.
97. For the list of Hamilton's affairs, see Joanne Freeman, *Affairs of Honor: National Politics in the New Republic* (New Haven, Conn., 2001), 326; for an account of the Church affair, see Kline, ed., *Burr Papers,* I: 410.

98. AB to ?, Oct. 6, 1799, Kline, ed., *Burr Papers,* I: 410.

99. *Ibid.*

100. AB to AH, June 20, 1804, Burr Papers, microfilm, reel 5.

101. AB to Theodosia Burr, Sept. 17, 1795, in Van Doren, ed., *Correspondence of Aaron Burr and his Daughter Theodosia,* 36; AB to James Monroe, Aug. 13, 1797, in Kline, ed., *Burr Papers,* I: 312 (italics added).

102. AB to AH, June 20, 1804, Burr Papers, microfilm, reel 5.

103. According to Burr, they had averted two other affairs. He claimed that Hamilton came forward voluntarily and made apologies, thus preempting Burr from initiating the *code duello*—see AB to Charles Biddle, July 18, 1804, in Kline, ed., *Burr Papers,* II: 887.

104. *Ibid.,* I: 314, 320–21. John Dawson, another friend drawn into the affair, reported Burr's comment that he disliked the "childish mode of writing" used by both men. See John Dawson to James Monroe, Dec. 24, 1797, in Syrett, ed., *Hamilton Papers,* XXI: 319; Ammon, *James Monroe,* 160.

105. James Monroe to James Madison, Oct. 15, 1797, and James Madison to James Monroe, Oct. 19, 1797, in Stagg, ed., *Papers of James Madison,* XVII: 50, 53; Syrett, ed., *Hamilton Papers,* XXI: 319; Kline, ed., *Burr Papers,* I: 320–21.

106. James Madison to Thomas Jefferson, Oct. 20, 1797, in Stagg, ed., *Papers of James Madison,* XXI: 54. Hamilton's pamphlet was published on Aug. 25 and entitled *Observations on Certain Documents Contained in No. V & VI of "The Hist. of the U.S. for the Year 1796," In Which the Charge of Speculation Against Alexander Hamilton, Late Secretary of the Treasury, is Fully Refuted. Written by Himself* (Philadelphia, 1796).

107. Hamilton portrayed himself as the seduced victim: he wrote that Mrs. Reynolds's "conduct, made it extremely difficult to disentangle myself. All the appearances of a violent attachment, and of agonizing distress at the idea of relinquishment, were played off with a most imposing art. This, though it did not make me entirely the dupe of the plot, yet kept me in a state of irresolution." See the *Observations on Certain Documents,* reprinted in Syrett, ed., *Hamilton Papers,* XXI: 238–85, esp. 252.

108. The female poet may have been a man using a female pseudonym. See Jemmima Spinningwheel [pseudo.], *Independent Chronicle,* Oct. 9, 1797, quoted in Cogan, "The Reynolds Affair," 406–08. New Yorker John Armstrong (a Federalist who later converted to Republicanism) made the disparaging comment about Hamilton hiding under Mrs. Reynolds's petticoats—see C. Edward Skeen, *John Armstrong, Jr., 1758–1843: A Biography* (Syracuse, N.Y., 1981), 41. See also Robert Troup to Rufus King, June 3, 1798, in King, ed., *The Life and Correspondence of Rufus King,* II: 330.

109. On the controversy over Hamilton's appointment, see Kurtz, *The Presidency of John Adams,* 280–81; and for a discussion of the sexual overtones of the XYZ Affair, see Nancy Isenberg, "Death and Satire: Dismembering the Body Politic,"

in Isenberg and Andrew Burstein, eds., *Mortal Remains: Death in Early America* (Philadelphia, 2003), 87–88. Even Hamilton wrote about the "mistresses," who "are appointed to intrigue our envoys." See his article "The Stand No. V" in the *Commercial Advertiser,* Apr. 16, 1798, reprinted in Syrett, ed., *Hamilton Papers,* XXI: 428, 431.

110. For the rumors about Knox, see Oliver Wolcott to AH, Oct. 10, 1798, in Gibbs, ed., *Memoirs of the Administration of Washington and Adams,* II: 101. Adams had no choice but to accept Hamilton, as Secretary of State Timothy Pickering explained to Rufus King: "You must know that the President wishes Knox to precede Hamilton whom he dislikes extremely, and whom he would have named first; but that the order of the names was designated by General Washington, who claimed as a condition of his accepting the Chief Command, the privilege of proposing his principal officers"—Timothy Pickering to Rufus King, Aug. 29, 1798, in *The Life and Correspondence of Rufus King,* II: 405.

111. The Military Committee was a "citizens' organization," and had no official standing or authority. See Syrett, ed., *Hamilton Papers,* XXI: 476; and Ebenezer Stevens to AB, Aug. 17, 1798, in Kline, ed., *Burr Papers,* I: 347–48, 353–54.

112. Hamilton also recommended the other member of the military committee, Ebenezer Stevens, for the position as naval agent, despite the fact that he, too, was not a Federalist. For his recommendation of Burr, see Alexander Hamilton to Oliver Wolcott, June 28, 1798; and for Stevens, see Alexander Hamilton to Oliver Wolcott, Junior, June 2, 1798, in Syrett, ed., *Hamilton Papers,* XXI:521–22, 480. For rumors, see Timothy Pickering to Oliver Wolcott, July 11, 1798, in Gibbs, ed., *Memoirs of the Administrations of Washington and John Adams,* II; 71; for his earlier attacks, see chapter four: "An Unprejudiced Mind."

113. See AH to John Jay, Feb. 12, 1799, in Syrett, ed., *Hamilton Papers,* XXII: 476–77.

114. John Adams to James Lloyd, 1815, *Works of John Adams,* X: 123–26. Adams's memory may be inaccurate, for according to Timothy Pickering, the president was suggesting Burr for quartermaster general—see Timothy Pickering to Oliver Wolcott, July 11, 1798, in Gibbs, ed., *Memoirs of the Administrations of Washington and Adams,* II: 71. It also appears that Washington had put Burr on his patronage list before the crisis over the Jay Treaty; and he had included other enemies of Hamilton like George Clinton. But we also know that Hamilton was reporting on Burr's political activities for the opposition party as early as 1792. See AH to George Washington, Sept. 23, 1792, in Syrett, ed., *Hamilton Papers,* XII: 418; see also Kurtz, *The Presidency of John Adams,* 244.

115. Robert Troup to Rufus King, Oct. 2, 1798, in King, ed., *The Life and Correspondence of Rufus King,* II: 431–32.

116. *Ibid.,* II: 431.

117. For Burr's revision of the final wording—expunging "French Directory" and replacing it with "all foreign nations"—see *New-York Journal,* Aug. 22, 1798. In

the notice of the meeting, Burr, his good friend David Gelston, Burrite John Broome, Dr. Samuel Mitchell, and Henry Rutgers all were appointed to a committee to draft an address to prevent further depredations on American commerce by the "British government, and any other nation." The meeting was held on June 13, and the notice was published in the *Argus,* June 15, 1798. This meeting was held just three days after Burr was appointed to the Military Committee on June 11, and it had been organized by the New York Democratic Society—see Foner, *The Democratic-Republican Societies,* 200; Helms, "An Uneasy Alliance," 25; and Kline, ed., *Burr Papers,* I: 347.

118. In his dedication, Burk claimed that Burr gave him the idea for the play. See John Burk, *Bunker-Hill; or the death of General Warren: An Historical Play in Five Acts* (New York, 1797). See also Joseph I. Shulim, "John Daly Burk: Irish Revolutionist and American Patriot," *Transactions of the American Philosophical Society* 54 (October 1964): 19–36; John Burk to Thomas Jefferson, June 19, 1801, Jefferson Papers, Library of Congress; AB to James Monroe, Dec. 25, 1798, in Kline, ed., *Burr Papers,* I: 361–62; and James Morton Smith, *Freedom's Fetters: The Alien and Sedition Laws and American Civil Liberties* (Ithaca, N.Y., 1956), 205–06, 211.

119. Burk was arrested before the passage of the Sedition Act on July 14, 1798. The federal district attorney, Richard Harison, relied on a common law indictment, but action was taken in anticipation of the passage of the new Sedition Act. Secretary of State Timothy Pickering had been watching *The Time Piece,* and wrote Harison to check Burk's status as a citizen. "If Burke be an alien," he wrote, then "no man is a fitter object for the operation of the alien act." So, Burk was considered a target under both the Alien and Sedition laws—Sharp, *American Politics in the Early Republic,* 177; and James Morton Smith, *Freedom's Fetters,* 210–11.

120. See Thomas Jefferson to James Madison, Apr. 26, 1798, and James Madison to Thomas Jefferson, May 20, 1798, in James Morton Smith, ed., *The Republic of Letters: The Correspondence of Thomas Jefferson and James Madison, 1776–1826,* 3 vols. (New York, 1994), II: 1042, 1050. At least twenty-one printers and editors were fined or imprisoned under the Sedition Act. See Smith, *Freedom's Fetters,* and F. M. Anderson, "The Enforcement of the Alien and Sedition Laws," *American Historical Association Annual Report* (1912), 115–26; Adams, *Life of Gallatin,* 204–06; and Sharp, *American Politics in the Early Republic,* 179, 183.

121. Margaret Bache was accused of running the paper like a bawdy house, promoting licentiousness instead of spreading the news. Federalist henchman William Cobbett provided the crudest insult; he claimed she published a protest against castration because she missed having sex with her husband. Duane was not only indicted under the Sedition Act, he was sued for libel, tried in state court for "riot and assault," and in 1799, he was beaten up by an angry group of

Federalist soldiers—see Jeffrey L. Pasley, *"The Tyranny of Printers": Newspaper Politics in the Early Republic* (Charlottesville, Va., 2001), 102–03, 189–90. Ann Greenleaf was indicted under the federal Sedition Act, and then Hamilton instituted a state libel prosecution that forced her to sell her paper. See Smith, *Freedom's Fetters,* 400; see also *New-York Gazette,* July 16, 1798; Shulim, "John Daly Burk," 31.

122. See Albert Gallatin to James Nicholson, Jan. 30, 1799, The Papers of Albert Gallatin, microfilm; also Walters, *Albert Gallatin,* 115; Adams, *Life of Albert Gallatin,* 191–92; and Smith, *Freedom's Fetters,* 221–46, esp. 243.

123. Burr's speech, along with the debates in the assembly, was reprinted in the *Albany Register*—see Kline, ed., *Burr Papers,* I: 371.

124. *Ibid.,* 366–67, 371.

125. *Ibid.,* 371.

126. *Ibid.,* 367.

127. *Ibid.,* 371.

128. Robert Troup to Rufus King, Jan. 23, 1799, in King, ed., *The Life and Correspondence of Rufus King,* II, 524; and *Aurora,* Jan. 18, 1799.

CHAPTER SIX

1. Parton, *Life and Times of Aaron Burr,* I: 320.

2. See AB to William Eustis, Oct. 20, 1797, in Kline, ed., *Burr Papers,* I, 315, 347; Theodosia Burr to John Bartow Prevost, Jan. 1798, Burr Papers, microfilm, reel 4.

3. See Robert Troup to Rufus King, May 6, 1799, and June 5, 1799, in *The Life and Correspondence of Rufus King,* III: 14, 35.

4. Young, *The Democratic Republicans,* 569; and Alfred Young, "The Mechanics and the Jeffersonians: New York, 1789–1801," *Labor History* 5 (1964): 262–63.

5. Young, "The Mechanics and the Jeffersonians," 247, 259, 267–68.

6. According to Mary-Jo Kline, the tax reform bill provided the "machinery for a modern system" of tax collection and "a fair and consistent tax program." It was intended to protect taxpayers from the "whims" of assessors by providing uniform guidelines and subjecting assessors to the supervision of state-appointed commissioners. It had one concrete advantage for mechanics, which Burr supported: it eliminated the duties on craftsmen. The bill became law on Apr. 1, 1799. In the same year, the municipal budget came under attack. The Republican *New-York Journal* argued that the municipal budget placed an unfair burden on city taxpayers. In the final bill, the amount was reduced from $150,000 to $110,000. Burr did his part to reduce the tax burden. He gathered information from his friend Charles Biddle on Philadelphia in order to compare that city's expenses to those of New York. The act for the city taxes became law on April 3, 1799. For a discussion of these two laws, see Kline, ed., *Burr Papers,* I: 376–83, 384–86.

7. John Swartwout married a relative of Melancton Smith, and he was one of the executors of Melancton Smith's will. Burr represented Swartwout and Smith's family in a legal case protecting the heir's estate. See Robin Brooks, "Melancton Smith," 277, 288; *Robert Troup and Peter Goelet v. Ezekiel Robins, John Swart-wout, Margaret Smith, Melancton Jr., Richbill, Sydney, and Pheobe,* June 3, 1799, in Burr Papers, microfilm, NYCC Cases, reel 20; and J. Scoville (Walter Barrett, pseudo), *The Old Merchants of New York* (New York, 1885), IV: 249. The Cayuga Bridge was spearheaded by Charles Williamson: he was the agent of the Pulteney associates (a group of British speculators) invested in developing the Genesee lands in central New York. Williamson was another one of Burr's allies in the assembly—see John W. Wells, *Cayuga Bridge* (Ithaca, N.Y., 1958), 2; Kline, ed., *Burr Papers,* I: 391–92.

8. John Coles, flour merchant and vice president of the Chamber of Commerce, had been involved in the appointment of the Military Committee on which Burr served. Coles also had an interest in the Boston Post Road project: he acquired a sixty-year charter to collect tolls on his section of the road in 1798. See Beatrice G. Reubens, "Burr, Hamilton and the Manhattan Company: Part I: Gaining the Charter," *Political Science Quarterly* 72 (Dec. 1957), 594, 596, 599; and "The Boston Road and Aaron Burr" (1921).

9. For Burr's efforts to ensure that the mechanics were paid, see AB to William W. Woolsey, Feb. 24, 1800, in Kline, ed., *Burr Papers,* I: 415–16.

10. Charles E. Brooks, *Frontier Settlement and Market Revolution: The Holland Land Purchase* (Ithaca, N.Y., 1996), 4, 12; Kline, ed., *Burr Papers,* I: 338–39; Paul Demund Evans, *The Holland Land Company* (Buffalo, N.Y., 1924), 206–07.

11. Evans, *The Holland Land Company,* 207–08, 212, Goebel, ed., *The Law Practice of Alexander Hamilton,* III: 627–28.

12. See "Holland Land C.: accounts, receipts, etc. for payment to AB, Josiah Ogden Hoffman, Thomas Morris, et al. for legal costs," Apr. 26–May 10, 1798, in Burr Papers, microfilm, reel 4; Evans, *The Holland Land Company,* 211–12; Goebel, ed., *The Law Practice of Alexander Hamilton,* III: 629–30.

13. Scholars have ignored the important role of David A. Ogden. "Mr. L." was most likely David Ogden's younger brother, Thomas Ludlow Ogden; he claimed to have played a major role in getting the Alien Landowners' Act passed. See Goebel, ed., *The Law Practice of Alexander Hamilton,* III: 629; Evans, *The Holland Land Company,* 224, 245; and "Background Note," Ogden Family Papers, William L. Clements Library, University of Mich., Ann Arbor, Mich.

14. Kline, ed., *Burr Papers,* I: 410.

15. "Holland Land C.: Cancellation of agreement to sell AB 100,000 acres of land," June 15, 1799, Burr Papers, reel 4; AB to ?, Oct. 6, 1799, Kline, ed., *Burr Papers,* I: 407–11; Goebel, ed., *The Law Practice of Alexander Hamilton,* III: 631; and Evans, *The Holland Land Company,* 209, 256.

16. See "The Anti-Revolutionist: No. IV," *Commercial Advertiser,* Apr. 29, 1799, and article signed "Julius," *Commercial Advertiser,* May 25, 1799.

17. For Browne's theory, see the Report from the Common Council, *Commercial Advertiser,* Jan. 26, 1799; see also *Minutes of the Common Council of the City of New York, 1784–1831* (New York, 1917), II: 486–89; and Pomerantz, *New York An American City,* 281–82.

18. For Burr's interest in bank charters, see AB to William Eustis, Dec. 16, 1796, and AB to Thomas Morris, Feb. 1, 1797, in Kline., ed., *Burr Papers,* I: 279–87; also Reubens, "Burr, Hamilton, and the Manhattan Company: Part I," 580–82. Both Federalist banks had "interlocking directories," which included a small circle of Hamilton's closest allies—see Young, *The Democratic Republicans,* 218–19.

19. See AH to Richard Varick (and enclosure), Feb. 26, 1799, in Syrett, ed., *Hamilton Papers,* XXII: 508–11, 448; and Richard Varick to John Jay, Mar. 1, 1799, The Papers of John Jay, Columbia University, New York, N.Y.

20. Ruebens, "Burr, Hamilton, and the Manhattan Company: Part I," 587.

21. *Ibid.,* 588, 592–93.

22. *Ibid.,* 596.

23. Kline, ed., *Burr Papers,* I: 401; Reubens, "Burr, Hamilton and the Manhattan Company: Part I," 599; Gregory S. Hunter, "The Manhattan Company: Managing a Multi-Unit Corporation in New York, 1799–1842," Ph.D. Dissertation, New York University, 1989, 44–45.

24. Hunter, "The Manhattan Company," 46–50.

25. See Robert E. Wright, "Artisans, Banks, Credit, and the Election of 1800," *Pennsylvania Magazine of History and Biography* 122 (July 1998): 227, 23; and Syrett, ed., *Hamilton Papers,* XXII: 510.

26. See "The American," signed "C.," *Commercial Advertiser,* Apr. 26, 1799.

27. See "The American," "The Anti-Revolutionist: No. II," "The Anti-Revolutionist: No. IV," *Commercial Advertiser,* Apr. 27, 29, 1799.

28. "The Anti-Revolutionist: No. II." For Robert Swartwout's introduction of the election reform bill, see *Commercial Advertiser,* Feb. 15, 1799.

29. "The Anti-Revolutionist: No. II."

30. See *ibid.,* "State of Manhattan," and "The Anti-Revolutionist: No. IV," *Commercial Advertiser,* Apr. 27, 29, May 22, 23, 1799. Burr was also accused of managing to "persuade some of the members and to intimidate and brow beat others," to get the bill passed in the assembly—see "The American," *Commercial Advertiser,* May 1, 1799.

31. See "To the Merchants of New York," *Commercial Advertiser,* June 8, 1799. Federalists made similar attacks against Burr's support of the Insolvent Act, claiming it would undermine the value of property, promote fraud, and disrupt the economy—see "The American," *Commercial Advertiser,* Apr. 29, 1799.

32. See Beatrice G. Reubens, "Burr, Hamilton and the Manhattan Company: Part II: Launching a Bank," *Political Science Quarterly* 73 (Mar. 1958), 105–08, 113, 116; Wright, "Artisans, Banks, and Credit," 229.

33. See Nicholas Low to AB, Sept. 10, 1799 (enclosing spurious letter from AB to Low, Sept. 9), Burr Papers, microfilm, reel 4. For Low's prominent role in opposing the Manhattan Company, see Reubens, "Burr, Hamilton and the Manhattan Company: Part II," 109–10. Low was one of the original directors of the Bank of New York and a large shareholder; he was also a director of the New York branch of the Bank of United States. He was president of the United Insurance Company, which gave him an added incentive to oppose the Manhattan Company: it starting selling insurance in 1800. See Young, *The Democratic Republicans,* 213, 218–19; *Longworth's American Almanac, New-York Register, and City Directory* (New York, 1800), 36; and an advertisement by the Manhattan Company for selling insurance in the *American Citizen and General Advertiser,* Mar. 15, 1800.

34. The Federalists won the election by 914 votes, and over 700 of those votes came from the Second and Third Wards. See election returns by ward in the *Commercial Advertiser,* May 4, 1799; see also John Dawson to James Madison, Dec. 12, 1799, in David B. Mattern, ed., *The Papers of James Madison* (Charlottesville, Va., 1991), XVII: 293.

35. Goebel, ed., *The Law Practice of Alexander Hamilton,* II: 50, 59.

36. Robert Troup to Nicholas Low, Feb. 7, 1800, Troup Papers, New York Public Library; Goebel, ed., *The Law Practice of Alexander Hamilton,* II: 86.

37. See Brockholst Livingston to Isaac Gouverneur, Nov. 2, 1797, Livingston Family Papers, New York Public Library; and Goebel, ed., *The Law Practice of Alexander Hamilton,* II: 73.

38. See "Alexander Hamilton, Esq.," *New-York Journal,* Jan. 10, 1798. The same letter and accompanying opinions were printed on Jan. 10 and 11 in the *Commercial Advertiser.*

39. Robert Troup to Nicholas Low, Jan. 25, Feb. 7, 1800, Troup Papers, New York Public Library; Robert Troup to Rufus King, Mar. 9, 1800, Rufus King Papers, New-York Historical Society; Goebel, ed., *The Law Practice of Alexander Hamilton,* II: 86, 88, 116–18; and Tripp, *Robert Troup,* 192–93.

40. Robert Troup to Rufus King, Mar. 9, 1800; Goebel, ed., *The Law Practice of Alexander Hamilton,* II: 83, 88.

41. Gouverneur Morris Diary, Gouverneur Morris Papers, Library of Congress; Goebel, ed., *The Law Practice of Alexander Hamilton,* II: 83–84. Later, Gouverneur Morris told Hamilton's son, James Hamilton, that "I never forgave your father for his speech on that occasion." See James Hamilton, *Reminiscences of James A. Hamilton* (New York, 1869), 12; and Tripp, *Robert Troup,* 192.

42. Gouverneur Morris Diary; Goebel, ed., *The Law Practice of Alexander Hamilton,* II: 83–84. Of course, Hamilton's relatives painted a very different portrait of the

battle between the two men. In his biography, Hamilton's grandson claimed that Morris supposedly said to Hamilton, "Before I have done I am confident I shall make my learned friend cry out, 'Help me, Cassius' (pointing to Burr) 'or I sink.'" If Morris did refer to Burr as Cassius, it underscores his impression that Burr was the counterbalance to Hamilton's excessive harangues. "Help me, Cassius, or I sink!" is a famous quotation from Shakespeare's *Julius Caesar,* Act I, scene 2. If Burr was Cassius, then Hamilton was Caesar. Morris's point was to mock Hamilton's hubris, acting godlike but depending on mere mortals like Cassius to save him. Morris's selection of this quote is interesting, because the real Cassius was one of the greatest lawyers in Roman history—see Allan McLane Hamilton, *The Intimate Life of Alexander Hamilton* (New York, 1911), 169–70.

43. Isaac Gouverneur died on Feb. 28—see AB to Louis Le Guen, Mar. 1, 1800, Burr Papers, microfilm, reel 4. And for the response to Gouverneur's death among the merchant community, see *New-York Gazette and General Advertiser,* Mar. 6, 1800, and Goebel, ed., *The Law Practice of Alexander Hamilton,* II: 87. In another announcement of his death, Gouverneur was praised as the beloved friend of merchants, mariners, and mechanics alike: "Ye hundreds!—Mechanics of every description—Mariners and all who have been employed by him, mingle your tears and sighs with mine, to waft the soul of your departed patron, into the harbor of peace"—*Commercial Advertiser,* Mar. 5, 1800.

44. See James Hardie, *An Impartial Account of the Trial of Mr. Levi Weeks, for the supposed number of Miss Julianna Elmore Sands* (New York, 1800), iii; Estelle Fox Kleiger, *The Trial of Levi Weeks or the Manhattan Well Mystery* (Chicago, 1989), 1, 201.

45. *Daily Advertiser,* Jan. 4, 1800; Kleiger, *The Trial of Levi Weeks,* 1–3; Goebel, ed., *The Law Practice of Alexander Hamilton,* I: 696.

46. Ezra was born in 1772; Levi in 1776. See Robert D. Weeks, *Genealogy of the Family of George Weeks, of Dorchester, Mass.* (Newark, N.J., 1885), 170–71; *Longworth's American Almanac, New-York Register, and City Directory* (New York, 1800), 369. Klieger includes a letter written by Levi Weeks in 1812, which demonstrates that he was well educated—see *The Trial of Mr. Levi Weeks,* 10–11, 207–22.

47. Hardie, *An Impartial Account of the trial of Mr. Levi Weeks,* v–vi; *A Brief Narrative of the Trial for the Bloody and Mysterious Murder of the Unfortunate Young Woman, in the Famous Manhattan Well* (New York, 1800), 5; Goebel, ed., *The Law Practice of Alexander Hamilton,* I: 697.

48. See *Daily Advertiser,* Jan. 9, 1800.

49. Burr and Brockholst Livingston had more experience than Hamilton in criminal cases. As attorney general, Burr had prosecuted a dozen murder and rape cases. Livingston had defended Henry Bedlow, in the most infamous rape trial in New York City during the 1790s. Burr alluded to the Bedlow trial in his opening remarks: the young woman had recanted her testimony, and it served

as reminder to the jury of the dangers of the public passions. A mob had formed after Bedlow's acquittal, destroying the bordello where the girl had claimed to have been raped; the same crowd threatened to destroy Livingston's house. See William Coleman, *Report of the Trial of Levi Weeks, on an Indictment for the Murder of Gulielma Sands, on Monday the Thirty-First day of March, and Tuesday the First day of Apr., 1800* (New York, 1800), 12, 67; Goebels, ed., *The Law Practice of Alexander Hamilton*, I: 698; Kleiger, *The Trial of Levi Weeks*, 29; and *Report of the Trial of Henry Bedlow, for committing a rape on Hannah Sawyer: Final arguments of counsel on each side* (New York, 1793).

50. See Colden's opening remarks for his strategy, and the testimony of her two cousins (Catherine Ring's was the longest testimony given in the trial) in Coleman, *Report of the Trial of Levi Weeks*, 13–14, 16, 18–39; see also Goebels, ed., *The Law Practice of Alexander Hamilton*, I: 698.

51. The Quaker was mocked by one of the jurors, who challenged his testimony by asking a humorous question. He also made a fool of himself earlier when he was asked to leave the courtroom during his wife's testimony (Catherine Ring, Gulielma's cousin), but snuck back in and stood behind her—Kleiger, *The Trial of Levi Weeks*, 70–71, 79, 83.

52. Croucher was defended by Brockholst Livingston in his rape trial—and his appearance was central to the case. See *Report of the Trial of Richard Croucher, on an indictment for the rape of Margaret Miller; on Tuesday, the 8th day of July, 1800* (New York, 1800), 20, 23; and *A Brief Narrative of the Trial for the Bloody and Mysterious Murder*, 14. The same pamphleteer confessed: "His appearance interested us greatly in his favor." For Croucher's fate, see Kleiger, *The Trial of Levi Weeks*, 197–98.

53. *Daily Advertiser*, Apr. 3, 1800. Burr's speech was the highlight of the trial. In one trial pamphlet, he was described as opening "in an eloquent and masterly manner"; in another, as giving "one of the most masterly speeches, both with respect to composition and oratory, which we have ever heard." See *A Brief Narrative of the Trial for the Bloody and Mysterious Murder*, 10, and Hardie, *An Impartial Account of the trial of Levi Weeks*, 21.

54. Chernow wrongly attributes the speech to the "grandeloquent" and "florid style" of Hamilton. See Ron Chernow, *Alexander Hamilton* (New York, 2004), 604. See also Coleman, *Report of the Trial of Levi Weeks*, 64; Kleiger, *The Trial of Levi Weeks*, 113.

55. See Merrill D. Peterson, *The Portable Thomas Jefferson* (New York, 1975), 291.

56. Coleman, *Report of the Trial of Levi Weeks*, 65–67.

57. *Ibid.*, 94–95, 98; *Daily Advertiser*, Apr. 3, 1800; *A Brief Narrative of the Trial for the Bloody and Mysterious Murder*, 14; Hardie, *An Impartial Account of the trial of Mr. Levi Weeks*, 33–34.

58. Hardie, *An Impartial Account of the trial of Mr. Levi Weeks*, vi; *Daily Advertiser*, Apr. 3, 1800; Klieger, *The Trial of Mr. Levi Weeks*, 202.

59. Thomas Jefferson to James Monroe, Jan. 12, 1800, in Paul Leicester Ford, ed., *The Works of Thomas Jefferson,* 12 vols. (New York, 1905), VII: 401–02; and Thomas Jefferson to James Madison, Mar. 4, 1800, in Andrew A. Lipscomb and Albert E. Bergh, eds., *The Writings of Thomas Jefferson,* 20 vols. (Washington, D.C., 1903), X: 158–59.

60. For Burr's "system" during the war years, see chapter two; for Burr's "lists of voters, and personal histories of each," see Parton, *Life and Times of Aaron Burr,* I: 250–51, and letter signed "Portius," *Commercial Advertiser,* May 4, 1800.

61. Jefferson to Monroe, Jan. 12, 1800, Jefferson to Madison, Mar. 4, 1800, in Ford, ed., *Works of Thomas Jefferson,* VII: 413, 429–34; Sharp, *American Politics in the Early Republic,* 245; and Kline, ed., *Burr Papers,* I: 42; also "To the People of the City and State of New York," *Commercial Advertiser,* Apr. 23, 1800.

62. Davis, ed., *Memoirs of Aaron Burr,* II: 57. For Davis's role in *The Time Piece,* see Shulim, *John Daly Burk,* 22; Philip Freneau, *The Carrier of the Time Piece, presenting the following Address to his patrons, with the compliments of the season* (New York, 1797); and Jerome Mushkat, "Matthew Livingston Davis and the Political Legacy of Aaron Burr," *New-York Historical Society Quarterly* 59 (1975): 125–27.

63. See "Republican Veterans," *Aurora,* Apr. 24, 1800. After his meeting with Burr, Jefferson also mentioned that "Clinton, General Gates, and some other old revolutionary characters, have been put on the ticket." See Jefferson to Madison, Mar. 4, 1800, in Lipscomb and Bergh, eds., *The Writing of Thomas Jefferson,* X: 158; and *American Citizen,* Apr. 22, 28, 1800.

64. Elias Nexsen (merchant), Thomas Storm (merchant), George Warner (mechanic: sailmaker), Philip Arcularius (mechanic: tanner), James Hunt (merchant), Ezekiel Robins (mechanic: hatter), and John Swartwout (merchant) had all been in the 1798 assembly with Burr. Of the three Manhattan Company directors, Samuel Osgood, the first U.S. postmaster, was the father-in-law of DeWitt Clinton, George Clinton's nephew; Brockholst Livingston was the son of William Livingston of Elizabethtown, N.J., and a cousin of Chancellor Livingston; and John Broome, merchant and war hero, was a friend of Burr. Broome and Burr had drafted the memorial from the New York Democratic Society protesting British depredations in 1798.

65. See Matthew L. Davis to Albert Gallatin, Mar. 29, Apr. 15, 1800, in Papers of Albert Gallatin, microfilm; and for reports of Hamilton storming out of meetings "in a rage," see *Aurora,* May 2, 1800.

66. Matthew L. Davis to Albert Gallatin, Apr. 15, 1800, Papers of Albert Gallatin, microfilm.

67. Journal of Benjamin Betterton Howell, New-York Historical Society; and Matthew Davis to Albert Gallatin, Mar. 29, May 1, 1800, Papers of Albert Gallatin, microfilm.

68. See Davis, ed., *Memoirs of Aaron Burr,* II: 56; also AB to Thomas Jefferson, May 3, 1800, in Kline, ed., *Burr Papers,* I: 426; Matthew L. Davis to Albert Gallatin,

Mar. 29, 1800, Papers of Albert Gallatin, microfilm; Schachner, *Alexander Hamilton,* 393.

69. James Nicholson to Albert Gallatin, May 6, 1800, Papers of Albert Gallatin, microfilm. Some examples of the sexual insults and taunting appeared in the newspapers. Federalists made a point of attacking the Republican slate as a group of old men, when "younger, and more active might be found." General Gates was ridiculed as a "doting, factious old man," who "retains no faculty in full vigor." Another article claimed that the "aged dotard" Gates had entered his "sixth age, and [was] already beginning a 'second childishness'" when 'his big, manly voice turning again toward a childish trouble, pipes and whistles in his sound.'" Federalists accused Republicans of engaging in similar taunts. One account had Henry Rutgers stationed at the polls on "orders of Burr," and challenging one voter by mocking his manhood. Rutgers supposedly said to one gentleman that he did not come "within the letter of the constitution," which granted the vote to "all *male* citizens." See "The Anti-Jacobin," "To the People of the City and State of New-York," and "A Neat Thing," *Commercial Advertiser,* Apr. 25, 30, 1800. Matthew Davis continued to celebrate the themes of patriotic memory and manly prowess in his Fourth of July oration. See Matthew L. Davis, *An Oration delivered in St. Paul's Church on the Fourth of July, 1800: being the 24th Anniversary of our Independence, before the General Society of Mechanics and Tradesmen, Tammany Society or Columbian Order, and other Associations of Citizens* (New York, 1800), 11–12.

70. See "Extract of a letter to the Editor, dated New-York, May 4th, 1800," *Aurora,* May 7, 1800; the *Aurora* reported that the Republicans had a clear majority of 440 in all the wards, and that in the Sixth Ward (filled with mostly poorer mechanics and Irish and French immigrant voters) the "federal ticket had not a single vote." Federalists complained that they had suffered a mysterious loss of votes in the Second Ward (heavily merchant), which they blamed on the Manhattan Bank. It is also clear from the lower turnout in the First and Second Wards (where Federalists had received the most support in 1799) that the traditional base of the Federalists had not rallied to support Hamilton or his party in this election. See *Aurora,* May 5, 1800; *Commercial Advertiser,* May 4, 1800; and for the 1799 returns, *Commercial Advertiser,* May 4, 1799.

71. AH to John Jay, May 7, 1800, in Syrett, ed., *Hamilton Papers,* XXIV: 465.

72. Schachner, *Aaron Burr,* 178; Alexander Hamilton to John Jay, May 7, 1800, in *ibid.,* ed., XXIV: 467.

73. Gallatin reported to his wife on May 12, that "we had last night a very large meeting of Republicans, in which it was unanimously agreed to support Burr for Vice President." Albert Gallatin to Hannah Gallatin, May 6, 1800, and Matthew Livingston Davis to Albert Gallatin, Mar. 29, 1800, in Papers of Albert Gallatin, microfilm; and Adams, *Life of Gallatin,* 243.

74. See James Nicholson to Albert Gallatin, May 6 and May 7 (letter with his report), 1800, in Gallatin Papers, microfilm.

75. Charles O. Lerche, Jr., "Jefferson and the Election of 1800: A Case Study in Political Smear," *William and Mary Quarterly* 5 (Oct. 1948): 470, 472, 479–81.

76. "A Traveller," Hartford *Connecticut Courant*, Sept. 8, 1800; "Extract of a Letter, from an American in Paris to his friend in this city, dated August 24, 1798," *Aurora*, Jan. 9, 1799.

77. AH to Theodore Sedgwick, May 10, 1800, in Syrett, ed., *Hamilton Papers*, XXIV: 475, 444–46.

78. Theodore Sedgwick to AH, May 13, 1800, in *ibid.*, XXIV: 482–83; Sharp, *American Politics in the Early Republic*, 235–36.

79. For Burr rumor, see Abigail Adams to John Adams, May 23, 1800, Adams Family Papers, Massachusetts Historical Society, and Timothy Phelps to Oliver Wolcott, July 15, 1800, in Gibbs, ed., *Memoirs of the Administrations of Washington and John Adams*, II: 380. On Smith, see Frank A. Cassell, *Merchant Congressman in the Young Republic: Samuel Smith of Maryland, 1752–1839* (Madison, Wis., 1971), 93–94; and for a newspaper account of the "visionary project" of the alliance between Adams and Jefferson, see "Correct Information," *Commercial Advertiser*, June 4, 1800.

80. See "Jersey Republican Meeting," *Aurora*, Oct. 4, 1800. For Burr's hopes for New Jersey, see AB to Pierpont Edwards, July 7, 1800, in Kline, ed., *Burr Papers*, I: 437–38, 444.

81. After he returned from his New England excursion, Burr wrote Robert Livingston that "Jefferson will have all the Votes of Rhode Island." See AB to Robert Livingston, Sept. 24, 1800; for his apologies, see AB to John Taylor of "Caroline," Dec. 18, 1800, and AB to Thomas Jefferson, Dec. 23, 1800, in Kline, ed., *Burr Papers*, I: 444, 472–73.

82. See Sharp, *American Politics in the Early Republic*, 245–47.

83. Hamilton's plans for distributing the pamphlet are not completely verifiable. At times, he claimed that he wanted to publish his views to a wider audience, while at other times he said that it would be limited to a select readership. The editors of the Burr Papers have concluded that Davis's interpretation (distributing the pamphlet in South Carolina) is the only one in which makes sense if Hamilton wished to avoid the devastating consequences of openly attacking Adams. But then again, Hamilton was not known for his discretion, and showed no remorse after publishing the pamphlet. See Syrett, ed., *Hamilton Papers*, XXV: 177–78, 182, 185, and 24: 451; Kline, ed., *Burr Papers*, I: 456–57.

84. For this secret proposition, see *Commercial Advertiser*, Dec. 19, 1800.

85. In the same article, Burr was praised as a great Republican Party leader in the U.S. Senate and New York State Assembly: he had been "obnoxious to the administration for his rigid and inflexible republicanism" while in the Senate,

and then retired from Congress, "advising the most influential republican members to follow his example; to go home, enlighten the minds of their constituents, and . . . correct the state governments." Finally, he is described as spreading republicanism throughout the northern states: the "activity and address of Colonel Burr have given it complete ascendancy in the formerly high federal states of New York and Rhode Island; and even in New Jersey and Connecticut." See "From the City Gazette," *Aurora*, Dec. 5, 1800.

86. On Kentucky, see *Commercial Advertiser*, Dec. 31, 1800; see also "Federalism!," *Aurora*, Dec. 30, 1800. On Tennessee giving Jefferson one more vote than Burr, see "Extract of a letter from one of the Senators of the state of Rhode Island, in Congress, dated Washington, Saturday afternoon, Dec. 20," *Commercial Advertiser*, Jan. 5, 1801; for the predictions after South Carolina's votes were known, see *"On the election of* PRESIDENT," *Commercial Advertiser*, Dec, 30, 1800.

87. Thomas Jefferson to AB, Dec. 15, 1800, in Kline, ed., *Burr Papers*, I: 469.

88. *Ibid*; Burr's biographer Milton Lomask interpreted Jefferson as trying to wring a concession; see Lomask, *Aaron Burr: The Years from Princeton to the Vice President*, 273.

89. Thomas Jefferson to AB, Dec. 15, 1800.

90. AB to Thomas Jefferson, Dec. 23, 1800, in Kline, ed., *Burr Papers*, I: 473–74.

91. John Francis Mercer to James Madison, Jan. 5, 1800, in Mattern, ed., *The Papers of James Madison*, XVII: 472. The Boston *Centinel* published a humorous barb concerning southern fears of a tie: "The Southern Jacobins are much afraid of Burr. They apprehend he will *stick* so close to the electors, as to prevent their *Idol* being elected." See *Aurora*, Dec. 13, 1800.

92. See "Newport (R.I.) Dec. 27," *Aurora*, Jan. 8, 1801; also *Commercial Advertiser*, Jan. 6, 1801; and Thomas Jefferson to AB, Dec. 15, 1800, AB to Thomas Jefferson, Dec. 23, 1800, and AB to Samuel Smith, Dec. 24, 1800, in Kline, ed., *Burr Papers*, I: 469, 473–75.

93. James Nicholson to Albert Gallatin, May 7, 1800, in Papers of Albert Gallatin, microfilm; Hannah Gallatin to Albert Gallatin, May 7, 1800, in Adams, *Life of Albert Gallatin*, 243.

94. AB to John Taylor of "Caroline," Oct. 23, 1800, in Kline, ed., *Burr Papers*, I: 451.

95. Theodore Sedgwick to AH, Dec. 17, 1800, in Syrett, ed., *Hamilton Papers*, XXV: 262.

96. Gouverneur Morris to AH, Dec. 19, 1800, in *ibid.*, XXV: 267; *Washington Federalist*, Feb. 4, 1801.

97. See AB to Samuel Smith, Dec. 16, 1800, in Kline, ed., *Burr Papers*, I: 471. For the publication of Burr's letter, see *National Intelligencer*, Dec. 31, 1800, and *Aurora*, Dec. 31, 1800. For his duty to accept, see "Read! Neighbors Read," *Aurora*, Jan. 10, 1801 (reprinted from the *Washington Federalist*). And on Fed-

eralists dismissing Burr's renunciation, see James McHenry to AH, Dec. 31, 1800, and James Bayard to AH, Jan. 7, 1800, in Syrett, ed., *Hamilton Papers,* XXV: 282–83, 300.

98. One article claimed that if Burr "would only be convinced of the fear of his party, particularly in Virginia, lest he should be elected President in preference to their IDOL Mr. Jefferson, he would quit them in disgust, and come over to our side"—see *Washington Federalist,* Nov. 24, 1800, reprinted in the New York *Daily Advertiser,* Dec. 1, 1800. For Burr being on the market, see Fisher Ames to Rufus King, July 15, 1800, in W.B. Allen, ed., *Works of Fisher Ames, as Published by Seth Allen* (Indianapolis, 1983), 2:1365; see also Lewis, "What Is to Become of Our Government?" in Onuf et al., eds., *The Revolution of 1800,* 8.

99. Harper's description of himself and his plan was recorded in the diary of Gouverneur Morris on Dec. 27; see Robert Goodloe Harper to AB, Dec. 24, 1800, in Kline, ed., *Burr Papers,* I: 474–75.

100. Morris also observed this arrogant posturing among his colleagues when he wrote to Hamilton: "Mr. Burr will it is said come hither, and some who pretend to know his views think he will *bargain* with the Federalists." The key phrase here is "pretend to know his views." See Harrison Gray Otis to AH, Dec. 17, 1800, AH to Oliver Wolcott, Jr., Dec. 16, 1800, and Gouverneur Morris to AH, Dec. 19, 1800, in Syrett, ed., *Hamilton Papers,* XXV:258–59, 267. See also Theodore Sedgwick to Theodore Sedgwick, Jr., Jan. 11, 1801, in Kline, ed., *Burr Papers,* I: 482; "From Washington," *Aurora,* Feb. 17, 1801.

101. See Gouverneur Morris to AH, Dec. 19, 1800, and Jan. 26, 1801, in Syrett, ed., *Hamilton Papers,* XXV: 267, 329; see also "Short and Plain Reasons why all those who are attached to the Federal Constitution, ought to prefer Col. Burr to Mr. Jefferson as President," *Washington Federalist,* Feb. 2, 1801, reprinted in the *Daily Advertiser,* Feb. 11, 1801. Theodore Sedgwick also made the argument that they should vote for Burr because he was not Jefferson; see Theodore Sedgwick to Theodore Sedgwick, Jr., in Kline, ed., *Burr Papers,* I: 482.

102. See "To the Federal Members of the House of Representatives" [signed "Lucius"], *Washington Federalist,* Feb. 6, 1801, reprinted in the *Daily Advertiser,* Feb. 16, 1801; see also "Who Shall Be President?" *Washington Federalist,* Jan. 12, 1801. For other defenses of Burr's manners and analytical mind, see "From the New York Gazette: No. III," "To the Federal member of the House of Representatives of the United States," [both signed "Epaminondas"], *Washington Federalist,* Jan. 21, 23, 1801.

103. AH to Theodore Sedgwick, Dec. 22, 1800, in Syrett, ed., *Hamilton Papers,* XXV: 270.

104. For references to Cataline, see AH to Oliver Wolcott, Jr., Dec. 16, 1800, and Alexander Hamilton to John Rutledge, Jan. 4, 1801; for his reference to Godwinism, see AH to James Bayard, Jan. 16, 1801; and for charges that Burr was using democracy while despising it, see AH to John Rutledge, Jan. 4, 1801,

and AH to James McHenry, Jan. 4, 1801, all in Syrett, ed., *Hamilton Papers,* XXV: 257, 287, 292, 297, 321.

105. Hamilton described his account to John Rutledge as a "faithful sketch of Mr. Burr's character," and he portrayed himself as an authority when writing James Bayard, James Ross, and John Marshall. For Burr's "extreme & irregular ambition," see AH to James Bayard, Jan. 19, 1801, and for establishing "supreme power in his own person," see AH to John Rutledge, Jan. 4, 1801. For Burr as a man who "loves nothing but himself," see AH to Harrison Gray Otis, Dec. 23, 1800; as a "bankrupt" and "voluptuary," and seeking war with Great Britain, see AH to Oliver Wolcott, Jr., Dec. 16, 1800, AH to Gouveneur Morris, Dec. 24, 1800, AH to James Bayard, Dec. 27, 1800, AH to James Ross, Dec. 29, 1800, and AH to John Rutledge, Jan. 4, 1801. For Burr attracting the worst men, the "young and profligate," laughing "in his sleeve," and signing a "death warrant" for the nation, see AH to James McHenry, Jan. 4, 1801, AH to John Rutledge, Jan. 4, 1801, AH to James Bayard, Dec. 27, 1800, AH to James Ross, Dec. 29, 1800, and AH to Oliver Wolcott, Dec. 1800. All in *ibid.,* XXV: 257, 271–72, 276–77, 280–81, 287, 292, 294–97, 320–21.

106. AH to John Rutledge, Jan. 4, 1801, AH to James Bayard, Jan. 16, 1801, and AH to James Bayard, Dec. 27, 1800, in *ibid.,* XXV: 276, 296, 323.

107. See Gouveneur Morris to AH, Dec. 19, 1800; and for Hamilton's harangue, see AH to Gouveneur Morris, Dec. 24, 1800, in *ibid.,* XXV: 267, 272.

108. AH to Gouveneur Morris, Dec. 26, 1800, and AH to Gouveneur Morris, in *ibid.,* XXV: 275.

109. John Marshall to AH, Jan. 1, 1801, James Bayard to AH, Jan. 7, 1801, John Rutledge to AH, Jan. 10, 1801, and Theodore Sedgwick to AH, Jan. 10, 1801, in *ibid.,* XXV: 290–91, 300–01, 308–09, 311–12.

110. See *Aurora,* Jan. 10, 1801; Thomas Jefferson to John Breckenridge [Breckinridge], Dec. 18, 1800, in Lipscomb and Bergh, eds., *The Writings of Thomas Jefferson,* X: 183; and "To the House of Representatives of the United States of America," *National Intelligencer,* Jan. 12, 1801, and *Washington Federalist,* Jan. 26, 1801. See also Joseph H. Nicholson to a constituent, Jan. 15, 1801, Nicholson MSS, Letter, Historical Society of Pennsylvania; and Sharp, *American Politics in the Early Republic,* 267–71.

111. This was the second fire in Washington; the first was in the War Department in November 1800, see *Aurora,* Jan. 26, 27, Feb. 19, 1801; Sharp, *American Politics in the Early Republic,* 250–52, 267–68.

112. Albert Gallatin to Hannah Gallatin, Jan. 22, 1801, in Papers of Albert Gallatin, microfilm; and Richard Mannix, "Albert Gallatin in Washington, 1801–1813," *Records of the Columbia Historical Society* (1971–72): 61, 64–65.

113. See Albert Gallatin to Hannah Gallatin, Jan. 22, Jan. 29, 1801, in Gallatin Papers, microfilm; James Madison to Thomas Jefferson, Jan. 10, 1801, in Mattern,

ed., *The Papers of James Madison,* XVII: 45–54; and Lewis, "What is to become of the Constitution?" in Onuf et al., eds., *The Revolution of 1800,* 37.

114. For the two plans, see James Hamilton to Albert Gallatin, Jan. 16, 1801, The Papers of Albert Gallatin, microfilm.

115. Albert Gallatin to Hannah Gallatin, Jan. 29, 1801, and Albert Gallatin to Thomas Jefferson and James Nicholson [ca. Jan. 29], in *ibid.*

116. Côté, *Theodosia,* 110–20; and Eleanor Parke Lewis to Mrs. Charles [Mary] Pinckney, [n.d.], in Lewis and Peter Papers, Special Collections, University of Virginia, Charlottesville, Va.

117. AB to Samuel Smith, Dec. 29, 1800, and for earlier declaration, see Burr to Samuel Smith, Dec. 16, 1800, in Kline, ed., *Burr Papers,* I: 478–79, 471.

118. AB to Samuel Smith, Dec. 29, 1800, and Burr to William Eustis, Jan. 16, 1801, in *ibid.,* I: 479, 490–91.

119. AB to Samuel Smith, Dec. 24, 1800, and Burr to Samuel Smith, Feb. 4, 1801, in *ibid.,* I: 475, 489.

120. The meeting between Burr and Smith is based on an account (given two years later) by one of Smith's Maryland colleagues of what Smith told him. The main thrust of the discussion centered on the fear of a deadlock, and whether Burr would resign to break it. See Gabriel Christie to Samuel Smith, Dec. 19, 1802, cited in Kline, ed., *Burr Papers,* I: 484; see also Albert Gallatin to Hannah Gallatin, Jan. 15, 1801, in Papers of Albert Gallatin, microfilm; Thomas Jefferson to Mary Jefferson Eppes, Jan. 4, 1801, in Edward Morris Betts and James Adam Bear, Jr., eds., *The Family Letters of Thomas Jefferson* (Charlottesville, Va., 1966), 190; and George Clinton to DeWitt Clinton, Jan. 13, 1801, in DeWitt Clinton Papers, Rare Book and Manuscript Library, Columbia University, New York, N.Y.

121. See AB to Albert Gallatin, Jan. 16, 1801, and AB to Samuel Smith, Jan. 16, 1801, in Kline, ed., *Burr Papers,* I: 492–93. For Hamilton spreading rumors about Livingston, see AH to Gouverneur Morris, Jan. 9, 1801, and Jan. 13, 1801, in Syrett, ed., *Hamilton Papers,* XXV: 305, 314. The only sources that make Edward Livingston into Burr's double agent are based on the gossip circulated by Federalists: Hamilton, Robert Troup, and James Bayard. Unlike the rumors, Livingston's letter to his brother, Chancellor Robert Livingston, conveyed his strong conviction to oppose the Federalist "usurpation," saying it "will be *firmly & Efficiently resisted.*" See Hatcher, *Edward Livingston,* 70. For Troup's letter, see Robert Troup to Rufus King, May 27, 1801, in King, ed., *Life and Correspondence of Rufus King,* III: 460; and Edward Livingston to Robert Livingston, Jan. 29, 1801, Robert Livingston Papers, New-York Historical Society; see also Kline, ed., *Burr Papers,* I: 504–05.

122. There were others: Timothy Green, Gideon Granger, Pierpont Edwards, and Abraham Bishop were accused for promoting Burr over Jefferson. David A. Ogden, Hamilton's law partner and protégé, shared a carriage ride with Burr

from New York to Trenton. He was approached by Federalists to talk to Burr; he later admitted that Burr had never engaged him as his agent, and that Burr flatly refused to make any deals. This is the same Ogden involved with the Holland Land Company. Linn was probably seen as a likely turncoat because he represented New Jersey, another delegation, like New York, that southern Republicans feared might switch sides. Virginian George Jackson wrote Madison that Linn was a "very Suspicious character," seeming to play both sides. Linn probably did know Burr: he attended Princeton around the same time, and married Mary Livingston, one of the daughters of William Livingston. But contrary to the rumors, the New York and New Jersey delegations made sure to reaffirm their commitment to Jefferson during a caucus meeting in anticipation of the balloting in the House. See "James Linn," in Harrison, ed., *Princetonians, 1769–1775,* II: 28–30; Kline, ed., *Burr Papers,* I: 489–90; and George Jackson to James Madison, Feb. 5, 1801, in Mattern, ed., *The Papers of James Madison,* XVII:461; see also Joanne Freeman, "Corruption and Compromise in the Election of 1800," in Onuf et al., eds., *The Revolution of 1800,* 108, 114.

123. AB to Albert Gallatin, Feb. 12, 1801, in Kline, ed., *Burr Papers,* I: 500; Edward Livingston to Matthew L. Davis, Feb. 5, 1801, in W. C. Ford, "Some Papers of Aaron Burr," *Proceedings of the American Antiquarian Society* (1919): 64.

124. For reports on the voting, see *Aurora,* Feb. 16, 1801.

125. Whether accurate or not, Federalists believed that Smith was the weak link among the Republicans; other Federalists besides Bayard approached him with offers for assurances from Jefferson. They assumed he would be more willing to make a deal. His biographer notes that they did not approach Gallatin. Federalists shared a negative view of Smith: James Gunn described him as "a man of small talents, but he has a passion for low intrigue, and wishes to be Secretary of the navy." Gallatin would later offer his own opinion that Smith had misled Bayard. He wrote: "One of our friends, who was very erroneously and improperly afraid of a defection on the part of some of our members, undertook to act as an intermediary, and confounding his own opinions and wishes with those of Mr. Jefferson, reported the result in such a manner as gave subsequently occasion for very unfounded surmises." Gallatin reacted as Burr did to those requesting that he resign: he thought Smith was guilty of impertinence, acting irrationally out of fear, and intentionally misleading Bayard. See Cassell, *Merchant Congressman,* 99, 100–01; and James Gunn to AH, Jan. 9, 1801, in Syrett, ed., *Hamilton Papers,* XXV: 303; Gallatin to Henry A. Muhlenberg, May 8, 1848, in Adams, *Life of Albert Gallatin,* 250–51; and depositions of James Bayard and Samuel Smith, 1806, in Elizabeth Donnan, ed., "Papers of James Bayard, 1796–1815," in *Annual Report of the American Historical Society for the Year 1913* (Washington, D.C., 1915), 128–29, *Aurora,* Feb. 17, 1801, and on voting, see John Ferling, *Adams vs. Jefferson: The Tumultuous Election of 1800* (New York: 2004), 193.

126. To his father-in-law, Bayard insisted that Burr did everything to stop the usurpation: "The election was in his power, but he was determined to come in as a Democrat. . . . We have been counteracted in the whole business by letters he has written to this place." See James A. Bayard to AH, Mar. 8, 1801, in Syrett, ed., *Hamilton Papers,* XXV: 345; James A. Bayard to Allen McClane, Feb. 17, 1801, Special Collections, University of Virginia, Charlottesville, Va.; see also James Bayard to Richard Bassett, Feb. 16, 1801, in Donnan, ed., "Papers of James Bayard," 126, 128–29.

CHAPTER SEVEN

1. See the New York *Daily Advertiser,* Mar. 6, 1801.
2. Dumas Malone, *Jefferson the President: The First Term, 1801–1805* (New York, 1970), 3–4; AB to Caesar A. Rodney, Mar. 3 and 4, 1801, in Kline, ed., *Burr Papers,* I: 518; New York *Daily Advertiser,* Mar. 12, 1801.
3. For church song, see Andrew Burstein, *Sentimental Democracy* (New York, 1999), 215; for toasts, see *Aurora,* Mar. 9, 10, 1801; and for Burr as Jefferson's successor, see "Jefferson and Burr," *Aurora,* Mar. 21, 1801; also New York *Daily Advertiser,* Mar. 4, 1801, and *American Citizen,* Mar. 5, 1801.
4. Malone, *Jefferson the President,* 46.
5. Jefferson claimed he was responsible for 316 offices. He did not include the military, judiciary, or the postmasters appointed by the postmaster general. See Malone, *Jefferson the President,* 51, 69–70, and Allgor, *Parlor Politics,* 4–5.
6. AB to Caesar Rodney, Mar. 5, 1801, in Kline, ed., *Burr Papers,* I; 519; and Noble E. Cunningham, Jr., *The Process of Government Under Jefferson* (Princeton, N.J., 1978), 12–17. In a letter to Dr. John Coats, another member of the Canadian expedition, Burr referred to Dearborn as "our fellow-traveller through the wilderness." So, there appears to have been some bond between the two men. See AB to Dr. John Coats, Feb. 23, 1803, in Davis, ed., *Memoirs of Aaron Burr,* II: 220.
7. For newspaper attacks on Gallatin, see New York *Daily Advertiser,* Mar. 16, Apr. 16, 1801; see also Albert Gallatin to Hannah Gallatin, Feb. 19, 1801, in Adams, *Life of Albert Gallatin,* 263; AB to Samuel Smith, Dec. 17, 1800, in Kline, ed., *Burr Papers,* I: 472, 519; and Cunningham, *The Process of Government,* 12–13.
8. See "Memoranda on Appointments," Mar. 17, 1801, in Kline, ed., *Burr Papers,* I: 537, 541–43.
9. Pierpont Edwards to Thomas Jefferson, May 12, 1801, in Gaillard Hunt, "Office-seeking During Jefferson's Administration," *American Historical* Review 3 (1898): 274–77; Pierpont Edwards and others to Levi Lincoln, June 4, 1801, enclosed in Lincoln to Jefferson, June 15, 1801, The Papers of Thomas Jefferson, microfilm; Noble E. Cunningham, *The Jeffersonian Republicans in Power:*

Party Operations, 1801–1809 (Chapel Hill, N.C., 1963), 18–21; AB to Pierpont Edwards, Mar. 9, 1801, in Kline, ed., *Burr Papers*, I: 526; and Thomas Jefferson to Wilson Cary Nicholas, June 11, 1801, in Ford, ed., *The Works of Thomas Jefferson*, IX: 266.

10. Thomas Jefferson to Wilson Cary Nicholas, June 11, 1801, in Ford, ed., *The Works of Thomas Jefferson*, IX: 266.

11. See AB to Edward Livingston, Feb. 12, 1801, in Kline, ed., *Burr Papers*, I: 502.

12. Clinton and Armstrong had a key friend in common: Ambrose Spenser, a Federalist turned Republican, who served on the Council of Appointment. See Steven Edwin Siry, "DeWitt Clinton and the American Political Economy: Sectionalism, Politics, and Republican Ideology, 1787–1828," Ph.D. Dissertation, University of Cincinnati, 1986, 43, 46–47, 56–57; Evan Cornog, *The Birth of Empire: DeWitt Clinton and the American Experience, 1769–1828* (New York, 1998), 6, 35, 37–40, 43; Dangerfield, *Chancellor Robert L. Livingston*, 305; and Skeen, *John Armstrong*, 44.

13. Skeen, *John Armstrong*, 42, 44–49; and Kline, ed., *Burr Papers*, I: 535–36.

14. Armstrong's biographer concludes: "Armstrong was indeed aggressive, not in the physical sense, but in the disputatious sense. Whether he delighted in his controversies or not is conjectural (more probably he did), but it can be said that he never side-stepped or avoided a dispute. He was also cynical and sarcastic and his demeanor was haughty and contemptuous—not endearing qualities"—Skeen, *John Armstrong*, 13, 16, 39–40, 49, 227.

15. The Council of Appointment began removing Federalists and appointing Livingston and Clinton supporters as early as August 1801. See Siry, "DeWitt Clinton and the American Political Economy," 45–47; Robert Livingston to Edward Livingston, Aug. 23, 1801, in Dangerfield, *Chancellor Robert L. Livingston*, 305; AB to Albert Gallatin, June 28, 1801, in Kline, ed., *Burr Papers*, II: 602–03; I: 538; James Nicholson to Albert Gallatin, Aug. 10, 1801, Papers of Albert Gallatin, microfilm; and Adams, *The Life of Albert Gallatin*, 282.

16. AB to Albert Gallatin, Sept. 8, 1801, in Kline, ed., *Burr Papers*, II: 620–22; also Cunningham, *The Jeffersonian Republicans in Power*, 40, 42, 44.

17. Albert Gallatin to Thomas Jefferson, Sept. 14, 1801, in Adams, *The Life of Albert Gallatin*, 287.

18. *Ibid.*, 287–88.

19. *Ibid.*

20. *Ibid.*, 288–89. In the *Anas*, Jefferson rationalizes his estrangement from Burr by stating: "I had never seen Colonel Burr till he came as a member of the Senate. His conduct soon inspired me with distrust. I habitually cautioned Mr. Madison against trusting him too much. . . . There never had been an intimacy between us, and but little association." The *Anas* was composed a decade after his retirement from the presidency, and it was a highly political document intended to shape the ex-president's legacy. This brief portion called "Conversations

with Aaron Burr" was meant to have taken place in 1804, by which time he had already decided to exclude Burr from national office. There is ample evidence that Jefferson courted Burr as much as Burr courted Jefferson in the late 1790s, and in 1801, they were still on good terms. See "Conversations with Aaron Burr," in Lipscomb and Bergh, eds., *The Writings of Thomas Jefferson,* I: 447–48.

21. *Aaron Burr!* (May 1801), in Burr Papers, microfilm, reel 4.

22. *Ibid.*

23. AB to William Eustis, May 13, 1801. Burr had used the same aphorism in an earlier letter to Jefferson during the election tie, in which he wrote, "I invariably pronounce to be a lie, every thing which ought not to be true"; see AB to Thomas Jefferson, Feb. 12, 1801, in Kline, ed., *Burr Papers,* I: 579, 501.

24. On prostitution, see Clara Anna Lyons, *Sex Among the Rabble: An Intimate History of Gender and Power in the Age of Revolution, Philadelphia, 1730–1830* (Chapel Hill, N.C., 2006), 107–08, 110, 188, 192; Timothy Gilfoyle, *City of Eros: New York City, Prostitution, and the Commercialization of Sex, 1790–1920* (New York, 1992), 24–26; Kenneth Roberts and Anna M. Roberts, eds., *Moreau de St. Méry's American Journal, 1793–1798* (Garden City, N.Y., 1947), 156; see also Rush's "Deaths of Persons of Note or Singular Character," in George W. Corner, ed., *The Autobiography of Benjamin Rush: His "Travels through Life" together with his Commonplace Book for 1789–1813* (Westport, Conn., 1948), 310–11. John Armstrong told Jefferson that Willett had lived in adultery, which he recorded in his *Anas;* see Kline, ed., *Burr Papers,* I: 536. Willett had an acknowledged illegitimate son, born in 1783, during his first marriage; see Howard Thomas, *Marinus Willett: Soldier, Patriot, 1740–1830* (New York, 1954), 95, 151, 184–87. For Burr's defense of Anne Livingston, see *Anne Horne Livingston v. Henry Beekman Livingston,* Dec. 7, 1790, NYCC Cases, in Burr Papers, microfilm, reel 19.

25. AB to Pierpont Edwards, May 5, 1798, in Burr Papers, microfilm, reel 4; for another letter suggestive of an intimate relationship, see Mrs. Hoyt to AB, Sept. 29, 1803, in Burr Papers, microfilm, reel 5; for contraceptives sold in bookstore, see *Moreau de St. Méry's American Journal,* 176–78.

26. See James Madison to Thomas Jefferson, Sept. 27, 1806, in Annette Gordon-Reed, *Thomas Jefferson and Sally Hemings: An American Controversy* (Charlottesville, Va., 1997), 231–32.

27. "The Old Bachelor's Masterpiece" (Fairhaven, Vt., 1797), 33–34. James Kent, Supreme Court justice and longtime admirer of Hamilton, described his friend Egbert Benson as an "invincible bachelor." See John D. Gordan III, "Egbert Benson: A Nationalist in Congress, 1789–1793," in Bowling and Kennon, eds., *Neither Separate Nor Equal: Congress in the 1790s,* 63.

28. For sexual euphemisms, see Peter Wagner, "The Pornographer in the Courtroom: Trial Reports About Cases of Sexual Crimes and Delinquencies as a

Genre of Eighteenth-Century Erotica," in Paul-Gabriel Boucé, ed., *Sexuality in Eighteenth-Century Britain* (Manchester, 1982), 135; and for the chancellor's brother, John R. Livingston, as New York City's "whoremaster," see Gilfoyle, *The City of Eros,* 43–44.

29. The diplomat in question was José Ignacio de Viar, who later was consul general under Yrujo. Sally McKean was the daughter of Governor McKean of Pennsylvania, and married Carlos Fernando Martínez de Yrujo in 1798; see Sally McKean to Dolley Madison, Aug. 3, 1797, in Mattern and Shulman, eds., *The Selected Letters of Dolley Payne Madison,* 34; see also Lyons, *Sex Among the Rabble,* 204.

30. For the story about Pinckney, see Cynthia D. Earman, "Messing Around: Entertaining and Accomodating Congress, 1800–1830" (personal paper in possession of the author).

31. Kline, ed., *Burr Papers,* I: lix.

32. See AB to William Eustis, Aug. 10, 1800, in Kline, ed., *Burr Papers,* I: 277–78, 442; and Theodosia Burr to William Eustis, Aug. 27, 1800, and for Eustis's invitation to the wedding, AB to William Eustis, Jan. 26, 1801, in Burr Papers, microfilm, reel 4. Eustis eventually married Caroline Langdon of New Hampshire (niece of Senator John Langdon) in 1810; he was fifty-seven, she twenty-nine. See Mattern and Shulman, eds., *The Selected Letters of Dolley Madison,* 400.

33. Robert Troup to Rufus King, May 27, 1801, in King, ed., *The Life and Correspondence of Rufus King,* III: 459; Porter, "Mixed Feelings: The Enlightenment and Sexuality in Eighteenth-Century Britain," 11; see also Barker-Benfield, *The Culture of Sensibility,* 291–93; and Wollstonecraft, *A Vindication of the Rights of Woman,* 234.

34. "Celeste" and "Inamorata" are discussed below. For "La Planche," and "Madame G.," see AB to Theodosia Burr Alston, Dec. 27, 1803, June 4–5, Feb. 8, 16, May 1, 8, June 11, July 20, 1804; and for the miserable marriage, see AB to Theodosia Burr Alston, Nov. 3, 1801, in Davis, ed., *Memoirs of Aaron Burr,* II: 156, 251, 267, 276–77, 285, 287, 289, 328.

35. For references to "sculpture," "statues," or "busts," see AB to Theodosia Burr Alston, Nov. 9, 26, Dec. 8, 1801, and Feb. 2, Feb. 23, 1802; in Davis, ed., *Memoirs of Aaron Burr,* II: 147, 157, 160–62, 172.

36. AB to Theodosia Burr Alston, June 13, 1804, in *ibid.,* II: 289.

37. The entire story included a series of letters from June 5 to June 12 in *ibid.,* II: 222–32, esp. 223, 224.

38. AB to Theodosia Burr Alston, June 8, 1803, in *ibid.,* II: 226.

39. See AB to Theodosia Burr Alston, June 10 and June 11, 1803 (entitled "Continuation of the Story of the Loves of Reubon and Celeste") in *ibid.,* II: 227, 229–30.

40. AB to Theodosia Burr Alston, Nov. 22, Dec. 27, 1803, May 1, May 8, June 24, July 20, 1804, in *ibid.,* II; 247, 251, 285, 287, 290, 328.

41. Susan Binney (1778–1849) was the daughter of Dr. Barnabas Binney of Boston, and the sister of Horace Binney, a lawyer in Philadelphia—see Kline, ed., *Burr Papers,* I: 436; see also Phillip S. Lapsansky, "Afro-Americana: Rediscovering Leonora Sansay," *Annual Report of the Library Company of Philadelphia for the Year 1992* (Philadelphia, 1993), 29–46.

42. AB to William Eustis, June 13, 1800, Dec. 5, 1800, Mar. 29, 1801, May 13, 1801, June 24, 1801, in Kline, ed., *Burr Papers,* I: 435, 464, 549, 579, 599.

43. AB to Susan Binney, Nov. 25, 1800, in Burr Papers, microfilm, reel 4.

44. Sansay may have been the daughter of William Hassall, who ran an inn near the State House in Philadelphia—see Lapsansky, "Afro-Americana: Rediscovering Leonora Sansay," 30; AB to Pierpont Edwards, Mar. 30, 1802, in Kline, ed., *Burr Papers,* II: 702–03; see also AB to William Eustis, July 16, 1797, and John Vanderlyn to AB, Apr. 8, 1802, in Burr Papers, microfilm, reels 4 and 5.

45. AB to Theodosia Burr Alston, July 10, 1804. Burr also made some provision for Leonora Sansay in his will, as he mentioned in his letter to Joseph Alston, July 10, 1804, in Davis, ed., *Memoirs of Aaron Burr,* II: 322–23, 326.

46. Sansay did not endorse the French way of seeking "only the gratification of their sensual appetites." She believed in the "union of hearts." See [Leonora Sansay], *Secret History; or, the Horrors of St. Domingo, in a series of letters, written by a lady at Cape Francois, to Colonel Burr* (Philadelphia, 1808), 79; see also Kline, ed., *Burr Papers,* II: 703.

47. AB to William Eustis, Dec. 1, 1800, in Kline, ed., *Burr Papers,* I: 463. Maria Reynolds divorced James Reynolds in 1793; she then married Reynolds's "former co-conspirator" in the extortions of Hamilton: Jacob Clingman. In 1800, she divorced him. See Cogan, "The Reynolds Affair and the Politics of Character," 416.

48. AB to William Eustis, Apr. 18, 1801, William Eustis to AB, July 31, Aug. 9, Aug. 11, 1803, in Kline, ed., *Burr Papers,* I: 561, II: 783–84, 788–89.

49. For the French version of this lifestyle, see Michel Feher, ed., *The Libertine Reader: Eroticism and Enlightenment in Eighteenth-Century France* (New York, 1977), 14, 20.

50. Grub Street was the famous haunt of hack writers in London. See "James Cheetham," *Dictionary of American Biography* (New York, 1930), 47; see also James Cheetham to Thomas Jefferson, Dec. 10, 1801, *Proceedings of the Massachusetts Historical Society,* 3rd ser. (1907–08) I: 46–52.

51. Matthew Livingston Davis, Memorandum Book, Vol. 57, Rufus King Papers, New-York Historical Society, New York; for Jefferson's patronage of Cheetham, see Cunningham, *The Jeffersonian Republicans in Power,* 254–55. Cheetham's letters are filled with his unctuous pleas to Jefferson for financial support. See James Cheetham to Thomas Jefferson, June 17, 1803, July 25, 1804, in *Proceedings of the Massachusetts Historical Society,* 59–63.

52. James Cheetham to the President [Thomas Jefferson], Dec. 10, 1801, in *Proceedings of the Massachusetts Historical Society*, 46–47.

53. *Ibid.*, 48–49, 51.

54. *Ibid.*, 49.

55. John Wood's book was titled *History of the Administration of John Adams Esq. Late President of the United States*. Mary-Jo Kline has called this episode, which ended the "lip service" that the Clintonians paid to their brief alliance with the Burrites, "bizarre even by the standards of N.Y. partisan politics." Burr seems to have had no role in the preparation of the manuscript, but became involved later when he first examined the book in Oct. 1801. William Duane, Republican editor of the Philadelphia *Aurora*, felt Wood's book was "a hasty, crude, and inconsistent production, calculated rather to produce evil than the least good." See William P. Van Ness to AB, Jan. 2, 1802, AB to William P. Van Ness, Mar. 17, 1802, and William Duane to AB, Apr. 15, 1802, Kline, ed., *Burr Papers*, II: 641–46, 698–98, 724–27; see also AB to William P. Van Ness, Mar. 18, 1802, in Burr Papers, microfilm, reel 5; and James Cheetham to Thomas Jefferson, Dec. 29, 1800, and Jan. 30, 1801, in *Proceedings of the Massachusetts Historical Society*, 51–58.

56. See James Cheetham, *A Narrative of the Suppression by Col. Burr, of the History of the Administration of John Adams, Late President of the United States* (New York, 1802), 11, 38–39; and James Cheetham, *A View of the Political Conduct of Aaron Burr, Esq., Vice President of the United States* (New York, 1802), 57.

57. Other prominent Republicans agreed with Burr, such as Alexander Dallas; he was the newly appointed U.S. Attorney for Pennsylvania's Eastern District, and felt strongly that the repeal threatened the independence of the judiciary. See AB's "Comment on a Motion to Repeal the Judiciary Act" (Jan. 27, 1802), AB to Barnabas Bidwell, Feb. 1, 1802, AB to Joseph Alston, Feb. 2, 1802, Alexander J. Dallas to AB, Feb. 3, 1802, and Nathaniel Niles to AB, Feb. 17, 1802, in Kline, ed., *Burr Papers*, II, 653–56, 659–61, 666–68, 678–79.

58. Robert Troup to Rufus King, Apr. 9, 1802, in King, ed., *The Life and Correspondence of Rufus King*, IV: 103; John P. Van Ness to William Van Ness, Apr. 2, 1802, Van Ness Papers, New York Public Library; see also Cunningham, *The Jeffersonian Republicans in Power*, 204–05.

59. See Gouverneur Morris to AH, Mar. 11, 1802, and AH to James Bayard, Apr. 6, 1802, and James Bayard to AH, Apr. 12, 1802, in Syrett, ed., *Hamilton Papers*, XXV: 561, 587–88, 600; Robert Troup to Rufus King, Apr. 9, 1802, in King, ed., *The Life and Correspondence of Rufus King*, IV: 102; and Cunningham, *The Jeffersonian Republicans in Power*, 205.

60. AB to Joseph Alston, Mar. 8, 1802, in Davis, ed., *Memoirs of Aaron Burr*, II: 185.

61. John P. Van Ness to William Van Ness, Apr. 2, 1802, William P. Van Ness Papers, New York Public Library; AB to Joseph Alston, July 3, 1802, in Davis,

ed., *Memoirs of Aaron Burr,* II: 205; and AB to Pierpont Edwards, July 15, 1802, in Kline, ed., *Burr Papers,* II: 728.

62. After the duel, Burr sent Alston a newspaper that detailed the affair of honor. He wrote that Clinton, according to the account, "indirectly acknowledges that he is an agent in the calumnies against me." See AB to Joseph Alston, Aug. 2, 1802, in Davis, ed., *Memoirs of Aaron Burr,* II: 209; see also Cornog, *The Birth of Empire,* 43–44; and Siry, "DeWitt Clinton and the American Political Economy," 50–53. And on using dueling for political advancement, see Freeman, *Affairs of Honor,* 184–87.

63. *American Citizen,* Aug. 16, Oct. 18, 25, Nov. 1, 1802; July 20, 22, 25, 1803.

64. See my essay "'The Little Emperor': Aaron Burr, Dandyism, and the Sexual Politics of Treason," in Jeffery I. Pasley, Andrew W. Robertson, and David Waldstreicher, eds., *Beyond the Founders: New Approaches to the Political History of the Early American Republic* (Chapel Hill, N.C., 2004), 129–58.

65. *American Citizen,* Dec. 20, 1802, June 20, Aug. 3, 1803, Jan. 17, 1804.

66. *American Citizen,* Jan. 24, Feb. 1, 9, 1803, Jan. 10, 1804. For the importance of the Cataline and the sodomite plot in eighteenth-century English political satire, see Cameron McFarlane, *The Sodomite in Fiction and Satire, 1660–1750* (New York, 1997), 30–31, 37, 101–02, 111, 114.

67. See Kline, ed., *Burr Papers,* I: xxxi, 412, 584, 2: 613, 896; and B. R. Brunson, *The Adventures of Samuel Swartwout in the Age of Jefferson and Jackson* (Lewiston, N.Y., 1989), 1–2. On Peter and Washington Irving, see Stanley T. Williams, *The Life of Washington Irving* (New York, 1935), 23, 25–26, 35–36; and Bruce I. Granger and Martha Hartzog, eds., *The Complete Works of Washington Irving: Letters of Jonathan Oldstyle, Gent./ Salmagundi* (Boston, 1978), xxiii.

68. Cheetham used several similar terms to describe Burr as demonic, treacherous, and elusive. He called him a "sort of a legerdemain," an "invisible spirit," a "serpent," a man "with the eye of a lynx," and one whose career displayed a "convenient versatility." He also referred to Burr's "refined system of intrigue and necromancy." See Charles Nolan, Jr., *Aaron Burr and the American Literary Imagination* (Westport, Conn., 1980), 50–52; *American Citizen,* Aug. 20, 1802; also James Cheetham, *On the Subject of Aaron Burr's Political Defection* (New York, 1803), 24. For Burr's opinion of Irving, see AB to Charles Biddle, Dec. 7, 12, 1802; and for Bloomfield's letter urging Burr to defend himself and Burr's published response, see Joseph Bloomfield to AB, Sept. 17, 1802, and AB to Joseph Bloomfield, Sept. 21, 1802, in Kline, ed., *Burr Papers,* II: 743–44, 737–39.

69. For Cheetham's defense of his lack of evidence, see "Letter Eight," *American Citizen,* Oct. 12, 1802.

70. Cheetham's two pamphlets, *A View of the Political Conduct of Aaron Burr, Esq., Vice President of the United States* (July 1802) and *Nine Letters on the Subject of Aaron Burr's Political Defection, with an Appendix* (Feb. 1803), included these

charges. The attacks made in his pamphlets also appeared in the *American Citizen*—see Kline, ed., *Burr Papers*, II: 738.

71. See "The Coach!!!," *Morning Chronicle Express*, Jan. 3, 1803; also a similar article mocking Cheetham's claims about the stage coach ride, *Morning Chronicle*, Jan. 27, 1803. Irving published an entire series of articles, entitled the "Rights of Editors," that pointed out all of Cheetham's journalist tricks, such as fake letters to the editor, circular logic, and his reliance on unsubstantiated gossip.

72. "Aristides" [William P. Van Ness], *An Examination of the Various Charges Exhibited Against Aaron Burr, Esq. Vice-President of the United States; and a Development of the Characters and View of the Political Opponents* (New York, 1803); there was also a southern edition of Van Ness's pamphlet published in Virginia. See also Kline, ed., *Burr Papers*, II: 812–13, 829; Cornog, *The Birth of Empire*, 42–43.

73. See Kline, ed., *Burr Papers*, II: 822–23; Siry, "DeWitt Clinton and the American Political Economy," 60.

74. Gideon Granger to DeWitt Clinton, Feb. 1, 1804, Clinton Papers, Columbia University Library, New York, N.Y., Thomas Jefferson to DeWitt Clinton, Dec. 2, 1803, in Ford, ed., *The Works of Thomas Jefferson*, VIII: 282.

75. Clinton received 67 out of 108 votes, the remaining votes were divided among five other candidates from western and northern states. See Wilson Cary Nicholas (ally of DeWitt Clinton) to DeWitt Clinton, Aug. 13, 1802, DeWitt Clinton Papers, Columbia University, New York, N.Y.; Littleton W. Tazewell to John Randolph, Mar. 4, 1804, Tazewell Family Papers, Virginia State Library, Richmond, Va.; Cunningham, *The Jeffersonian Republicans in Power*, 103–07, 208; *Morning Chronicle*, Mar. 2, 1804; and Kline, ed., *Burr Papers*, II: 840.

76. Lansing had a distinguished career: he was a veteran of the Revolutionary War, a lawyer, and a delegate to the Constitutional Convention in 1787, and the New York ratifying convention in 1788. He was appointed to the state Supreme Court in 1790 and made chief justice in 1798; he became chancellor in 1801. See Kline, ed., *Burr Papers*, II: 830, and Syrett, ed., *Hamilton Papers*, XXVI: 122.

77. Kline, ed., *Burr Papers*, II: 830–31; Cornog, *The Birth of Empire*, 51, 53. Morgan Lewis was a classmate of Burr's at Princeton, graduating one year after Burr, as a member of the class of 1773. He had attended the same grammar school as Burr in Elizabethtown, when Burr's future brother-in-law, Tapping Reeve, was the instructor. He married Gertrude Livingston, the sister of Robert R. Livingston. Clinton had tried to woo Lewis, as he had Burr, by appointing him state attorney general in 1791, and later he appointed him to the state Supreme Court in 1792. He became chief justice in 1801 when John Lancing became chancellor. See "Morgan Lewis," in Harrison, ed., *Princetonians: 1769–1775*, II: 308–12.

78. See Hamilton's "Speech at a Meeting of Federalists in Albany," Feb. 10, 1804, and AH to Robert G. Harper, Feb. 19, 1804, in Syrett, ed., *Hamilton Papers*, XXVI: 187–93.

79. See Cunningham, *The Jeffersonian Republicans in Power,* 212–13; Everett Somerville Brown, ed., *William Plumer's Memorandum of the Proceedings in the United States Senate, 1803–1807* (New York, 1923), 517–18; and "Rufus King: Memorandum of a Conversation between Burr and Rufus Griswold," Apr. 5, 1804, in Kline, ed., *Burr Papers,* II: 862–65.

80. See Kline, ed., *Burr Papers,* II: 828; Chilton Williamson, *American Suffrage: From Property to Democracy, 1760–1860* (Princeton, N.J., 1960), 162–64; and Pomerantz, *New York, an American City,* 145–47.

81. Oliver Phelps to Thomas Jefferson, Apr. 10, 1804, Jefferson Papers, microfilm; John P. Van Ness to William Van Ness, Apr. 2, 1802, William P. Van Ness Papers, New York Public Library; Kline, ed., *Burr Papers,* II: 838–39; and Cunningham, *Jeffersonian Republicans in Power,* 210–11. Irving also criticized Jefferson for supporting Cheetham; see *Chronicle Express,* Dec. 29, 1803, Jan. 9, 1804.

82. *Chronicle Express,* Dec. 29, Mar. 14, 1803, Jan. 30, Feb. 2, 16, 20, 28, Mar. 14, 22, and Apr. 5, 1804. For his independence from "family connections," see "To the Republican Electors of the State," [1804] broadside, American Antiquarian Society, Worcester, Mass.; and Kline, ed., *Burr Papers,* II: 832–33.

83. *American Citizen,* Jan. 10, Feb. 25, Mar. 20, Mar. 30, Apr. 19, Apr. 28, Apr. 30, 1804. Sardanapalus was a ruler circa 822 B.C. who dressed in woman's attire, wore makeup, and lived in seclusion with his concubines and eunuchs. Antoninus Heliogabalus was Roman emperor in 218–222; he was known for sending out his agents in Rome to search for young men with large penises that he might "enjoy their vigour." See Aelius Lampridius, *The Life of Antoninus Heliogabalus,* trans. David Magie (1924).

84. *American Citizen,* Apr. 28, 1804. Burr wrote Theodosia before the more lurid attacks appeared; see AB to Theodosia Burr Alston, Mar. 28, 1804, in Davis, ed., *Memoirs of Aaron Burr,* II: 281.

85. AB to Theodosia Burr Alston, Apr. 25, May 1, 1804, in Davis, ed., *Memoirs of Aaron Burr,* II: 284–85; *New-York Evening Post,* May 3, 1804; and Kline, ed., *Burr Papers,* II: 837, 842.

86. Kline, ed., *Burr Papers,* II: 877.

87. AB to AH, June 18, 1804 (and enclosure), in Syrett, ed., *Hamilton Papers,* XXVI: 242–46.

88. See "William P. Van Ness's Narrative of the Events of June 18, 1804," in *ibid.,* XXVI: 241; AB to Charles Biddle, July 18, 1804, in Kline, ed., *Burr Papers,* II: 887.

89. "William P. Van Ness's Narrative of the Events of June 18–21, 1804," and AH to AB, June 20, 1804, in Syrett, ed., *Hamilton Papers,* XXVI: 246–49.

90. AB to AH, June 21, 1804, in *ibid.,* XXVI: 249–51.

91. "William P. Van Ness's Narrative of the Events of June 22, 1804," in *ibid.,* XXVI: 251–52.

92. "Nathaniel Pendleton's Narrative of the Events of June 22, 1804," "William P. Van Ness's Narrative of the Events of June 25, 1804," "Nathaniel Pendleton's

Second Account of Alexander Hamilton's Conversation at John Taylor's House," all in *ibid.*, XXVI: 252, 261–63.

93. AH to AB, June 22, 1804, "William P. Van Ness's Narrative of Later Events of June 25, 1804," *ibid.*, XXVI: 253–54, 264–65.

94. AB to William P. Van Ness, June 26, 1804, and "William P. Van Ness's Narrative of the Events of June 26, 1804" and "William P. Van Ness to Nathaniel Pendleton, June 26, 1804, in *ibid.*, XXVI: 266–69.

95. See AB to AH, June 22, 1804, "Nathaniel Pendleton to William P. Van Ness, June 26, 1804," and "William P. Van Ness to Nathaniel Pendleton, June 27, 1804" in *ibid.*, XXVI: 255–56, 270–73.

96. John Randolph to Joseph H. Nicholson, Aug. 27, 1804, in Robert McColley, ed., *John Randolph: A Biography by Henry Adams* (Armonk, N.Y.), 83–84.

97. For Burr's views on honor, see "Aaron Burr's Instructions to William P. Van Ness," in Syrett, ed., *Hamilton Papers*, XXVI: 256–57; see also Charles Biddle, *Autobiography of Charles Biddle, Vice-President of the Supreme Executive Council of Pennsylvania: 1745–1821* (Philadelphia, 1883), 303.

98. Syrett, ed., *Hamilton Papers*, XXVI: 294. Nineteen-year-old Philip Hamilton had engaged in a duel with George Eacker on Nov. 23, 1801, and Hamilton's eldest son died the following day. Hamilton was deeply affected by the duel, especially since his son died defending his father's honor (Eacker had attacked Hamilton's economic and military policies)—*ibid.*, XXV: 435–37.

99. For the publication history of Hamilton's "Statement on Impending Duel with Aaron Burr" (a title given it by the editors of the *Hamilton Papers*), *ibid.*, XXVI: 281.

100. *Ibid.*, XXVI: 278–29.

101. *Ibid.*, XXVI: 279.

102. *Ibid.*, XXVI: 279; see chapter six for Hamilton's attacks on Burr during the election tie in 1801.

103. Syrett, ed., *Hamilton Papers*, XXVI: 280.

104. AB to Joseph Alston, July 10, 1804, in Davis, ed., *Memoirs of Aaron Burr*, II: 324; and Hamilton, "Statement of my property and Debts July 1, 1804," in Syrett, ed., *Hamilton Papers*, XXVI: 283–86; Schachner, *Alexander Hamilton*, 432.

105. AB to Theodosia Burr Alston, July 10, 1804, in Davis, ed., *Memoirs of Aaron Burr*, II: 322–23.

106. W. J. Rorabaugh, "The Political Duel in the Early American Republic: Burr v. Hamilton," *Journal of the Early Republic* 15 (Spring 1995): 1.

107. As Merrill Lindsey has noted, Hamilton owned a correct pair of dueling pistols but chose to use Church's pistols with the hair trigger. His selection of trick pistols violated the code of honor. "Joint Statement by William P. Van Ness and Nathaniel Pendleton on the Duel between Alexander Hamilton and Aaron Burr," July 17, 1804, and William Van Ness to Charles Biddle, [undated], and

David Hosack to William Coleman, Aug. 17, 1804, in Syrett, ed., *Hamilton Papers,* XXVI: 333–36, 344; Biddle, *Autobiography of Charles Biddle,* 304; Rorabaugh, "The Political Duel," 2–3; and Merrill Lindsay, "Pistols Shed Light on Famed Duel," *Smithsonian* 6 (Nov. 1971): 96.

108. AB to Charles Biddle, July 18, 1804, AB to William Van Ness, July 20–21, 1804, in Kline, ed., *Papers of Aaron Burr,* II: 887–89; Syrett, ed., *Hamilton Papers,* XXVI: 335; Biddle, *Autobiography of Charles Biddle,* 304.

109. AB to David Hosack, July 12, 1804, and Benjamin Moore to William Coleman, July 12, 1804, in Syrett, ed., *Hamilton Papers,* XXVI: 312, 315–17; and Douglass Adair and Marvin Harvey, "Was Alexander Hamilton a Christian Statesman?" *William and Mary Quarterly* 12 (Apr. 1955): 328–29.

110. "General Hamilton's Death," *American Citizen,* July 21, 23; see also Aug. 7, Aug. 16, 1804; *New-York Evening Post,* Aug. 4, 1804; Schachner, *Aaron Burr,* 254–55.

111. See "The Funeral," *New-York Evening Post,* July 14, 1804, in Syrett, ed., *Hamilton Papers,* XXVI: 322–23.

112. "Funeral Oration," in Syrett, ed., *Hamilton Papers,* XXVI: 324–25, 328–29.

113. Gouverneur Morris's Diary, July 13, 1804, in *ibid.,* XXVI: 324.

114. AB to Joseph Alston, July 13, 18, 1804, John Swartwout to AB, Aug. 2, 1804, in Davis, ed., *Memoirs of Aaron Burr,* II; 327, 329; AB to Charles Biddle, July 18, 1804 [two letters, same date], in Kline, ed., *Burr Papers,* II: 885–87.

115. AB to Joseph Alston, July 29, 1804, AB to Theodosia Alston, Aug. 3, 1804, in Davis, ed., *Memoirs of Aaron Burr,* II: 328–29, 331; Kline, ed., *Burr Papers,* II: 886, 890.

116. AB to Theodosia, Dec. 4, 1804, in Davis, ed., *Memoirs of Aaron Burr,* II; 351–52. Elisha Boudinot, Hamilton's mentor and an ardent Federalist, was the judge presiding over the hearings in New Jersey where Burr was indicted for murder. See AB to Charles Biddle, Jan. 31, 1805, in Kline, ed., *Burr Papers,* II; 886, 905–06; and *The People v. Aaron Burr,* Aug. 14, 1804, in Syrett, ed., *Hamilton Papers,* XXVI: 341–44.

117. AB to Joseph Alston, July 13, 1804, and AB to Joseph Alston, July 29, 1804, in Davis, ed., *Memoirs of Aaron Burr,* II: 327, 329; *New-York Evening Post,* Aug. 4, 1804.

118. For Burr's travel plans and his friend Pierce Butler, see AB to Charles Biddle, Aug. 11, 1804, in Kline, ed., *Burr Papers,* II: 624, 893–94; AB to Theodosia Burr Alston, Aug. 11, 1804, in Davis, ed., *Memoirs of Aaron Burr,* II: 331.

119. AB to Joseph Alston, Aug. 11, 1804, AB to Theodosia Burr Alston, Aug. 28, 1804, see also his journal/letter to Theodosia (Aug. 31–Sept. 26, 1804), esp. AB to Theodosia Burr Alston, Sept. 15, 1804, in Davis, ed., *Memoirs of Aaron Burr,* II; 332–43.

120. AB to Theodosia Burr Alston, Aug. 28, 1804, in Davis, ed., *Memoirs of Aaron Burr,* II: 333; Lomask, *Aaron Burr: The Years from Princeton to the Vice President,* 358.

CHAPTER EIGHT

1. Schachner, *Aaron Burr*, 261; Brown, ed., *William Plumer's Memorandum*, 203–4; Albert Gallatin to James Nicholson, July 19, 1804, in Papers of Albert Gallatin, microfilm.

2. Brown, ed., *William Plumer's Memorandum*, 203–04, 213.

3. Thomas Jefferson to J. H. Nicholson, May 13, 1803, The Papers of Thomas Jefferson, Library of Congress; Jane Shaffer Elsmere, *Justice Samuel Chase* (Muncie, Ind., 1980), 149–50, 161, 165–67, 175–76; James F. Simon, *What Kind of Nation: Thomas Jefferson, John Marshall, and the Epic Struggle to Create a United States* (New York, 2002), 148, 195–97, 199; Peter Charles Hoffer and N. E. H. Hull, *Impeachment in America, 1635–1805* (New Haven, Conn., 1984), 206, 216–17; Malone, *Jefferson the President: First Term*, 466, 469; and Eleanore Bushnell, *Crimes, Follies, and Misfortunes: The Federal Impeachment Trials* (Urbana, Ill., 1992), 46, 49. The sixty-three-old Pickering was widely known to have been "deranged" (in modern terms, clinically insane); he was impeached on grounds of his drunkenness and incompetence.

4. Elsmere, *Justice Samuel Chase*, 162; Hoffer and Hull, *Impeachment in America*, 182; and Malone, *Jefferson the President: First Term*, 228–30. In 1806, Jefferson approved a series of prosecutions for sedition in Connecticut. Ironically, one of the Federalists indicted there was Burr's brother-in-law, Judge Tapping Reeve. Even more perverse, Connecticut's District Judge Pierpont Edwards (Burr's uncle), until he dismissed the indictment, was almost forced to preside over the case. See Charles Heckman, "A Jeffersonian Lawyer and Judge in Federalist Connecticut: The Career of Pierpont Edwards," *Connecticut Law Review* 28 (Spring 1996): 697–706, and Robert Wetmore, "Seditious Libel Prosecutions in 1806 in the Federal Court in Connecticut: United States v. Tapping Reeve, and Companion Cases," *Connecticut Bar Journal* (1983): 196–204.

5. Thomas Jefferson to Joseph H. Nicholson, May 13, 1803; Hoffer and Hull, *Impeachment in America*, 182; Simon, *What Kind of Nation*, 199.

6. Elsmere, *Justice Samuel Chase*, 170, 175, 181.

7. Burstein, *America's Jubilee: July 26, 1826: A Generation Remembers the Revolution After Fifty Years of Independence* (New York, 2001), 171–74, 202–03. For a contemporary account of Randolph as the only orator worth listening to in Congress, see *Journal of Alexander Dick, 1806–1809*, Special Collections, University of Virginia, Charlottesville, Va.; Elsmere, *Justice Samuel Chase*, 168–69.

8. Elsmere, *Justice Samuel Chase*, 231.

9. *Trial of Samuel Chase, an Associate Justice of the Supreme Court of the United States, impeached by the House of Representatives. For High Crimes and Misdemeanors, before the Senate of the United States*, 2 vols. (Washington City, 1805; New York, 1970), I: 14–18; Elsmere, *Justice Samuel Chase*, 215, 217–18; Brown, ed., *William Plumer's Memorandum*, 236–39.

10. Brown, ed., *William Plumer's Memorandum*, 239; *Trial of Samuel Chase*, I: 6.

11. *Trial of Samuel Chase,* I: 22–23; Uriah Tracy to James Gould, Feb. 4, 1805, in Elsmere, *Justice Samuel Chase,* 225–26.

12. Brown, ed., *Memorandum of William Plumer,* 238, 274; Elsmere, *Justice Samuel Chase,* 216. For the letter to Governor Bloomfield, see *Autobiography of Charles Biddle,* 306–08; see also AB to Charles Biddle, Nov. 22, 1804, in Kline, ed., *Burr Papers,* II: 897–98.

13. Brown, ed., *Memorandum of William Plumer,* 283–85.

14. Elsmere, *Justice Samuel Chase,* 26.

15. *Ibid.,* 269–70; Samuel Taggart to John Taylor, Feb. 18, 25, 1805, Samuel Taggart Papers, American Antiquarian Society, Worcester, Mass.; Manasseh Cutler to Dr. Torrey, Mar. 1, 1805, in Schachner, *Aaron Burr,* 265.

16. "Charles Lee," in Harrison, ed., *Princetonians: 1769–1775,* II: 493–97; Elsmere, *Justice Samuel Chase,* 203, 254, 279, 282.

17. Harper had been the defense attorney for the son of Judge Pickering; see Robert Goodloe Harper to AB, Mar. 5, 1804, in Kline, ed., *Burr Papers,* II: 813–14, 847–48; see also *The Trial of Samuel Chase,* II: 247, and Elsmere, *Justice Samuel Chase,* 285, 291–92.

18. See Elsmere, *Justice Samuel Chase,* 296–99; *The Trial of Samuel Chase,* II: 492–93.

19. Simon, *What Kind of Nation,* 217; Elsmere, *Justice Samuel Chase,* 301–02, 309–10.

20. See "John Quincy Adams's Notes on Burr's Farewell Address to the Senate," in Kline, ed., *Burr Papers,* II: 912; and *Monthly Register, Magazine, and Review of the United States* (1805): 115. The Senate body as a whole "*Resolved unanimously,*" thanking Burr for his "impartiality, dignity and ability, with which he presided over their deliberations," and then praised him by extending "entire approbation of his conduct" in the discharge of "the arduous and important duties, assigned him as President of the Senate." See *Journal of the Senate of the United States of America; being the Second Session of the Eighth Congress, begun and held at the City of Washington, November 5, 1804, and on the twenty-ninth year of the sovereignty of said United States* (Washington City, 1804), 191.

21. Samuel Latham Mitchell to wife, Mar. 2, 1805, in *Harper's Magazine* 58 (1879): 749–50; see also Kline, ed., *Burr Papers,* II: 910–11.

22. *Washington Federalist,* Mar. 13, 1805; see also Kline, ed., *Burr Papers,* II: 917.

23. *Ibid.*

24. Schachner, *Aaron Burr,* 267. On some of Burr's favorite books, see Wandell and Minnegerode, *Aaron Burr,* I: 126.

25. "Farewell Address to the Senate," in Kline, ed., *Burr Papers,* II: 915.

26. William Godwin, *Enquiry Concerning Political Justice* (1793; New York, 1985), 140; Dorothy Hale, "Profits of Altruism: *Caleb Williams* and *Arthur Mervyn,*" *Eighteenth-Century Studies* 22 (1988): 58.

27. William Godwin, *Caleb Williams, or Things as They Are,* ed. Maurice Hindle (London, 1794; New York, 1988), 334–35.

28. "Farewell Address to Senate," Kline, ed., *Burr Papers,* II: 916.

29. *Ibid.,* and *Journal of the Senate of the United States,* 191.

30. *American Citizen,* Mar. 22, 1805, *Morning Chronicle,* Mar. 11, 19, 1805; Kline, ed., *Burr Papers,* II: 911.

31. AB to Theodosia Burr Alston, Mar. 13, 1805, in Davis, ed., *Memoirs of Aaron Burr,* II: 360.

32. For Burr's interest in land speculation in New Orleans, see Richard Platt to AB, Dec. 3, 1803; see also Jonathan Dayton to AB, Oct. 27, 1803, Burr Papers, microfilm, reel 5.

33. See Amy S. Greenberg, *Manifest Manhood and the Antebellum American Empire* (New York, 2005), 5; and Hoffer and Hull, *Impeachment in America,* 154.

34. See Robert E. May, *Manifest Destiny's Underworld: Filibustering in Antebellum America* (Chapel Hill, N.C., 2002), 4; Alan Taylor, "A Northern Revolution of 1800? Upper Canada and Thomas Jefferson," in Onuf et al., eds., *The Revolution of 1800,* 383–409.

35. Sharp, *American Politics in the Early Republic,* 106–07; May, *Manifest Destiny's Underworld,* 4; and William Masterson, *William Blount* (Baton Rouge, La., 1954), 307; see also AH to Rufus King, Aug. 22, 1798, and AH to Francisco de Miranda, Aug. 22, 1798, in Syrett, ed., *Hamilton Papers,* XXII: 154–56; and Charles H. Brown, *Agents of Manifest Destiny: The Lives and Times of the Filibusters* (Chapel Hill, N.C., 1980), 3–5.

36. James R. Sofka, "Thomas Jefferson and the Problem of World Politics," in Peter J. Kastor, ed., *The Louisiana Purchase: Emergence of an American Nation* (Washington, D.C., 2002), 57–59; see also Peter J. Kastor, *The Nation's Crucible: The Louisiana Purchase and the Creation of America* (New Haven, Conn., 2004), 37.

37. E. Wilson Lyon, *Louisiana in French Diplomacy* (Oklahoma City, 1934), 183; Kastor, *The Nation's Crucible,* 38.

38. For pro-invasion sentiments, see the *Morning Chronicle,* Nov. 18, 1802, and *Chronicle Express,* Feb. 3, 1803; also Walter McCaleb, *The Aaron Burr Conspiracy and New Light on Aaron Burr* (reprint 1903; New York, 1966), 19; Kastor, *The Nation's Crucible,* 38; and Thomas Robson Hay and M. R. Werner, *The Admirable Trumpeter: A Biography of General James Wilkinson* (New York, 1941), 196.

39. For Burr's efforts to secure information from the U.S. consul to London, see George W. Erving to AB, Apr. 5, 1803, in Kline, ed., *Burr Papers,* II: 753, 767; and Charles Biddle to AB, Feb. 3, 1803, in Davis, ed., *Memoirs of Aaron Burr,* II: 235.

40. Kastor, *The Nation's Crucible,* 40, 42.

41. James Madison to Charles Pinckney, Oct. 12, 1803, in Gaillard Hunt, ed., *Writings of James Madison;* 9 vols. (New York, 1900–10), VII: 74; see also Sofka, "Thomas Jefferson and the Problem of World Politics," 60.

42. Thomas Jefferson to James Bowdoin, Apr. 2, 1807, in Lipscomb and Bergh, eds., *The Writings of Thomas Jefferson,* XI: 185.

43. See Jack D. L. Holmes, "Showdown on the Sabine: General James Wilkinson vs. Lieutenant-Colonel Simon De Herrera," *Louisiana Studies* 3 (1964): 46–76.

44. See AB to Charles Biddle, Nov. 18, 1800, Mar. 3, 1802, and James Wilkinson to AB, May 16, 1802, in Kline, ed., *Burr Papers,* I: 458–59, II: 682–84, 720–22, 921–22; see also Hay and Werner, *The Admirable Trumpeter,* 109, 113, 156–57, 186–87, 189, 191.

45. James Wilkinson to AB, May 23, 26, 1804, in *Burr Papers,* microfilm, reel 5; Isaac J. Cox, "General Wilkinson and His Later Intrigues with the Spaniards," *American Historical Review* 19 (July 1914): 800.

46. Albert Gallatin to Thomas Jefferson, Feb. 12, 1806, in Henry Adams, ed., *The Writings of Albert Gallatin,* 3 vols. (New York, 1879), I: 290.

47. On Burr and Dayton's connection to Clark, see Jonathan Dayton to AB, May 12, 1804, Burr Papers, microfilm, reel 5; also AB to Abraham R. Ellery, in Davis, ed., *Memoirs of Aaron Burr,* II: 274–75. Some historians have supposed that Jefferson made a corrupt bargain with Burr in acceding to these appointments, ensuring Burr's support during the Chase trial. There is, however, no evidence to support this claim. For Burr's support of Browne, see AB to Thomas Jefferson, Mar. 10, 1805 (a letter sent after the Chase trial and after Burr was no longer vice president), in Kline, ed., *Burr Papers,* II: 918. On Wilkinson's appointment, see William Foley, "James A. Wilkinson: Territorial Governor," *Missouri Historical Society Bulletin* 25 (1968): 4, 16. For the corrupt bargain, see Henry Adams (the originator of this interpretation), *History of the United States During the First Administration of Thomas Jefferson* (New York, 1889), II: 220–21; and Schachner, *Aaron Burr,* 263; Milton Lomask, *Aaron Burr: The Conspiracy and Years of Exile, 1805–1836* (New York, 1982), 27; and Thomas Perkins Abernethy, *The Burr Conspiracy* (New York, 1954), 21–22

48. For Burr's efforts to meet Humboldt, see Andrew Ellicott to AB, June 11, 1804, and Alexander von Humboldt to AB, June 27, 1804, in Burr Papers, microfilm, reel 5; on Burr making a copy of Humboldt's map, see also Isaac J. Cox, "General Wilkinson and His Later Intrigues with the Spaniards," *American Historical Review* 19 (July 1914): 800. On Burr making a copy of Humboldt's map, see Statement by Henry Lee, in Henry Lee's correspondence, 1781–1818, Curtis-Lee Family Papers, box 2, n.d., Library of Congress. I would like to thank Manuscript Reference Librarian Bruce Kirby for locating this source. For those who see Burr as getting the map, see Abernethy, *The Burr Conspiracy,* 20; and Thomas Robson Hay, "Charles Williamson and the Burr Conspiracy," *Journal of Southern History* 2 (May 1936): 183. Other historians have Wilkinson pumping Humboldt for information, and both Burr and Wilkinson securing the map—see Jacobs, *Tarnished Warrior,* 212; and Isaac J. Cox, "Hispanic-American Phases of the 'Burr Conspiracy,'" *Hispanic-American Review* XII (May 1932): 154.

49. For the mythology that Burr headed west out of desperation, combined with the audacity to conquer a new empire, see Abernethy, *The Burr Conspiracy,* 15;

for the same image of a restless and embittered man, see James Ripley Jacobs, *Tarnished Warrior: Major-General James Wilkinson* (New York, 1938), 214–15. Even his biographer, who sees Burr's actions in a more positive light, concluded that he was "dejected, gloomy," and as an outcast from New York and Washington society, had to head west. See Schachner, *Aaron Burr,* 269; and for the persistence of this portrait in a recent study, see Buckner F. Melton, Jr., *Aaron Burr: Conspiracy to Treason* (New York, 2002), 38.

50. Abernethy, *The Burr Conspiracy,* 10–11.
51. There was no official oath of allegiance to Spain, but Wilkinson gave the Spanish official the impression that he wished to become a Spanish subject. See Hay and Werner, *The Admirable Trumpeter,* 83–88, 91, 95–96; Malone, *Jefferson the President: Second Term,* 218, 362–67; and John Thornton Posey, "Rascality Revisited: In Defense of General James Wilkinson," *Filson Club Quarterly* 74 (2000): 343–45. Judith O'Hare Smith concludes that Wilkinson easily imagined Kentucky as a colony of Spain—see "The Spanish Conspiracy, 1783–1792: A Quest for Equality," Ph.D. dissertation, University of California, San Diego, 1983, 159.
52. Cox, "General Wilkinson and His Later Intrigues with the Spaniards," 795–98.
53. For those questioning the value of Wilkinson's "Reflections," see Jacobs, *Tarnished Warrior,* 206; Hay and Werner, *The Admirable Trumpeter,* 213. Abernethy makes nothing of the memorial; see Abernethy, *The Burr Conspiracy,* 13. The historian with the best grasp of Wilkinson's motives is Isaac Cox. He finds it odd that the Spanish would trust, let alone pay Wilkinson for his "obvious suggestions," but he does see the general as trying to exert pressure on the Spanish by encouraging Jefferson to insist on the Rio Grande boundary. My point is that Wilkinson was more than willing to manipulate both sides—and provoke war—if it made him more valuable—see Cox, "General Wilkinson and His Later Intrigues with the Spaniards," 799–801. For a translated version of Wilkinson's "Reflections on Louisiana," though incorrectly attributed to Vicente Folch, see James Alexander Robertson, ed., *Louisiana Under the Rule of Spain, France, and the United States 1785–1807* (Cleveland, 1911), 332, 333, 339, 341–45.
54. "Reflections on Louisiana," in Robertson, ed., *Louisiana Under the Rule of Spain,* 325–27, 330, 333–35, 339–40, 342, esp. 337–38.
55. Charles Biddle to James Wilkinson, Mar. 18, 1805, in Jacobs, *Tarnished Warrior,* 215; "Reflections on Louisiana," in Robertson, ed., *Louisiana Under the Rule of Spain,* 334; John Adair to James Wilkinson, Dec. 10, 1804, in Isaac J. Cox, "Western Reactions to the Burr Conspiracy," *Transactions of the Illinois State Historical Society* (1928), 75.
56. Cox, "General Wilkinson and His Later Intrigues with the Spaniards," 801; Abernethy, *The Burr Conspiracy,* 28; see Andrew Jackson to George Washing-

ton Campbell, Jan. 15, 1807, and "Testimony Before the Grand Jury in the Case of Aaron Burr," June 25, 1807, in Harold Moser, Sharon Macpherson, and Charles F. Bryan, Jr., eds., *The Papers of Andrew Jackson*. Vol II: 1804–1813 (Knoxville, Tenn., 1984), 147–49, 168–69.

57. See Anthony Merry to Lord Harrowby, Aug. 6, 1804, in Kline, ed., *Burr Papers*, II: 891–92; Adams, *History of the United States, 1801–1805*, 11, 394–95, 402–03.

58. Williamson knew about Burr's plan before his duel with Hamilton; see Charles Williamson to AB, May 16, 1804, in Burr Papers, microfilm, reel 5; see also Hay, "Charles Williams and the Burr Conspiracy," 175–78. Burr and William-son were both in involved in the Cayuga Bridge Company—see John W. Wells, *Cayuga Bridge* (Ithaca, N.Y.), 2–3; Kline, ed., *Burr Papers*, I: 391–92.

59. Hay, "Charles Williamson and the Burr Conspiracy," 180; Raymond A. Mohl, "Britain and the Aaron Burr Conspiracy," *History Today* 21 (1971): 391, 392–95.

60. Malcolm Lester, *Anthony Merry Redivivus: A Reappraisal of the British Minister to the United States, 1803–06* (Charlottesville, Va., 1978), 22, 30–37, 41–42, 101–02, 110–11; Mohl, "Britain and the Aaron Burr Conspiracy," 393; Lo-mask, *Aaron Burr: The Conspiracy*, 35, 38, 49.

61. Henry Adams concluded that Merry cared little about Hamilton's death, but the British minister still used High Federalist language to describe "what is generally known of the Profligacy of Mr. Burr's Character." See Anthony Merry to Lord Harrowby, Aug. 6, 1804, in Kline, ed., *Burr Papers*, II: 891–92; and Adams, *History of the United States, 1801–1805*, 394.

62. See Charles Williamson to Lord Justice of Scotland (Charles Hope of Grafton), Jan. 6, 1806, a letter intended for Lord Melville; see also Williamson to same, Jan. 3, 1806, and Williamson to Sir Evan Nepean, Feb. 2, 1805, Charles Wil-liamson Papers, Newberry Library, Chicago.

63. AB to Theodosia Burr Alston, Mar. 29, 1805, in Davis, ed., *Memoirs of Aaron Burr*, II: 366–67.

64. AB's abbreviated journal sent to Theodosia (entries from May 23, 1805, to Sept. 2, 1805) in *ibid.*, II: 370, 373.

65. AB to Theodosia Burr Alston, Apr. 30, 1805, and extracts from his journal, in *ibid.*, II: 368–69; Kline, ed., *Burr Papers*, II: 934.

66. Ray Swick, "Aaron Burr's Visit to Blennerhassett Island," *West Virginia History* 35 (1974): 205–12, 214, and his *An Island Called Eden: The Story of Harman and Margaret Blennerhassett* (Parkersburg, W. Va., 2000), 16–22, 26–27; and Raymond Fitch, ed., *Breaking with Burr: Harman Blennerhassett's Journal, 1807* (Athens, Ohio, 1988), xi.

67. See Swick, "Aaron Burr's Visit to Blennerhassett Island," 217; Swick, *An Island Called Eden*, 38–39; and Kline, ed., *Burr Papers*, II: 949–52.

68. Isaac Cox, "The Conspiracy in Indiana," *Indiana Magazine of History* 25 (Dec. 1929): 258–60, 262–65; and Stuart Seely Sprague, "The Louisville Canal: Key

to Aaron Burr's Western Trip of 1805," *Register of the Kentucky Historical Society* 73 (1973): 71–73, 76–78. The canal company took shape in Washington, when its backers petitioned Congress for a charter. This effort failed, but the company eventually secured a state charter from the Indiana legislature. Brown, along with Dayton and John Smith, was on a Senate committee that favored the canal project—see AB to John Brown, May 8, 1805, in Kline, ed., *Burr Papers,* II: 933–35. Burr also tried to recruit Benjamin Henry Latrobe to design the canal—see Benjamin Henry Latrobe to AB, Apr. 7, 1805, *Burr Papers,* microfilm, reel 6.

69. Sprague, "Louisville Canal," 76–78; William G. Leger, "The Public Life of John Adair," Ph.D. Dissertation, University of Kentucky, 1960; AB to James Wilkinson, Mar. 26, 1805, in Kline, ed., *Burr Papers,* II: 922–24, 926, 934; "John Brown," in Harrison, ed., *Princetonians, 1776–83,* III: 221; Lomask, *Aaron Burr: The Conspiracy,* 67–68; Hay and Werner, *The Admirable Trumpeter,* 241.

70. Andrew Burstein, *The Passions of Andrew Jackson* (New York, 2003), 34, 48–49, 55, 56–57, 62–67, 72, 129, 131–33.

71. Burr was born in 1756; Brown in 1757; Adair in 1757; Dayton in 1760; Jackson in 1767. Smith's age is difficult to determine, but he may have been the oldest member of the group. Lyon was born in 1750. Because little is known of Smith's life before he came to the Northwest Territory in 1790, he is the only one without a record of military service. For Smith's and Lyon's military contracts, see Leland R. Johnson, "Aaron Burr: Treason in Kentucky?" *Filson Club History Quarterly* 75 (2001): 5, 7–8; see also Robert W. Wilhelmy, "Senator John Smith and the Aaron Burr Conspiracy," *Cincinnati Historical Society Bulletin* 28 (1970): 39–43.

72. See AB's journal to Theodosia Burr Alston, June 6–June 10, 1805, in Davis, ed., *Memoirs of Aaron Burr,* II: 370; AB to James Wilkinson, May 19, 1805, and Edward Livingston to AB, July 27, 1802, in Kline, ed., *Burr Papers,* II: 732, 937; Hatcher, *Edward Livingston,* 108, 110, 123–24, 127; McCaleb, *The Aaron Burr Conspiracy,* 32–34.

73. AB's journal to Theodosia Burr Alston, June 17–July 10, 1805, in Davis, ed., *Memoirs of Aaron Burr,* II: 370–71; Abernethy, *Burr Conspiracy,* 25–26, 28; Kastor, *The Nation's Crucible,* 59–61, 70, 72–75; McCaleb, *The Aaron Burr Conspiracy,* 35; and Hay and Werner, *The Admirable Trumpeter,* 217.

74. AB to James Wilkinson, Sept. 26, 1805, and AB to ?, Oct. 7, 1805, in Kline, ed., *Burr Papers,* II: 940–43; McCaleb, *The Aaron Burr Conspiracy,* 36–37.

75. *United States Gazette,* Aug. 2, 1805.

76. Most studies simply quote the queries, without analyzing the argument. See Abernethy, *The Burr Conspiracy,* 32–34; McCaleb, *The Aaron Burr Conspiracy,* 38–39; Lomask, *Aaron Burr: The Conspiracy,* 75–76.

77. Scholars have missed the unique feature of the Burr Conspiracy: it was imagined as an eastern invasion of the West. For a discussion of the traditional

concerns of disunion, see James Lewis, "The Burr Conspiracy and the Problem of Loyalty," in Kastor, ed., *The Louisiana Purchase,* 64–73.

78. For the claim that Yrujo wrote the *Gazette* "queries," see Cox, "Western Reactions to the Burr Conspiracy," 78–79; Lomask, *Aaron Burr: The Conspiracy,* 76; and Joseph Wheelan, *Jefferson's Vendetta: The Pursuit of Aaron Burr and the Judiciary* (New York, 2005), 128.

79. See Philadelphia *Aurora,* Mar. 26, 1805, and another *Aurora* article, commenting on Burr's recent departure west, claiming that Burr planned to run for governor of Louisiana once it became a state. This idea was dismissed as the wishful thinking of supporters of "quidism"; it was reprinted in the *American Citizen,* May 1, 1805. On the meaning of the Quids, see Noble E. Cunningham, Jr., "Who Were the Quids?" *Mississippi Valley Historical Review* 50 (Sept. 1963): 253–54. And for articles associating Burr with quidism, see the Pittsburgh *Commonwealth* quoted in the *American Citizen,* Jan. 6, 1807; Philadelphia *Aurora,* Jan. 3, 1807; *Lancaster* [Pa] *Intelligencer,* Dec. 10, 1806, quoted in *Aurora,* Jan. 9, 1807; *Richmond Enquirer,* Dec. 9, 1806; *American Citizen,* Dec. 15, 20, 1806; and *National Intelligencer,* Jan. 12, 1807.

80. See *Lancaster* [Pa] *Intelligencer,* Dec. 10, 1806. For example, during the 1804 governor's election, the *American Citizen* reprinted an address that claimed the "nomination of Col. Burr as the first leading attempt to effect a separation of the United States." Here Burr is associated with the New England Federalist plot of disunion, but he is also condemned for his ruthless desire for the presidency. His plan to steal the election in 1800 was a clear step toward his desire for the "dissolution of the American empire"—*American Citizen,* May 1, 1804.

81. For articles connecting Federalists with Burr's conspiracy, see *American Citizen,* Nov. 21, 1806; and for a list of all the Federalists (incorrectly identifies some men as Federalists who were not), see *Aurora,* Jan. 6, 1807.

82. *American Citizen,* Sept. 17, 1804.

83. See Anonymous. Philadelphia postmark, received Dec. 1, 1805, in The Papers of Thomas Jefferson, microfilm; the second anonymous letter was sent on Dec. 5, 1805; see Abernethy, *The Burr Conspiracy,* 38. This letter (unlike the queries) was probably written by the Marquis de Casa Yrujo. Why? The author used the Latin spelling for Cataline ("Catalina"), which was identical to the Spanish usage. The grammatical style of this letter is completely different from the queries, indicating that Yrujo most likely did not write the "queries."

84. Mushkat, "Matthew Livingston Davis and the Political Legacy of Aaron Burr," 131–34; Cornog, *The Birth of Empire,* 74–77; Kline, *Burr Papers,* II: 958. Some scholars believe that Burr and Jefferson met in Feb., while others think it was in Mar.. See "Thomas Jefferson: Memorandum of a Conversation with Burr," Kline, *Burr Papers,* II: 958, 962–64, 972–73; Lomask, *Aaron Burr: The Conspiracy,* 106.

85. For Burr's view that there would be no war, see AB to Joseph Alston, Nov. 29, 180[5], in Davis, ed., *Memoirs of Aaron Burr,* II: 375; see also AB to James

Wilkinson, Jan. 6, 1806, and AB to Andrew Jackson, Mar. 24, 1806, in Kline, ed., *Burr Papers,* II: 958, 956. On Jefferson's foreign policy, see Sofka, "Thomas Jefferson and the Problem of World Politics," 61; and McCaleb, *The Aaron Burr Conspiracy,* 50. And for his dealings with Merry, see Anthony Merry to Lord Mulgrave, Nov. 25, 1805, in Kline, ed., *Burr Papers,* II: 943–47, and Lester, *Anthony Merry,* 104–08.

86. Burr probably discussed the Bastrop property with Edward Livingston, who was one of the investors, during his visit to New Orleans in the summer of 1805. The property was tied up in legal disputes until the fall of 1805, so Burr probably did not make any definite plans for the settlement until after that date. He was discussing the plan of resettlement in Louisiana as early as December 1805, when he corresponded with Harman Blennerhassett—see Harman Blennerhassett to AB, Dec. 21, 1805, and AB to Albert Gallatin, July 31, 1806, in Kline, ed., *Burr Papers,* II: 950, 992–93.

87. Marquis de Casa Yrujo to Don Pedro Cevallos, Dec. 5, 1805, Jan. 1, 1806, Feb. 13, 1806, in Henry Adams Transcripts from the *Spanish State Papers: Casa Yrujo, 1801–1807,* Library of Congress; see also McCaleb, *The Aaron Burr Conspiracy,* 52–58, 64; Abernethy, *Burr Conspiracy,* 39–40; and Lomask, *Aaron Burr: The Conspiracy,* 102–05.

88. Abernethy, *Burr Conspiracy,* 40.

89. Kline, ed., *Burr Papers,* II: 870–71.

90. Max Savelle, *George Morgan: Colony Builder* (New York, 1932), 203–33; Abernethy, *Burr Conspiracy,* 58, 61; Kline, ed., *Burr Papers,* II: 1039.

91. Savelle, *George Morgan,* 234–35; Kline, *Burr Papers,* II: 1039.

92. *American Citizen,* Jan. 6, 1807 (quoting the Pittsburgh *Commonwealth* from an earlier date).

93. Joshua V. H. Clark, *From Onondaga; or Reminiscences of Earlier and Later Times* (Syracuse, N.Y., 1849), I: 365–78; and *American Citizen,* Sept. 23, 1806 (quoting the *Farmer's Monitor* of Herkimer, N.Y.); *National Intelligencer,* Nov. 18, Dec. 19, 1806.

94. See William H. Safford, *The Life of Harman Blennerhassett* (1850; Freeport, N.Y., 1972), 74–75; Abernethy, *Burr Conspiracy,* 66–67, 69–71; and Burstein, *Passions of Andrew Jackson,* 73–74. Burr placed a great deal of trust in Rachel Jackson's nephew, Stokely Hays. See AB to Harman Blennerhassett, Dec. 20, 1806, in Burr Papers, microfilm, reel 6; see also Andrew Jackson to James Winchester, Oct. 4, 1806, and "Order to the Brigadier Generals of the 2nd Division," [Oct. 4, 1806], in Moser et al., eds., *The Papers of Andrew Jackson,* II: 110–14.

95. For Dearborn's instructions to Wilkinson, to act with force and repel the Spanish in case of an invasion, see Henry Dearborn to James Wilkinson, May 6, 1806, in James Wilkinson Papers, Chicago Historical Society; see also Jacobs, *Tarnished Warrior,* 229; Holmes, "Showdown on the Sabine," 56–57, 59–60;

and Jared W. Bradley, "W. C. C. Claiborne and Spain: Foreign Affairs Under Jefferson and Madison," *Louisiana History* 12 (1971): 313–14.

96. See Wilkinson to John Adair, Sept. 28, 1806, and James Wilkinson to John Smith, Sept. 26, 1806, in McCaleb, *The Aaron Burr Conspiracy,* 107, 112–14; Abernethy, *Burr Conspiracy,* 142–43.

97. AB to William Henry Harrison, Oct. 24, 1806, and, for Burr's payment for the Bastrop property, AB to William Wilkins, Oct. 21, 1806 in Kline, ed., *Burr Papers,* II: 994–98; AB to Benjamin Henry Latrobe, Oct. 26, 1806, Burr Papers, microfilm, reel 6. Abernethy concludes that Burr primarily intended to have his settlers build the two roads. The importance of the roads is evident from a map that Burr sent Wilkins. See the enclosure in AB to Wilkins, Oct. 21, 1806, in Burr Papers, microfilm, reel 6; and Abernethy, *Burr Conspiracy,* 72, 76–77.

98. Kline, ed., *Burr Papers,* II: 998; Abernethy, *Burr Conspiracy,* 80, 83.

99. See Ronald Rayman, "Frontier Journalism in Kentucky: Joseph Monfort Street and the Western World, 1806–1809," *Register of the Kentucky Historical Society* 76 (1978): 98, 100–01.

100. Rayman, "Frontier Journalism in Kentucky," 101–02; Abernethy, *Burr Conspiracy,* 93–94.

101. Rayman, "Frontier Journalism in Kentucky," 101, 105; Abernethy, *Burr Conspiracy,* 91–92, 95.

102. Samuel Edwards, *Barbary General: The Life of William H. Eaton* (Englewood Cliffs, N.J., 1968), 3–4, 184–85, 203, 213–18, 227, 231; Abernethy, *Burr Conspiracy,* 85.

103. For rumors connecting Granger to Burr, see *American Citizen,* Nov. 8, 1806; Cunningham, *The Jeffersonian Republicans in Power,* 226; Abernethy, *Burr Conspiracy,* 85–86; Malone, *Jefferson the President: Second Term,* 240–41; Lomask, *Aaron Burr: The Conspiracy,* 109–11; and Edwards, *Barbary General,* 254.

104. Jefferson's *Anas,* in Lipscomb and Bergh, eds., *The Writings of Thomas Jefferson,* I: 458–60.

105. "Thomas Jefferson: Memorandum of a Conversation with Burr," in Kline, ed., *Burr Papers,* II: 962.

106. *The Anas,* in *The Writings of Thomas Jefferson,* I: 460–61.

107. *Ibid.,* 461–62.

108. *Ibid.,* 462.

109. Abernethy, *Burr Conspiracy,* 95–96.

110. *Ibid.,* 96; Kline, ed., *Burr Papers,* II: 999–1000.

111. See Wilhelmy, "Senator John Smith," 46–47; AB to Harmon Blennerhassett, Nov. 6, 1806, and AB to William Henry Harrison, Oct. 24, Nov. 27, 1806, in Kline, ed., *Burr Papers,* II: 996–99, 1000–06; and Moser, et al., eds., *The Papers of Andrew Jackson,* II: 115–16; AB to Henry Clay, Dec. 1, 1806, in Burr Papers, microfilm, reel 6. For Clay's explanation that he felt "there might be something

in the nature of his enterprise that would militate against his duty as senator— & therefore improper for him to engage as council," see Brown, ed., *William Plumer's Memorandum,* 547.

112. Abernethy, *Burr Conspiracy,* 98–99; Kline, ed., *Burr Papers,* II: 1000; see "Col. Burr Before the Federal Court," reprinted from the *Western World* [Dec. 18], in *National Intelligencer,* Jan. 12, 1807. Clay's conviction of Burr's innocence was genuine. Clay later told Senator William Plumer (to whom he had explained his concerns) that "his own opinion was that Mr. Burr was unjustly accused. That if there was any evidence ag[ains]t him he had not been able to discover it." See Brown, ed., *William Plumer's Memorandum,* 549.

113. John Wood, *A Full Statement of the Trial and Acquittal of Aaron Burr, esq.: containing, all the proceedings and debates that took place before the federal court at Frankfort, Kentucky, November 25, 1806* (Alexandria, Va., 1807), 34–35; Abernethy, *Burr Conspiracy,* 99; Raymon, "Frontier Journalism in Kentucky," 108; McCaleb, *The Aaron Burr Conspiracy,* 162.

114. Samuel M. Wilson, "The Court Proceedings of 1806 in Kentucky Against Aaron Burr and John Adair," *Filson Club History Quarterly* 10 (1936): 39–40; Abernethy, *Burr Conspiracy,* 99; "Col. Burr Before the Federal Court."

115. "Col. Burr Before the Federal Court;" Raymon, "Frontier Journalism in Kentucky," 108.

116. Raymon, "Frontier Journalism in Kentucky," 110; see also Joseph Hamilton Daveiss, *A View of the President's Conduct, Concerning the Conspiracy of 1806* (Frankfort, Ky., 1807), 24, 28.

117. Holmes, "Showdown on the Sabine," 65.

118. James Workman, *A Letter to the Respectable Citizens, inhabitants of the county of Orleans: together with several letters to His Excellency Governor Claiborne, and other documents relative to the extraordinary measures lately pursued in this territory* (New Orleans, 1807), v; see also Henry Carey, *Chrononhotonthologos, the Most Tragical Tragedy that ever was Tragedized by any Company of Tragedians* (London, 1743).

119. On Machiavelli and deception, see Wendy Brown, *Manhood and Politics: A Feminist Reading in Political Theory* (Totowa, N.J., 1988), 84, 96, 101–04, 115.

120. James Wilkinson to Thomas Jefferson, Oct. 20, 1806 (and enclosed report), Burr Conspiracy Papers, Library of Congress; Abernethy, *Burr Conspiracy,* 150–52.

121. Smith deposition in James Wilkinson, *Memoirs of my own Times,* 3 vols. (Philadelphia, 1816), II: 94.

122. Machiavelli employed the fox as his symbol for justifying the political need for using deception. And he advised that the "best fox" does not simply avoid snares, he sets them. This captures Wilkinson's approach for dealing with Burr perfectly. See Ruth Weissbourd Grant, *Hypocrisy and Integrity: Machiavelli,*

Rousseau and the Ethics of Politics (Chicago, 1999), 24. See also Brown, *Manhood and Politics*, 106–07, 115.

123. Kline, ed., *Burr Papers*, II: 974, 985.

124. See cipher letter, To James Wilkinson [July 22–29], in Kline, ed, *Burr Papers*, II: 975, 983–84, 86–97.

125. James Wilkinson to Colonel Freeman, Nov. 7, 1806, and to Colonel Cushing, Nov. 7, 1806, in Wilkinson, *Memoirs*, II: 99; James Wilkinson to Governor Claiborne, Nov. 12, 1806, in Rowland, *Official Letter Books of W. C. C. Claiborne* (Jackson, Miss., 1917), IV: 55–56; and McCaleb, *The Aaron Burr Conspiracy*, 135–36, 139–40.

126. James Wilkinson to Thomas Jefferson, Nov. 12, 1806, in Wilkinson, *Memoirs*, II: 100; McCaleb, *The Aaron Burr Conspiracy*, 181–82.

127. McCaleb, *The Aaron Burr Conspiracy*, 175–76; Abernethy, *Burr Conspiracy*, 174; Edward Livingston, *Faithful Picture of the Political Situation in New Orleans* (Boston, 1808), 14–15. See also report on meeting in *Washington Federalist*, Jan. 17, 1807.

128. Livingston, *A Faithful Picture*, 18–21; see also account from the *New Orleans Gazette*, Dec. 30, 1806, in *Washington Federalist*, Feb. 11, 1807; and Abernethy, *Burr Conspiracy*, 178–79, 196.

129. Livingston, *A Faithful Picture*, 23, 27, 31–33; see Judge James Workman's letters to Claiborne in Workman, *A Letter to the Respectable Citizens*, 2–3, 7–8, 17–18, 28–29; McCaleb, *The Aaron Burr Conspiracy*, 186–87.

130. President Jefferson's Proclamation of Nov. 27, 1806, in Ford, ed., *The Works of Thomas Jefferson*, VIII: 481; Abernethy, *Burr Conspiracy*, 188, 190.

131. Kline, ed., *Burr Papers*, II: 982; "Special Message to Congress, Jan. 22, 1807," in Ford, ed., *The Works of Thomas Jefferson*, IX: 14–20, esp. 14–15.

132. "Special Message to Congress," in Ford, ed., *The Works of Thomas Jefferson*, IX: 16; Kline, ed., *Burr Papers*, II: 982–83.

133. See *Supplemental Journal of Such Proceedings of the First Session of the Fifth General Assembly of the State of Ohio, as during the time they were depending, were considered confidential* (Chillicothe, Ohio, 1806), 1–2, 23, 41–42; Abernethy, *Burr Conspiracy*, 105–08; Lomask, *Aaron Burr: The Conspiracy*, 186–92; and McCaleb, *The Aaron Burr Conspiracy*, 204–09. See also report with rumors of Burr's army of 20,000 sent from Cincinnati, Dec. 23, published in the *National Intelligencer*, Jan. 16, 1806; and Safford, *Life of Harmon Blennerhassett*, 112; and Swick, *An Island Called Eden*, 42–43.

134. AB to Cowles Mead, Jan. 12, 1807, in Kline, ed., *Burr Papers*, II: 1007–09.

135. See *Aurora*, Jan. 22, 1807; and "Special Message to Congress," in Ford, ed., *The Works of Thomas Jefferson*, IX: 15; Abernethy, *Burr Conspiracy*, 175, 218; Isaac Cox, *The West Florida Controversy, 1798–1813* (Baltimore, 1918), 202–03; McCaleb, *The Aaron Burr Conspiracy*, 230.

CHAPTER NINE

1. See the exchange of letters between Burr and Cowles Mead and Thomas Fitz-patrick, Jan. 12–16, in Kline, ed., *Burr Papers*, II: 1008–16. The search party found few weapons: three muskets, six fusees, eleven rifles, two blunderbusses, thirteen brace of pistols, and five swords. For the trunks of books, see letter from Washington, M.T., Jan. 19, in *National Intelligencer*, Feb. 23, 1807; and "Extract of letter from Cowles Mead, secretary and acting governor of the Mississippi Territory, to the department of war, dated Washington, M.T. Jan. 19th, 1807," in the *American Citizen*, Feb. 24, 1807.

2. For a report on the grand jury verdict, see the *Mississippi Messenger*, Feb. 27, 1807, reprinted in *Third Annual Report of the Director of the Department of Archives and History of the State of Mississippi*, Oct. 1, 1903–Oct. 1, 1904 (Nashville, Tenn., 1905), 101; and *National Intelligencer*, Mar. 18, 1807. See also T. A. Smith, Lt., to General Wilkinson, Feb. 1807, James Wilkinson Papers, Chicago Historical Society, Chicago; and Abernethy, *Burr Conspiracy*, 217–18.

3. See AB to Robert Williams [Feb. 7, 1807] and Feb. 12, 1807, and Robert Williams to AB, Feb. 13, 1807, in Kline, ed., *Burr Papers*, II: 1022–24; Abernethy, *Burr Conspiracy*, 218–19. See also Report of army officers, under order of Wilkinson to arrest Burr, from Washington, Miss., Feb. 16, 1807, in James Wilkinson Papers; and Cox, *The West Florida Controversy, 1798–1813*, 202–03.

4. For the most accurate account of Burr's capture, see Nicholas Perkins to C. A. Rodney, Statement relating to the capture of Aaron Burr [1807], Nicholas Perkins Papers, Tennessee Historical Society, Nashville, Tenn. This document is reprinted in Stuart O. Stumpf, ed., "The Arrest of Aaron Burr: A Documentary Record," *Alabama Historical Quarterly* (Fall & Winter 1980): 113–23, esp. 117–18.

5. "The Arrest of Aaron Burr," 118–19.

6. *Ibid.*, 119; see also *The Examination of Aaron Burr before the Chief Justice of the United States: upon the charges of high misdemeanor, and of treason against the United States; together with the arguments of counsel and opinion of the judge* (Richmond, Va., 1807), 4.

7. "The Arrest of Aaron Burr," 119–20. For one of the first newspaper accounts to describe his arrest in more dramatic terms, see *Richmond Enquirer*, Mar. 27, 1807.

8. Kline, ed., *Burr Papers*, II: 1026.

9. See "The Arrest of Aaron Burr," 121–22; and copy of letter sent by Edmund P. Gaines to General James Wilkinson and Governor Robert Williams, Feb. 19, 1807, and Edmund P. Gaines to Nicholas Perkins, Feb. 19, 1807, in "The Capture of Aaron Burr," *American Historical Magazine* (Jan. 1896): 146–48. See also "The following extract of a letter from Lt. Gaines, dated Fort Stoddert, Feb. 22, 1807, furnishes some interesting circumstances relative to the arrest of Aaron Burr," *National Intelligencer*, Apr. 8, 1807; Kline, ed., *Burr Papers*, II: 1026–27.

10. Kline, ed., *Burr Papers*, II: 1028.

11. "The Arrest of Aaron Burr," 123; *The Examination of Aaron Burr,* 4.

12. "The Arrest of Aaron Burr," 114; Kline, ed., *Burr Papers,* II: 1029; and John Randolph to Joseph H. Nicholson, Mar. 25, 1807, in McColley, ed., *John Randolph,* 147. And for the two descriptions sent to Jefferson, see William Tatham to Thomas Jefferson, Mar. 27, 1807, and Caesar A. Rodney to Thomas Jefferson, Mar. 27, 1807, Thomas Jefferson Papers, Library of Congress.

13. For the reference to Burr's capture being more exciting than the "page of romance," see *National Intelligencer,* Apr. 1, 1807; for the debate on Burr's disguise, see *Richmond Enquirer,* Apr. 21, 1807; and for the reference to "old Virginia leggins," see William Tatham to Thomas Jefferson, Mar. 27, 1807.

14. Return J. Meigs, who issued the warrant for Blennerhassett's arrest, claimed that around fifty men fled from the island, but other reports set the number of men at thirty. See "Extract of a letter from Return J. Meigs, Esq.," dated Marietta, Dec. 17, in *American Citizen,* Jan. 6, 1807; and Abernethy, *Burr Conspiracy,* 108.

15. For reports of French transporting arms, see "Extract of a letter, dated Cincinnati, Nov. 24, 1806," and another report about Burr arriving in Cincinnati at the same time as the French men, in *National Intelligencer,* Dec. 24, 1806; and for a report of 20,000 men, see report from Cincinnati, Dec. 23, in *National Intelligencer,* Jan. 16, 1807. For the governor's message to the assembly, which also reported on the French men carrying arms, and the heavily armed flotilla on Blennerhassett Island, see *Supplemental Journal of Such Proceedings of the Fifth General Assembly of the State of Ohio,* 1–2, 41–42; and for the governor's messages in the newspapers, *National Intelligencer,* Dec. 29, 1806. For the rumors of Blennerhassett publishing treasonous articles, see "Mr. Burr," in *American Citizen,* Mar. 19, 1807; and for Blennerhassett as a Irish royalist, see "Cognitions," in the *National Intelligencer,* Dec. 5, 1806.

16. See letter in the *National Intelligencer,* Jan. 16, 1807.

17. See John Ross to Peter Ross, Jan. 18, 1807, in Special Collections, University of Virginia Libraries, Charlottesville, Va.

18. For the transformation of Burr's reputation to "rascal, villain, thief and highway robber," see "Extract of the Letter from West Chester (K[entucky])," dated Jan. 8, 1807, in *National Intelligencer,* Feb. 2, 1807; see also "Armistice," *American Citizen,* Jan. 27, 1807.

19. For the publication of Burr's letter to Cowles Mead, see *National Intelligencer,* Mar. 6, 1807; and *American Citizen,* Mar. 12, 1807; see also criticism of Wilkinson ("military despotism in New Orleans") in the *Mississippi Messenger,* Jan. 20, 1807, reprinted in *Third Annual Report of the Directors of the Department of Archives and History of the State of Mississippi,* 99.

20. See "Edward Livingston's Address to the Public," New Orleans, Dec. 30, in *National Intelligencer,* Feb. 9 and 13, 1807; John Smith's deposition, taken in Chillicothe, Ohio, Feb. 12, in the *National Intelligencer,* Feb. 27, 1807. For

John Adair, see report on his letter from Wilkinson, inviting him to come to New Orleans and join Adair in the conquest of the Spanish territories; and for his criticism of Wilkinson, which he prepared on Mar. 1, 1807, see *National Intelligencer*, Feb. 23, Mar. 4, 1807; see also McCaleb, *The Aaron Burr Conspiracy*, 249–50.

21. Abernethy, *Burr Conspiracy*, 196.

22. Bradley Chapin, *The American Law of Treason: Revolutionary and Early National Origins* (Seattle, 1964), 101–03.

23. See proceedings of the House of Representatives, Feb. 18, in *Washington Federalist*, Feb. 21, 1807.

24. For Eaton's first account of Burr's conspiracy, see *American Citizen*, Dec. 5, 1806, and *National Intelligencer*, Dec. 5, 1806, both reprinted from the *Boston Repertory*. For articles contending that Eaton's disclosure made it "impossible not to believe Burr's guilt," see *National Intelligencer*, Jan. 23, Mar. 13, 1807, *American Citizen*, Jan. 24, Mar. 19, *Morning Chronicle*, Mar. 21, 1807, and a defense of Eaton in the *Washington Federalist*, Feb. 28, 1807. For the publication of Eaton's deposition from the Bollman and Swartwout trial, see *Washington Federalist*, Jan. 31, Feb. 4, 1807; see also Matthew Livingston Davis to William Van Ness, Feb. 11, 1807, in Miscellaneous Manuscripts, Matthew Livingston Davis, New-York Historical Society, New York, N.Y.

25. For Jefferson's "Message" and the accompanying documents, see *National Intelligencer*, Jan. 23, Jan. 28, 1807; broadside, "Message of the President of the United States, Containing a Development of the Conspiracy," Jan. 28, 1807 (Washington City), in Special Collections, University Virginia Library, Charlottesville, Va.; and John Adams to Benjamin Rush, Feb. 2, 1807, in Schultz and Adair, eds., *The Spur of Fame*, 76.

26. See Thomas Jefferson to Governor Edward Tiffin, Feb. 2, 1807, and Thomas Jefferson to General James Wilkinson, Feb. 3, 1807, in Lipscomb and Bergh, eds., *The Writings of Thomas Jefferson*, XI: 146–50.

27. See Thomas Jefferson to William B. Giles, Apr. 20, 1807, and Thomas Jefferson to George Hay, May 26, Aug. 20, 1807, in *ibid.*, XI: 188, 209, 341.

28. See "Thomas Jefferson: Memorandum of a Conversation with Burr [Apr. 15, 1806]," in Kline, ed., *Burr Papers*, II: 962.

29. See *The Examination of Col. Aaron Burr*, 3; "John Wickham (1763–1839)," in *Richmond Portraits: In an Exhibition of Makers of Richmond, 1737–1860* (Richmond, Va., 1949), 206–07; Ruth Doumlele, "Treasonable Doubt: Aaron Burr on Trial," *Richmond*, Mar. 1995; and Mary Newton Standard, *Richmond: Its People and Its Story* (Philadelphia, 1923), 98.

30. *The Examination of Col. Aaron Burr*, 3–5.

31. *Ibid.*, 6–7.

32. See "The Deposition of William Eaton," *Washington Federalist*, Jan. 31, 1807; also *The Life of the Late Gen. William Eaton* (Brookfield, Mass., 1813), 397–98.

33. *The Life of the Late Gen. William Eaton,* 399.

34. "The Deposition of William Eaton, Esq. (concluded)," *Washington Federalist,* Feb. 4, 1807; *The Life of the Late Gen. William Eaton,* 401–03.

35. *The Examination of Col. Aaron Burr,* 15; Brown, ed., *William Plumer's Memorandum,* 542; *American Citizen,* Dec. 5, 1806.

36. See Edwards, *Barbary General,* 100, 175–80, 224, 231, 238–49.

37. See William Eaton to Stephen Bradley, Mar. 18, 1808 and Eaton to Bradley [1808], in Papers of William Eaton, 1764–1811, Huntington Library, Pasadena, Calif. See also *The Life of the Late Gen. William Eaton,* 53–54; Edwards, *Barbary General,* 54–56.

38. Eaton persisted in believing that Burr's conspiracy was gaining momentum in the winter of 1806–07, when the president and others in Washington felt it was "blasted." Here, again, is another indication of his tendency to misconstrue the facts and exaggerate his own importance in saving the country—see William Eaton to Amos A. Brewster, Feb. 5, 1807, in the Papers of William Eaton. And for Eaton's obsession with honor, accusations of his disordered fancy, and his drinking and gambling problems, see *The Life of the Late Gen. William Eaton,* 44, 46, 229, 408–10, 428; and Edwards, *Barbary General,* 254. Reports of Eaton's drunkenness circulated in December 1806. John Quincy Adams showed a letter from his wife in Boston, noting that Eaton "was frequently in a state of intoxication—that the better sort of people avoided him." See Brown, ed., *William Plumer's Memorandum,* 542, 550; for a similar view of Burr's known discretion, see *National Intelligencer,* Dec. 5, 1805.

39. *The Examination of Col. Aaron Burr,* 6–8.

40. *Ibid.,* 9–10.

41. *Ibid.,* 12–13.

42. *Ibid.,* 13–14.

43. *Ibid.,* 14–15.

44. *Ibid.,* 17, 20.

45. *Ibid.,* 23.

46. *Ibid.*

47. *Ibid.,* 24.

48. *Ibid.,* 24–28.

49. See notice of death of Mrs. Rebecca Hay, wife of George Hay, on Mar. 21, in *Richmond Inquirer,* Mar. 24, 1807.

50. *The Examination of Col. Aaron Burr,* 32.

51. *Ibid.,* 33–34.

52. *Ibid.,* 34–35.

53. *Ibid.,* 35.

54. *Ibid.,* 38.

55. See Thomas Jefferson to James Bowdoin, Apr. 2, 1807, Thomas Jefferson to William B. Giles, Apr. 20, 1807, and Thomas Jefferson to W. C. C. Claiborne,

Feb. 3, 1807, in Lipscomb and Bergh, eds., *The Writings of Thomas Jefferson,* XI: 151, 186–87.

56. See Thomas Jefferson to James Bowdoin, Apr. 2, 1807, and Thomas Jefferson to William B. Giles, Apr. 20, 1807, in *ibid.,* XI: 186–87; Malone, *Jefferson the President: The Second Term,* 80–81, 86–88; and Brown, *Agents of Manifest Destiny,* 3–5. Though Burr and Miranda never worked together, they did share some of the same backers, such as John Swartwout of New York. Burr went out of his way to make sure that he had no connection with Miranda; he later denied having any ill feelings for him, but it is clear that Miranda disliked Burr. Even so, Burr made no attempt to befriend the rival filibusterer. See AB to Jeremy Bentham, Oct. 16, 1811, in Kline, ed, *Burr Papers,* II: 948, 1134–35.

57. Andrew Burstein, *Jefferson's Secrets: Death and Desire at Monticello* (New York, 2005), 212–13, 216–17.

58. Thomas Jefferson to William B. Giles, Apr. 20, 1807, in Lipscomb and Bergh, eds., *The Writings of Thomas Jefferson,* IX: 188–90; for the dinner, see the *Richmond Enquirer,* Apr. 10, 28, 1807.

59. Thomas Jefferson to William B. Giles, Apr. 20, 1807, in Lipscomb and Bergh, eds., *The Writings of Thomas Jefferson,* IX: 190–91.

60. Albert J. Beveridge, *The Life of John Marshall,* 3 vols. (Boston, 1919), III: 390–93.

61. AB to Theodosia Alston, May 15, 1807, in Davis, ed., *Memoirs of Aaron Burr,* II: 406.

62. Paul S. Clarkson and R. Samuel Jett, *Luther Martin of Maryland* (Baltimore, 1970), 246–47; Thomas Jefferson to George Hay, June 19, 1807, in Lipscomb and Bergh, eds., *The Writings of Thomas Jefferson,* XI: 235.

63. "Alexander McRae (1765–1840)," in *Richmond Portraits,* 113. On Wirt, see Andrew Burstein, *America's Jubilee,* 34–37; William Wirt, *Letters of the British Spy* (Richmond, 1832; Chapel Hill, N.C., 1970), 135, 142, 183; and John Kennedy, *Memoirs of the Life of William Wirt* (Philadelphia, 1850), 140; and Fillmore Norfleet, *Saint-Mémin in Virginia: Portraits and Biographies* (Richmond, Va., 1943), 38, 135.

64. David Robertson, *Report of the Trials of Colonel Aaron Burr,* 2 vols. (Philadelphia, 1808; New York, 1969), I: 31–43; and Burr to Theodosia Burr Alston, May 15, 1807, in Davis, ed., *Memoirs of Aaron Burr,* II: 405.

65. For the political composition of the jury, see AB to Theodosia Burr Alston, May 15, 1807, in Davis, ed., *Memoirs of Aaron Burr,* II: 405.

66. AB to Theodosia Burr Alston, Apr. 26, 1807, in *ibid.*; Robertson, *Report of the Trials of Colonel Aaron Burr,* I: 46–47.

67. For Wickham throwing the affidavit, see "Statement of Miles Seloen," James Wickham Papers, Special Collections, University of Virginia, Charlottesville, Va.; Robertson, *Report of the Trials of Colonel Aaron Burr,* I: 50–66. There were even bets taken on whether Burr would abscond; see Washington Irving to

James K. Paulding, June 22, 1807, in Pierre M. Irving, *The Life and Letters of Washington Irving* (New York, 1862), I: 194.

68. Robertson, *Report of the Trials of Colonel Aaron Burr,* I: 67, 69–76.
69. *Ibid.,* I: 58–62.
70. *Ibid.,* I: 77–78.
71. *Ibid.,* I: 78.
72. AB to Theodosia Burr Alston, June 3, 1807, in Davis, ed., *Memoirs of Aaron Burr,* II: 406; Robertson, *Report of the Trials of Colonel Aaron Burr,* I: 111.
73. Robertson, *Report of the Trials of Colonel Aaron Burr,* I: 115–16, 119, 122.
74. *Ibid.,* I: 128.
75. *Ibid.,* I: 128–129.
76. *Ibid.,* I: 138–39, 144.
77. *Ibid.,* I: 146.
78. *Ibid.*
79. *Ibid.,* I: 155–57, 159–60.
80. *Ibid.,* I: 169–70.
81. *Ibid.,* I: 177–89; Thomas Jefferson to George Hay, June 19, 1807, in Lipscomb and Bergh, eds., *The Writings of Thomas Jefferson,* XI: 235–36; Simon, *What a Nation,* 242.
82. AB to Theodosia Burr Alston, June 18, 1807, in Davis, ed., *Memoirs of Aaron Burr,* I: 406–07; Robertson, *Report of the Trials of Colonel Aaron Burr,* I: 190.
83. Malone, *Jefferson the President: The Second Term,* 269–271; Abernethy, *Burr Conspiracy,* 196; Thomas Jefferson to George Hay, May 20, 1807, in Lipscomb and Bergh, eds., *The Writings of Thomas Jefferson,* XI: 205. For Bollman's later statement to the newspapers, see *National Intelligencer,* July 22, 1807.
84. AB to Theodosia Burr Alston, June 18, 1807, in Davis, ed., *Memoirs of Aaron Burr,* II: 407; Robertson, *Report of the Trials of Colonel Aaron Burr,* I: 190–91, 193.
85. Robertson, *Report of the Trials of Colonel Aaron Burr,* I, 196.
86. Jacobs, *Tarnished Warrior,* 213; AB to Theodosia Burr Alston, June 18, 1807, in Davis, ed., *Memoirs of Aaron Burr,* II: 406; Beveridge, *John Marshall,* III: 456.
87. James Wilkinson to Thomas Jefferson, June 17, 1807, in The Papers of Thomas Jefferson, Library of Congress.
88. Washington Irving to James Paulding, June 22, 1807, in Irving, ed., *The Life and Letters of Washington Irving,* I: 194–95.
89. On Brummell, see Ellen Moers, *The Dandy: Brummell to Beerholm* (London, 1960), 17–19; on the "effortless effort," see Anne Hollander, *Sex and Suits* (New York, 1994), 92, 100; and see Rhonda K. Garelick, *Rising Star: Dandyism, Gender, and Performance in the Fin de Siècle* (Princeton, N. J., 1998), 6, 19, 21.
90. John Randolph to Joseph H. Nicholson, June 25, 1807, in McColley, ed., *John Randolph,* 147; Abernethy, *Burr Conspiracy,* 239; and Kline, ed., *Burr Papers,* II:

1036–37. Rumors circulated that Wilkinson was almost indicted for treason, but a juryman who wrote to the *Virginia Gazette* claimed that he was almost indicted for misprision of treason. See the *National Intelligencer*, Aug. 3, 1807.

91. John Randolph to Joseph H. Nicholson, June 25, 1807, in McColley, ed., *John Randolph*, 147.

92. Abernethy, *Burr Conspiracy*, 240; Beveridge, *John Marshall*, III: 458, 462, 465.

93. Robertson, *Report of the Trials of Colonel Aaron Burr*, I: 306, 330.

94. See *ibid.*, I: 83, 85, 311, 351–52. For the original indictment, see Aaron Burr Papers, Miscellaneous Manuscripts Collection, Library of Congress; and AB to Theodosia Burr Alston, June 24, 1807, in Davis, ed., *Memoirs of Aaron Burr*, II: 408.

95. Robertson, *Report of the Trials of Colonel Aaron Burr*, I: 312, 351.

96. *Ibid.*, I: 357–59; Abernethy, *Burr Conspiracy*, 242; AB to Theodosia Burr Alston, June 30, 1807, in Davis, ed., *Memoirs of Aaron Burr*, II: 409. For Wirt's mother-in-law, see "Mrs. Robert Gamble," in *Richmond Portraits*, 74–75; Washington Irving to Miss Mary Fairlie, July 7, 1807, in Irving, *The Life and Letters of Washington Irving*, I: 201–02; Fitch, ed., *Breaking with Burr*, 22; and article reprinted from the *Aurora* in the *National Intelligencer*, July 22, 1807.

97. See Andrew Jackson to William Preston Anderson, June 16, 1807, and Andrew Jackson to Daniel Smith, Nov. 28, 1807, in Moser et al., eds., *The Papers of Andrew Jackson*, II: 164–65, 176; and George Hay to Thomas Jefferson, June 14, 1807, in The Papers of Thomas Jefferson, Library of Congress.

98. For the rumors of Wilkinson stealing Swartwout's watch—a story Swartwout himself circulated—see William Allen [Jr.] to William Allen, Mar. 9, 1807, in "Letters of William Henry Allen, 1800–1813," *Huntington Quarterly* I (Jan. 1938): 204–05. And for his published insults, see the *American Citizen*, Oct. 30, 1807; Fitch, ed., *Breaking with Burr*, 169; and Abernethy, *Burr Conspiracy*, 243.

99. For Alston's letter to the governor, see *National Intelligencer*, Feb. 25, 1807, and his pamphlet, *A Short Review of the Late Proceedings at New Orleans; and some remarks upon the bill for the suspension of Habeas Corpus, which passed the Senate of the United States, during the last session of Congress; in two letters to the Printer. By Agrestis* (S.C., 1807); and see Schachner, *Aaron Burr*, 426.

100. Robertson, *Report of the Trials of Colonel Aaron Burr*, I: 361–62, 382, 397, 420–23.

101. *Ibid.*, I: 430, 436–40.

102. *Ibid.*, 447–49.

103. *Ibid.*, 447–48.

104. *Ibid.*, I: 449–50; and see "The Examination of Col. Aaron Burr," 6, and Brown, *Manhood and Politics*, 80, 88.

105. Robertson, *Report of the Trials of Colonel Aaron Burr*, I: 452, 454, 462.

106. *Ibid.*, I: 472.

107. *Ibid.*, I: 474–76, 482–83.

108. Fitch, ed., *Breaking with Burr*, 14; and Edwards, *Barbary General*, 254–55.

109. See Suzanne B. Geissler, "The Commodore Goes to Court," *Naval History* 11 (1997): 32–35; AB to Charles Biddle, Apr. 18, 1807, in Kline, ed., *Burr Papers*, II: 1030–31.

110. Robertson, *Report of the Trials of Colonel Aaron Burr*, I: 486–89. Truxton's views were known before the treason trial, appearing in a published excerpt of a letter from Truxton to Burr's son-in-law, Joseph Alston; see *National Intelligencer*, Apr. 15, 1807.

111. Robertson, *Report of the Trials of Colonel Aaron Burr*, I: 486, 488–91.

112. *Ibid.*, I: 492–94.

113. *Ibid.*, I: 494–95.

114. William H. Sanford, ed., *The Blennerhassett Papers, embodying the Private Journal of Harman Blennerhassett, and the hitherto unpublished correspondence of Burr, Alston, Comfort Tyler, Devereaux, Dayton, Adair, Miro, Emmett, Theodosia Burr Alston, Mrs. Blennerhassett, and others, their contemporaries; developing the purposes and aims of those engaged in the attempted Wilkinson and Burr Revolution; embracing also the first account of the "Spanish Association of Kentucky," and Memoir of Blennerhassett*. (Cincinnati, 1891), 252; Theodosia Burr Alston to AB, Dec. 5, 1808, in Van Doren, ed., *Correspondence of Aaron Burr and his Daughter Theodosia*, 270.

115. Robertson, *Report of the Trials of Colonel Aaron Burr*, I: 372; Sanford, ed., *The Blennerhassett Papers*, 317, 323; and see *The Amorous Intrigues and Adventures of Aaron Burr* (New York, 1861), 99.

116. The militia did more than destroy property; they demanded that the black servants wait on them. Margaret and her children, who were still in the house, described the uncouth militiamen as transforming themselves into lords and masters. See William H. Sanford, *The Life of Harman Blennerhassett* (Cincinnati, 1850), 46–47; and Swick, *An Island Called Eden*, 22–23, 25, 28, 41, 43. That the attack on the island was seen as a class war was echoed by members of Burr's expedition. Silas Brown, who was one of Burr's recruits, explained that—on the night of Dec. 10—the men did "not flee from the hand of Justice, but to escape the hands of the infamous Ruffians, Kenhaway Mobs and Robbers." He further stated that since the "Kanahawa [sic] Militia and Wood County Mobs were to be at the Island early the next morning for the purpose of exhibiting their *True Patriotism* and taking us with force and arms—it was thought expedient to be out of their way, and, if possible, not to engage in any contest with such a low, mean set of beings." See Silas Brown to his Cousin, Mar. 7, 1807, and Silas Brown to Ephraim Brown, Oct. 26, 1807, in *The Aaron Burr Expedition: Letters to Ephraim Brown from Silas Brown, 1805–1815* (Mansfield, Ohio, 19__), 7, 20.

117. Robertson, *Report of the Trials of Colonel Aaron Burr*, I: 497–98, 501–03, 505; see also Eaton's deposition, in Prentiss, *The Life of the Late Gen. William Eaton*, 399. This also explains why prosecutor Hay was upset when Eaton omitted from his

testimony the account of overthrowing the government in Washington. He wanted the jurors to see the similarity between Eaton's and the Morgans' testimony. Wirt later asserted that the Morgans' testimony confirmed Eaton's—see Robertson, *Report of the Trials of Colonel Aaron Burr,* I: 476, II: 58.

118. See George Morgan to Presley Neville, Sept. 2, 1806, and "Memorandum," dated Nov. 19, 1806, recorded by Justice William Tilgham, in Burr Conspiracy documents, Special Collections, University of Virginia, Charlottesville, Va. George Morgan sent his own warning to Jefferson, and Presley Neville and Judge Roberts sent a letter about the interview to James Madison. Though Jefferson later wrote to Morgan (incorrectly) that Morgan's was the first "intimation" he had of Burr's plot, at the time he did not react to the warning. Interestingly, General Neville's son had joined Burr's expedition. See Abernethy, *Burr Conspiracy,* 84; Malone, *Jefferson the President: Second Term,* 239; and Thomas Jefferson to George Morgan, Mar. 26, 1807, in Lipscomb and Bergh, eds., *The Writings of Thomas Jefferson,* IX: 174. Eaton's involvement in the Burr trial was not the first time he viewed himself as defeating a conspiracy. In 1797, he had been charged with a confidential commission from the secretary of state to arrest New Yorker D. Nicholas Romayne, then considered Tennessean William Blount's major accomplice in the attempt to seize Spanish lands. See *The Life of the Late Gen. William,* 53–54; and Edwards, *Barbary General,* 54–56.

119. "Memorandum" dated Nov. 19, 1806; Robertson, *Report of the Trials of Colonel Aaron Burr,* I: 504. See also Presley Neville and Samuel Roberts to James Madison, Oct. 7, 1806 (this letter also reported on the same meeting with the Morgans and there was no mention of the offensive remark), James Madison Papers, Library of Congress; and AB to Jonathan Rhea, July 25, 1807, in Kline, ed., *Burr Papers,* II: 1037.

120. Robertson, *Report of the Trials of Colonel Aaron Burr,* I: 509–10.

121. *Ibid.,* I: 508, 513–18, 526–29.

122. *Ibid.,* I: 518–19, 521, 532.

123. *Ibid.,* I: 529, 533, 578. Henry Tazewell, a member of the grand jury, and a lawyer, praised Wickham's address—see Schachner, *Aaron Burr,* 432.

124. Robertson, *Report of the Trials of Colonel Aaron Burr,* I: 534–39, 542, 558.

125. *Ibid.,* I: 562–63.

126. *Ibid.,* I: 568–69, 578, 582.

127. See *New York Herald,* Oct. 3, 1807; *American Citizen,* Oct. 5, 1807; Parton, *Life and Times of Aaron Burr,* 2: 146; Burstein, *America's Jubilee,* 39; and Robertson, *Report of the Trials of Colonel Aaron Burr,* II: 58, 95.

128. Robertson, *Report of the Trials of Colonel Aaron Burr,* II: 96–97.

129. Amazingly, because Blennerhassett had become so important to the prosecution's case, just two days before Wirt's speech, William Duane, editor of the *Aurora,* tried to bribe the prisoner with a promise of a presidential pardon if he

agreed to turn state's evidence against Burr—see Sanford, ed., *The Blennerhas-sett Papers,* 356–58; see also Robertson, *Report of the Trials of Colonel Aaron Burr,* II: 64–65.

130. Robertson, *Report of the Trials of Colonel Aaron Burr,* II: 123–24; Beveridge, *The Life of John Marshall,* III: 498.

131. Robertson, *Report of the Trials of Colonel Aaron Burr,* II: 336–37.

132. *Ibid.,* II: 425, 428–29, 439, 445–47.

133. William Wirt to Dabney Carr, Sept. 7, 1807, in William Wirt Papers, Maryland Historical Society, Baltimore; Thomas Ritchie to Joseph C. Cabell, Aug. 31, 1807, Cabell Papers, Special Collections, University of Virginia, Charlottes-ville, Va.; Robertson, *Report of the Trials of Colonel Aaron Burr,* II: 539; Beveridge, *The Life of John Marshall,* III: 523–24; Malone, *Jefferson the President: The Second Term,* 345; and AB to Theodosia Burr Alston, Sept. 26, 1807, in Davis, ed., *Memoirs of Aaron Burr,* II: 411.

134. In the end, Burr gave a bond for $5,000, but the state of Ohio declined to prosecute him—see Beveridge, *The Life of John Marshall,* III: 517, 527–28; and George Hay to Thomas Jefferson, Oct. 15, 1807, The Papers of Thomas Jeffer-son, Library of Congress. Joseph Cabell, who took notes on the trial, wrote that toward the end of the proceedings, Wilkinson was "secretly given up by Hay and Wirt"—Joseph C. Cabell to Isaac Coles, Nov. 6, 1807, Cabell Papers, Spe-cial Collections, University of Virginia, Charlottesville, Va.

135. Mary-Jo Kline, editor of the *Burr Papers,* compared handwriting and discov-ered the true authorship of the cipher letter—see Kline, ed., *Burr Papers,* II: 985; see also Charles Biddle to Nicholas Biddle, July 18, 1807, Nicholas Biddle Letters, Historical Society of Pennsylvania, Philadelphia.

136. Thomas Jefferson to James Monroe, Jan. 11, 1812, in Ford, ed., *The Works of Thomas Jefferson,* IX: 120.

137. Jefferson also wrote to the marquis de Lafayette that Burr's "conspiracy has been one of the most flagitious of which history will ever furnish an example," and that the "man who could expect to effect this, with American materials, must be a fit subject for Bedlam." See Thomas Jefferson to Charles Clay, Jan. 11, 1807, Thomas Jefferson to Robert Livingston, Mar. 24, 1807, Thomas Jef-ferson to ?, Mar. 25, 1807, Thomas Jefferson to Colonel George Morgan, Mar. 26, 1807, Thomas Jefferson to William B. Giles, Apr. 20, 1807, and Thomas Jefferson to Marquis de La Fayette, July 14, 1807, in Lipscomb and Bergh, eds., *The Writings of Thomas* Jefferson, XI: 133, 171–72, 174, 191, 277.

138. Burr dined with Jefferson at the President's House on Nov. 19, 1805, Feb. 22, 1806, and Apr. 9, 1806. His private conference with Burr is believed to have occurred in Mar.—see Kline, ed., *Burr Papers,* II: 964; see also Jefferson's din-ner records in Mary Ellen Scofield, "The Fatigues of His Table: The Politics of Presidential Dining During the Jefferson Administration," *Journal of the Early Republic* 16 (Fall 2006): 466–467.

139. John Adams to Benjamin Rush, Feb. 2, 1807, in Schultz and Adair, eds., *The Spur of Fame*, 76.

CHAPTER TEN

1. Kline, ed., *Burr Papers*, II: 1042.
2. See reprinting of the handbill in *American Citizen*, Nov. 9, 1807.
3. See other reports in *American Citizen*, Nov. 9, Dec. 5, 1807; and Sanford, ed., *Blennerhassett Papers*, 478–82; Clarkson and Jett, *Luther Martin*, 274.
4. For the tragic portrait, which comes from Charles Biddle's reminiscences, see Schachner, *Aaron Burr*, 445–46; Lomask, *Aaron Burr: The Conspiracy*, 293; and *The Autobiography of Charles Biddle*, 323. For reports on Burr's movements, see *National Intelligencer*, Nov. 18, 1807; and Sanford, ed., *Blennerhassett Papers*, 518.
5. Sanford, ed., *Blennerhassett Papers*, 535–38. For Alston's repayment, see Côté, *Theodosia*, 255–56; and Theodosia Burr Alston to AB, May 10, 1811, in Van Doren, ed., *Correspondence of Aaron Burr and his Daughter Theodosia*, 327–28; see also Ronald Ray Swick, "Harman Blennerhassett: Irish Aristocrat and Frontier Entrepreneur," in *Essays in History* 14 (Charlottesville, Va., 1968–69): 65–66, 68, 70–71.
6. Nicholas and his older brother William provided legal assistance to Burr. See AB to William S. Biddle, Nov. 19, 1807, AB to Nicholas Biddle, Dec. 1, 1807, AB to Nicholas Biddle [ca. December 1807], and AB to Nicholas Biddle [1807–08], in Burr Papers, microfilm, reel 6. For Burr's patronage of and affection for Biddle's sons, see AB to Samuel Smith, Mar. 31, 1804, Charles Biddle to AB, Mar. 13, 1812, and AB to Charles Biddle, July 18, 1804, in Kline, ed., *Burr Papers*, I: 550; II: 687, 885–86; see also Thomas Payne Govan, *Nicholas Biddle: Nationalist and Public Banker, 1786–1844* (Chicago, 1959), 19–22, 59, 78.
7. See AB to Charles Williamson, Nov. 25, 1807, in Burr Papers, microfilm, reel 6; Charles Williamson to Lord Justice Clerk, June 5, 1807, in Williamson Papers, Newberry Library, Chicago.
8. Williamson wrote that one informant told him: "If we had let Burr alone he would have attacked Mexico I have no doubt, & the opinion is very much abroad that Wilkinson deceived him—and instead of joining him as he had reason to believe he would, from some cause or other (some think bribed by the Spaniards) took part against him—and overact the whole." See Charles Williamson to Lord Justice Clerk, July 12, 1807, Williamson Papers.
9. Swartwout kept in regular contact with Williamson from Feb. to May 1808, sending him several letters and arranging meetings. See Charles Williamson to Lord Melville, Feb. 9, 1808, and Swartwout to Williamson, Mar. 8, Mar. 20, Mar. 29, Apr. 26, May 14, 1808, in Williamson Papers; see also Cox, "Hispanic-American Phases of the 'Burr Conspiracy,'" 170–71; and Kline, ed., *Burr Papers*, II: 1045.

10. The court-martial of Wilkinson began on Jan. 11 and lasted until June 28, 1808. See Thomas Jefferson to Edward Tiffin, Jan. 30, 1808, in Lipscomb and Bergh, eds., *The Writings of Thomas Jefferson,* XI: 435; and Abernethy, *Burr Conspiracy,* 260, 265–67.

11. AB to Theodosia Burr Alston [ante June 1, 1808], in Matthew Livingston Davis, ed., *The Private Journal of Aaron Burr* (New York, 1838), I: 20–21; William K. Bixby, ed., *The Private Journal of Aaron Burr* (Rochester, N.Y., 1903), I: 1–2.

12. Davis, ed., *Private Journal,* I: 121.

13. Bixby, ed., *Private Journal,* I: 2; William Pinckney to James Madison, Aug. 2, 1808, The Papers of James Madison, Library of Congress.

14. AB to Colonel Charles Williamson, July 19, 1808, in Burr Papers, microfilm, reel 6; and "Declaration before John Reeves" [August 10, 1808], in Kline, ed., *Burr Papers,* II: 1047–48.

15. AB to Charles Williamson, July 19, 1808; Charles Williamson to AB, June 19, 1808, in Kline, ed., *Burr Papers,* II: 1046–47; and Hay, "Charles Williamson and the Burr Conspiracy," 205–06. See also William W. Kaufman, *British Policy and the Independence of Latin America, 1804–1828* (New Haven, Conn., 1951), 36–40.

16. See William Spence Robertson, "The Juntas of 1808 and the Spanish Colonies," *English History Review* 31 (1916): 573–85; and Kline, ed., *Burr Papers,* II: 1052.

17. AB to Samuel Swartwout, Aug. 19, 1808, Kline, ed., *Burr Papers,* II: 1049, 1053.

18. For Burr's interest in Bentham's writings, see George W. Erving to AB, Apr. 5, 1803, and Jeremy Bentham to Samuel Bentham, Aug. 29, 1808, in Kline, ed., *Burr Papers,* II: 767, 1057.

19. See AB to Theodosia Burr Alston, Sept. 9 and 10, 1808, AB to Jeremy Bentham, Sept. 12, 1808, and Theodosia Burr Alston to AB, Dec. 5, 1808, in Davis, ed., *Private Journal of Aaron Burr,* I: 46–49, 50–52; and AB to Jeremy Bentham, Sept. 7, 1808, in Kline, ed., *Burr Papers,* II: 1059. See also Williford, "Bentham on the Rights of Women," 168–72; Bixby, ed., *Private Journal of Aaron Burr,* I: 12.

20. See David Armitage, "The Declaration of Independence," *William and Mary Quarterly* 59 (2002); and John Dinwiddy, *Bentham* (Oxford, 1989), 20–21, 39–42, 49–51.

21. Burr owned Beccaria's writings; see Burr's inventory of his book collection, Burr Papers, reel 3; see also my discussions of Burr's attraction to Utilitarianism in chapters one and four.

22. One expert on Bentham stresses that 1809 was a crucial turning point for the philosopher. He overcame his fears of the French Revolution and began to look to America as the democratic model of the future. Some scholars have noted the influence of James Mill, who met Bentham in 1807. But most scholars have either ignored Burr or downplayed his influence, probably because of his scandalous reputation. But Burr (as he no doubt told Bentham at this time)

saw himself as having "superior knowledge" on American democracy, which, of course, he did. See AB to David Randolph, Aug. 21, 1808, in Kline, ed., *Burr Papers,* II:1051–52. See also H. L. A. Hart, "Bentham and the United States of America," *Journal of Law and Economics* 19 (1976): 560–61; and Chilton Williamson, "Bentham Looks at America," *Political Science Quarterly* 70 (Dec. 1955): 544; Dinwiddy, *Bentham,* 81–82; Williford, "Bentham on the Rights of Women," 168–69.

23. Dinwiddy, *Bentham,* 92.

24. Burr even collected drawings from Bentham's brother Samuel, who had helped design the revolutionary prison—AB to Theodosia Burr Alston, Sept. 10, 1808, and Theodosia Burr Alston to AB, Dec. 5, 1808, in Van Doren, ed., *Correspondence of Aaron Burr and his Daughter Theodosia,* 243–44, 269; AB to Jeremy Bentham, Sept. 2, 1808, in Kline, ed., *Burr Papers,* II: 1056–57.

25. The memorandum was to be delivered to the Marquis de Casa Yrujo by fellow American David Randolph—see AB to David Randolph, Aug. 21 and Aug. 28, 1808, and AB to Jeremy Bentham, Sept. 1, 1808, in Kline, ed., *Burr Papers,* II: 1051–52, 1054–55.

26. AB to Jeremy Bentham, Sept. 2, 1808, AB to Anthony Merry, [Nov. 6, 1808], in Kline, ed., *Burr Papers,* II: 1057, 1064–65; Bixby, ed., *Private Journal of Aaron Burr,* I: 9.

27. See Theodosia Burr Alston to William Eustis, Oct. 3, 1808. For her other correspondence with the doctor, see her July 20, Oct. 6, 1808, letters to him in the Burr Papers, reel 6; see also Côté, *Theodosia,* 249–50.

28. AB to Theodosia Burr Alston, Oct. 24, Nov. 9, 10, 1808, Theodosia Burr Alston to AB, Oct. 31, 1808, , in Van Doren, ed., *Correspondence of Aaron Burr and his Daughter Theodosia,* 249–50, 252, 254, 258–60; AB to Joseph Alston, Nov. 10, 1808, in Davis, ed., *Private Journal of Aaron Burr,* I: 82–83.

29. AB to Timothy Green, Sept. 9, 1808, in Burr Papers, microfilm, reel 6; AB to Theodosia Burr Alston, Sept. 9,1808, and Theodosia Burr Alston to AB, Oct. 31, 1808, in Van Doren, ed., *Correspondence of Aaron Burr and his Daughter Theodosia,* 245, 251; and AB to Jeremy Bentham, Oct. 14, 1808, in Kline, ed., *Burr Papers,* II: 1063.

30. See "Declaration before John Reeves," in Kline, ed., *Burr Papers,* I: 1048–49, 1068; and Theodosia Burr Alston to AB, Aug. 31, 1809, in Van Doren, ed., *Private Correspondence of Aaron Burr and his Daughter Theodosia,* 308; Bixby, ed., *Journal of Aaron Burr,* I: 15–16.

31. AB to Jeremy Bentham, Jan. 13, 1809, AB to Theodosia Burr Alston, Feb. 12, 1809, in Davis, ed., *Private Journal of Aaron Burr,* I: 135. In his journal, Burr incorrectly identified Henry Mackenzie as Alexander M'Kenzie—Bixby, ed., *Private Journal of Aaron Burr,* I: 47.

32. Burr also felt that his Journal "is only a memorandum to talk from. The most interesting and amusing incidents are not noted at all, because I am sure to remember them"—Bixby, ed., *Private Journal of Aaron Burr,* I: 165.

33. *Ibid.*, I: 16–17.
34. The second editor of Burr's journal, William Bixby, compiled a glossary of seventeen foreign language words or phrases that described sex or women—see *ibid.*, I: 116, 125, II: 485–503.
35. *Ibid.*, I: 40–41, 75–76, 415, 468, II: 207.
36. *Ibid.*, II: 73–74; Burstein, *Jefferson's Secrets*, 29–30. James Wilson's pocket diary for 1773 can be found in the American Philosophical Society, Philadelphia; I would like to thank Mary McCarthy for bringing this document to my attention. Professor Brendan McConville has developed a convincing case for why the sexual entries were added later by Wilson's enemies, discovering that not only was different ink used but the handwriting is different. That a prominent man could be attacked for keeping a sexual diary confirms that fact that Americans, in the late eighteenth and early nineteenth century, knew that elite men did keep this kind of record. I would like to thank Brendan McConville for sharing his research with me. See also Benjamin Franklin, *The Autobiography,* intro. Daniel Aaron (New York, 1990), 81, and Sisman, *Boswell's Presumptuous Task,* 28–29.
37. Bixby, ed., *Private Journal of Aaron Burr,* I: 199.
38. AB to Jeremy Bentham, Jan. 23, 1809, and Jeremy Bentham to AB, Mar. 1, 1809, in Davis, ed., *Private Journal of Aaron Burr,* I: 166–69; and AB to Theodosia Burr Alston, Feb. 15, 1809, in Van Doren, ed., *Correspondence of Aaron Burr and his Daughter Theodosia,* 286.
39. For AB's interviews with Lord Melville, see AB to Charles Hope, Mar. 1, 1809, in Kline, ed., *Burr Papers,* II: 1077–78; for Melville's "bold, manly character," see also David Williamson to AB, Feb. 1, 1809, in Davis, ed., *Private Journal of Aaron Burr,* I:157. For titling his trip "Adventures of Gil Blas Moheagungk [sic] De Manhattan," see Bixby, ed., *Private Journal of Aaron Burr,* I: 40. His story was based on *Gil Blas* by Alain-René Le Sage, which was written between 1700 and 1730; it was translated into English by Tobias Smollett and popular among English and American readers alike. Manhattan is not only a reference to New York but to its Indian name, and Moheigungk was one of the nations inhabiting the island. Burr also referred to himself as Moheigungk in his letter to Bentham. See AB to Bentham, Jan. 23, 1809, in Davis, ed., *Private Journal of Aaron Burr,* I: 166–68.
40. See Bixby, ed., *Private Journal of Aaron Burr,* I: 93–95; and AB to John Reeves, Apr. 5, 1809, and "Memorandum for Lord Liverpool," in Kline, ed., *Burr Papers,* II: 1083–85.
41. AB to Jeremy Bentham, Apr. 19, 1809, AB to Mrs.———, N.Y., Apr. 25, 1809, in Davis, ed., *Private Journal of Aaron Burr,* I: 202–03, 212; AB to Lord Liverpool, Apr. 20, 1809, in Kline, ed., *Burr Papers,* II: 1090–92.
42. See AB to Mary Jane Clairmont (Mrs. Willliam) Godwin, Mar. 29, Apr. 21, 1809, and AB to Ann Onslow, Apr. 21, 1809, in Davis, ed., *Private Journal of*

Aaron Burr, I: 186–87, 205–06. For Burr's references to himself as a state pris-
oner, see AB to Theodosia Burr Alston, Apr. 22, 1809, in Van Doren, ed.,
Correspondence of Aaron Burr and his Daughter Theodosia, 293, and Kline, ed.,
Burr Papers, II: 1092.

43. Kline, ed., *Burr Papers,* II: 1092–93; Bixby, ed., *Private Journal of Aaron Burr,* I:
    107, 110–11, 128; Schachner, *Aaron Burr,* 462.

44. AB to Theodosia Burr Alston, Oct. 13, 1809, in Van Doren, ed., *Correspondence
    of Aaron Burr and his Daughter Theodosia,* 311; AB to Henry Gahn, Oct. 12,
    1809, in Davis, ed., *Private Journal of Aaron Burr,* I: 312–13; Bixby, ed., *Private
    Journal of Aaron Burr,* I: 122–23.

45. Kline, ed., *Burr Papers,* II: 1093; Lynn Hudson Parsons, *John Quincy Adams*
    (Madison, Wis., 1998), 88–89, 91–92, 96.

46. Diedrich Lünning to AB, Oct. 21, 1809, and AB to Alexandre Maurice Blanc de
    Lanautte, comte d'Hauterive, Sept. 10, 1809, in Davis, ed., *Private Journal of
    Aaron Burr,* I: 332, 305; Bixby, ed., *Private Journal of Aaron Burr,* I: 254–55,
    76–77.

47. See AB to comte d'Hauterive, Jan. 29, 1810, in Kline, ed., *Burr Papers,* II:
    1093–94, 1096.

48. AB to comte de Volney, Jan. 29, 1810, in Kline, ed., *Burr Papers,* II: 1097–98;
    Bixby, ed., *Private Journal of Aaron Burr,* I: 338; and Erwin G. Gudde, "Aaron
    Burr in Weimar," *South Atlantic Quarterly* 40 (1941): 361–63.

49. Kline, ed., *Burr Papers,* II: 1096, 1099; Bixby, ed., *Private Journal of Aaron Burr,*
    I: 410.

50. See "Documents Delivered to the Ministry of Foreign Affairs," [Mar. 1–13,
    1810], and Louis Roux: Report to the duc de Cadore, Mar. 13, 1810, and
    Louis Roux to the duc de Cadore, July 29, 1810, in Kline, ed., *Burr Papers,* II:
    1100–01, 1105, 1110–11, 1113–15, 1117–19, 1124–25.

51. Bixby, ed., *Private Journal of Aaron Burr,* I: 430–31, 454; Kline, ed., *Burr Pa-
    pers,* II: 1101–02.

52. See Louise Hunt Averill, "John Vanderlyn, American Painter (1775–1852),"
    Ph.D. Dissertation, Yale University, 1949, 82, 91; AB to Madame——, May 9,
    1810, Madame "Z." to AB, July 20, 1811, and AB to Madame "Z.," Aug. 28,
    1811, in Davis, ed., *Private Journal of Aaron Burr,* II: 15, 237–38. See also AB
    to [a lady] (also Madame "Z."), Mar. 28, 1811, in Burr Papers, microfilm, reel
    6; and Bixby, ed., *Private Journal of Aaron Burr,* I: 468, II: 87–88.

53. AB to comte de Volney, Aug. 5, 1810, in Davis, ed., *Private Journal of Aaron
    Burr,* II: 30–31; Jonathan Russell to AB, Oct. 25, 1810, AB to Alexander McRae,
    Oct. 29, 1810, and Alexander McRae to AB, Oct. 29, 1810, in Kline, ed., *Burr
    Papers,* II: 1128–29; Bixby, ed., *Private Journal of Aaron Burr,* II: 22, 25, 28–29;
    and Averill, "John Vanderlyn," 88.

54. Kline, ed., *Burr Papers,* II: 1131–33.

55. Bixby, ed., *Private Journal of Aaron Burr,* 244; Theodosia Burr Alston to Dolley

Madison, June 24, 1809, in the Dolley Madison Papers, Special Collections, Alderman Library, University of Virginia. See AB to Theodosia Burr Alston, May 31, Oct. 13, 1809, Theodosia Burr Alston to AB, Aug. 1, 1809, in Van Doren, ed., *Correspondence of Aaron Burr and his Daughter Theodosia,* 296, 304, 312; and Theodosia Burr Alston to Frederick Prevost, Sept. 12, 1809, in Côté, *Theodosia,* 253.

56. Theodosia Burr Alston to AB, Feb. 14, 1811, in Van Doren, ed., *Correspondence of Aaron Burr and his Daughter Theodosia,* 321; see also Mattern and Shulman, eds., *The Selected Letters of Dolley Madison,* 400.

57. Theodosia Burr Alston to Albert Gallatin, Mar. 9, 1811, in Davis, ed., *Private Journal of Aaron Burr,* II: 155–56.

58. See Natalie Sumter to Mary Hooper, Aug. 2, 1809, in Côté, *Theodosia,* 253–54; Catherine D. Westcott to AB, Dec. 8, 30, 1812, in Burr Papers, microfilm, reel 7.

59. Theodosia Burr Alston to AB, Feb. 14, 1811, May 10, 1811, in Van Doren, ed., *Correspondence of Aaron Burr and his Daughter Theodosia,* 322, 326.

60. AB to John Reeves, Oct. 5, 1811, in Davis, ed., *Private Journal of Aaron Burr,* II: 241–42; and AB to David Williamson, Mar. 4, 1812, in Kline, ed., *Burr Papers,* II: 1133–34, 1139–41.

61. AB to David Williamson, Mar. 4, 1812, in Kline, ed., *Burr Papers,* II: 1140–41, 1144–45; Bixby, ed., *Private Journal of Aaron* Burr, II: 401.

62. AB to George Gardner, July 5, 1812, AB to Edward Livingston, July 10, 1812, AB and Timothy Green: Catalogue of Books, Aug. 1, 1812, in Burr Papers, microfilm, reel 7; AB to [J.] Wickham, Mar. 10, 1812, in Davis, ed., *Private Journal of Aaron Burr,* II: 373; J. Wickham to Samuel Swartwout, July 4, 1812, The Historical Society of Pennsylvania, Philadelphia; Kline, ed., *Burr Papers,* II: 1146.

63. Theodosia Burr Alston to AB, July 12, 1812, and AB to Jeremy Bentham, Aug. 27, 1812, in Burr Papers, microfilm, reel 7; Joseph Alston to AB, July 26, 1812, in Davis, ed., *Memoirs of Aaron Burr,* II: 426–27.

64. Joseph Alston to AB, July 26, 1812, and Timothy Green to AB, Dec. 7, 22, 1812, in Davis, ed., *Memoirs of Aaron Burr,* II: 427–28; Côté, *Theodosia,* 260, 63.

65. Joseph Alston to AB, Jan. 19, Feb. 25, 1813, in Davis, ed., *Memoirs of Aaron Burr,* II: 429–32; AB to Kate, Feb. 7, 1813, and AB to Lenora Fenwick, Dec. 26, 1814, in Burr Papers, microfilm, reel 7; Côté, *Theodosia,* 261–65, 268, 271, 274.

66. AB to Oliver Phelps, Aug. 13, 1812, in Burr Papers, microfilm, reel 7.

67. Burr was helping the couple make financial arrangements for John's mother, the widow Jane Yates; and another acquaintance of Burr's, Catherine Thompson, referred to "Recorder Yates" as Burr's friend—see Catherine B. Thompson to AB, July 21, 1814, Eliza Yates to AB, Aug. 11, Sept. 18, 30, Oct. 1, [Oct. 1813], Nov. 12, John V. N. and Eliza Yates to AB, [1814–15?]. See also AB to

Kate, Aug. 21, 1812, [P.M.B.] and "K" to AB, Apr. 17, 1814, P.M.B. to AB, June 16, 1814, in Burr Papers, microfilm, reel 7; and AB to Theodosia Burr Alston, Nov. 3, 1801, in Davis, ed., *Memoirs of Aaron Burr,* II: 156; Bixby, ed., *Private Journal of Aaron Burr,* II: 22; "Robert Yates," in James Grant Wilson and John Fiskeels, *Appletons Encyclopedia of American Biography* (New York, 1887–89).

68. Catherine Thompson was born in 1779—she was three years older than Theodosia. She later became a schoolteacher in Beaufort, S.C., and in 1818, she married a man ten year her junior. See Catherine B. Thompson to AB, Sept. 8, 17, 30, 1813, Feb. 14, 17, Mar. 8, 29, May 5, June 7, July 21, Sept, 29, Dec. 19, 1814, and July 8, 1817, and Arabella Seymour (Catherine's sister) to AB, Feb. 24, 1818, in Burr Papers, microfilm, reels 7, 8. For family history, see census records for Dutchess County, N.Y., 1810, in *The Dutchess,* vol. 11, no. 3 (Spring 1984): 21, 89; and "Will of Alexander Thompson, 1813," Will Book D, 185.

69. See Mrs. Jenkins to AB, Sept. 16 or 18, 1813; Isabella Mix to AB, [Feb. 4, 1814], [Dec. 27, 1814], and Mar. 18, 14, 1814. Other women wrote him for money or advice; see Ann Spear to AB, Jan. 18, 1813, Mrs. M. Green to AB, Mar. 19, 1813, Madame M. to AB, May 1814. For his handlings of the case of Mrs. Denton, see AB to Gurdon Lathrop, Mar. 28 and 29, 1814, and Mar. 1, 1815, in Burr Papers, microfilm, reel 7; see also *Isabella Mix v. Marvin P. Mix,* Apr. 30, 1814, in NYCC Cases. In Burr's other divorce cases at this time, he only represented women: see *Williamson v. Parisien,* Apr. 8, 1815, *Esther Smith v. Robert C. Smith,* May 15, 1815, *Adelaide Lindsley v. Abraham Lindsley,* July 8, 1815, and *Martha Codd v. Matthew Codd,* May 29, 1816, in NYCC Cases, Burr Papers, microfilm, reel 21.

70. "Samuel Blodget, Jr.," *American National Biography* (New York, 1999), III: 38–40; and Kenneth Hafertepe, "Banking Houses in the United States: The First Generation, 1781–1811," *Winterthur Portfolio* 35 (Spring 2000): 9–13.

71. Appendix C, "Guide to the William Smith Papers," University Archives and Record Center, University of Pennsylvania, Philadelphia; Shields, *Civil Tongues and Polite Letters in British America,* 126; and "Samuel Blodget," *Dictionary of American Biography* (New York, 1929), II: 380–81.

72. Rebecca Blodget to AB, June 10, 1814, and AB to Burdon W. Lathrop, Aug. 1814, Burr Papers, microfilm, reel 7.

73. Rebecca Blodget to AB, June 17, 1814, and July 15, 1814, Sept. 6, 1814, Nov. 21, 1814, Burr Papers, microfilm, reel 7.

74. AB to Joseph Alston, Oct. 16, 1815, in Davis, ed., *Memoirs of Aaron Burr,* II: 433; *David Gelston v. AB,* Oct. 1814, *Louis Le Guen v. AB,* July 31, 1817, and *John Berry v. AB,* Jan. 17, 1818, NYSC Cases, Burr Papers, microfilm, reel 16; and Clarkson and Jett, *Luther Martin,* 292.

75. AB to Gurdon Lathrop, Feb. 15, 1814, in Burr Papers, microfilm, reel 7; and AB to Arthur Breese, Mar. 11, 1814, in Kline, ed., *Burr Papers,* II: 1150. See also Royster, *A Revolutionary People at War,* 123–25.

76. AB to [Gurdon W. Lathrop], Apr. 4, 1814, and AB to Martin Van Buren, [Jan. 31–Mar. 25, 1815], in Kline, ed., *Burr Papers*, II: 1153–55; Martin Van Buren to AB, July 23, 1814, in Burr Papers, microfilm, reel 7; Donald B. Cole, *Martin Van Buren and the American Political System* (Princeton, N.J., 1984), 43–45; John Niven, *Martin Van Buren: The Romantic Age of American Politics* (New York, 1983), 45–46; John C. Fitzpatrick, ed., "The Autobiography of Martin Van Buren," *American Historical Association, Annual Report of the American Historical Association for the Year 1918* (1920), 2: 55–56; and Kline, ed., *Burr Papers*, II: 1156.

77. Catherine B. Thompson to AB, May 5, 1814, in Burr Papers, microfilm, reel 7; AB to [Gurdon W. Lathrop], Apr. 4, 1815, in Kline, ed., *Burr Papers*, II: 1163–64.

78. Cole, *Martin Van Buren and the American Political System*, 45; Donald M. Roper, "Martin Van Buren as Tocqueville's Lawyer: The Jurisprudence of Politics," *Journal of the Early Republic* 2 (1982): 169–89; Jerome Mushkat and Joseph G. Rayback, *Martin Van Buren: Law, Politics, and the Shaping of Republican Ideology* (DeKalb, Ill., 1997), 21–22; John Brooke, "Columbia: Civil Life in the World of Martin Van Buren's Emergence, 1776–1821," unpublished MS, 2005; and Fitzpatrick, ed., "The Autobiography of Martin Van Buren," 2: 13–14.

79. Theodosia Burr Alston to AB, Feb. 14, May 10, 1811, in Van Doren, ed., *Correspondence of Aaron Burr and his Daughter Theodosia*, 321–22, 325–26; Erich Bollmann to AB, Mar. 5, 1811, in Davis, ed., *Private Journal of Aaron Burr*, II: 154; Bixby, ed., *Private Journal of Aaron Burr*, II: 402.

80. J. C. A. Stagg, *Mr. Madison's War: Politics, Diplomacy, and Warfare in the Early Republic, 1783–1830* (Princeton, N.J., 1983), 278–79, 504–05.

81. AB to Joseph Alston, Nov. 15, 1815, in Kline, ed., *Burr Papers*, II: 1165–66.

82. *Ibid.*; see also Solomon Nadler, "Federal Patronage and New York Politics, 1801–1830," Ph.D. Dissertation, New York University, 1973.

83. AB to Joseph Alston, Nov. 15, 1815, in Kline, ed., *Burr Papers*, II: 1166. Writing much later in life, and offering a kinder but similar assessment of Monroe, Van Buren noted in his autobiography: "Mr. Monroe's character was that of an honest man, with fair, but not very marked capacities,"—Fitzpatrick, ed., *The Autobiography of Martin Van Buren*, II: 119.

84. AB to Joseph Alston, Nov. 15, 1815, in Kline, ed., *Burr Papers*, II: 1166–67.

85. Cole, *Martin Van Buren*, 46–48; Burstein, *Passions of Andrew Jackson*, 124.

86. Joseph Alston to AB, Feb. 16, 1816, in Davis, ed., *Memoirs of Aaron Burr*, II: 437; Côté, *Theodosia*, 277.

87. José Alvárez de Toledo to AB, Sept. 20, 1816, in Davis, ed., *Memoirs of Aaron Burr*, II: 442–43.

88. John Alderson to AB, Oct. 16, 1817, in Kline, ed., *Burr Papers*, II: 1170–72.

89. Robert Cartmel to AB, July 31, 1817, in Burr Papers, microfilm, reel 8; Kline, ed., *Burr Papers*, II: 1175–1177.

90. Reid commanded the *John Armstrong*, a privateer that fought off an attack by

the Royal Navy at Fayal in the Azores in 1814. This battle delayed the British attack on Louisiana, which contributed to Jackson's victory at New Orleans. Samuel Reid to AB, Oct. 22, 1823, AB to Samuel Reid, Dec. 28, 1823, Robert Cartmel to AB, Mar. 31, 1824, in Kline, ed., *Burr Papers*, II: 1177–80, 1182–84; AB to Samuel Reid, Aug. 27, 1824, in Burr Papers, microfilm, reel 8. And for the connection between Ruggles, Reid, and Burr, see AB to Ruggles Hubbard, Feb. 25, 1815, in Burr Papers, microfilm, reel 7, and AB to Samuel C. Reid, Mar. 2, 1815, in Kline, ed., *Burr Papers,* II: 1156–57.

91. AB to Gurdon Lathrop, Mar. 9, 1814, AB to Benjamin Butler, Oct. 17, 1818, Burr Papers, microfilm, reel 7; *Maria and Jacob Morton v. John Miller, George W. and Augustine J. Prevost et al.,* Jan. 13, 1815, and *Levi Phillips and Leah and Belah Cohen,* Jan. 26, 1818, NYSC, reel 16; *Daniel Coxe v. William Goldsborough, Rebecca Blodget. . . ,* Oct. 13, 1815, NYCC, reel 21; AB to [Gurdon W. Lathrop], Apr. 4, 1814, in Kline, ed., *Burr Papers,* II: 1153.

92. "Eden Family," in Mary-Jo Kline, ed., *The Guide and Index to the Microfilm Edition of the Papers of Aaron Burr 1756–1836* (New York, 1978), 27; *John Wood v. AB,* July 20, 1825, NYCC, 16–17.

93. "Eden Family," in Kline, ed, *Guide,* 27; *John Wood v. AB,* 1825, NYCC, 5,13–15, 20–28.

94. *Wood v. AB,* 1825, NYCC, 7–8, 10, 23. See also *Morton v, Miller,* 1815, *Phillips v. Prevost,* 1818, NYSC, reel 22; *Cox v. Goldsborough,* 1815, NYCC, *John Wood v. AB, Eden,* May 2, 1828, NY Ct. of Errors, Burr Papers, microfilm, reel 21, 26. Benjamin Bulter to AB, June 24, 1818, AB to Daniel Webster, Jan. 27, 1827, and Elizabeth Eden to AB, Jan. 25, 1827, in Burr Papers, microfilm, reels 8, 11; and Mushkat and Rayback, *Martin Van Buren,* 168–69, 174–75.

95. For Burr's reputation as a lawyer, see "The Traveller," *New-York Mirror, and Ladies' Literary Gazette,* Nov. 5, 1825, 119; "Eden Family," in Kline, ed., *Guide,* 27. See also the prenuptial agreement draw up by Burr for Isadore Guillet and Elizabeth Eden, Mar. 15, 1828, Elizabeth Eden to AB, Sept. 27, 1826, Rebecca Eden to AB, Oct. 6, 1826, Elizabeth Eden to AB, [Nov. 1826], [AB?] to Mr. H., Oct. 13, 1833, and AB to Rebecca M. Eden Wilson, Dec. 15, 1833, in Burr Papers, microfilm, reel 11.

96. Jane L. Coryell, "'The Lincoln Colony': Aaron Columbus Burr's Proposed Colonization of British Honduras," *Civil War History* 43 (1997): 5–16; Aaron Burr Columbus to AB, Dec. 30, 1817, and Leonora Fenwick to AB, July 24, 1818, in Burr Papers, microfilm, reel 8.

97. AB to Captain James Biddle, July 5, 1829, in Burr Papers, microfilm, reel 11; AB to Peter Buell Porter [Secretary of War], Feb. 18, 1829, in Kline, ed., *Burr Papers,* II: 1195–97.

98. For Burr's historical ambitions, see Benjamin D. Silliman to Edward F. De Lancy, Jan. 22, 1876, in Thomas Jones, *History of New York during the Revolutionary War, and of the Leading Events in the Other Colonies at that Period* (New

York, 1879): I: 608–09; and Darius Hawkins to AB, Oct. 23, 1820, Burr Papers, microfilm, reel 9.

99. Richard H. Bayard to AB, Mar. 8, Apr. 22, 1830, AB to Richard Bayard, Mar. 10, 1830, AB to Matthew Livingston Davis, Mar. 15, 1830, and Matthew Livingston Davis to AB, Mar. 18, 1830, in Kline, ed., *Burr Papers*, II: 1197–04. Bayard felt his rendition of the facts offered "the most exact history of the matter"—see Richard Bayard to John W. Williams, Dec. 31, 1836, in Special Collections, University of Virginia, Charlottesville, Va. We know that Jefferson was well aware of James Bayard's letter to Allen McLane, in which Bayard promised that Jefferson would not dismiss him from his office. This letter was in Jefferson's private papers, but it is not clear when he received this copy. It may have been in 1806 or earlier. What we do know is that Jefferson had every reason to deny the secret deal in the *Anas*. Jefferson had a habit of rewriting history for posterity. See the copy of James Bayard to Allen McLane, Feb. 17, 1801, with Jefferson Note, in Barbara Oberg, ed., *The Papers of Thomas Jefferson* (Princeton, N.J., 2006).

100. Davis began reading Jefferson's Papers on May 30, 1830. See Matthew Livingston Davis, Memorandum Book, vol. 51, Rufus King Papers, New-York Historical Society, New York. I want to thank Jeff Pasley for referring this source to me. See also Kline, ed., *Burr Papers*, I: xxx.

101. AB to Aaron Ogden, Dec. 19, 1828, "Declaration of Military Service," Feb. 11, 1829, "Supplementary Declaration of Military Service," Feb. 5, 1833, AB to Jared Sparks, Feb. 28, 1833, "Supplementary Declaration of Military Service," [Mar. 1833], AB to Nelson Chase, Jan. 20, 21, Feb. 5, May 17, 1834, and AB to Martin Van Buren, Mar. 25, 1834, "Declaration of Military Service," [Apr. 5, 1834], in Kline, ed., *Burr Papers*, II: 1192–95, 1212–27; Aaron Ogden to AB, Jan. 8, 1832, in Burr Papers, microfilm, reel 11.

102. Ogden had been ruined by a protracted legal battle over his steamboat ferry monopoly. This suit against him came before the Supreme Court in 1824; it was the most celebrated anti-monopoly case of the time, *Gibbons v. Ogden*. More troubling for their relationship, Burr had prepared a brief for Gibbons, calling Ogden's monopoly "highly absurd & tyrannical." This case became particularly vicious and personal, because it pitted Ogden against Thomas Gibbons, his former partner, whose son was married to Jonathan Dayton's only child. See "Aaron Ogden," *Princetonians, 1769–1775* (Princeton, N.J., 1980), 332–334; "Jonathan Dayton," *Princetonians, 1776–1783* (Princeton, N.J., 1981), 40–41; AB: Brief on Fulton-Livingston steamboat monopoly (*Gibbons v. Ogden*), [ca. 1815?], in *Burr Papers*, microfilm, reel 7; One historian dates Burr's opinion as July 31, 1817, see Herbert A. Johnson, "*Gibbons v. Ogden* Before Marshall," in Leo Hershkowitz and Milton M. Klein, eds., *Courts and Law in Early New York* (Port Washington, N.Y., 1978), 108,147; and Maurice G. Baxter, *The Steamboat Monopoly: Gibbons v. Ogden, 1824* (New York, 1972), 29–32.

103. "Aaron Ogden," *Princetonians, 1769–1775,* II: 331, 333–34.
104. Clarkson and Jett, *Luther Martin,* 302–03; AB, "Agreement with Alexander L. Botts on behalf of John Pelletrau," Jan. 31, 1833, and AB to Rebecca Blodget, Nov. 10, 1834, in Burr Papers, microfilm, reel 11. And on Benjamin Botts's tragic death, see "John Minor Botts," *Richmond Portraits,* 20.
105. See description of "Eliza Bowen Jumel" in the guide to the Fuller Collection of Aaron Burr (1756–1836), Manuscripts Division, Department of Rare Books and Special Collections, Princeton University Library, Princeton, N.J; see also Lomask, *Aaron Burr: The Conspiracy,* 395–96. And for the unreliability of Jumel's self-invented past, see "Eliza Bowen Jumel," *American National Biography* 12, 317–18.
106. See Dianne Sachko Macleod, "Eliza Bowen Jumel: Collecting and Cultural Politics in Early America," *Journal of the History of Collections* 13 (2001): 60–61; "Eliza Bowen Jumel," *ANB.*
107. Macleod, "Eliza Bowen Jumel," 61–72. For her nasty comments about her husband, see a recorded conversation she had with Washington Irving in 1824, in Washington Irving, *Journals and Notebooks* (Boston, 1984), III: 430.
108. AB to John P. Bigelow, Sept. 9, 1833; for another letter of congratulation, see Margaret B. Sage to AB, Sept. 29, 1833, in Burr Papers, microfilm, reel 11; and Kline, ed., *Burr Papers,* II: 1218.
109. *Eliza B. Burr v. AB,* July 11, 1834, NYCC, 301, 303, 306, 322, 326, 330–34.
110. *Ibid.,* 291, 370, 372–76.
111. *Ibid.,* 375–76, 378. Mariah Johnson's testimony did meet the criteria of the courts, however. It became standard practice in divorce cases to rely on the testimony of witnesses, especially servants. Because of rigid divorce laws allowing adultery as the sole legally recognized cause, lawyers relied on strategic behavior. As the legal historian Henrik Hartog has argued, "if you needed a persuasive witness, then you would find or create a persuasive witness." The courts were more concerned with making the divorce fit a formula than actually finding out the truth—see Hartog, *Man and Wife in America: A History* (Cambridge, Mass., 2000), 64–66, 74–75. As Milton Lomask points out, Johnson's testimony was inaccurate, claiming that Burr did not have palsy at the time of his liaisons with McManus in August 1833. But there is clear evidence that Burr had a tremor in his hand as early as 1824. Johnson seemed more than willing to twist the facts, eliminating any detail that made Burr look less guilty. See Lomask, *Aaron Burr:The Conspiracy,* 402; also editor's commentary in AB to Thomas H. Flandrau, Feb. 13, 1824, in Burr Papers, microfilm, reel 10.
112. AB to Jane McManus, Nov. 17, 1832, in Burr Papers, microfilm, reel 11; and Linda S. Hudson, *Mistress of Manifest Destiny: A Biography of Jane McManus Storm Cazneau, 1807–1878* (Austin, Tex., 2001), 14–15, 17, 28–31.
113. AB to Jane McManus, Nov. 17, 1832, Enclosure: AB to Judge Workman, Nov. 16, 1832, in Burr Papers, microfilm, reel 11. Jane was in New York in early

July 1834 (when Eliza Jumel presented her bill to the court), but by the end of the month she was back in Texas. See Hudson, *Mistress of Manifest Destiny,* 32–33; *Eliza B. Burr v. AB,* NYCC, 318, 361–63.

114. Eliza Jumel's behavior in later years is consistent with this reading. The gay divorcée returned to Europe proclaiming herself the widow of the former U.S. vice president. She apparently felt there was a power in widowhood, translatable into social capital; but she enjoyed her independence more than she actually enjoyed being married to the seventy-seven-year-old Burr. See *Eliza B. Burr v. AB,* NYCC, 291, 301–02, 306–13, 354. For Burr's reference to "Madame of the Heights," see AB to Nelson Chase, Jan. 20, 1834, in Kline, ed., *Burr Papers,* II: 1218. And for Jumel spreading gossip about Burr's reckless spending, see *Diary of William Dunlap (1766–1839): The Memoirs of a Dramatist, Theatrical Manager, Painter, Critic, Novelist, and Historian* (New York, 1930), III: 796; and Constance M. Greiff, *The Morris-Jumel Mansion: A Documentary History* (Rocky Hill, N.J., 1995), 56.

115. *Eliza B. Burr v. AB,* NYCC, 291, 382–83; and *People v. Johnson,* 1837, and AB: Last Will and Testament, with codicils of Jan. 11, July 26, Dec. 27, 1835, in Burr Papers, microfilm, reel 11; Hudson, *Mistress of Manifest Destiny,* 37.

116. Ogden Edwards, the son of Pierpont Edwards, took care of the funeral arrangements. See Samuel Lewis Southard to Ogden Edwards, Sept. 16, 1836, in Papers of Pierpont Edwards Collection, 1756–1876, Huntington Library, San Marino, Calif.; Kline, ed., *Burr Papers,* II: 1228; Davis, ed., *Memoirs of Aaron Burr,* II: 446–49.

EPILOGUE

1. For Burr's lost papers, see Mary-Jo Kline, ed., *Burr Papers,* I, xxx. For Jefferson's concerted effort to shape his historical legacy, see Burstein, *Jefferson's Secrets,* 211–34. And for Jefferson's family, who did everything possible to preserve his memory, see Jan Ellen Lewis, "The White Jeffersons," in Jan Ellen Lewis and Peter S. Onuf, eds., *Sally Hemings and Thomas Jefferson: History, Memory, and Civic Culture* (Charlottesville, Va., 1999), 127–60; and Elizabeth Chew, " 'Our Pioneering Way': Monticello, the Randolph Family, and Jefferson's Memoirs of 1829," Paper given at the Thomas Jefferson in Retirement Conference, Mar. 4, 2005. For the importance of Hamilton's wife and family, and the publication of his papers, for protecting and enhancing his reputation, see Stephen F. Knott, *Alexander Hamilton and the Persistence of Myth* (Lawrence, Kans., 2002), 21–23, 154.

2. From a paper read by Judge John Greenwood before the Long Island, N.Y., Historical Society, on Sept. 24, 1863, reprinted in Parton, *Life and Times of Aaron Burr,* II: 403–14.

3. *The Conspiracy; or, the Western Island: A Drama in Five Acts* (1838) was published anonymously. Tarkington's play was performed at the Fulton Theatre in

New York City on Jan. 10, 1931—see Samuel H. Wandell, *Aaron Burr in Literature* (London, 1936), 232; and Charles J. Nolan, Jr., *Aaron Burr and the American Literary Imagination* (Westport, Conn., 1980), 189. Atherton also has a mysterious Madame La Croix (later Madame Jumel), a French spy and Jacobin, funding Burr's political career in 1800; later, out of revenge against Hamilton for not leaving his family for her, she convinces Burr to challenge him to a duel—see Gertrude Franklin Horn Atherton, *The Conqueror; A Dramatized Biography of Alexander Hamilton* (New York, 1902), 459, 500, 509, 512–13; Thomas B. Sweeney, *Aaron Burr's Dream for the Southwest: A Drama for the Library* (San Antonio, Tex., 1955), 3, 5, 116, 163, 173, 186–67, 193–94.

4. Chernow, *Alexander Hamilton,* 682, 704, 716.

5. Joseph Holt Ingraham, *Burton; or, The Sieges: A Romance,* 2 vols. (New York, 1838); for an obituary that claimed "as a successful ladies' man there never was parallel to Aaron Burr in this country," see *New York Herald,* July 12, 1836.

6. Virginia Tatnall Peacock, "Theodosia Burr (Mrs. Joseph Alston)," in *Famous Belles of the Nineteenth Century* (Philadelphia, 1901), 19; Emerson Hough, *The Magnificent Adventure, this being the story of the world's greatest exploration, and the romance of a very gallant gentleman; a novel* (New York, 1916). And see Judge Champ Clark, "Address on Aaron Burr," in *Modern Eloquence,* VII: 230; Anya Seaton, *My Theodosia* (Boston, 1941), 63, 117, 363–64; and Gore Vidal, *Burr* (New York, 1973), 137.

7. Jerome Dowd, *Burr and Hamilton: A New York Tragedy* (New York, 1884); Charles Frederic Nirdlinger, *The First Lady of the Land: A Play in Four Acts* (Boston, 1914), 12, 25, 32–33, 49, 51–54, 63–64, 78, 99–100, and 145. The same theme of Burr as the elegant but honorable suitor of Dolley Madison appears in David Nevins's novel *Treason* (New York, 2003); see also Nolan, *Aaron Burr and the American Literary Imagination,* 77–78, 94–95.

8. Kennedy's take on Jefferson is no less far-fetched than his take on the relationship between Hamilton and Burr. Reminiscent of Nirdlinger's work of 1914, Kennedy's Jefferson is jealous of Burr for having come between Madison and him, that is, for ruining their "bachelor partnership." This time Jefferson is the closeted gay lover, who resents that Burr introduced Dolley to Madison. The suicide argument (Hamilton's death wish) can be traced back to an article published in the *Journal of Psychohistory* in 1980. Atherton (see note 3 above) also relied on sexual jealousy as the reason for the duel. See Roger Kennedy, *Burr, Hamilton, and Jefferson: A Study in Character* (New York, 1999), 42, 368; Arnold A. Rogow, *A Fatal Friendship: Alexander Hamilton and Aaron Burr* (New York, 1998), xiv, 266–67; also Knott, *Alexander Hamilton and the Persistence of Myth,* 196.

9. William Henry Venable, *A Dream of Empire, or the House of Blennerhassett* (New York, 1901), 83; Eudora Welty, "First Love" (1943) from *The Wide Net and*

Other Stories, in *The Collected Stories of Eudora Welty* (New York, 1983), 154, 159, 166.

10. See "Portrait of Burr," *Port Folio*, May 16, 1807, 314–15.

11. Joseph J. Ellis, *Founding Brothers: The Revolutionary Generation* (New York, 2000), 18. Other accomplished historians of the early period err in similar ways through a lack of thoroughness in researching Burr's political conduct. John Ferling and Joanne Freeman both call Burr an "enigma," and a man without principles; Freeman describes him in Chesterfieldian terms. She also contends that "Burr was a most unfounderlike Founder, and those who force him into the traditional 'Founder' model deny his very essence." This skewed view of Burr's character matches that of a Hamilton biographer, the politically conservative Forrest McDonald, who merely repeats what Hamilton said about Burr's ambition, but makes no effort to obtain real proof. Two other conservative defenders of Federalism, Stanley Elkins and Eric McKitrick, distort Burr's character in their massive study of the 1790s. They describe him as a "consummate liar, less than the first rank of the Republic's founders' generation," and again as an "enigma." Elkins and McKitrick conclude that he was "*not* a representative man of his time. He was clearly a deviant type; whether he represented anything or anyone beyond himself is at best debatable." In his 1994 presidential address before the Society for Historians of the Early Republic, William J. Rorabaugh observed that "Burr's self-centeredness was legendary." Gordon Wood, in his new book *Revolutionary Characters*, continues this reductionist tradition, claiming that Burr was the only founder who rejected the prevailing notion of virtue. In effect, Wood contends that Burr lacked both moral and political principle and was devoid of all the positive qualities that the other founders possessed. No one but Alfred Young stopped to investigate Burr's role in state politics, wherein he clearly emerges as a legitimate actor. See John Ferling, *Adams vs. Jefferson: The Tumultuous Election of 1800* (New York, 2004), 9, 95; Freeman, *Affairs of Honor: National Politics in the New Republic*, 205, 211; and Freeman, "History as Told by the Devil Incarnate: Gore Vidal's *Burr*," in Mark C. Carnes, ed., *Novel History: Historians and Novelists Confront America's Past (and Each Other)* (New York, 2001), 32; Forrest McDonald, *Alexander Hamilton: A Biography* (New York, 1982), 360; Stanley Elkins and Eric McKitrick, *Age of Federalism: The Early American Republic, 1788–1800* (New York, 1993), 743–44; W. J. Rorabaugh, "The Political Duel in the Early Republic: Burr v. Hamilton," *Journal of the Early Republic* 15 (Spring 1995): 5; Gordon Wood, *Revolutionary Characters: What Made the Founders Different* (New York, 2006); and Alfred Young, *The Democratic Republicans of New York: The Origins, 1763–1797* (Chapel Hill, N.C., 1967).

12. *The Federalist Papers*, ed. Clinton Rossiter (New York, 1961), 54–55.

13. Kline, ed., *Burr Papers*, II: 367.

INDEX